Race, Social Class, and Individual Differences in I. Q.

Sandra Scarr
Yale University

Commentaries by
Leon J. Kamin
Arthur R. Jensen

LEA LAWRENCE ERLBAUM ASSOCIATES, PUBLISHERS
1981 Hillsdale, New Jersey

Lawrence Erlbaum Associates, Inc., Publishers
365 Broadway
Hillsdale, New Jersey 07642

Library of Congress Cataloging in Publication Data
Main entry under title:

Race, social class, and individual differences in I.Q.;
   new studies of old issues.

   Bibliography: p.
   Includes index.
   1. Intellect. 2. Intelligence levels. 3. Socioeconomic status and intelligence. 4. Ethnopsychology.
5. Nature and nurture. I. Scarr, Sandra.
BF432.A1R33   153.9′2   80-29591
ISBN 0-89859-055-8

Printed in the United States of America

Contents

Preface

The role—indeed the very existence—of genetic differences in human behavior has long been a matter of heated debate in the social sciences. That the relative weights to be awarded to nature and nurture are still disputed is demonstrated by the following papers, comments upon them, and replies to the criticisms. At last, however, I think that more light than heat is produced by the new designs, methods, and samples that my collaborators and I have used to study genetic and environmental differences in human behavior.

The major theme that integrates all the chapters is the question: "Why do people differ from one another in intellectual performance?" The first issue is how to define, measure, and explain why individuals and groups differ in test scores: Are the tests valid measures for all people? The second issue is the contrast between the study of individual and group variability. In this book, studies of individual variability are complemented by unusual research on average differences among people by race and social class.

From a theoretical point of view, individual and group differences in intellect follow the same evolutionary laws of variation and selection. From a methodological point of view, however, group differences must be studied very differently from individual variability. And social classes—among which there is some individual mobility—must be treated in a different fashion from racial groups—among which individual mobility is unlikely.

Both developmental and quantitative genetics bear on behavioral differences, but their implications are quite different. The necessary partnership of genes and environments in producing developmental change has often been confused with the potentially separable effects of genetic and environmental differences in producing human variation. Principles of developmental genetics—such as malleability and canalization—and of quantitative genetics—such as selection and polygenic effects—are explained in the several chapters of Part I. The two subsequent parts provide empirical studies of genetic theories as they relate to racial, social-class, and individual variability. The implications of these studies for the behavioral sciences and for society are discussed in the final part.

The series of studies reported in the book is unique. With the collaboration of Solomon H. Katz and William B. Barker at the University of Pennsylvania, the first large-scale studies of genetic individual differences among blacks were done. Also, we collaborated on the only study of the (lack of) relationship between African ancestry and intellectual performance. With Richard A. Weinberg at Minnesota, the only studies of the intellectual effects of transracial adoption and of adopted children in late adolescence were performed. Because so few of these studies have any counterparts in the social or biological science literature, I feel that collecting them together in a coherent volume accomplishes two goals: to make the theoretical and empirical integrity of the research program more apparent, and to allow colleagues and students to assess the state of our knowledge in a more comprehensive way.

A PERSONAL HISTORY OF THE RESEARCH PROGRAM AND THE BOOK

The potentially dangerous results and implications that might have been obtained from these studies may raise questions in readers' minds about the motivation for undertaking the research. Why would anyone want to study genetic differences in human behavior, particularly racial and social-class differences?

My interest in the possibility of genetic behavioral differences began when, as an undergraduate, I was told that there were none. The Sociology Department at Vassar agreed with the social science view of the time that genetics set limits on behavioral development in the human species, but that all individuals and groups were equally endowed with everything important, such as genes for intelligence (whatever those might be). My own observation about human differences made me curious about the department's certainty on this matter, particularly when I noticed the lack of evidence for such a view. It seemed more important to me to understand human differences than to stifle research for fear of unpopular results. (I joined the ACLU in my senior year.)

In graduate school, I decided to have a closer look at human individuality and did a dissertation on genetic differences in motivation and personality (not represented in this book). After moving to the University of Pennsylvania in 1966, a quick glance at the local scene told me that the most interesting question of practical import was: "Why do black children perform so poorly in school and on intellectual tests?" This question had been addressed in hundreds of studies that merely charted the magnitude of the performance differences between blacks and whites at many age levels and in many locales. There must be, I thought, more analytically powerful ways to get at the causes of these performance differences. Two logically possible hypotheses had been offered to explain why black children score badly on tests and do poorly in school—sociocultural disadvantage and racial genetic differences. The advocates of both views asserted their positions with vehemence, but there were no critical tests of either hypothesis.

Thus, in 1967, I began a program of research with three previously unused strategies to study the sources of racial difference in intellectual performance: (1) studies of genetic individual variability *within* the black population by the twin method; (2) the study of genetic markers of individual degrees of African ancestry and the possible relationship of ancestry to intellectual differences among blacks; and (3) the study of transracial adoption by which socially classified black children were reared in the cultural environment sampled by the tests and the schools. The evidence against a genetic racial-differences hypothesis, and in favor of a sociocultural hypothesis, has been a convergent operation from these three sources of data, reported in Part II.

My interest in individual differences continued at the University of Minnesota in 1970. A unique study of adolescents who were adopted in the 1st year of life was launched with the collaboration of Richard A. Weinberg. If environmental advantages and disadvantages were the major determinants of intellectual differences, we reasoned, then adopted children in the late adolescent years ought to provide the best opportunity to observe those effects. At the end of the child-rearing period, children ought to show the cumulative effects of the various opportunities afforded or not afforded them by their parents. What we observed was little systematic environmental variability in the intellectual differences of adopted children and considerable genetic variability when correlations among adoptees were compared to those in a similar biological-family sample. These data are in Part III.

The lack of systematic individual variability based on differences among adoptive families led us to examine social-class effects. What difference does it make to have been reared in a working-class family or a professional family if one is genetically unrelated to those parents? The answer is "very little," whereas in the comparable biological-family sample, social-class differences in intellectual performance are much larger. This result had previously been reported by Leahy and Burks from their adoption studies in the 1920s and 1930s, but was largely forgotten in the massive sociological and economic literature on family effects. These data and similar social-class analyses from the transracial adoption study are reported in Part III.

The implications that I draw from the series of studies on racial, social-class, and individual differences in IQ are described in Part IV (although conclusions appear elsewhere in the chapters and in replies to criticisms). The chapter on testing minority children spells out the implications of our research on racial differences for intellectual assessment. And the final chapter, "From Evolution to Larry P.,'' recapitulates the evolutionary theory presented in the first part of the book and the genetic research reported in the three empirical parts; and it relates them to the social policy questions of testing, schooling, and equality. The final part, therefore, is a summary and a statement of the larger social implications of the research program as I see them.

Many of the chapters in this book appeared first as journal articles. They have not been changed, because the critiques and comments they generated have been reprinted with them. It would have been unfair to the authors of the comments to change the objects of their criticisms. More selfishly, reprinting the criticisms allowed me to add our published replies, which—with the comments—I consider the most enlightening parts of the debate. Thus, the original articles, comments, and replies appear here together, so that the reader can follow the varied lines of argument about racial, social-class, and individual variability in intelligence. I did not always fare as well as I would have liked in these debates, but they are presented in full as part of the intellectual history of research on these touchy issues.

In Part V, commentaries on the research were invited from the leading advocates of opposing positions in the Great IQ Debate. Leon Kamin best represents the political and scientific groups who oppose the use of IQ tests and who resist any genetic interpretation of individual and group differences in intelligence. On the other side is Arthur Jensen, whose writings on the probability of racial genetic differences in intelligence have inflamed public opinion in scientific and lay communities. My replies to their criticisms, the effectiveness of which the reader should judge, are aimed at general issues in scientific inquiry and constitute my "last word" about research on the genetic bases of human differences. Part V contains some of the most illuminating discussion of the book, because of the overt and covert disagreements among Jensen, Kamin, and me. The objective reader—if such exists on matters of genetic differences in human behavior—will find a certain humor, I hope, in the very seriousness of the debate.

Finally, the book is an example of scientific debate in a politically explosive arena. The debate has stretched across many journals and many more popular publications. One could hardly expect that the participants would display detached objectivity in their reasoning or their writing, but some of the excesses of political motivation are lamentable. Nevertheless, I conclude that we have learned from the research and from the public debate over genetic differences in human behavior.

ACKNOWLEDGMENTS

Colleagues and graduate students at several institutions have contributed to the research in this book. Most notable is Richard Weinberg, with whom the two adoptive studies were done. His skills as a school psychologist and sensitive assessor of human abilities were invaluable. With us at the University of Minnesota were Louise Carter, Harold D. Grotevant, and Patricia Webber, whose dissertations were parts of the adoption studies. Joanne Bergman scheduled families and kept order.

The twin studies were done at the University of Pennsylvania, Graduate School of Education and Dental School. With William B. Barker and Solomon Katz, hundreds of pairs of twins were given psychological assessments, anthropometric and dental measurements. The management of the exhausting data collection was principally the labor of Valerie Lindstrom and David Armstrong. The Philadelphia School District cooperated by supplying the names, addresses, and school test data of all of the twins in the school system. Without their help the samples would be much less representative.

Most of all, we all thank the thousands of families and children who participated in the studies and the many who are still cooperating in follow-up research, presently being conducted at Yale.

I would also like to thank the publishers who permitted me to reprint their materials.

Sandra Scarr
Yale University

GENETICS AND
INTELLIGENCE

I.1 Genetics and the Development of Intelligence*

IN THIS CHAPTER the three terms of the title, "genetics," "development," and "intelligence," will be defined and interrelated in several ways. The term "genetics" subsumes the two broad theoretical and methodological areas of Mendelian and biometrical genetics. Both are important to the study of intellectual development. "Development" is defined as a change over time in the direction of greater differentiation and integration of structure and function; developmental changes at biochemical, morphological, and behavioral levels are all important to the study of genetics and intelligence. "Intelligence" is a behavioral construct for which everyone can give many examples at all developmental stages but which often evades definition. A lack of consensus on the necessary and sufficient criteria for definition is the source of controversy. In this chapter psychometric, cognitive developmental, and cross-cultural approaches to intelligence will be related to genetic principles.

This chapter will explore the development of normal, human intelligence from a behavior-genetic point of view. The review is perforce largely theoretical because there is only a small (but growing) literature on the genetics of human intellectual development in the normal range. Two major goals of the chapter are to clarify behavior-genetic concepts of intellectual development and to frame questions about genetic aspects of intelligence that can be productively investigated.

There are several other goals which this chapter will *not* attempt to achieve. First, it will not describe in detail the basic principles of Mendelian and quantitative genetics, for which other sources are readily available (see Cavalli-Sforza and Bodmer 1972, for a particularly good

My deepest gratitude to Professors William Charlesworth, John Flavell, Irving I. Gottesman, Frances D. Horowitz, Anne D. Pick, Steven G. Vandenberg, and Ronald Wilson for their suggestions on the manuscript for this chapter. They are in no way responsible, however, for its content or conclusions. I received support during the period of research from the Grant Foundation and the National Institute of Child Health and Human Development (HD-06502, HD-08016).

treatment). Second, it will not review the endless controversy over the measurement of intelligence, for which recent sources are also available (see Cancro 1971; Butcher 1968). Third, it will not describe the growing literature on genetic anomalies in intellectual development, which are well reviewed by Reed in this volume (chapter 2). Fourth, this chapter will not recapitulate a half-century of the nature-nurture controversy, even as it pertains to intelligence; however, some of the research on foster children and related individuals will be discussed where relevant.

Lastly, this chapter will not offer a primary review of the excellent behavior-genetic literature on infrahuman species, which is well-represented in Manosevitz, Lindzey, and Thiessen (1969), Hirsch (1967), and Thiessen (1972a). Elegant experiments on strain and species differences in behavior development have value in demonstrating some of the mechanisms of development from genotype to phenotype, both theoretically and particularly for the populations studied. But the analogue to the mechanisms and course of development of human intelligence is tenuous indeed. Other surveys on behavior genetics and development have appeared that have reviewed the extensive animal literature (Lindzey, Loehlin, Manosevitz, and Thiessen 1971; McClearn 1964, 1970; Thiessen 1970).

Intelligence is a very complex phenotype with a very complex developmental sequence. For those reasons it is not an ideal phenotype for behavior-genetic analysis (Hirsch 1967, 1971). The importance of human intellect in human affairs is so great, however, that an abdication of the pursuit is not excusable either. The relative lack of information on human intelligence, compared to simpler genetic mechanisms in simpler organisms, is not surprising in light of the difficulty of analyzing phenotypes that arise from many genes and many pathways in varied environments.

Biases and Controversies

Theoretical and empirical controversies abound in the area of genetics and intelligence. Any chapter on the subject is necessarily biased by the author's interpretation of what we already know, what we need to discover, how research questions should be theoretically framed, and what inferences can be made from the findings. It is not possible to write a chapter on genetics and intelligence without these factors affecting the presentation of the topic. The following is a brief outline of the author's beliefs through which the material in this chapter has been filtered.

1. Our present knowledge of genetic factors in normal human intellectual development is primarily in the area of individual differences. The study of genetic and environmental contributions to individual differ-

ences is valuable, both in its own right and as an indication of where genetic research should be concentrated.

2. Generalizations from research on genetic and environmental differences are limited to the distributions of genotypes, environments, and measures actually sampled. The finding of substantial genetic variance in one population with one set of environments and one set of measures does not guarantee finding the same proportion in another.

3. At present we know that perhaps half of the variance of intellectual tests in the white population can be attributed to individual genetic differences. We know little or nothing about different populations reared under different sets of environments. Despite some assertions to the contrary, we know nothing about the sources of average intellectual differences between populations because appropriate methods have never been used to study these differences.

4. The application of genetic theory to normal intelligence has been limited to the analysis of variance and to biometrical models which assume that the phenotype is a static entity. Development is a dynamic concept that requires theoretical accounts of both stability and change in the organization of behavior and the plasticity of the developing phenotype.

5. Genetic theory has too often been applied to human behavioral development in a reductionist, linear manner. The necessary transactions between genotypes and environments have been paid lip service but have seldom been measured in research on developing phenotypes.

6. The methods of animal behavior-genetic research (e.g., selective breeding, uniform environments) have avoided many of the pitfalls cited above but are not themselves directly applicable to human studies. New models and methods are badly needed for the study of normal human development.

7. Knowledge gained from research on the abnormal development of abnormal genotypes is of limited use for the construction of models of normal development. Although it is very important to trace the effects of a single blocked pathway from gene action to mental retardation, knowing one source of error does not inform us of the other hundreds of pathways that must also function properly and together for normal intellectual development to occur.

8. The measurement of intelligent behavior at different developmental stages is fraught with so many conceptual and methodological problems that an open mind on IQ tests, operational measures, cross-cultural strategies, and possible psychophysical measures is absolutely required. Inferences from behaviors observed, under similar or different testing conditions, to the construct intelligence should be cautious and circumscribed.

Intelligence is a value-laden inference from behaviors that are generally considered to belong in the intellectual domain: problem-solving, concept formation, symbolic reasoning, hierarchical classification, and the like. Humphreys (1971, p. 36) defines intelligence as "the totality of responses available to the organism at any one period of time for the solution of intellectual problems." The domain of intellectual problems is defined by a consensus among psychologists.

It is possible to debunk operational definitions of intelligence as "what IQ tests measure," but in doing so one is surely ignoring the demonstrated value of the construct. There *is* some consensus among psychologists, and even people in general, as to what skills fall in the intellectual domain. There is substantial disagreement on how best to measure intelligent behavior: e.g., differential versus general ability (Butcher 1968), empirically-based normative versus theoretically-based operational tests (Almy, Chittenden, and Miller 1966; Cancro 1971; Pinard and Laurendreau 1964; Tuddenham 1970), culture-fair versus situation-specific behavior samples (Cattell 1971; Cole and Bruner 1971; Labov 1966).

A distinction between competence and performance in studies of intelligence, as in language, has assumed considerable importance for cognitive development. Competence is necessarily an inference from performance, and the crucial question concerns the basis of that inference. Shall intellectual competence be estimated from the best performance given by an individual in any situation (Cole, Gay, Glick and Sharp 1972; Labov 1970), by a specific performance under comparable conditions among individuals (IQ tests), or by an average of performances across many situations?

The distinction between cognitive competence and performance is like the distinction between intelligence and IQ scores. Both distinctions depend upon the latter being used as an estimate of the former. Although one can argue extensively for and against the various bases for estimation, the issue cannot be settled here.

Situational factors can influence the production of responses to intellectual problems, so that performances by the same individual may vary considerably from one situation to another. In cross-cultural research the best intellectual performance a person can give may not be sampled in unfamiliar testing or experimental situations posed by investigators (Cole, Gay, Glick and Sharp 1972; Ervin-Tripp 1972). Labov has argued that many U.S. black children who use cognitively and linguistically complex codes with their peers fail to perform well on IQ tests primarily because the testing situation elicits hostility and suspicion rather than motivation to perform well (Labov 1970). In contrast, Jensen (1973) has shown that the motivation to perform well on tests is equally high in black and white children.

A possible explanation for the conflicting results is that, apart from the motivation to behave appropriately and the competence to perform well, children learn to select and apply one of several alternative behaviors in any situation. Non-Western subjects and some U.S. black children may want to behave appropriately in the testing situation, may have the competence to do so, but may not have learned that categorization and complex problem-solving skills are appropriately applied to artificial testing situations. Their ability to perform at a higher intellectual level in other situations would suggest this conclusion. On the other hand, Jensen (1969, 1971b) has made a compelling argument for at least two factors in intelligence: one, conceptual ability, which we generally call IQ; the other, associative ability. High levels of the latter can account for the frequent finding of adequate social skills among people who perform poorly on tests of conceptual abilities. One must be careful, therefore, that the mental operations inferred from samples of social behaviors are actually the same conceptual skills sampled by IQ tests.

Interpretations of standard IQ tests and cognitive developmental measures should be restricted to statements about performance under given conditions. These performances have important implications and make quite good predictions of performance in school, job, and similar situations which call for conceptual skills. But they should not be used to infer "native ability" or ability to perform more or less adequately in situations that differ greatly from the testing conditions. *In this chapter, IQ tests and other operational measures will be used to infer intelligence, with the limitations noted above.*

The usefulness of IQ scores in behavior-genetic studies will be evident from the regular fit between polygenic theory and phenotypic IQ correlations among related individuals, from the fit between the theoretical and demonstrated effects of inbreeding, from the application of the reaction-range model to available IQ data, and from the prediction of parent-offspring regression. The usefulness of cognitive developmental measures and cross-cultural strategies in behavior-genetic research can be shown in a few recent studies. As in many other instances, seemingly competing and conflicting approaches turn out to provide complementary data.

GENETIC MECHANISMS IN DEVELOPMENT

Development is the process by which the genotype comes to be expressed as a phenotype. Development in any one case is the expression of only one of many alternative phenotypes in the genotype's range of reaction (Ginsburg and Laughlin 1971; Hirsch 1971). The degree to which an individual's genotype is expressed in his or her intellectual development depends upon many environmental factors that are critically present in adequate or inadequate amounts during the developmental process.

Genes are a primary part of the cellular system, being segments of chromosomes in the nucleus of every cell. Genes act, however, as constituents in all hierarchically organized systems from cellular to behavioral levels. Developmentally, gene action both initiates growth and is regulated by the growth of other constituents in the systems. To understand genetic factors in development is to know the ways in which gene action regulates and is regulated at every level and at every point in development, and to understand how individual variation develops.

The ultimate goal in behavior-genetic research is to understand the developmental pathways between genotypes and phenotypes. A complete knowledge of the biochemical-physiological-behavioral links from genotype to behavioral phenotype would encompass the understanding of both its Mendelian determinants and its individual variation.

This goal is far from being realized. At present, behavior-genetic studies of human intellectual development are primarily concerned with variation rather than with the role of genes in development. This section will outline what is known about genetic mechanisms in development. The third section will concentrate on genetic variation.

Mendelian and Biometrical Genetics

Mather (1971) has contrasted Mendelian and biometrical genetic analysis:

The Mendelian approach depends on the successful recognition of clearly distinguishable phenotypic classes from which the relevant genetical constitution can be inferred. It is at its most powerful when there is a one-to-one correspondence of phenotype and genotype, though some ambiguity of the relationship, as when complete dominance results in heterozygote and one homozygote having the same phenotype, is acceptable (p. 351). The biometrical approach is from a different direction starting with the character rather than the individual determinant. It makes no requirement that the determinants be traceable individually in either transmission or action. It seeks to measure variation in a character and then, by comparing individuals and families of varying relationship, to partition the differences observed into fractions ascribable to the various genetical (or for that matter non-genetical) phenomena . . . (p. 352).

The two methods are entirely complementary (although they are often seen as competing) and, in fact, have somewhat different applications.

For polygenic traits like intelligence in the normal range of variation, the biometrical method has been applied almost exclusively because too many genes and pathways are involved to allow for Mendelian analysis. In the case of abnormalities, Mendelian analysis is used to establish the genotype-phenotype pathways. In some cases where major genes are involved in a polygenic system, Mendelian and biometrical analysis will give similar results (Mather 1971).

Both Mendelian and biometrical approaches depend ultimately upon a knowledge of environmental factors which regulate gene expression. The behavior-genetic analysis of intellectual development must proceed with knowledge of the many gene-action pathways, gene regulatory mechanisms, and environmental factors that affect the expression of the genotype in the phenotype for intelligence.

Gene Action and Behavioral Development

If gene-action pathways in human development were known, this chapter would be simple reporting rather than speculative construction. In fact, only bits and pieces of the genetics of developmental processes are known. The basic DNA-RNA, protein-synthesis code is well established. Knowledge of fetal development at a morphological level is fairly complete. But how does morphological development over the fetal period, and indeed the life span, relate to protein synthesis at a cellular level? What causes some cells to differentiate and develop into the cortex and others into hemoglobin? And how do gene action and morphological development relate to intellectual development from birth to senescense? How do cells, which all originate from the same fertilized ovum and all carry the same genetic information, come to program development into different organs and systems and in different behavioral stages of development?

The relation between gene action and behavioral development has been well summarized by Thiessen (1972a, p. 87).

The lengthy, often tortuous, path from DNA specificity to metabolic synchrony explains why behavior must be considered a pleiotropic reflection of physiological processes. Gene influence in behavior is always indirect. Hence the regulatory processes of a behavior can be assigned to structural and physiological consequences of gene action and developmental canalization. The blueprint for behavior may be a heritable characteristic of DNA, but its ultimate architecture is a problem for biochemistry and physiology. Explaining gene-behavior relations entails knowing every aspect of the developmental pattern: its inception, its relation to the environment, its biochemical individuality, and its adaptiveness. When these things are known, it is possible to enter an experimental wedge at any level and to adjust gene expression anywhere within the limits of modification.

It has been hypothesized (Jacob and Monod, 1961) that several kinds of genes exist: structural genes to specify the proteins to be synthesized, operator genes to turn protein synthesis on and off in adjacent structural genes, and regulator genes to repress or activate the operator and structural genes in a larger system (Jacob and Monod 1961; Lerner 1968; Martin and Ames 1964). The instructions that a cell receives must be under regulatory control that differentiates the activity of that cell at several points in development.

Genes and chromosome segments are "turned on" at some but not other points in development. Enlargements of a chromosome section (called "puffs") have been observed to coincide with RNA synthesis in the cell. Puffs occur on different portions of the chromosomes at different times in different cells, indicating the existence of regulatory mechanisms in development.

Regulatory genes are probably the ones responsible for species and individual differentiation through control of the expression of structural genes. Most of the structural genes, which are directly concerned with enzyme formation, are common to a wide array of species and function in approximately the same way. They provide the fundamental identity of life systems. The diversity of individuals and species is due in large part to the regulatory genes, which modify the expression of basic biochemical processes (Thiessen 1972a).

In other words, the greatest proportion of phenotypic variance, at least in mammalian species, is probably due to regulatory rather than structural genes—genes that activate, deactivate, or otherwise alter the expression of a finite number of structural genes (p. 124).

Several cellular regulatory mechanisms have been suggested (Lerner 1968). First, the cytoplasms of different cells contain different amounts of material and may contain different materials. As cell division proceeds, daughter cells receive unequal amounts of cytoplasm, and this may relate to their progressive differentiation. Second, the position of the developing cells may influence their course. Outer cells may have different potentialities for development than those surrounded by other cells.

Third, the cell nuclei become increasingly differentiated in the developmental process. Progressively older nuclei have a more limited range of available functions; they become more specialized in the cell activities they can direct. Specialization of nuclei is related to the differentiation of organs and functions in different portions of the developing organism.

The regulation of developmental processes over the life span is accomplished through the gene-encoded production of hundreds of thousands of enzymes and hormones. During embryogenesis there are precise correlations between changes in enzyme concentrations and development (Hsia, 1968).

For example, *cholinesterase* activity shows particularly close relationships with neural development. As early as the closure of the neural tube, high cholinesterase activity has been found in association with morphogenesis of the neuraxis. . . . Nachmansohn has shown that *cholinesterase* is synthesized in the developing nervous system of the chick embryo exactly at the time that synapses and nerve endings appear (pp. 96–97).

Any behavior represented phenotypically by the organism *must,* by definition, have a genetic and organismic representation. It does not appear without CNS regulation, and CNS regulation does not occur without brain myelenization, synaptic transmission, and previous experience encoded chemically in the brain.

Enzymatic differentiation is specific to the stage of development, the specific organ, specific regions within organs, and the type of enzyme. Development proceeds on a gene-regulated path by way of enzymatic activity. Generalizations are very risky from one point in time to another and from one organ part to another.

There are several enzyme systems that are active in the embryo but that disappear with the cessation of growth. Other enzymes that are absent or present in low activity in the embryo greatly increase in activity at the time an organ becomes functionally mature. These enzymes then remain active throughout life to regulate functional organ activity. A third class of enzymes is activated only with maturation and remains active the rest of adult life (Hsia 1968, pp. 96–107).

Interference with regulatory mechanisms at a cellular or organ-system level can result in a variety of phenotypic abnormalities. The result of interference is often related to the time it occurs during development. For example, male rabbit fetuses castrated on the nineteenth day of gestation resemble a female at birth. Castration on any day up to the twenty-fourth results in a gradation of femininity, but if castration is performed on the twenty-fifth day or later, there is no effect on the development of male genitalia. Figure 1 is a schematic presentation of the biochemical development of the embryo and the influence of environment at all levels of development.

Hormonal activity is critically important to the stimulation of protein synthesis and to the differentiation of male embryos from the basic female form. Minute quantities of fetal testosterone at critical periods in development affect genital differentiation as well as CNS differences that seem

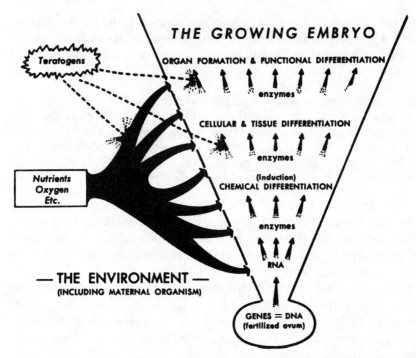

Fig. 1. Model of the biochemical development of the growing embryo and the influence of environment at all levels of development. (From Hsia 1968, after Wilson.)

to last a lifetime (Levine 1967). The variety of hormones that stimulate protein synthesis includes growth hormones as well as sex hormones, cortisone, insulin, and thyroxine (Thiessen 1972a, p. 95). A model of hormone-gene flow is presented by Thiessen, as shown in figure 2.

There are many known ways in which normal development can be

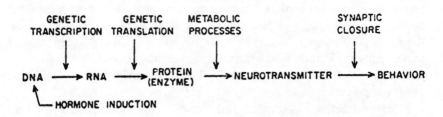

Fig. 2. Model of hormone-gene flow from cellular to behavioral levels. (From Thiessen 1972b.)

disrupted at a biochemical level. Defects in the biochemical pathways between gene action and normal cell metabolism number in the hundreds. In the glucose to glycogen pathway alone, there are seven independent genetic errors that result in different genetic anomalies (Hsia 1968).

Environmental pathogens can, of course, intervene in normal development. Radiation, infectious diseases, drugs, and other specific environmental factors are responsible for some congenital abnormalities in the developing fetus.

The effect of ionizing radiation on CNS development is detailed in figure 3. Rubella, mumps, toxoplasmosis, and viral infections produce

TIMETABLE OF RADIATION MALFORMATIONS IN MICE AND MAN

AGE (DAYS) Mouse	AGE (DAYS) Man	EMBRYO (mm.)	NERVOUS SYSTEM	OTHER
0–9	0–25		No damage	
9	25½	2.4	Anencephaly (extreme defect of forebrain)	Severe head defects
10	28½	4.2	Forebrain, brain stem, or cord defects	Skull, jaw, skeletal, visceral defects, anophthalmia
11	33½	7.0	Hydrocephalus, narrow aqueduct, encephalocele, cord, and brain stem defects	Retinal, skull, skeletal defects
12	36½	9.0	Decreasing encephalocele; microcephaly, porencephaly	Retinal, skull, skeletal defects
13	38	12.0	Microcephaly, bizarre defects of cortex, hippocarpus, callosum, basal ganglia, decreasing toward term	Decreasing skeletal defects

Fig. 3. Timetable of radiation malformations in mice and man. (From Hsia 1968, after Hicks.)

characteristic anomalies when contracted by the fetus in the first trimester of pregnancy. Mental retardation is a prominent feature of many genetic and environmental disturbances in the developmental process (see chapter 2 in this volume).

Another genetic pathway that has received considerable attention is that of phenylalanine. While many behavioral scientists recognize that a block in this pathway can produce PKU (phenylketonuria), most are not aware that four other identifiable genetic syndromes result from additional blocks in the same pathway, as shown in figure 4.

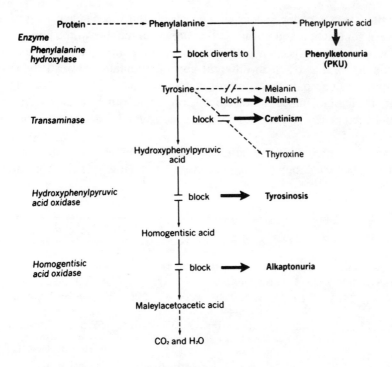

Fig. 4. Genetic blocks in the metabolism of phenylalanine. (From *Heredity, Evolution, and Society* by I. Michael Lerner [W. H. Freeman and Company. Copyright © 1968].)

Genetic Canalization

The concept of canalization in development accounts for many phenotypic phenomena. Canalization is the restriction of alternative phenotypes to one or a few outcomes. The developing phenotype is represented as more or less difficult to deflect from a growth path (creode), depending upon the degree of genotypic control, the force of the deflection, and the timing of the deflection. Waddington's epigenetic landscape, as shown in figure 5, is a model of the varying canalization in the development of different aspects of the organism (Waddington 1957, 1962).

The ball is the developing phenotype which rolls through valleys of varying widths and depths. At some points a minor deflection can send the phenotype into a different channel of development; at other points a major deflection would be required to change the course of development because genetic canalization (represented by a narrow, deep valley) is very strong.

Lesser canalization means greater modifiability. Greater canalization

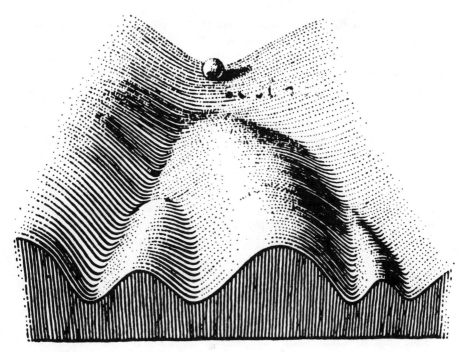

Fig. 5. Waddington's epigenetic landscape: a model of genetic canalization in development. (From Waddington 1957.)

means that a large array of environmental events may have little or no effect on the development of the phenotype. It has been suggested (Wilson 1972) that infant intellectual development has strong canalization, whereas later intelligence may be more easily modified. Similarly, infant babbling seems to be strongly canalized since even congenitally deaf infants babble (Lenneberg 1967).

The Concept of Expression

Phenotypic intelligence is an outcome of the developmental process by which genes were expressed in environments from the cellular to the fetal to the postnatal stages of growth.

The concept of *expression* is extremely important in developmental genetics. For example, the same genes that produce clinical diabetes in some people do not achieve clinical expression in others due to the modifying effects of environments and other genes during development. A common-sense example can be found in physical growth. The expression of height depends on a variety of growth hormones, protein and caloric intake, and many other regulatory mechanisms in growth. Final stature may be limited by many diseases, and by nutritional and biochemical deficiencies that affect the expression of the genotype.

Another polygenic characteristic, skin color, is not fully expressed when a single recessive locus for albinism blocks melanin production, even though normal genes for skin color are present. The expression of skin color is also affected by the amount of sunlight received shortly before the time of measurement. The same genotype will generally be expressed as a lighter phenotype as distance from the equator increases. It cannot be said, however, that skin color is any less genetically *determined* at greater, than at less, distances from the tropical sun. It is simply that many genotypes for skin color are less fully expressed in colder climates. Some genotypes, however, achieve pale phenotypes in most locations and, therefore, can be said to have a limited range of reaction.

The genotypic expression of intellectual development apparently works the same way, under better and worse environmental conditions. Intelligence can be said to be genetically determined, as is skin color, but the phenotypes achieved by the same genotype can vary, depending upon important features of the environment that affect the expression of the genotype.

One important feature of the child's environment is his or her mother. Maternal effects have been shown to affect the expression of familial mental retardation. Children reared by their retarded mothers but with normal IQ fathers have two and one-half times the rate of retardation found among children with equally retarded fathers and normal IQ mothers (Reed and Reed 1965). Whether the maternal effect is entirely postnatal can only be discovered through large studies of adopted children with a retarded natural parent.

Willerman's recent study of maternal effects (1972) shows that college students whose mothers are more highly educated than their fathers have higher aptitude scores than those whose fathers are more highly educated than their mothers, even though the socioeconomic status of the latter significantly exceeds the former. One is tempted to conclude that mothers have a greater effect on children's intellectual development in this society because they spend far greater amounts of time with children than do most fathers. Maternal effects on the development of IQ may influence the expression of genotypes by setting the intellectual level of the environment.

The Range of Reaction: A Developmental Model

The expression of the genotype in the phenotype can be shown in an adaptation of the *reaction range* model (fig. 6). The concept of reaction range refers to the quantitatively different phenotypes that can develop

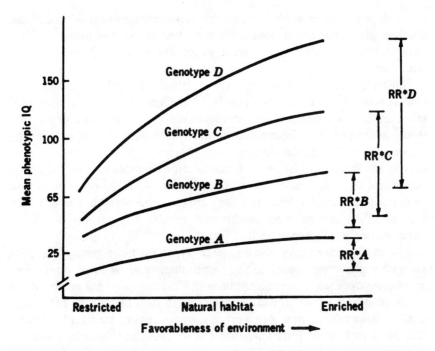

Fig. 6. The intellectual reaction ranges of several genotypes in more and less favorable environments. The phenotypic range of each genotype is indicated by RR. Genotype A, which achieves a very low phenotypic IQ under excellent conditions, is not part of the normal IQ range. The other curves represent genotypically unique responses to the changing favorableness of the environment. (From Gottesman 1963.)

from the same genotype under varying environmental conditions (Gottesman 1963).

The potential for development into any one of a number of phenotypes is called the *genomic repertoire* (Ginsburg and Laughlin 1971). A given genotype has only those degrees of freedom that are inherent in its genes. The actual phenotype that develops is achieved through genotypic expression in a set of environments over the entire span of development.

Every genotype has a unique range of reaction to a given set of environmental conditions, which accounts for the broad range of intellectual differences among children in the same family. It is not correct, however, to say that heredity sets the limits on development while environment determines the extent of development. Both are half-truths because they ignore the constant transaction between genotype and environment during development.

Under different environmental conditions the same genotype can become different phenotypes; under the same environmental conditions, different genotypes can become different phenotypes; and under uniform environmental conditions, different genotypes may result in the same phenotype.

Ginsburg and his colleagues (1966, 1968, 1971) have summarized evidence on the genomic repertoires of a number of inbred strains of mice. Since each strain is essentially made up of identical genotypes, strain differences can be treated as individual human differences. The important developmental findings are (1) genotype-environment inter-actions are frequent, (2) environmental circumstances that will alter the behavioral development of one strain will have no effect on another and an opposite effect on a third, (3) the period during development at which a given effect can be most readily induced by a given environmental circumstance is genotype-specific.

Just as there are many possible phenotypes for most genotypes, there are many genotypic routes to the same phenotype. A large number of genetic-environmental combinations will yield the same IQ score. Much of the genotypic variation within species is, in fact, masked by the strong canalization of development in a given range of environments. Phenotypes that apparently have little variation can, in fact, be shown in other en-vironments to be based on different genotypes, whose differences were simply not expressed in the first set of environments (Thiessen 1972b).

There are no general laws of reaction range that can predict a priori the development of individuals. Only for certain abnormal genotypes can the reaction range be roughly specified under existing environments. As Hirsch (1971, p. 94) has said,

The more varied the conditions, the more diverse might be the phenotypes developed from any one genotype. Of course, different genotypes should not be expected to have the same norm of reaction; unfortunately, psy-cology's attention was diverted from appreciating this basic fact of biology by half a century of misguided environmentalism. Just as we see that, except for monozygotes, no two human faces are alike, so we must expect norms of reaction to show genotypic uniqueness. . . . Extreme environmentalists were wrong to hope that one law or set of laws described universal features of modifiability. Extreme hereditarians were wrong to ignore the norm of reaction.

Identical twins reared apart provide the best human data on reaction ranges in intelligence. Since monozygotic twins have the same genotype, all differences between co-twins must arise from environmental sources beginning at the first cell division and including pre- and postnatal events. If monozygotic twins are separated at birth into different families, how different can they become in intellectual level?

Jensen (1971a) combined the results of four published studies on a total of 122 MZ pairs separated in early childhood and reared apart.

TABLE 1.   STATISTICS ON IQs OF MZ TWINS REARED APART

Study	N (Pairs)	Mean IQ	SD	$/\overline{d}/$	$SD_{/\overline{d}/}$	r_t	r_d
Burt	53	97.7	14.8	5.96	4.44	.88	.88
Shields	38	93.0	13.4	6.72	5.80	.78	.84
Newman et al.	19	95.7	13.0	8.21	6.65	.67	.76
Juel-Nielsen	12	106.8	9.0	6.46	3.22	.68	.86
Combined	122	96.8	14.2	6.60	5.20	.82	.85

SOURCE: Jensen 1971a.

The average absolute difference ($/\overline{d}/$) in IQ scores between MZ twins reared apart is about 6.5 points; between MZ twins reared together it is about 5 points; and between dizygotic twins reared together the difference is about 11 IQ points. Rearing in different families per se does not increase the average IQ differences between MZ twins by very much and certainly not to the level obtained from DZ twins reared together.

How different were the families in which co-twins were reared? This question has been answered anecdotally from the case histories of the separated twins. In general, between-family differences were within the average range of the population sampled, from working to upper-middle-class environments. The largest IQ differences between separated twins were associated with the largest life history differences, but there is no linear correlation between the phenotypic differences of co-twins and social class differences of the adoptive families.

Gottesman (1968) has estimated that the IQ reaction range under natural habitat conditions is about ± 12 points for average genotypes. Similarly, DeFries (1971) estimated that the IQ scores of children presently reared by parents with IQs of 80 could be raised by 25 points if they were reared under the best .01 percent of conditions. Thus, the reaction range of most genotypes probably falls in the ± 10 to 12 point range depending upon rearing conditions of low to high average values.

Very poor environments can radically lower IQ scores (Skeels 1966). Intellectually superior environments, such as those provided in intensive tutoring programs (Heber 1969) and kibbutzim (Smilansky, personal communication), may be able to radically raise IQ scores, at least for disadvantaged children. New interventions are conceivable. If the gene-action pathways to normal intellectual development were known, intervention would probably be possible at a biochemical level, especially for many forms of familial retardation, which do not now respond well to educational treatment.

Another line of evidence on reaction range comes from studies of adopted children (Burks 1928; Skodak and Skeels 1949). While a great deal of attention has been given to the greater *correlation* between adopted children's IQ and their natural parents' intellectual level, an equally important fact is the substantially higher mean of the adopted children's IQ scores compared to their natural mothers' average IQs. The children might well have had IQs in the low 90s (by regression toward the mean) instead of the average of 106 which was actually obtained (Skodak and Skeels 1949). Similarly, Burks' (1928) and Leahy's (1935) studies found the average IQs of adopted children well above the population mean. Burks' sample of 214 adopted children averaged IQ 107.4, and Leahy's 194 children averaged 110.5. Adopted children are unlikely to be retarded because they are a selected group, but it is also true that the greater environmental enrichment provided by the adoptive parents, in comparison to that given by the natural parents, acted on the reaction range of each genotype to produce higher than expected phenotypes for IQ. Further, the adopted children's IQ scores were correlated ($r \simeq .20$ to .30) with the adoptive families' socioeconomic characteristics, even though adoptive families constitute an attenuated sample of the SES range.

Based on the data from separated monozygotic twins and adopted children, a reasonable reaction range model for most genotypes (not severely retarded or extremely gifted) would include phenotypes in a 25-point IQ range. This figure is based only on currently existing environments, not on innovations that could shift the whole distribution of IQ scores to an unknown degree.

Intelligence as Species-Specific Development

The evolution of human intelligence is often presented in a phylogenetic frame with appropriate accounts of the increasing brain capacities of our progenitors. The crucial interplay of behavioral adaptation and morphological changes in the cortex have been well reviewed (Alland 1967; Washburn and Howells 1960): culture, language, and intelligence evolved together as genetic, species-specific characteristics.

The intellectual genotypes of man have changed through natural selection, i.e., the differential reproductive rate of better-adapted members of the species. Selection acts at a phenotypic level, but changes in the genotype are necessary for a continuation of the new adaptation.

It is not simply the final, adult phenotype that is the subject of selection. Selection can act at all points in a developmental sequence. In the human case, selection has acted to extend infancy and to increase the role of cultural learning in man's ontogeny (Dobzhansky 1962; La Barre 1965).

The ontogenesis of intelligence should be seen as an evolved pattern of development. The modal sequence of intellectual stages described extensively by Piaget and his colleagues (see Flavell 1963, 1970) can be understood as the development of normal human genotypes under a range of average to superior human environments. The modal progression from sensorimotor to preoperational, concrete, and perhaps formal operational stages is found in every normal member of the species who is exposed to a natural human environment. It is, of course, the *form* of the behavior, not the *content,* that is the evolved pattern of development.

Cross-cultural studies on conservation and related concepts find an invariant order for the major stages of intellectual development but not necessarily for their timing (Cole et al. 1972; deLacey 1970, 1971*a,* 1971*b;* DeLemos 1969; Hyde 1969; Price-Williams 1961; Prince (1968). The timing is doubtless influenced by the cultural milieux. The universality of cognitive developmental stages led Price-Williams (1961) to conclude, "As these children have had no formal instruction in abstract numbers, there is much to be said for the neuro-physiological interpretation for dealing with such concepts" (p. 303).

The normal human genotype is programmed for this sequence of development, having been adapted under rearing conditions of a family, peers, and a larger social group. The evolution of prolonged brain development in postnatal life and a prolonged learning period is as much a part of species history as is the evolution of the opposable thumb.

The gene-action pathways to the normal stages of intellectual development are not known. But one can reason backwards from observed development to genotype and be fairly sure that this regular species-specific progression in cognitive development has CNS representation and that CNS development is genetically programmed through enzymatic, hormonal, and other regulatory mechanisms.

"Much behavior that we see may be controlled by regulatory genes open to processes of canalization, early and later experiences, and natural selection" (Thiessen 1972*b,* p. 124). For intellectual development this means that, as the CNS matures, previously irrelevant aspects of the environment become relevant, learning occurs, and the CNS develops. The constant transaction between organismic development and environmental features produces intellectual, behavioral development.

Inbreeding Effects

One test for the effects of genes on intellectual development is the study of inbreeding. If some gene combinations are important for the development of high IQ, and others for low IQ, then IQ ought to be a sensitive measure of the generally depressing effects of inbreeding. It is. When two related individuals mate, their offspring have an increased chance of receiving at many loci the same genes twice from the same ancestor. They are homozygous at these loci. Homozygocity at many loci increases the probability that some deleterious recessive characteristics will be expressed in the offspring. In some cases, however, particularly desirable combinations may result from homozygous genes at some loci, which explains the frequent use of brother-sister and parent-offspring matings by breeders of domestic animals. But the cost of inbreeding is increased fetal mortality, congenital defects, and depressed physical and intellectual growth for other offspring.

An extreme form of inbreeding in man is found in incestuous matings between brothers and sisters and between parents and their children. Carter (1967) reported the outcome of thirteen such unions: three of the children had died of rare recessive diseases, one was severely retarded, and four more had IQ scores between 59 and 76. The remaining five had IQs in the normal range. A second study turned up eighteen offspring of incestuous matings (Adams, Davidson, and Cornell 1967; Adams and Neel 1967). Three of the eighteen children had died in infancy, two were severely retarded, three had IQ scores between 60 and 70, and ten fell in the normal range of intelligence-test scores. Six of the ten children with normal IQs ranged from 110 to 119, which supports the notion that inbreeding does not always have bad to disastrous outcomes. The fact that eight of the eighteen children had serious mental impairments, however, demonstrates the dangers of severe inbreeding.

Less severe forms of inbreeding include the cousin marriages and uncle-niece unions that are common in some parts of the world. Three studies of cousin marriages have shown depression of IQ scores to be the most consistent outcome for offspring. Böök (1957) reported a mental retardation rate of 4.6 percent for offspring of cousin marriages, compared to 1.3 percent for the controls. Cohen and his colleagues (1963) found depression of all subtest scores on the WAIS for the offspring of cousin marriages, compared to matched controls.

In the largest study to date, Schull and Neel (1965) used the Japanese form of the WISC to evaluate 865 children of cousin marriages (first cousins, first cousins once removed, and second cousins) and 989 children of unrelated parents. The effects of socioeconomic class, age, and inbreeding were evaluated in a multivariate analysis. Inbreeding was found to depress IQ scores independent of socioeconomic status and the age of the child. Vandenberg (1971) has arranged the Japanese data to express inbreeding depression as a percentage of the mean of non-inbred children for each subtest in the WISC, as shown in table 2.

Since the IQ mean of the outbred group (children of unrelated parents) is about 100, the inbred children averaged only about IQ 93 on

TABLE 2.   EFFECT ON CONSANGUINITY ON
WISC IQ SCORES

| | Depression as percent of outbred mean | |
	Boys	Girls
Information	8.1	8.5
Comprehension	6.0	6.1
Arithmetic	5.0	5.1
Similarities	9.7	10.2
Vocabulary	11.2	11.7
Picture completion	5.6	6.2
Picture arrangement	9.3	9.5
Block design	5.3	5.4
Object assembly	5.8	6.3
Coding	4.3	4.6
Mazes	5.3	5.4
Verbal score	8.0	8.0
Performance score	5.1	5.1
Total IQ	7.0	7.1

SOURCE: Vandenberg 1971, based on Schull and Neel 1965.

the basis of inbreeding alone. Increased fetal mortality and congenital defects, as expected, have also been reported for the offspring of cousin marriages (Böök 1957).

A Polygenic Model of Intelligence

Intelligence, like many human characteristics that vary quantitatively among people, is probably determined by many genes acting together with the environment to produce the phenotype. Polygenic systems are assumed to be composed of many genes, each of which adds a little to the development of the trait. There may also be a few major genes, or ones with larger effects, that substantially reduce or increase intellectual levels beyond the additive effects of the polygenes (Bock and Kolakowski 1973; Jinks and Fulker 1970).

There are no genes specifically for behavior; all genes act at a more molecular level on the development and maintenance of structures that have consequences for behavior. Genes have pleiotropic (many) effects, and genes at one locus act on the expression of genes at other loci (epistasis). No one knows how many genes affect the development of intelligent behavior or how many pleiotropic and epistatic effects there are within the polygenic system.

The fact that at least twenty genes (Gottesman 1963) or as many as several hundred (Dewey et al. 1965; Wall 1967) are involved in intelligence, makes the inheritance of intelligence a quantitative matter. Li (1971) has presented a simple but comprehensive polygenic model for intelligence which explains parent-child regression, variability within families, and the other phenomena observed for phenotypic IQ. The most important single consequence of the genetic model is that, for any given class of parents, their offspring will be scattered in various classes; conversely, for any given class of offspring, their parents will have come from various classes. This effect is shown in figure 7.

Parents at the high and low *extremes* of the distribution contribute offspring primarily to the upper or the lower *halves* of the distributions, while

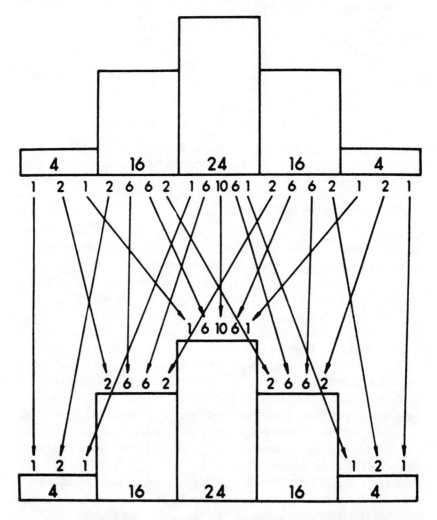

Fig. 7. The distributions of offspring and parents in five phenotypic classes in a random mating population. (From C. C. Li, in R. Cancro, ed., *Intelligence: Genetic and Environmental Influences* [Grune and Stratton 1971]. Used by permission.)

parents in the middle of the distribution contribute children to all classes in the distribution. On the average, the children will have less extreme scores than their parents, but the total distribution of phenotypic IQ will remain relatively constant from one generation to another (unless selective forces intervene).

To the redistribution of offspring from parental to offspring classes in each generation, Li adds the Markov property of populations: "The properties of an individual depend upon the state (in this case, genotype) in which he finds himself and not upon the state from which he is derived. A state is a state; it has no memory" (Li 1971, p. 173).

TABLE 3. TRANSITIONAL PROBABILITIES FROM ANCESTOR TO DESCENDANT

State of ancestor	State of descendant				
	0	1	2	3	4
T					
0	.2500	.5000	.2500	0	0
1	.1250	.3750	.3750	.1250	0
2	.0417	.2500	.4167	.2500	.0417
3	0	.1250	.3750	.3750	.1250
4	0	0	.2500	.5000	.2500
T^2					
0	.1354	.3750	.3542	.1250	.0104
1	.0937	.3125	.3750	.1875	.0312
2	.0590	.2500	.3819	.2500	.0590
3	.0312	.1875	.3750	.3125	.0937
4	.0104	.1250	.3542	.3750	.1354
T^4					
0	.0784	.2812	.3744	.2187	.0472
1	.0703	.2656	.3750	.2344	.0547
2	.0624	.2500	.3752	.2500	.0624
3	.0547	.2344	.3750	.2656	.0703
4	.0472	.2187	.3744	.2812	.0784
T^8					
0	.0635	.2520	.3750	.2480	.0615
1	.0603	.2510	.3750	.2490	.0620
2	.0625	.2500	.3750	.2500	.0625
3	.0620	.2490	.3750	.2510	.0630
4	.0615	.2480	.3750	.2520	.0635

SOURCE: Li 1971.

Under conditions of random mating, successive generations form a Markov chain of probabilities (T, T^2, T^4, T^8) from parent state to offspring state. In table 3, the ancestors and descendants are divided into five classes (0–4). In the case of intelligence, the classes would correspond to IQ groups from retarded to very superior levels. Parents of class 0 (retarded) have children in the T generation, whose IQs are distributed in classes 0, 1, and 2 but not 3 or 4. Parents of class 4 have children distributed in classes 2, 3, and 4 but not 0 or 1. In the next generation (T^2), however, the grandchildren of class 0 ancestors are distributed in all classes, as are the grandchildren of class 4 ancestors, albeit in unequal proportions. By the eighth generation (T^8), the descendants of classes 0 and 4 are distributed about equally in all five classes.

Environmentalists sometimes misunderstand the implications of population genetics, thinking that heredity would imply "like class begets like class." Probably the opposite is true. Only very strong social and environmental forces can perpetrate an artificial class; heredity does not (Li 1971, p. 172).

Whether present-day family groups and social classes are entirely artificial groups is debatable (Herrnstein 1971) because one assumption of Li's model is random mating, which is violated by an IQ correlation of about .40 between parents. The topic of assortative mating will be taken up in the next section.

Even under conditions of high assortative mating, however, there is considerable regression of offspring scores toward the population mean and considerable IQ variation among the offspring of the same parents. Burt's (1961) classic study of the IQ scores of some forty thousand adults and their children illustrates the polygenic system in IQ very nicely.[1] Tables 4 and 5 give his results. When the fathers are grouped by occupational status, their mean IQs range from 140 in the highest professional groups to 85 in the unskilled occupations. Their children's IQ scores, however, varied from only 121 to 93 over the same social class range, thereby illustrating the regression effect predicted from a polygenic model of IQ.

The children had considerably more varied IQ scores within each occupational class than had their fathers ($\sigma = 14$ and 9.6 respectively), as Li (1971) has described. If one followed a single family line through several generations, one would find great variation in IQ scores and occupational achievements. It would be impossible to predict exactly a grandchild's score from the grandparents' scores, and vice versa.

The polygenic nature of familial retardation was explored by Roberts (1952) using sibling comparisons. Institutionalized retardates were divided into two groups of severely retarded and less severely retarded on the basis of IQ scores. In each group correlations were then calculated between the IQ scores of the retardates and their siblings. The IQ scores of severely retarded children (IQ < 50) showed no correlation at all with

---

[1] It is with some retrospective embarrassment that this laudatory citation of Burt's study is reprinted. Since 1977, serious doubts have been cast upon the reliability of Burt's reports and even on the existence of these data. If I were to write the chapter again in 1981, I would omit reference to Burt's study and include our own findings on social-class variation that appear in Section III of this book.

TABLE 4. DISTRIBUTION OF INTELLIGENCE ACCORDING TO OCCUPATIONAL CLASS: ADULTS

IQ	Professional Higher I	Professional Lower II	Clerical III	Skilled IV	Semi-skilled V	Un-skilled VI	Total
50–60						1	1
60–70					5	18	23
70–80				2	15	52	69
80–90			1	11	31	117	160
90–100			8	51	135	53	247
100–110			16	101	120	11	248
110–120		2	56	78	17	9	162
120–130		13	38	14	2		67
130–40	2	15	3	1			21
140+	1	1					2
Total	3	31	122	258	325	261	1000
Mean IQ	139.7	130.6	115.9	108.2	97.8	84.9	100

SOURCE: Burt 1961.
N = 40,000, converted to a base of 1,000.

TABLE 5. DISTRIBUTION OF INTELLIGENCE OF CHILDREN ACCORDING TO FATHER'S OCCUPATIONAL CLASS

IQ	Professional Higher I	Professional Lower II	Clerical III	Skilled IV	Semi-skilled V	Un-skilled VI	Total
50–60					1	1	2
60–70				1	6	15	22
70–80			3	12	23	32	70
80–90		1	8	33	55	62	159
90–100		2	21	53	99	75	250
100–110	1	6	31	70	85	54	247
110–120		12	35	59	38	16	160
120–130	1	8	18	22	13	6	68
130–140	1	2	6	7	5		21
140+				1			1
Total	3	31	122	258	325	261	1000
Mean IQ	120.8	114.7	107.8	104.6	98.9	92.6	100

SOURCE: Burt 1961.
N = 40,000, converted to a base of 1,000.

those of their siblings, whose average IQ was 100. The IQ scores of the less severe retardates, however, correlated about .50 with those of their siblings, whose scores averaged only 85. The distribution of the siblings' IQ scores is shown in figure 8.

These data support the important distinction between single-gene and chromosomal anomalies, which produce severe retardation in a few children but which leave most sibs completely unaffected, and polygenic retardation, which may occur in various degrees of severity in other members of the same family.

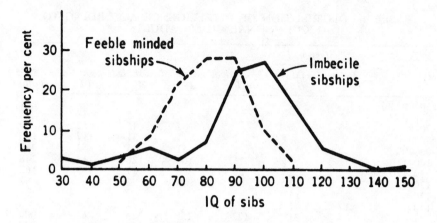

Fig. 8. Frequency distributions of the IQs of siblings of severe (imbecile) and less severe (feebleminded) retardates. (From Roberts 1952.)

Summary

In this section the basic genetic mechanisms have been reviewed. From the current state of knowledge in this field, it can be concluded that:

1. The role of genes in human behavioral development is poorly understood at present. A speculative construction of gene effects on development emphasized the mutual regulation of genes and environments acting in systems from cellular to behavioral levels.

2. The concepts of canalization, gene expression, and range of reaction are important in understanding the regulation of genotype-to-phenotype development. There is no one-to-one correspondence between genotypes and behavioral phenotypes; rather, there is a complex set of transactions between genotypic, physiological, and environmental factors that leads to the development of one of many possible phenotypes.

3. A polygenic model of intelligence accounts for the distribution of IQ values in a population, for the regression from parent to offspring IQ, and for the effects of inbreeding. Although there may be a few major genes that affect intellectual development, a multigene model fits the data very well.

4. Normal intellectual development can be seen as a species-specific, evolved pattern of development. The stage-sequence model described by Piaget and others may be modal for the species. All normal members of the human group with environments in the normal range show the same progressive development of intelligence.

VARIATION IN THE DEVELOPMENT OF INTELLIGENCE

The statement that variability in a given trait depends, in part, upon genetic variation implies necessarily that genetic variation contributed to differences *in the development of that trait*. McClearn (1970, p. 65) summarized the point:

In a very real sense it is the case that any demonstrated genetic control over an adult characteristic is, at the same time, an implication of genetic control over the developmental processes that culminated in that characteristic. Research aimed explicitly at studying the genetic control of behavioral development unfortunately has been rare, particularly with respect to man.

Since Mendelian models of genetics have not yet been fitted to the complex polygenic system of normal human intelligence, the only substantial literature to review concerns the determinants of *variation* of intelligence. Studies of environmental differences within and between families, social class, and ethnic groups try to account for portions of the variance in IQ scores, just as studies of genetic differences do. There is sometimes great confusion of meaning when authors of studies in *variation* call their variables *determinants* of intelligence. Certainly, some of the genotypic differences between people are also important determinants of intellectual development, but there must be many genes that produce little or no variation which are also important determinants of intelligence.

An example of a genetic characteristic that shows little genetic variation is human birth-weight (Morton 1955). Almost 90 percent of the variation in birth-weight does *not* depend on genotypic differences among fetuses. Most of the variation is environmental in origin even though the narrow range of normal birth-weight is clearly a species-specific, genetically determined characteristic.

It is a principle of genetic variation that characteristics particularly close to reproductive fitness and viability are allowed little variability within the species. Variants that are less fit or viable are selected out rapidly. Thus, birth-weight has a narrow range of largely nonheritable variation.

It is likely that many gene loci for normal intellectual development also have little polygenic variability within the species and that a minority of regulatory genes control most of the individual variation in the normal range (Thiessen 1972*b*).

Given some genetic and environmental variation, individual differences in phenotypic intelligence can be analyzed into genetic and environmental components of variance by appropriatic behavior-genetic methods. Most of the variation that has been studied has been individual variation *within* a population or breeding group. There is strong interest, however, in analyzing the phenotypic variations in IQ *between* populations (Jensen, 1973). The latter requires quite different assumptions: i.e., about distributions and values of genotypes and environments within and between different populations. In the first part of this section, variation within a population will be considered, followed by between-group comparisons.

Individual Variation within a Population

The relative contributions of genetic and environmental differences to phenotypic diversity within a population depend upon six major parameters: (1) range of genotypes; (2) range of environments; (3) favorableness of genotypes; (4) favorableness of environments; (5) covariance of genotypes and environments; (6) interactions of genotypes and environments.

The range of genotypes and environments can independently and together affect the total variance of a behavioral, polygenic trait in a population. The mean favorableness of genotypes and environments can independently and together affect the mean values of phenotypes.

Two separate problems are involved in understanding the effects of mean favorableness and ranges of genotypes in a population: gene frequencies, and the distribution of genes among the genotypes. Gene frequencies are affected by two principal processes: differential reproduction, or *natural selection,* and *sampling errors.* Genotype frequencies are affected by *assortative mating.* Two populations (or two generations of the same population) may have equal gene frequencies but different genotype frequencies if assortative mating for a behavioral trait is greater in one population than the other.

1. *Genotypic range and favorableness.* a. Natural selection. Changing environmental conditions, such as the introduction of more complex technology, may affect the rate of reproduction in different segments of the IQ distribution in a generation. We know, for example, that severely mentally retarded persons in the contemporary white populations of Europe and the United States do not reproduce as frequently as those who can hold jobs and maintain independent adult lives (Bajema 1968; Higgins, Reed, and Reed 1962). Severe retardation renders one less likely to be chosen as a mate and less likely to produce progeny for the next generation.

If one segment of the phenotypic IQ range has been strongly and consistently selected against, as severely mentally retarded persons are in contemporary industrial populations, then the range and favorableness of the total gene distribution will be slowly changed. If, in another population, high phenotypic IQ were disadvantageous for mate selection and reproduction, then the genic distribution would be reduced at that end. It is probably true that systematic selection against high phenotypic IQ does not occur frequently. In any case, selection against polygenic characteristics is probably very slow (Stern 1960), especially when many gene loci are involved.

b. Sampling. Gene frequencies can also be affected by genetic drift, a random sampling error. Not every allele at every gene locus is equally sampled in every generation through reproduction. Rare genes, especially, may disappear through random failure to be passed on to the next generation, and the frequencies of other alleles may be randomly increased or decreased from generation to generation.

A special case of restriction in genic range is nonrandom sampling from a larger gene pool in the formation of a smaller breeding group. If, for example, an above-median sample from the IQ group migrated to a distant locale and bred primarily among themselves, the gene frequencies within the migrant group might vary considerably from those of the nonmigrant group, all other things being equal.

c. Assortative mating. The distribution of genes in genotypic classes within a population can vary because of assortative mating. To the extent that "likes" marry "likes," genetic variability is decreased within families and increased between families. At the present time, within the U.S. white population, the assortative mating correlation for parental IQ is approximately .40, which increases the sibling correlation for phenotypic IQ to about .55 instead of the .50 expected, since they share, on the average, one-half of their genes in common (Jensen 1968, 1969). Assortative mating for IQ also increases the standard deviation of IQ scores within the total (white) population by increasing the frequency of extremely high and extremely low genotypes for phenotypic IQ. On a random mating basis, the probability of producing extreme genotypes is greatly reduced because extreme parental genotypes are unlikely to find each other by chance. The sheer frequency of middle-range genotypes makes an average mate the most likely random choice of an extreme genotype for both high or low IQ.

Since children's IQ values are distributed around the mean parental value (with some regression toward the population mean), the offspring of such matings will tend to be closer to the population mean than offspring of extreme parental combinations. The phenotypic distribution under conditions of random mating will tend to have a leptokurtic shape with a large modal class and low total variance.

2. *Environmental range and favorableness.* The range of environments within a population can also affect phenotypic variability. Uniform environments can restrict phenotypic diversity by eliminating a major source of variation. Since environments can be observed and manipulated, there are many studies on infrahuman populations to demonstrate the restriction of variability through uniform environments (Manosevitz, Lindzey, and Thiessen 1969).

Far more important, however, for the present discussion is the favorableness dimension of the environment. Environments which do not support the development of a trait can greatly alter the mean value of the trait. If environments in the unfavorable range are common to all or most members of a population, then the phenotypic variance of the population can be slightly reduced while the mean can be drastically lowered.

The most likely effects of very suppressive environments are that they lower the mean of the population, decrease phenotypic variability, and consequently reduce the correlation between genotype and phenotype (Henderson 1970; Scarr-Salapatek 1971b). A contrast can be made between uniform environments which support the development of a particular behavior and suppressive environments which may also be uniform but not supportive of optimal development (Nichols 1970). Uniform environments of good quality may reduce variability and raise the mean of the population.

The ranges of genotypes and environments and the favorableness of the environment control a large portion of the total phenotypic variance in IQ. The two additional factors—covariance and interaction—are probably less important (Jinks and Fulker 1970), at least within the white North American and European populations.

3. *Covariation.* Covariance between genotypes and environments is expressed as a correlation between certain genotypic characteristics and certain environmental features which affect phenotypic outcome: e.g., the covariance between the IQs of children of bright parents, which is likely to be higher than average, and the educationally advantaged environment offered by those same parents to their bright children. Retarded parents, on the other hand, may have less bright children under any environmental circumstances but also may supply those children with educationally deprived environments. Covariation between genotype and environment may also depend upon the genotype and the kind of response it evokes from the environment. If bright children receive continual reward for their educationally superior performance, while duller children receive fewer rewards, environmental rewards can be said to covary with IQ. The fact that the giving of rewards in this example depends upon the genotype of the child in a significant way does not remove covariance from the environmental side of the equation.

4. *Interaction.* Covariance is sometimes confused with interaction but they are quite different terms. When psychologists speak of genetic-environment interaction, they are usually referring to the reciprocal relationship that exists between an organism and its surroundings. The organism brings to the situation a set of characteristics that affects the environment, which in turn affects the further development of the organism, and vice versa. This is not what quantitative geneticists mean by interaction. A better term for the psychologists would be "transaction" between orga-

nism and environment because the statistical term "interaction" refers to the *differential* effects of various òrganism-environment transactions on development.

Behavioral geneticists, whose experimental work is primarily with mouse strains and drosophila, often find genotype-environmental interactions of considerable importance. The differential response of two or more genotypes or two or more environments is interaction. In general, m genotypes in n environments yield $\dfrac{(mn)!}{m!n!}$ types of interaction; for example, ten genotypes in ten environments can generate 10^{144} kinds of interaction (Hirsch 1971). In studies of animal learning, where both genotypes and environmental conditions can be manipulated, so-called maze-dull rats who were bred for poor performance in Tryon's mazes were shown to perform as well as so-called maze-bright rats when given enriched environments (Cooper and Zubec 1958) and when given distributed rather than massed practice (McGaugh, Jennings, and Thompson 1962). The interaction of learning conditions with genotypes is obvious in figure 9.

Studies of genotype-environment interaction in human populations are quite limited. Biometrical methods that include an analysis for interaction have failed to show any substantial variance attributable to nonlinear effects on human intelligence (Jinks and Fulker 1970; Jensen 1973). This is not to say that genotype-environment interaction may not account for some portion of the variance in IQ scores in other populations or in other segments of white populations (e.g., the disadvantaged).

5. *Total phenotypic variance.* Jensen (1969) has offered an array of variance terms that combine to produce total phenotypic variance in studies of human characteristics.

$$V_p = [(V_g + V_{AM}) + V_D + V_i] + [V_E + 2\,\mathrm{Cov}_{HE} + V_I + V_e]$$

where: V_p = phenotypic variance in the population
        V_g = genic (or additive) variance
        V_{AM} = variance due to assortative mating, $V_{AM} = 0$ under random mating
        V_D = dominance deviation variance
        V_i = epistatis (interaction among genes at two or more loci)
        V_E = environmental variance
        Cov_{HE} = covariance of heredity and environment
        V_I = true statistical interaction of genetic and environmental factors
        V_e = error of measurement (unreliability)

The first bracket contains the terms usually grouped under total genetic

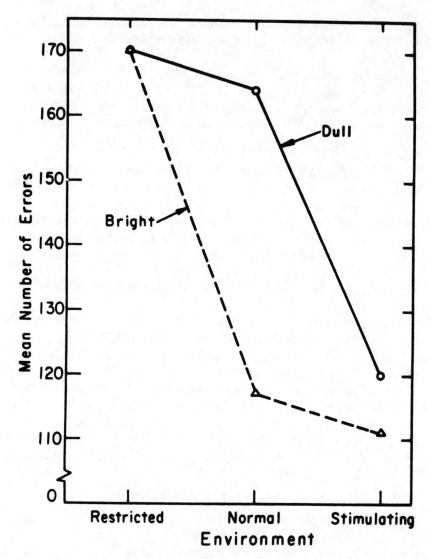

Fig. 9. Error scores in maze learning by Tryon "bright" and "dull" rats reared in restricted, average, and stimulating environments. (From Cooper and Zubek 1958.)

variance, the second those usually grouped as total environmental variance. The estimation of genetic variance leads to estimates of heritability.

6. Heritability is a summary statement of the proportion of the total phenotypic variance that is due to additive genetic variance (narrow heritability) or to total genetic variance (broad heritability). Heritability (h^2) is a *population statistic,* not a property of a trait (Fuller and Thompson 1960). Estimates of h^2 vary from population to population as genetic

variance varies as a proportion of the total variance. (For the calculation of various kinds of heritability estimates see Falconer 1960).

TABLE 6. CORRELATIONS FOR INTELLECTUAL ABILITY: OBTAINED AND THEORETICAL VALUES

Correlations Between	Number of Studies	Obtained Median r^a	Theoretical Value[b]	Theoretical Value[c]
Unrelated Persons				
Children reared apart	4	−.01	.00	.00
Foster parent and child	3	+.20	.00	.00
Children reared together	5	+.24	.00	.00
Collaterals				
Second cousins	1	+.16	+ .14	+ .063
First cousins	3	+.26	+ .18	+ .125
Uncle (or aunt) and nephew (or niece)	1	+.34	+ .31	+ .25
Siblings, reared apart	3	+.47	+ .52	+ .50
Siblings, reared together	36	+.55	+ .52	+ .50
Dizygotic twins, different sex	9	+.49	+ .50	+ .50
Dizygotic twins, same sex	11	+.56	+ .54	+ .50
Monozygotic twins, reared apart	4	+.75	+1.00	+1.00
Monozygotic twins, reared together	14	+.87	+1.00	+1.00
Direct Line				
Grandparent and grandchild	3	+.27	+ .31	+ .25
Parent (as adult) and child	13	+.50	+ .49	+ .50
Parent (as child) and child	1	+.56	+ .49	+ .50

SOURCE: Jensen 1969, adapted from Burt 1961.
[a] Correlations not corrected for attenuation (unreliability).
[b] Assuming assortative mating and partial dominance.
[c] Assuming random mating and only additive genes, i.e., the simplest possible polygenic model.

The six parameters of individual variation within a population noted at the beginning of this section are the major contributors to the total phenotypic variance in any population. The proportions of genetic variance (additive, assortative mating, dominance, and epistasis) and environmental variance (biological-social, covariance, interaction) may well vary from one population to another depending upon the ranges and favorableness of the two sets of variables, their covariances and interactions. The variance terms and heritability statistics are frequently used in family studies to estimate the relative importance of genetic and environmental differences to account for phenotypic IQ differences.

7. *Family studies of IQ variation.* A number of excellent reviews of the behavior genetic literature on intelligence have appeared in the last five or six years.[2] The data shown in table 6 are representative of results from family studies.

[2] Readers who wish to pursue the methodological and substantive issue of IQ heritability should see Lindzey et al. 1971; Hirsch 1967; Huntley 1966; Jarvik and Erlenmeyer-Kimling 1967; Jensen 1969, 1973; Vandenberg 1966, 1967, 1968, 1971; Scarr-Salapatek 1971a, 1971b; Bouchard 1972.

There is increasing similarity in IQ scores as genetic relatedness increases. Rearing together has a relatively small effect on IQ correlations, as shown in figure 10.

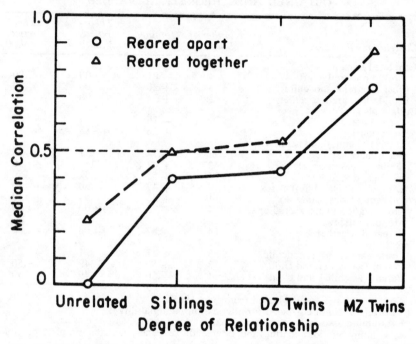

Fig. 10. Median values of all correlations reported in the literature up to 1963 for the indicated kinships. (From Jensen 1969, adapted from Erlenmeyer-Kimling and Jarvik, "Genetics and Intelligence: A Review," *Science* 142 [December 1963]: 1477–79, copyright © 1963 by the American Association for the Advancement of Science.)

When intellectual abilities are tested differentially, rather than as a summary IQ score, there emerge different heritabilities for different factors, over and above the heritability of general intelligence (Nichols 1965; Vandenberg 1965). Verbal and spatial abilities appear to be more highly heritable than other factors like numerical reasoning and memory. Multivariate analyses (see Vandenberg 1971) have shown that *separate* genetic variances are involved in spatial and verbal skills. Thus, besides general IQ, with which most research has been concerned, there are differential abilities that have still other degrees of heritability. Spatial abilities may, in fact, have a sex-related pattern of inheritance (Bock and Kolakowski, in press; Money 1968).

The research literature on genetic and environmental contributions to variation in IQ test scores is substantial. Within North American and European Caucasian populations, individual differences in IQ seem to be due more to genotypic differences than to measured environmental variation. (This may be due, in part, to failure to measure environmental differences as well as genetic differences.) Most biometrical and family studies suggest that half to three-quarters of the individual variation in the IQ arises from genotypic variation in those populations. The particular gene-action pathways and environmental determinants that create the developmental differences in IQ are unknown.

In less advantaged populations, particularly lower social-class groups, the full genotypic range may not be expressed in the distribution of their phenotypic IQ scores. Environments that limit the expression of genotypic differences can reduce phenotypic variability, lower the mean phenotypic value, and reduce the statistical contribution of the genotype to the phenotypic development (Scarr-Salapatek 1971a, 1971b).

There are many ways to produce a poor phenotype for intelligence. Neonatal starvation, prenatal rubella, extreme parental abuse, deprivation of learning opportunities are examples. Genotypic intelligence is not well expressed under these conditions. In the socially advantaged ranges of environmental variation, phenotypes may reflect more genotypic variability; in less advantaged ranges, genotypic expression may be reduced and environmental variation increased. New research on this issue will be forthcoming.

Between-group Differences

Mean differences in IQ scores between racial, ethnic, and social-class groups are too well known to be restated at any length (see Jensen 1969, 1973; Weyl 1969). Briefly, there is often found an average difference of 10 to 20 points on IQ tests between black and white samples, between lower- and upper-middle-class white samples, and between various ethnic groups, such as Irish and Jews. There is also a growing literature on population differences in cognitive developmental skills that reports similar results (Berry 1966; deLacey 1970, 1971a, 1971b; DeLemos 1969; Gaudia 1972; MacArthur 1968, 1969; Price-Williams 1961). In general, Caucasian, American Indian, Eskimo, and Oriental children are shown to have higher IQ scores and more rapid cognitive development than children of African or Australian aboriginal origin, particularly after the first two years of life (Bayley 1965; Geber 1958).

The finding of average differences between populations does not favor either a genetic or environmental explanation. Even if the heritabilities of intellectual performance *within* each of two populations have been shown to be high, there is practically no connection between within-group heritability and between-group heritability (DeFries 1971; Lewontin 1970; Scarr-Salapatek 1971a). Intelligence score differences within two populations can be related primarily to genetic differences among individuals while average differences between groups can be related primarily to environmental differences.

While most investigators prefer an environmental hypothesis to account for between-population differences (Jensen 1973), there is no a priori scientific basis for this stance (Scarr-Salapatek 1971a). Variation between populations on many characteristics like blood groups, skin color, height, physique, and so on are thought to be evolutionary adaptations to different environments. It is unlikely that any two relatively isolated populations have maintained exactly the same gene or genotype frequencies for any characteristic. This does not mean, however, that their reaction ranges for intellectual development need differ significantly, because important human qualities have tended to show convergent evolution among temporarily isolated groups (Gottesman 1968).

1. *Race and social class.* These are terms that refer to socially defined subgroups of the human population. Reproduction is more likely to occur between people in the same subgroup than between persons from different subgroups. There is no question that races are partially closed breeding groups with a great deal more mating within the group (endogamy) than mating outside of the group (exogamy). It is also true in modern times that social-class groups (groups whose members have attained a certain educational and occupational status) within races practice more endogamy than exogamy (Gottesman 1968; Kiser 1968).

Social mobility, based on IQ, from generation to generation actually helps to define social classes more sharply as rather distinct breeding groups with different average IQ levels. In older times, when social status was gratuitously ascribed because of family origin and when there was less social mobility, social-class groups were probably less distinct in their average IQ levels.

Because of social mobility in contemporary society, the IQ distribution within each social-class level tends to be reestablished in each generation of adults (Burt 1966; Herrnstein 1971). Brighter children in families at all but the top social levels tend to be upwardly mobile, whereas duller siblings at all but the bottom class level tend to be downwardly mobile (Waller 1971). Social-class groups may be thought of as endogamous primarily for IQ (as expressed in occupational and educational achievements).

The mean differences by social class in children's IQ reflect differences in both parental genotypes and rearing environments, which covary to a large extent in the development of IQ. Crucial evidence on the genetic and environmental components from adopted children is very limited, but, as mentioned before, Skodak and Skeels (1949) revealed a 20-point rise in the IQ of adopted children over that of their biological mothers.

The distribution of adopted children's IQs was even shifted beyond the values expected by regression to a mean above the average of the population, presumably by their better social environments.

Social-class groups, then, are subdivisions of the total population and represent different distributions of parental genotypes, as well as different rearing environments. There is no comparable statement that can be made about racial groups: whereas races represent different rearing environments, no statements can be made concerning different distributions of parental genotypes for IQ. Since there is no direct test possible for distributions of genotypic IQ (Thoday 1969), it is impossible to assert that such distributions for the two races are "equal" or "different."

The same six parameters of individual variation within a population describe the sources of variation between populations. The mechanisms that can produce population differences in gene and genotype frequencies are the same. The major difference, and the importance of this difference cannot be exaggerated, is that comparisons between racial populations require a set of assumptions different from comparisons between individuals and social-class groups within a population.

Only if one assumes that within the two populations the same environmental factors affect the development of intelligence in the same way, is it possible to make between-race comparisons. If one is unwilling to assume a complete identity in the distribution of environmental variables and in the ways they affect development, then between-race comparisons are not justifiable (Scarr-Salapatek 1971b). Jensen (in press) calls this reluctance to make quantitative comparisons between races "the factor X" hypothesis—one which proposes that some unknown environmental factor (like racial discrimination) affects one group and not the other or affects one group in a different way from the other (Chinese versus blacks). The reader must judge for himself which assumptions seem justified.

2. *Admixture studies.* To avoid direct comparisons between racial or ethnic groups, there is a better research strategy that uses hybrid populations: the study of admixture. Suppose that groups of children reared under comparable conditions but differing in racial admixture rates were also found to differ in mean IQ scores. Such evidence would suggest a genetic basis for at least part of the phenotypic differences between races.

Negro Americans and aboriginal Australians are examples of populations with varying degrees of Caucasian admixture that have accumulated over the several centuries. Since visible amounts of African and aboriginal ancestry cause the bearer to be classified as nonwhite, most of the persons of mixed ancestry have remained in these groups rather than in the populations of European ancestry (Reed 1969).

DeLemos (1969) presented Piagetian conservation tasks to full aboriginal and part-aboriginal children in the same mission. The part-aboriginal children had small percentages of Caucasian ancestry, most being
classified from mission records as seven-eighths aboriginal. The European ancestry was, therefore, several generations removed from the present group:

There were no apparent differences in the present environment of part-
Aboriginal and full-Aboriginal children in the Hermannsburg groups.
Part-Aborigines and full-Aborigines formed a single integrated community, and the children were brought up under the same mission conditions
and attended the same school (p. 257).

The results for several conservation tasks are presented in table 7.
Children with some Caucasian ancestry performed significantly better
than full-aboriginal children on four of the six tasks. DeLemos claims
that an environmental hypothesis cannot account for these results.

TABLE 7.   COMPARISON OF THE NUMBER OF PART-
ABORIGINAL AND FULL-ABORIGINAL CHILDREN
SHOWING CONSERVATION

Test	Full-Abor. $N = 38$	Part.-Abor. $N = 34$	X^2	p
Quantity	4	18	15.214	$< .001$
Weight	16	25	7.227	$< .01$
Volume	2	8	3.595	$.05 < p < .10$
Length	12	20	5.365	$< .05$
Area	3	10	4.225	$< .05$
Number	3	9	3.22	$.05 < p < .10$
Total	40	90	36.141	$< .001$

SOURCE: DeLemos 1969.

DeLemos's results have not been replicated in several other studies. De-
Lacey (1970, 1971a, 1971b) has studied verbal intelligence, classificatory ability, and operational thinking in aboriginal, part-aboriginal, and
white Australian children. Within each population, social-class differences
have been shown to affect scores on all measures. Between the groups,
smaller average differences were found on performance than on verbal
tasks. From two separate reports it is possible to compare full- with part-
aboriginal samples, both in schools with white children. On the Peabody
Picture Vocabulary Test (PPVT), forty full-aboriginal children from six
to twelve years of age scored an average of IQ 63.5 (S.D.=12.3). Thirteen part-aboriginal children scored an average of IQ 69.3 (S.D.=14.5).
One hundred and five low SES white children scored an average of 94.1

(S.D.=12.6). There is no question that white Australian children scored higher on verbal IQ tests in English than aboriginal children, but there was no clear difference between the part- and full-aboriginals.

For Piagetian operational tasks, deLacey (1971a) found no differences between aboriginal and white Australian children. Although the samples are small (three to ten at each age level) the data in table 8 show that increases in the percentage of children giving operational responses on classification tasks were similar in the two groups.

TABLE 8. PERCENTAGE OF ITEMS ANSWERED OPERATIONALLY ON TWO CLASSIFICATION TESTS BY ABORIGINAL AND LOW SOCIOECONOMIC WHITE CHILDREN

	Age groupings						
Tests	6	7	8	9	10	11	12
Nixon Test[a]							
Aboriginals	26	52	67	64	89	88	95
Whites	35	48	72	77	90	90	
Matrices Test[b]							
Aboriginals	5	10	25	38	49	57	68
Whites	4	8	26	36	44	71	78

SOURCE: DeLacey 1971a.
[a] Chi square = 3.24, df 6, $p > .50$.
[b] Chi square = 2.48, df 6, $p > .50$.

DeLemos's samples also showed marked increases in cognitive skills with age. It is possible that age was confounded with full- and part-aboriginal background in DeLemos's study, thereby giving false positive results for the background variable. From his report (1969), it is impossible to find the age distributions in the full- and part-aboriginal groups. If more full-aboriginal children were in the younger age-groups, the results can be explained by age alone.

Unless more quantitative approaches are used in studies of racial admixture, it is difficult to form any firm conclusions about the effects of genotypic differences on intellectual differences between racial groups. A better method would use *degree* of white ancestry as a correlate of intellectual performance, where degree of ancestry would be measured from pedigree studies or from independent estimates of admixture obtained from blood group phenotypes. No studies of this sort have yet been done.

Studies of children from interracial marriages in the U.S. (Willerman, Naylor, and Myrianthropoulos 1970, 1971) have suggested substantial maternal effects on the development of intelligence. The children of white mothers and black fathers develop higher IQ scores over the first four years of life than the children of black mothers and white fathers. The educational levels of the parents in both types of interracial matings were quite comparable, but there was still a maternal effect on intellectual development.

3. *Cross-fostering studies.* The rearing of offspring from one group by mothers from another group is known as cross-fostering, a technique that is often used in animal behavior genetics to separate maternal environmental effects from genotypic effects. Cross-fostering periods can include the prenatal and postnatal environments, the former by means of ova transplants.

In human populations, cross-fostering is not arranged for experimental convenience, of course, but sometimes occurs naturally in adoptive families. To separate possible genetic racial differences from the effects of environments provided by the racial groups, one could compare the development of children reared by parents of their own race with those reared by parents of another race. A complete design would include children of both racial groups reared by same- and different-race parents, as follows:

		Race of parents	
		A	B
Race of child	A^1	A^1A	A^1B
	B^1	B^1A	B^1B

The reader can immediately see the pitfalls of a cross-fostering approach if average intellectual differences were found among the offspring groups. Racial classifications are primarily social—not genetic—categories and depend upon identifiably different phenotypes. Thus, the offspring of race A are identifiably different from the offspring of race B; and even though reared by parents from a different group, they may be treated by others as members of their own race. Any finding of average intellectual differences would not discriminate between a genetic-difference hypothesis and a social-discrimination hypothesis.

The finding of *no difference,* however, between the children of races A and B when reared by parents of a single race would be an interesting result, suggesting that the reaction range of the two racial groups included the same IQ values under similar rearing conditions. In other words, if combinations of child and parent $A^1A = B^1A > A^1B = B^1B$, then environmental differences between races A and B becomes the preferred hypothesis. The result $A^1A = A^1B > B^1A = B^1B$ does not discriminate between genetic differences and environmental differences. Several patterns of results would suggest interaction effects between race of child and race of parents: $A^1A > A^1B > B^1A > B^1B$, or $A^1A > B^1B > A^1B > B^1B$, and so forth.

Adoptive families may be seen as providing cross-fostering for many characteristics on which they differ from the natural parents. Children of retarded parents may be seen as cross-fostered when reared by adoptive families of normal IQ. Children of psychotic parents, when adopted, are reared in nonpsychotic environments. Children whose natural parents are alcoholic, drug addicted, psychopathic, and so forth are often adopted into families without those characteristics. Comparisons can then be made between the adopted children and others reared by similar natural parents. To complete the cross-fostering design one can also study the children of nonpsychotic, nonretarded, nonalcoholic natural parents reared by psychotic or retarded or alcoholic adoptive parents. (Since adoptive families are selected by social agencies for their virtues, however, pathological adoptive parents are probably a very small group.) The last group would be nonpathological families who rear their own offspring. For a review of the use of this design in studies of psychopathology, see Rosenthal (1970).

To my knowledge, there have been no studies of the effects of cross-fostering on the intellectual development of children from different racial or ethnic groups. Nor have there been any systematic studies on the postnatal effects of normal-IQ adoptive parents on the children of retarded natural parents. Only Skodak and Skeels (1949) considered the intellectual outcomes of adopted children with natural mothers of higher or lower IQs. The children of lower-IQ natural mothers did not achieve as high phenotypic levels of IQ as the children of higher-IQ mothers, regardless of adoptive family characteristics. Eleven adopted children whose natural mothers had IQs of less than 70 (mean = 63) had an average IQ of 104. Eight adopted children, whose mothers had IQs above 105 (mean = 111) had an average IQ of 129. Although the number of cases is very small, the results suggest (1) that there is a considerable reaction range shown by the children's IQ scores, and (2) that genotypic differences between groups of children with retarded natural mothers and those with above-average natural mothers were important in determining the rank order of the children's IQ scores. Note, however, that even the children with retarded natural mothers scored above the average IQ level of the population, a fact that demonstrates the importance of the adoptive home environments in raising the IQ level of the adopted children.

Developmental Differences in Intelligence

How malleable is the genotypic response to variations in the environment? How severe or prolonged must environmental effects be to deflect the developing phenotype from its genetically canalized, "normal" course of growth? How far above and below the average range of environments must treatments be to have substantial effects on raising or lowering IQ? Heritability tells us nothing about malleability (Crow 1969). For this we must look to the reaction ranges of genotypes under different environments, as in cross-fostering and intervention studies.

Tentative answers, or at least new questions, are provided by three current lines of developmental research: longitudinal studies on the intellectual development of related individuals (Honzik 1971; McCall 1970; Wilson 1972), life-span research on intellectual similarity in twins (Jarvik et al. 1971; Jarvik, Blum, and Varna 1972; Jarvik et al. 1957; Jarvik and Kato 1970; Kallman 1961), and new intervention studies on children of predictable intellectual level (Heber 1969; Rynders 1972; Smilansky and Smilansky, 1968).

With the exceptions noted above, nearly all studies of naturally occurring "environmental" variations have failed to separate genetic from environmental components of variance. Seemingly environmental measures such as socioeconomic status, parental education, number of books in the home, and the like reflect the parents' IQ level. The parents' IQs not only contribute to the child's environmental enrichment but are an indication of what the child received genetically from his parents. There is a confounding of genotypes and environments in sociological studies of the "environmental" variation among unselected families and unknown genotypes.

Similarly, psychological studies of maternal styles of child rearing fail to separate maternal contributions to the child's genotype from maternal behavior toward the child (Brophy 1970; Hess and Shipman 1965). If there is a substantial maternal-style effect in the development of IQ *differences,* then it must be demonstrated after eliminating genetic components of variance. When mothers taught their twins to sort blocks by one of several possible criteria, Fischer (1972) and Waterhouse (1972) failed to find any maternal-style effect on the magnitude of cognitive differences between MZ or DZ co-twins.

Better studies of maternal-style effects and the like can be accomplished by either controlling for genetic relatedness, as in twin and sibling studies, or by eliminating relatedness, as in studies of mothers with adopted children. Studies of larger social-class variation can be made more interpretable by equating parents for IQ while varying socioeconomic status, and vice versa, in order to compare the two components of variation. Behavior genetic methods can improve studies of true environmental variation by controlling for genetic variation.

Experimental treatment or training studies on intellectual or cognitive acceleration usually escape the covariance problem by randomly assigning genotypes to environments. Treatment effects are averaged across the varied genotypes, often lumping large with small, and even reverse, effects. What is to be learned from studies on just any group of fifty six-year olds, that show, for example, that a certain form of concrete manipulation accelerates the acquisition of a conservation concept? While one learns one way to increase average performance on that task in that sample, one learns nothing about the varied ways in which individual children learn conservation concepts (even under the artificial training conditions, and especially not in the real world). Behavior genetic methods of selecting children of known relatedness from stipulated populations would make experimental studies somewhat more meaningful.

1. *Longitudinal family studies.* The Louisville Twin Study, organized by Vandenberg (1968b), has collected data on the development of intelligence in the first two years. Wilson (1972) separated environmental and genetic variation in infant mental development. The 261 pairs of monozygotic and dizygotic twins were measured repeatedly with the Bayley Mental Scales. Over the first two years of life, both absolute level of mental development and pattern of development were very similar for both MZ and DZ twins. Mental development was more similar for MZ than DZ twins, as shown in table 9.

Socioeconomic variables in Wilson's average white sample correlated

TABLE 9. ANALYSIS OF BAYLEY MENTAL SCALE SCORES
FOR TWINS IN FIRST AND SECOND YEARS

Source of variance	Within-pair correlations (R)	Test for MZ > DZ (P)	Range of 98 percent level of confidence	Mean square Between pairs	Within pairs	Degrees of freedom
		Ages 3, 6, 9, and 12 months				
Overall level						
MZ pairs	.90	< .01	.80—.95	645.5	35.6	44/45
DZ pairs	.75		.57—.86	871.8	122.4	50/51
Profile contour						
MZ pairs	.75	< .01	.65—.83	280.0	39.1	132/135
DZ pairs	.50		.34—.63	228.5	76.0	150/153
		Ages 12, 18, and 24 months				
Overall level						
MZ pairs	.89	< .05	.79—.94	677.8	40.7	50/51
DZ pairs	.79		.62—.89	614.5	71.0	45/46
Profile contour						
MZ pairs	.67	< .05	.53—.78	272.4	53.1	100/102
DZ pairs	.52		.33—.68	200.7	62.4	90/92

Source: Wilson 1972.
Note: The within-pair correlation is given by $R = (MS_b - MS_w)/(MS_b + MS_w)$, where MS_b is the mean square between pairs and MS_w is the mean square within pairs.

only slightly ($r \simeq .11$ for the first year, $r \simeq .20$ for the second year) with intellectual status. Wilson concluded,

Therefore, the hypothesis is proposed that these socioeconomic and maternal care variables serve to modulate the primary determinant of developmental capability, namely the genetic blueprint supplied by the parents. . . .

Further, while there is a continuing interaction between the genetically determined gradient of development and the life circumstances under which each pair of twins is born and raised, it required unusual environmental conditions to impose a major deflection upon the gradient of infant development. . . . For the great majority of pairs, life circumstances fall within the broad limits of sufficiency that permit the genetic blueprint to control the course of infant mental development (p. 917).

These conclusions are very strong in light of the only moderate heritabilities that could be calculated from them both. The fact that DZ correlations are very high suggests a strong similarity of twins' gestation and early environment rather than genetic similarity. Note also that Wilson does *not* say that extraordinary environmental factors cannot have disastrous or extremely beneficial effects upon the course of intellectual development. But in a population of cooperative parents, who varied from welfare to upper-middle-class status, differences in their infants' mental development depended more upon genotypic differences than upon environmental differences.

At older ages, both genetic and social environmental differences between families may assume greater importance than in infancy. It is well known (Burks 1928; Honzik 1957; Jensen 1969) that children's IQ scores increasingly resemble their parents' scores over the preschool and early school years. The increasing similarity between parents and their children could be due to any of the following: (1) greater similarity of tasks on IQ tests at older ages, (2) increasing expression of genetic individual differences, and (3) longer and more effective exposure of the children to the parental environment. Studies of adopted children's increasing resemblance to their natural parents can only be interpreted as support for explanations 1 and 2. The extent to which their resemblance to natural, and not adoptive parents, increases with age, can only support 2, the increasing expression of genetic differences (Honzik 1957).

The *level* of IQ scores at any one age shows more genetic variation than does the *pattern* of IQ development over time. Wilson found correlations between .80 and .90 for level of IQ in MZ twins and around .70 for pattern of development. One MZ twin's IQ score was a better predictor of his co-twin's score at a single age than it was of his own score at another age. In other words, the patterning of development has two variable aspects: it is probably genotype-specific, so that MZ twins are fairly similar in their patterns of development in similar environments, but it is also environmentally variable depending upon prenatal effects, illnesses, preferential maternal care, and the like. The profiles of two MZ twins may be somewhat "offset" in time, so that their correlations are reduced. Absolute level of IQ score, however, takes into account the wide differences between families, which make MZ co-twins comparatively very similar.

McCall (1970) studied the levels and patterns of development in siblings and parents (as children) and their children. The IQs of one hundred pairs of siblings correlated around .55 consistently across ages from three and a half to eleven years. The thirty-five pairs of parents and children, who share half their genes in common, had lower correlation ($r \simeq .30$) than the expected .50, for unexplained reasons.[3] Differences in patterns of development for siblings and parents and children did not show substantial genetic variation. This again supports the reaction range model: that patterns of intellectual growth may be genotype-specific and environmentally variable. Since parent-child and sibling pairs receive only half of their genome by identical descent, and since their pre- and postnatal environments vary more than those of fraternal twins, they may have quite different patterns of growth. The resemblance of their phenotypic levels of IQ at any one age suggests some similarity in their reactions to similar environments, but they need not have achieved that intellectual status by the same profile of growth over the preceding years.

Wilson (1972) found significant correlations for patterns of intellectual growth between DZ co-twins ($r \simeq .51$). Although DZ co-twins share the same percentage of their genome in common as ordinary siblings, they are products of the same pregnancy and are reared at the same time. Environmental variation within families, therefore, seems to influence profiles of growth more than phenotypic levels of IQ within families.

Honzik (1971) reported WAIS correlations for three generations of family members (grandparents, parents, and children). Besides correlating the levels of IQ, as has been done in many studies (see table 6 from Burt), she used rank order correlations to ascertain their similarity in patterns of ability on the WAIS subtests, without regard to overall IQ level. To summarize the results of more than five hundred rhos, the percentage of positive and significantly positive rhos was computed (50 percent will be positive by chance if the expectation is zero correlation). These are shown in table 10.

---

[3] Correlations between parents and children are often found to be lower than those of siblings. Both parent-child pairs and siblings share about half of their genome in common, but only siblings can share dominance variance (see Mather and Jinks 1971). That can increase their similarities over those of the purely additive effects shared by parents and children. In addition, siblings share a common rearing environment which parents and their children cannot share.

TABLE 10. THE PERCENT OF POSITIVE AND SIGNIFICANTLY
POSITIVE RANK ORDER CORRELATIONS FOR WAIS SUB-
TEST SCORES AMONG GRANDPARENTS, PARENTS,
AND THEIR CHILDREN

Relationship	N (Pairs)	% Positive	% Positive, p < .05
Father-son	12	92	
Father-daughter	20	85	21
Mother-daughter	27	89	
Mother-son	15	67	
Grandfather-grandson	26	54	
Grandfather-granddaughter	21	43	5
Grandmother-granddaughter	39	59	
Grandmother-grandson	36	58	
Mother-father (assortative mating)	81	81	17

SOURCE: Honzik 1971.

The finding of a positive rho is dependent upon variability in subtest scores. "In other words a significant rho tells us something (about similar patterns of abilities regardless of IQ level) but the large proportion of low positive and negative rhos are not informative" (p. 6). Significant parent-child similarity in WAIS pattern of ability is based on relatively higher vocabulary than block design scores, for example, not on level of performance in either. The study of pattern similarity suggests that children significantly reflect their parents' patterns of ability, probably on both genetic and environmental grounds. Parental correlations reflect assortative mating. Similar studies of siblings, adopted children, half-siblings, cousins, and so on would permit the analysis of the pattern differences into genetic and environmental components. In the Honzik study, however, the greater parent-child than grandparent-grandchild pattern similarity fits the polygenic model presented by Li (1971).

2. *Life-span genetic differences.* The control of the genotype over development throughout life is often ignored. Genetic influences on the acquisition *and maintenance* of intellectual level have now been shown to persist from infancy to the ninth decade of life. In their studies of 134 pairs of aging twins, first tested in their 60s (Kallman, 1961), Jarvik and her associates have shown that genotypic differences continue into late life to be highly related to phenotypic differences in intellectual skills. In the most recent publication (Jarvik et al. 1972) nineteen surviving intact pairs, with a mean age of 83.5 years, were evaluated. Among aging twins there is considerable concordance for survival in MZ pairs and much less similarity of life span in DZ pairs; hence, the 2:1 ratio of MZ:DZ intact pairs. Interestingly enough, the survivors had *not* deteriorated in intellectual level over the twenty-year period despite a decline in speeded motor performance. Test results for the survivors are given in tables 11 and 12.

TABLE 11. INTRACLASS CORRELATIONS[a] OF TEST SCORES FOR
13 MONOZYGOTIC (MZ) AND 6 DIZYGOTIC (DZ) PAIRS
TESTING INITIALLY IN 1947 AND RETESTED IN 1967

Tests	1947		1967		Tests	1967	
	MZ	DZ	MZ	DZ		MZ	DZ
Vocabulary	0.89[b]	−0.31	0.87[b]	0.29	Stroop card 1	0.98[b]	0.24
Similarities	0.76[b]	−0.02	0.71[b]	0.38	Stroop card 2	0.70[b]	−0.29
Digits forward	0.23	0.09	0.42	0.24	Stroop card 3	−0.19	0.32
Digits backward	0.59[c]	−0.47	0.52[c]	0.19	Stroop card 3-card 2	−0.39	0.33
Tapping	0.77[b]	0.47	0.33	0.55	Graham-Kendall	0.08	0.10
Block design	0.77[b]	0.86[b]	0.56[c]	0.68[c]	Picture arrangement	0.35	0.32
Digit symbol substitution	0.87[b]	0.27	0.46	−0.38	Picture completion	−0.39	0.55

SOURCE: Jarvik et al. 1972.
[a] Fisher (1938)
[b] p < 0.01
[c] p < 0.05

TABLE 12. COMPARATIVE MEAN RAW SCORES OF AGING
MONOZYGOTIC (MZ) AND DIZYGOTIC (DZ) TWINS
TESTED IN 1947 AND 1967

	Original sample (N = 240)		Surviving subgroup (N = 38)			
	1947		1947		1967	
	MZ	DZ	MZ	DZ	MZ	DZ
Tests						
Vocabulary	29.18	27.09	30.25	29.42	29.38	29.92
Similarities	9.24	8.21	11.38	11.08	9.81	9.92
Digits forward	5.94	5.69	6.29	6.00	5.71	6.08
Digits backward	4.15	4.10	4.32	4.58	3.82	4.00
Tapping	67.72	63.23	71.00[a]	74.00[a]	48.32[a]	54.92[a]
Block design	13.18	13.80	13.94[a, b]	18.80[b]	9.33[a,b]	15.30[b]
Digit symbol substitution	28.25	26.88	33.25[a]	33.50	21.66[a]	24.40
No. of subjects	150	90	26	12	26	12
Mean age	68.08	70.75	66.08	61.21	85.00	80.35

SOURCE: Jarvik et al. 1972.
[a] Difference within zygosity groups 1947–1967: significant (p < 0.01)
[b] Difference between zygosity groups: significant (p < 0.05)

Although the sample sizes are very small (hardly surprising at an average age of 83), at ages 60 and 80 the MZ pairs were clearly more similar in verbal intellectual skills than the DZ survivors. From the 60s to the 80s, however, there was a steep decline in the similarity of MZ twins in speeded motor tasks, "suggesting that there comes an age (possibly in the 70s) when nongenetic factors modify the genetic influences on motor performance to a significant extent" (Jarvik et al., 1972, p. 166). Verbal reasoning and vocabulary skills continued to show strong genetic variation near the end of life.

3. *Intervention studies.* Another strategy for behavior genetic research is the intervention study with children of known genetic relatedness or at

least predictable phenotypic outcome. A seldom-used strategy is the co-twin control study in which monozygotic twins are separated into different treatment conditions to evaluate the efficacy of various training procedures with the same genotypes. A few pairs of MZ twins have been used in this way to evaluate training in motor development (Dennis 1941). Provided the samples were large enough, excellent studies of educational treatments could be done by separating pairs of co-twins and exposing them to two curricula. Statistical tests for main and interaction effects can be done across treatment groups, controlling for genotypic differences. Reversals in the treatment effects for some pairs could lead to hypotheses about the limitations of the treatments on a much more economical basis than usually occurs in curriculum studies. This strategy is also more likely to show treatment $\times$ ability interactions than the usual one.

Another strategy is to provide treatments for children of predictable intellectual outcome. For those with poor prognoses the research strategy is to calculate the gain of actual over expected values. (One needn't expect a mean IQ of 100 in every group.)

Heber (1969) has tutored a group of infants whose mothers have tested IQs of less than 70. Their fathers IQ scores are unknown. One may generously assume the fathers' IQs to average 95 and the mothers' to average 65. The midparent IQ is, therefore, 80. By calculating the expected regression of offspring scores with a conservative heritability figure of .5, the expected average children's score is 90 if reared by their own mothers. The task of the experimental treatment, therefore, is to raise the average above 90 and not to beat the mothers' figure of 70 nor the population average of 100. The infants in Heber's group, whose intensive tutoring had extended from birth to three years by 1971, have average IQs in excess of 120, a very significant difference from the expected 90.

Rynders (1972) has successfully tutored a group of twenty-five Down's syndrome infants from birth. Their expected intellectual level was at severe retardation. The predicted IQ is less than 50, based on untreated samples of Down's children. The group now averages 85 at the age of three years. A control group of Down's infants in other treatment programs has an average IQ of 68. In the case of chromosomal anomalies, the midparent IQ is not important because the regressions expected for normal children may not occur predictably in case of abnormality.[4]

---

[4] In fact, I do not know of any study that has tried to regress mid-parent IQ scores on the scores of children with Down's Syndrome. It may be that some systematic depression of the children's IQ scores would be revealed by a sizeable parent-child correlation. A lack of parent-child correlation would suggest that the child's abnormal IQ level is not affected by the normal range of genotypic differences among parents.

An Israeli study (Smilansky, personal communication) reported on the IQ scores of children from Oriental and European Jewish families living on kibbutzim. Child-rearing on the 129 kibbutzim sampled was handled from shortly after birth to adolescence in communal nurseries and in small groups of children with their caretakers. Children visited with their parents daily for about two hours but resided in the children's groups. Their education was handled entirely within their communal setting.

Home-reared Oriental Jewish children are often found to have tested IQs of about 92 on the average, compared to about 108 for children of European Jewish parents. The populations from which the Oriental and European groups come have been separated for so many thousands of years that they constitute very different gene pools. In addition, they are culturally very different. Thus, the home-reared Oriental Jewish children probably differ both genetically and environmentally from home-reared European Jewish children.

Within each kibbutz the rearing conditions are uniform for all children, regardless of descent. The Smilanskys matched each of 670 Oriental children with a European child within the same kibbutz, controlling for parental educational level, length of residence in Israel, and several other factors. The children were tested with the Stanford-Binet (four- to five-year-olds) or the Wechsler Intelligence Scale for Children (six to fourteen).

At both kindergarten age and at elementary ages (six to fourteen), the two groups of children had equivalent, and high, average IQs ($\simeq 115$). Since kibbutz residents are self-selected, one cannot conclude that all Israeli children would be as bright if they were similarly reared. But one can conclude that the reaction ranges of the present kibbutz children include the same IQ values whether they come from the Oriental or European Jewish populations.

Within each population, parental educational level correlated significantly ($r \simeq .25-.45$) with children's IQs. In part, the parent-child correlations may be due to parental environmental influence, although this is attenuated by the communal rearing. A probably more important fact is that parental education reflects parental IQ to a considerable extent (Jencks 1972) and that IQ has moderate heritability within Israeli, as well as other, populations.

Even if the heritability of IQ is substantial *within* each of two populations, and even if there are sizeable *average differences between* the populations, uniformly good rearing conditions can act on the reaction ranges of children in both populations and result in similar distributions of phenotypes.

Treatment studies of children whose phenotypic outcomes under environmental conditions are predictable can supply important data on the reaction ranges of various genotypes when other conditions are provided. (For a general review of the intervention-study literature, see Horowitz and Paden 1973.) Studies of twins and siblings, one of whom is provided with the treatment, can provide still better comparisons than ordinary control or comparison groups.

A sibling study on the effects of extremely low birth-weight (Dann, Levine, and New 1964) is an example of the use of related persons to evaluate the effects of a naturally occurring "treatment." The IQ scores of fifty low birth-weight children (< 1,000 grams at birth) and their normal-weight sibs differed by 13 IQ points on the average (94 vs. 107). Since genotypes can be assumed to be randomly distributed between the two siblings and since they are reared in the same families, the decrement in IQ scores for the low birth-weight babies can be attributed to the sequelae of low birth-weight rather than to possible genetic and environmental differences between the families of prematures and normal birth-weight infants.

There is a great need for developmental studies that attend to genetic as well as environmental parameters of variation. The individual child, with his or her unique genotype and unique response to environmental contingencies, is the datum to be understood. Until we build theoretical models to better account for the individual child, our generalities based on average values will always dissolve into a mass of conflicting trends. Evolutionary theory, polygenic models of intelligence, and the reaction range concept suggest many approaches to the study of intellectual development. We should capitalize on the opportunities.

Summary

1. Individual variation in IQ has been extensively studied at the phenotypic level by variance analysis techniques. Studies of related and unrelated persons, living together and apart, suggest that the majority of the variance in IQ scores in white populations is due to genetic differences.

2. Little is known about the sources of variation in nonwhite populations.

3. Little is known about the sources of between-group average differences on IQ tests because appropriate methods have not been used.

4. The development of intellectual skills has been studied longitudinally in a few samples of twins, siblings, and parent-child pairs. The results suggest that the level of IQ is moderately heritable, and that the pattern of intellectual development is more variable than the level within families.

5. Behavior genetic methods can be profitably applied to developmental problems in intervention research, in longitudinal studies, and in

many other areas where it is important to separate genotypic from environmental effects.

CONCLUSIONS

Trends in Psychological Explanation

Psychology seems to be in the midst of an aperiodic swing between extreme forms of environmentalism and hereditarianism. More biological assumptions, variables, methods, and conclusions have crept into child development during the past ten years than in the preceding twenty-five. This trend must be critically evaluated. We must, first, be alert to the dangers of the reductionist thinking inherent in biological explanations of behavioral phenomena. Second, we must avoid an extreme form of hereditarianism that ignores the necessary transactions between genotypes and environments throughout the life-span development of human intelligence. A serious appraisal of the new genetics avoids both of these errors.

Much of the confusion in earlier hereditarian eras arose from the failure to distinguish between determinism and differences. Although genetic studies of intelligence were most often concerned with apportioning the sources of individual *differences,* some faulty conclusions were drawn concerning the importance of genes in *determining* intelligence. The conclusions from twin, family, and adoptive studies apply only to the sources of differences, not to the importance of genes in determining development. Even though environmental differences were found to be less important sources of IQ variation than genetic differences, there is no reason to conclude that the environment is less important than genes in determining intellectual development. It may simply be the case that all members in the population studied had functionally equivalent environments, but they all had environments!

A related, and equally faulty, conclusion is that, if genetic differences contribute more than environmental differences to the variance in IQ scores, then IQ is considered to be not very malleable. The myth of heritability limiting malleability seems to die hard. Until recently, the importance of the genotype's reaction range was underestimated; it provides alternative phenotypes for the same individual, depending upon crucial environmental factors in the development of that individual. There is no one-to-one correspondence between genotype and behavioral phenotype, regardless of the heritability of a characteristic. Even if the heritability for IQ in a population were one, meaning that present environmental differences contributed nothing to individual phenotypic differences, a change in the environments could dramatically shift the mean of the entire phenotypic distribution.

Studies of reaction ranges, canalization, genetic expression, and related issues have barely begun in human populations. From a developmental point of view, these are the critical concepts because they lead to research on the malleability of intellectual development and to questions about genetic mechanisms underlying that development.

An Overview

Studies of genetics and human intelligence have concentrated on the apportionment of statistical variation in IQ scores into environmental components. Although we still know virtually nothing about the sources of intellectual variation within nonwhite and disadvantaged populations, the methods are available to be applied. Further refinements of the variance theme will come from more careful studies of covariance and interaction effects, with samples of adoptive families and separated relatives. From the many twin and family studies of IQ variation, it is necessary to conclude that genotypic differences are a more important source of IQ differences than are environmental differences, within white U.S. and European populations. Most investigators estimate genetic sources of variation to account for half to three-quarters of the phenotypic differences in these populations. Covariance and interaction effects have not been well studied yet.

Although studies of variation are important, they are barely a prelude to the research that needs to be done before we will have any substantial knowledge of genetic differences in normal intellectual development and of genetic mechanisms in development. Some strategies for developmental genetic research have been suggested: Studies of interventions with groups of predictable phenotypic level, co-twin control strategies, longitudinal family studies, cross-fostering studies, admixture studies, and life-span genetic research. Many of the research studies now being done in child development can be improved by the inclusion of behavior-genetic strategies.

In this chapter there has been an attempt to review previous research on normal, human intellectual development, to construct a coherent account of the relation of genetics to human intellectual development, to evaluate the present state of our knowledge, and, primarily, to indicate our lack of knowledge. Perhaps a later volume in this series can include a more conclusive chapter on the subject.

REFERENCES

Adams, M. S., Davidson, R. T., & Cornell, P. Adoptive risks of the children of incest —a preliminary report. *Child Welfare*, 1967, *46*, 137–142.

Adams, M. S. & Neel, J. V. Children of incest. *Pediatrics*, 1967, *40*, 55–62.
Alland, A. *The Evolution of Human Behavior*. New York: American Museum of Natural History, 1967.
Almy, M., Chittenden, E., & Miller, P. *Young Children's Thinking: Studies of Some Aspects of Piaget's Thinking*. New York: Teacher's College Press, 1966.
Bajema, C. J. Relation of fertility to occupational status, IQ, educational attainments, and size of family of origin: a follow-up study of a male Kalamazoo public school population. *Eugenics Quarterly*, 1968, *15*, 198–203.
Bayley, N. Comparison of mental and motor test scores for ages 1–15 months by sex, birth order, race, geographical location, and education of parents. *Child Development*, 1965, *36*, 379–411.
Berry, J. W. Tenne and Eskimo perceptual skills. *International Journal of Psychology*, 1966, *1*, 207–222.
Bock, R. D. & Kolakowski, D. F. Further evidence of a major-gene influence on human spatial abilities. *American Journal of Behavior Genetics*, 1973, *25*, 1–14.
Böök, J. A. Genetical investigation in a north Swedish population: The offspring of first-cousin marriages. *Annals of Human Genetics*, 1957, *21*, 191–221.
Bouchard, T. J. Genetic factors in intelligence. In A. R. Kaplan, ed., *Human Behavior Genetics*. Springfield: Thomas, 1972.
Brophy, J. E. Mothers as teachers of their own preschool children: the influence of socioeconomic status and task structure on teaching specificity. *Child Development*, 1970, *41*, 79–94.
Burks, B. S. The relative influence of nature and nurture upon mental development: a comparative study of foster parent–foster child and true parent–true child resemblance. *Twenty-seventh Yearbook of the National Society for the Study of Education*, 1928, 219–316.
Burt, C. Intelligence and social mobility. *British Journal of Statistical Psychology*, 1961, *14*, 3–24.
———. The genetic determination of differences in intelligence: a study of monozygotic twins reared together and apart. *British Journal of Psychology*, 1966, *57*, 137–153.
Butcher, H. J. *Human Intelligence*. London: Methuen, 1968.
Cancro, R., ed. *Intelligence: Genetic and Environmental Influences*. New York: Grune & Stratton, 1971.
Carter, C. O. Risk to offspring of incest. *Lancet*, 1967, *1*, 436.
Cattell, R. B. The structure of intelligence in relation to the nature-nurture controversy. In R. Cancro, ed., *Intelligence: Genetic and Environmental Influences*. New York: Grune & Stratton, 1971, 3–30.
Cavalli-Sforza, L. L. & Bodmer, W. F. *The Genetics of Human Populations*. San Francisco: W. H. Freeman, 1972.
Cohen, T., Block, N., Flum, Y., Kadar, M., & Goltschmidt, E. School attainments in an immigrant village. In F. Goldschmidt, ed., *The Genetics of Migrant and Isolate Populations*. Baltimore: Williams & Wilkens, 1963.
Cole, M. & Bruner, J. S. Cultural differences and inferences about psychological processes. *American Psychologist*, 1971, *26*, 867–876.
Cole, M., Gay, J., Glick, J. A., & Sharp, D. W. *The Cultural Context of Learning and Thinking*. New York: Basic Books, 1972.
Cooper, R. & Zubek, J. Effects of enriched and restricted early environments on the learning ability of bright and dull rats. *Canadian Journal of Psychology*, 1958, *12*, 159–164.
Crow, J. Genetic theories and influences: comments on the value of diversity. *Harvard Educational Review*, 1969, *39*, 153–170.
Dann, M., Levine, S. Z., & New, E. V. A long-term follow-up study of small, premature infants. *Pediatrics*, 1964, *33*, 945–955.
DeFries, J. C. Quantitative aspects of genetics and environment in the determination of behavior. Paper presented at the C.O.B.R.E. Research Workshop on Genetic

Endowment and Environment in the Determination of Behavior. Rye, New York, October 3–8, 1971.

deLacey, P. R. A cross-cultural study of classificatory skills in Australia. *Journal of Cross-Cultural Psychology*, 1970, *1*, 293–304.

———. Classificatory ability and verbal intelligence among high-contact aboriginal and low socio-economic white Australian children. *Journal of Cross-Cultural Psychology*, 1971a, *2*, 393–396.

———. Verbal intelligence, operational thinking and environment in part-aboriginal children. *Australian Journal of Psychology*, 1971b, *23*, 145–149.

DeLemos, M. M. The development of conservation in aboriginal children. *International Journal of Psychology*, 1969, *4*, 255–269.

Dennis, W. Infant development under conditions of restricted practice and minimum social stimulation. *Genetic Psychology Monographs*, 1941, *23*, 143–191.

Dewey, W. J., Barrai, I., Morton, N. E., & Mi, M. P. Recessive genes in severe mental defect. *Amercian Journal of Human Genetics*, 1965, *17*, 237–256.

Dobzhansky, T. *Mankind Evolving*. New Haven: Yale University Press, 1962.

Ervin-Tripp, S. Personal communication. February, 1972.

Falconer, D. S. *Introduction to Quantitative Genetics*. New York: Ronald, 1960.

Fischer, K. Genetic aspects of individual differences in language development. Ph.D. dissertation, University of Pennsylvania, 1972.

Flavell, J. H. *The Developmental Psychology of Jean Piaget*. Princeton: Van Nostrand, 1963.

———. Concept development. In P. H. Mussen, ed., *Carmichael's Manual of Child Psychology*. Vol. 1. New York: Wiley, 1970, 983–1059.

Fuller, J. L. & Thompson, W. R. *Behavior Genetics*. New York: John Wiley, 1960.

Gaudia, G. Race, social class, and age of achievement of conservation on Piaget's tasks. *Developmental Psychology*, 1972, *6*, 158–165.

Geber, M. The psycho-motor development of African children in the first year, and the influence of maternal behavior. *Journal of Social Psychology*, 1958, *47*, 185–195.

Ginsburg, B. E. & Laughlin, W. The multiple bases of human adaptability and achievement: A species point of view. *Eugenics Quarterly*, 1966, *13*, 240–257.

Ginsburg, B. E. Genotypic factors in the ontogeny of behavior. *Science and Psychoanalysis*, 1968, *12*, 12–17.

Ginsburg, B. E. & Laughlin, W. Race and intelligence, what do we really know? In R. Cancro, ed., *Intelligence: Genetic and Environmental Influences*. New York: Grune & Stratton, 1971, 77–87.

Gottesman, I. I. Biogenetics of race and class. In M. Deutsch, I. Katz, & A. R. Jensen, eds., *Social Class, Race, and Psychological Development*. New York: Holt, Rinehart & Winston, 1968.

———. Genetic aspects of intelligent behavior. In N. Ellis, ed., *Handbook of Mental Deficiency*. New York: McGraw-Hill, 1963, 253–296.

Heber, R. *Rehabilitation of Families at Risk for Mental Retardation*. Regional Rehabilitation Center, University of Wisconsin, 1969.

Henderson, N. D. Genetic influences on the behavior of mice as can be obscured by laboratory rearing. *Journal of Comparative and Physiological Psychology*, 1970, *3*, 505–511.

Herrnstein, R. IQ. *Atlantic Monthly*, 1971, *228* (September), 44–64.

Hess, R. D. & Shipman, V. Early experience and the socialization of cognitive modes in children. *Child Development*, 1965, *36*, 869–886.

Higgins, J., Reed, E. W., & Reed, S. Intelligence and family size: a paradox resolved. *Eugenics Quarterly*, 1962, *9*, 84–90.

Hirsch, J., ed. *Behavior-Genetic Analysis*. New York: McGraw-Hill, 1967.

Hirsch, J. Behavior-genetic analysis and its biosocial consequences. In R. Cancro, ed., *Intelligence: Genetic and Environmental Influences*. New York: Grune & Stratton, 1971.

Honzik, M. P. Developmental studies of parent-child resemblance in intelligence. *Child Development*, 1957, *28*, 215–228.

———. Resemblance in Wechsler Patterns in Three Generations. Paper presented at the Biennial Meetings of the Society for Research in Child Development, Minneapolis, April 2, 1971.

Horowitz, F. D. & Paden, L. Y. The effects of environmental intervention programs. In B. Caldwell & H. Riccuti, eds., *Review of Child Development Research*. Vol. 3. Chicago: University of Chicago Press, 1973.

Hsia, D. Y. Y. *Human Developmental Genetics*. Chicago: Yearbook Medical Publishers, 1968.

Humphreys, L. G. Theory of intelligence. In R. Cancro, ed., *Intelligence: Genetic and Environmental Influences*. New York: Grune & Stratton, 1971, 31–42.

Huntley, R. M. C. Heritability of intelligence: In J. E. Meade & A. S. Parkes, eds., *Genetic and Environmental Factors in Human Ability*. Edinburgh: Oliver & Boyd, 1966, 201–218.

Hyde, D. M. An investigation of Piaget's theories of the development of the concept of number as reported in DeLemos (1969).

Jacob, F. & Monod, J. Genetic regulatory mechanisms in the synthesis of proteins. *Journal of Molecular Biology*, 1961, *3*, 318–356.

Jarvik, L. F., Altschuler, K. Z., Kato, T., & Blummer, B. Organic brain syndrome and chromosome loss in aged twins. *Diseases of the Nervous System*, 1971, *32*, 159–170.

Jarvik, L. F., Blum, J. E., & Varna, A. O. Genetic components and intellectual functioning during senescence: A 20-year study of aging twins. *Behavior Genetics*, 1972, *2*, 159–171.

Jarvik, L. F. & Erlenmeyer-Kimling, L. Survey of family correlations in measured intellectual functions. In J. Zubin & G. Jervis, eds., *Psychopathology of Mental Development*. New York: Grune & Stratton, 1967, 447–459.

Jarvik, L. F., Kallman, F. J., Falek, A., & Klaber, M. M. Changing intellectual functions in senescent twins. *Acta Genetica Statistica Medica*, 1957, *7*, 421–430.

Jarvik, L. F. & Kato, T. Chromosome examinations in aged twins. *American Journal of Human Genetics*, 1970, *22*, 562–572.

Jencks, C. *Inequality: A Reassessment of the Effect of Family and Schooling in America*. New York: Basic Books, 1972.

Jensen, A. R. *Educability, and Group Differences*. New York: Harper & Row, 1973.

———. Social class and verbal learning. In M. Deutsch, I. Katz, & A. R. Jensen, eds., *Social Class, Race, and Psychological Development*. New York: Holt, Rinehart & Winston, 1968.

———. How much can we boost IQ and scholastic achievement? *Harvard Educational Review*, 1969, *39*, 1–123.

———. The IQs of MZ twins reared apart. *Behavior Genetics*, 1971a, *2*, 1–10.

———. A Two-Factor Theory of Familial Mental Retardation. Paper presented at the Fourth International Congress of Human Genetics, Paris, 1971b.

Jinks, J. L. & Fulker, D. W. Comparison of the biometrical, genetical, MAVA, and classical approaches to the analysis of human behavior. *Psychological Bulletin*, 1970, *73*, 311–349.

Kallman, F. J. Genetic factors in aging: comparative and longitudinal observations on a senescent twin population. In P. H. Hoch & J. Zubin, eds., *Psychopathology of Aging*. New York: Grune & Stratton, 1961, 227–247.

Kiser, C. V. Assortative mating by educational attainment in relation to fertility. *Eugenics Quarterly*, 1968, *15*, 98–112.

LaBarre, W. *The Human Animal*. Chicago: University of Chicago Press, 1965.

Labov, W. *The Social Stratification of English in New York City*. Washington, D.C.: Center for Applied English, 1966.

———. The logic of nonstandard English. In F. Williams, ed., *Language and Poverty*. Chicago: Markham, 1970, 153–189.

Leahy, A. M. Nature-nurture and intelligence. *Genetic Psychology Monographs*, 1935, *17*, 235–307.

Lenneberg, E. H. *Biological Foundations of Language*. New York: John Wiley, 1967.

Lerner, I. M. *Heredity, Evolution, and Society*. San Francisco: Freeman, 1968.

Levine, S. Sex differences in the brain. In J. L. McGaugh, N. M. Weinberger, & R. E. Whalen, eds., *Psychobiology*. San Francisco: Freeman, 1967.

Lewontin, R. C. Race and intelligence. *Bulletin of the Atomic Scientists*, 1970, *26*, 2–8.

Li, C. C. A tale of two thermos bottles: properties of a genetic model for human intelligence. In R. Cancro, ed., *Intelligence: Genetic and Environmental Influences*. New York: Grune & Stratton, 1971.

Lindzey, G., Loehlin, J., Manosevitz, M., & Thiessen, D. Behavioral genetics. *Annual Review of Psychology*. Palo Alto: Annual Reviews, 1971.

MacArthur, R. S. Some differential abilities of northern Canadian native youth. *International Journal of Psychology*, 1968, *3*, 43–51.

———. Some cognitive abilities of Eskimo, White and Indian-Metis pupils age 9 to 12 years. *Canadian Journal of Behavior Sciences*, 1969, *1*, 50–59.

Manosevitz, M., Lindzey, G., & Thiessen, D., eds. *Behavioral Genetics*. New York: Appleton-Century-Crofts, 1969.

Martin, R. G. & Ames, B. N. Biochemical aspects of genetics. *Annual Review of Biochemistry*, 1964, *33*, 235–256.

Mather, K. On biometrical genetics. *Heredity*, 1971, *26*, 349–364.

Mather, K. & Jinks, J. L. *Biometrical Genetics*. Ithaca, New York: Cornell University, 1971.

McCall, R. Intelligence quotient patterns over age: Comparisons among sibling and parent-child pairs. *Science*, 1970, 644–648.

McClearn, G. E. Genetics and behavior development. In M. L. Hoffman & L. W. Hoffman, eds., *Review of Child Development Research*. Vol. 1. New York: Russell Sage, 1964.

———. Genetic influences on behavior and development. In P. H. Mussen, ed., *Carmichael's Manual of Child Psychology*. New York: John Wiley, 1970, 39–76.

McGaugh, J. L., Jennings, R. D., & Thompson, C. W. Effect of distribution of practice on the maze learning of descendants of Tryon maze bright and maze dull strains. *Psychological Reports*, 1962, *10*, 147–150.

Money, J. Cognitive deficits in Turner's syndrome. In S. G. Vandenberg, ed., *Progress in Human Behavior Genetics*. Baltimore: Johns Hopkins, 1968.

Morton, N. E. The inheritance of human birth weight. *Annals of Human Genetics*, 1955, *20*, 125–134.

Nichols, P. The effects of heredity and environment on intelligence test performance on 4- and 7-year-old white and Negro sibling pairs. Ph.D. dissertation, University of Minnesota, 1970.

Nichols, R. C. The National Merit twin study. In S. G. Vandenberg, ed., *Methods and Goals in Human Behavior Genetics*. New York: Academic Press, 1965, 231–243.

Pinard, A. & Laurendreau, M. A scale of mental development based on the theory of Piaget. *Journal of Research in Science Teaching*, 1964, *2*, 253–260.

Price-Williams, D. R. A study concerning concepts of conservation of quantities among premature children. *Acta Psychologica*, 1961, *18*, 297–305.

Prince, J. R. The effect of Western education on science conceptualization in New Guinea. *British Journal of Educational Psychology*, 1968, *38*, 64–74.

Reed, E. W. & Reed, S. C. *Mental Retardation: A Family Study*. Philadelphia: W. B. Saunders, 1965.

Reed, T. E. Caucasian genes in American Negroes. *Science*, 1969, 762–768.

Roberts, J. A. F. The genetics of mental deficiency. *Eugenics Review*, 1952, *44*, 71–83.

Rosenthal, D. *Genetic Theory and Abnormal Behavior*. New York: McGraw-Hill, 1970.

Rynders, J. Personal Communication, November, 1972, University of Minnesota.

Scarr-Salapatek, S. Unknowns in the IQ equation. *Science*, 1971*a*, *174*, 1223–1228.

———. Race, social class, and IQ *Science*, 1971*b*, *174*, 1285–1295.

Schull, W. J. & Neel, J. V. *The Effects of Inbreeding on Japanese Children*. New York: Harper & Row, 1965.

Skeels, H. M. Adult status of children with contrasting early life experience. *Monographs of the Society for Research in Child Development*, 1966, *31*, (whole no. 105).

Skodak, M. & Skeels, H. M. A final follow-up of one hundred adopted children. *Journal of Genetic Psychology*, 1949, *75*, 85–125.

Smilansky, M. Personal communication, June 12, 1973.

Stern, C. *Principles of Human Genetics*. 2d ed. San Francisco: Freeman, 1960.

Thiessen, D. D. Philosophy and method in behavior genetics. In A. R. Gilgen, ed., *Scientific Psychology: Some Perspectives*. New York: Academic Press, 1970.

———. *Gene Organization and Behavior*. New York: Random House, 1972*a*.

———. A move toward a species-specific analysis in behavior genetics. *Behavior Genetics*, 1972*b*, *2*, 115–126.

Thoday, J. M. Limitations to genetic comparisons of populations. *Journal of Biosocial Science*, 1969, Supplement, 3–14.

Tuddenham, R. A "Piagetian" test of cognitive development. In B. Dockrell, ed., *On Intelligence*. Toronto: Ontario Institute for Studies in Education, 1970, 49–70.

Vandenberg, S. G. Contributions of twin research to psychology. *Psychological Bulletin*, 1966, *66*, 327–352.

Vandenberg, S. G., ed. *Methods and Goals in Human Behavior Genetics*. New York: Academic Press, 1965.

Waddington, C. H. *The Strategy of the Genes*. London: Allen & Unwin, 1957.

———. *New Patterns in Genetics and Development*. New York: Columbia University Press, 1962.

Wall, C. Paper presented at the Fourth International Congress of Human Genetics, Paris, September 6–10, 1967.

Waller, J. H. Achievement and social mobility: relationship among IQ score, education and occupation in two generations. *Social Biology*, 1971, *18*, 252–259.

Washburn, S. L., & Howells, F. C. Human evolution and culture. In S. Tax, ed., *Evolution after Darwin: The Evolution of Man*. Vol. 2. Chicago: University of Chicago Press, 1960, pp. 33–57.

Waterhouse, L. H. Genetic and sociocultural influence on language development. Ph.D. dissertation, University of Pennsylvania, 1972.

Weyl, N. Some comparative performance indexes of American ethnic minorities. *Mankind Quarterly*, 1969, *9*, 194–199.

Willerman, L. Personal communication. August, 1972.

Willerman, L., Naylor, A. F., & Myrianthropoulos, N. C. Intellectual development of children from interracial matings. *Science*, 1970, *170*, 1329–1331.

———. Children of interracial matings: evidence for environmental effects on intellectual performance. Paper presented at the Fourth International Congress of Human Genetics, Paris, September, 6–11, 1971.

Wilson, R. S. Twins: Early mental development. *Science*, 1972, *175*, 914–917.

1.2 Unknowns in the IQ Equation*

IQ scores have been repeatedly estimated to have a large heritable component in United States and Northern European white populations (*1*). Individual differences in IQ, many authors have concluded, arise far more from genetic than from environmental differences among people in these populations, at the present time, and under present environmental conditions. It has also been known for many years that white lower-class and black groups have lower IQ's, on the average, than white middle-class groups. Most behavioral scientists comfortably "explained" these group differences by appealing to obvious environmental differences between the groups in standards of living, educational opportunities, and the like. But recently an explosive controversy has developed over the heritability of between-group differences in IQ, the question at issue being: If individual differences within the white population as a whole can be attributed largely to heredity, is it not plausible that the average differences between social-class groups and between racial groups also reflect significant genetic differences? Can the former data be used to explain the latter?

To propose genetically based racial and social-class differences is anathema to most behavioral scientists, who fear any scientific confirmation of the pernicious racial and ethnic prejudices that abound in our society. But now that the issue has been openly raised, and has been projected into the public context of social and educational policies, a hard scientific look must be taken at what is known and at what inferences can be drawn from that knowledge.

---

*This chapter by Sandra Scarr-Salapatek was originally published in *Science*, 1971, *174*, 1223–1228. Copyright © 1971 by the American Association for the Advancement of Science. Reprinted by permission of the American Association for the Advancement of Science.

The public controversy began when A. R. Jensen, in a long paper in the *Harvard Educational Review,* persuasively juxtaposed data on the heritability of IQ and the observed differences between groups. Jensen suggested that current large-scale educational attempts to raise the IQ's of lower-class children, white and black, were failing because of the high heritability of IQ. In a series of papers and rebuttals to criticism, in the same journal and elsewhere (2), Jensen put forth the hypothesis that social-class and racial differences in mean IQ were due largely to differences in the gene distributions of these populations. At least, he said, the genetic differences hypothesis was no less likely, and probably more likely, than a simple environmental hypothesis to explain the mean difference of 15 IQ points between blacks and whites (3) and the even larger average IQ differences between professionals and manual laborers within the white population.

Jensen's articles have been directed primarily at an academic audience. Herrnstein's article in the *Atlantic* and Eysenck's book (first published in England) have brought the argument to the attention of the wider lay audience. Both Herrnstein and Eysenck agree with Jensen's genetic-differences hypothesis as it pertains to individual differences and to social-class groups, but Eysenck centers his attention on the genetic explanation of racial-group differences, which Herrnstein only touches on. Needless to say, many other scientists will take issue with them.

EYSENCK'S RACIAL THESIS

Eysenck has written a popular account of the race, social-class, and IQ controversy in a generally inflammatory book. The provocative title and the disturbing cover picture of a forlorn black boy are clearly designed to tempt the lay reader into a pseudo-battle between Truth and Ignorance. In this case Truth is genetic–environmental interactionism (4) and Ignorance is naive environmentalism. For the careful reader, the battle fades out inconclusively as Eysenck admits that scientific evidence to date does not permit a clear choice of the genetic-differences interpretation of black inferiority on intelligence tests. A quick reading of the book, however, is sure to leave the reader believing that scientific evidence today strongly supports the conclusion that U.S. blacks are genetically inferior to whites in IQ.

The basic theses of the book are as follows:

1. IQ is a highly heritable characteristic in the U.S. white population and probably equally heritable in the U.S. black population.
2. On the average, blacks score considerably lower than whites on IQ tests.
3. U.S. blacks are probably a non-random, lower-IQ, sample of native African populations.

4. The average IQ difference between blacks and whites probably represents important genetic differences between the races.
5. Drastic environmental changes will have to be made to improve the poor phenotypes that U.S. blacks now achieve.

The evidence and nonevidence that Eysenck cites to support his genetic hypothesis of racial differences make a curious assortment. Audrey Shuey's review (5) of hundreds of studies showing mean phenotypic differences between black and white IQ's leads Eysenck to conclude:

All the evidence to date suggests the strong and indeed overwhelming importance of genetic factors in producing the great variety of intellectual differences which we observe in our culture, and much of the difference observed between certain racial groups. This evidence cannot be argued away by niggling and very minor criticisms of details which do not really throw doubts on the major points made in this book [p. 126].

To "explain" the genetic origins of these mean IQ differences he offers these suppositions:

White slavers wanted dull beasts of burden, ready to work themselves to death in the plantations, and under those conditions intelligence would have been counter-selective. Thus there is every reason to expect that the particular sub-sample of the Negro race which is constituted of American Negroes is not an unselected sample of Negroes, but has been selected throughout history according to criteria which would put the highly intelligent at a disadvantage. The inevitable outcome of such selection would of course be a gene pool lacking some of the genes making for higher intelligence [p. 42).

Other ethnic minorities in the U.S. are also, in his view, genetically inferior, again because of the selective migration of lower IQ genotypes:

It is known [*sic*] that many other groups came to the U.S.A. due to pressures which made them very poor samples of the original population. Italians, Spaniards, and Portuguese, as well as Greeks, are examples where the less able, less intelligent were forced through circumstances to emigrate, and where their American progeny showed significantly lower IQ's than would have been shown by a random sample of the original population [p. 43].

Although Eysenck is careful to say that these are not established facts (because no IQ tests were given to the immigrants or nonimmigrants in question?), the tone of his writing leaves no doubt about his judgment. There is something in this book to insult almost everyone except WASP's and Jews.

Despite his conviction that U.S. blacks are genetically inferior in IQ to whites, Eysenck is optimistic about the potential effects of radical environmental changes on the present array of Negro IQ phenotypes. He points to the very large IQ gains produced by intensive one-to-one tutoring of black urban children with low-IQ mothers, contrasting large environmental changes and large IQ gains in intensive programs of this sort with insignificant environmental improvements and small IQ changes obtained by Headstart and related programs. He correctly observes that, whatever the heritability of IQ (or, it should be added, of any characteristic), large phenotypic changes may be produced by creating appropriate, radically different environments never before encountered by those genotypes. On this basis, Eysenck calls for further research to determine the requisites of such environments.

Since Eysenck comes to this relatively benign position regarding potential improvement in IQ's, why, one may ask, is he at such pains to "prove" the genetic inferiority of blacks? Surprisingly, he expects that new environments, such as that provided by intensive educational tutoring, will not affect the black–white IQ differential, because black children and white will probably profit equally from such treatment. Since many middle-class white children already have learning environments similar to that provided by tutors for the urban black children, we must suppose that Eysenck expects great IQ gains from relatively small changes in white, middle-class environments.

This book is an uncritical popularization of Jensen's ideas without the nuances and qualifiers that make much of Jensen's writing credible or at least responsible. Both authors rely on Shuey's review (5), but Eysenck's way of doing it is to devote some 25 pages to quotes and paraphrases of her chapter summaries. For readers to whom the original Jensen article is accessible, Eysenck's book is a poor substitute; although he defends Jensen and Shuey, he does neither a service.

It is a maddeningly inconsistent book filled with contradictory caution and incaution; with hypotheses stated both as hypotheses and as conclusions; with both accurate and inaccurate statements on matters of fact. For example, Eysenck thinks evoked potentials offer a better measure of "innate" intelligence than IQ tests. But on what basis? Recently F. B. Davis (6) has failed to find any relationship whatsoever between evoked potentials and either IQ scores or scholastic achievement, to which intelligence is supposed to be related. Another example is Eysenck's curious use of data to support a peculiar line of reasoning about the evolutionary inferiority of blacks: First, he reports that African and U.S. Negro babies have been shown to have precocious sensorimotor development by white norms (the difference, by several accounts, appears only in gross motor skills and even there is slight). Second, he notes that by three years of age U.S. white exceed U.S. black children in mean IQ scores. Finally he cites a (very slight) negative correlation, found in an early study, between sensorimotor intelligence in the first year of life and later IQ. From exaggerated statements of these various data, he concludes:

> These findings are important because of a very general view in biology according to which the more prolonged the infancy the greater in general are the cognitive or

intellectual abilities of the species. This law appears to work even within a given species [p. 79].

Eysenck would apparently have us believe that Africans and their relatives in the U.S. are less highly evolved than Caucasians, whose longer infancy is related to later higher intelligence. I am aware of no evidence whatsoever to support a within-species relationship between longer infancy and higher adult capacities.

The book is carelessly put together, with no index; few references, and those not keyed to the text; and long, inadequately cited quotes that carry over several pages without clear beginnings and ends. Furthermore, considering the gravity of Eysenck's theses, the book has an occasional jocularity of tone that is offensive. A careful book on the genetic hypothesis, written for a lay audience, would have merited publication. This one, however, has been publicly disowned as irresponsible by the entire editorial staff of its London publisher, New Society. But never mind, the American publisher has used that and other condemnations to balance the accolades and make its advertisement (7) of the book more titillating.

HERRNSTEIN'S SOCIAL THESIS

Thanks to Jensen's provocative article, many academic psychologists who thought IQ tests belonged in the closet with the Rorschach inkblots have now explored the psychometric literature and found it to be a trove of scientific treasure. One of these is Richard Herrnstein, who from a Skinnerian background has become an admirer of intelligence tests—a considerable leap from shaping the behavior of pigeons and rats. In contrast to Eysenck's book, Herrnstein's popular account in the *Atlantic* of IQ testing and its values is generally responsible, if overly enthusiastic in parts.

Herrnstein unabashedly espouses IQ testing as "psychology's most telling accomplishment to date," despite the current controversy over the fairness of testing poor and minority-group children with IQ items devised by middle-class whites. His historical review of IQ test development, including tests of general intelligence and multiple abilities, is interesting and accurate. His account of the validity and usefulness of the tests centers on the fairly accurate prediction that can be made from IQ scores to academic and occupational achievement and income level. He clarifies the pattern of relationship between IQ and these criterion variables; High IQ is a necessary but not sufficient condition for high achievement, while low IQ virtually assures failure at high academic and occupational levels. About the usefulness of the tests, he concludes:

An IQ test can be given in an hour or two to a child, and from this infinitesimally small sample of his output, deeply important predictions follow—about schoolwork, occupation, income, satisfaction with life, and even life expectancy. The predictions are not perfect, for other factors always enter in, but no other single factor matters as much in as many spheres of life [p. 53].

One must assume that Herrnstein's enthusiasm for intelligence tests rests on population statistics, not on predictions for a particular child, because many children studied longitudinally have been shown to change IQ scores by 20 points or more from childhood to adulthood. It is likely that extremes of giftedness and retardation can be sorted out relatively early by IQ tests, but what about the 95 percent of the population in between? Their IQ scores may vary from dull to bright normal for many years. Important variations in IQ can occur up to late adolescence (8). On a population basis Herrnstein is correct; the best early predictors of later achievement are ability measures taken from age five on. Predictions are based on correlations, however, which are not sensitive to absolute changes in value, only to rank orders. This is an important point to be discussed later.

After reviewing the evidence for average IQ differences by social class and race, Herrnstein poses the nature–nurture problem of "which is primary" in determining phenotypic differences in IQ. For racial groups, he explains, the origins of mean IQ differences are indeterminate at the present time because we have no information from heritability studies in the black population or from other, unspecified, lines of research which could favor primarily genetic or primarily environmental hypotheses. He is thoroughly convinced, however, that individual differences and social-class differences in IQ are highly heritable at the present time, and are destined, by environmental improvements, to become even more so:

> If we make the relevant environment much more uniform (by making it as good as we can for everyone), then an even larger proportion of the variation in IQ will be attributable to the genes. The average person would be smarter, but intelligence would run in families even more obviously and with less regression toward the mean than we see today [p. 58].

For Herrnstein, society is, and will be even more strongly, a meritocracy based largely on inherited differences in IQ. He presents a "syllogism" (p. 58) to make his message clear:

1. If differences in mental abilities are inherited, and
2. If success requires those abilities, and
3. If earnings and prestige depend on success,
4. Then social standing (which reflects earnings and prestige) will be based to some extent on inherited differences among people.

Five "corollaries" for the future predict that the heritability of IQ will rise; that social mobility will become more strongly related to inherited IQ differences; that most bright people will be gathered in the top of the social structure, with the IQ dregs at the bottom; that many at the bottom will not have the intelligence needed for new jobs; and that the meritocracy will be built not just on inherited intelligence but on all inherited traits affecting success, which will presumably become correlated characters. Thus from the successful realization of our most precious, egalitarian, political and social goals there will arise a much more rigidly stratified society, a "virtual caste system" based on inborn ability.

To ameliorate this effect, society may have to move toward the socialist dictum, "From each according to his abilities, to each according to his needs," but Herrnstein sees complete equality of earnings and prestige as impossible because high-grade intelligence is scarce and must be recruited into those critical jobs that require it, by the promise of high earnings and high prestige. Although garbage collecting is critical to the health of the society, almost anyone can do it; to waste high-IQ persons on such jobs is to misallocate scarce resources at society's peril.

Herrnstein points to an ironic contrast between the effects of caste and class systems. Castes, which established artificial hereditary limits on social mobility, guarantee the inequality of opportunity that preserves IQ heterogeneity at all levels of the system. Many bright people are arbitrarily kept down and many unintelligent people are artificially maintained at the top. When arbitrary bounds on mobility are removed, as in our class system, most of the bright rise to the top and most of the dull fall to the bottom of the social system, and IQ differences between top and bottom become increasingly hereditary. The greater the environmental equality, the greater the hereditary differences between levels in the social structure. The thesis of egalitarianism surely leads to its antithesis in a way that Karl Marx never anticipated.

Herrnstein proposes that our best strategy, in the face of increasing biological stratification, is publicly to recognize genetic human differences but to reallocate wealth to a considerable extent. The IQ have-nots need not be poor. Herrnstein does not delve into the psychological consequences of being publicly marked as genetically inferior.

Does the evidence support Herrnstein's view of hereditary social classes, now or in some future Utopia? Given his assumptions about the high heritability of IQ, the importance of IQ to social mobility, and the increasing environmental equality of rearing and opportunity, hereditary social classes are to some extent inevitable. But one can question the limits of genetic homogeneity in social-class groups and the evidence for his syllogism at present.

Is IQ as highly heritable throughout the social structure as Herrnstein assumes? Probably not. In a recent study of IQ heritability in various racial and social-class groups (9), I found much lower proportions of genetic variance that would account for aptitude differences among lower-class than among middle-class children, in both black and white groups. Social disadvantage in prenatal and postnatal development can substantially lower phenotypic IQ and reduce the genotype–phenotype correlation. Thus, average phenotypic IQ differences between the social classes may be considerably larger than the genotypic differences.

Are social classes largely based on hereditary IQ differences now? Probably not as much as Herrnstein believes. Since opportunities for social mobility act at the phenotypic level, there still may be considerable genetic diversity for IQ at the bottom of the social structure. In earlier days arbitrary social barriers maintained genetic variability throughout the social structure. At present, individuals with high phenotypic IQ's are often upwardly mobile; but inherited wealth acts to maintain genetic diversity at the top, and nongenetic biological and social barriers to phenotypic development act to maintain a considerable genetic diversity of intelligence in the lower classes.

As P. E. Vernon has pointed out (10), we are inclined to forget that the majority of gifted children in recent generations have come from working-class, not middle-class, families. A larger percentage of middle-class children are gifted, but the working and lower classes produce gifted children in larger numbers. How many more disadvantaged children would have been bright if they had had middle-class gestation and rearing conditions?

I am inclined to think that intergenerational class mobility will always be with us, for three reasons. First, since normal IQ is a polygenic characteristic, various recombinations of parental genotypes will always produce more variable genotypes in the offspring than in the parents of all social-class groups, especially the extremes. Even if both parents, instead of primarily the male, achieved social-class status based on their IQ's, recombinations of their genes would always produce a range of offspring, who would be upwardly or downwardly mobile relative to their families of origin.

Second, since, as Herrnstein acknowledges, factors other than IQ—motivational, personality, and undetermined—also contribute to success or the lack of it, high IQ's will always be found among lower-class adults, in combination with schizophrenia, alcoholism, drug addiction, psychopathy, and other limiting factors. When recombined in offspring, high IQ can readily segregate with facilitating motivational and personality characteristics, thereby leading to upward mobility for many offspring. Similarly, middle-class parents will always produce some offspring with debilitating personal characteristics which lead to downward mobility.

Third, for all children to develop phenotypes that represent their best genotypic outcome (in current environments) would require enormous changes in the present social system. To improve and equalize all rearing environments would involve such massive intervention as to make Herrnstein's view of the future more problematic than he seems to believe.

RACE AS CASTE

Races are castes between which there is very little mobility. Unlike the social-class system, where mobility based on IQ is sanctioned, the racial caste system, like the hereditary aristocracy of medieval Europe and the caste system of India, preserves within each group its full range of genetic diversity of intelligence. The Indian caste system was, according to Dobzhansky (*11*), a colossal genetic failure—or success, according to egalitarian values. After the abolition of castes at independence, Brahmins and untouchables were found to be equally educable despite—or because of—their many generations of segregated reproduction.

While we may tentatively conclude that there are some genetic IQ differences between social-class groups, we can make only wild speculations about racial groups. Average phenotypic IQ differences between races are not evidence for genetic differences (any more than they are evidence for environmental differences). Even if the heritabilities of IQ are extremely high in all races, there is still no warrant for equating within-group and between-group heritabilities (*12*). There are examples in agricultural experiments of within-group differences that are highly heritable but between-group differences that are entirely environmental. Draw two random samples of seeds from the same genetically heterogeneous population. Plant one sample in uniformly good conditions, the other in uniformly poor conditions. The average height difference between the populations of plants will be entirely environmental, although the individual differences in height within each sample will be entirely genetic. With known genotypes for seeds and known environments, genetic and environmental variances between groups can be studied. But racial groups are not random samples from the same population, nor are members reared in uniform conditions within each race. Racial groups are of unknown genetic equivalence for polygenic characteristics like IQ, and the differences in environments within and between the races may have as yet unquantified effects.

There is little to be gained from approaching the nature–nurture problem of race differences in IQ directly (*13*). Direct comparisons of estimated within-group heritabilities and the calculation of between-group heritabilities require assumptions that few investigators are willing to make, such as that all environmental differences are quantifiable, that differences in the environments of blacks and whites can be assumed to affect IQ in the same way in the two groups, and that differences in environments between groups can be "statistically controlled." A direct assault on race differences in IQ is vulnerable to many criticisms.

Indirect approaches may be less vulnerable. These include predictions of parent–child regression effects and admixture studies. Regression effects can be predicted to differ for blacks and whites if the two races indeed have genetically different population means. If the population mean for blacks is 15 IQ points lower than that of whites, then the offspring of high-IQ black parents should show greater regression (toward a lower population mean) than the offspring of whites of equally high IQ. Similarly, the offspring of low-IQ black parents should show less regression than those of white parents of equally low IQ. This hypothesis assumes that assortative mating for IQ is equal in the two races, which could be empirically determined but has not been studied as yet. Interpretable results from a parent–child regression study would also depend upon careful attention to intergenerational environmental changes, which could be greater in one race than the other.

Studies based on correlations between degree of white admixture and IQ scores *within* the black group would avoid many of the pitfalls of between-group comparisons. If serological genotypes can be used to identify persons with more and less white admixture, and if estimates of admixture based on blood groups are relatively independent of visible characteristics like skin color, then any positive correlation between degree of admixture and IQ would suggest genetic racial differences in IQ. Since blood groups have not been used directly as the basis of racial discrimination, positive findings would be relatively immune from environmentalist criticisms. The trick is to estimate individual admixture reliably. Several loci which have fairly different distributions of alleles in contemporary African and white populations have been proposed (*14*). No one has yet attempted a study of this sort.

h^2 AND PHENOTYPE

Suppose that the heritabilities of IQ differences within all racial and social-class groups were .80, as Jensen estimates, and suppose that the children in all groups were reared under an equal range of conditions. Now, suppose that racial and social-class differences in mean IQ still remained. We would probably infer some degree of genetic difference between the groups. So what? The question now turns from a strictly scientific one to one of science and social policy.

As Eysenck, Jensen, and others (*14*) have noted, eugenic and euthenic strategies are both possible interventions to reduce the number of low-IQ individuals in all populations. Eugenic policies could be advanced to encourage or require reproductive abstinence by people who fall below a certain level of intelligence. The Reeds (*15*) have determined that one-fifth of the mental retardation among whites of the next generation could be prevented if no mentally retarded persons of this generation reproduced. There is no question that a eugenic program applied at the phenotypic level of parents' IQ would substantially reduce the number of low-IQ children in the future white population. I am aware of no studies in the black population to support a similar program, but some proportion of future retardation could surely be eliminated. It would be extremely important, however, to sort out genetic and environmental sources of low IQ both in racial and in social-class groups before advancing a eugenic program. The request or demand that some persons refrain from any reproduction should be a last resort, based on sure knowledge that their retardation is caused primarily by genetic factors and is not easily remedied by environmental intervention. Studies of the IQ levels of adopted children with mentally retarded natural parents would be most instructive, since some of the retardation observed among children of retarded parents may stem from the rearing environments provided by the parents.

In a pioneering study of adopted children and their adoptive and natural parents, Skodak (*16*) reported greater *correlations* of children's IQ's with their natural than with their adoptive parents' IQ's. This statement has been often misunderstood to mean that the children's *levels* of intelligence more closely resembled their natural parents', which is completely false. Although the rank order of the children's IQ's resembled that of their mothers' IQ's, the children's IQ's were higher, being distributed, like those of the adoptive parents, around a mean above 100, whereas their natural mothers' IQ's averaged only 85. The children, in fact, averaged 21 IQ points higher than their natural mothers. If the (unstudied) natural fathers' IQ's averaged around the population mean of 100, the mean of the children's would be expected to be 94, or 12 points lower than the mean obtained. The unexpected boost in IQ was presumably due to the better social environments provided by the adoptive families. Does this mean that phenotypic IQ can be substantially changed?

Even under existing conditions of child rearing, phenotypes of children reared by low-IQ parents could be markedly changed by giving them the same rearing environment as the top IQ group provide for their children. According to DeFries (*17*), if children whose parents average 20 IQ points below the population mean were reared in environments such as usually are provided only by parents in the top .01 percent of the population, these same children would average 5 points *above* the population mean instead of 15 points below, as they do when reared by their own families.

Euthenic policies depend upon the demonstration that different rearing conditions can change phenotypic IQ sufficiently to enable most people in a social class or racial group to function in future society. I think there is great promise in this line of research and practice, although its efficacy will depend ultimately on the cost and feasibility of implementing radical intervention programs. Regardless of the present heritability of IQ in any population, phenotypes can be changed by the introduction of new and different environments. (One merit of Eysenck's book is the attention he gives to this point.) Furthermore, it is impossible to predict phenotypic outcomes under very different conditions. For example, in the Milwaukee Project (*18*), in which the subjects are ghetto children whose mothers' IQ's are less than 70, intervention began soon after the children were born. Over a four-year period Heber has intensively tutored the children for several hours every day and has produced an enormous IQ difference between the experimental group (mean IQ 127) and a control group (mean IQ 90). If the tutored children continue to advance in environments which are radically different from their homes with retarded mothers, we shall have some measure of the present phenotypic range of reaction (*19*) of children whose average IQ's might have been in the 80 to 90 range. These data support Crow's comment on h^2 in his contribution to the *Harvard Educational Review* discussion (p. 158):

It does not directly tell us how much improvement in IQ to expect from a given change in the environment. In particular, it offers no guidance as to the consequences of a new kind of environmental influence. For example, conventional heritability measures for height show a value of nearly 1. Yet, because of unidentified environmental influences, the mean height in the United States and in Japan has risen by a spectacular amount. Another kind of illustration is provided by the discovery of a cure for a hereditary disease. In such cases, any information on prior heritability may become irrelevant. Furthermore, heritability predictions are less dependable at the tails of the distribution.

To illustrate the phenotypic changes that can be produced by radically different environments for children with clear genetic anomalies, Rynders (20) has provided daily intensive tutoring for Down's syndrome infants. At the age of two, these children have average IQ's of 85 while control-group children, who are enrolled in a variety of other programs, average 68. Untreated children have even lower average IQ scores.

The efficacy of intervention programs for children whose expected IQ's are too low to permit full participation in society depends on their long-term effects on intelligence. Early childhood programs may be necessary but insufficient to produce functioning adults. There are critical research questions yet to be answered about euthenic programs, including what kinds, how much, how long, how soon, and toward what goals?

DOES h^2 MATTER?

There is growing disillusionment with the concept of heritability, as it is understood and misunderstood. Some who understand it very well would like to eliminate h^2 from human studies for at least two reasons. First, the usefulness of h^2 estimates in animal and plant genetics pertains to decisions about the efficacy of selective breeding to produce more desirable phenotypes. Selective breeding does not apply to the human case, at least so far. Second, if important phenotypic changes can be produced by radically different environments, then, it is asked, who cares about the heritability of IQ? Morton (21) has expressed these sentiments well:

> Considerable popular interest attaches to such questions as "is one class or ethnic group innately superior to another on a particular test?" The reasons are entirely emotional, since such a difference, if established, would serve as no better guide to provision of educational or other facilities than an unpretentious assessment of phenotypic differences.

I disagree. The simple assessment of phenotypic performance does not suggest any particular intervention strategy. Heritability estimates can have merit as indicators of the effects to be expected from various types of intervention programs. If, for example, IQ tests, which predict well to achievements in the larger society, show low heritabilities in a population, then it is probable that simply providing better environments which now exist will improve average performance in that population. If h^2 is high but environments sampled in that population are largely unfavorable, then (again) simple environmental improvement will probably change the mean phenotypic level. If h^2 is high and the environments sampled are largely favorable, then novel environmental manipulations are probably required to change phenotypes, and eugenic programs may be advocated.

The most common misunderstanding of the concept "heritability" relates to the myth of fixed intelligence: If h^2 is high, this reasoning goes, then intelligence is genetically fixed and unchangeable at the phenotypic level. This misconception ignores the fact that h^2 is a population statistic, bound to a given set of environmental conditions at a given point in time. Neither intelligence nor h^2 estimates are fixed.

It is absurd to deny that the frequencies of genes for behavior may vary between populations. For individual differences within populations, and for social-class differences, a genetic hypothesis is almost a necessity to explain some of the variance in IQ, especially among adults in contemporary white populations living in average or better environments. But what Jensen, Shuey, and Eysenck (and others) propose is that genetic racial differences are necessary to account for the current phenotypic differences in mean IQ between populations. That may be so, but it would be extremely difficult, given current methodological limitations, to gather evidence that would dislodge an environmental hypothesis to account for the same data. And to assert, despite the absence of evidence, and in the present social climate, that a particular race is genetically disfavored in intelligence is to scream "FIRE! . . . I think" in a crowded theater. Given that so little is known, further scientific study seems far more justifiable than public speculations.

ACKNOWLEDGMENTS

I thank Philip Salapatek, Richard Weinberg, I. I. Gottesman, and Leonard I. Heston for their critical reading of this paper. They are not in any way responsible for its content, however.

REFERENCES AND NOTES

1. For a review of studies, see L. Erlenmeyer-Kimling and L. F. Jarvik, *Science* **142,** 1477 (1963). Heritability is the ratio of genetic variance to total phenotypic variance. For human studies, heritability is used in its broad sense of total genetic variance/total phenotypic variance.

2. The *Harvard Educational Review* compilation includes Jensen's paper, "How much can we boost IQ and scholastic achievement?," comments on it by J. S. Kagan, J. McV Hunt, J. F. Crow, C. Bereiter, D. Elkind, L. J. Cronbach, and W. F. Brazziel, and a rejoinder by Jensen. See also A. R. Jensen, in J. Hellmuth, *Disadvantaged Child,* vol. 3 (Special Child Publ., Seattle, Wash., 1970).

3. P. L. Nichols, thesis, University of Minnesota (1970). Nichols reports that in two large samples of black and white children, seven-year WISC IQ scores showed the same means and distributions for the two racial groups, once social-class variables were equated. These results are unlike those of several other studies, which found that matching socio-economic status did not create equal means in the two racial groups (A. Shuey (5); A. B. Wilson, *Racial Isolation in the Public Schools,* vol. 2 (Government Printing Office, Washington, D.C., 1967)]. In Nichols's samples, prenatal and postnatal medical care was equally available to blacks and whites, which may have contributed to the relatively high IQ scores of the blacks in these samples.

4. By interaction, Eysenck means simply $P = G + E$, or "Heredity and environment acting together to produce the observed phenotype" (p. 111). He does not mean what most geneticists and behavior geneticists mean by interaction; that is, the *differential* phenotypic effects produced by various combinations of genotypes and environments, as in the interaction term of analysis-of-variance statistics. Few thinking people are not interactionists in Eysenck's sense of the term, because that's the only way to get the organism and the environment into the same equation to account for variance in any phenotypic trait. How much of the phenotypic variance is accounted for by each of the terms in the equation is the real issue.

5. A. Shuey, *The Testing of Negro Intelligence* (Social Science Press, New York, 1966), pp. 499–519.

6. F. B. Davis, *The Measurement of Mental Capacity through Evoked-Potential Recordings* (Educational Records Bureau, Greenwich, Conn., 1971). "As it turned out, no evidence was found that the latency periods obtained . . . displayed serviceable utility for predicting school performance or level of mental ability among pupils in preschool through grade 8" (p. v).

7. *New York Times,* 8 Oct. 1971, p. 41.

8. J. Kagan and H. A. Moss, *Birth to Maturity* (Wiley, New York, 1962).

9. S. Scarr-Salapetek, *Science,* in press.

10. P. E. Vernon, *Intelligence and Cultural Environment* (Methuen, London, 1969).

11. T. Dobzhansky, *Mankind Evolving* (Yale Univ. Press, New Haven, 1962), pp. 234–238.

12. J. Thoday, *J. Biosocial Science* **1,** suppl. 3, 4 (1969).

13. L. L. Cavalli-Sforza and W. F. Bodmer, *The Genetics of Human Populations* (Freeman, San Francisco, 1971), pp. 753–804. They propose that the study of racial differences is useless and not scientifically supportable at the present time.

14. T. E. Reed, *Science* **165,** 762 (1969); *Am. J. Hum. Genet.* **21,** 1 (1969); C. MacLean and P. L. Workman, paper at a meeting of the American Society of Human Genetics (1970), Indianapolis).

15. E. W. Reed and S. C. Reed, *Mental Retardation: A Family Study* (Saunders, Philadelphia, 1965); *Social Biol.* **18,** suppl., 42 (1971).

16. M. Skodak and H. M. Skeels, *J. Genet. Psychol.* **75,** 85 (1949).

17. J. C. DeFries, paper for the C.O.B.R.E. Research Workshop on Genetic Endowment and Environment in the Determination of Behavior (3–8 Oct. 1971, Rye, N.Y.).

18. R. Heber, *Rehabilitation of Families at Risk for Mental Retardation* (Regional Rehabilitation Center, Univ. of Wisconsin, 1969). S. P. Strickland, *Am. Ed.* **7,** 3 (1971).

19. I. I. Gottesman, in *Social Class, Race, and Psychological Development,* M. Deutsch, I. Katz, and A. R. Jensen, Eds. (Holt, Rinehart, and Winston, New York, 1968), pp. 11–51.

20. J. Rynders, personal communication, November 1971.

21. N. E. Morton, paper for the C.O.B.R.E. Research Workshop on Genetic Endowment and Environment in the Determination of Behavior (3–8 Oct. 1971, Rye, N.Y.).

An Evolutionary Perspective on Infant Intelligence: Species Patterns and Individual Variations*

I.3

Since selection can and did occur in terms of developments at all ontogenetic points, the entire life span is a product of evolutionary adaptation, and a psychologist interested in causes of behavior must simultaneously consider phylogeny and ontogeny, difficult as it may seem. [Freedman, 1967, p. 489]

Any attempt to construct an evolutionary view of infant intelligence should raise a certain skepticism in the reader's mind. What, after all, is the nature of intelligence in infancy? And how shall the validity of an evolutionary account be judged? Not, certainly, by its predictive power for the future evolution of infant behavior! On the first question I shall defer largely to Piaget (1952), whose descriptions and explanations of infant intelligence I find consistent with an evolutionary view. On the second question, a few words about evolutionary theory may be helpful.

The central tenet of evolutionary theory is natural selection, an exceedingly simple idea. Organisms differ from one another. They produce more young than the available resources can sustain. Those best adapted survive to pass on their genetic characteristics to their offspring, while others perish with fewer or no offspring. Subsequent generations therefore are more like their better-adapted ancestors. The result is evolutionary change (Ghiselin, 1969, p. 46). Elaborations of the

---

*This chapter by Sandra Scarr-Salapatek originally appeared in M. Lewis (Ed.), *Origins of Intelligence: Infancy and Early Childhood*. New York: Plenum, 1976. Copyright © 1976. Reprinted by permission of Plenum Press.

idea of natural selection, as it applies to periods in the life span, learned characteristics, and speciation, appear throughout this chapter.

An evolutionary account of any human behavior is by definition a historical reconstruction. We cannot observe our behavioral past. There are limits, however, to the fancifulness of a useful evolutionary construction: the known facts must fit and contrary facts must be few and isolated. Most important, the hypothetical account must be open to falsification; it cannot contain statements that could explain every possible outcome—and thus be unfalsifiable. These criteria are especially important for *ad hoc* theories, since predictions about human evolution cannot be tested within the life span of any investigator. Some testable hypotheses can be generated, however, about phenomena not directly used to construct the account. The implications of the theoretical construction will, hopefully, extend beyond the immediate boundaries of its most central facts. In these ways evolutionary views can be scientifically tested.

Within an evolutionary framework I want to make a radical argument about the natural history of human, infant intelligence. The argument revolves around the primary nature of early intelligence—a nonverbal, practical kind of adaptation. Sensorimotor behaviors must, I think, have emerged very early in primate evolution, certainly before man split off from the great apes. There is simply too high a degree of parallelism in the early intelligence of apes and man to suggest independent, convergent evolution. The phylogeny of infant intelligence seems to be very ancient history.

The ontogeny of infant intelligence has a distinctive pattern and timing. The species pattern, I would argue, is not an unfolding of some genetic program but a dynamic interplay of genetic preadaptations and developmental adaptations to features of the caretaking environment. Individual variation is limited by canalization, on the one hand, and by common human environments, on the other. From the common behavioral elements to be seen among individuals, one can abstract a species pattern to describe and contrast with the patterns of other species. One must be ever mindful, however, that what exists are individuals, each different from the other; a species-typical pattern is an abstraction from reality. The development of infant intelligence has both a species-typical pattern and individual variation. How and why the species theme and individual differences exist is the subject of this chapter.

Four hypotheses about the nature and evolution of human infant intelligence are basic to my argument:

1. That infant intelligence evolved earlier in our primate past than ontoge-
    netically later forms of intelligent behavior and remains virtually
    unchanged from the time that hominids emerged.
2. That selection pressures that resulted in the present pattern of sensori-
    motor intelligence acted both on the infant himself and on the caretak-
    ing behaviors of his parents.
3. That infant intelligence is phenotypically less variable than later intelli-
    gent behavior because it has been subjected to longer and stronger
    natural selection.
4. That the phenotypic development of infant intelligence is governed
    both by genetic preadaptation (canalization) and by developmental
    adaptation to human physical and caretaking environments.

AN EVOLUTIONARY VIEW OF INFANT INTELLIGENCE

The Nature of the Sensorimotor Period

The primary tasks of infant primates are to survive the first two
years and to learn to operate effectively in the physical and social
environment. The attachment system is of critical importance to survival
and to learning species-appropriate social interactions. Sensorimotor
skills are critical to survival and to adaptation in the physical and social
worlds. As several authors have noted (e.g., Bell, 1970; Bowlby, 1969,
1973), the development of social attachments is intertwined with increasing cognitive skills, such as object or person permanence. I divide
the cognitive and affective domains here more for convenience of discussion than for any good conceptual reasons. Infant primates' survival
depends upon the protection of their caretakers while they become
competent to explore and learn. The increasing distance permitted
between infant and mother is correlated with increasing sensorimotor
skills. Both serve survival and adaptation.

Infant primates are remarkably curious and open to learning how to
be practical experimenters. The presymbolic skills of human infancy that
Piaget has so richly described also characterize our nearest primate
relatives. The great apes and even Old World monkeys master sensorimotor skills that are very like those of human infants.* Later in the life

* I do not claim that other mammals are not capable of some aspects of sensorimotor
  intelligence, such as object permanence. The manipulative, tool-using skills, however,
  are largely limited to species with good prehension.

span human and nonhuman primates show different forms of adaptation. Different selective pressures, particularly those that led to man's cultural revolution, have produced quite dissimilar forms of childhood and adult intelligence.

Man's gradual accumulation of culture has great relevance to his evolution past infancy. Culture provided new environments to which childhood and adult adaptations could occur. As McClearn (1972) said:

> First steps toward culture provided a new environment in which some individuals were more fit, in the Darwinian sense, than others; their offspring were better adapted to culture and capable of further innovations; and so on. The argument can be made that, far from removing mankind from the process of evolution, culture has provided the most salient natural selection pressure to which man has been subject in his recent evolutionary past. (p. 57)

The pressures of culture on intelligence are self-evident. The greater the ability of some individuals to learn and to innovate, the more likely they were to survive to reproduce, and the more likely it was in the long run that their progeny would have even greater fitness in the new environment. But I would argue that the symbolic cultural revolution had practically no effect on the evolution of infant intelligence.

The distinctly different nature of infant intelligence was recognized by Florence Goodenough, who noted:

> The unsettled question as to whether or not true intelligence may be said to have emerged before symbolic processes exemplified in speech may have become established. Attempting to measure infantile intelligence may be like trying to measure a boy's beard at the age of three. (quoted by Elkind, 1967)

Sensorimotor intelligence is qualitatively different from later symbolic operations, whose evolution may have quite a different history. I do not propose a common primate history for formal operations, or even for concrete operations, although some symbolic and conceptual skills are shared by apes and man (e.g., Premack, 1971). I do propose that the natural history of sensorimotor intelligence is independent of skills that evolved later and that there is no logically necessary connection between them.

Indeed, the empirical connection between sensorimotor skills and later intellectual development is very tenuous (Stott and Ball, 1965). Children with severe motor impairments, whose sensorimotor practice has been extremely limited, have been shown to develop normal symbolic function (Kopp and Shaperman, 1973). The purported dependence of symbolic activity on sensorimotor action has not been demonstrated. One reason for the lack of correlation may be different sources of individual variation. If sensorimotor and symbolic skills have different genetic bases, they could well be uncorrelated. Sensorimotor skills are best seen as a criterion achievement; that is, individual differences are found in the *rate* but not the final *level* of sensorimotor development. Symbolic intelligence has individual differences in both rate and level of achievement, and the rate of development is correlated with the final level (witness the substantial correlations between IQ at ages 5 and 15). Infant intelligence is characterized by universal attainment by all nondefective species members. Its evolution is more ancient history than symbolic reasoning, and individual differences do not have the predictive significance of variations in later intelligence.

Infant Learning

The fact that human infants learn is of paramount importance to understanding the evolution of infancy and infant development. All normal babies interact with their social and physical worlds, structure and interpret their experiences, and modify their subsequent interactions. As Piaget has described, human infants set about learning in a graded sequence of intellectual stages that reflect their growing awareness of the effects of their actions and of the properties of the physical and social worlds around them.

A critical feature of human learning is its flexibility. In infancy we see the major transitions from reflex organization to a flexible, experimental approach to the world. By 1–1½ years babies have become impressive, practical experimenters. The rapid development of practical intelligence leaves the rest of the preadolescent period for mental adaptations. While formal operational thought may not develop in all normal species members, sensorimotor intelligence does.

In a brilliant and provocative paper Bruner (1972) outlined the nature and uses of immaturity for human development. He identified the "tutor-proneness" of the young, their readiness to learn through observation and instruction. Infants are ever ready to respond to novelties provided by the adult world. Further, they use play, according to Bruner, as an opportunity to work out their knowledge in safety—without the consequences that would befall adults who were in the initial stages of learning sensorimotor skills and how to be a responsible social animal. The distinctive pattern of immaturity lends itself to more flexible adaptation for the species. The usefulness of opportunities for learning depends upon the behavioral flexibility of the infant to acquire by learning what has not been "built into" the genome.

Two facts of human evolutionary history are particularly salient for infancy: the necessity of infant–mother dyads and the consistent availability of a larger human group into which the dyad is integrated. No surviving infant was without a social context throughout human history.* The evolution of infant development has occurred, therefore, in the context of normal infant environments. This context has, I think, profound implications for the lack of developmental fixity (Lehrman, 1970) in infant behavior. Foremost, it has been unnecessary for selection to build into the genotype those behaviors that all infants would develop experientially in their human groups. All normal infants would have close contact with mothers and other conspecifics and with tools and material culture, thus giving them opportunities to learn object manipulation, social bonds, and a human language. What has evolved genotypically is a bias toward acquiring these forms of behavior, a bias that Dobzhansky (1967) calls human educability.

The Evolution of Infancy

Infancy is a mammalian theme. A period of suckling the dependent young evolved as an efficient way to increase the survival chances of fewer and fewer offspring. Extended care of the dependent young is a burden and a risk for their parents, however, but it is of greatest evolutionary importance to the mammalian pattern of reproduction and parental behavior. The more an organism is protected from the vicissitudes of the environment, the greater the role of intraspecific competition. What one offspring requires of its parents are energy and resources not available to another offspring of those same parents. It became advantageous to have fewer and better-equipped offspring rather than many offspring and to have long life spans. Both competition for females and demands for long parental care put a premium on long life

---

* The few reported cases of feral children, even if they are believed, have contributed little to the human gene pool and the subsequent evolution of infant behaviors.

span, and this again decreased the number of offspring still further (Mayr, 1970, pp. 338–340).

Primate infancy is an elaboration (exaggeration?) of the mammalian pattern: A single infant born not more than once a year and requiring years of parental care. What advantages can such a pattern confer? Highly developed parental care allows a fundamental change in the genetics of behavioral development. Primate infants have a more "open program" for learning than other mammals. Such an open program requires a far larger brain in the adults who provide the care and in the infants who must learn what information is needed. Primate intelligence is a coadapted product of evolutionary changes in the duration and the intensity of infant dependence and parental care. No one product could have evolved independently of the others.

I would argue, however, that the pattern of development for human infants in the sensorimotor period was basically established in common with other closely related primates. The later evolutionary history of apes and man led to species differences in the degree of immaturity at birth, the degree of flexibility in learning, and the length of the socialization period. In considering infancy alone, however, I am struck by incredible similarities in the sensorimotor period, similarities that should be considered apart from the later, more obvious differences. Prolonged infancy evolved as a primate variation on the mammalian theme. Human infancy is a further evolution of the primate pattern. Contemporary apes have evolved patterns of infant development that still share much with the human species. These similarities originated in our common primate past.

Every period of the human life span is a product of selection (Mayr, 1970, p. 84). Multiple pressures, which we can only speculate about *post hoc*, must have played interacting roles in the evolution of prolonged infancy. LaBarre (1954) argued for an increasing specialization of human infants in *brains*. One-seventh of the newborn's weight is brain. With limitations to the female pelvic girth infants were born less and less mature to assure the safe passage of the big-brained fetus into the world. Changes in adult behaviors must have accompanied the increasingly long dependence of a less mature infant:

> Curiously enough, as human females became better mammals (through sexual availability and permanent breasts) and as human males increased in constancy of sexual drive, the human infant seems simultaneously to be specializing in mammalian infancy. In helplessness and dependency, human

babies and children are about as infantile as mammalian infants come.
(LaBarre, 1973, p. 29)

LaBarre's account of the coordinated changes in adult male, adult
female, and infant adaptations includes the structure of the family,
which, he says, depends upon the sexual availability of the female to
keep the father home, on the father's strong sexual drive, and on the
infant's attachment relation with his mother (LaBarre, 1954). LaBarre's
account of the evolution of human immaturity is highly speculative.
Mayr (1970, p. 407) argued that brain size could have increased still
further if (1) the female pelvic size increased; (2) pregnancy were shortened; or (3) more brain growth were postnatal. Any of these adaptations
would permit further evolution of brain size (although no increase in
brain size has occurred in the last 30,000 years of man's evolution,
presumably because there is no longer a selective premium on it).
Omenn and Motulsky (1972) noted that human newborns are delivered
at a less advanced stage of development than newborn apes and monkeys, a fact that they attribute to two adaptational differences. First, the
female pelvis narrowed with the adaptation to bipedal locomotion, and
the restriction in the bony birth canal required earlier birth of fetuses.
Second, the slow maturation of human infants is ideally adapted to the
molding of species-specific behaviors by social input.

It is impossible at present to decide which set of factors in evolutionary history accounted for the correlated shifts in infant intelligence,
immaturity, and parental behaviors. They are coadapted. The total
phenotype is, after all, a compromise of all selection pressures, some of
which are opposed to each other (Mayr, 1970, p. 112). The evolution of
neoteny and infant intelligence most likely represents a compromise
solution among pressures on adults to provide increased infant care (a
liability), pressures for increasing brain size and flexible learning ability
(a benefit, we presume), reproductive economy, and other factors we
can only guess.

Restrictions on Phenotypic Variability

In the case of infant intelligence, the flexibility in learning that is
typical of humans must have some bounds. Species adaptation depends
upon a rather limited range of behavioral phenotypes. Some character-

istically human patterns need to emerge in every individual. There are two principal mechanisms for limiting the possible number of phenotypes that develop: *canalization* by genetic preadaptation and *developmental adaptation*.

Canalization is a genetic predisposition for the development of a certain form of adaptation, guided along internally regulated lines. Environmental features are necessary for complete development or for the full expression of the adaptation, but the direction of the development is difficult to deflect. Environmental inputs that are necessary for canalized development to occur must be universally available to the species, else this form of adaptation would not work.

Embryologists, particularly Waddington (1957, 1962, 1971), have long recognized the "self-righting" tendencies of many aspects of growth. The difficulty of deflecting an organism from its growth path (which Waddington calls a *creod*) is expressed in the idea of canalization. Canalization restricts phenotypic diversity to a limited species range while maintaining desirable genetic diversity. If all genetic diversity were phenotypically expressed, there would be such enormous behavioral differences among people that it is difficult to see how any population could reproduce and survive (Vale and Vale, 1969). There are obviously functional equivalences in many genotypes (they produce similar phenotypes) for the most basic human characteristics.

Canalization is a very conservative force in evolutionary history. A well-knit system of canalization tends to restrict evolutionary potential quite severely. It accounts for the maintenance of particular phenotypes throughout a family of related species for no obvious reason, since a different phenotype seems to serve another taxon equally well in the same environment (Mayr, 1970, p. 174). In the case of infant intelligence the similarities among primate species suggest a relative immunity to recent evolutionary pressures.

A major reason for the perseverence of particular phenotypes is that new characters or traits are produced not by isolated mutations but by a reorganization of the genotype. It requires a genetic revolution to break up a well-buffered developmental pattern. Second, most genetic variability can be hidden by canalized development and therefore be immune to selective pressures:

> A tight system of developmental homeostasis helps to shield the organism against environmental fluctuations. However much genetic variation

there is in a gene pool the less of it penetrates into the phenotype, the smaller
the point of attack it offers to selection. (Mayr, 1970, p. 39)

The total genome is a "physiological team." No genes are soloists;
they must play harmoniously with others to achieve selective advantage
because selection works on the whole person and on whole coadapted
gene complexes in the population. As Dobzhansky (1955) has said,
evolution favors genes that are "good mixers," ones that make the most
positive contributions to fitness against the greatest number of genetic
backgrounds.

Selection is always for coadapted gene complexes that fit a developmental pattern. The sheer number of gene differences between individuals or species is not a good measure of overall difference. To express
individual or population differences as differences in the number of
nucleotide pairs of the DNA is like trying to express the difference
between the Bible and Dante's *Divine Comedy* in terms of the frequency
of letters used in the two works (Mayr, 1970, p. 322). The developmental
pattern of infant intelligence is, I would argue, a strongly buffered
epigenotype that is shared by our closest primate relatives. To break it
up would require multiple rewritings of the primate manuscript.

Compared with canalization, *developmental adaptation* is a more flexible arrangement to ensure survival in varied possible environments. The
genetic program does not specify a particular *response* to any environment, but it specifies a generalized *responsiveness* to the distinctive
features of environments within a permissible range of variation. In
practice it is very difficult to distinguish between *developmental adaptation*
and *genetic preadaptation* (through selection) because they serve the same
goal, i.e., to limit the possible behavioral phenotypes that develop.

The contrast between canalization and developmental adaptation is
not a distinction between genetic and environmental determinants of
development. Every human characteristic is genetically based (because
the entire organism is), but a useful distinction can be made between
genetic differences and nongenetic differences. *Nongenetic* means simply
that the differences between two phenotypes are not caused by genetic
differences. The capacity of a single genotype to produce two or more
phenotypes is itself genetically controlled, of course (Mayr, 1970). The
notion of a genetic blueprint for ontogeny means that each genotype has
its own canalized course of development, from which it is difficult to
deflect. In the case of strong genetic canalization, individual phenotypic

differences are presumably genetic because one genotype cannot produce a variety of phenotypes. In the case of weak canalization, one genotype can and does produce multiple phenotypes among which the differences are not genetic.

Two puzzling examples of human adaptation illustrate the difference between genetic adaptation as a result of natural selection and developmental adaptation as a result of genetic flexibility (strong versus weak canalization). Milk "intolerance" normally develops in most humans after the preschool years. The ability to digest large quantities of milk in adulthood is the result of prolonged lactase activity in some populations that have practiced dairying for the past several thousand years. Is the continued secretion of lactase in adulthood a developmental adaptation to continued milk drinking past weaning? Or is it a result of natural selection for lactase activity in those peoples for whom some selective advantage was derived from milk in their adult diets?

The second example is adaptation to life at high altitudes. One feature of high altitudes is reduced oxygen concentrations in the air. Peoples in Ethiopia and in the Andes at elevations above 10,000 feet typically have large lung capacities and deep "barrel chests." Peoples who live at lower altitudes have smaller chests and lung capacities. Is this primarily a developmental adaptation or a result of natural selection for adaptation to a high-altitude niche?

In both cases, either a developmental or a selective adaptation would accomplish the same goal of better utilization of the available resources—in one case nutrition, in the other case oxygen. For reasons beyond the comprehension of this author, the case of milk "intolerance" seems to be primarily the result of natural selection acting on the gene frequencies for lactase activity past childhood (Gottesman and Heston, 1972). The second case—adaptation at high altitudes—is primarily a developmental phenomenon. We know these explanations to be the primary ones because in the case of lactase activity, continued milk drinking into later childhood does not maintain lactase activity in intolerant people at levels adequate for comfortable absorption of a significant portion of one's nutrition through milk, and discontinued milk drinking does not terminate lactase activity in people who are genetically tolerant of milk. In the lactose-tolerant group loading the stomach with milk at any time results in renewed lactase activity. In the lactose-intolerant case lactase activity declines despite continued stimulation through milk consumption.

The high-altitude example could well have represented genetic selection for life under unusual oxygen tension (Baker, 1969). After 15,000 years in the high Andes, however, Peruvian Indians who descend to the lowlands have children with little evidence of barrel-chestedness, and Indians who migrate from lowland to highland areas have children who exhibit the phenomenon. Harrison (1967) reported that Amharic Ethiopians who migrate from 5000- to 10,000-foot altitudes develop some chest enlargement even in adulthood.

What kinds of human behavioral characteristics are likely to show developmental adaptation more than genetic preadaptation? Omenn and Motulsky (1972) proposed that older (in an evolutionary sense) forms of adaptation are more likely to have limited genetic variability and a higher degree of canalization. Specifically, the brain stem, the midbrain, and the limbic structures that evolved earlier are less polymorphic than cortical areas of the brain. Behavioral characteristics associated with higher cortical centers are newer evolutionary phenomena and likely to develop more variable phenotypes. Behaviors associated with older areas of the brain, those we share with other primates, are genotypically and phenotypically less variable. Their development is more highly canalized. This hypothesis has clear implications for infant intelligence, as contrasted with later forms of intelligence.

Evidence on Canalization at Species, Population, and Individual Levels of Analysis

To evaluate the research evidence on the canalization of infant intelligence, we must coordinate the data gathered with several methodological approaches. Ethological and comparative studies of primates speak to the canalization of infant intelligence at a species level. Behavior genetic studies of variation analyze sources of individual differences within populations, and cross-cultural studies deal with population differences in development. Four operational definitions (or primitive models) are proposed to integrate comparative and ethological descriptions of species patterns with analytical studies of variation, including population and individual levels of analyses. Predictions can be made from any of the four:

1. Functional equivalencies in both genotypes and environments are interpreted as strong canalization at a species level. If neither geno-

typic nor environmental differences contribute much to phenotypic diversity, there will be a restricted range of individual differences, moderate heritability, and a distinctive species pattern.

2. Functional differences in genotypes but equivalencies in environments are interpreted as strong canalization at an individual, not a species, level. If genetic differences are the primary contributors to phenotypic differences, then heritability will be high within a population and between populations, if the distribution of genotypes is different.

3. Functional equivalencies of genotypes but not environments are interpreted as weak canalization at individual and population levels, with low heritabilities and a weak species pattern.

4. Functional equivalencies of neither genotypes nor environments will yield extreme individual phenotypic variation and moderate heritabilities within and between populations, if genotypes are differently distributed.

The implications of an evolutionary account for varied data on infant intelligence can now be tested. If infant intelligence indeed evolved early in primate history, if its development is to some extent canalized, and if both genotypes and environments are largely functionally equivalent, then contemporary primates should share a similar pattern of infant intelligence, individual diversity within the human species should be restricted, and the heritability of sensorimotor intelligence should be moderate, not high.

Infant Intelligence as Species-Specific Behavior

The notion of species-specific behavior is an abstraction from the reality of individual variation. Some behavioral geneticists deny the concept of "species-typical" any heuristic value (Bruell, 1970); others would support its usefulness as a statement about the highly leptokurtic shape of the distribution of individual differences within a species, measured on a species-comparative scale. Genetically conditioned homogeneity within a species is seen as a species-specific character; genetically conditioned heterogeneity is seen as individual variation within a species (Gottesman and Heston, 1972).

There is confusion inherent in the contrast between genetically conditioned homogeneity and heterogeneity in behavioral characteristics because (1) the notion of species-specific behavior is always an abstraction; (2) complex behaviors are always polygenic and to some degree phenotypically heterogeneous; and (3) the degree of phenotypic homogeneity is always relative to the scale on which the phenotype is measured. For example, take linear height. In the human population adult heights vary between, say, 3 feet and 7 feet, with the median height being about 5 feet 6 inches. From a within-species vantage point the distribution is somewhat leptokurtic, with perhaps 95% of the world population distributed between 5 feet and 6 feet 2 inches. If we scale human heights on a species-comparative scale from 0.01 inches to 240 inches (from protozoans to giraffes), the human distribution appears strongly leptokurtic. A "species-typical" height of about 5½ feet represents a useful value in relation to other species. Actually, of course, the human variation is quite large if one's perspective is intraspecific. And so it is with nearly all human behaviors.

Robin Fox (1970) has argued for the usefulness of the species-specific concept. Language capacity is one obvious example, but kinship, courtship and marriage arrangements, political behaviors, and male groups that exclude females appear to be other species-specific human traits. There are limits, he argues, to what the human species can do and to what we can understand in another's behavior. There must be "wired-in" ranges for the information-processing capacity that responds only to certain kinds of inputs. Our ability to process information and to respond to the inputs of another's behavior are strongly tied to our phylogeny and to timing in the life cycle.

We are faced with an apparent paradox: that species-specific behaviors do not exist but are an abstraction from the reality of individual variation, yet the concept of species-typical does have heuristic value on a species-comparative scale. We can better approach the problem of variation and the species-typical concept, I believe, by looking at what limitations there are on variability within species, and by what mechanisms variation is limited.

Biases in Learning

Though it hardly needs saying, human infants tend to learn some things rather than others. One example is language acquisition, for which underlying sensitivities to speech sounds, both comprehension and production, combine with the stimulation of a language environment to produce a speaking human child. Another example is hand–eye coordination. At around 3 months normal infants gaze extendedly at their hands as though they were detached objects. One might think that visually guided reaching followed from such accidental experiences. In fact, blind infants "gaze" at their hands in prolonged fashion at about the same age as seeing infants (Freedman, 1974). The canalization of arm–hand motor development seems to bring all infants' hands within their visual range at that point in development. Experience with hand regard doubtless plays a role in subsequent coordinations, but the opportunity for hand–eye coordination to develop has not been left to experiential chance.

Seligman (1970) has shown that mammals come to a learning situation with a good deal of built-in bias to learn particular things. It is simply not the case that any stimulus can be equally well associated with any response or reinforcement. I would argue that human infants have built-in biases to acquire certain kinds of intelligent behaviors that are consonant with primate evolutionary history, that these biases are programmed by the epigenotype, and that human environments guarantee the development of these behaviors through the provision of material objects that are assimilated to them.

We seldom emphasize the role of common human environments in development, being attuned as we are to look at distinctive features. The environments for highly canalized behaviors like walking are seldom even studied. Lipsitt (1971, p. 499) gave a charming description of an infant who is "ready" to walk being propped up on his legs and flopped back and forth between adults. The acquisition of walking undoubtedly has experiential components that can be studied (Zelazo, 1974). On the other hand, all human environments seem to provide the necessary and sufficient conditions for walking to begin between 10 and 15 months. Only physically infirm infants (handicapped, malnourished) and those deprived of firm support (Dennis, 1960) fail to walk during infancy.

A similar point can be made about language acquisition. All normal, hearing infants have a human language environment, regardless of which language is spoken, that provides the necessary and sufficient conditions for acquisition. Infant intellectual development has some of the same properties in that it follows a species pattern of sensorimotor skills that assimilate whatever material objects the culture offers. The overall species patterns for motor, language, and cognitive development seem to be well ordered by the chromosomes and the common human environment. While experimental interventions may accelerate the acquisition of these behaviors, all normal infants acquire them in due time, and it is not clear that acceleration has any lasting impact on subsequent development.

Deprivation Effects

If infant intelligence is highly canalized at a species level, one would predict that environmentally caused retardations of sensorimotor development would be overcome once the environmental causes were eliminated. Canalization implies such an outcome. Recently Kagan and Klein (1973) published a cross-sectional study of infant and childhood development in Guatemala. Their assessment of infant development in an Indian village suggested to them that the children were behaviorally quite retarded at the end of the first year. Older children in the same setting, however, approached the performance levels of United States children on a variety of learning and perceptual tasks. From the observation of "retarded" infants and intellectually "normal" older children, they concluded that human development is inherently resilient, that is, highly canalized at the species level:

> This corpus of data implies that absolute retardation in the time of emergence of universal cognitive competences during infancy is not predictive of comparable deficits for memory, perceptual analysis, and inference during preadolescence. Although the rural Guatemalan infants were retarded with respect to activation of hypotheses, alertness, and onset of stranger anxiety and object permanence, the preadolescents' performance . . . were comparable to American middle class norms. Infant retardation seems to be partially reversible and cognitive development during the early years more resilient than had been supposed. (p. 957)

What Kagan and Klein (1973) suggested about canalization is that the caretaking practices of rural Guatemalans significantly retard the rate of infant development but that this deflection is only temporary because later child-rearing practices compensate for the early deprivation. In Waddington's terms the Guatemalan infants' mental development is asserted to have been temporarily deflected from its canalized course by environmental deprivations but to have exhibited the same kind of "catch-up" phenomenon claimed for physical growth among children who have been ill or malnourished for brief periods of time. Unfortunately, serious ceiling effects on the later tests make it difficult to judge whether or not the older Guatemalan children have intellectual skills typical of United States white children. Thus arguments for the canalization of infant intelligence at a species level are not well supported by this study.

The Guatemalan data do suggest that environmental deprivation can retard sensorimotor development. Studies of institutionalized infants (White, 1971; Dennis, 1960) also support the conclusion that social and physical deprivation retard infant intelligence. One can question, however, whether or not sensorimotor skills fail to emerge eventually in even moderately deprived infants. While there is no question that the rate of acquisition is affected, is there any evidence that infants who have any contact with physical and social objects fail to develop criterion-level sensorimotor skills by 2–3 years of age?

Clearly one could design a featureless, contactless environment that would turn any infant into a human vegetable. Extreme deprivation will prevent the emergence of the species-typical pattern. But the more interesting questions are how much input is necessary for adequate sensorimotor development and how many naturally occurring environments fail to provide the necessary conditions for criterion level development.

The proposal that sensorimotor intelligence is to some degree a canalized form of development does not require that the behaviors emerge in an environmental vacuum. *Canalization does not imply that species-typical development will occur under conditions that are atypical of those under which their evolution occurred.* It does imply that within the range of natural human environments most genotypes will develop similarly in most environments.

The Guatemalan data suggest that in at least one naturally occurring human environment the rate of sensorimotor development is slower than in some other conditions. An alternate explanation is also available, however: that the differences observed are due to genetic differences between groups in the rate of sensorimotor development. Whether the differences between Guatemalan and United States infants are genetic and/or environmental, the data provide some evidence against an extreme canalization position. There must be some developmental adaptation to enriched or impoverished environments and/or some group differences in genotypic responsiveness to sensorimotor environments that affect the rate of infant intellectual development. There is no evidence, however, that nondefective genotypes and naturally occurring environments are not equivalent in producing, eventually, the species-typical pattern.

Other Primates

The ethological, comparative evidence suggests that we share with at least the great apes a primate form of infant intelligence. The homologous, intelligent behaviors of infant apes and humans strongly suggest common origins in our primate past. During the first 18 months of human life there are few intellectual accomplishments that are not paralleled in nonhuman primates, particularly the apes. Both develop object concept, imitation, spatial concepts, cause–effect relations, and means–ends reasoning. In brief, both young apes and young humans become skillful, practical experimenters.

Our knowledge of chimp intellectual development comes primarily from home-reared animals, whose progress on form-board problems and the like exceeds that of their human infant companions in the first year of life (Hayes and Nissen, 1971). Even at the age of 3, Viki, the Hayeses' chimp, closely resembled a human child of 3 on those items of the Gesell, Merrill–Palmer, and Kuhlmann tests that do not require language:

> Viki's formal education began at 21 weeks with string-pulling problems. At 1 year she learned her first size, form, and color discriminations. By 2½ years of age she could match with an accuracy of 90% even when a 10-second delay was imposed. (Hayes and Nissen, 1971, p. 61)

Viki was reared in a human child's environment, and her nonlinguistic attainments are impressive. Certainly her sensorimotor intelligence was as adequate as that of a human infant. In the wild Van Lawick-Goodall's (1971) observations confirm the excellent sensorimotor intelligence of chimps at later ages, but few data are available on their intellectual development in the first year of life.

Hamburg (1969) noted the many similarities between man and chimpanzees in the number and form of chromosomes, in blood proteins, in immune responses, in brain structure, and in behavior. The more we see of their behavior, he said, the more impressed we are by their resemblance to man: "This is not to imply that we inherit fixed action patterns. The chimpanzee's adaptation depends heavily on learning, and ours does even more so!" (p. 143).

Hamburg further suggested that there are probably important biases in what chimps and humans learn: "Our question is: Has natural selection operated on early interests and preferences so that the attention of the developing organism is drawn more to some kinds of experiences than others?" (p. 144). Both chimp and human infants attend to physical problem-solving tasks and to relational problems in their environments.

The nature of learning processes in chimp and human infants is virtually the same. Both profit particularly from observational learning, a skill that is a forte of primate adaptation. From observing the behavior of conspecifics, primates imitate and then practice the observed sequences of behavior over and over again:

> The chief mode of learning for the non-human primate is a sequence that goes from observation to imitation, then to practice. They have full access to virtually the whole repertoire of adult behavior with respect to aggression, sex, feeding, and all other activities. The young observe intently, and then imitate, cautiously at first, all the sequences they see. Then they may be seen practicing these sequences minutes or hours after they have occurred. This observational learning in a social context becomes extremely important for the young primates. It takes the place of active instruction on the part of adults, which never seems to occur. (Hamburg, 1969, p. 146)

The active instruction of human infants by adults probably exceeds that provided by other primate parents. In most parts of the world, however, infants are not instructed on the development or use of sensorimotor schemes. Although both home-reared chimps and human infants may profit from active instruction, it is not clear that the normal development of sensorimotor intelligence requires more than *opportunities* for exploration and learning.

The Gardner's chimp, Washoe, exhibited observational learning of even the most "unnatural" behaviors, like signs, although most of the signs were deliberately taught to her. She learned the sign for "sweet" from the Gardners' use of it in connection with her baby-food desserts. Later reinforcement of her use of the sign increased the reliability of her use of "sweet," but she acquired it from observation (Gardner and Gardner, 1971). She freely combined signs in novel utterances, reflecting her primate ability to make flexible combinations.

What differences, then, exist between the chimp and the human infant in sensorimotor intelligence? I would argue that the differences are in degree, not in kind. As Bruner (1972) has said, the difference between apes, monkeys, and man is in the *flexible use* and *combinatorial quality* of schemes, not in the schemes themselves. This is especially true in infancy, in which the greater cortical development of the human species has only barely begun to show its eventual effects. Human infants may exceed chimps in the combinatorial quality of their schemes, but the evidence is not so striking that observers of chimpanzee infants have noticed any great differences from human infants.

There is no question that after the age of 3, chimps and human children are intellectually different. Despite extensive tutoring in sign language and conceptual skills, Washoe's and Viki's problem-solving skills at 4 years were hardly a match for those of an ordinary 4-year-old child. In infancy, however, their skills were entirely comparable to those of a normal human infant.

The commonalities between apes and man in sensorimotor intelligence suggest that within each species most genotypes and environments are functionally equivalent in producing the recognizable species (perhaps, panprimate) form of development. The commonalities also suggest that this ancient phylogenetic adaptation has been highly resistant to evolutionary change—a characteristic of canalized behaviors.

Early forms of development are always more similar to other species' early forms than later, more differentiated forms. The most extreme statement of this point of view is that ontogeny recapitulates phylogeny. Although we have all been taught to reject this rigid view, there is a perfectly good observation that has been thrown out in the process. Embryologists can tell the difference between a human embryo and a fish embryo even though both have gill slits, but the embryonic forms share more in common than adult forms of the two taxons. It is not too great a leap, I hope, to note that early behavioral forms among primates share more in common than later behavioral forms. This is not to say that chimps and human infants have identical forms of behavior, only that they share more in common in the first 18 months than they do in later life.

An elaboration of this view, suggested by John Flavell, would propose that early human behavior has qualities that are pan-mammalian (e.g., sucking); later in the sensorimotor period, we can no longer refer to pan-mammalian but only to pan-primate forms of behavior. By adolescence, human intelligence is uniquely human, and other primate intelligence is unique to those species. The progressive divergence of intellectual development is analogous to the progressive differentiation of embryos. At no point are species forms indistinguishable, but early forms share more in common than later ones.

The restricted range of individual variation is another characteristic of canalization at a species level. Such individual differences as exist arise in the *rate* of sensorimotor development, not in the level eventually attained. Differences in the rate of sensorimotor development are small, relative to later intellectual differences. The overall pattern of sensorimotor intelligence is quite homogeneous for the species since criterion performance is accomplished in 15 to 20 months for the vast majority of human infants. When one compares this restricted range of phenotypic variation with the range of intellectual skills of children between 11 and 12 years, for example, it is readily apparent that sensorimotor skills are a remarkably uniform behavioral phenomenon.

The hypothesis that infant intelligence is a more highly canalized form of development than later intelligence does not mean that environmental influences are inconsequential, either for development or for individual differences. Even strongly canalized behaviors respond to experience. Learning strongly affects the subsequent sexual behavior of castrated male cats, whose normal sexual development requires only opportunities to perform. Male cats castrated after copulatory experience are vastly superior in sexual performance to inexperienced castrates. Nest building in rabbits improves steadily over the first three litters, even though the differences among strains of rabbits in nest-building skills are largely due to genetic differences (Petit, 1972). Rather, I would argue that infant intelligence shows some signs of canalization in the timing and the general outline of its program but clearly develops in response to the sensorimotor environment. Later intellectual development, particularly around adolescence, seems to have a far less definite form and timing for all members of the species.

All nondefective infants reared in natural human environments achieve all of the sensorimotor skills that Piaget has described. (Do you know anyone who didn't make it to preoperational thought?) This is not a trivial observation, or at least no more trivial than the observations that all nondefective human beings learn a language, are attached to at least one caretaker, achieve sexual maturity, and die in old age, if not before. One cannot say that all nondefective human beings develop formal operational logic, learn a second language, are attracted to the opposite sex, or have musical talent. There is a fundamental difference between these two sets of observations: in the first case, everyone does it; in the second case, only some do.

Uniformity of achievement may be due to limited genetic variability, to canalized development that hides genetic variability, to uniform environments, or to some combination of the three causes. The evidence suggests to me that there is less genetic variability in infant than in later intelligence, that much of the genetic variability that exists is hidden in a well-buffered, epigenetic system, and that many environments are indeed functionally equivalent for the development of sensorimotor skills. I would argue that the genetic preadaptation in sensorimotor intelligence is a strong bias toward learning the typical schemes of infancy and toward combining them in innovative, flexible ways. What human environments do is to provide the materials and the opportunities to learn. For the development of sensorimotor skills, nearly any natural, human environment will suffice to produce criterion-level performance.

Canalization at the Individual Level

Wilson (1972a, 1972b) has argued, on the basis of his data on twins' development, that infant mental development is highly canalized at the individual level, difficult to deflect from its genotypic course, and unaffected by differences in an average range of home environments. If Wilson is correct, the heritability of infant intelligence scores should be very high, phenotype variation fairly large, and the data should fit canalization model 2 (p. 87 of this chapter):

> Therefore, the hypothesis is proposed that these socioeconomic and maternal care variables serve to modulate the primary determinant of developmental capability, namely, the genetic blueprint supplied by the parents. On this view, the differences between twin pairs and the similarities within twin pairs in the course of infant mental development are primarily a function of the shared genetic blueprint.
>
> Further, while there is a continuing interaction between the genetically determined gradient of development and the life circumstances under which each pair of twins is born and raised, it requires unusual conditions to impose a major deflection upon the gradient of infant development. (Wilson, 1972b, p. 917)

The primacy of "genetic blueprints" for development is a view shared by Sperry (1971). With respect to the importance of infancy and early childhood, Sperry said:

> The commonly drawn inference in this connection is that the experiences to which an infant is subjected during these years are primary. I would like again to suggest that there might be another interpretation here, namely, that it is the developmental and maturational processes primarily that make these years so determinative.
>
> During the first few years, the maturational program is unraveling at great speed. A lot of this determination seems to be inbuilt in nature; this is becoming increasingly clear from infant studies. I think we ought to keep our

minds open to the possibility that the impression these first years are so critical is based to a considerable extent on the rapid unraveling of the individual's innate character. (p. 527)

Two lines of evidence have been used to support a strong canalization position on individual differences in infant mental development: family correlations and studies of individual consistency over time.

Family Studies

Table I shows the results of four family studies of twins and siblings, using infant mental tests.

Wilson's conclusion about the "genetic blueprint" for development is based on the very high monozygotic (MZ) correlations obtained on the same day by co-twins (Wilson and Harpring, 1972). The co-twin correlations at the same point in time were much higher, in fact, than the month-to-month correlations for the same infant.

Nichols and Broman's (1974) data from the Collaborative Study support Wilson's findings of high MZ correlations. Monozygotic twins could hardly have been more similar. The two studies differ, however, in their results for dizygotic (DZ) pairs. The genetic correlation between DZ co-twins is estimated to be between 0.50 and 0.55, the larger figure based on parental assortative mating. But note that Wilson's DZ pairs were considerably more similar than expected. Wachs (1972) replied that "This degree of correlation indicates the operation of nongenetic factors in the dizygotic twins' mental test performance." Indeed, Nichols and Broman's dizygotic twins displayed the level of similarity predicted by a genetic model. Both same- and opposite-sexed twins have correlations of 0.50 ± 0.09, which are well within the 95% confidence interval around 0.5 in this study.

Now look at the siblings. Although they share the same percentage of genes in common, on the average, as dizygotic twins, the Fels study and the Collaborative Study found them to be far less similar in mental development during infancy. With sample sizes between 656 and 939 pairs, Nichols and Broman reported average correlations of about 0.20 for siblings; McCall reported 0.24. There is no question that sibs are less similar than DZ twins and that the explanation must be based on the greater environmental similarity of twins, both pre- and postnatally.

The comparison of sibling and DZ twin results is puzzling. The maximum heritability that can be obtained for any characteristic is twice

TABLE I

Infant Mental Scale Correlations for Related Pairs in the First Year of Life

Author	Date	Test	Age (months)	Twins						Siblings				Estimates of genetic variance	
				MZ	(N)	SSDZ	(N)	OSDZ	(N)	SS	(N)	OS	(N)	Twins 2(riMZ−riDZ)	Sibs 2(ri)
Wilson	(1972b)	Bayley	3	0.84		0.67								0.34	
			6	0.82		0.74								0.16	
			9	0.81	(~82)	0.69	(~101)[a]							0.24	
			12	0.82		0.61								0.42	
Nichols and Broman	(1974)	Bayley													
		Whites	8	0.83	(48)	0.51	(41)	0.56	(62)	0.17	(887)	0.22	(939)	0.64	0.39
		Blacks	8	0.85	(74)	0.43	(47)	0.57	(78)	0.22	(656)	0.16	(745)	0.84	0.38
		Total	8	0.84	(122)	0.46	(88)	0.58	(140)	0.21	(1543)	0.20	(1684)	0.76	0.41
McCall	(1972a)	Gesell	6 & 12							0.24	(142)	—			0.48
Freedman and Keller	(1963)	Bayley	2–12	Variance within MZ pairs significantly lower than variance within DZ pairs (N = 20)											

[a] There were a few opposite-sex pairs included.

the sibling correlation (Falconer, 1960). This calculation assumes that *all* of the variance between sibs is genetic and that no environmental variance is present. For behavioral traits this is an absurd assumption, and the heritability should most often be less than twice the sib correlation. A comparison of the McCall and the Nichols and Broman sibling data with the latter's twin results quickly shows a substantial difference in calculated heritability. Twice the sibling correlation varies around 0.40; heritabilities based on the twin results are much higher, around 0.75.

Since twins are nearly always tested on the same day, while sibs may be tested at slightly different ages, Nichols and Broman (1974) examined their data for age differences between sibs at testing, which were inconsequential. Then they tested for uniform correlations across the range of scores to assess the influence of extremely low scores. Extreme scores, which are much more frequent for twins in general, also showed greater concordance than higher scores among MZ twins. After eliminating the twin pairs in which one or both scored less than 50, Nichols and Broman found that the MZ correlation was reduced to 0.63, while the DZ correlation increased slightly to 0.57. Low scores had inflated the heritability estimate by a factor of 6! Although the best estimate of heritability for a population should include some low scores, the distribution of scores in a twin sample should represent the population distribution. Nichols and Broman concluded:

> These results suggest that the influence of genetics (differences) on scores on the Bayley Mental exam is greatest at the low end of the distribution, and underline the need for caution when interpreting twin correlations. (p. 5)

The hypothesis that a "genetic blueprint" programs individual infant mental development does not stand up as well as the high MZ correlations would lead us to believe.

Canalization of Patterns of Infant Mental Development

There is an additional hypothesis that deserves mention: that patterns of change in infant mental development are programmed by the individual genotype. Waddington (1971) proposed that the degree of canalization can vary depending upon the alleles present at relevant loci, which would suggest that some genotypes are better buffered than others. Wilson (1972a) found that the profiles of scores obtained from the MZ twins over the first two years were significantly more similar than those obtained from DZ pairs, that is, that MZ co-twins show more similar responses to their common environments. McCall (1970) found no similarity in sibling profiles of intellectual development. Apart from the methodological arguments, which I will not detail here (see McCall, 1970, 1972b; McCall et al., 1973; Wilson, 1972b; Wilson and Harpring, 1972), there is a substantive question again about the interpretation of twin data. Co-twins must share very common rearing environments as well as genotypes. In infancy the effects of shared prenatal environments may be more important than they are at later ages. Sibling data provide a crucial check on the generalization of twin results.

Continuity in Development

Continuity in developmental levels and profiles has been used as evidence for canalization. In longitudinal studies of singletons less continuity of intellectual level has been found in infancy than in later years (Bayley, 1965). Although one recent study with a small sample failed to find any continuity (Lewis and McGurk, 1972), there are most often correlations of 0.2–0.6 in mental levels across the first two years. Wilson (1972a; Wilson and Harpring, 1972) has attributed the lower correlations among ages under 2 to the genetic blueprint, which has genotypically different spurts and lags in its course. Others have argued for discontinuities in the skills being tested at various ages (Stott and Ball, 1965; McCall et al., 1973).

Continuity from infant to later development can be observed for some infants who score poorly on infant mental scales. They more often remain retarded than others who are not impaired in early life. But the prediction from the first year to later childhood is greatly enhanced by consideration of the caretaking environment, which, if poor, increases the risks for poor development of "retarded" infants (Willerman et al., 1970; Scarr-Salapatek and Williams, 1973; Sameroff and Chandler, 1975). Infants who perform poorly in the first year but who have middle-class families are rarely retarded by school age. Infants at risk for retardation whose families are lower class show greater continuity in poor development (Willerman et al., 1970; Scarr-Salapatek and Williams, 1973).

The reasons for later retardation may vary between middle-class and lower-class groups, but the continuous caretaking environment is at least one apparent difference. Sameroff and Chandler (1975) presented a transactional model that ascribes consistency both to organismic variables and to caretaking environments that support and maintain responses in the system. For example, infants with "difficult" temperaments are more likely to evoke assaultative behavior from their caretakers, whose battering increases the probability of more maladaptive behavior by the infants, and so forth. It is not clear that continuity in infant mental development can be attributed primarily to individual genetic blueprints.

Canalization at the Population Level: Group Differences

If infant development is highly canalized at a species level, one might expect to find universal patterns and rates of infant behavioral development, regardless of differences in child-rearing practices. No one has recently argued that the *sequences* of infant behavioral acquisitions are different across cultures. Piaget's descriptions of the important sensorimotor stages seem to apply to all normal infants. Differences in *rates* of development, however, have been noted for infants and older children of various cultural groups.

There are at least three problems with the cross-cultural paradigm in studies of canalization. First, genetic differences in rates of development may exist between populations. Relatively isolated gene pools may have evolved somewhat different patterns of infant development. Second, cross-cultural studies are fraught with methodological problems (Pick, in press; Warren, 1972) that may apply less to infant studies than to studies of older children but that cannot be ruled out entirely. Third, the cultural practices that may, in fact, affect rates of infant development may not be identified by investigators, who may be at a loss to know what comparisons to make. These three problems—possible genetic differences, methodological problems, and identification of relevant environmental contingencies—make the interpretation of cross-cultural research on infant development difficult. Nevertheless, what has been observed?

Compared to United States white infants, those reared in other groups have been observed to be accelerated or retarded in sensorimotor development. African infants have often been found to be precocious (Warren, 1972; Freedman, in press), particularly in the early appearance of major motor milestones, such as sitting, standing alone, and walking.

Although some investigators have related the precocity of African infants to child-rearing practices (Geber, 1958), U. S. black infants have also been found to be precocious in the same ways (Bayley, 1965; Nichols and Broman, 1975; Knobloch and Pasamanick, 1953). The similar pattern of precocity of urban United States black infants and rural African infants would seem to reduce the efficacy of a cultural argument to explain the phenomenon.

Navaho infants have been reported to be somewhat retarded in motor development, an observation that has been attributed to the cradle board but that may reflect gene pool differences. The latter explanation is particularly interesting in light of Freedman's (1974) report of the flaccid muscle tone and paucity of lower limb reflexes in Navaho newborns.

Several other reports of behavioral differences among newborns from different populations are suggestive of gene pool differences (Brazelton et al., 1969; Freedman, 1974), although prenatal differences are not easily ruled out. In a particularly well-designed study Freedman and Freedman (1969) did show differences between small samples of Chinese-American and Caucasian-American newborns whose mothers were members of the same Kaiser-Permanente hospital group. Presumably many possible differences in prenatal life could be ruled out as competitive hypotheses.

There are few comparable studies of infant mental or language development cross-culturally. We do not know when object permanence or first words appear in various groups; a first step toward studies of canalization at a population level should certainly include the simple description of the existing group variation.

The evidence from cross-cultural studies suggests that there are variations among groups in the rates of infant development. The origins of these differences are possibly cultural in part and probably genetic in part. Further studies at a descriptive level would clarify the degree of variation among groups in developmental patterns. Studies of infants from two gene pools—some of whom were reared by members of their own culture, compared to others adopted into families of a different group—would clarify the roles of genetic and environmental differences among groups. If canalization is strong for infant development in both groups, then rearing conditions should not affect the differences among infants from different gene pools nor the similarities among infants from the same gene pool. Opportunities for such studies exist, as in the cases of black and Asian infants adopted into United States Caucasian families. Is their rate of infant development similar to Caucasian infants in the same families or to infants from the same gene pool reared by members of their own group?

Whither Studies of Canalization?

Hypotheses about the strong canalization of infant development at species, population, or individual levels have not been thoroughly investigated as yet. Studies of canalization at an individual level can benefit from several research strategies. Adoptive studies also provide a useful technique to examine the influence of shared genotypes and shared environments. Comparisons of infants with their biological relatives can be made for groups reared by their own parents and others reared by adoptive families. Further family studies of siblings and half siblings, reared together and apart, would enhance our knowledge of genotypic differences in development. An ingenious natural experiment can be found in the families of adult monozygotic twins. In the family constellations are MZ twins, siblings, parents and their children, half sibs, and separated "parent"–child pairs (composed of the MZ twin with the co-twin's children). A beautiful part of the design is the intactness and normality of the families who are related in all of those varied ways.

High heritabilities of infant development within a population would suggest that the environments sampled are functionally equivalent and that genotypic differences are important sources of variation. This would be evidence for the canalization of that development within the context of average infant environments. Current evidence from twin and sibling studies of mental development leaves this model in doubt, however, even for the one population studied. There is even less evidence available for the canalization of mental development at a population level.

At a species level an argument can be made for considerable restriction in phenotypic variation and for a recognizable species pattern, a pattern shared with our closest primate relatives. Whatever the sources of variation, there is a typical form of sensorimotor intelligence that develops over the first 18 months of human life. This pattern, I would argue, depends upon the functional equivalence of most genotypes and environments within the species. Canalization of infant sensorimotor intelligence is not a genetic blueprint for the emergence of particular responses. It is , rather, a preadapted responsiveness to certain learning opportunities. The full development of the sensorimotor skills depends upon the infants' encountering the appropriate learning opportunities, but most human environments are rich in the physical and social stimuli that infant intelligence requires. Differences in rates of sensorimotor development are not yet assignable to genetic or environmental causes, but they are relatively unimportant variations on a strong primate theme.

ACKNOWLEDGMENTS

I want to express my gratitude to Professors William Charlesworth and John Flavell for their careful, critical reviews of the manuscript. Their challenging ideas have been sometimes incorporated in the chapter, but they are not responsible for any errors of presentation. The research and review were supported by the Grant Foundation and the National Institute of Child Health and Human Development (HD-06502 and HD-08016).

REFERENCES

Baker, P. Human adaptation to high altitude. *Science,* 1969, *163,* 1149.

Baker, P., & Weiner, J. *The Biology of Human Adaptability.* New York: Oxford, 1966.

Bayley, N. Comparisons of mental and motor test scores for ages 1–15 months by sex, birth order, race, geographical location, and education of parents. *Child Development,* 1965, *36,* 379.

Bell, S. M. The development of the concept of the object and its relationship to infant-mother attachment. *Child development,* 1970, *41,* 291.

Bowlby, J. *Attachment and Loss (Vol. 1: Attachment).* New York: Basic Books, 1969.

Bowlby, J. *Attachment and Loss (Vol. 2: Separation).* New York: Basic Books, 1973.

Brazelton, T. B., Robey, J. S., & Collier, G. A. Infant development in the Zincanteco Indians of southern Mexico. *Pediatrics,* 1969, *44,* 274.

Bruell, J. Behavioral population genetics and wild *Mus musculus.* In G. Lindzey and D. D. Thiessen (Eds.), *Contributions to behavior genetic analysis: The mouse as a prototype.* New York: Appleton, 1970.

Bruner, J. S. The nature and uses of immaturity. *American psychologist,* 1972, *27,* 687.

Dennis, W. Causes of retardation among institutional children: Iran. *Journal of genetic psychology,* 1960, *96,* 47.

Dobzhansky, T. A review of some fundamental concepts and problems of population genetics. *Cold spring harbor symposium on quantitative biology,* 1955, *20,* 1.

Dobzhansky, T. On types, genotypes, and the genetic diversity in populations. In J. Spuhler (Ed.), *Genetic diversity and human behavior.* Chicago: Aldine, 1967.

Elkind, D. Cognitive development. In Y. Brackbill (Ed.), *Infancy and early childhood.* New York: Free Press, 1967.

Falconer, D. S. *Introduction to quantitative genetics.* New York: Ronald Press, 1960.

Fox, R. The cultural animal. *Encounter,* 1970, *42,* 31.

Freedman, D. G. A biological approach to personality development. In Y. Brackbill (Ed.), *Infancy and early childhood.* New York: Free Press, 1967.

Freedman, D. G. *An ethological perspective on human infancy.* New York: Erlbaum, 1974.

Freedman, D. G., & Freedman, N. C. Behavioral differences between Chinese-American and European-Americal newborns. *Nature,* 1969, *24,* 1227.

Freedman, D. G., & Keller, B. Inheritance of behavior in infants. *Science,* 1963, 140, 196–198.

Gardner, B. T., and Gardner, R. A. Two-way communication with an infant chimpanzee. In A. M. Schrier & F. Stollnitz (eds.), *Behavior of Non-Human Primates.* New York: Academic Press, 1971.

Geber, M. The psychomotor development of African children in the first year, and the influence of maternal behavior. *Journal of social psychology,* 1958, *47,* 185.

Ghiselin, M. *The triumph of the darwinian method.* Berkeley: University of California Press, 1969.

Gottesman, I. I., & Heston, L. I. Human behavior adaptations: speculations on their genesis. In L. Ehrman, G. S. Omenn, & E. Caspari (Eds.), *Genetics, environment, and behavior.* New York: Academic Press, 1972.

Hamburg, D. A. Sexual differentiation and the evelution of agressive behavior in primates. In N. Kretchmer & D. N. Walcher (Eds.), *Environmental Influences on Genetic Expression.* Washington, D. C.: United States Government Printing Office, 1969.

Harrison, G. A. Human evelution and ecology. In *Proceedings of the third international congress of human genetics.* Baltimore: Johns Hopkins University, 1967.

Hayes, J. J., & Nissen, C. H. Higher mental functions of a home-raised chimpanzee. In A. M. Schrier & F. Stollnitz (eds.), *Behavior of non-human primates.* New York: Academic Press, 1971.

Kagan, J., & Klein, R. E. Cross-cultural perspectives on early development. *American psychologist,* 1973, *28,* 947.

Knobloch, H., & Pasamanick, B. Further observations on the behavioral development of Negro children. *The journal of genetic psychology,* 1953, *83,* 137.

Kopp, C. B., & Shaperman, J. Cognitive development in the absence of object manipulation during infancy. *Developmental psychology,* 1973, *9,* 430.

LaBarre, W. *The human animal.* Chicago: University of Chicago Press, 1954.

LaBarre, W. The development of mind in man in primitive cultures. In F. Richardson (Ed.), *Brain and Intelligence.* 1973.

Lehrman, D. Semantic and conceptual issues in the nature-nurture problem. In L. R. Aronson, E. Tobach, & E. Shaw (Eds.), *Development and Evolution of Behavior.* San Francisco: Freeman, 1970.

Lewis, M. & McGurk, H. Evaluation of infant intelligence. *Science,* 1972, *178,* 1174.

Lipsitt, L. P. Discussion of paper by Harris. In E. Tobach, L. R. Aronson, & E. Shaw (Eds.), *The Biopsychology of development.* New York: Academic Press, 1971.

Mayr, E. *Populations, species, and evolution.* Cambridge: Harvard University Press, 1970.

McCall, R. B. IQ pattern over age: Comparisons among siblings and parent-child pairs. *Science,* 1970, 170, 644.

McCall, R. B. Paper presented at the meeting of the American Psychological Association, Honolulu, 1972a.

McCall, R. B. Similarity in developmental profile among related pairs. *Science,* 1972b, *178,* 1004.

McCall, R. B., Appelbaum, M. I., & Hogarty, P. S. Developmental changes in mental performance. *Monographs of the society for research in child development,* 1973, *38*(3, Whole No. 150).

McClearn, G. E. Genetic determination of behavior (animal). In L. Ehrman, G. S. Omenn, & E. Caspari (Eds.), *Genetics, environment, and behavior.* New York: Academic Press, 1972.

Nichols, P. L., & Broman, S. H. Familial resemblance in infant mental development. *Developmental psychology,* 1974, *10,* 442.

Nichols, P. L., & Broman, S. H. *Preschool IQ: Prenatal and early developmental correlates.* New York: Wiley, 1975.

Omenn, G. S., & Motulsky, A. G. Biochemical genetics and the evolution of human behavior. In L. Ehrman, G. S. Omenn, & E. Caspari (Eds.), *Genetics, environment, and behavior*. New York: Academic Press, 1972.

Petit, C. Qualitative aspects of genetics and environment in the determination of behavior. In L. Ehrman, G. S. Omenn, & E. Caspari (Eds.), *Genetics, environment, and behavior*. New York: Academic Press, 1972.

Piaget, J. *The origins of intelligence in children*. New York: International Universities Press, 1952.

Pick, A. D. The games experimenters play: a review of methods and concepts of cross-cultural studies of cognition and development. In E. C. Carterette, & M. P. Friedman (Eds.), *Handbook of perception*. New York: Academic Press, 1975.

Polansky, N. A., Borgman, R. D., DeSaix, C., and Smith, B. J. Mental organization and maternal adequacy in rural Applachia. *American journal of orthopsychiatry*, 1969, *39*, 246.

Premack, D. On the assessment of language competence in the chimpanzee. In A. M. Schrier, & F. Stollnitz (Eds.), *Behavior of nonhuman primates*. New York: Academic Press, 1971.

Sameroff, A. J., & Chandler, M. J. Reproductive risk and the continuum of caretaking casualty. In F. D. Horowitz, M. Hetherington, S. Scarr-Salapatek, & G. Siegel (Eds.), *Review of child development research (Vol. 4)*. Chicago: University of Chicago Press, 1975.

Scarr-Salapatek, S., & Williams, M. L. The effects of early stimulation on low-birth-weight infants. *Child development*, 1973, *44*, 94.

Seligman, M. E. P. On the generality of laws of learning. *Psychological review*, 1970, *77*, 406.

Sperry, R. W. How a developing brain gets itself properly wired for adaptive function. In E. Tobach, L. R. Aronson, & E. Shaw (Eds.) *The biopsychology of development*. New York: Academic Press, 1971.

Stott, L. H., & Ball, R. S. Infant and preschool mental tests: review and evaluation. *Monographs of the society for research in child development*, 1965, *30* (Whole No. 101).

Vale, J. R., and Vale, C. A. Individual differences and general laws in psychology. *American psychologist*, 1969, *24*, 1093.

Van Lawick-Goodall, J. *In the shadow of man*. New York: Dell, 1971.

Wachs, T. Technical comment. *Science*, 1972, *178*, 1005.

Waddington, C. H. *The strategy of the genes*. London: Allen & Son, 1957.

Waddington, C. H. *New patterns in genetics and development*. New York: Columbia University Press, 1962.

Waddington, C. H. Concepts of development. In E. Tobach, L. R. Aronson, & E. Shaw (Eds.), *The biopsychology of development*. New York: Academic Press, 1971.

Warren, N. African infant precocity. *Psychological bulletin*, 1972, *78*, 353.

White, B. L. *Human Infants: Experience and psychological development*. Englewood Cliffs, New Jersey: Prentice-Hall, 1971.

Willerman, L., Broman, S. H., & Fiedler, M. Infant development, preschool IQ, and social class. *Child development*, 1970, *41*, 69.

Wilson, R. S. Twins: early mental development. *Science*, 1972a, *175*, 914.

Wilson, R. S. Similarity in developmental profile among related pairs of human infants. *Science*, 1972b, *178*, 1005.

Wilson, R. S., & Harpring, E. B. Mental and motor development in infant twins. *Developmental psychology*, 1972, *7*, 277.

Zelazo, P. R. *Newborn walking: from reflexive to instrumental behavior*. Paper presented at the annual meetings of the AAAS, Symposium on psychobiology: The significance of infancy, San Francisco, 1974.

RACE AND IQ

II.1 IQ Test Performance of Black Children Adopted by White Families*

ABSTRACT

The poor performance of black children on IQ tests and in school has been hypothesized to arise from (a) genetic racial differences or (b) cultural/environmental disadvantages. To separate genetic factors from rearing conditions, 130 black/interracial children adopted by advantaged white families were studied. The socially classified black adoptees, whose natural parents were educationally average, scored above the IQ and the school achievement mean of the *white* population. Biological children of the adoptive parents scored even higher. Genetic and environmental determinants of differences among the black/interracial adoptees were largely confounded. The high IQ scores of the socially classified black adoptees indicate malleability for IQ under rearing conditions that are relevant to the tests and the schools.

INTRODUCTION

It is well known that black children reared by their own families achieve IQ scores that average about a standard deviation (15 points) below whites (Jensen, 1973; Loehlin, Lindzey, & Spuhler, 1975). This finding is at the heart of a continuing controversy in the educational arena. Recent studies (Cleary, Hum-

---

*This chapter by Sandra Scarr and Richard A. Weinberg originally appeared in *American Psychologist*, 1976, *31*, 726–739. Copyright © 1976 by the American Psychological Association, Inc. Reprinted by permission.

phreys, Kendrick, & Wesman, 1975) confirm the hypothesis that low IQ scores predict poor school performance, regardless of race. Thus, more black children than white children fail to achieve academically and to earn the credentials required by higher occupational status, with its concomitant social prestige and economic security (Husén, 1974; Jencks, 1972).

In an attempt to remedy the alarming rate of school failure, compensatory educational programs, which were directed particularly at black children, were introduced in the 1960s. At the same time, but for different reasons, a more intensive intervention began: the adoption of black children by white families. Whereas compensatory educational programs involve the child for a few hours per day, transracial adoption alters the entire social ecology of the child. Parents, siblings, home, peers, school, neighborhood, and community—the child's rearing environment—are transformed by adoption.

The existence of transracial families offers much to the scientific study of social milieus and intellectual performance (Grow & Shapiro, 1974; Loehlin et al., 1975). Transracial adoption is the human analog of the cross-fostering design, commonly used in animal behavior genetics research (e.g., Manosevitz, Lindzey, & Thiessen, 1969). The study of transracial adoption can yield estimates of biological and sociocultural effects on the IQ test performance of cross-fostered children.

The results of a transracial or cross-fostering study require careful interpretation. Black children reared in white homes are socially labeled as black and therefore may suffer racial discrimination. Because of the unmeasured effects of racism, poor IQ test performance by black children in white homes cannot be uncritically interpreted as a result of genetic limitations. In addition, equal performance by black and other adoptees cannot be interpreted as an indication of the *same* range of reaction for all groups. Again, the unknown effects of racism may inhibit the intellectual development of the black adoptees. However, equally high IQs for black and other adoptees would imply that IQ performance is considerably malleable.

Upper-middle-class white families have an excellent reputation for rearing children who perform well on IQ tests and in school. When such families adopt white children, the adoptees have been found to score above average on IQ tests, but not as highly as the biological offspring of the same and similar families (Burks, 1928; Freeman, Holzinger, & Mitchell, 1928; Leahy, 1935; Munsinger, 1975b; Skodak & Skeels, 1949). How do the IQ test scores of black children adopted by white families compare to the scores of both white adoptees and the biological children of these parents?

If black children have genetically limited intellectual potential, as some have claimed (Jensen, 1973; Shockley, 1971, 1972), their IQ performance will fall below that of other children reared in white upper-middle-class homes. On the other hand, if black children have a range of reaction similar to other adoptees, their IQ scores should have a similar distribution. The concept, range of reaction, refers to the fact that genotypes do not usually specify a single phenotype. Rather, genotypes specify a range of phenotypic responses that the organism can make to a variety of environmental conditions.

This is an investigation of the IQ test performance of black and interracial black children adopted by white families in Minnesota. The present study is part of a larger investigation of the psychosocial functioning of transracial adoptive families. Intellectual, personality, and attitudinal tests were administered to the parents and all children over the age of 4 years. Extensive interviews were conducted with the parents, and ratings of the home environment were made.

Minnesota has been in the forefront of interracial adoption. Although the black population of the state is small (.9% in 1970), there were too many black and interracial children available for adoption and too few black families to absorb them. Minority group children—black, American Indian, Korean, and Vietnamese—have consequently been adopted by white families in large numbers. Furthermore, in recent years, many nonwhite children have been adopted from other states.

The climate for interracial adoption changed dramatically in the late 1950s and early 1960s because of the efforts of public and private agencies and the pioneering white adoptive parents. Several agency and parent organizations were formed to promote the adoption of black and interracial black children. The most influential, continuing organization is the Open Door Society of Minnesota, formed in 1966 by adoptive parents of socially classified black children. The founding president of the Open Door Society is a leading columnist on one of the Minneapolis daily newspapers who frequently writes about his multiracial family. The intellectual and social climate of Minnesota is generally conducive to liberal and humanitarian movements such as interracial adoption.

GOALS OF THE STUDY

We posed five major questions in the study:

1. What is the estimated reaction range for IQ scores of black/interracial children reared in typical black environments or in white adoptive homes?

2. Do interracial children (with one black and one white parent) perform at higher levels on IQ tests than do children with two black parents; that is, does the degree of white ancestry affect IQ scores?

3. How do the IQ scores of socially classified black children reared in white homes compare to those of other adopted children and biological white children within the same families; that is, do different racial groups, when exposed to similar environments, have similar distributions of IQ scores?

4. How well do socially classified black children reared in white families perform in school?

5. How accurately can we predict the IQ test performance of adopted children from the educational characteristics of their natural parents, from the educational, intellectual, and other characteristics of their adoptive homes, and from their placement histories?

THE FAMILIES

The 101 participating families were recruited through the Newsletter of the Open Door Society and by letters from the State Department of Public Welfare Adoption Unit to families with black adopted children, 4 years of age and older, who were adopted throughout the state of Minnesota through Lutheran Social Service and Children's Home Society. These agencies have placed the majority of black

TABLE 1

Recruitment of Families

Method	*n*
Department of Public Welfare letters	
Not eligible to participate	46[a]
Unknown	
Letter undelivered	43
No response	41
Eligible	
Not participating	
In another study	3
Don't approve of study	2
Child appears white	3
Personal reasons	3
No reason given	3
Live too far away	10
Yes, but changed their minds	6
Participating	68
Total letters sent	228
Open Door Society	
Not eligible to participate	19[a]
Eligible	
Not participating	
Live too far away	4
Yes, but changed their minds	1
Participating	33
Total responses	57

[a] Most because their black children were under 4 years of age.

TABLE 2

Out-of-State Origins of the Adopted Children

Origin	n
Other adopted	
Korea	7
Vietnam	1
Canada (Indian)	5
Ecuador (Indian)	2
Black and interracial adopted	
Illinois	4
Iowa	1
Kentucky	9
Massachusetts	11
New York	3
North Dakota	1
Ohio	2
Texas	2
Utah	1
Washington	2
Wisconsin	16
White adopted	
Massachusetts	1
Total	68

and interracial children in the state. We were unable to ascertain how many transracial adoptive families learned about the study from the Newsletter, because the mailing list of about 300 includes agencies, social workers, and interested citizens. In addition, we do not know how many of these families were also contacted by the State Department of Public Welfare. The support of the Open Door Society was important, however, in affirming the legitimacy of the study.

The State Department of Public Welfare mailed 228 letters to transracial adoptive families. In some cases a family received more than one letter if they had adopted more than one child. Table 1 describes the results of the mailing. Of the 136 families known to be eligible for participation in the study, 74% did participate.

The 101 participating families included 321 children 4 years of age and older: 145 biological children (81 males, 64 females) and 176 adopted children (101 males, 75 females), of whom 130 are socially classified as black and 25 as white. The remaining 21 included Asian, North American Indian, and Latin American Indian children.

All of the adopted children were unrelated to the adoptive parents. Adopted children reared in the same home were unrelated, with the exception of four sibling pairs and one triad adopted by the same families.

The sample of families live within a 150-mile radius of the Twin Cities (Minneapolis–St. Paul) metropolitan area. Although nearly all of the children were adopted in Minnesota, 68 were born outside of the state. Through interstate cooperation, the child placement agencies arranged for the adoption of many nonwhite children from other states. Table 2 gives the out-of-state origins of the sample.

PROCEDURES

Most of the information was obtained directly from members of the adoptive families. Some additional data on the natural parents and the children's preadoption history were obtained by State Department of Public Welfare personnel from the adoption records. Achievement and aptitude test scores were supplied by school districts for all of the school-aged children to whom such tests had been administered.

The IQ Assessment

Both parents and all children in the family over 4 years of age were administered an age-appropriate IQ test as part of an extensive battery of intellectual, personality, attitudinal, and demographic measures. Children under 4 years of age were excluded because IQ tests are less predictive of later IQ at younger ages. By 4, the correlation of IQ with adolescent scores is about .7. The tests were administered in the family home during two visits by a team of trained testers. The examiners were all graduate students who had completed at least a year-long course in psychoeducational assessment and who had participated in a training session on assessment for this study. Among the 21 examiners were 6 males and 15 females, including 2 blacks. Testers were assigned randomly to members of the family.

Both parents and all children 16 years of age and older were administered the Wechsler Adult Intelligence Scale (WAIS; Wechsler, 1955). Children between 8 and 15 were given the Wechsler Intelligence Scale for Children (WISC; Wechsler, 1949), and children between 4 and 7 were administered the Stanford-Binet Intelligence Scale, Form L-M. (Terman & Merrill, 1972).

All scoring of protocols and computations of IQ scores were done by a graduate student with extensive experience in administering and scoring IQ measures. This student had no contact with the families and with the examiners except to clarify questionable responses. In no case was the scorer aware of the child's race or adoptive status.

The Adoption Records

The Director of the Adoption Unit, State Department of Public Welfare, abstracted the following information from the records of the adopted children and their families:

1. The child: (a) birthdate; (b) number and dates of preadoption placements, unless the child was in the adoptive home at 2 months of age; (c) evaluation of the quality of preadoption placements, rated by the authors on a scale of 1 = poor to 3 = good; 4 = placement only in the adoptive home; (d) date of placement in adoptive home.
2. The natural parents: (a) age at birth of child; (b) educational level at birth of child as an estimate of intellectual functioning, since IQ scores were not available; (c) occupation of mother; (d) race.

The race of the two natural parents was used to classify their child's race. If a child had one or two black parents, he was considered socially black.

Family Demographics

As part of the interview portion of the testing session, each parent was asked his or her birthdate, last school grade completed, occupation and whether it was full time or part time, range of income, and date of marriage. Occupations were coded for prestige using the scale development from the National Opinion Research Center (NORC) survey (Reiss, 1961).

The School Data

With parental consent, forms requesting recent aptitude and achievement test scores were mailed to the schools of all school-aged children participating in the study; 100% of the forms were returned. Because school districts use a variety of tests,[1] comparable scores were combined across tests. For aptitude tests, a total score was generated. For achievement tests, a vocabulary, a composite reading, and an arithmetic score were used.

RESULTS

Since the major focus of the study was to estimate the level of IQ performance of the black adoptees and to account for that performance level, the nature and quality of the children's adoptive experience were examined.

---

[1] Eight aptitude and 11 achievement tests were used by the various school districts.

Family Characteristics

The adoptive families who participated in the study can be characterized as highly educated and above average in occupational status and income. Table 3 is a summary of selected demographic characteristics of the adoptive and natural parents.

The educational level of the adoptive parents exceeded that of the adopted children's natural parents by 4–5 years. The typical occupations of the adoptive fathers were clergyman, engineer, and teacher. Nearly half (46.5%) of the adoptive mothers were employed at least part time, typically as teachers, nurses, and secretaries. The mean educational level of the natural parents was high school graduation, which is close to the median for that age cohort of the general population. Actually, the black mothers had one year less education than the black females in their age group (25–44). Fathers of the early-adopted black children had slightly more. Table 4 shows the average educational level of the white mothers of interracial black children, the black mothers, and the black fathers, compared to local and regional norms. (Because there were only two white fathers of interracial children, they have been omitted from the table.) In contrast, the mean educational level of the adoptive parents was atypically high. Typical occupations of the natural mothers were office workers, nurse's aides,

TABLE 3

Demographic Characteristics of the Adoptive and Natural Parents

Characteristic	n	M	SD	Range
Income				
Adoptive	100	$15,000–17,500	$5,000	$5,000–>$35,000
Education				
Adoptive father	101	16.9	3.0	9–22
Adoptive mother	101	15.1	2.2	12–21
Natural father	46	12.1	2.0	8–17
Natural mother[a]	135	12.0	2.2	6–18
Age				
Adoptive fathers[b]	100	37.3	6.7	28–59
Adoptive mothers[b]	100	35.5	5.8	26–53
Natural fathers[c]	55	26.3	6.6	16–44
Natural mothers[c]	150	21.6	5.3	12–40

[a] If the 40 students are excluded, the mean is the same.
[b] Current.
[c] At birth of child.

TABLE 4

*Educational Levels of the Natural Parents of
Adopted Children, Compared to Their Populations*

	Natural parents of the adopted children	Natural parents of the early-adopted children	North Central region	Minneapolis– St. Paul[a]
Black mothers	10.8	10.8	11.9	12.0
White mothers of interracial children	12.4	12.6	12.5	12.5
Black fathers	12.3	12.6	12.0	12.0

Note. Levels given in years.
[a] Men or women, aged 25–44 years.

and students. Insufficient information was available on the occupations of the natural fathers.

Preadoptive Experience

Table 5 includes two measures of the children's preadoptive placements: number and quality. The information is presented for all adoptees and by race.

Forty-four children were placed in their adoptive homes by 2 months of age and were considered to have had no previous placements. The remaining adopted children had from one to six previous placements. Black children had a smaller number of preadoption placements, and the quality of their placements was better than that of the Asian/Indian adoptees. Fewer black children were in institutions or were removed from homes for neglect or abuse, and more were in agency foster homes.

Only 18 of the 176 adopted children had ever lived with their biological parents: 7 of the Asian/Indian adoptees, for an average of 85 months; 3 of the white children, for an average of 28 months; and 8 of the black children, for an average of 36 months.

The Adoptive Experience

As shown in Table 5, the average age of placement in the adoptive homes was 22 months, but the median age of placement was 6 months. One hundred and eleven children, including 99 black and interracial adoptees, were placed in their adoptive homes during the first year of life. The Asian and Indian children were placed significantly later than either white or black children. The socially classified black children, however, had lived with their adoptive families for

TABLE 5

The Adopted Children

	All adopted (n = 176)	White (n = 25)	Black/inter-racial (n = 130)	Asian/Indian (n = 21)
Preadoption				
Number of placements[a]				
M	1.06	.77	1.02	1.57
SD	1.04	1.24	.93	1.12
Range	0–6	0–4	0–6	0–4
Quality of placements[a,b]				
M	3.17	3.46	3.18	2.50
SD	.63	.84	.50	.73
Range	1–4	1–4	2–4	1–4
Adoptive placement				
Age of placement[c]				
M	22.48	19.04	17.97	60.71
SD	34.20	32.80	24.70	56.90
Range	0–189	0–94	0–124	1–189
Time in adoptive home[c]				
M	64.70	104.20	57.25	63.81
SD	33.50	39.30	25.50	38.20
Range	8–199	22–187	8–199	9–137
Current age[c]				
M	87.18	123.24	74.22	124.52
SD	40.80	48.00	29.60	44.40
Range	48–257	69–257	48–201	52–218

[a] Information available for 156 children: 22 white; 120 black/interracial; 14 Asian/Indian.
[b] Quality of placement was rated: 1 = poor to 3 = good; 4 = placed when less than 2 months old.
[c] In months.

fewer years than the others, particularly than the white adoptees. Also shown in Table 5, black and interracial children were currently younger, on the average, than the others.

IQ Scores of Adoptive Parents

As indicated in Table 6, the mean WAIS IQ scores of the adoptive parents were in the high average to superior range of intellectual functioning. The distribution

TABLE 6

WAIS IQ Scores of Adoptive Parents

WAIS	Mother				Father			
	n	M	SD	Range	n	M	SD	Range
Verbal	100	118.3	10.4	92–144	99	120.7	10.6	92–140
Performance	99	115.9	11.4	86–143	99	118.2	10.9	91–149
Full Scale	99	118.2	10.1	96–143	99	120.8	10.0	93–140

of scores extends from the low average to the very superior, with considerable restriction of range. The scores were congruent with the very high educational level of the group.

IQ Scores of the Natural Children of the Adoptive Parents

The mean IQ scores of the natural children of the adoptive families were in the high average to superior range of intellectual functioning. As expected from polygenic theory, when both parents have high IQ scores, there is less regression toward the population mean than under conditions of random mating. Table 7 gives the Stanford–Binet, WISC, and WAIS results for the natural children. Only the Wechsler scores had a restricted range. With tests combined, the total IQ score of the natural children averaged 116.7 with a standard deviation of 14.0.

The IQ Scores of Adopted Children

The mean IQ scores of the adopted children were in the average range. As shown in Table 8, the scores on the three IQ tests, although for children at different age levels, were highly comparable. The adopted children did not perform as well as either the adoptive parents or their biological children.

For all of the groups of children, the Stanford–Binet (1972 norms) yielded a slightly lower mean score than did the WISC or WAIS. Had the 1960 Stanford–Binet norms been used, the average IQ scores of the children would have been 7 points higher.

IQ Scores of Adopted Children by Race

Although adopted children of various ages were administered different tests, their performance was sufficiently comparable that we could combine the IQ scores across the three tests. Table 9 gives the mean IQ scores by race.

Although all groups had comparable ranges and were performing within the average range of intellectual functioning, the black and interracial children scored, on the average, between the white and Asian/Indian adopted groups. The scores of the socially classified black and white groups were significantly above the mean of the general population. The Asian/Indian adopted children scored exactly at the population mean. The means of the three groups of adopted children differ significantly ($p < .005$). The children adopted during the first year of life scored higher than those adopted after the first year. The average score for the 111 early-adopted group was an IQ of 111; for the 65 later adoptees, the mean IQ score was 97.5.

For those who hypothesize that blacks have lower IQ scores than whites because of their African ancestry, we compared socially classified black children with one versus two black natural parents. On the average, children with two

TABLE 7
IQ Scores of the Natural Children of the Adoptive Parents

Scale	Total				Males				Females			
	n	M	SD	Range	n	M	SD	Range	n	M	SD	Range
Stanford-Binet	48	113.8	16.7	81–148	26	111.6	16.5	81–148	22	116.3	16.9	88–140
WISC												
Verbal	82	113.5	13.1	84–147	50	114.0	12.8	89–147	32	112.8	13.6	84–144
Performance	82	119.5	14.9	68–147	50	120.5	12.5	82–143	32	117.8	18.1	68–147
Full Scale	82	117.9	12.7	87–150	50	118.5	10.8	96–145	32	117.0	15.3	87–150
WAIS												
Verbal	14	117.5	11.0	100–139	5	121.6	13.9	103–139	9	115.2	9.2	100–125
Performance	14	117.1	10.8	103–137	5	121.8	14.6	104–137	9	115.4	8.1	103–125
Full Scale	14	118.9	11.2	101–141	5	123.0	14.9	104–141	9	116.6	8.6	101–126

Note. WISC = Wechsler Intelligence Scale for Children. WAIS = Wechsler Adult Intelligence Scale.

TABLE 8
IQ Scores of Adopted Children

Scale	Total			Males			Females		
	n	M	SD	Range	n	M	SD	Range	n	M	SD	Range
Stanford-Binet	122	106.5	13.9	68–144	69	107.1	12.6	80–144	53	105.6	15.5	68–136
WISC												
Verbal	48	101.2	15.6	66–142	30	101.9	14.4	71–139	18	100.2	17.9	66–142
Performance	48	109.7	17.7	62–143	30	111.0	18.3	62–143	18	107.5	17.0	80–142
Full Scale	48	105.8	16.1	64–140	30	106.9	15.8	64–140	18	104.1	16.8	80–133
WAIS												
Verbal	6	98.3	7.0	86–107	3	95.3	8.7	86–107	3	101.3	2.1	99–103
Performance	6	113.5	6.5	107–119	3	113.0	4.9	107–119	3	114.0	9.5	108–125
Full Scale	6	105.2	6.3	94–113	3	102.7	7.8	94–113	3	107.7	2.9	106–111

Note. WISC = Wechsler Intelligence Scale for Children. WAIS = Wechsler Adult Intelligence Scale.

TABLE 9

IQ Scores for Adopted Children by Race,
with Tests Combined

Children		IQ scores		
	n	*M*	*SD*	Range
All adopted				
Black and interracial	130	106.3	13.9	68–144
White	25	111.5	16.1	62–143
Asian/Indian	21	99.9	13.3	66–129
Early-adopted				
Black and interracial	99	110.4	11.2	86–136
White	9	116.8	13.4	99–138
Asian/Indian[a]				

[a] Only 3 cases.

black parents have a higher degree of African ancestry than those with one black and one white parent. Table 10 compares the IQ scores, placement histories, and natural-parent education of children with one or two black parents. Socially classified black children with one parent of unknown, Asian, Indian, or other racial background have been eliminated from this analysis.

The 29 children with two black parents achieved a mean IQ score of 96.8. The 68 with only one black parent scored on the average 109.0. It is essential to note, however, that the groups also differed significantly ($p < .05$) in their placement histories and natural mother's education. Children with two black parents were significantly older at adoption, had been in the adoptive home a shorter time, and had experienced a greater number of preadoption placements. The natural parents of the black/black group also averaged a year less of education than those of the black/white group, which suggests an average difference between the groups in intellectual ability. There were also significant differences between the adoptive families of black/black and black/white children in father's education and mother's IQ. One can see in Table 10 that the children with two black parents had poorer histories and had natural and adoptive parents with lower educational levels and abilities. It will be shown in the section on IQ variance that these characteristics largely account for the IQ differences between black children with one or two black parents.

Expectancy Effect

It is possible, though not likely, that the adoptive parents' belief about the child's racial background could influence the child's intellectual development. If parents expected interracial children to score higher than children with two black parents,

TABLE 10
Comparison of Adopted Children with One or Two Black Natural Parents

Variable	Black/black				Black/white[a]			
	n	M	SD	Range	n	M	SD	Range
IQ	29	96.8	12.8	80–130	68	109.0	11.5	86–136
Age at adoption[b]	29	32.3	33.1	1–124	68	8.9	11.2	0–52
Time in home[b]	29	42.2	14.3	8–120	68	60.6	17.4	33–199
Quality of placement	27	2.9	.4	2–4	64	3.3	.5	3–4
Number of placements	27	1.2	.7	0–3	64	.8	.9	0–6
Natural mother's education	22	10.9	1.9	6–14	66	12.4	1.8	7–18
Natural father's education	15	12.1	1.4	10–16	20	12.5	2.2	8–17
Adoptive father's education	29	16.5	2.7	12–21	68	17.2	2.8	12–21
Adoptive mother's education	29	14.9	2.3	12–20	68	15.3	2.0	11–20
Adoptive father's IQ	29	119.5	10.3	106–137	66	121.4	10.1	93–140
Adoptive mother's IQ	28	116.4	7.5	100–129	68	119.2	10.5	96–143

[a] 66 black fathers, 2 black mothers.

[b] In months.

there could be an expectancy effect. Twelve interracial children were believed by their adoptive parents to be black/black. Only two black/black children were believed to be interracial, and they have been omitted from the analysis.

Interracial children believed to be the offspring of two black parents scored on the average at the same level as interracial children correctly classified by their adoptive parents. The mean IQ score of 43 correctly identified interracial children was 108.4 ($SD = 12.6$). The average IQ score of 12 interracial children believed to be black/black was 108.6 ($SD = 10.2$). There was no evidence for an expectancy effect.

The Criticism of Self-Selection

Self-selection has been used to criticize the above-average IQ scores obtained in other adoption studies. Munsinger (1975a) noted that obviously retarded and damaged infants are not likely to be adopted, a fact which raises the mean IQ of adoptees above the population average. This bias is slight, however: If all infants with eventual IQ scores of less than 60 (at most 3% of children) were eliminated from the adoption pool, the mean IQ of adoptees would be raised by only 1 IQ point.

Another bias could be the self-selection of families whose children appear normal in intelligence and school work. The range of IQ scores in this study contraindicates a strong bias in this regard, because 15 of the 176 adopted children have IQ scores of 85 and below. Furthermore, since 74% of those families known to be eligible did participate and the average IQ of all adoptees was 106, the average IQ of children in the 26% of the families who did not participate would have to be unreasonably low to explain mean results. If we consider the sample to be composed entirely of interracial children, with white adoptees offsetting those with two black parents, their average IQ should fall between those of black and white children in the region.

To lower the average adoptee's IQ to a hypothetical average of 95 for interracial children, the nonparticipants would have to have IQ scores that average 64, or in the retarded range. This is highly unlikely for any sample of adopted children.

School Achievement

The IQ assessments of the present study should bear a meaningful relationship to school achievement. Slightly above average IQ test performance should predict to slightly above average school achievement. The school data are also important because they come from many different school districts and are uncontaminated by any biases that may have inadvertently influenced testing in our study. Most importantly, they represent a "real-life" criterion of intellectual achievement.

Table 11 gives the mean national percentile scores for vocabulary, reading, and mathematics achievement, and a total aptitude score expressed in IQ form, for the socially classified black adopted and natural children of the adoptive families. Although the sample sizes were rather small, the black children in school were performing slightly above the national norms on standard scholastic

TABLE 11

School Achievement Test Scores of Black/
Interracial Adopted and Natural Children:
Mean National Percentiles

Test	M %ile	SD	n
Black adoptees			
Vocabulary	57.2	29.1	20
Reading	55.0	28.6	24
Mathematics	55.2	29.9	19
Aptitude (IQ)	108.8	5.9	5
Natural children			
Vocabulary	73.1	11.7	48
Reading	74.5	25.8	77
Mathematics	71.3	22.6	69
Aptitude (IQ)	119.6	11.7	39

achievement tests, just as their IQ scores would predict. The average IQ of the children with achievement test scores was 104.9. The mean aptitude scores of the 5 black adoptees who had been given school-administered group IQ tests were quite close to their average scores on the WISC and Stanford–Binet. The correlation between aptitude and individual IQ scores could not be calculated because of small sample size.

The natural children of the adoptive parents scored higher than the adopted children on scholastic achievement tests, as predicted by their individual IQ test scores. Furthermore, their group-tested IQ performance was also very close to their average IQ as assessed in this study with individual tests. The correlation between the individual and group test scores of the 39 natural children was .78 ($p < .001$).

SOURCES OF VARIANCE IN BLACK ADOPTEES' IQ SCORES

The possible effects of the adoptive experience and of natural and adoptive family variables on IQ scores were explored in correlational and regression analyses. To account both for the differences between black/black and black/white children and for the above-average performance of the black adopted children on the IQ tests, we intercorrelated their natural parents' education, natural mother's race, their adoptive experience, adoptive family characteristics, and IQ scores. We were particularly concerned about the confounding of racial variables with preadoptive and adoptive family variables that could affect the children's IQ performance. Selective placement of the children of better educated (presumably brighter) natural mothers with better educated adoptive families—a situation that creates genotype-environment correlations–also needed to be examined. The correlation matrix is presented in Table 12.[2]

Natural Parents and the Child's Adoptive Experience

The educational and racial characteristics of the natural mothers of the adopted children had a great deal to do with when and by whom the children were adopted. Less well educated mothers, who were more often black, had children who were placed later for adoption, had spent less time in the adoptive homes, and were adopted by families with lower educational and income levels. The same pattern held for natural fathers' education. (Since all but two of the known natural fathers were black, father's race was omitted from the analysis.)

The black children's IQ scores were significantly correlated with the same

---

[2]The age of the child and the race and sex of the examiner are omitted from the tables because they are uncorrelated with the children's IQ scores ($rs = .01, .06,$ and $.01$, respectively).

TABLE 12

Correlations of Natural Parent Characteristics, Child's Adoptive Experience, Adoptive Family Characteristics, and Child's IQ Scores for Black/Interracial Children

	1	2	3	4	5	6	7	8	9	10	11	12	13
Natural parent characteristics													
1. Natural mother's race (117)													
2. Natural mother's education (107)[a]	-.36												
3. Natural father's education (37)	-.19	.27											
Adoptive experience													
4. Age at placement (130)	.36	-.34	-.27										
5. Time in home (130)	-.45	.27	.37	-.31									
6. Number of placements (112)	.22	-.17	-.31	.50	-.21								
7. Quality of placements (112)	-.30	.26	.17	-.37	.15	-.65							
Adoptive family characteristics													
8. Adoptive mother's education (130)	-.10	.22	.12	-.10	.12	-.13	.02						
9. Adoptive father's education (130)	-.13	.26	.25	-.27	.26	-.14	.04	.56					
10. Adoptive father's occupation (129)	.01	.07	.04	.00	.09	.01	-.05	.31	.29				
11. Family income (129)	.08	.16	-.06	.16	.12	-.04	-.06	.31	.04	.45			
12. Adoptive father's IQ (127)	-.01	.12	.33	-.19	.06	-.33	.08	.26	.47	.18	-.07		
13. Adoptive mother's IQ (128)	-.18	.09	.29	-.01	.26	-.05	-.05	.53	.30	.21	.27	.21	
Child's IQ													
14. Black adoptees (130)	-.41	.31	.45	-.36	.30	-.36	.38	.22	.34	-.01	-.00	.18	.17

Note. Total $N = 130$. Numbers in parentheses are *ns*. Also, in the correlation and regression analyses (Tables 12–14), natural mothers who were students at the time of the child's birth were included. Of the 107 mothers of black children for whom we had educational data, 34 were students in high school or college. Since the mean educational level of the natural mothers, with and without the students, was the same and since the correlation of natural mother's education and child's IQ was higher when students were included, we decided to present the tables based on the larger *ns*.

[a] Students included.

placement and adoptive family variables. Children who were adopted earlier, who had spent more years in the adoptive homes, who had fewer preadoptive placements, and who had better quality placements had higher IQ scores. In addition, adopted black and interracial children who had better educated and higher-IQ adoptive parents had higher IQs. Thus, there was an important confounding of the characteristics of the natural parents, the preadoption experience, and the adoptive family, all of which affected the level of the black/interracial children's intellectual functioning.

Selective Placement

Selective placement further confuses the sources of variance in the black children's intellectual functioning. As Table 12 indicates, the natural mother's educational level is correlated with the adoptive parents' educational level, between .22 and .26, suggesting that the adoption agencies practiced selective placement, based on the educational information they had available. The correlations of natural mother's education and adoptive parents' IQ scores are not as high (.09 and .12), presumably because the agencies did not have the IQ data available. Selective placement increases the similarity between natural parents and their (adopted) children and between the adoptive family and their adopted children.

The biological and social factors, many of which separately and together can affect IQ scores, were largely confounded in the sample of black and interracial adoptees. Therefore, we did not attempt to estimate point values for the genetic and environmental contributions to IQ differences. Instead, we decided to present two regression analyses.

When the *biological* variables were put into the regression first, we could find out how much of the remaining variance would be accounted for by the social variables. When the *social* variables were put into the regression equation first, we could determine how much of the remaining variance would be determined by the biological variables. Tables 13 and 14 present the two regression analyses (see Footnote 2).

In Table 13, the social variables, including placement and adoptive family measures, were stepped in first. The natural family data, called biological variables, were entered second into the regression equation. In Table 14, the biological variables were entered first, the social variables second. Both steps were statistically significant in both tables.

When the social variables were entered first, they accounted for 31% of the total variance in the IQ scores of socially classified black adopted children. The biological variables added 4% of the variance without natural father's education and 11% with father's education. (Because the sample of black children with natural father information was small, $n = 37$, a separate regression including only those children was done. The results for the other variables were very

TABLE 13
Two-Step Multiple Regression of Biological and Adoptive Family
Variables on the IQ Scores of Black/Interracial Children, Adoptive
Variables First

Step	Multiple R	R^2	R^2 change	Simple r	p <
1. Social variables					
Adoptive mother's education	.22	.05	.05	.22	.001
Quality of placements	.44	.19	.14	.38	
Adoptive father's IQ	.45	.20	.01	.18	
Adoptive father's occupation	.46	.21	.00	−.01	
Family income	.46	.21	.00	−.00	
Adoptive mother's IQ	.46	.21	.01	.17	
Age at placement	.53	.28	.07	−.36	
Adoptive father's education	.56	.31	.03	.34	
Number of placements	.56	.31	.00	−.36	
Time in home	.56	.31	.00	.30	
2. Biological variables					
Natural mother's education[a]	.57	.32	.01	.31	.001
Natural mother's race	.59	.35	.03	−.41	

[a] Students included; natural mother's education entered first to leave residual variance for race.

TABLE 14
Two-Step Multiple Regression of Biological and Adoptive Family
Variables on the IQ Scores of Black/Interracial Children, Biological
Variables First

Step	Multiple R	R^2	R^2 change	Simple r	p <
1. Biological variables					
Natural mother's education[a]	.31	.09	.09	.31	.001
Natural mother's race	.44	.20	.10	−.41	
2. Social variables					
Adoptive father's occupation	.44	.20	.00	−.01	.001
Adoptive father's IQ	.47	.22	.03	.18	
Adoptive mother's IQ	.48	.23	.01	.17	
Quality of placements	.54	.29	.06	.38	
Adoptive father's education	.58	.34	.05	.34	
Family income	.58	.34	.00	−.00	
Adoptive mother's education	.58	.34	.00	.22	
Number of placements	.59	.35	.01	−.36	
Age at placement	.59	.35	.00	−.36	
Time in home	.59	.35	.00	.30	

[a] Students included; natural mother's education entered first to leave residual variance for race.

similar, and father's education accounted for an additional 7% of the total IQ variance.)

When the biological variables were entered into the regression analysis first, natural mother's education and race accounted for 20% of the variance in the black children's IQ scores. (Natural father's education added 11%, but the sample size was too small to include in the full analysis.) The social variables, stepped in second, added 15% of the IQ variance.

It is impossible to distinguish the effects of the separate social and biological variables, because 24.5 of the 35% of the variance accounted for was shared by the so-called biological and social variables. Using part correlations, we found that natural mother's race and adopted father's education each contributed 3% to the variance of the socially classified black adoptee's IQ scores, and the quality of the children's preadoptive placements contributed 2%. The remaining 1.4% of the unique variance was contributed almost equally by the other "biological" and "social" variables.

In the case of natural mother's race, it is unwarranted to conclude that race stands solely for genetic differences between the races. In this sample, natural mother's race was correlated with many measured social variables; it is conceivably correlated with other *unmeasured* social variables. Race does make a small contribution to the socially classified black children's IQ variance, independent of the other measures, but not necessarily independent of other environmental variables.

Another consideration in the interpretation of the regression analyses is the restricted range of variation in adoptive family characteristics. Parental education, IQ scores, income, occupational status, and other unmeasured family variables, such as child-rearing practices, varied over half or less of their normal range in the general population. Thus, the adoptive family variables accounted for less of the IQ variance among black and interracial adoptees than they would in a more varied adoptive population. The importance of the social variables is very likely to be underestimated.

DISCUSSION

This study attempted to answer five questions about the impact of transracial adoption on the IQ performance of black and interracial children adopted into white homes. The first question focused on the reaction range of IQ scores within the black population. Would socially classified black children reared in economically advantaged white homes score above those reared in black environments?

The average IQ score of black and interracial children, adopted by advantaged white families, was found to be 106. Early-adopted black and interracial children performed at an even higher level. This mean represents an increase of 1 standard deviation above the average IQ of 90 usually achieved by black children reared in their own homes in the North Central region (Kaufman & Doppelt, in press). Furthermore, in the Minneapolis public school district, the average performance of 4th-grade children on the Gates–MacGinitee vocabulary test at a school with 87% black and interracial enrollment in 1973 was about the 21st national percentile, which translates to an IQ equivalent of about 90.

Since 68 of the 130 black children were known to have one white parent and only 29 were known to have had two black parents (the remainder were of other mixed or unknown parentage), it may seem misleading to compare the adoptees to black children in the general population. Even if all of the black children were interracial offspring, however, a strong genetic hypothesis should not predict that they would score well above the white population average. Nor should they score as highly as white adoptees. In fact, the black and interracial children of this sample scored as highly on IQ tests as did white adoptees in previous studies with large samples (Burks, 1928; Leahy, 1935).

In other words, the range of reaction of socially classified black children's IQ scores from average (black) to advantaged (white) environments is at least 1 standard deviation. Conservatively, if we consider only the adopted children with two black parents (and late and less favorable adoptive experiences), the IQ reaction range is at least 10 points between these environments. If we consider the early-adopted group, the IQ range may be as large as 20 points. The level of school achievements among the black and interracial adoptees is further evidence of their above-average performance on standard intellectual measures.

The dramatic increase in the IQ mean and the additional finding that placement and adoptive family characteristics account for a major portion of the IQ differences among the socially classified black children strongly suggest that the IQ scores of these children are environmentally malleable.

One reason for the substantial increase in test performance of the black and interracial adoptees is that their rearing environments are culturally relevant to the tests and to the school. Amid the IQ controversy, some have argued that standardized measures are inappropriate for children whose cultural background is different from that of the tests. While the rejection of IQ tests as predictors of academic success, on the basis of their cultural bias, is untenable (Jensen, 1974), we believe that the tests and the schools share a common culture to which black children are not as fully acculturated as are white children. However, the socially classified black children in this study have been fully exposed to the culture of the tests and the school, although they are still socially defined as black.

IQ Comparisons within the Black Group

The second question concerned a comparison of the IQ scores of children whose parents were both black with black children of interracial parentage. The interracial children scored about 12 points higher than those with two black parents, but this difference was associated with large differences in maternal education and preplacement history. The part correlations suggested that variation in the race of mothers accounted for 3% of the children's IQ variance, but even this percentage of variance probably includes some additional and unmeasured environmental differences between the groups.

For example, black mothers are known to be at greater risk than white mothers for nutritional deficiencies, maternal death, infant mortality, and other reproductive casualties (Scarr-Salapatek & Williams, 1973). The prematurity rate among black mothers is more than double that of whites. These antenatal risks are often found to be associated with long-term developmental problems among the children. The interracial children, all but two of whom have white mothers, were less likely to have suffered any of these problems.

Comparisons of Black/Interracial, Asian/Indian, and Natural Children of the Adoptive Families

The third question asked for comparisons among the IQ scores of black/interracial, Asian/Indian adoptees, and the biological children of the adoptive families. There were significant differences in IQ scores among the groups. The socially classified black children scored on the average between the white and Asian/Indian adoptees, but these results were confounded with placement variables. Among the early adoptees, there were too few white and Asian/Indian children to make meaningful comparisons. The black/interracial early adoptees, however, performed at IQ 110, on the average.

Compared to adopted children in previous studies, the average IQ of 110 for the 99 early-adopted black/interracial children compares well with the 112.6 reported by Leahy (1935, p. 285) for white adoptees in professional families.

The above-average IQ level of adopted children, reported in all adoption studies, reflects both their better-than-average environments and the elimination of severely retarded children from the pool of potential adoptees. Although Munsinger's (1975a) review concluded that adoptive family environments have little or no impact on the intellectual development of adoptees, past studies have not adequately tested this hypothesis. Because children who are selected for adoption are not grossly defective, their predicted IQ level is slightly above that of the general population. In this study, however, the adopted *black/interracial* children could not have been predicted to have average IQ scores above the mean of the *white* population unless adoptive family environments have considerable impact.

The biological children of the adoptive families scored above the average of the black/interracial early adoptees. Not only have the biological children been in their families since birth, but their natural parents are considerably brighter than those of the adopted children, regardless of race.

School Achievement

A fourth question focused on the school achievement of the black/interracial adoptees and the biological children in the adoptive families. Black/interracial adoptees were found to score slightly above average on school-administered achievement and aptitude tests, as predicted by their IQ scores. The natural children of the adoptive families scored higher than the socially classified black adoptees on school achievement measures, a finding which is congruent with their higher IQ scores. The school achievement data provided validation for our IQ assessment.

Genetic and Environmental Sources of IQ Variance

The final question posed by the study dealt with the relative contributions of biological and social environmental measures to IQ differences among the socially classified black children. The placement variables, adoptive family characteristics, and genetic background all contributed to the IQ differences among the black/interracial adoptees. Because the social and biological variables were confounded, it is very difficult to make a clear comparison. Although this study has an unusual sample of children, we propose that genetic and social variables are usually confounded in families. Indeed, we suspect that genotype–environment correlations are the rule and that they account for a sizable portion of the IQ variance in the general population.

In making any comparison between biological and social variables, we must be concerned about the quality of those measures. Although the adoptive family variables are only indices of the qualities of the environment that have an impact on children, the natural parent data are even more limited. It would have been advantageous to have comparable IQ scores for the natural parents, rather than educational levels, although the latter correlate about .7 with IQ in the general population (Jencks, 1972).

Because the social variables accounted for a substantial portion of the IQ variance among black/interracial adoptees, it is likely that IQ performance is malleable within the range of existing environments. If all black children had environments such as those provided by the adoptive families in this study, we would predict that their IQ scores would be 10–20 points higher than the scores are under current rearing conditions.

Social Implications of the Study

Given the above-average IQ scores of black/interracial children adopted transracially, it may seem that we are endorsing the adoption of black children by white families as a social policy. There is no question that adoption constitutes a massive intervention, as noted earlier, and that it has a favorable impact on IQ scores. However, there is good reason why transracial adoption is not a panacea for low IQ scores among black children. Only an infinitesimally small proportion of black children will ever be available for adoption, and of those, many will and *should be* adopted by black families.

What we do endorse is that *if* higher IQ scores are considered important for educational and occupational successs, then there is need for social action that will provide black children with home environments that facilitate the acquisition of intellectual skills tapped by IQ measures. Although there has been some research describing the immediate environments of middle-, working-, and lower-class homes (Hess & Shipman, 1965; Kohn, 1959; White & Watts, 1973), there is still a need to investigate how families, such as these transracial adoptive families, constitute an ecological system in which IQ skills are developed. The physical environment, the amount and quality of parent–child interaction, the parents' attitudes and practices in child rearing, the neighborhood and community settings of the family, and the larger social contexts of employment, economic security, and cultural values must be all considered in describing the parameters of family effects.

Educational interventions alone are unlikely to have the effects reported here for adoption. Schools, as presently constituted, cannot have the far-reaching, intensive impact of the family and home.

Our emphasis on IQ scores in this study is not an endorsement of IQ as the ultimate human value. Although important for functioning in middle-class educational environments, IQ tests do not sample a huge spectrum of human characteristics that are requisite for social adjustment. Empathy, sociability, and altruism, to name a few, are important human attributes that are not guaranteed by a high IQ. Furthermore, successful adaptation within ethnic subgroups may be less dependent on the intellectual skills tapped by IQ measures than is adaptation in middle-class white settings.

This study was not designed to address the social issues we have just highlighted. Rather, it was intended to examine the effects of cross-fostering on the IQ scores of black/interracial children. The major questions of the study concerned the relative effects of genetic background and social environment on IQ levels and variations among socially classified black children. The major findings of the study support the view that the social environment plays a dominant role in determining the average IQ level of black children and that both social and genetic variables contribute to individual variation among them.

ACKNOWLEDGMENTS

The present study was supported by the Grant Foundation and the National Institute of Child Health and Human Development (HD-08016).

This study was conducted with the full collaboration of the Minnesota State Department of Public Welfare, Adoption Unit, directed by Ruth Weidell and assisted by Marjorie Flowers. Their help was invaluable. The additional support of the Open Door Society, Lutheran Social Service, and The Children's Home Society, all of Minnesota, facilitated the study.

We are very grateful for the assistance of Louise Carter-Saltzman, Harold Grotevant, Margaret Getman, Marsha Sargrad, Patricia Webber, Joanne Bergman, William Thompson, and Carol Nelson.

REFERENCES

Burks, B. S. The relative influence of nature and nurture upon mental development; a comparative study of foster parent–foster child resemblance and true parent–true child resemblance. *Yearbook of the National Society for the Study of Education*, 1928, *27*, 219–316.

Cleary, T. A., Humphreys, L. G., Kendrick, S. A., & Wesman, A. Educational uses of tests with disadvantaged students. *American Psychologist*, 1975, *30*, 15–41.

Freeman, F. N., Holzinger, K. J., & Mitchell, B. C. The influence of environment on the intelligence, school achievement and conduct of foster children. *Yearbook of the National Society for the Study of Education*, 1928, *27*, 101–217.

Grow, L. J., & Shapiro, D. *Black children–white parents.* New York: Child Welfare League of America, 1974.

Hess, R. D., & Shipman, V. C. Early experience and the socialization of cognitive modes in children. *Child Development*, 1965, *36*, 869–886.

Husén, T. *Talent, equality, and meritocracy.* The Hague: Martinue Nijhoff, 1974.

Jencks, C. *Inequality: A reassessment of the effects of family and schooling in America.* New York: Basic Books, 1972.

Jensen, A. R. *Educability and group differences.* New York: Basic Books, 1973.

Jensen, A. R. How biased are culture-loaded tests? *Genetic Psychology Monographs*, 1974, *90*, 185–244.

Kaufman, A. S., & Doppelt, J. E. Analysis of WISC-R standardization data in terms of the stratification variables. *Child Development*, in press.

Kohn, M. L. Social class and the exercise of parental authority. *American Sociological Review*, 1959, *24*, 352–366.

Leahy, A. M. Nature–nurture and intelligence. *Genetic Psychology Monographs*, 1935, *17*, 237–307.

Loehlin, J., Lindzey, G., & Spuhler, J. N. *Race differences in intelligence.* San Francisco, Calif.: Freeman, 1975.

Manosevitz, M., Lindzey, G., & Thiessen, D. *Behavioral genetics: Method and research.* New York: Appleton-Century-Crofts, 1969.

Munsinger, H. The adopted child's IQ: A critical review. *Psychological Bulletin*, 1975, *82*, 623–659. (a)

Munsinger, H. Children's resemblance to their biological and adopting parents in two ethnic groups. *Behavior Genetics*, 1975, *5*, 239–254. (b)

Reiss, A. J., Jr. *Occupations and social status.* New York: Free Press, 1961.

Scarr-Salapatek, S., & Williams, M. L. The effects of early stimulation on low-birth-weight infants. *Child Development*, 1973, *44*, 94–101.

Shockley, W. Morals, mathematics, and the moral obligation to diagnose the origin of Negro IQ deficits. *Review of Educational Research*, 1971, *41*, 369–377.

Shockley, W. Dysgenics, geneticity, raciology: A challenge to the intellectual responsibility of educators. *Phi Delta Kappan*, 1972, *53*, 297–307.

Skodak, M., & Skeels, H. M. A final follow-up study of one hundred children. *The Journal of Genetic Psychology*, 1949, *75*, 85–125.

Terman, L. M., & Merrill, M. *Stanford–Binet Intelligence Scale*. Boston, Mass.: Houghton Mifflin, 1972.

Wechsler, D. *Wechsler Intelligence Scale for Children*. New York: Psychological Corporation, 1949.

Wechsler, D. *Wechsler Adult Intelligence Scale*. New York: Psychological Corporation, 1955.

White, B. L., & Watts, J. C. *Experience and environment*. Englewood Cliffs, N.J.: Prentice-Hall, 1973.

Comments and Replies

COMMENT: IQ, RACE, AND ADOPTION*

In their article, Scarr and Weinberg (October 1976) stated that their results "support the view that the social environment plays a dominant role in determining the average IQ level of black children and that both social and genetic variables contribute to individual variation among them" (p. 739). Surely the authors are not suggesting that the factors influencing the IQs of individuals are different from those affecting the mean IQ of the population. The mean, after all, is just an abstraction from individual scores. Perhaps what Scarr and Weinberg meant was that their data support the view that the difference between the black IQ mean and the white IQ mean is due to social factors, while individual differences within the populations are a function of both social and genetic variables. While their results are consistent with the position that race differences in IQ are environmental, we believe that the genetic and social variables in this study were sufficiently confounded so that the results are consistent with virtually any theory of race differences in IQ.

The study does demonstrate rather convincingly that the IQs of black children are environmentally malleable. It does not, however, contradict the results of studies showing that IQ is highly heritable (Jensen, 1967; Munsinger, 1975). As has been pointed out by Jensen (1969) and others (McCall, Appelbaum, & Hogarty, 1973), even if the heritability of IQ is as high as .80, large changes in

---

*The comments by Werner, Lane, and Mohanty; Nichols; and McNemar; and the reply by Scarr and Weinberg originally appeared in *American Psychologist,* 1977, *32,* 677–683. Copyright © 1977 by the American Psychological Association. Reprinted by permission.

the environment (within the range occurring in the population) could result in substantial changes in IQ. To wit: If the standard deviation in IQ test performance is 15, then the variance is 225. Twenty percent, or 45, would be the variance attributable to nongenetic factors. Therefore, with a 1 standard deviation change in environmental quality, a change as large as $\sqrt{45}$ or 6.71 IQ points would not be unexpected (cf. Jensen, 1973). Considering the descriptions provided by Scarr and Weinberg of the adopting families (see their Table 3) and preplacement histories (Table 5), it is not unreasonable to assume that the adopted children were provided with an environment about 3 standard deviations above what they would have received had they not been adopted. An increase of about 20 IQ points would, therefore, not be unexpected. They found that the average IQ of black and interracially adopted children was 106, an increase of about 16 points above the average black child in the same region of the country. Clearly, their data are consistent with a heritability estimate of .80.

The finding that children with two black parents scored 12 IQ points lower than children with only one black parent is, at first, quite striking. The authors correctly point out that most, but not all, of the difference is confounded with the social variables. They interpret this to mean that the difference in the two groups is due to differences on the social variables (both measured and unmeasured). There is no way of determining, however, whether differences in racial ancestry are related to IQ because of their mutual correlation with the social variables or whether the relation of the social variables to IQ is due to their mutual correlation with racial ancestry. These data simply do not differentiate between the various theories of race differences in IQ performance.

The social and biological variables in this study were confounded, thus making it impossible to draw any unambiguous conclusions. It is clear that Scarr and Weinberg are aware of this drawback: "we propose that genetic and social variables are usually confounded in families" (p. 738). Nevertheless, they attempt to determine the relative contribution of social and genetic factors to the variance in IQ scores of the adopted children. Their analysis is uninformative because the estimates are not meaningful outside this particular sample. The degree to which the adoptive parents provided differing environments and the degree to which the natural parents differed genetically were probably the main contributing factors in the estimates of variance explained. The problem is similar to that encountered in estimating variance components with a fixed-effects design (Dooling & Danks, 1975). Even ignoring this statistical problem, the analysis of the relative contributions of social and genetic factors is not convincing. Only 2 biological variables are pitted against 10 social variables. Further, one of the biological variables, mother's race, is dichotomous and hence its predictive power is quite limited. The other variable, mother's education, is not an adequate measure of her IQ. The inadequacy of this measure is accentuated for black females who probably have had limited educational opportunities. Still, in spite of these biases against the biological variables, they appear to make a strong contribution. With father's education added to the 2 biological variables, the unique variance attributable to the 10 social variables and the 3 biological variables is approximately equal. Scarr and Weinberg make a case for the significance of other *"unmeasured* social variables," but an even stronger case can be made for a number of important and unmeasured biological variables. We are not advocating a genetic model, we only want to note that it is one of many alternatives that fit the data.

Finally, Scarr and Weinberg suggest that their data may be of social significance. This contention is hard to follow. It is difficult to see any value, either scientific or applied, in transracial adoption studies. If one is interested in the genetics of intelligence, then there must be better ways of investigating the topic. There is probably no other area in psychology in which so many variables are confounded. As far as practical differences are concerned, we think most would agree that the best policy is to provide every child with the best possible environment. Neither genetic differences between groups nor heritability as high as .80 would preclude the possibility of intervention programs having substantial beneficial effects. Questions about the possibility of race differences do not have to be answered to justify these programs.

REFERENCES

Dooling, D. J., & Danks, J. H. Going beyond tests of significance: Is psychology ready? *Bulletin of the Psychonomic Society,* 1975, *5,* 15–17.

Jensen, A. R. Estimation of the limits of heritability of traits by comparison of monozygotic and dizygotic twins. *Proceedings of the National Academy of Sciences,* 1967, *58,* 149–156.

Jensen, A. R. Reducing the heredity–environment uncertainty: A reply. *Harvard Educational Review,* 1969, *39,* 449–483.

Jensen, A. R. Let's understand Skodak and Skeels finally. *Educational Psychologist,* 1973, *10,* 30–35.

McCall, R. B., Applebaum, M. I., & Hogarty, P. S. Developmental changes in mental performance. *Monographs of the Society for Research in Child Development,* 1973, *38*(3, Serial No. 150).

Munsinger, H. The adopted child's IQ: A critical review. *Psychological Bulletin,* 1975, *82,* 623–659.

Scarr, S., & Weinberg, R. A. IQ test performance of black children adopted by white families. *American Psychologist,* 1976, *31,* 726–739.

JOHN WERNER
Brown University

DAVID LANE
Tulane University

AJIT MOHANTY
University of Alberta

COMMENT: BLACK CHILDREN ADOPTED BY WHITE FAMILIES

The interesting data on black children adopted by white families, provided by Scarr and Weinberg (October 1976), unfortunately suffer from the trade-off, so frequently encountered in the behavioral sciences, between the social relevance and the methodological adequacy of data. The part of their data that most lends itself to rigorous analysis and interpretation is the correlation among the characteristics of the biological parents, the adoptive experience, the adoptive family, and the child's IQ for the 130 black and interracial adopted children. The complete matrix of intercorrelations of these 14 variables was given in Scarr and Weinberg's Table 12 (p. 734). Since there were substantial correlations between the characteristics of the biological mother and the adoptive experience, Scarr and Weinberg performed a regression analysis in an attempt to disentangle some of the confounding. Although they did not identify it as such, their analysis was essentially a partitioning of variance or commonality analysis in which the predictable variance of the child's IQ was partitioned into a part uniquely associated with the characteristics of the biological mother (biological variables), a part uniquely associated with the characteristics of the adoptive family and adoptive experience (social variables), and a part jointly associated with the two sets of variables. The joint part, or commonality, results from the confounding of the two sets of variables, and cannot, from the present data, be attributed to either. This type of analysis was introduced by Mood (1971) and has since been discussed favorably in several respected methodological texts (Cooley & Lohnes, 1976, pp. 218–223; Kerlinger & Pedhazur, 1973, pp. 297–305).

The partitioning of variance presented by Scarr and Weinberg is shown in the first column of Table 1. On the basis of these results they concluded:

> Because the social variables accounted for a substantial portion of the IQ variance among black/interracial adoptees, it is likely that IQ performance is malleable within the range of existing environments. If all black children had environments such as those provided by the adoptive families in this study, we would predict that their IQ scores would be 10–20 points higher than the scores are under current rearing conditions. (p. 738)

The partitioning of variance performed by Scarr and Weinberg, however, neglected the fact that multiple regression capitalizes on chance relationships in the sample and, thus, overestimates the multiple correlation prevailing in the population. The degree of overestimation increases with the number of variables in the equation. Since there were 10 social variables and only 2 biological variables, the overestimation was greater for the social variables than for the biological variables. This bias may be eliminated by basing the partitioning of variance on estimated-population multiple correlations instead of on the sample values used by Scarr and Weinberg. Darlington (1968) has provided formulas for

TABLE 1

Partitioning of Variance of Adopted Child's IQ

	Proportions of variance	
Variance partitions	Reported by Scarr and Weinberg[a]	Based on estimated-population multiple correlations[b]
Unique variance		
2 biological variables	.04	.023
10 social variables	.15	.029
Commonality		
Biological and social	.16[e]	.134
Variance accounted for	.35	.186
Estimated error of measurement[d]	.10	.100
Unexplained variance	.55	.714
Total variance of child's IQ	1.00	1.000

Note. Data from Scarr and Weinberg (1976).
   [a] Scarr and Weinberg reported only the first four numbers in this column. The last three were added for completeness.
   [b] Proportions of variance are reported to three decimal places to better reveal the small differences among some partitions. It is not intended to convey a spurious indication of accuracy.
   [e] In the text (p. 736), Scarr and Weinberg reported the shared variance to be 24.5%. It is not clear how they arrived at this figure. My calculations from their correlations show a shared variance of 15.5%.
   [d] A reliability of .90 was somewhat arbitrarily assumed for the IQ tests.

obtaining these estimates from the number of variables, the number of cases, and the sample multiple correlation (Formulas 12 and 14). The partitions of variance shown in the second column of Table 1 were based on these estimated population values. The effect of this correction was to increase the unexplained variance, as would be expected, to reduce the unique variance of the social variables to a value about equal to that of the biological variables, and to increase the relative importance of the commonality. These results show the confounding of biological and social variables to be so great that little should be said about their unique contributions other than that they are quite small.

The 10 social variables consisted of six characteristics of the adoptive family (e.g., education and IQ of the adoptive parents) and four characteristics of the adoptive experience (e.g., age at placement and number of previous placements), which were combined for the partitioning of variance. Yet these two types of social variables, which were identified separately in the correlation matrix, represent different kinds of environmental influences on the adopted child, and they should be studied separately. Fortunately, partitioning of variance is not limited to two sets of variables.

Table 2 shows a partitioning of the variance of the adopted children's IQs that separates the effects of the two types of social variables. The calculations in this table were based on estimated-population multiple correlations, since the number of variables in the three sets was unequal. Thus, it is a redistribution of the same proportion of variance accounted for (.186) in the second column of Table 1. These results show more clearly where the confounding lies and with what influences the unique contribution of the social variables is associated.

The confounding of the race and education of the mother with the social variables was with the characteristics of the adoption itself rather than with the characteristics of the adoptive family. A close look at the correlation matrix reveals that the confounding consisted almost entirely of the interracial children of white mothers experiencing the more favorable adoption circumstances. They were adopted at a younger age, they had fewer placements before adoption, the quality of their placements was better, and they had spent more time in the adoptive family than had the children of black mothers. The confounding of these two variables—race of mother and favorableness of placement—accounted for over half of the total explained variance, since these variables had among the highest correlations with the child's IQ. Children of white mothers and those with more favorable placements tended to obtain the higher scores. It is unfortunate that the data do not allow further separation of these two quite different and heuristically titillating variables. I have computed numerous partial correlations in the attempt, but the confounding seems to be in the nature of the sample rather than in the indicators.

TABLE 2

Additional Partitioning of Variance of Adopted Child's IQ

Variance partitions	Proportions of variance based on estimated-population multiple correlations[a]	
Unique variance		
2 characteristics of the biological mother (BM)	.023	
4 characteristics of the adoptive experience (AE)	.029	
6 characteristics of the adoptive family (AF)	.000[b]	
Commonalities		
BM × AE	.107	
BM × AF	.006	
AE × AF	.014	
BM × AE × AF	.007	
Variance accounted for		.186
Estimated error of measurement[c]	.100	
Unexplained variance	.714	
Total variance of child's IQ	1.000	

[a] Proportions of variance are reported to three decimal places to better reveal the small differences among some partitions. It is not intended to convey a spurious indication of accuracy.
[b] The calculated value for this unique variance was −.014, which was changed to zero because unique variances cannot be negative (although commonalities can). The estimation of population multiple correlations can result in negative values, which should then be changed to zero. See Darlington (1968) for an explanation. Because of missing data for many variables, the correlations in Scarr and Weinberg's Table 12 were calculated on varying Ns. An average value for N of 120 was used in calculating the estimated-population multiple correlations.
[c] A reliability of .90 was somewhat arbitrarily assumed for the IQ tests.

The unique contributions to explained variance were small relative to the commonality, but, as Scarr and Weinberg indicated, they were highly significant statistically.[1] The partitioning of variance attributed no unique contribution to the characteristics of the adoptive family, but instead assigned all of the unique social variance to the circumstances of adoption. The characteristics of the biological mother, of course, retained the same unique contribution that was shown in Table 1. Other things being equal, these uniquenesses indicate that both the characteristics of the biological mother and the circumstances of the adoption significantly influenced the IQ of the child. However, since these unique contributions to variance were approximately equal and were quite small relative to the commonality, they give little help in apportioning the joint variance.

The absence of a unique contribution or even a substantial commonality for the characteristics of the adoptive family leaves some of Scarr and Weinberg's more sanguine conclusions without adequate empirical support. For example, they stated that "one reason for the substantial increase in test performance of the black and interracial adoptees is that their rearing environments are culturally relevant to the tests and to the school" (p. 737). This statement seems to have been prompted by the relatively large uniqueness observed for the social variables in their partitioning of variance. However, we have seen that the part of this unique variance that was not due to capitalization on chance was associated with the circumstances of the adoption, not with the culture of the adoptive family.

The "substantial increase in test performance" mentioned in the above quotation referred to the finding of an average IQ of 106 for the black and interracial adopted children. Scarr and Weinberg claimed that "this mean represents an increase of 1 standard deviation above the average IQ of 90 usually achieved by black children reared in their own homes in the North Central region" (p. 736). Regional norms leave something to be desired as a control group for these unusual adopted children. They were selected at an average age of 18 months by adoptive parents of above-average intelligence and education at a time when there was a surplus of available black children from which to choose. Fifty-six percent of the biological mothers were white. It seems quite reasonable that under such circumstances, an above-average group of children would be selected—if not by the parents then by the agencies who were attempting to promote interracial adoption at the time. At least this is a plausible rival hypothesis that cannot be ruled out from the data presented.

---

[1]The fact that variance components are greater than zero, when based on estimated-population multiple correlations, is, in itself, an indication of statistical significance. My experience has been that when multiple correlations are not significant at somewhere between the .05 and .01 levels by conventional F tests, the estimated-population multiple correlation, derived from the Darlington formulas, is zero.

REFERENCES

Cooley, W. W., & Lohnes, P. R. *Evaluation research in education.* New York: Irvington, 1976.
Darlington, R. B. Multiple regression in psychological research and practice, *Psychological Bulletin*, 1968, *69*, 161–182.
Kerlinger, F. N., & Pedhazur, E. J. *Multiple regression in behavioral research.* New York: Holt, Rinehart & Winston, 1973.
Mood, A. M. Partitioning variance in multiple regression analyses as a tool for developing learning models. *American Educational Research Journal*, 1971, *8*, 191–202.
Scarr, S., & Weinberg, R. A. IQ test performance of black children adopted by white families. *American Psychologist*, 1976, 31, 726–739.

ROBERT C. NICHOLS
State University of New York at Buffalo

COMMENT: STATISTICS CAN MISLEAD

Sandra Scarr and Richard A. Weinberg (October 1976) provide yet another example of how statistics can mislead. In brief, these authors attempted, among other things, to ascertain the relative contributions of 10 "social" and 2 (3 if natural father's education is included) "biological" variables to the IQ variance of 130 socially classified black children who had been adopted by, and had resided an average of 5 years with, white families. The statistical treatment involved two "2-step" multiple regression analyses. In the first analysis, R^2 was calculated for the social (soc.) variables as Step 1, then with the biological (biol.) variables included as Step 2 (i.e., soc. add biol.); in the second, R^2 was calculated for the biological variables as Step 1, then with the social variables included as Step 2 (i.e., biol. add soc.). Whichever set of variables, when added to the regression equation as Step 2, increased R^2 the most was declared the winner in the genetic–environment sweepstakes. The results, without natural father's education (excluded because of small $N = 37$), were:

Soc. add biol., R^2, .31 up to .35
Biol. add soc., R^2, .20 up to .35,

and with natural father's education included:

Soc. add biol., R^2, .31 up to .42
Biol. add soc., R^2, .31 up to .42

The authors say that "the social variables accounted for a substantial portion of the IQ variance" (p. 738) and that "these [social] characteristics largely account for the IQ differences between black children'' (p. 732). This claim was apparently based on the first set of four R^2 values (15% more variance by adding the social variables, contrasted with only 4% by adding the biological variables), a claim that ignores the equal increments when natural father's education was included.

But my main concern is about two serious statistical problems in this type of stepwise multiple regression analysis, the first of which has to do with the differentially biasing effect on R^2 when one starts with 10 variables and then adds 2 variables versus starting with 2 variables and then adding 10 variables (as holds for the first four R^2 values; 10 and 3 versus 3 and 10 for the second set). When I use the so-called shrinkage formula as a very nearly unbiased estimator, I get the following:

Soc. add biol., R^2, .25 up to .28
Biol. add soc., R^2, .19 up to .28,

and for natural father's education included:

Soc. add biol., R^2, .25 up to .35
Biol. add soc., R^2, .29 up to .35.

By the authors' way of interpreting results, the first set of unbiased R^2s would still seem to support their claim, because the increment of variance is 9% for the social versus 3% for the biological variables, but now the seemingly forgotten contribution of natural father's education reverses the relative incremental contribution to variance: 6% for social versus 10% for biological. Note also that for both the biased and the corrected sets of R^2s, the inclusion of natural father's education explains 7% more variance.

The second difficulty with this type of incremental analysis is the fact that no statistical significance test is available for the difference between increments, such as 9% − 3% = 6% (or 10% − 6% = 4%). True, a separate increment can be tested as the difference between two R^2 values, but that does not yield the needed single probability for the chance occurrence of as large a difference between two increments as 6% (or 4%).

The actual results based on the necessarily corrected, or unbiased, R^2s show opposing ''trends.'' The ''naturite'' who seizes onto the analysis that includes natural father's education should not forget that low N of 37. The ''nurturite'' who thinks the first set, unbiased and based on larger $N(s)$, is indicative of something should beware of the obvious fact, admitted and then ignored by Scarr and Weinberg, that selective placement was operative. Then there is the question: What would the results have been if the IQs of the natural parents had been available and included among the ''biological'' variables? After all, biology was represented only by the natural mother's (and father's) education and the mother's race (70% white, 30% black).

REFERENCE

Scarr, S., & Weinberg, R. C. IQ test performance of black children adopted by white families. *American Psychologist*, 1976, *31*, 726–739.

QUINN McNEMAR
Stanford University

REPLY: REDISCOVERING OLD TRUTHS, OR A WORD BY THE WISE IS SOMETIMES LOST

Each generation of psychologists rediscovers the nature–nurture problem. Contemporary students of the issue have been handicapped, however, by a chasm in intellectual history between the present group of middle-aged, behavioral scientists who ruled the issue out of polite discourse, and older generations of scholars, who actually did research on the problem. Those of us who were educated in the 1950s and early 1960s were taught, for the most part, an environmentalism-run-amok. From the mid-1960s on, the nature–nurture problem took on new life, but, alas, few of us were in contact with the wisdom of earlier generations.

To rediscover what used to be widely known about nature and nurture, let us examine some wisdom in Woodworth's (1941, pp. 30–31) classic book:

These two statements—(1) that differences in environment can produce substantial differences in intelligence, and (2) that the differences actually present in a community are *not* due mostly to differences in environment—may appear mutually contradictory. That they are not contradictory has been emphatically pointed out by several students of the nature–nurture problem. For example:

Thorndike (1914): "If the environments are alike with respect to a trait, the differences in respect to it are due entirely to original nature;... if the original natures are alike with respect to a trait, the differences in respect to it are due entirely to differences of training. . . . Many disagreements spring from a confusion of what may be called absolute achievement with what may be called relative achievement. A man may move up a long distance from zero and nevertheless be lower down than before in comparison with other men who have moved up still farther. The commonest error . . . is that of concluding from the importance of . . . heredity that education and social control in general are futile. . . . To the real work of man for man,—the increase of achievement through improvement of the environment,—the influence of heredity offers no barrier."

Shuttleworth (1935): "The data of Burks indicate very clearly that interfamily environmental differences account for a much smaller proportion . . . of the variance . . . in intelligence than do hereditary differences. . . . The inferiority complex which many educators and environmentalists have created for themselves by the misinterpretation of these and similar data is a most bizarre phenomenon. It *does not follow* that the *general level* of the environment is a relatively unimportant factor in determining the *general level* of intelligence, *but only* that environmental *differences* are relatively small in comparison with hereditary *differences* in determining individual *differences* in intelligence. Even if environmental differences accounted for zero per cent and hereditary differences accounted for one hundred per cent of the individual differences in intelligence, it would still be true that the general level of the environment would be a most important factor determining the general level of intelligence.''

Shuttleworth's statement bears particular emphasis in light of the comments by Werner et al., Nichols, and McNemar. These comments focus on heritabilities or the partitioning of variance to account for individual differences within the sample of adopted children. The major import of the Scarr and Weinberg (1976) study, however, was to demonstrate the malleability of IQ scores for the entire group of black and interracial children, reared in homes that are socioeconomically advantaged and culturally relevant to IQ test and school performance.

Are Individual Differences Genetic?

Nothing in our paper denied the importance of genetic differences for variation in IQ scores. As Thorndike (1914) reminded us, there may be considerable improvement in the absolute achievement level of the whole group without implication for the sources of individual variation. Unfortunately, it is hopeless to try to estimate the relative importance of hereditary and environmental differences from this sample of adopted children. Theoretically, a group of children unrelated to their rearing parents could provide a direct estimate of the effects of environmental differences between families, but in fact, adoptive families alone are insufficient for this purpose because environmental variation within adoptive families is quite restricted, compared to the population. (Adoptive homes are all socioeconomically advantaged, as we said, although not 3 standard deviations above the natural parents.) Adoptive samples will always have restricted environmental variation, because they are selected by agencies for their virtues. One cannot estimate the true effects of variation-in-virtues from a sample that hardly varies in virtues. Only the comparison of the adopted parent–child similarity with that of equally selected biologically related parents and children can begin to estimate the relative effects of genetic and environmental differences, and then only under a massive set of tenuous assumptions, too arcane to discuss in this context. (It so happens that the adoptive parents of the black and interracial children also have many biological offspring. We will report variance analyses and heritability estimates [Scarr & Weinberg, 1977, 1979] based on the *same* families.)

The regression analyses reported in our October 1976 article reflected our curiosity about the sources of individual differences among the children in this sample. We wanted to know to what extent their individual differences were influenced by genetic differences, by differences in early experience, and by differences in their rearing environments. We did not attempt to generalize the regression analyses to any broader population.

SES and Cultural Differences

One excellent reason for not generalizing the regression equations from this sample is that the rearing environments of the adoptive homes are not at all representative of the usual rearing environments of black children. The differences between the adoptive and typical homes of such children are not merely socioeconomic advantages in the former, as both comments propose, but also cultural differences—in the sense that these adoptive families foster very effectively the development of skills and knowledge that are sampled by standardized tests and reflected in school performance. Support for this view of cultural differences comes from the study of interracial children reared by their black or white mothers (Willerman, Naylor, & Myrianthopoulos, 1970). The interracial offspring of white mothers and black fathers scored about 8 IQ points higher than the comparably interracial offspring of black mothers and white fathers reared by their black mothers. (The parents in the two kinds of pairings had similar educational levels.)

Racial Versus Individual Differences

Although the unusual array of environments for black children in the adoptive families limits what one can conclude about the sources of individual differences in the black population, the adoptive sample provides a quasi-experimental treatment (called socioeconomically advantaged and test-school-relevant rearing environment) for a group of children who do not usually experience such environments. As we stated, transracial adoption is a human analog to the cross-fostering design. This is one of the few ways to study racial differences, as opposed to individual differences within races. Another is to study variation in degree of African ancestry (Scarr, Pakstis, Katz, & Barker, in press). Degree of African ancestry was found to be uncorrelated with differences in intellectual skills within a black population.

The study of racial differences cannot use an individual-differences approach to sort out possible genetic from environmental differences. The two quasi-experimental designs, suggested above, permit inferences about the sources of racial differences because they capitalize on naturally occurring variation in one parameter, holding the other (more or less) constant. In the study of transracial adoption of black children, racial background is held constant and sociocultural environment of the home is varied in relation to the criteria of tests and schools. In the ancestry study, the sociocultural milieu is held constant (all individuals are socially classified as black) and racial background is varied. Loehlin, Lindzey, and Spuhler (1975) provide a valuable review of research strategies for racial differences.

On the value of such studies: we believe that new information is always preferable to old rumors.

Factual Errors

Nichols refers to an average age of adoption as 18 months, but he neglects the median age of adoption of 6 months, as stated on page 117 of our chapter. Since the 99 black and interracial children adopted in the first year of life have average IQ scores of 110, it is hard to argue that their mean is not above the mean of the black or white populations in the area. In addition, Nichols states that there was an excess of black children from whom to choose; this is simply not true. No adoptive parents were given their choice of one among several children. In fact, of all the black children adopted in the state of Minnesota, we could find only two who had been adopted by black families; all the rest were adopted by white families, and the only selective factors among those white families were whether or not they were willing to accept an older or handicapped child (as in any other adoption). Most families had to wait quite awhile before the agency located a child for them to adopt, especially an infant. Only in the early 1960s was there a group of black children in the state awaiting adoption for whom no black families could be found. At that time the agencies began to recruit white families, and all 75 or so black children in foster homes were placed quickly.

Statistical Problems

Nichols has misconstrued Darlington's (1968) formulas, which do not in fact provide an estimate of "the multiple correlation prevailing in the population." Such an estimate is provided by the conventional adjustment for shrinkage, for example, Cohen and Cohen (1975, pp. 106–107). For our data, the shrunken R^2 is .28, instead of the .19 in Nichols' Table 1.

It is possible to play around with the sets and subsets of social and biological variables and to produce different regression results, as Nichols did. If one subdivides the social variables into two sets instead of entering them into the regression equation as a single set, of course, the results are different. We published the correlations, means, and standard deviations, so that one and all may play that game. We will not argue with Nichols about his results, but we do question the wisdom of focusing so much attention on the sources of variation among the adopted children and so little on the high average intellectual level of the group.

REFERENCES

Cohen, J., & Cohen, P. *Applied multiple regression/correlation analysis for the behavioral sciences.* Hillsdale, N.J.: Erlbaum, 1975.

Darlington, R. B. Multiple regression in psychological research and practice. *Psychological Bulletin,* 1968, *69,* 161–182.

Loehlin, J. C., Lindzey, G., & Spuhler, L. N. *Race differences in intelligence.* San Francisco: Freeman, 1975.

McNemar, Q. Statistics can mislead. *American Psychologist,* 1977, *32,* 680–681.

Nichols, R. C. Black children adopted by white families. *American Psychologist,* 1977, *32,* 678–680.

Scarr, S., Pakstis, A., Katz, S., & Barker, W. The absence of a relation between ancestry and intellectual skills in a black population. *Human Genetics,* in press.

Scarr, S., & Weinberg, R. A. IQ test performance of black children adopted by white families. *American Psychologist,* 1976, *31,* 726–739.

Scarr, S., & Weinberg, R. A. Intellectual similarities within families of both adopted and biological children. *Intelligence,* 1977, *1,* 170–191.

Scarr, S., & Weinberg, R. A. Nature and nurture strike (out) again. *Intelligence,* 1979, *3,* 31–39.

Shuttleworth, F. K. The nature *versus* nurture problem: II. The contributions of nature and nurture to individual differences in intelligence. *Journal of Educational Psychology,* 1935, *26,* 655–681.

Thorndike, E. L. *Educational psychology* (Vol. 3). New York: Teachers College, 1914.

Werner, J., Lane, D., & Mohanty, A. IQ, race, and adoption. *American Psychologist,* 1977, *32,* 677–678.

Willerman, L., Naylor, A. F., & Myrianthopoulos, N. C. Intellectual development of children from interracial matings. *Science,* 1970, *170,* 1329–1331.

Woodworth, R. S. *Heredity and environment.* New York: Social Science Research Council, 1941.

SANDRA SCARR
RICHARD A. WEINBERG
University of Minnesota

COMMENT: THE RIP IN SOCIAL SCIENTIFIC REPORTING*

We respect the American tradition of freedom of the press. Or is it the relative freedom? Complete freedom of the press would be chaotic. Many of us have sent articles, books, plays, and poems to editors and have experienced them being rejected—silences as we may choose to conceive it. From an editor's point of view, however, our literary creations may be incomprehensible, boring, poorly conceived, or lacking in scientific merit. Denial of access to the press, as it turns out, often serves a more noble purpose than hushing worthy material from an

---

*This comment by Oden & MacDonald and the reply by Scarr & Weinberg originally appeared in *American Psychologist,* 1978, *33,* 952–957. Copyright © 1978 by the American Psychological Association. Reprinted by permission.

awaiting audience. Responsible selection assists the reader in the job of wading through rivers of drivel to reach worthwhile articles and, incidentally, keeps our journals down to a reasonable size. We agree with the practice of editorial selection. Freedom of the press implies some literary standards, and in our profession, reporting requires scientific criteria as minima for publication.

In this comment, we are calling for editorial criteria. Some may call it censorship. The call reflects our concern for a raising of consciousness regarding scientific reporting. All scientists must be careful to report results objectively and accurately, of course. But in addition, social scientists reporting on human studies must report work such that readers of many levels of sophistication will come to reasonable conclusions and not unwarranted ones.

The awareness we are trying to raise regards reasonable inferential process (RIP), and we are concerned about it not only in the sense that the social scientist keep discussions related to data, but also that discussions and implications be presented such that the reader will not be misled. It was, in fact, our reading of an article in the *American Psychologist* which led to the drafting of this comment. The article was "IQ Test Performance of Black Children Adopted by White Families" by Sandra Scarr and Richard A. Weinberg in the October 1976 *American Psychologist*. The article exemplifies what we regard as reasonable social scientific procedure followed by unreasonable social commentary which, unfortunately, carries with it the smack of scientific authority.

At the outset, the authors describe "transracial adoption" and assert that such adoption is "the human analog of the cross-fostering design commonly used in animal behavior genetics research" (Scarr & Weinberg, 1976, p. 726). The article actually describes a study in which black, "interracial," and Indian/Oriental children adopted by middle-class white families are compared on IQ and school performance tests to the natural children of the adoptive parents.

The authors mention fostering in rather inclusive terms, but the particular families represented in this study may well practice a style of fostering that is, in itself, rather unusual (Kribs, 1972; Skeels, 1966). Cross-fostering studies control both the environment and the genetics of the subjects (Manosevitz, Lindzey, & Thiessen, 1969). This study did neither. Unfortunately, the study does not consider what black, interracial, or Indian/Oriental children would do in middle-class families with their own ethnic origin, nor do they include data regarding white children fostered in nonwhite homes. We say "unfortunately" because the original goals of the cited study can only be answered by a truly "cross-fostering" study with the controls of such a procedure.

It is not just the methodology, however, to which we address our remarks. Rather, it is to the inferences that are so readily available from the article, although not always specifically stated by the authors. For example, in developing the article, "race" seems to be an independent variable although no definition of race is presented. It appears, from the way the sample was developed, that the authors of the article did not know, in fact, the genealogy of the black or interracial adoptees. From what our historians tell us (Reuter, 1931; Washington, 1970), the vast majority of what we refer to as blacks in America are actually the progeny of many degrees of miscegenation. Genetically, the "interracial" children (one white and one black parent) are probably genotypically a good deal more white than black. In short, the Scarr-Weinberg sample of adoptees is what we might call a racial hodge-podge, rather than a well-defined sample. It might be more appropriate to relabel the dimension "ethnic" and recognize that these adoptees come from different *social* backgrounds. But even then, a good argument could be made that the "interracial" adoptees (from one socially classed black parent and one white parent) come from neither the black nor the white culture (Crow & Shapiro, 1974). But let us not dwell on whether "black" is a genetic or ethnic variable. We do not want to continue a ho-hum discussion in which, once again, black (ethnic) children are shown to be responsive to the social conditions in which they are raised (Munsinger, 1975; Scott & Smith, 1972; Tobias, 1974).

After a detailed and what we consider well-laid-out explanation of what was done and found, the theme advocating transracial adoption, begun in the opening discussion, is picked up again on page 132 of the chapter: "If all black children had environments such as those provided by the adoptive families . . . IQ scores would be 10 to 20 points higher." It could also be said that the same number of IQ points would be added if the children of the study were adopted by black families of similar social means and status. But the latter is not said. Again, while the statements may well be innocent enough, they maintain a lopsided presentation in favor of the inference that white (implying race) parents, rather than advantaged parents (implying social class) is the potent variable. In the next paragraphs the authors seem to imply cross-adoption as a "remedial" action: "There is no question that adoption constitutes a massive intervention" and "*if* higher IQ scores are considered important . . . then there is need for social action that will provide black children with home environments that facilitate the acquisition of intellectual skills tapped by IQ measures" (p. 133). But Scarr and Weinberg deny the suggestion of a pat solution to the problem of certain black children of low IQs and the undesirable social sequelae related to IQs. They state that "transracial adoption is not a panacea for low IQ scores among black children" and that "only an infinitesimally small proportion of black children would ever be available for adoption, and of those, many will and *should be* adopted by black families" (p. 133, emphasis in original). Scarr and Weinberg later state that they are aware that the "intervention" they suggest at two points in their article is not a solution to the problem of black students with low IQs. Perhaps the problem with the article is similar to that of a positive afterimage. Scarr and Weinberg present a suggestion and then withdraw it from our view. But the positive afterimage of the presentation does not disappear with the removal of the suggestion via belated disclaimer.

For the brief time that we are confronted with the afterimage that transracial adoption is a favorable solution to the low-IQ problems of some black children, we are reminded that the suggestion suffers many flaws, of which we shall mention three. First is the defining of transracial adoption as an "intervention." An intervention, as we understand the word, refers to a well-defined procedure for altering the behavior, attitude, or condition of a specified deficiency in the recipient. Transracial adoption remedies the undesirable condition of a homeless child. The second issue that may introduce a constant bias in the inferences of the reader suggests that transracial adoption is patently desirable. Many authorities in the field, both black and white, have brought the process under serious question (Chestang, 1972; Chimezie, 1975; Simon, 1974). The third objection is the consistent implicit assumption that the white-culture-derived IQ is an adequate (the only?) gauge for the development of nonwhite children. Again, the authors recognize this in stating that "we believe that the tests and the schools share a common culture to which black children are not as fully acculturated as are white children" (p. 737). The continued use of IQ, however, suggests that they do not weigh this caveat in their major considerations. It would be useful if there were some device that measured the IQ of all persons regardless of language and ethnic background. But there is none (Anastasi, 1976). The notion of IQ as measured by IQ tests is valued differently by various ethnic groups, so that it might be lauded in some white groups, but valued less in some nonwhite groups. Up to now, the Wechsler Intelligence Scale for Children (WISC) and similar tests have been, but should not be, the preferred gauge regarding the development of children.

The underlying sentiment of the Scarr-Weinberg article seems to be the equal sharing of employment opportunities and societal rewards with all persons, regardless of background. However, the authors seem to be addressing the wrong problem. Their implicit reasoning seems to be that the white community, which distributes most of the resources in our society, values high IQs, and that therefore, if blacks want to share in the benefits, they must display the credentials of WISC-type intelligence and standardized school excellence. The theme continues: High IQ predicts school achievement, and school achievement permits access to prized jobs and rewards. Thus, this article is a statement of white values. As such, it infers that the white style of school orientation, competition, and emphasis on displays of intellectual virtuosity is the best for all persons, regardless of their backgrounds. This stand is apparently justified on the grounds that those persons lacking in this style of life do not do well in school and do not get the desired jobs and rewards.

To share in the fruits of the promised land, blacks, already having been stripped of their African family tree of culture, are now asked to undergo another pruning of their current culture, developed through three centuries in a homeland thrust upon them. Now they are to permit a graft upon their remaining rootstock of practices found in white adoptive families. While the objective of making accessible to minorities employment and social opportunities equal to those of whites is commendable, the alteration of black culture and traditions appears to be the grisly price to pay.

That minority members achieve in schools at levels below their white counterparts and do not enjoy the same vocational opportunities is of central concern to Scarr and Weinberg, as it is to the nation as a whole. The article, however, takes the one of the three options available that is the most punishing to blacks and other minorities and the least troublesome to the white majority culture. That is, when it becomes clear that an ethnic group (or other interest group) is not faring as well as the dominant white majority, then at least three alternatives are available: (1) locate the problem within the minority class itself, which is called "blaming the victim" (Ryan, 1971), (2) locate the problem in the majority group, and (3) locate the problem in the system that embraces all persons in the society (a strategy used by the Supreme Court and other agencies). It seems to us that the Scarr-Weinberg article is a sophisticated version of the first alternative. The article focuses on black child rearing and calls for its alteration. It suggests that the family atmosphere is the cause of black children with low IQs and seems to imply removal of children from that environment—or a changing of the environment. It infers that IQ tests and low achievement in school are the social problem, and that the children should adjust to the school (rather than vice versa). What started out as a scientific article becomes social commentary on the plight of disadvantaged children but then takes the most punishing position toward the disadvantaged people possible. We hope that those responsible for publication of the official organ of the APA will redouble their efforts to present objective discussions in ways that do not punish the very group for which proposals would seem to be directed.

In responding to the Scarr-Weinberg article, we are sympathetic to the intent of the authors and to the difficult task of the editors. However, we are also concerned with the impact that the publishing of such articles may have on the sophisticated readers of the *American Psychologist* and upon the lay audience that is indirectly influenced by such discussion. We suggest that editors of journals who publish data-bound articles that speculate about social action observe the following guidelines: (a) Editors of articles that have social implications should be particularly careful in examining the proposals when they are implicitly or explicitly making invidious comparisons between one social group and another. Such comparisons usually sacrifice benefits for both interest groups, and a broader perspective is called for. (b) Editorial staffs that read and review materials for possible publication should include minority members from the group to which the writing refers. (c) Editors of the social science journals, themselves, should undergo self-examination and self-initiated training in becoming sensitive to issues involving cross-cultural, cross-racial, and cross-sexual issues in the social sciences so they will be alerted to potential biasing of social science literature. (d) Editors should insist that authors of articles that talk about members from more than one interest group (be it a sex, age, race, or ethnic one) identify the origin of the instruments used and indicate whether or not the instruments reflect the values and standards of each of the groups or whether they favor one or the other.

While these proposals in no way guarantee unbiased design, implementation, and reporting of social science research, they do point out the ease with which science can become biased and fall into the unwitting trap of using white middle-class standards and values as an appropriate context for discussion of issues pertaining to minority groups, when in fact they are inappropriate.

We are concerned that a reasonable piece of field research can be published when the discussion is a combination of RIP and unfounded social commentary. How did such remarks get past the desks of alert and sharp-eyed editors? How did it escape the blue pencils of editors of periodicals who pride themselves on RIP? It would be advantageous if the editors were to use RIP in the sense of reasonable inferential process, rather than as a headstone inscription for a minority culture.

ACKNOWLEDGMENTS

For their critical comments, insights, and suggestions, the authors wish to acknowledge the contributions of James Ballard, Bruce Balow, Mark Davison, Reginald Jones, Geoffrey Maruyama, and Frank Wilderson.

REFERENCES

Anastasi, A. *Psychological testing*. New York: Macmillan, 1976.

Chestang, L. The dilemma of biracial adoption. *Social Work*, 1972, *17*, 100–105.

Chimezie, A. Transracial adoption of black children. *Social Work*, 1975, *20*, 296–301.

Crow, L. J., & Shapiro, D. *Black children–white parents: A study of transracial adoption*. New York: Child Welfare League of America, 1974.

Kribs, N. A comparison of characteristics of women who have adopted a black child and women who state an unwillingness to adopt a black child. *Dissertation Abstracts International*, 1972, *33*, 192.

Manosevitz, M., Lindzey, G., & Thiessen, D. *Behavioral genetics: Method and research*. New York: Appleton-Century-Crofts, 1969.

Munsinger, H. The adopted child's IQ: A critical review. *Psychological Bulletin*, 1975, *82*, 623–659.

Reuter, E. B. *Race mixture*. New York: McGraw-Hill, 1931.

Ryan, W. *Blaming the victim*. New York: Random House, 1971.

Scarr, S., & Weinberg, R. IQ test performance of black children adopted by white families. *American Psychologist*, 1976, *31*, 726–739.

Scott, R., & Smith, J. Ethnic and demographic variables and achievement scores on preschool children. *Psychology in the Schools*, 1972, *9*, 174–182.

Simon, R. An assessment of racial awareness, preference, and self-identity among white and adopted nonwhite children. *Social Problems*, 1974, *22*, 43–57.

Skeels, H. Headstart on headstart: A thirty-year evaluation. In J. F. Magary & R. B. McIntyre

(Eds.), *Fifth Annual Distinguished Lectures in Special Education: Summer Sessions*, 1966, pp. 1–23.

Tobias, P. IQ and the nature–nurture controversy. *Journal of Behavioral Science*, 1974, 2.

Washington, J. R. *Marriage in black and white.* Boston: Beacon Press, 1970.

CHESTER W. ODEN, JR.
W. SCOTT MacDONALD
University of Minnesota
(Minneapolis)

REPLY: THE RIGHTS AND RESPONSIBILITIES OF THE SOCIAL SCIENTIST

Oden and MacDonald (this issue) raise three kinds of issues with our article on transracial adoption (Scarr & Weinberg, 1976): (1) methodological issues, (2) the explicit and implicit implications of the results, and (3) the alleged benefits of editorial censorship of scientific reports. The first set is largely uncontroversial; the second, one of values in social science; and the third, a red flag for civil liberties.

Research Design

The authors are correct that we could not manipulate either genotypes or environments in the study of adopted black/interracial children. Such manipulations are ethical and technical impossibilities. But we did *measure* characteristics of both: The children were shown to have educationally average natural parents, and many characteristics of the adoptive environments were reported. Most human research of important and enduring traits, like much evolutionary and astronomical research, must depend on naturally occurring experiments. Cross-fostering designs in the human case depend on the offspring of one gene pool (here, U.S. blacks) being reared by parents of another (here, U.S. whites). Proper comparisons can be made with reciprocally cross-fostered groups, and with offspring reared by parents of their own gene pool. The children in the transracial study were shown to be scoring far higher on IQ and school achievement tests than black children reared by their own parents, higher than the average of white children, and as highly as white adoptees reared by similar white families (Scarr & Weinberg, 1978).

For completeness, we, too, wish for studies of white children adopted by black families and of black children reared by black adoptive families of social and educational status comparable to those of the transracial families. The first is so rare as to be unavailable as a comparison. The second is possible but has never been done. Contrary to the assertion of Oden and MacDonald, the intellectual development of black children adopted by advantaged black families has not been studied. Although they further assert that such children would be found to score as well as our transracial adoptees on IQ tests, there is good reason not to expect that result. Black children reared by "middle" class black families have repeatedly been found to score lower on IQ and school-achievement tests than have "lower" status white children (Jensen, 1973; Scarr-Salapatek, 1971; Wilson, 1967). This seemingly anomalous result is best explained by the overall cultural differences between black and white groups and by the fact that schools and tests sample almost exclusively from the skills and knowledge of white culture.

What Is Race?

The term *race* was repeatedly defined as a social classification in this study. In the United States, anyone with visible marks of African ancestry is socially classified as black. As a group, U.S. blacks are approximately 80% African and 20% European in ancestry, as estimated from blood-group markers. U.S. whites have less than .01% African ancestry (Reed, 1969). Individuals within the socially classified U.S. black group can vary from having more than 95% African ancestry to less than 40 percent. It goes without saying that the U.S. dichotomy of black–white is a case of simplemindedness not followed everywhere (e.g., Brazil and Cuba).

We refused to estimate degrees of African ancestry for the black children in this study, because the research rationale did not require it and blood samples would have been required, an unnecessary intrusion in our view. The major questions could be answered without individual estimates of ancestry: Do children with substantial amounts of African ancestry score as well as other adopted children without African ancestry, and do those children with one black parent and one from another racial group outscore those with two socially classified black parents (and on the average more African ancestry)?

In a companion study, however, all of the black children were reared within the black community and were culturally black. For this group of twins, we used blood-group and serum-protein markers to establish zygosity and to estimate degree of African ancestry. A racial, genetic-differences hypothesis would have to predict that those blacks with less African and more European ancestry will score higher on intellectual tests than those with more African ancestry. The results (Scarr, Pakstis, Katz, & Barker, 1977) showed that intellectual test scores are unrelated to degrees of African ancestry within a socially classified black group in which individuals vary in the degree of their African ancestry.

The strategies of the two studies are complementary: In the transracial adoption study, genetic-racial background was averaged among socially classified black children, and culture of rearing was varied from that usually experienced by such a group; in the ancestry study, rearing background was held constant and genetic-racial background varied among socially classified blacks.

Explicit and Implicit Implications of the Results

We suspect that on matters of social goals, there is little or no disagreement between our critics and ourselves. We, too, are concerned about the degree of cultural monotheism in the United States and the lack of representation of minority cultural practices and views in the social and economic life of the country (see Chapter IV-2). We do not think that identifying the cultural roots of IQ tests and school achievement and showing that children with more than half African ancestry can learn that culture as effectively as children of European ancestry constitutes ''blaming the victim.'' On the contrary, we showed that the victim is not genetically inferior in ''intelligence'' by the same standard of IQ that is used for whites, once access to the culture sampled by the tests is assured. If the diminution of the genetic-differences hypothesis suggests to others some unpalatable social implications (that we did not draw), they have the responsibility and right to say so, as they have done here. We are free to respond that we disagree with the implications they assert, particularly regarding black families.

The more important issues, however, are not the particular implications that we, they, or others may wish to draw from this research, but the more general problem of values in social science and scientific reporting. Oden and Mac-Donald propose censorship to eliminate implications they find unacceptable. We propose that their treatment is based on a mistaken diagnosis of the problem and will kill the patient.

On Editorial Censorship

Who can doubt that minority groups have been underrepresented in every arena of social, political, and scientific life, or that their points of view have not had a proper hearing? Agreement that minorities are underrepresented should lead to efforts to improve their representation, however, *not* to an endorsement of minority censorship of others' writings, even those about minorities.

With Right on one's side, it is too easy to advocate the suppression of Wrong. The 20th century abounds with examples of such convictions translated into political action, usually at the expense of others' freedoms. It is too easy to forget that to plead for the representation of one's own ideas in the intellectual marketplace is necessarily to guarantee others the same right. The proper exercise of one's own first-amendment rights requires one to advocate the open debate of all points of view, even those one may deplore.

Advocates of minority views have to appeal to a benign majority for their political rights, *guaranteed* by the Constitution but *implemented* by majority adherence to laws governing the exercise of those rights. From the perspective of social psychology, it is not surprising that these advocates of minority views are often the first to deny others the same rights. From a political point of view, however, such authoritarianism cannot be permitted. And certainly not in social science.

Ugly denials of the right to speak have marred university campuses over the past decade, as political radicals and blacks mobilized to deny Jensen, Herrnstein, and Shockley their right to speak. In decades, before, it was these same groups who were themselves illegally denied free expression. Now it is the Nazis in St. Louis and Skokie. If we fail to see the identity of these cases, we are blind to the most precious right guaranteed by our Constitution.

We are unalterably opposed to any form of scientific censorship, however much we disagree with the view expressed. One can ignore the communication, urge others to do so, present counterevidence and opinion, and rally others to a different flag. But one may not prevent the presentation of opposing views.

To advocate editorial censorship (blue penciling) of authors' views of the implications of their research is just as surely a denial of free speech as the noisy demonstration to prevent Arthur Jensen from speaking at the University of Minnesota in May 1976.

The Dilemma of Values in Social Science

Nearly everyone would agree that investigators bring their social–political beliefs to the formation of research questions. Few believe that the subsequent research is completely determined by the investigators' prior views. There is nonetheless an unavoidable infusion of values into social science research (Packenham, 1978; Rein, 1976). It is important, therefore, to identify *where* in the research process and *how much* the investigators' values affect the research outcomes.

Those of us who believe in the possibility of objectivity rely on several standards of conduct for investigators. Besides honesty, we look for the reproducibility of the results, preferably by others with different views; the testing of competing hypotheses, preferably within the same study; and several standards of research reporting that make objectivity more likely.

The largely unwritten ethics of research reporting demand that two standards be met: (a) that the methods section be written in such detail that another investigator, perhaps with a different bias, can repeat the study, with the possibility of same or different results; and (b) that the results section of the report be given in as full detail as possible to insure that readers, particularly those with different points of view, can examine the results and reach their own conclusions.

The introduction to the research report has to meet the standard of a not-too-selective review of past work in the same and related areas. Judgments of the adequacy of introductory materials are more subjective, but not hopelessly so, as there is general agreement in most fields as to the network of ideas that gives rise to new investigations. Investigators ignore this network at their manuscripts' peril.

The discussion section of a research report, however, is not merely a recitation of the results, even in light of the introduction. Particularly in the reporting of socially or politically sensitive research, investigators have the responsibility to spell out the implications of the results, *as they see them*. Reviewers of the manuscript are free to *suggest* that report writers consider other implications, but it is not right to demand that authors adopt the reviewers' views in order to secure publication of the manuscript. This is censorship.

In the face of disagreements over the implications of the results of a research report, an editor can and should invite comments from opposing sides, to be published with the research report or subsequently. The *American Psychologist* maintains a lively *Comment* section for just this purpose. It is gratifying to see this opportunity used to represent alternative views and interpretations of data.

REFERENCES

Jensen, A. R. *Educability and group differences*. New York: Basic Books, 1973.

Oden, C. W., Jr., & MacDonald, W. S. The RIP in social scientific reporting. *American Psychologist*, 1978, *33*, 952–954.

Packenham, R. A. Social science and public policy. In S. Verba & L. Pye (Eds.), *The citizen and the state: A comparative perspective*. Stamford, Conn.: Greylock Publishers, 1978.

Reed, T. E. Caucasian genes in American Negroes. *Science*, 1969, *165*, 762–768.

Rein, M. *Social science and public policy*. New York: Penguin Books, 1976.

Scarr, S. From evolution to Larry P., or what shall we do about IQ tests? Editorial. *Intelligence*, 1978, *2*, 325–342.

Scarr, S., Pakstis, A. J., Katz, S. H., & Barker, W. B. The absence of a relationship between degree of white ancestry and intellectual skills within a black population. *Human Genetics*, 1977, *39*, 69–86.

Scarr, S., & Weinberg, R. A. IQ test performance of black children adopted by white families. *American Psychologist*, 1976, *31*, 726–739.

Scarr, S., & Weinberg, R. A. Attitudes, interests, and IQ. *Human Nature*, 1978, *1*(4), 29–36.

Scarr-Salapatek, S. Race, social class and IQ. *Science*, 1971, *174*, 1285–1295.

Wilson, A. Educational consequences of segregation in a California community. In *Racial isolation in the public schools* (Vol. II, App. C-3). Washington, D.C.: U.S. Government Printing Office, 1967.

SANDRA SCARR
Yale University

RICHARD A. WEINBERG
University of Minnesota

II. 2
Absence of a Relationship between Degree of White Ancestry and Intellectual Skills within a Black Population*

Introduction

Genetic differences have been offered as an hypothesis to explain the average IQ difference usually found between US black and white populations (Jensen, 1973; Shockley, 1972). While most behavioral scientists would choose to ignore the hypothesis as distasteful, there is little direct evidence against it (Scarr and Weinberg, 1976). Those who prefer an environmental hypothesis to account for the average difference between black and white groups on intellectual tests have not succeeded in accounting for the magnitude of the effect, nor have those who hold a genetic hypothesis been able to refute an environmental stance. No direct comparisons of black and white samples will settle the issue of possible genetic differences, because obvious environmental differences are confounded with any genetic differences between the populations that are socially classified as black and white (Scarr-Salapatek, 1971a, 1971b, 1972, 1973, 1974; Scarr and Weinberg, 1976).

The fact that US blacks are a hybrid population[1] makes the study of admixture a potential method to evaluate the effects of racial genetic differences. Those environmental differences between the races that affect *all* blacks equally, but no whites, will not contaminate the possible relationship between genetic racial differences and intellectual performance within the hybrid group. Thus, if genetic, racial differences do contribute to average intellectual differences between blacks and whites, then those blacks with higher degrees of white ancestry should perform better on intellectual tests than those with lesser degrees of admixture (Jensen, 1973; Shuey, 1966).

Even within the hybrid group, the effects of environmental differences cannot be ignored. The amount of racial discrimination may be related to the degree of

---

*This chapter by Sandra Scarr, Andrew J. Pakstis, Solomon H. Katz, and William B. Barker originally appeared in *Human Genetics*, 1977, *39*, 69–86. Copyright © 1977 by Springer-Verlag. Reprinted by permission.

[1] In the United States, any person with visible signs of African ancestry is socially classified as black. This social classification of race provides the basis for Reed's (1969a; 1969b; 1973) report that blacks in the Oakland, California area have about 22% European ancestry, whereas socially classified whites in the same area have less than 0.1% African ancestry

African ancestry (Klineberg, 1963). Invisible markers for ancestry, such as blood group loci, are likely to be correlated with visible markers for discrimination, such as skin color, nose and lip width, hair texture, and the like. Great care must be taken to separate the effects of correlated genetic and environmental variables on intellectual performance.

This study will evaluate the hypothesized effects of genetic racial differences, estimated from blood group and serum protein loci, on intellectual performance in a sample of black twins. Social, environmental effects will be considered apart from genetic differences between the racial groups. The construct validity of two measures of ancestry will be examined.

Admixture Estimates for US Blacks. Estimates of the degree to which contemporary black gene frequencies derive from ancestral African and Caucasian populations vary, depending upon the region of the country, the gene loci used to estimate admixture, and the sampling procedures (Adams and Ward, 1973; Glass and Li, 1953; Pollitzer, 1972; Reed, 1969a, 1969b, 1973). There is general agreement, however, that the Duffy (Fy) locus offers the best estimates of about 22% of Caucasian admixture in Northern urban populations.

Population admixture estimates are an *average* of the individuals in the hybrid population. Individual ancestry can vary from near zero to near one when the admixture has continued over ten generations. Independent assortment and mating that is random with respect to admixture serve to distribute Caucasian genes throughout the hybrid population; assortative mating with respect to admixture tends to restrict gene flow within the population. Because there are no accurate pedigrees over ten generations and because the population parameters that affect the distribution of admixture cannot be measured historically, it is very difficult to estimate the distribution of Caucasian genes among individuals in the contemporary black population. Recently, MacLean and his colleagues (1974) estimated the distribution of admixture in a large black sample from upstate New York. The individual Caucasian admixture values ranged from less than 10% to more than 60%, with a mean around 20%. The standard error of estimate for their admixture value (θ), based on nine blood group systems, is so large ($\pm 2\,SE = \pm 0.16$) that point estimates of admixture were not really achieved. They did find, however, a significant relationship between θ and hypertension in the black group.

Correlates of Ancestry and Intellectual Skills. Any positive or negative relationship between blood group estimates of ancestry and intellectual skills will be confounded with correlates of the two variables. For example, blood group estimates of ancestry are likely to be correlated with skin color, another set of genetic markers. If skin color depends upon a few gene loci (Stern, 1970), then a large set of independent blood group markers drawn from the same ancestral population should be correlated with skin color. The magnitude of the correlation will depend upon the degree of reassortment and the dispersion of admixture in the black population. But skin color is also a visible marker for racial discrimination and has in the past been associated with socioeconomic status within the US black population. The darker one is, the lower one's social status (Klineberg, 1963). Socioeconomic status is usually positively correlated with intellectual achieve-

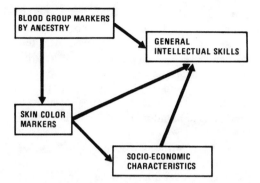

Fig. 1. A model for the effects of ancestry and socioeconomic status on the intellectual skills of US blacks

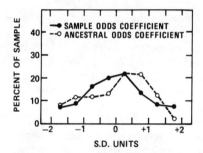

Fig. 2. The distribution of ancestral and sample odds coefficients in the sample of Philadelphia blacks

ments. Thus, skin color and socioeconomic characteristics must be considered as correlates of any estimate of ancestry and intellectual skills in the black population.

The path model shown in Figure 1 specifics the genetic and environmental contributions of ancestry (blood groups and skin color) and life chances (socioeconomic status and skin color) to intellectual skills.

Blood Group Markers. Blood group loci, including red cell antigens and serum proteins, are the most reliable markers of population differences. While 90% of the variance in blood group phenotypes occurs within populations, some 10% occurs between populations (Nei and Roychoudhury, 1972). At some loci, such as Duffy and Gm, alternate alleles are found in some populations and not others; for most loci, however, only allelic frequencies vary among populations.

Known blood group loci are a very small sample of the total genome, which is estimated to contain from 15 000 to 100 000 loci. It is possible that blood group markers do not sample those segments of the genome associated with cognitive abilities (Loehlin et al., 1973). If independent assortment has occurred repeatedly over many generations, one might not expect any association among genes from the same ancestral population, except those that are closely linked.

On the other hand, if reassortment is limited by low crossover rates and by assortative mating with respect to admixture, genetic markers from an ancestral population will not be totally dissociated in the hybrid group, even after ten generations. Evidence on the nonindependence of population markers can be found in the correlations among blood groups and between blood groups and other genetic markers, such as skin color. If unlinked genetic markers are still associated, then there is some reason to believe that other genes (those associated with cognitive skills) from the same ancestral population are still associated with the blood group markers.

It should be clear nonetheless that even without assortative mating for admixture to maintain a high degree of association of Caucasian genes, the use of genetic loci to index the proportion of Caucasian ancestry—contrary to what some authors seem to suggest (Loehlin et al., 1973)—is not invalidated. From a sampling perspective, if 40% of an individual's genome derives from the white population, then an adequate, random sample of genetic markers discriminating ancestral origin of the alleles should *on the average* reflect that actual percentage. This in turn should also be the best estimate of the proportion of genes influencing cognitive phenotypes that derive from one or other ancestral group.

An even greater problem in producing reliable estimates of individual admixture is the high degree of overlap in gene frequencies among contemporary human populations. MacLean and Workman (1973) proposed a method by which individual admixture estimates in a hybrid population can be calculated. Reed (1973) noted, however, that at least 18 loci that discriminate perfectly between the two ancestral populations would be required to obtain point estimates of individual admixture with acceptable standard errors. There are only two nearly perfect loci and many which yield far less information about ancestry. Given the paucity of blood group loci that discriminate African from Caucasian populations, we reject the possibility of *point* estimates of admixture at the present time.

We propose instead an *odds coefficient*[2] that establishes a rank order of individuals depending upon their resemblance at several blood group loci to one of two populations. By using phenotype[3] frequency estimates for populations A and B, the odds that an individual's phenotype came from population A can be estimated with the following formula:

$$O_A = \log \left[\frac{A_1 A_2 A_3 \ldots A_n}{B_1 B_2 B_3 \ldots B_n} \right]$$

---

[2]   Other coefficients were assessed for their efficiency in discriminating individual differences in ancestry within the black population. An additive model $\left[\frac{A_1 - B_1}{A_1 + B_1} + \frac{A_2 - B_2}{A_2 + B_2} + \cdots + \frac{A_n - B_n}{A_n + B_n} \right]$, a model that weighted the loci by the combined phenotypic frequencies for populations A and B $\left[\log \left(\frac{A_1 A_2 \ldots A_n}{A_1 A_2 \ldots A_n + B_{12} \ldots B_n} \right) \right]$, and several others were tried. The coefficients were all highly correlated (> 0.9) unless their distributions were very poor. We chose the simplest odds coefficient with a good distribution

[3]   Phenotype frequencies were chosen instead of genotypes because, for many loci, estimating individual genotypes is another tentative step away from the data. For loci without co-dominant alleles, particularly complex ones such as Rhesus, estimating individual genotypes seemed unnecessarily combersome. The use of individual phenotypes and phenotypic frequencies avoided this problem

where A_1 is the frequency of the individual's phenotype at locus 1 in population A, B_1 is the frequency of his phenotype at locus 1 in population B, etc.

The odds coefficient is not an admixture estimate; it is merely an expression of the combined probabilities across n loci that an individual's blood group alleles come from population A, given the frequency to those alleles in populations A and B. The size of the odds coefficient, when considering only one marker locus, depends on how dissimilar the phenotype frequencies are in the presumed ancestral populations. Thus, perfect discrimination occurs when a gene exists in one ancestral population but not the other. The more similar the frequencies are, the less reliably the origin of the genetic marker can be predicted and consequently the smaller the odds. The formula can be used to express the relative odds that an individual comes from either one of two populations with contrasting phenotype frequencies.

African and Caucasian Populations: The Putative Parents. Many African groups contributed to the US black gene pool over several centuries. The estimation of an historical ancestral population from contemporary African populations is fraught with pitfalls. There is considerable heterogeneity in gene frequencies among contemporary African ethnic groups; no one knows the exact proportions of slaves that were brought to the USA from these varied groups, or even if the contemporary groups are the same ones that inhabited the regions from which slaves were brought. Further, no one knows if the slaves were a random sample of the African populations, or if survival and reproductive rates were equal across the African groups that became slaves. Possible selection trends and genetic drift complicate the estimation problem still more. Thus, the gene frequencies for any putative African 'parent' population for contemporary US blacks makes many tenuous assumptions (Adams and Ward, 1973).

Estimates of gene frequencies for European populations that contributed to the US black population pose similar problems, but there is less heterogeneity in gene frequencies among the Northern European groups that are thought to have contributed the majority of genes to the hybrid blacks. This putative parent population is probably more accurately estimated than the former.

Given the severe reservations that any reasonable person would have about our ability to estimate 'parent' populations for contemporary US blacks, we attempted to develop construct validity for two odds coefficients: one based on estimated ancestral frequencies and one based on contemporary samples of blacks and whites. The odds coefficients were then tested for relationships with measures of intellectual skills.

Material and Methods

Subjects. The subjects of this report are same-sex twins who were sampled from black and white populations in Philadelphia, Pennsylvania, for the study of genetic variability in physical, mental, and personality development from 10 to 16 years of age. The fact that the subjects are twins is not directly relevant to the study of ancestry or admixture. The black twins were drawn from 181 different families, each of whom is represented by two offspring. About 59% of the black pairs are dizygotic (DZ), and the remaining 41% monozygotic (MZ).

Table 1. Twin pairs by race, sex, and zygosity

Zygosity	Black		White		Total pairs
	Male	Female	Male	Female	
Monozygotic	34	43	67	63	209
Dizygotic	44	60[a]	52	42	196
Total	78	103[a]	119	105	405

[a]   includes 2 sets of triplets

The major effect of using twin pairs in the study of ancestry is to confuse the issue of how many degrees of freedom ought to be allowed in the statistical analyses (Elston, personal communication 1974). In the case of monozygotic pairs, they have the same ancestry, as estimated by genetic markers, but they seldom have exactly the same mental test scores. Dizygotic twins have neither the same ancestry nor the same test scores. We would have used only one twin from each family and thereby eliminated the confusion about degrees of freedom, but the analyses would have lost some information in the reduced sample. We could have averaged the test scores of the co-twins, but it was not clear that this was an equally appropriate procedure for both MZ and DZ pairs. Therefore, after discussions with several statisticians, we decided to use both members of the twin pair but to reduce the degrees of freedom to a range between the number of independently sampled families and the number of individuals. In the tables, however, the number of families and twin pairs are both given.

The samples of black and white twins are described in Table 1. Of the black twin pairs, 157 come from the city public schools, the remainder from the city parochial schools. Socio-economic characteristics of their neighborhoods were taken from census tracts. The median income of the tracts in which black twins reside is $7910, and the median adult educational level is 10.2 years. Both figures are very close to the average 1970 census figures for urban black families. The subjects ranged in age from 10 years to 15 years, 11 months.

The actual sample sizes available for the several analyses to be reported in this paper varied from about 300 individuals from 160 twin pairs to 288 individuals in 144 pairs on whom we had complete blood group data on the 12 systems used for estimation of ancestry and nearly complete mental test data. The largest reduction in sample size occurred for the paired-associate learning task, because the established instructions were not sufficiently understood by the inner-city black children, resulting in the elimination of many of their results. The other mental test results have more valid pairs, as indicated in the tables.

Procedures. The children were each paid $10 to participate, and they received a free dental check up, physical growth assessment, and refreshments. They were brought after lunch by chartered bus from the elementary school nearest their homes and returned to the school after approximately 5 h at the Dental School, University of Pennsylvania.

Co-twins were separated into different small groups, each with an adult leader who explained the procedures, answered questions, and gave assistance. An average of 28 children, divided into four small groups, were tested each weekday afternoon from early July to early August, 1972.

For the psychologic assessments the small groups were assembled in a large auditorium. Seating was arranged in alternate seats and rows. Test materials were presented by 35 mm slides on a large screen. Instructions and test items were presented by audio tape and coordinated automatically with the slide presentations. No reading skills were required. All of the materials had been pretested with 30 black, inner-city children who were paid a consultant fee to criticize the procedures and tests. Based on the pretest, all test instructions were made more redundant than standard instructions to help the disadvantaged black children to understand the nature of tasks. Group leaders monitored the children's use of the simplified answer sheets for the tests.

Blood samples were drawn at the end of the day, just before the payments were given out. Although some children were reluctant to have blood drawn, peer pressure at the promise of ten dollars produced excellent cooperation and minimal distress.

Intellectual Skills. Five measures of intellectual skills were administered as parts of two $1\frac{1}{4}$ h psychologic assessments that also included personality and self-esteem measures. The two sessions were separated by approximately 1 h, in which dental, taste, dermatoglyphic, radiologic, physical growth, and other assessments were made. Refreshments were served during a break between sessions.

The Raven Standard Progressive Matrices, Sets A, B, C, and D were included to measure abstract reasoning skills. Seventy items from the Peabody Picture Vocabulary Test were used to measure knowledge of standard English vocabulary. Thirty items from the Columbia Test of Mental Maturity were used to assess conceptual skills. The Revised Figural Memory Test was included to test conceptual memory for designs. Finally, a paired-associate task was included to test rote, associative learning skills.[4]

The matrices, vocabulary, and conceptual skills tests were all found to have high internal consistencies, ranging from 0.82 to 0.95 in the black sample (Kuder-Richardson, Formula 20). The Figural Memory Test and the paired-associate task are not suited to consistency analysis, but their expected correlations with the other cognitive measures (~ 0.5 and 0.3 respectively) were observed. Factor analysis of the first four cognitive tests showed similar high loadings (0.75 to 0.79) on a first principal component, accounting for half of the variance in separate analyses on the black and white samples. There is every reason to believe that the first four tests are valid, reliable measures of intellectual skills in a black sample. The paired-associate test is less related to the others, both theoretically and empirically. The scores used in this paper were standardized by 1-year age intervals to eliminate age variance.

Socioeconomic Status. Two measures of socioeconomic status were obtained. The Home Index (Gough, 1949), a 24-item measure of family SES, was administered as part of the first test battery. It was found to be unreliable for black children because co-twins often disagreed about information on their families (Carter-Saltzman et al., 1975). A revised scale of the ten most reliable items was included in this study. Census tract median values for educational level and income were obtained on all census tracts in which black twins lived. The census tract in an urban area is fairly homogeneous with respect to socioeconomic characteristics, but it is an imperfect measure of individual SES. It is a good measure of some neighborhood and school characteristics that are related to children's intellectual development.

Skin Color Reflectance. Both black and white twins were measured on skin reflectance. Three filters (red, blue, green) and three locations (forehead, medial aspect of the lower arm, and inside of the upper arm) combined to produce nine measures of skin color reflectance. The reflectance values were so highly intercorrelated ($r > 0.8$) that only one, red filter-forehead, will be reported here. The reliability of the skin color measures is reflected in the very high heritabilities, between 0.85 and 0.98.

Blood Group Markers. Two 10-cm^3 blood samples were obtained from each child, one in EDC solution, one in a clot tube. Blood samples were shipped daily by air in refrigerated cartons to the Minneapolis War Memorial Blood Bank for typing. The following marker loci were assessed: AB0 (A_1, A_2, B, 0) MNSs, Kidd (Jk^a, Jk^b), Kell (K, k), Rhesus (r, r', R^0, R^1, R^2), Ceruloplasmin (Cp^a, Cp^b, Cp^c), Group Specific (Gc^1, Gc^2), Transferrin (Tf^C, Tf^D), Duffy (Fy^a, Fy^b), Hemoglobin (Hb^A, Hb^S, Hb^C), Haptoglobin (Hp^1, Hp^2), Adenylate kinase (AK^1, AK^2) Gm (a, x, b, c), and Inv(1). The distribution of the blood group phenotypes and the intellectual test scores are available from the American Documentation Service.

---

[4]   J. C. Raven, *Standard Progressive Matrices:* Sets A, B, C, D, and E (H. K. Lewis and Co., London, 1958); L. M. Dunn, Peabody picture vocabulary test (American Guidance Service, Inc., Circle Pines, Minnesota, 1959); Columbia Test of Mental Maturity (Harcourt, Brace, and Winston, New York, 1959); A. L. Benton, The revised visual retention test, Form C (William C. Brown Co., Inc., Dubuque, Iowa, 1963); H. W. Stevenson, G. A. Hale, R. E. Klein, and L. K. Miller, Monographs of the society for research in child development, **33**, Whole No. 123 (1968)

Twin zygosity was established by comparing co-twin's blood groups at each of the loci. If dizygosity was determined by only one blood group difference, the tests for that locus were redone to affirm the diagnosis.

Ancestral Phenotype Frequencies. To calculate the ancestral African frequencies different weighting schemes were applied to the available data from different regions of sub-Saharan Africa. Curtin's (1969) speculative estimates of the proportion of slaves originating from eight arbitrary African regions is reproduced in row a of Table 2. Curtin based his calculations on records from colonial Virginia and South Carolina as well as the total British slave trade. Two other weighting schemes were used in this study. That shown in row b of Table 2 gives equal weighting to each region while row c is a modification of Curtin's estimates to give greater weight to regions VI, VII, and VIII.

Gene frequency estimates for each region were obtained from an extensive review of the published literature on African gene frequencies. Unlike earlier estimates, greater weight was given where possible to groups within 200 miles of the coast than to inland groups, who probably contributed less to the slave trade. The phenotype frequency estimates for the eight regions are given in Table 3.[5] While these data represents information on many thousands of individuals, the many empty cells emphasize the fragmentary nature of our knowledge of modern African populations, especially for those genetic loci of greatest value for the present study.

The three weights were combined with the eight regional phenotype frequency estimates to produce three possible ancestral populations.

---

[5]   The ancestral Caucasian and African gene frequencies used are found in the following sources. The same references were used as are found in footnote 18 of J. Adams and R. H. Ward, Science, **180**, 1137 (1973) plus these additional sources where they do not overlap: R. E. G. Armattoe, Am. J. Phys. Anthrop., n.s. **9**, 371 (1950); R. E. G. Armattoe, E. W. Ikin, and A. E. Mourant, W. Afr. Med. J. **2**, 89 (1953); S. H. Boyer and E. J. Watson-Williams, Nature (Lond.) **190**, 456 (1961); J. Buettner-Janusch, R. Reisman, D. Coppenhaver, G. A. Mason, and V. Buettner-Janusch, Am. J. Phys. Anthrop. **38**, 661 (1973); L. L. Cavalli-Sforza and W. F. Bodmer, The genetics of human populations (Freeman and Co., San Francisco, 1971), pp. 267—268; H. Cleve and A. G. Bearn, in Progr. Med. Genet., Vol. 2, A. G. Steinberg and A. G. Bearn, eds. (1962); G. M. Edington, G. Afr. Med. J. **5**, 71 (1956); A. Eyquem, L. Podliachouk, and J. Presles, Vox Sang. (Basel) **6**, 120 (1961); I. Faye, H. Ruscher, M. P. Tsala, and G. Bloc, Bull. Soc. Med. Afr. Noire lang. franç. **16**, 551 (1971); E. R. Giblett, in Progr. Med. Genet., Vol. 2, A. G. Steinberg and A. G. Bearn, eds. (1962); E. R. Giblett, Genetic markers in human blood (F. A. Davis Co., Philadelphia, 1969); G. Holmgren and K. G. Gotestam, Hum. Hered. **20**, 433 (1970); T. Jenkins, A. Zoutendyk, and A. G. Steinberg, Am. J. Phys. Antrop. **32**, 197 (1970); G. Kellermann and H. Walter, Humangenetik **15**, 84 (1972); F. D. Kitchin and A. G. Bearn, Nature (Lond.) **202**, 827 (1964); J. Lambotte-Legrand and C. Lambotte-Legrand, Ann. Soc. belg. méd. trop. **30**, 547 (1950); V. T. Matznetter and W. Spielmann, Z. Morph. Anthrop. **61**, 57 (1969); J. Moullec, J. M. Fine, C. Henry, and C. Silverie, Proc. 7th Cong. Internatl. Soc. Bl. Transf. (Rome, September 3—6, 1958), pp. 881—883, P. Moureau and J. Brocteur, Bull. Acad. roy. Méd. Belg. 7 (No. 2), 147 (1962; W. C. Parker and A. G. Bearn, Ann. hum. Genet. **25**, 227 (1961); R. R. Race and R. Sanger, Blood Groups in Man, 5th edition (Blackwell, Oxford, 1968); L. Reys, C. Manso, G. Stamatoyannopoules, and E. Giblett, Humangenetik **16**, 227 (1972); L. Rivat, M. Blanc, C. Rivat, C. Ropartz, and J. Ruffie, Humangenetik **13**, 108 (1971); H. Sagnet, J. Thomas, L. Vovan, C. Jesserand, A. Marie-Nelly, and A. Orsini, Pediatrie **26**, 611 (1971); M. H. K. Shokeir and D. C. Shreffler, Biochem. Genet. **4**, 517 (1970); A. G. A. Simbeye, Hum. Hered. **22**, 286 (1972); W. Spielmann, H. Ruppin, L. Schilling, and D. Teixidor, Dtsch. Z. ges. gerichtl. Med. **64**, 186 (1968); A. G. Steinberg, Am. J. hum. Genet. **18**, (1), 109 (1966); D. Tills, J. L. Van den Branden, V. R. Clements, and A. E. Mourant, Hum. Hered. **20**, 517 (1970) and Hum. Hered. **21**, 302 (1971); P. V. Tobias, in The biology of human adaptability, P. T. Baker and J. S. Weiner, eds. (1966); R. M. Winston, W. Afr. Med. J. **3**, 17 (1954). Although a small amount of American Indian admixture has been found in some local black populations (B. Glass, Am. J. hum. Genet. **7**, 368 (1955), the contribution is small enough to be safely ignored when so many other sources of error are more obvious

Table 2. Weighting schemes used to obtain the ancestral African frequencies

	I	II	III	IV	V	VI	VII	VIII
a	0.13	0.06	0.11	0.16	0.04	0.23	0.25	0.02
b	0.125	0.125	0.125	0.125	0.125	0.125	0.125	0.125
c	0.05	0.05	0.05	0.10	0.15	0.30	0.20	0.10

Caucasian phenotype frequencies for England, Ireland, Scotland, and Wales were used for the Caucasian ancestral population. While we recognize that other European groups also contributed to the contemporary US black population, no weighting scheme exists for the white ancestral populations comparable to the one Curtin provides for African groups. Besides, most of the US black population resided in the southeastern states during the time that hybrid group was forming and in that region the white population derived predominantly from British Isles' settlers. Table 3 also gives the Caucasian phenotype frequencies used as the second ancestral population.

Phenotype frequencies from the three estimated African ancestral populations and the Caucasian ancestral populations were inserted in Formula (1) to calculate the three *ancestral odds coefficients*. High values indicate closer resemblance to African phenotype frequencies.

Sample Frequencies. Since we were not concerned with an individual admixture estimate but with a rank order coefficient, the phenotype frequencies actually obtained in the black and white samples in Philadelphia could be used to rank order socially classified blacks according to their degree of resemblance to the white sample. Those individual phenotypes that closely resemble the black sample values, especially at those loci with large differences in phenotype frequencies between the black and white samples, will receive higher rank order values than those phenotypes that closely resemble the white sample frequencies. Using Formula (1), we calculated a *sample odds coefficient*.

Construct Validation of the Odds Coefficient. If these odds coefficients are valid measures of racial genetic variability, then they should meet two criteria. First, they should correlate with skin color, which also reflects racial genetic variability. Second, the correlation for the odds coefficients between dizygotic twins should be around 0.5 or a little higher if there is assortative mating for characteristics such as skin color that are related to admixture. DZ twins share half of their genes on the average.

Results

Ancestral Odds. The three putative African ancestral populations produced indistinguishable ancestral odds coefficients. Although the phenotype frequencies varied somewhat, the rank orders of black children were essentially the same. Thus, we chose to use Curtin's (1969) weighted values as the final measure.

Validity of the Odds Coefficients. The DZ twin correlations for ancestral and sample odds were 0.55 and 0.61 respectively (SE = 0.11). These intraclass correlations are in the expected range for a valid coefficient based on genetic variability. Plots of the co-twin values for the odds indicated that variability between co-twins was equally distributed across the range of the sample odds coefficient. Variability in ancestral odds was greater for low values that represent less African ancestry. Thus, a greater number of individuals with higher degrees of Caucasian ancestry are discriminated than there are in the range of the

Table 3. Phenotype frequencies used in computing ancestral and sample odds coefficients

Phenotypes		Regions[b] of Africa								Composite[a] ancestral African	Black sample	White sample	Ancestral Caucasian
		I	II	III	IV	V	VI	VII	VIII				
AB0	0	0.50	0.47	0.50	0.50	0.54	0.52	0.50	0.56	0.51	0.46	0.46	0.47
	A	0.24	0.24	0.22	0.21	0.21	0.25	0.27	0.22	0.24	0.25	0.35	0.42
	B	0.21	0.24	0.24	0.24	0.22	0.18	0.19	0.18	0.21	0.25	0.12	0.09
	AB	0.04	0.05	0.04	0.09	0.04	0.04	0.04	0.03	0.04	0.04	0.07	0.03
Adenylate kinase	1				1.00	1.00			0.99	1.0	0.98	0.96	0.91
	1–2				0.00	0.00			0.01	0.00	0.02	0.04	0.09
Ceruloplasmin	B						0.70	0.87	0.78	0.74	0.90	0.98	0.98
	BA						0.25	0.10	0.10	0.21	0.10	0.01	0.02
	BC						0.01	0.01	0.00	0.01	0.00	0.00	0.00
Duffy	A			0.01				0.07	0.00	0.04	0.13	0.23	0.20
	AB							0.01	0.00	0.00	0.03	0.40	0.46
	B							0.02	0.01	0.02	0.17	0.36	0.33
	A–B–							0.90	0.99	0.94	0.66	0.01	0.00
Group specific	1					0.89		0.82	0.90	0.88	0.76	0.51	0.51
	1–1					0.10		0.17	0.10	0.12	0.22	0.43	0.41
	2					0.00		0.01	0.00	0.00	0.02	0.06	0.08
Haptoglobin	1	0.40	0.44	0.51		0.52	0.38	0.36	0.25	0.42	0.32	0.15	0.16
	1–2	0.47	0.45	0.41		0.40	0.47	0.48	0.50	0.45	0.44	0.50	0.48
Inv(1)	(1+)	0.57						0.58	0.59	0.57	0.51	0.19	0.18
	(1–)	0.43						0.42	0.41	0.43	0.49	0.81	0.82
Kell	K			0.05	0.01	0.01	0.01			0.02	0.01	0.05	0.09
	k			0.94	0.98	0.98	0.98			0.97	0.99	0.95	0.91
MN	M	0.13	0.21	0.21	0.30	0.23	0.18	0.24	0.25	0.22	0.24	0.26	0.28
	MN	0.45	0.49	0.50	0.49	0.50	0.49	0.50	0.50	0.49	0.44	0.55	0.50
	N	0.39	0.30	0.29	0.20	0.27	0.33	0.26	0.25	0.29	0.32	0.20	0.22

Rhesus	rh	0.07	0.07	0.06	0.10	0.05	0.06	0.06	0.02	0.07	0.04	0.12	0.15
	rh'rh	0.00	0.00	0.01	0.03	0.01	0.01	0.00	0.01	0.02	0.00	0.00	0.01
	Rh_0	0.74	0.64	0.67	0.53	0.52	0.60	0.67	0.71	0.64	0.49	0.03	0.02
	Rh_1rh	0.09	0.10	0.13	0.18	0.22	0.04	0.11	0.03	0.11	0.28	0.34	0.35
	Rh_1Rh_1	0.00	0.00	0.00	0.01	0.01	0.00	0.01	0.00	0.00	0.01	0.20	0.19
	Rh_2rh	0.07	0.17	0.11	0.07	0.11	0.22	0.14	0.11	0.13	0.12	0.12	0.12
	Rh_2Rh_2	0.00	0.01	0.00	0.00	0.01	0.02	0.01	0.00	0.01	0.02	0.02	0.02
	Rh_2Rh_0	0.00	0.01	0.01	0.01	0.02	0.01	0.01	0.01	0.01	0.04	0.16	0.13
Transferrin	C	0.96	0.94	0.92	0.88	0.88	0.86	0.94	0.92	0.91	0.93	0.99	0.99
	CD	0.04	0.05	0.07	0.11	0.11	0.12	0.05	0.08	0.08	0.07	0.01	0.00
	D	0.00	0.00	0.00	0.00	0.00	0.00	0.00	0.00	0.00	0.00	0.00	0.00
Gm	a−, x−, b^1+, c^3−									0.00	0.02	0.50	0.53
	a+, x−, b^1+, c^3−									0.41	0.65	0.35	0.21
	a+, x+, b^1+, c^3−									0.07	0.03	0.08	0.18
	a+, x−, b^1+, c^3+									0.49	0.25	0.00	0.00
	a+, x−, b^1−, c^3−									0.00	0.03	0.03	0.00
	a+, x+, b^1−, c^3−									0.00	0.01	0.03	0.02
	a+, x+, b^1+, c^3+									0.03	0.01	0.00	0.06

Note: All zero frequencies were made equal to 0.0001 since the log of zero is undefined

[a] Using 'a' weights of Table 2, Curtin's (1969) speculative estimates

[b] The regional phenotype frequencies are pooled estimates and not simple averages

African nations corresponding to eight regions:

I   Senegal, Gambia
II Sierra Leone, Guinea (Bissau), Guinea
III Liberia, Ivory Coast
IV Ghana
V   Dahomey, Western Nigeria, Togo
VI Cameroons, Eastern Nigeria
VII Angola, Equatorial Guinea, Gabon, Congo, Zaire
VIII Malagasy, Mozambique

Table 4. Correlations among skin color, ancestral and sample odds coefficients, based on three and nine marker loci

	SC	AO(3)	AO(9)	SO(3)	SO(9)
Skin color reflectance	X				
Ancestral odds (3)	0.16	X			
Ancestral odds (9)	0.11	0.11	X		
Sample odds (3)	0.22	(0.58)	0.11	X	
Sample odds (9)	0.18	0.09	(0.76)	0.10	X

$n \cong 300$ individuals from ~ 160 twin pairs; If $n = 160$ and $r \geq 0.15$, $P \leq 0.05$

distribution reflecting higher degrees of African ancestry when the ancestral odds coefficient is used.

Both the ancestral and sample odds coefficients were found to be significantly correlated with the skin color measure, 0.21 and 0.27 respectively ($P < 0.01$). Although we were unable to make a point prediction for the correlations (because little is known about the distribution of admixture in the black population) we anticipated a low positive relationship that is consonant with the power of the genetic marker loci used to index degree of ancestry.

There is another hypothesis, however, to explain the correlation between skin color and blood group markers: that one skin color locus is closely linked to Gm and/or Fy (Gershowitz and Reed, 1972; Cavalli-Sforza, personal communication 1974). Indeed, skin color was found to be more highly correlated with Gm than any other single locus ($r = 0.20$), followed by Duffy, Transferrin ($r = 0.13$ for each) and AB0 ($r = 0.11$). These loci are good markers for ancestry, however, and could be correlated with skin color for that reason.

Skin color variation probably depends upon a few good markers of ancestry. If skin color phenotypes correlate with ancestral odds, because ancestral genes have not been dispersed throughout the black population, then any three good blood group markers ought to correlate positively with other markers from the same ancestral population. If, instead, the relationship between skin color and ancestry depends upon the close linkage between a skin color locus and Fy/Gm, then three blood group markers should not correlate positively with the rest, and skin color should not correlate with any set of blood groups lacking the linked marker.

To test the competing hypotheses we selected three good blood group markers (gm, Fy, AB0) to correlate with the remaining nine and to compare with the correlation of skin color to odds coefficients calculated on the set of three and the set of nine. The correlations are given in Table 4.

All of the correlations among skin color and the odds coefficients were in a positive direction. Three of the eight were statistically significant, including the correlations between skin color and the sample odds, with and without Gm and Duffy ($r = 0.22$ and 0.18 respectively). The correlations between the sets of three and nine blood group markers were not statistically significant. While no firm conclusions can be drawn, the relationship between skin color and the blood

Table 5. The distributions of ancestral and sample odds coefficients calculated separately for co-twins 1 and 2

	Co-twin 1	Co-twin 2
Ancestral odds		
Mean	4.13	4.22
SD	3.00	2.96
SE	0.26	0.24
Skewness	−0.93	−0.94
Kurtosis	1.67	1.46
Range	−8.3 to 10.1	−8.3 to 9.9
Sample odds		
Mean	2.96	2.98
SD	2.15	2.07
SE	0.19	0.17
Skewness	0.09	0.14
Kurtosis	0.18	−0.07
Range	−3.0 to 8.7	−3.0 to 8.4

group markers does not depend solely upon a hypothesized linkage with Gm. The data are consistent with a hypothesis of partial nondispersion of ancestry.

As a further test of the validity of the odds coefficients, the ancestral and sample frequencies were used to calculate 'admixture' for the white sample. Since African populations are not significant progenitors of the contemporary US white group, we did not expect the odds coefficients to correlate with skin color within the white sample. Although both skin color reflectance and the odds coefficients were sufficiently variable and reliable to produce the expected DZ twin coefficients of about 0.5 (red filter-forehead $r_{DZ} = 0.51$; ancestral odds $r_{DZ} = 0.48$; sample odds $r_{DZ} = 0.54$), the genetic variability in skin color and blood group markers were unrelated to African ancestry within the white sample (skin color, ancestral odds $r = 0.04$; sample odds $r = 0.05$).

In the black sample the distributions of the ancestral and sample odds coefficients were calculated separately for co-twins, randomly designated 1 and 2. The statistical characteristics of the four odds coefficients are given in Table 5.

Co-twins, separated into two samples, do not constitute a traditional replication study, but they do provide two related samples on which to test the distributional qualities of the proposed statistic. The odds coefficients for co-twins 1 and 2 are very similarly distributed. As shown in Figure 2, the ancestral and sample odds coefficients differed in the shapes of their distributions. The sample odds coefficient produced more individuals with low degrees of estimated African ancestry, and the ancestral odds produced a greater number of individuals in the high ranges of estimated African ancestry.

Relationships of Odds Coefficients to Social Variables. There were negligible correlations between the two measures of socioeconomic status and the odds coefficients. The census tract data correlate negatively with increasing resemblance to the black or African groups. (The higher SES, the less the resemblance to black or

SES	Ancestral odds	Sample odds
Census	−0.10	−0.12
Individual	+0.09	+0.07

Table 6. Correlations of the odds coefficients and SES

Table 7. Correlations of ancestral and sample odds coefficients with intellectual skills

	Ancestral odds	Sample odds
Raven standard progressive matrices	−0.08	−0.13
Peabody picture vocabulary test	−0.06	0.00
Columbia test of mental maturity	0.02	−0.04
Revised test of figural memory	−0.12	−0.10
Paired-associate test	0.15	0.12
First principal component	−0.03	−0.05

$n \cong 144$ pairs; $r \leq -0.14$, one-tailed test, $P \leq 0.05$; SE = 0.083

African groups.) The individual SES measure correlates positively with the odds coefficients. None of the coefficients is statistically different from zero, but they are given in Table 6.

Skin color is only slightly related to SES characteristics, in the same directions as the odds coefficients. The darker children tend to live in lower SES neighborhoods ($r = 0.15$) but do not tend to have lower SES families ($r = 0.03$). There are no significant correlations between skin color and SES.

The Odds Coefficients and Intellectual Skills. None of the correlations between the ancestral or sample odds and the five intellectual skills was significantly different from zero. There was no association between our estimates of ancestry and intellectual performance within the sample of black twins. The first principal component from the four cognitive tests, which most psychologists would call g, is the set of intellectual skills that is general to intellectual measures. The first principal component was significantly related to socioeconomic status ($r = -0.20$; $P < 0.05$) and tended to be related to skin color ($r = 0.155$), but general intellectual skills were not correlated with ancestry. Table 7 gives the results before social variables were partialled out of the correlations. A scatter plot of one of the correlations, that of sample odds and the first principal component, is given in Figure 3. It is clear that no statistically significant relationship exists.

Allthough the social correlates of the odds coefficients account for very little of the variance in intellectual performance, we computed the correlations between the odds coefficients and the intellectual skills holding skin color and SES (census tracts) constant. Since social discrimination can be based on visible markers of ancestry, it seemed advisable to partial out the social effects. Table 8 gives the results.

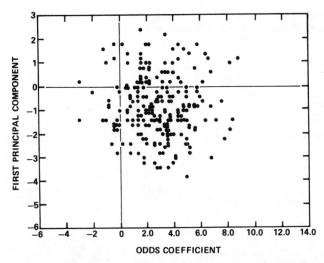

Fig. 3. A scatterplot of scores on the first principal component of four cognitive tests and the sample odds coefficient of ancestry within a sample of Philadelphia blacks

Table 8. Correlations of ancestral and sample odds with intellectual skills: SES (census tracts) and skin color partialled out

	Ancestral odds	Sample odds
Raven standard progressive matrices	−0.09	−0.10
Peabody picture vocabulary test	−0.03	0.04
Columbia test of mental maturity	0.03	−0.02
Revised test of figural memory	−0.10	−0.06
Paired-associate test	0.14	0.10
First principal component	−0.01	−0.02

$n \cong 144$ pairs; $r \leq -0.14$, one-tailed test, $P \leq 0.05$; SE = 0.083

To test further the relationships between the odds coefficients and intellectual performance, extreme groups were contrasted. The distributions of ancestral and sample odds coefficients were divided into thirds. The test scores of the group with the highest odds for African ancestry were compared to those of the group with the lowest. Skin color and social class differences are confounded in these contrasts, and the sample sizes are overestimated. Despite the confounding of social variables, in only one case out of 12 did extreme group contrasts achieve statistical significance with a sample size inflated to the number of individuals instead of the number of families independently sampled. These results are given in Table 9.

On the Revised Test of Figural Memory, the third of the sample with the least African ancestry had higher scores than the third with the most, but this result was not replicated with the sample odds coefficient. Most importantly, the

Table 9. Contrasts between extreme thirds of the ancestral and sample odds distributions on intellectual test scores (least black minus most black in standard deviation units)

	Sample odds				Ancestral odds			
	m diff.	SE[a]	*t*	*P*	*m*diff.	SE[a]	*t*	*P*
Raven standard progressive matrices	0.21	0.13	1.60	0.11	0.16	0.13		
Columbia test of mental maturity	0.09	0.13			0.06	0.13		
Peabody picture vocabulary test	−0.08	0.13			0.08	0.13		
Revised test of figural memory	0.07	0.12			0.31	0.12	2.31	0.02
Paired-associate test	−0.06	0.15			−0.23	0.15	1.63	0.11
First principal component	0.11	0.21			0.13	0.22		

[a]   Assumes that individuals are independently sampled and $n \cong 280$. In fact, n is best considered between 280 individuals and 140 independent families

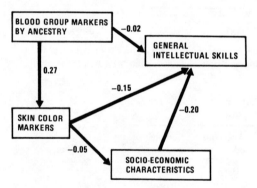

Fig. 4. Path coefficients of the effects of ancestry and socioeconomic status on the intellectual skills of a sample of Philadelphia blacks

general factor of the intellectual tests was not related to ancestry. Although intellectual skills were not consistently related to estimated ancestry in the extreme thirds, skin color was. The group with the highest estimated African ancestry was significantly darker than the group with the lowest (ancestral odds, $t = 2.05$, $P < 0.05$; sample odds, $t = 3.25$, $P < 0.001$).

To summarize the results, Figure 4 presents a path analysis of the model underlying this research, presented earlier as Figure 1. The path coefficients of ancestry (skin color and blood group markers) and life chances (skin color and socioeconomic status) with general intellectual skills support the stronger effects of life chances than ancestry on intellectual performance.

Discussion

The test of a relationship between degree of African ancestry, estimated with the odds coefficients, and intellectual skills failed to provide evidence for genetic racial differences in intelligence. Jensen (1973) predicted the correlation between the degree of Caucasian admixture and intellectual ability as around 0.50, under the assumptions of his proposal that half to three-quarters of the IQ difference between races is due to genetic differences (Jensen, 1973). In the correlational analyses presented in this paper, no evidence at all can be found for a correlation of that magnitude (Tables 7 and 8). In fact, none of the correlations was reliably different from zero in the expected direction, given the sample size involved (a correlation of about -0.14 would be different from zero at $P \leq 0.05$, one-tailed test). Even if the correlations between ancestry and intellectual skills could not exceed those between skin color and ancestry, because of less than perfect reliabilities, they would have been detected by this study.

Now, if we look as well at the differences between the averages of the upper and lower thirds of the black group on the various intellectual measures rather than rely solely on a correlational analysis, no consistent support for Jensen's hypothesis emerges either. The average difference between blacks and whites in this study on intellectual measures is around 0.9 standard deviations (SD). If we assume that the most extreme third of the black group averages 35% Caucasian ancestry, while the least admixed third averages 15% (based on data of MacLean et al., 1974), the average difference between extreme thirds should be about one-fourth of a standard deviation on the intellectual dimension.[6]

The sample size in this study is sufficient to detect a mean difference in intellectual skills of 0.26 between the extreme thirds of the distribution arrayed by estimated degree of ancestry, with a standard error of 0.13, when $p = 0.05$. If we let $p = 0.10$, an average difference of 0.22 achieves statistical significance. With a relaxed alpha value, one of the twelve mean differences between extreme thirds was statistically significant, and two others approached statistical significance— one in the direction of high to low degree of black ancestry and the other in the direction of low to high degree of black ancestry (see Table 9). An extrapolation from the contrast between extremes within the hybrid group to the average difference between the races predicts that not more than one-third of the observed difference between the races could be due to genetic differences. In view of the negligible correlations between estimated ancestry and intellectual skills, even this seems unlikely.

We suggest that stronger tests of the hypothesis of genetic racial differences can be provided by increased sample sizes, improved estimates of the ancestral population gene frequencies, and a larger number of polymorphisms that discriminate ancestral origin. Other approaches to the problem, such as the study of transracial adoption, have shown that black and interracial children reared by middle-class white families achieve IQ scores well above the average of white children in the US (Scarr and Weinberg, 1976). Neither the study of transracial adoption nor the present study provide any support for a strong hypothesis of genetic racial differences in intelligence.

---

[6]   The rough calculation for the estimate of the difference between upper and lower thirds of the black group proceeds as follows. If the resultant difference in standard deviations is 0.9 between the races when the mean difference in degree of Caucasian ancestry is about $(0.99 - 0.22 = 0.77$, then the difference between upper and lower thirds of the black group alone should be about 0.23 SD when the difference in Caucasian ancestry is about $(0.35 - 0.15) = 0.20$. Furthermore, if three-fourths of that mean difference is due to racial genetic differences alone the smallest expected difference is $(0.75 \times 0.23) = 0.18$. So, about one-fifth to one-fourth of a SD would be the expected mean difference between upper an lower thirds of the black group.

Acknowledgements. Our deepest appreciation to the many people who assisted in this research: to Dr. Herbert Polesky, Director of the Minneapolis War Memorial Blood Bank, for all of the blood analyses; to William Thompson, who helped to fomulate the odds coefficients, wrote the computer programs, and analyzed the data; to Louise Carter-Saltzman, who edited the psychologic test protocols; to Valerie Lindstrom, who supervised much of the data collection; to Professors Julian Adams, V. Elving Anderson, Luigi Cavalli-Sforza, T. E. Reed, and Peter Workman for consultation on the design and analysis of the study. None of them is responsible in any way for the conclusions drawn from the research by the authors. The research was supported by the Grant Foundation and by NICHHD (HD-08016) and in part by Mental Health Training Grant (MH 10679).

References

Adams, J., Ward, R. H.: Admixture studies and the detection of selection. Science **180**, 1137—1143 (1973)

Carter-Saltzman, L., Scarr-Salapatek, S., Barker, W. B.: Do these co-twins really live together? An assessment of the validity of the Home Index as a measure of family socioeconomic status. Educational and Psychological Measurement **56**, 1021—1025 (1975)

Curtin, P.: The Atlantic slave trade. Madison: University of Wisconsin 1969

Gershowitz, H., Reed, T. E.: Hardy-Weinberg disequilibrium of the Fy system in four American Negro populations. Amer. J. hum. Genet. **24**, 38—42 (1972)

Glass, B., Li, C. C.: The dynamics of racial intermixture—an analysis based on the American Negro. Amer. J. hum. Genet. **5**, 1—20 (1953)

Jensen, A. R.: Educability and group differences. New York: Harper & Row 1973

Klineberg, O.: Negro-White differences in intelligence test performance: A new look at an old problem. Amer. Psychol. **18**, 198—203 (1963)

Loehlin, J. C., Vandenberg, S. G., Osborne, R. T.: Blood group genes and Negro-White ability differences. Behav. Genet. **3**, 263—270 (1973)

MacLean, C., Workman, P.: Genetic studies on hybrid populations. II. Estimation of the distribution of ancestry. Ann. hum. Genet. **36**, 459—465 (1973)

MacLean, C. J., Adams, M. S., Leyshon, W. C., Workman, P. L., Reed, T. E., Gershowitz, H., Weitkamp, L. R.: Genetic studies on hybrid populations. III. Blood pressure in an American black community. Amer. J. hum. Genet. **26**, 614—626 (1974)

Nei, M., Roychoudhury, A. K.: Gene differences between Caucasian, Negro, and Japanese populations. Science **177**, 434—436 (1972)

Pollitzer, W. S.: Problems in admixture estimates from different genetic loci. Haematologia **6**, 193—198 (1972)

Reed, T. E.: Caucasian genes in American Negros. Science **165**, 762—768 (1969 a)

Reed, T. E.: Critical tests of hypotheses for race mixture using Gm data on American Caucasians and Negros. Amer. J. hum. Genet. **21**, 71—83 (1969 b)

Reed, T. E.: Number of gene loci required for accurate estimation of ancestral population proportions in individual human hybrids. Nature **244**, 575—576 (1973)

Scarr-Salapatek, S.: Unknowns in the IQ equation. Science **174**, 1223—1228 (1971 a)

Scarr-Salapatek, S.: Race, social class, and IQ. Science **174**, 1285—1295 (1971 b)

Scarr-Salapatek, S.: IQ: Methodological and other issues. Sciences **178**, 229—240 (1972)

Scarr-Salapatek, S.: Heritability of IQ by social class: Evidence inconclusive. Science **182**, 1045—1047 (1973)

Scarr-Salapatek, S.: Some myths about heritability and IQ. Nature **251**, 463—464 (1974)

Scarr, S., Weinberg, R. A.: IQ test performance of black children adopted by white families. Amer. Psychol. **31**, 726—739 (1976)

Shockley, W.: Dysgenesis, geneticity, raceology: A challenge to the intellectual responsibility of educators. Phi Delta Kappan **53**, 297—307 (1972)

Shuey, A.: The testing of negro intelligence. New York: Social Science 1966

Stern, C.: Model estimates of the number of gene pairs involved in pigmentation variation of the Negro American. Hum. Hered. **20**, 165—168 (1970)

Received November 11, 1976 / April 12, 1977

Comments and Replies

COMMENT: THE USE OF RACIAL ADMIXTURE AS
EVIDENCE IN INTELLIGENCE RESEARCH: A CRITIQUE*

On standard measures of IQ the average black usually scores approximately 1 standard deviation below the average white (e.g., Scarr, Scarr, Pakstis, Katz, & Barker, 1977). There is an ongoing controversy whether this is due primarily to environmental or genetic differences between the two populations.[1] Scarr et al. (1977) state that "if genetic, racial differences do contribute to average intellectual differences between black and whites, then those blacks with higher degrees of white ancestry should perform better on intellectual tasks than those with lesser degrees of admixture [p. 161]." They then design a study wherein the degree of white ancestry of black children, as determined by gene markers, is compared to their performance on intellectual tasks.

Would finding a positive correlation lend convincing support to notions of white genetic superiority? No—for the study design of Scarr et al. rests upon a fundamental, untestable assumption. They assume that in terms of intellectual function, those whites who contributed to black ancestry were a random sample of all whites. A genetic interpretation of a positive correlation assumes that miscegenous whites had genetic IQs superior to blacks because they were a representative sample of the general white population—which, in turn, assumes

---

*This comment by Centerwall originally appeared in *Human Genetics,* 1978, *45,* 237–238. Copyright © 1978. Reprinted by permission.

[1]For clarity of argument, an either/or approach is taken. Intermediate positions can be entertained.

that whites have superior genetic IQs. Thus, to conclude from a positive correlation that whites have superior genetic IQs, it is necessary to assume that whites have superior genetic IQs.

Suppose miscegenous whites were not a random collection of whites. If their IQs were similar to blacks—and lower than whites—there should be no genetic correlation between degree of white ancestry and intellectual skills. Therefore, any positive correlation would be *ipso facto* attributable to environmental forces. Would this necessarily mean that miscegenous whites had less genetic mental endowment than other whites? Of course not. Environmental theory assumes that group differences in IQ are due to environmental forces. Thus, if it is assumed that blacks have lower apparent IQs due to environmental forces, it can as well be assumed that miscegenous whites also had lower apparent IQs for the same reasons—for example, social stigma, poor schooling, poverty.

Unfortunately, these arguments cut both ways. If no correlation is found between degree of white ancestry and intellectual skills (Chapter II-2), it would be tempting to infer that there are no general black–white differences in genetic IQ. However, a lack of correlation only demonstrates that there was no significant difference in genetic IQ between ancestral blacks and ancestral miscegenous whites. To complete the syllogism, it is necessary to demonstrate that there was no significant difference in IQ between ancestral miscegenous whites and other whites, or—if there was—to demonstrate that the difference was due to environmental rather than genetic causes. Since most of the principals are dead and the historical data almost nonexistent, neither demonstration is possible.

In attempting to resolve the genes-versus-environment controversy, Scarr et al. have designed a study where any result can be explained by either hypothesis. From an ethical and social viewpoint, their findings were most fortunate. However, resting as they do on an untestable assumption, any inferences are scientifically invalid. The same will hold for any future studies of the same design.

REFERENCE

Scarr, S., Pakstis, A. J., Katz, S. H., & Barker, W. B. Absence of a relationship between degree of white ancestry and intellectual skills within a black population. *Human Genetics,* 1977, *39,* 69–86.

BRANDON S. CENTERWALL
School of Medicine
University of California, San Diego

REPLY TO CENTERWALL*

As we noted in the original article (Scarr, Pakstis, Katz, & Barker, 1977, p. 73), there are no records of the intellectual achievements of either the African or European ancestors who contributed their genes to the contemporary black population. There is no a priori reason to expect, however, that they deviated intellectually from the more general populations from which they were drawn.

Very little of the racial admixture that occurred between the early 1600s and 1950 was produced by legally married couples. Historians of slavery—for example, Johnston (1970)—depict a completely different world—one of illicit sexual liaisons resulting in large numbers of mulatto children during colonial times.

> The colonial English aristocrat married with those of his own caste. . . . Nevertheless, some of the men of this class maintained permanent relations with Negro women to a more or less open extent. Also, on the large plantations rumors often involved the planters' sons in affairs with Negro girls. . . .
>
> The planter policy with regard to the intermixture of the races, as it concerns the Negro, was as follows: to prohibit the marriage of the Negro and the white race but to tolerate illicit union of the Negro woman and the white man, provided always that the mulatto offspring should follow the condition of its mother. Possibly the planter had decided that under the existing system the prevention of intermixture was humanly impossible. Without doubt, he believed that more of evil would result from the mulatto reared by a white mother than reared by slave mothers, and if the mulatto child of the Negro mother were . . . kept in the same status as his Negro kindred, dangers to planter society would be averted [pp. 183–184].

Johnston also describes several other cross-racial liaisons in which mulatto offspring were produced: Indentured white servants and slaves; free Negroes and whites of varied social background in the North; and a few marriages of free blacks and whites, including men and women of both groups. In other words, there is no evidence in Johnston's material that the *intellectual* level of the whites who contributed genes to the black population was atypically high or low. Even the social level of miscegenous whites was not clearly skewed toward the lower groups in the colonial era, and in those days of lesser social mobility, the correlation of class and IQ was surely less than it is today.

In brief, there is no evidence that whites who contributed genes to the ancestral black population constitute a biased sample of European populations; nor is there any positive evidence that they were a random sample. There are only the blind processes of slave capture and survival, the lack of social mobility in plantation society, and the absence of intellectual measurement at the time that

---

*This reply by Scarr, Pakstis, Katz, & Barker originally appeared in *Human Genetics*, 1979, 47, 225–226. Copyright © 1979. Reprinted by permission.

lead us to believe that little intellectual bias could have crept into the process of creating a new hybrid population.

REFERENCES

Johnston, J. H. *Race relations in Virginia & miscegenation in the South 1776–1860.* Amherst: University of Massachusetts Press, 1970.
Scarr, S., Pakstis, A. J., Katz, S. H., & Barker, W. B. Absence of a relationship between degree of white ancestry and intellectual skills within a black population. *Human Genetics,* 1977, *39,* 69–86.

SANDRA SCARR
A. J. PAKSTIS
University of Minnesota

S. H. KATZ
W. B. BARKER
University of Pennsylvania

II.3 Race, Social Class, and IQ*

The heritability of intelligence in white, middle-class populations of school-aged children and adults has been repeatedly estimated to account for 60 to 80 percent of the total variance in general intelligence scores, however measured (*1-4*). Yet Jensen (*3*, pp. 64–65) has noted many limitations to the available data on heritability.

> It is sometimes forgotten that such [heritability] estimates actually represent *average* values in a population that has been sampled and that they do not necessarily apply either to differences *within* various subpopulations or to differences *between* subpopulations.... All the major heritability studies have been based on samples of white European and North American populations, and our knowledge of intelligence in different racial and cultural groups within these populations is nil. For example, no adequate heritability studies have been based on samples of the Negro population of the United States [italics added].

After carefully examining the intelligence data on the black and white populations, Jensen (*3,4*) hypothesized that the average genetic potential of the black population may not be equal to that of the white population. Others (*5, 6*) have interpreted the same racial differences in mean IQ (intelligence quotient) within an environmental framework, often naively and without good evidence for their competing hypotheses. Dislike of a genetic hypothesis to account for racial differences in mean IQ scores does not equal disproof of that hypothesis. Evidence for genetic

*This chapter by Sandra Scarr-Salapatek originally appeared in *Science*, 1971, *174*, 1285–1295. Copyright © 1971 by the American Association for the Advancement of Science. Reprinted by permission.

or environmental hypotheses must come from a critical examination of both explanations, with data that support one.

As every behavioral geneticist knows, the heritability of a behavioral characteristic is a function of the population in which it is measured (7, 8). There is no reason to assume that behaviors measured in one population will show the same proportion of genetic and environmental variances when measured in a second population whose distributions of genetic or environmental characteristics, or both, differ in any way from those of the first population. Racial and social class groups are, for many purposes, sufficiently different populations to make a generalization from one to another highly questionable (9–11).

The sociological literature on social class and racial differences in style of life, nutrition, child-rearing practices, and the like describes *population* differences in distributions of environments. These population differences must affect the development of phenotypic (observed) IQ (12) and the relative proportions of genetic and environmental variances in IQ scores.

Distributions of genotypes for the development of behavioral characteristics may also vary from one population to another. Except for single-gene characteristics such as Huntington's chorea, microcephaly, and the like, we know very little about genotypic variability among populations for behavioral development. Because identified single-gene characteristics are known to occur with varying frequencies among populations, it is assumed that genes for polygenic characteristics may also be distributed somewhat differently among groups.

The sources of within-group and between-group variation can be assessed, although they are seldom effectively studied. Thoday (13, pp. 4–5) reviewed the problems of cross-population studies and concluded:

> While discontinuous variables such as blood groups present us with little difficulty [in studying differences between populations], continuous variables such as IQ are a different matter, for it is not possible with these to identify specific genotypes and it is therefore not possible to determine gene frequencies. Furthermore, there are always environmental as well as genetic causes of variation. We may measure the relative importance of environmental as well as genetic causes of variation or heritability within a population, and if the heritabilities are very high, that is, variation is almost entirely a consequence of genetic variety, we may know more than if they are low. But even if they are high, as with fingerprint ridge counts, we are already in difficulties with population comparisons, for there is no warrant for equating within-group heritabilities and between-group heritabilities.

In this article, I outline important concepts and methods in the study of individual and group variation and describe a new study of genetic and environmental variances in aptitude scores in black and white, and advantaged and disadvantaged populations.

TWO MODELS OF IQ,
SOCIAL CLASS, AND RACE

There are two major, competing hypotheses for predicting the relation among social class, race, and IQ—the environmental disadvantage hypothesis and the genotype distribution hypothesis. Both hypotheses make differential predictions about the proportions of genetic and environmental variance in IQ within lower and higher social class groups.

The term "environmental disadvantage" refers to the largely unspecified complex of environmental factors associated with poverty that prevents an organism from achieving its optimum development. The biological environmental disadvantages have been reviewed by Birch and Gussow (*14*), and references to social environmental disadvantages have been reviewed by Deutsch, Katz, and Jensen (*15*).

Race and social class are terms that refer to socially defined subgroups of the human population. Reproduction is more likely to occur between people in the same subgroup than between people in different subgroups. There is no question that races are partially closed breeding groups with a great deal more endogamy than exogamy (*10*). It is also true that social class groups (groups whose members have attained a certain educational and occupational status) within races practice more endogamy than exogamy (*11*). Social mobility from generation to generation does not upset the notion of social classes as somewhat different breeding groups, in terms of IQ levels, because the distribution of IQ's within each occupational level is reestablished in each generation of adults (*16*). Brighter children in families at all but the top social levels tend to be upwardly mobile, whereas duller siblings at all but the bottom class level tend to be downwardly mobile (*17*). Social class groups may be thought of as endogamous primarily for IQ (as expressed in occupational and educational achievements).

Social class groups may represent both different distributions of parental genotypes for IQ and different rearing environments for children. Although fathers' average IQ scores may vary by 50 points or more from top professional groups to unskilled laborers, their children's average IQ's differ by 25 points or less (*16, 17*).

The mean differences in children's IQ's by social class reflect differences in both parental genotypes and rearing environments, which covary to a large extent in the development of IQ. Crucial evidence on the genetic and environmental components from adopted children is very limited, but Skodak and Skeels (*18*) revealed a 20-point rise in the IQ of adopted children over that of their biological mothers. The distribution of adopted children's IQ's was also shifted beyond the values expected by regression to a mean above the average of the population, presumably by their better social environments.

Social class groups, then, are subdivisions of races and represent different distributions of parental genotypes, as well as different rearing environments. There is no comparable statement that can be made about racial groups: whereas races represent different rearing environments, no statements can be made concerning different distributions of parental genotypes for IQ. Since there is no direct test possible for distributions of genotypic IQ (*13*), it is impossible to assert that such distributions for the two races are "equal" or "different." Races do constitute different rearing environments in two respects. First, proportionately more blacks than whites are socially disadvantaged, thus more black children are reared under lower-class conditions; second, being black in the United States may carry with it a social burden not inflicted on any white.

The environmental disadvantage hypothesis assumes that lower-class whites and most blacks live under suppressive (*19, 20*) conditions for the development of IQ. In brief, the disadvantage hypothesis states: (i) unspecified environmental factors affect the development of IQ, thereby causing the observed differences in mean IQ levels among children of different social classes and races; (ii) blacks are more often biologically and socially disadvantaged than whites; and (iii) if disadvantage were equally distributed across social class and racial groups, the social class and racial correlations with IQ would disappear. The environmental disadvantage hypothesis predicts that IQ scores within advantaged groups will show larger proportions of genetic variance and smaller proportions of environmental variance than IQ scores for disadvantaged groups. Environmental disadvantage is predicated to reduce the genotype–phenotype correlation (*21*) in lower-class groups and in the black group as a whole.

The genetic differences hypothesis, as it applies to social class groups within races, centers on the issues of assortative mating by IQ and selective migration, based on intelligence, within the social structure. Social class differences in mean IQ are assumed to be principally genetic in origin and to result from the high heritability of IQ throughout the population, assortative mating for IQ, and a small covariance term that includes those educational advantages that brighter parents may provide for their brighter children (*3, 10*). Social class differences in phenotypic IQ are assumed to reflect primarily the mean differences in genotype distribution by social class; environmental differences between social class groups (and races) are seen as insignificant in determining total phenotypic variance in IQ. Therefore, the proportion of genetic variance in IQ scores is predicted to be equally high for all social class groups (and for both races). Figures 1 and 2 present models 1 and 2, respectively, as they apply to social class.

In model 1, there are assumed to be equal distributions of genotypes across social classes. In model 2, there are assumed to be unequal distributions of genotypes for IQ, the lower class having proportionally more genotypes for low IQ and the upper social groups having proportionally more genotypes for high IQ. Environmental effects of social class are posited to be strong in model 1 and very weak in model 2.

Model 1: Environmental advantage as the
determinant of group differences in IQ.

Assumptions:

1. Genotypic distribution by social class for phenotypic
IQ of children (no differences).

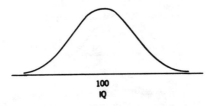

2. Environmental effects on the development of IQ
by SES (large effect).

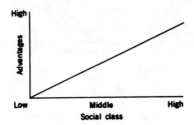

Prediction: Lower h^2 in disadvantaged groups.

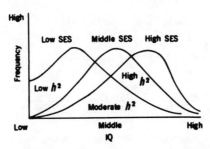

FIG. 1.   Environmental disadvantage, model 1 (h^2 is heritability for twins; SES is socioeconomic status).

COMPETING PREDICTIONS

Both models account for the observed social class data on IQ, but they make competing predictions about the proportion of genetic variance. In model 1, environmental factors are predicted to reduce the mean and the heritability of IQ in the lower social class groups and raise both in the higher social groups. Model

**Model 2: Genetic differences as the primary
determinant of group differences in IQ.**

Assumptions:

1. Genotypic distribution by social class for phenotypic
   IQ of children (differences).

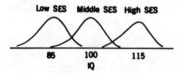

2. Environmental effects on the development of IQ
   by SES (small effect).

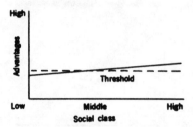

Prediction: Equal h^2 in all groups.

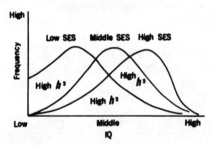

FIG. 2. Genetic differences, model 2 (h^2 is heritability for twins; SES is socioeconomic status).

2 predicts equally high heritabilities for all groups, regardless of rearing environments and regardless of mean scores. Estimated heritabilities by social class and race provide a new way of evaluating the adequacy with which the two hypotheses account for observed differences in mean IQ by social class. Racial differences may also be examined if the following rationale is always considered.

To the extent that the *same* environmental factors are assumed to affect the development of IQ in the same way in both black and white populations, predictions can be made about the sources of racial differences in mean IQ scores. If certain biological deprivations (such as low weight at birth, poor nutrition) are known to be more prevalent in lower class groups of both populations and more prevalent among blacks than whites, then the two models can make differential predictions about the effects of these sources of environmental variance on the proportion of genetic variance in each population. Given a larger proportion of disadvantaged children within the black group, the environmental disadvantage hypothesis must predict smaller proportions of genetic variance to account for differences in phenotypic IQ among blacks than among whites, as whole populations. Since the genotype distribution hypothesis predicts no differences in the proportion of genetic variance for social class groups within the races, it should predict the same proportions of genetic variance in the two races.

To the extent that *different* environmental factors are assumed to affect the development of IQ in black and white populations, or the same environmental factors are assumed not to affect the development of IQ in the same way, or both, no differential predictions about the origin of racial differences can be made by the two models. If all black children are disadvantaged to an unknown degree by being reared as blacks in a white-dominated society, and no white children are so disadvantaged, it is impossible to estimate genetic and environmental variances between the races. Only if black children could be reared as though they were white, and vice versa, could the effects of different rearing environments on the genotype distribution of the two races be estimated.

Some combinations of models 1 and 2 may be found to account best for phenotypic variability within and between groups. The clear opposition of models 1 and 2 as explanations for the same IQ, racial, and social class data was presented to demonstrate the differential predictions that can be generated about proportions of genetic variance in different populations.

TWIN SAMPLE

An alphabetic roster of all students enrolled in the Philadelphia public schools in April 1968 was examined for children with the same last name, the same birth dates, and the same home address. Children who met the three criteria were identified as twins.

Of the 250,258 children in kindergarten through grade 12, 3042 were identified as twins, including 493 opposite-sex pairs and 1028 same-sex pairs.

The racial distribution of these twins was 36 percent white and 64 percent black. The corresponding figures for the entire public school population were 41 percent white and 59 percent black. The twins' racial distribution was discrepant from the total population by 5 percent, which can be accounted for by the substantially higher rate of fraternal twinning among blacks (22).

In a large sample of twins it is tactically difficult to differentiate the monozygotic and dizygotic groups directly. Direct approaches to zygosity could be discarded in favor of the indirect, statistical approach, which is advocated by Burt (2), Vandenberg (23), Sandon (24), and Husen (25). The reasoning is as follows: the percentage of opposite-sex pairs is known in any complete population survey. By applying the Weinberg formula, the proportion of monozygotic twins can be easily obtained (21). There will always be approximately the same proportion of same-sex pairs as opposite-sex pairs because of the distribution of sexes. It is then a simple matter to estimate the percentage of monozygotic pairs as follows: 100 − 2 (percent of opposite-sex pairs) = percent of monozygotic pairs. Percentage estimates for monozygotic and dizygotic groups were done separately for each racial group.

Once the proportion of monozygotic and dizygotic twins is known, the correlations for same-sex and opposite-sex groups can be used to estimate the correlation coefficients for monozygotic and dizygotic twins within the same-sex sample. By converting correlation coefficients to z scores, the same-sex intraclass coefficient can be apportioned according to the percentages of monozygotic pairs in the same-sex group, so that:

$$r_{iss} = \frac{\% \ SS_{dz} \ (r_{ios}) \ + \ \% \ SS_{mz} \ (X)}{\% \ SS_{mz+dz}}$$

On the basis of seven independent studies including more than 1000 pairs of same-sex and 100 pairs of opposite-sex twins, Burt (2) found the average correlations for intelligence to be .76 and .57, respectively. From these coefficients, he was able to estimate the correlation for monozygotic and dizygotic groups as .89 and .56, respectively. These estimates match very closely the correlations found for intelligence in samples of monozygotic and dizygotic twins whose zygosity had been determined by blood-grouping procedures.

In the Philadelphia sample, 30 percent of the white pairs and 34 percent of the black pairs were found to be of opposite sexes. Therefore, by the Weinberg formula, 40 percent of the whites and 32 percent of the blacks were estimated to be monozygotic pairs. The higher proportion of monozygotic twins in the white population matched the figures reported (24) for a complete age-group of British children taking the 11+ examinations.

The final samples were considerably smaller than the original 1521 pairs found, for several reasons. First, since standardized tests were not administered to the kindergarten or first-grade groups, 282 pairs were lost. Second, one or both members of 124 pairs were found to be enrolled in special classes, to whom the tests used in this study were not given (26). Third, the absence of one or both twins on the days that tests were administered eliminated an additional 123 pairs. Combined losses of 529 pairs reduced the final sample to 992 pairs with aptitude or achievement scores, or both, for each twin, as shown in Table 1.

Table 1. Final sample pairs by race and test scores.

Test scores	Black	White
Aptitude only	315	194
Achievement only	129	75
Aptitude and achievement	191	88
Total pairs	635	357

SOCIAL CLASS MEASURES

Within both the black and white groups, social class variables were used to assign pairs to relatively advantaged and disadvantaged groups. The public school data on parental occupation, income, and education were incomplete and too unreliable for these purposes. Instead, census tract information from the 1960 U.S. Census was used.

Every pair had a census tract designation for which median income and educational data were available. Although census tracts in an urban area are designed to provide maximum homogeneity within tracts, they are still imperfect measures of individual SES (socioeconomic status) characteristics. Relatively advantaged and disadvantaged groups could be designated by neighborhood SES, however, since peer associations and school characteristics would be reflected in the census tract data. To the extent that the social disadvantage hypothesis pertains to the life-style, in addition to within-family environment, the census tract data were appropriate.

Social-class assignment was made by establishing a median level of income and educational characteristics for the total number of census tracts from which the twin sample was drawn, regardless of race. Cross-tabulations of above- and below-median levels of income and education provided three groups: one below the census tract medians for both income and education; one above the medians of both; and a third above in one and below in the other. On this basis, the three groups were designated as below median, above median, and middle status.

APTITUDE AND ACHIEVEMENT TESTS

Results from several tests were available in the 1968–69 school year for children in the Philadelphia school district from second through twelfth grade (27). All children in grades three through eight who were in regular academic classrooms were given the Iowa Tests of Basic Skills, which test long-term development of intellectual skills (28). These are highly reliable group tests (29) that are used to measure scholastic achievement in many school districts across the nation. The vocabulary, reading, language total, arithmetic total, and composite scores were obtained. A total of 319 black and 163 white pairs had scores on all subtests for each twin.

Since a different aptitude test was given in every second school grade, it was impossible to obtain a sufficiently large number of pairs for reliable test-by-test results. It was decided, therefore, to combine aptitude test results across tests and age ranges, and to treat them as age-appropriate, equivalent forms of the same test. This radical decision was based primarily on the roughly equivalent structure of the aptitude tests. All have at least two principal subtests, a verbal and a nonverbal (or numerical), as well as a total score. Some tests, such as the Differential Abilities Test, have additional subtests to measure spatial, mechanical, and other abilities not included in more scholastically oriented tests, such as the School and College Ability Tests. Thus, the total scores based on all subtests are not strictly equivalent; nor are the nonverbal tests, which may be based primarily on arithmetic reasoning or may include abstract reasoning as well. The verbal scores are the most nearly equivalent from test to test, and thus are the most reliable for comparisons across grades.

No a priori assumptions were made about the appropriateness of standardized aptitude tests for different social-class and racial groups. Although there exists a popular notion that standardized tests are less predictive of scholastic achievement in disadvantaged groups, this has generally been unsupported by research (30). This hypothesis was tested, however, by examining the correlations between aptitude and achievement scores for each racial and social-class group.

Since the generalizations were never intended to exceed the limits of aptitude test and IQ scores, no extensive discussion of the epistemological issue, "What do IQ tests measure?" will be attempted here. Suffice it to say that variance in IQ and aptitude test scores have been shown to have strong genetic components in other studies of white populations, and that the appropriateness of these measures for other racial and social-class samples will be considered in the results section.

STATISTICS

Statistics in studies of twins are based on the variances in scores among individuals of different genetic and environmental relatedness. The total phenotypic variance in the populations studied can be apportioned into between-family and within-family variances for both same- and opposite-sex twins. The comparison of between- and within-family mean squares is usually expressed as an F ratio

$$F = \frac{\sigma_b^2}{\sigma_w^2}$$

The intraclass correlation expresses the proportion of variance arising from family influences, both genetic and environmental. It compares the between-family variances minus the within-family variances to the total phenotypic variance in the population from which the related persons are drawn.

$$r_t = \frac{\sigma_b^2 - \sigma_w^2}{\sigma_b^2 + \sigma_w^2} = \frac{F - 1}{F + 1}$$

where σ_b^2 is the mean squares between pairs, and σ_w^2 is the mean squares within pairs.

The comparison of intraclass correlation coefficients and variance ratios for two or more related sets of individuals leads to the calculation of heritability estimates. The heritability of a trait is an expression of the ratio of total genetic variance to total phenotypic variance.

In the simplest form for studies of twins, the restricted model for broad heritability (h^2) was defined by

$$h_r^2 = \frac{2(r_{ims} - r_{ids})}{1 - \sigma_E^2}$$

where r_{imz} is the intraclass correlation for monozygotic pairs, r_{idz} is the intraclass correlation for dizygotic pairs, and σ_E^2 is the percentage of variance due to errors in measurement. In this study, σ_E^2 was estimated to be .073, or the minimum unreliability for group aptitude tests.

Another version of the h^2 statistic for broad heritability using twins was offered by Jensen (31) to include the available data on assortative mating for IQ in the white population. The assortative-mating model for data on twins takes into account the positive correlation between IQ scores of parents, which are generally found to be around .40. Nonrandom mating patterns produce a genetic correlation between siblings that is somewhat higher than the .50 expected under mating patterns that are random with respect to IQ. The formula for computing the heritability coefficient with assortative mating (h_a^2) is

$$h_a^2 = \frac{c(r_{ims} - r_{ids})}{1 - \sigma_E^2}$$

where $c = 1 / 1 - p$, or 2.222, when $p = .55$; and σ_E^2 is the percentage of variance due to errors in measurement.

If the heritability of a trait is known, the total variance can be apportioned into four major components; within-family genetic variance (σ_{wg}^2), within-family environmental variance (σ_{we}^2), between-family genetic variance (σ_{bg}^2 and between-family environmental variance (σ_{be}^2). Regardless of the absolute size of the total variance, the proportions of variance can be estimated (32).

DISTRIBUTIONS OF SCORES

An initial look at the distribution of scores within the samples of twins from Philadelphia indicated that the scores were far from normal. The low mean value especially in the black population, and the skew of the distributions required careful normalization of the scores before any heritability analyses could be attempted. Thus, the results are reported in three sections: first, the distributions of scores and their transformations; second, the analyses of data on twins; and third, the heritability and estimated proportions of variance in the scores by race and social class.

The distributions of aptitude scores, based on national norms were divided first by race and then by race and social class. The means and standard deviations of the scores were markedly different by race; the mean aptitude scores of whites were slightly below the national mean of 50, while the mean aptitude scores of blacks were one standard deviation ($\sigma = 19$) below the national mean. There was almost one standard deviation between the means of the two races. The standard deviations of the whites were slightly higher than those of the blacks, as Jensen (3,4) and others have noted; but the ratios of standard deviations to the means (proportional variance) were higher in the black that in the white groups (see Table 2).

On measures of aptitude, the racial groups had surprisingly large differences, once social class was considered (Table 3). The mean of the below-median (in income and education) white group equalled or surpassed the mean of the above-median black children on verbal, nonverbal, and total aptitude scores. The quartile (Q) boundaries showed the distributions of below-median whites and above-median blacks to have similar properties, except that the total variance among advantaged black children was somewhat higher than that among disadvantaged whites.

The social-class divisions among whites separated the aptitude means of the subpopulations by approximately four-fifths of a standard deviation. The com-

Table 2. Means and standard deviations (σ) of national scores for individuals by race.

Aptitude test	Black (N = 1006)		White (N = 560)	
	Mean	σ	Mean	σ
Verbal	30.3	18.2	45.9	21.2
Nonverbal	32.7	19.1	47.9	21.8
Total	28.9	18.5	46.1	20.8

Table 3. Mean and standard deviations (σ) of national scores on combined aptitude tests for individuals by race and social class (Q indicates quartile).

Statistics	Black			White		
	Below (N = 634)	Middle (N = 236)	Above (N = 134)	Below (N = 114)	Middle (N = 106)	Above (N = 340)
			Verbal			
Mean	29.0	30.9	35.3	36.4	43.9	49.8
σ	(17.7)	(17.2)	(20.8)	(18.6)	(22.6)	(20.4)
Q	15-28-39	19-31-43	23-32-46	22-38-50	28-42-56	38-41-63
			Nonverbal			
Mean	32.0	32.7	35.9	38.3	44.5	52.2
σ	(19.2)	(18.7)	(19.3)	(18.0)	(22.5)	(21.5)
Q	17-32-44	20-32-46	20-34-50	25-39-50	29-43-59	36-51-68
			Total			
Mean	27.7	29.7	33.0	34.8	43.4	50.9
σ	(18.1)	(18.1)	(20.3)	(16.9)	(21.4)	(20.2)
Q	15-26-39	15-30-41	19-29-47	23-37-47	29-42-56	38-52-65

parable divisions among blacks produced a difference of one-quarter of a standard deviation between children below and above the medians for the 280 census tracts in which the twins lived. Social-class groups of children were far more differentiated among whites than among blacks, despite the same criteria for assignment.

Comparisons across racial groups showed that disadvantaged white children scored in a pattern similar to that of black children, while the middle and above-median white groups had much higher means. Variances were not reliably different across races.

Compared to the national distribution, the twins in Philadelphia scored poorly. Instead of mean scores of 50, all black groups and white groups of below-median and middle status had mean performance scores in the 20 to 40 range. Only the above-median whites had mean scores close to the national average. A comparison of the means and variances of the twins' scores with those of all Philadelphia children showed that the twins were indeed representative of their respective racial and social-class groups, and were only slightly handicapped by their twinship.

Since the scores based on national norms were skewed within the Philadelphia samples, the scores for each test were normalized, separately by racial groups, to a mean of 50 and a standard deviation of 10, in order to develop comparable data for blacks and whites. Since the means and variances of the two racial groups were arbitrarily set as equal, there was no longer any difference based on race in the distributions of scores. In every test, there were significant social-class differences and significant class-by-race interaction terms, which reflected the fact that social-class differences in mean scores were much greater among whites than blacks.

Correlational analyses of all test scores by race and social class were done to

TABLE 4
Intercorrelations of Test Scores by Race and Social Class [Nonverbal (NV), Total (T), Vocabulary (Vo), Reading (R), Language (L), Arithmetic (A), Composite (C)]

Black

Test	Aptitude			Achievement			
	Verbal	Nonverbal	Total	Vocabulary	Reading	Language	Arithmetic
Below-median group (N = 351)							
NV	.57						
T	.84	.87					
Vo	.56	.44	.54				
R	.56	.47	.59	.64			
L	.59	.54	.64	.67	.67		
A	.53	.58	.62	.57	.66	.67	
C	.64	.57	.67	.82	.84	.86	.83
Middle group (N = 125)							
NV	.71						
T	.90	.89					
Vo	.54	.47	.56				
R	.64	.56	.66	.66			
L	.67	.54	.65	.66	.75		
A	.60	.53	.60	.64	.72	.73	
C	.70	.59	.70	.83	.89	.90	.85
Above-median group (N = 51)							
NV	.53						
T	.82	.86					
Vo	.60	.35	.53				
R	.62	.56	.68	.71			
L	.68	.55	.71	.74	.87		
A	.55	.65	.68	.61	.81	.77	
C	.67	.57	.71	.83	.94	.93	.87

White

Test	Aptitude			Achievement			
	Verbal	Nonverbal	Total	Vocabulary	Reading	Language	Arithmetic
Below-median group (N = 60)							
NV	.44						
T	.81	.83					
Vo	.53	-.04	.31				
R	.62	.30	.51	.61			
L	.76	.28	.61	.69	.79		
A	.67	.37	.59	.58	.77	.79	
C	.75	.26	.58	.81	.87	.92	.89
Middle group (N = 43)							
NV	.57						
T	.88	.85					
Vo	.81	.49	.71				
R	.84	.59	.79	.88			
L	.71	.51	.69	.75	.85		
A	.60	.52	.63	.64	.71	.77	
C	.78	.61	.77	.86	.93	.94	.85
Above-median group (N = 147)							
NV	.66						
T	.81	.88					
Vo	.71	.49	.59				
R	.68	.53	.60	.78			
L	.69	.61	.66	.73	.74		
A	.70	.70	.74	.66	.71	.78	
C	.77	.64	.72	.87	.90	.88	.87

examine the equivalence of measurement among groups. As Table 4 shows, the patterns of correlation among aptitude and achievement scores were quite similar in all groups, regardless of race or social class. It is difficult to argue that the dimensions of performance measured in the different racial and social-class groups were not comparable. The most parsimonious explanation of similar patterns of correlations is that there are similar underlying dimensions. It is impossible to argue that ''nothing'' is being measured by these tests in disadvantaged groups, because the prediction from aptitude to achievement scores is approximately as good in the below-median as in the middle black groups, and is certainly as good in the black groups as it is in the white groups.

ANALYSES OF TWINS BY RACE

The four major groups of same-sex and opposite-sex, black and white twins were treated separately for the first set of analyses. Analyses of variance comparing within-pair and between-pair variances were applied to each test score in the four groups. Table 5 gives the twins' results by race for the three aptitude scores.

TABLE 5
Analysis of Variance of Aptitude Scores of Twin Pairs by Race

Mean squares	Black		White	
	Same sex	Opposite sex	Same sex	Opposite sex
		Verbal		
	(N = 333)	(N = 169)	(N = 192)	(N = 82)
σ_b^2	129.1	113.7	149.4	133.2
σ_w^2	38.2	44.8	29.6	33.9
F	3.38	2.54	5.05	3.93
r_i	0.543	0.435	0.669	0.594
r_{ims}		0.653		0.719
		Nonverbal		
	(N = 332)	(N = 169)	(N = 192)	(N = 82)
σ_b^2	130.5	115.2	149.7	131.7
σ_w^2	39.6	39.4	33.8	26.8
F	3.30	2.92	4.42	4.92
r_i	0.535	0.490	0.631	0.662
r_{ims}		0.594		0.601
		Total		
	(N = 334)	(N = 169)	(N =193)	(N = 82)
σ_b^2	127.4	119.2	168.0	156.9
σ_w^2	35.1	31.2	23.7	28.4
F	3.62	3.82	7.10	5.53
r_i	0.567	0.585	0.753	0.694
r_{ims}		0.544		0.791

Intraclass correlations for the monozygotic group are estimated by the method described earlier.

Same-sex twins were, in general, more similar than were opposite-sex pairs. In both the black and white groups, the presence of monozygotic pairs in the same-sex group increased their correlation above that of the opposite-sex dizygotic pairs, so that the estimated monozygotic correlation was higher than the dizygotic correlation for four of the six comparisons. The two exceptions are total aptitude score for the blacks and nonverbal aptitude for the whites. Correlations between the two children in each same-sex and opposite-sex black pair were consistently lower than for their white counterparts. Black twins were not found to be as similar to each other as white twins, when compared to randomly paired members of the same groups.

ANALYSES OF TWINS
BY RACE AND SOCIAL CLASS

It was hypothesized in model 1 that social-class conditions of life would affect twin similarities and resulting estimates of genetic variances. The potentially restricting effects of lower-class life on the development of genetically based individual differences could tend to reduce within-pair correlation co-efficients in the lower-class groups, whereas better environmental opportunities could allow a greater range of phenotypic individual differences in the middle-class groups. Model 2 predicted that similar proportions of genetic variance would be found across social-class groups because mean differences in scores were assumed to arise from differences in genotype distributions.

Within-pair similarities were analyzed for those pairs below the median and then for those of middle and above status combined—the small number of black

Table 6. Analysis of variance of verbal aptitude scores of twin pairs by race and social class.

Mean squares	Black		White	
	Same sex	Opposite sex	Same sex	Opposite sex
	Below-median group			
	$(N = 211)$	$(N = 107)$	$(N = 41)$	$(N = 16)$
σ_b^2	120.7	102.9	81.8	105.8
σ_w^2	41.7	42.1	28.7	31.0
F	2.89	2.44	2.85	3.41
r_i	0.486	0.419	0.481	0.546
r_{ims}		0.558		0.430
	Middle and above-median group			
	$(N = 123)$	$(N = 62)$	$(N = 153)$	$(N = 70)$
σ_b^2	136.0	134.0	154.1	119.9
σ_w^2	32.2	49.4	29.8	34.5
F	4.23	2.71	5.17	3.47
r_i	0.618	0.460	0.676	0.553
r_{ims}		0.753		0.749

Table 7. Analysis of variance of nonverbal aptitude scores of twin pairs by race and social class.

Mean squares	Black		White	
	Same sex	Opposite sex	Same sex	Opposite sex
	Below-median group			
	(N = 211)	(N = 107)	(N = 41)	(N = 16)
σ_b^2	128.9	120.3	111.1	87.8
σ_w^2	41.4	37.8	34.8	20.7
F	3.11	3.19	3.20	4.25
r_1	0.513	0.523	0.524	0.619
r_{1ms}		0.508		0.445
	Middle and above-median group			
	(N = 123)	(N = 62)	(N = 152)	(N = 68)
σ_b^2	132.5	107.8	149.9	122.3
σ_w^2	36.3	42.2	33.6	28.1
F	3.65	2.55	4.46	4.34
r_1	0.570	0.437	0.634	0.625
r_{1ms}		0.698		0.642

pairs above the median made it advantageous to combine the latter two groups. Tables 6, 7, and 8 give the analysis of variance results of the aptitude tests for the below-median and the combined middle and above-median groups for both races.

In the below-median SES groups of both races, the same-sex correlation exceeded the opposite-sex coefficient only once (black verbal aptitude). The failure of opposite-sex correlations to exceed same-sex cofficients left the estimated monozygotic correlations and heritability statistics indeterminant. It is unlikely that the correlations for monozygotic twins were lower than those for the same-sex dizygotic twins, but it is senseless to assign a value when r_{ios} is greater than r_{iss}. The most likely interpretation of this result is that the greater genetic correlation between monozygotic twins was not sufficient to increase the same-sex correlations above the values obtained for opposite-sex twins. Thus, genetic

Table 8. Analysis of variance of total aptitude scores of twin pairs by race and social class.

Mean squares	Black		White	
	Same sex	Opposite sex	Same sex	Opposite sex
	Below-median group			
	(N = 212)	(N = 107)	(N = 41)	(N = 16)
σ_b^2	122.7	109.7	83.1	109.1
σ_w^2	38.1	27.5	20.5	24.7
F	3.22	3.99	4.05	4.42
r_1	0.526	0.599	0.604	0.631
r_{1ms}		0.434		0.585
	Middle and above-median group			
	(N = 123)	(N = 62)	(N = 155)	(N = 70)
σ_b^2	130.6	137.4	174.7	139.1
σ_w^2	30.1	37.5	24.5	29.2
F	4.34	3.66	7.13	4.76
r_1	0.625	0.571	0.754	0.653
r_{1ms}		0.680		0.813

factors cannot be seen as strong determinants of aptitude scores in the disadvantaged groups of either race.

In the middle- to above-median SES groups, the same-sex correlations exceeded the opposite-sex correlations for all three aptitude scores in both races. The most likely inference from these data is that both genetic and environmental components of variance contributed to the similarity of within-pair scores in the advantaged group. For the disadvantaged group, the failure of same-sex correlations to exceed opposite-sex coefficients makes it doubtful that the proportion of genetic variance in the lower-class group equals that of the advantaged group.

Total variance was generally larger in the advantaged than in the disadvantaged groups of both races. For whites, total variance was larger in all six comparisons of advantaged and disadvantaged groups. For blacks, total variance was larger in four of six comparisons. This finding reflects the greater phenotypic variability of advantaged children, as predicted in model 1. The intraclass correlations were found to be comparable for blacks and whites within classes (see Table 9).

Assuming that the comparison of estimated monozygotic correlations and opposite-sex dizygotic correlations can be used to estimate heritability ratios, the proportion of genetic to total variance was calculated by the restricted and assortative mating formulas. Table 10 gives the intraclass correlations and estimated heritabilities for aptitude scores by race and social class.

As noted earlier, the proportion of genetic variance in disadvantaged groups was low, but indeterminant—except for verbal aptitude among blacks. Aptitude scores in advantaged groups all showed heritability estimates of greater than zero, except in the nonverbal scores of whites. Verbal aptitude scores had the highest heritability for both blacks and whites.

Table 9. Estimated heritability ratios by race and social class for aptitude scores.

Aptitude test scores	Black					White				
	r_{los}	r_{lss}	r_{lms}	h_r^2	h_a^2	r_{los}	r_{lss}	r_{lms}	h_r^2	h_a^2
Below-median group										
Verbal	0.419	0.486	0.558	0.309	0.343	0.546	0.481	*	*	*
Nonverbal	0.523	0.513	*	*	*	0.619	0.524	*	*	*
Total	0.599	0.526	*	*	*	0.631	0.604	*	*	*
Middle and above-median group										
Verbal	0.460	0.618	0.753	0.651	0.723	0.553	0.676	0.749	0.436	0.484
Nonverbal	0.437	0.570	0.698	0.580	0.644	0.625	0.634	0.642	0.038	0.042
Total	0.571	0.625	0.680	0.242	0.269	0.653	0.754	0.813	0.356	0.395
All										
Verbal	0.435	0.543	0.653	0.470	0.522	0.594	0.669	0.719	0.270	0.299
Nonverbal	0.490	0.535	0.594	0.224	0.249	0.662	0.631	*	*	*
Total	0.585	0.567	*	*	*	0.694	0.753	0.791	0.209	0.232

* Cannot be estimated.

Table 10. Percentage of variance in verbal aptitude scores for opposite-sex twins by race and social class.

Source	Disadvantaged			Advantaged		
	Between family	Within family	Total	Between family	Within family	Total
			Black			
Genetic	18.8	15.5	34.3	39.7	32.6	72.3
Environmental	23.1	42.6	65.7	6.3	21.4	27.7
Total	41.9	58.1	100.0	46.0	54.0	100.0
			White			
Genetic	*	*	*	24.0	19.6	43.6
Environmental	54.6	45.4	*	31.3	25.1	56.4
Total	54.6	45.4	*	55.3	44.7	100.0

* Cannot be estimated.

Table 11. Percentages of variance in nonverbal aptitude scores for opposite-sex twins by race and social class.

Source	Disadvantaged			Advantaged		
	Between family	Within family	Total	Between family	Within family	Total
			Black			
Genetic	*	*	*	35.4	29.0	64.4
Environmental	52.3	47.7	*	8.3	27.3	35.6
Total	52.3	47.7	*	43.7	56.3	100.0
			White			
Genetic	*	*	*	2.3	1.9	4.2
Environmental	61.9	38.1	*	60.2	35.6	95.8
Total	61.9	38.1	*	62.5	37.5	100.0

* Cannot be estimated.

Table 12. Percentages of variance in total aptitude for opposite-sex twins by race and social class.

Source	Disadvantaged			Advantaged		
	Between family	Within family	Total	Between family	Within family	Total
			Black			
Genetic	*	*	*	14.3	11.7	26.0
Environmental	59.9	40.1	*	42.7	31.3	74.0
Total	59.9	40.1	*	57.0	43.0	100.0
			White			
Genetic	*	*	*	21.5	17.5	39.0
Environmental	63.1	36.9	*	43.5	17.5	61.0
Total	63.1	36.9	*	65.0	35.0	100.0

* Cannot be estimated.

Table 13. Analysis of variance of aptitude scores for same-sex pairs by race.

Mean squares	Black		White	
	Male ($N = 139$)	Female ($N = 194$)	Male ($N = 96$)	Female ($N = 96$)
	Verbal			
σ_b^2	144.3	119.0	162.5	134.8
σ_w^2	43.1	34.7	34.7	24.4
F	3.35	3.43	4.68	5.52
r_1	0.540	0.549	0.648	0.693
	Nonverbal			
σ_b^2	131.6	129.1	156.3	144.6
σ_w^2	47.6	33.7	28.7	39.0
F	2.76	3.83	5.45	3.71
r_1	0.468	0.586	0.690	0.575
	Total			
σ_b^2	127.6	127.3	202.0	135.0
σ_w^2	43.0	29.5	26.1	21.2
F	2.97	4.31	7.75	6.36
r_1	0.496	0.623	0.771	0.728

Based on the estimated heritability ratios, genetic and environmental variances can be apportioned. The apportionment between and within families is based on the ratio of between-family to total variance, expressed in the intraclass correlation. Only opposite-sex pairs were used, because their correlations were known to be based on a common inheritance of about 55 percent.

From Tables 11, 12, and 13, one can see that the percentage of total variance attributable to genetic sources was always higher in the advantaged groups of both races. In most cases, genetic variance could not be estimated for the aptitude scores of lower-class children. For both advantaged and disadvantaged children,

Table 14. Analysis of variance of white, advantaged, opposite-sex twins, by aptitude level.

Mean squares	Both < 50 ($N = 22$)	Both ≥ 50 ($N = 31$)
	Verbal	
σ_b^2	54.8	65.7
σ_w^2	30.1	20.3
F	1.82	3.24
r_1	0.291	0.528
	Nonverbal	
σ_b^2	44.7	59.4
σ_w^2	18.7	20.9
F	2.39	2.84
r_1	0.410	0.479
	Total	
σ_b^2	34.6	57.5
σ_w^2	17.8	19.8
F	1.94	2.90
r_1	0.320	0.487

however, there were approximately equal variances between and within families, the between-family variance being somewhat larger more often. Thus, the major finding of the analysis of variance is that advantaged and disadvantaged children differ primarily in what proportion of variance in aptitude scores can be attributed to environmental sources.

To check on the validity of the findings, the aptitude data were analyzed separately for male–male and female–female pairs who were found to have correlations of similar magnitude. The overall results of the study were not due to the greater similarity of male or female pairs, as seen in Table 14.

GENOTYPE–ENVIRONMENT INTERACTION

While neither model 1 nor model 2 predicted statistical interaction, a combination of the two models could predict an interaction between genotypes and environments in producing phenotypic ability. Wiseman (*33*) has suggested that children with lower IQ's are less affected by environmental deprivations than are children with higher IQ's. If lower IQ children are less affected by differential family environments, then the between-family variance and the correlations between siblings with lower IQ's will be smaller than among siblings with higher IQ's, on whom family environment presumably has a greater effect. Burt (*34*) reported a correlation of .61 between siblings both of whose IQ's were above 100, and a correlation of .43 between siblings with IQ's below 100.

The possible explanations for these findings include (i) restriction of total variance in the group with lower IQ's because of a "floor effect" in the tests used; (ii) larger within-pair variances for children with lower IQ's as a function of a poor family environment; and (iii) smaller between-pair variances for children with lower IQ's as a function of less responsiveness to different family environments.

A test for restriction in total variance was made by dividing all opposite-sex pairs into those with both twins above the mean of 50 and those with both twins below. Mixed cases were eliminated from the samples. Neither black nor white twins with aptitude scores below the mean had lower total variances than the above-mean groups. Since total variances were equal in the two groups, a test of the interaction hypothesis could be made.

To test for the effects of lower IQ alone on patterns of sibling correlation in the white group, only those children with social class ratings at the median and above were included. Intraclass correlations for the 22 white, advantaged, opposite-sex pairs with aptitude scores below 50, and the 31 above 50 were found to be consistently different. As Table 14 shows, siblings below the aptitude mean had consistently lower correlations between their scores than siblings above the mean. The lower correlations between siblings with lower IQ's were not a function of social class, but a smaller between-pair variances, primarily.

This suggests that white children with lower IQ's are less susceptible to environmental differences between families than are children with higher IQ's, even in an advantaged population. There was no evidence of interaction between IQ and environment in the black population.

MEAN SCORES AND GENETIC VARIANCE

The lower mean scores of disadvantaged children of both races can be explained in large part by the lower genetic variance in their scores. A "deprived" or unfavorable environment for the development of phenotypic IQ unfavorably affects mean scores, phenotypic variability, genetic variance in phenotypes, and the expression of individual differences (19, pp. 64–65). No study of human family correlations to date has looked at all of these effects of suppressive environments. In a landmark study of mice, however, Henderson (8) has demonstrated that suppressive environments reduce the amount of genetic variance in performance, reduce phenotypic variability, and reduce mean performance scores. The percentage of genetic variance in the scores of standard-cage-reared animals was one-fourth that of animals with enriched environments (10 percent versus 40 percent). Not only did genetic variance account for a larger portion of the variance among animals with enriched environments, but their performance on the learning task was vastly superior to that of their relatively deprived littermates.

Although generalizations from genetic studies of the behavior of mice to genetic studies of the behavior of human beings are generally unwarranted (because mechanisms of development vary greatly among species), the role that a better rearing environment played in the development of genetic individual differences among Henderson's mice finds an obvious parallel with the effects of advantaged SES homes in this study.

From studies of middle-class white populations, investigators have reached the conclusion that genetic variability accounts for about 75 percent of the total variance in IQ scores of whites. A closer look at children reared under different conditions shows that the percentage of genetic variance and the mean scores are very much a function of the rearing conditions of the population. A first look at the black population suggests that genetic variability is important in advantaged groups, but much less important in the disadvantaged. Since most blacks are socially disadvantaged, the proportion of genetic variance in the aptitude scores of black children is considerably less than that of the white children, as predicted by model 1.

"Disadvantage" has been used as a term throughout this paper to connote all of the biological and social deficits associated with poverty, regardless of race. As long as these environmental factors were considered to be the same, and to act in the same way on children of both races, then racial differences in scores could be discussed. Unquantified environmental differences between the races—either different factors or the same factors acting in different ways—preclude cross-racial comparisons. Informed speculation is not out of order at this point, however.

Those cultural differences between races that affect the *relevance* of home experience to scholastic aptitudes and achievement may be of primary importance in understanding the remaining racial differences in scores, once environmental deficits have been accounted for. In a series of studies of African children's scholastic performance, Irvine found that many sources of variation that are important for European and American scores are irrelevant for African children (*35*, p. 93).

> Of environmental varibles studied in population samples, including socio-economic status, family size, family position, and school quality, only school quality showed significant and consistent relation to ability and attainment tests. Other sources of variation were irrelevant to the skills being learned.

For the black child in Philadelphia, the relevance of extrascholastic experience is surely greater than it is for the tribal African. But one may question the equivalence of black and white cultural environments in their support for the development of scholastic aptitudes. As many authors of an environmental persuasion has indicated (*6, 36*), the black child learns a different, not a deficient, set of language rules, and he may learn a different style of thought. The transfer of training from home to school performance is probably less direct for black children than for white children.

The hypothesis of cultural differences in no way detracts from the predictive validity of aptitude tests for the scholastic achievement of black children. The correlations between aptitude and achievement are equally good in both racial groups. But the cultural differences hypothesis does speak to the issue of genetic and environmental components of variance. If most black children have limited experience with environmental features that contribute to the development of scholastic skills, then genetic variation will not be as prominent a source of individual phenotypic variation: nor will other between-family differences, such as SES level, be as important as they are in a white population. School-related experiences will be proportionately more important for black children than for white children in the development of scholastic aptitudes. The Coleman report (*37*) suggested that scholastic environment does have more influence on the performance of black children than it does on the performance of white children. The generally lower scores of black children can be fit adequately to the model 1 hypothesis, with the additional interpretation of cultural differences to account for the lower scores of black children at each social-class level.

The differences in mean IQ between the races can be affected by giving young black children rearing environments that are more conducive to the development of scholastic aptitudes. Or the differences in performance can simply be accepted as differences, and not as deficits. If there are alternate ways of being successful within the society, then differences can be valued variations on the human theme (*38*), regardless of their environmental or genetic origins. Haldane (*39*) has suggested that, ideally, different human genotypes would be found to respond most favorably to different environmental conditions—that genotype–environment interactions would exist for many human characteristics. From a genetic point of view, varied adaptations are useful to the species and permit the greatest flowering of individual differences. Socially invidious comparisons, however, can destroy the usefulness of such differences.

Group differences in mean scores and phenotypic variability that exist because of environmental deprivation can and should be ameliorated. To the extent that children are not given supportive environments for the full development of their individual genetic differences, changes can be made in their prenatal and post-natal environments to improve both their overall performance and the genetic variance in their scores. If all children had optimal environments for development, then genetic differences would account for most of the variance in behavior. To the extent that better, more supportive environments can be provided for all children, genetic variance and mean scores will increase for all groups. Contrary to the views of many naive environmentalists, equality of opportunity leads to bigger and better genotype–phenotype correlations. It is toward this goal that socially concerned citizens should work.

ACKNOWLEDGMENTS

My gratitude goes to Heidelise Rivinus and Marsha Friefelder, who collected much of the data; to William Barker and Melvin Kuhbander, who ran many of the analyses; to Professors I. I. Gottesman, Arthur R. Jensen, Harold W. Stevenson, Leonard Heston, V. Elving Anderson, Steven G. Vandenberg, and Lee Willerman, and to Dr. Paul Nichols, all of whom critically read an earlier draft of this article. The research was supported by a grant from the National Institute of Child Health and Human Development (HD-04751).

REFERENCES AND NOTES

1. L. Erlenmeyer-Kimling and L. F. Jarvik, *Science* **142**, 1477 (1963); S. G. Vandenberg, in *Genetics*, D. Glass, Ed. (Rockefeller Univ. Press, New York, 1968), pp. 3–58; *Acta Genet. Med. Gemellol.* **19**, 280 (1970).
2. C. Burt, *Brit. J. Psychol.* **57**, 137 (1966).
3. A. R. Jensen, *Harv. Educ. Rev.* **39**, (1969a).
4. _____, in *Disadvantaged Child*, J. Hellmuth, Ed. (Brunner-Mazel, New York 1970), vol. 3, pp. 124–157.
5. T. F. Pettigrew, *A Profile of the Negro American* (Van Nostrand, Princeton, N.J., 1964).
6. S. Baratz and J. Baratz, *Harv. Educ. Rev.* **40**, 29 (1970).

7. M. Manosevitz, G. Lindzey, D. Thiessen, *Behavioral Genetics: Method and Research* (Appleton-Century-Corfts, New York, 1969).

8. N. Henderson, *J. Comp. Physiol. Psychol.* **3,** 505 (1970).

9. I. Gottesman, in *Handbook of Mental Deficiency: Psychological Theory and Research,* N. Ellis, Ed. (McGraw-Hill, New York, 1963), pp. 253–295; F. Weizmann, *Science* **171,** 589 (1971).

10. I. Gottesman, in *Social Class, Race, and Psychological Development,* M. Deutsch, I. Katz, A. Jensen, Eds. (Holt, Rinehart & Winston, New York, 1968), pp. 11–51.

11. C. V. Kiser, *Eugen. Quart.* **15,** 98 (1968).

12. A genotype is the genetic makeup of an individual. The term may refer to one, several, or all loci. Genetic variance refers to the differences among individuals that arise from differences in genotypes. A phenotype is the sum total of all observable characteristics of an individual. Phenotypic variance refers to the observable differences among individuals.

13. J. Thoday, *J. Biosoc. Sci.* **1** (Suppl.), 3 (1969).

14. H. Birch and J. Gussow, *Disadvantaged Children: Health, Nutrition and School Failure* (Harcourt, Brace & World, New York, 1970).

15. M. Deutsch, I. Katz, A. Jensen, Eds., *Social Class, Race and Psychological Development* (Holt, Rinehart & Winston, New York, 1968).

16. C. Burt, *Brit, J. Statist, Psychol.* **14,** 3 (1961); R. Herrnstein *Atl. Mon.* **228,** 43 (September 1971).

17. J. Waller, thesis, University of Minnesota (1970).

18. M. Skodak and H. Skeels, *J. Genet. Psychol.* **75,** 85 (1949).

19. Suppressive environments are those which do not permit or evoke the development of a genetic characteristic. "Suppose, for example, that early experience in the manipulation of objects is essential for inducing hoarding behavior. Genetic differences in this form of behavior will not be detected in animals reared without such experience" (*21,* p. 65).

20. J. L. Fuller and W. R. Thompson, *Behavior Genetics* (Wiley, New York, 1960).

21. The genotype–phenotype correlation is generally expressed as the square root of the heritability of a characteristic in a given population ($p_{pg} = \sqrt{h^2}$).

22. H. Strandskov and E. Edelen, *Genetics* **31,** 438 (1946).

23. S. G. Vandenberg, quoted in C. Burt (*2*).

24. F. Sandon, *Brit, J. Statist. Psychol.* **12,** 133 (1959).

25. T. Husen, *Psychological Twin Research* (Almquist and Wiksele, Stockholm, 1959).

26. Of the 124 pairs in special classes, one or both members of 99 pairs were enrolled in "retarded educable" and "retarded trainable" classes. The racial distribution of the "retarded" twins was 80 percent black and 20 percent white, which represents a 15 percent discrepancy from the racial distribution of twins in the public schools. The exclusion of "retarded" twins attenuates the sample and restricts the conclusions of the study to children in normal classrooms.

27. Aptitude tests used in this study are Primary Mental Abilities (2nd grade): *verbal meaning, perceptual speed, *number facility, spatial relations, and *total; Lorge–Thorndike Intelligence Tests (4th grade): *verbal, *nonverbal, and *total; Academic Promise Tests (6th grade): abstract reasoning, numerical, *nonverbal total, language usage, verbal, *verbal total, and *total; Differential Abilities Tests (8th grade): *verbal reasoning, *numerical ability, abstract reasoning, space relations, mechanical reasoning, clerical speed and accuracy, language usage, and *total (scholastic aptitude); School and College Ability Tests (10th grade): *verbal, *quantitative, and *total; Test of Academic Progress (12th grade): *verbal, *numerical, and *total. Achievement tests used are Iowa Tests of Basic Skills (3rd through 8th grades): *vocabulary, *reading comprehension, *language total, work-study skills, *arithmetic total, and *composite (average of five scores). Asterisks indicate scores reported.

28. H. Stevenson, A. Friedrichs, W. Simpson, *Child Develop.* **41,** 625 (1970).

29. O. Buros, Ed. *The Sixth Mental Measurements Yearbook* (Gryphon Press, Highland Park, N.J., 1965).

30. J. Stanley, *Science* **171**, 640 (1971).
31. A. Jensen, *Proc. Nat. Acad. Sci. U.S.* **58**, 149 (1967).
32. My gratitude to Prof. V. Elving Anderson and Dr. Paul Nichols for suggesting this analysis.
33. S. Wiseman, in *Genetic and Environmental Factors in Human Ability*, J. Meade and A. Parkes, Eds. (Oliver and Boyd, London, 1966), pp. 64–80.
34. C. Burt, *Brit. J. Educ. Psychol.* **13**, 83 (1943).
35. S. Irvine, *J. Biosoc. Sci.* **1**, (Suppl.), 91 (1969).
36. S. Houston, *Child Develop.* **41**, 947 (1970); F. Williams, in *Language and Poverty*, F. Williams, Ed. (Markham, Chicago, 1970). pp. 1–10; C. Cazden, *ibid.*, pp. 81–101.
37. U. S. Commission on Civil Rights, *Racial Isolation in the Public Schools* (Government Printing Office, Washington, D.C., 1967).
38. D. Freedman, in *Progress in Human Behavior Genetics*, S. G. Vandenburg, Ed. (Johns Hopkins Press, Baltimore, 1968), pp. 1–5.
39. J. B. S. Haldane, *Ann. Eugen.* **13**, 197 (1946).

Comments and Replies

IQ: METHODOLOGICAL
AND OTHER ISSUES*

COMMENTS

In the United States, the average IQ of blacks is 85 rather than 100. A number of investigators—most notably Jensen and Eysenck, on whose writings Scarr-Salapatek comments in her book review (Chapter I-2 in this volume), and Scarr-Salapatek herself (Chapter II-3 in this volume)—have attempted to determine the degree to which this discrepancy is due to (i) *genetic differences* between blacks and whites or (ii) the racist nature of U.S. society. The degree of genetic contribution cannot be determined directly by methods based on assuming a non-systematic relationship between genes and environment, or on sorting out genetic and environmental influences within groups, because it is clear that racial discrimination in the United States has led to a confounding of black genes with an environment not conducive to intellectual development. In Scarr-Salapatek's words (p. 189),

> If all black children are disadvantaged to an unknown degree by being reared as blacks in a white-dominated society, and no white children are so disadvantaged, it is impossible to estimate genetic and environmental variances between the races.

and (p. 69),

*The following comments by Dawes; Willerman; Calloway; Hubbard; Powers; Eysenck; and Shucard and reply by Scarr-Salapatek originally appeared in *Science*, 1972, *178*, 229–240. Copyright © 1972 by the American Association for the Advancement of Science. Reprinted by permission.

> Direct comparisons of estimated within-group heritabilities and the calculation of between-group heritabilities require assumptions [about environmental effects] that few investigators are willing to make. . . .

Instead, in her book review she proposes some "indirect approaches" [*see next letter*]; and her own study describes still another way of exploring the source of racial differences in IQ—a method based on comparing correlation coefficients. The purpose of this letter is both to raise a question about specific findings in her study and to point out a common problem with studies based on the comparison of correlation coefficients.

Scarr-Salapatek derives estimates of the heritability of IQ in blacks and in whites, in upper and lower classes, on the basis of the degree to which the correlation of IQ between same-sex twins differs from that between opposite-sex twins, and examines whether the results are better predicted by an "environmental-disadvantage" model or a "genetic-differences" model (pp. 188–189):

> To the extent that the *same* environmental factors are assumed to affect the development of IQ in the same way in both black and white populations, predictions can be made about the sources of racial differences in mean IQ scores. If certain biological deprivations (such as low weight at birth, poor nutrition) are known to be more prevalent in lower class groups of both populations and more prevalent among blacks than whites, then the two models can make differential predictions about the effects of these sources of environmental variance on the proportion of genetic variance in each population. Given a larger proportion of disadvantaged children within the black group, the environmental disadvantage hypothesis must predict smaller proportions of genetic variance to account for differences in phenotypic IQ among blacks than among whites, as whole populations. Since the genotype distribution hypothesis predicts no differences in the proportion of genetic variance for social class groups within the races, it should predict the same proportions of genetic variance in the two races.

She appears to interpret her findings as supportive of a smaller proportion of genetic variance among blacks than among whites. But the proportions she obtains are highly questionable.

Twelve heritabilities are evaluated. Each combination of test (verbal, nonverbal, and total) by race (black, white), by social class (below median, and middle and above median) yields an estimate of heritability based on the difference between the correlation between same-sex twins and that between opposite-sex twins. Yet in 5 of the 12 instances heritability "cannot be estimated"—because the correlation between the IQ's of opposite-sex twins is higher than that between same-sex twins! If genetic disposition determines phenotypic intelligence to *any* extent, opposite-sex twins—all of whom are dizygotic—simply cannot have more similar IQ's than do same-sex twins, some of whom are monozygotic. The finding that in virtually half the contexts studied there is a higher correlation between opposite-sex twins sheds severe doubt on the degree to which the correlations that Scarr-Salapatek computes are representative of the population from which she sampled. Since the sample values do not perfectly reflect the population values of the correlation coefficients, statistical tests to determine the significance of the differences between the correlations would be desirable. (Testing the differences between the correlations for the same-sex twins and for the opposite-sex twins by a method proposed by Fisher (1) reveals that there are no significant differences; however, this does not test differences between dizygotic and monozygotic correlations, because some same-sex twins are dizygotic.)

But suppose the differences were statistically reliable. Could we then conclude that blacks have lower heritability than do whites? Could we not equally well conclude that the heritability of intelligence is equal for blacks and for whites, and that the particular tests she used were simply more precise indices of intelligence for whites than for blacks? The point is that the value of a correlation between any two variables will be dependent on the precision with which they are measured—the greater the precision, the higher the absolute value of the correlation. (Of course, it is always possible to take a nominalist position and maintain that variables are synonymous with the techniques devised to assess them—that "intelligence is whatever an intelligence test measures"—but then any question about race, social class, and intelligence must be phrased in terms of a specific test and interest in the answer diminishes rapidly.) Much the same objection may be raised to "genetic" interpretations of Skodak and Skeels's (2) finding that IQ's of adopted children are more highly correlated with those of their natural parents than with those of their adoptive parents; an alternative interpretation is that the IQ of the adoptive parent is simply a weaker measure of environmental enrichment than the IQ of the natural parent is of genetic disposition. Or consider Astin's (3) often-quoted assertion that students' innate ability is a more important determinant of scholastic achievement than is college environment; his measure of student intellectual endowment was a very carefully devised measure based on years of refinement, one meant specifically to correlate with academic achievement; on the other hand his measures of educational environment—as extensive as they were—were to a large extent ad hoc and only tangentially related to important psychological and phenomenological differences between colleges. It is therefore not at all surprising to find that the intellectual input measures correlate more highly with the academic output measures than do the environmental measures.

In short, conclusions based on correlational measures—and differences between correlations—must be evaluated in terms of (i) the statistical reliability of the correlation coefficients and (ii) the precision with which the variables involved in the correlations are measured—that is, the extent to which the numbers are valid indices of the target phenomena. While the main criticisms in this note are of Scarr-Salapatek's failure to take into account these two factors, she is by no means alone. I hope that other people who wish to investigate or interpret correlational studies of race, social class, and intelligence will take them into account.

The assertion that the discrepancy between the average white and average black IQ in the United States is due in some part to genetic differences is equivalent to the assertion that if there were no differences in the environments of whites and blacks there would still be a difference in their average intelligence. It may not be productive to examine this assertion with correlational studies of samples drawn from United States society as it exists. Perhaps a better method would be to attempt experimental evaluation of how IQ differences would change if in fact the environments of blacks and whites were equivalent. In other words, the best way to settle this controversy might be to eliminate racism.

REFERENCES AND NOTES

1. R. A. Fisher, *Statistical Methods for Research Workers* (Oliver & Boyd, Edinburgh, 1925, 1958).
2. M. Skodak and H. M. Skeels, *J. Genet. Psychol.* **75,** 85 (1949).
3. A. W. Astin, *Science* **161,** 661 (1968).
4. I thank my colleagues at Oregon Research Institute, especially the "Judgment Group" and William Chaplin and Daniel Kahneman in particular, for their interest in and insights about the problem discussed in this letter.

ROBYN M. DAWES
Oregon Research Institute,
P. O. Box 3196, Eugene 97403,
and *Department of Psychology,*
University of Oregon, Eugene

. . . I want to take issue with the two research designs which, in her thoughtful book review, Scarr-Salapatek suggests for helping to solve the riddle of genetic and environmental influences on intellectual functioning.

One of her proposed solutions is to take advantage of the fact that there are racial differences in gene frequencies for various blood groups. By correlating the "degree of white admixture and IQ scores *within* the black group," she hopes to separate the genetic and environmental components in the IQ scores of blacks.

Aside from the formidabile difficulties of making statistically independent the visible (such as skin color) from the nonvisible (blood group), the results of such a study are likely to be ambiguous regardless of outcome. If we assume only positive assortative mating for intelligence, an intelligent black would have increased probability of mating with a white partner. Their 50 percent admixed child could have a high IQ for either genetic or environmental reasons—that is, because of the high admixture or because of being reared in a family with an intelligent parent who provides a favorable environment.

The second proposed solution is based on the notion that "regression effects can be predicted to differ for blacks and whites if the two races indeed have genetically different population means." Thus, according to the author's interpretation, if high IQ black parents had children whose IQ's showed greater regression than the offspring of white parents of equally high IQ, it could be because the black children are regressing back to the black population mean which is below the population mean for the whites.

On the contrary, results of this sort would be precisely the opposite of what would be predicted genetically and, if anything, would be suggestive of lower heritability for IQ among blacks. The "population mean" is irrelevant for the actual genetic makeup of high IQ parents, whether black or white, and their children would be expected to fall at the midparent average. The fact that regression commonly occurs is typically due to the *nonheritable* components of the trait and to chance failures to reproduce in the children unusually good genetic interactions that each parent was fortunate enough to have.

The last point I wish to raise concerns the limits of population-genetic methodologies alone to solve the problem of racial differences in IQ. Acknowledging that genetic influences play a role in intellectual functioning means, in fact, acknowledging that biochemical products are related to IQ. Whether heritability is ultimately 0.01 or 1.00, the solution will come when we learn the functional relationships between these gene products and intellectual functioning. When the quantity or quality of these biochemical products can be related to intelligence regardless of race, we will have made real progress.

LEE WILLERMAN
Department of Psychology,
University of Texas, Austin 78712

After 40 years in science and 30 years in medicine as a black scientist, I can say without any equivocation that scientists are no more bigoted than the general public, but neither are they less so. The excellent book review by Scarr-Salapatek brings to mind some seldom-discussed aspects of the controversy over black-versus-white achievement often referred to in a trite fashion as IQ equivalence. . . .

Since race represents a social class in America, unfortunately, those who are identified as blacks are relegated to a social situation that by its nature forces them into an inferior position. This cannot be denied, since racism is the strongest social force in America. All aspects of democracy take a second place to it. Witness the remark of Senator Muskie that a black could not be elected vice president of the United States.

Thus the lower social class finds difficulty in producing individuals that can reach high achievement levels, since they carry their badge of identification, like the scarlet letter A, always with them. It is impossible to test IQ in the newborn. By the time the child reaches the age at which he can be tested reliably, he has already absorbed imprints of cultural inferiority. The black child is taught from birth that he has no chance, he has no opportunity. He is taught that such things as haste only work for the white man, and therefore the black should slow down. It is not possible, therefore, to equate blacks and whites on the basis of income or educational background. The black child basically is taught to see things, hear things, and say nothing. He is taught that successful competition will be met by physical damage, embarrassment, failure of recognition, or ridicule. Therefore timed examinations are meaningless for most ghetto children and indeed after 6 or 7 years of age the child is so deeply imbued with the concept of the hopelessness of the situation that the vast majority could not care less about competitive intellectual pursuits.

Unfortunately, these children have heard discussions of such trivia as have been written by Jensen and Eysenck, discussions which ignore all complexities and blame everything on some unidentified, mysterious African gene. In medicine, a defect in ideation in which the individual sets out with a false premise and then collects all data relevant or irrelevant to prove a point is known as paranoia. . . .

It is rather remarkable that an entire language has been developed by American blacks that American whites never hear. This is the ability, produced and nurtured by the necessity of slave communication, to use the English language in such a fashion that it is unintelligible except to those who thoroughly understand. This has been spoken of as ghetto language. It is not really that. It has existed ever since the black was brought to America. I find that when necessary in class I can talk with double meanings, those for the whites, who hear what I say in English, and those for the blacks, who hear what I say in the underground language. The words are exactly the same, and of course are spoken but once. Certainly the scientist of the IQ argument would deny that the white students are stupid because they do not have the ability to understand all that is really being said!

N. O. CALLOWAY
1103 Regent Street,
Madison, Wisconsin 53715

Though Scarr-Salapatek considers in her review many of the social implications of the current IQ controversy, she does not mention the one that to me seems most important: whether our society should continue to set such great store by those attributes that are conveniently measured by IQ tests.

The kinds of verbal and mathematical problem-solving skills that make some people score well on such tests constitute only part of our human repertory. The IQ tests ignore much in us that is artistic, contemplative, and nonverbal. They were constructed to predict success in the kinds of schools that have prevailed in Europe and the United States. Many of us have been losing faith in what these schools have done to us and are currently doing to our children. Yet we continue to accept the notion that IQ tests measure qualities we like to see developed in our children.

I should like to see a better analysis, not of the heritability of IQ but of what qualities it measures, so that we can decide whether we want to go on stressing and encouraging them.

RUTH HUBBARD
Biological Laboratories,
Harvard University,
Cambridge, Massachusetts 02138

The debate over the meaning of racial differences in test scores continues still (I believe) without an attack on the basic moral question: Is it not a perversion of statistics to apply mass measures to individuals? I would like to ask those who are qualified to do so to consider the uses of statistical tests—not just in terms of within-group or between-group variances but in terms of game theory.

A psychological testing service never promises to evaluate each individual correctly. Whether the results are used by employers, schools, or therapists, some degree of accuracy less than 100 percent is considered worth the effort—and the fee. That is because organizations evaluate their own achievements statistically. If the testing service improves the record over the long run, the service is worth x dollars per individual tested.

On the other hand, the individual who is being tested does not have a variance and a mean. He has only the properties he has, in his own individual mix. When he undergoes a test, he is exposed to a certain risk of being misevaluated and thus either being denied a lucrative position within his capacities or being placed in a position where he will suffer the consequences of conspicuous failure. Such misevaluations carry penalties that must be weighed against the risk.

It would be highly pertinent, therefore, to investigate the payoff matrix for this "game." Perhaps this approach would provide a common language in which well-intentioned individuals on both sides of the race–IQ question, and many similar debates, could reach an acceptable compromise on what is ethically "right." One of our (hypothetical) national ideals is to respect individual rights before the rights of artificial entities such as corporations or governments, yet we all recognize that certain organizations must have some rights for the common good. Any approach that tends toward a solution of this conflict would be preferable to ignoring science or ignoring individual rights—which all too often seems to be the choice that is presented.

WILLIAM T. POWERS
1138 Whitfield Road,
Northbrook, Illinois 60062

... Scarr-Salapatek in her review of my book *The IQ Argument* states as an example of my "inaccurate statements" that "Eysenck thinks evoked potentials offer a better measure of 'innate' intelligence than IQ tests. But on what basis?" She then quotes a study by F. B. Davis (*1*), published after my book was written, to the effect that "no evidence was found that the latency periods obtained . . . displayed serviceable utility for predicting school performance or level of mental ability." As a matter of simple fact, I never stated (or thought) that evoked potentials offered a better measure of intelligence than IQ tests; I said that "it may become possible, in due course, to measure intelligence in . . . physiological terms." I added: "This is already possible to some extent," referring to a well-known figure taken from a paper by Ertl and Schafer (*2*). They found correlations of around .4 between IQ tests and evoked potential latencies; we repeated their experiment and obtained similar results. I did not then, nor do I now, claim that such physiological measurements display *serviceable utility* for predicting school performance. . . .

REFERENCES

1. F. B. Davis, *The Measurement of Mental Capacity through Evoked-Potential Recordings* (Educational Records Bureau, Greenwich, Conn., 1971).
2. J. P. Ertl and E. W. P. Schafer, *Nature* **223**, 421 (1969).

H. J. EYSENCK
Institute of Psychiatry, DeCrespigny
Park. Denmark Hill, London, S.E.5

... A number of investigations (*1*) have found statistically significant correlations between evoked potential measures and human intelligence measures, generally fluctuating between .2 and .5. These findings have been replicated in a number of different laboratories. Scarr-Salapatek's reliance on the Davis report . . . , in view of the preponderance of evidence to the contrary, does not do the issue justice. At present I believe it is fair to conclude that there is a weak but reliable relationship between certain evoked potential measures and measures of human intelligence. Whether the evoked potential is a better index of "innate" intelligence than IQ tests is yet to be answered, and indeed depends entirely on one's definition of intelligence (2).

REFERENCES AND NOTES

1. J. Ertl and E. W. P. Schafer, *Nature* **223**, 421 (1969); A. Plum, thesis, University of Florida (1969); G. Galbraith, J. B. Gliddon, J. Bush, *Am. J. Ment. Defic.* **75**, 341 (1970); D. W. Shucard and J. L. Horn, *J. Comp. Physiol. Psychol.* **78**, 59 (1972).
2. I thank Robert Kinsman for his helpful comments.

DAVID W. SHUCARD
Department of Behavioral Science,
National Jewish Hospital,
Denver, Colorado 80106, and
Department of Psychiatry, University
of Colorado Medical Center, Denver

REPLY

Before replying directly to any of the preceding letters, I feel compelled to assert my cherished beliefs in human virtues other than high IQ, in the value of human diversity, in racial and economic justice, and in the essential goodness of man (as a species, of course). I am also in favor of additional research on any problem, including evoked potentials, test item bias, the use of psychological tests, and various human characteristics of a nonintellective nature.

I am against overgeneralizing the results of any one study, particularly mine. The limits of generalizability should not exceed similar populations, similar group aptitude tests, and similar points in time. And replications (or failures thereof) are essential before firm conclusions can be drawn on matters of population differences in the heritability of IQ.

Some Methodological Questions

Dawes's letter makes three major criticisms of my article "Race, social class, and IQ": (i) that the heritability coefficients obtained for the black and the white disadvantaged and advantaged groups are statistically unreliable; (ii) that the correlation coefficients are probably not representative of the populations sampled; (iii) that the aptitude tests given by the schools are more precise measures of IQ for whites than for blacks, and that the lower intraclass correlations obtained for black children result from the imprecision of aptitude measurement in that group.

In connection with his first point, Dawes correctly notes that heritabilities could not be calculated for five of the six scores in the disadvantaged groups (both black and white) because the same-sex coefficient did not exceed the opposite-sex correlation. (In no case did the opposite-sex coefficient significantly exceed the same-sex coefficient.) In cases where the same-sex did exceed the opposites-sex correlation, estimated monozygotic correlations were calculated, and from the comparison of these estimates with obtained dizygotic (opposite-sex) correlations heritability estimates were made. (Since blood-group information was not available, zygosity could not be determined directly.)

Statistical tests of the differences between estimated MZ and obtained DZ coefficients could have been calculated by Fisher's method, but I hesitated to guess what the standard error of an *estimated* intraclass correlation coefficient might be. I know of no established statistical technique for calculating the reliability of an estimated coefficient. Dawes's calculation of the significance of differences between the obtained same- and opposite-sex correlations is practically meaningless, since about half the same-sex group was estimated to be DZ pairs. Such a comparison is too dilute a test of any genetic differences hypothesis, depending upon very large sample sizes to yield $r_{DZ} + {}_{MZ} > r_{DZ}$.

If we ignore, for a moment, the problem of unknown reliability in estimated MZ correlations, the pattern of significant results is just what I said it was: the advantaged groups had significantly higher MZ than DZ correlations, and the disadvantaged groups did not. Four of the six estimated MZ correlations significantly exceed the DZ coefficients in the advantaged groups of both races, while none of the differences between MZ and DZ correlations were significant in the disadvantaged groups. This pattern of findings does not depend on relative sample sizes in the social-class groups since black disadvantaged pairs comprise the largest group, for whom no MZ:DZ comparison even approached significance.

Dawes can certainly disagree with my interpretation of the results, although I gather that he too prefers an environmental disadvantage hypothesis. More secure conclusions must depend on further studies of genotypic expression in phenotypes that develop under a variety of racial and social-class environments.

Dawes's second criticism is that the obtained correlation coefficients may not be representative of the population of black and white twins from which I sampled. One basis of his doubt is his belief that "genetic disposition determines phenotypic intelligence" to such an extent that it should manifest itself in all social-class and racial environments. Unfortunately, this argument assumes the hypothesis to be tested, that is, that in various populations genetic differences are expressed to the same extent in the phenotypic correlations of MZ and DZ twins. One cannot reject empirical results because they contradict one's assumptions. Perhaps we can agree that genes must program phenotypic development to a considerable extent, but the issue here is the expression of genotypic differences, not genetic determinism.

The obtained correlations could be unrepresentative of the twin populations in several ways. First, the 992 pairs of twins could be unrepresentative of the twin populations from which they were sampled. A total of 247 pairs were lost because scores were unavailable (123 pairs) and because one or both members were in special classes (124 pairs). Certainly the low-aptitude end of the distribution was lost, and results on the 992 pairs must be limited to the population of children in normal classrooms. As for the other 123 pairs who had no scores, one can only caution that the sample represents 89 rather than 100 percent of the regular public school twin population between 7 and 18 years of age.

A second possible source of unrepresentativeness lies in the correlation coefficients themselves, as sampled from a universe of coefficients that could be obtained from the same tests on the same populations at other points in time. Since the analyses were done on only one sample of tests, it is impossible to show empirically how reliable the coefficients are in representing possible results. The magnitude of the sample, however, increases the probability of obtaining similar results on other occasions.

Third, the pattern of results in the disadvantaged groups seems unrepresentative of the general twin study literature, which always reports higher MZ than DZ correlations for measures of intelligence. At least three possible explanations occur to me: first, no other study has specifically dealt with genetic variance in the IQ scores of lower-class twins, and therefore there are no other studies with which to compare this one; second, heritability studies of IQ with no results are not published; and, third, the results of my study have more limited generalizability than Dawes thinks I impute to them.

The first point is simply true to my knowledge. There are no other reports of genetic variance in the IQ scores of disadvantaged groups. The second point is true in nearly all fields; there are few published reports of null results unless a major theoretical point is at issue. I, for one, obtained the same correlation (.61) for blood-grouped MZ and DZ twins on an individually administered test of nonverbal IQ and did not submit the results for publication (because no one would believe that MZ twins were not more similar than DZ twins, there were only 60 pairs, and so on).

The third point of self-criticism is more serious: How generalizable to other measures are the results of a study whose scores were obtained from teacher-administered group tests of scholastic aptitude? Dawes believes that if questions of race, social class, and IQ must be phrased in terms of specific tests, then interest in the answers diminishes rapidly. I am far more conservative than that. In behavior genetic studies, results are always specific to the measures, the population, and a point in time. I tried extensively to explain the composition of the tests, precisely in order to limit the generalizability of any results to teacher-administered group tests, of Philadelphia children (or at most children in an Eastern urban area) in 1969 (maybe 1968 and 1970 as well).

Does the specificity of the results cause most people to lose interest in them? Perhaps. That is a matter of personal taste. I am tempted to caution patience until more results are available from which to generalize. The fact is that millions of school children are given group intelligence tests yearly, and decisions about their futures are made on the basis of their scores. I would suggest that information on the (low) proportion of genetic variance in the (low) scores of disadvantaged urban children may be encouraging to those who would act to improve their educational environments and their aptitude scores. Interest in the results of this and similar studies is probably greater than Dawes suggests.

Validity of IQ Tests

Dawes's third major criticism raises the question of whether "the particular tests she used were simply more precise indices of intelligence for whites than for blacks." The issue of precision can refer to the statistical measurement characteristics of the tests or to more metaphysical concerns with what IQ tests "really" measure in various populations. I dealt with measurement validity by correlating aptitude test scores with criterion tests of academic achievement. The results, as reported in table 4, showed similar correlations for the two racial groups and for the social-class groups within each race. (Only the white below-median group had somewhat lower correlations between aptitude and achievement scores.) Many would like to claim that the low average IQ scores of disadvantaged children result from measurement invalidity, but I find no support whatsoever in my data for this assertion. The fact is that children who score poorly on aptitude tests also tend to score poorly on achievement tests, as is to be expected when the criteria for successful performance are so similar.

Distress over low aptitude scores comes primarily, I think, from the erroneous belief that IQ tests measure a fixed level of "native intelligence" (a slippery construct if there ever was one). IQ tests are a sample of problem-solving behavior and cultural knowledge at a specific point of time. They are simply indicators of current levels of performance on intellectual tasks designed to predict to similar criterion situations in school, jobs, and the like. One could argue that IQ scores *ought* to show heritable differences in all populations because the lack of heritability indicates either a less-than-optimum expression of genotypes in phenotypes or a social environment that is less relevant for the development of important skills. I suggested both these explanations in the discussion section.

An expansion of the cultural differences argument may speak to the issue of test precision. If the content of the test items is inappropriate for some children because they speak a different language, or if the test situation is inhibiting, then one could argue that the "precision" of the test is reduced. Cross-cultural studies

(*1*) often search for culturally appropriate methods, materials, and settings in which to test intellectual behavior. The goal is to estimate intellectual competence, which can be inferred from behaviors in any setting that optimizes performance.

There are severe limitations to what can be learned from the different-test strategy, as there are in the same-test strategy. The use of different tests in every group, or with every child, makes comparisons of performance by different children and groups very difficult. The use of the same test in every group, and with every child, makes inferences about what the test measures very difficult. These two strategies represent two profoundly different approaches to the study of intelligence.

The most important contrasts, I think, between cognitive-developmental approaches to intelligence and psychometric ones are that (i) the former concern themselves with the stage-sequence model of development with little attention to individual variation from the modal pattern, whereas the latter concern themselves particularly with the distribution of individual differences; (ii) the former attempt to explain qualitative changes in intelligence over time, the latter seek to minimize qualitative changes in favor of predicting consistent levels of intelligence over time; (iii) the former are incidentally concerned with rate of acquisition and speed of performance, the latter are primarily concerned with these aspects of intelligent behavior, especially as they relate to school achievement. The more sophisticated psychometric people know that much of the consistency in the rank order of children's scores over time rests on (i) the consistency of both their genotypes and their environments (which if poor when the children are four years old are likely to be poor when they are ten) and on (ii) nonintellective aspects of performance.

From a psychometric point of view, nonintellective factors are all part of performance on IQ tests, as they are of performance in school. From a cognitive-developmental point of view, intellectual organization is conceptually distinct from situational and personal factors which may detract from performance. Thus, cognitive-developmental measures are usually given repeatedly, with varied materials, and under the best possible conditions to elicit the child's optimum performance. IQ tests are typically timed and given in a stereotyped and impersonal manner. The contrast in administration rests not on the sadism of psychometricians but on the predictive validity that can be achieved by standard conditions approximating traditional academic conditions. To the extent that academic and occupational performance in this society are better predicted by IQ tests, they remain important measures of "effective intelligence." Even if adequate cognitive competencies can be shown to exist in nontest situations, the intellectual performance of some children may still be deficient in socially important settings like jobs and schools.

One conclusion that might be drawn is that schools should be changed to give every child an optimum setting in which to use his cognitive competence; for example, rate of acquisition should be de-emphasized, varied modes of learning should be available, criterion measures of progress should be given priority, and everyone should appreciate the blessings of diverse talents. In that case cognitive-developmental measures might be better predictors of achievement. If cognitive-developmental measures could be constructed within a more rigorous psychometric frame, then their theory base would make them infinitely preferable to the empirically selected items of present IQ tests. If a child passed items at a given level of cognitive development, then we might be able to predict which skills he could be helped to develop next.

A related point, and an extremely important one, has been raised by Kagan (2). Can we not assume that almost all children are able to learn the basic skills that society seems to require? Reading at a fourth-grade level, elementary arithmetic, and a complete grasp of concrete operational thought should be within the ability of 98 percent of the population. Yet many children do not acquire these minimum skills either at home or in school. There seems to be no excuse for the failure of any but defective children to reach minimum performance levels.

Indirect Approaches to Racial Studies

Willerman criticizes the two indirect approaches to the study of racial differences: the admixture and regression methods, which were proposed in my book review.

The admixture approach, he says, will probably yield ambiguous results because of a sizable covariance between high degrees of Caucasian admixture and the provision of good rearing environments. In the rare case which he cites of a contemporary interracial mating, disentangling social-environmental factors from genetic ones is difficult but possible. Children with one white parent could vary in admixture from 50 to more than 90 percent, because the black parent is unlikely to have total African ancestry. The children of interracial matings are, however, a socially different population from the children of two black parents, even though they fall within the same admixture distribution. One could meet Willerman's objections by correlating variations in admixture, skin color, and IQ within the population of interracial children, but their numbers are so few and the range of admixture variation so restricted that the study would be less valuable than a similar study of children with two black parents.

Let us look at the other 99 percent of the children socially defined as black. Their degrees of white admixture can vary from less than 10 percent to more than 90 percent even though both parents call themselves black. The children will vary in serological estimates of admixture, in skin color, and in IQ scores; it is not a difficult statistical problem to intercorrelate three linear variables partialing out one at a time.

One could still argue, as Willerman suggests, that higher degrees of white admixture in children may covary with better rearing environments, and that good environments, not admixture, may produce higher IQ scores. The hypothesized covariance is subject to empirical test. Within the contemporary black population, the slogan "Black is beautiful" connotes a far greater acceptance of black heritage than was true some years ago. I am not at all sure that higher-IQ blacks tend to marry whites or only light-skinned blacks.

In any case, a control for the effects of family-rearing environments can be provided. An interesting test of the genetic hypothesis on admixture could be made on within-family variation, using DZ twins. Members of a DZ pair may vary in skin color, IQ scores, and serological estimates of admixture; they vary little in rearing environments.

From a genetic point of view, partialing out the correlation (if any) between skin color and IQ from the correlation (if any) between serological admixture and IQ can result in the loss of some genetic variance as well as environmental effects. Skin color is not only a visible marker for social discrimination, but also an independent genetic marker for admixture. Thus, the first method proposed to study racial differences in IQ is fairly conservative and unambiguous, I think. Its feasibility depends on the constantly increasing number of blood loci for which population differences between African and European populations are known. I was not advocating its feasibility so much as its logic.

Regarding the second indirect method I proposed, Willerman is correct in stating that regression from parent to offspring results from nonheritable portions of variance in IQ, or any trait. But he errs in his interpretation of different regression effects in the two racial groups at the two ends of the IQ distribution.

First, I specifically cited the need for regression to be calculated at the high *and low* ends of the IQ distribution. It is essential that the offspring of parents of equal midparent IQ's in the two racial groups be compared above and below the observed population mean. Second, I assumed that the heritabilities of IQ scores in the two racial groups would have been calculated, because without them the formulas for predicting regression effects are not soluble. I also assumed that the assortative mating coefficient was known.

The prediction of the null hypothesis is that no differences in regression will be found between blacks and whites at any point in the IQ curve. The null hypothesis could be rejected in several ways.

First, the heritabilities for IQ could differ in the two populations, so that regression effects from parent to offspring would be greater both above and below the empirical population mean in one or the other racial group (Fig. 1:

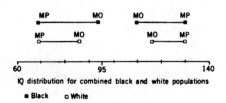

FIG. 1. A hypothetical regression of midoffspring (*MO*) IQ from midparent (*MP*) IQ in black and white populations where heritabilities are unequal.

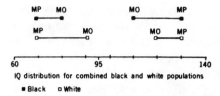

FIG. 2. A hypothetical regression of midoffspring (*MO*) IQ from midparent (*MP*) IQ in black and white populations where heritabilities are equal.

since the more likely hypothesis is that heritabilities are somewhat lower in the black than in the white population, that is the one illustrated). The result shown would indicate lower heritability in the black population but a similar population mean. Other charts could be drawn to indicate unequal regression and unequal population means.

Second, the heritabilities for IQ could be approximately equal in the two racial groups but the regression effects could be unequal both above and below the population mean (Fig. 2). Since regression effects are greater at the extremes of a distribution, this result would indicate that similar midparent IQ's represent different points on the IQ distributions of the respective populations. The most likely interpretation of these results is that the two populations have different means. The different means, as hypothesized in Fig. 2, would suggest genetic racial differences, in part for the reason Willerman gives: "chance failures to reproduce in the children unusually good [or bad] genetic interactions that each parent was fortunate [or unfortunate] enough to have."

It is possible, however, to interpret Fig. 2 as showing exclusively environmental effects. To the extent that racial discrimination and the multiple disadvantages of minority group status affect the development of IQ, high-IQ black parents can be said to be less able than whites of comparable IQ to give their children favorable rearing conditions. Similarly, low-IQ black parents may give their offspring an even less favorable environment than equally low-IQ white parents give theirs. Thus, the regression effects observed to be greater at the high-IQ end for blacks and at the low-IQ end for whites could be the result of complex and unquantified environmental differences between the groups. The environmental explanation lacks the parsimony of simple genetic principles like independent assortment, but may be true nonetheless.

Many other models of regression effects for the two racial groups could be suggested, but these are illustrative of possible results. I am led by additional thought to conclude that the results of regression studies, while interesting, are probably ambiguous when considered apart from other data. Only acceptance of the null hypothesis of no differences in regression would be an unambiguous outcome.

In his last paragraph Willerman touches on an extremely important point that is often misunderstood. The study of genetic differences is not the study of genetic determination. Studies of genetic differences ask questions about genetic and environmental contributions to *variance* among us, without respect to known gene loci and specific gene action pathways. Studies of genetic determination can ask questions about the links between gene loci, biochemical pathways, anatomy, and behavior, without respect to variation among us. As Willerman suggests, knowledge of biochemical pathways to brain development is crucial, presumably because such knowledge will lead to effective treatment for retardation and other intellectual problems. Studies of genetic differences cannot supply this information.

REFERENCES

1. For example, M. Cole, J. Gay, J. Glick, D. Sharp, *The Cultural Context of Learning and Thinking* (Basic Books, New York, 1972).
2. J. S. Kagan, *Harvard Educ. Rev.* **39**, 126 (1969).

SANDRA SCARR-SALAPATEK
Institute of Child Development,
University of Minnesota, Minneapolis

HERITABILITY OF IQ BY SOCIAL CLASS: EVIDENCE INCONCLUSIVE*

COMMENTS

In her provocative article on race and intelligence (*1*), Scarr-Salapatek may give the mistaken impression that "two major, competing hypotheses," or some combination of them, are the only plausible explanations of the relation among social class, race, and IQ (intelligence quotient). Either (i) racial differences in intelligence result from environmental disadvantage that simultaneously retards mental development and prevents full expression of genetic differences or (ii) racial differences reflect genetic differences that contribute a similar proportion of variance in all social classes. Scarr-Salapatek attempts to exclude the second hypothesis and thereby, perhaps, to strengthen the environmental explanation of race differences.

It is sometimes supposed that an optimum environment will result in maximum expression of genetic factors, but the fallacy of this view becomes apparent when one asks, "Optimum for what?" or "Expression of which genetic factors?" Different environments elicit the expression of different sets of genes.

*The following comments by Allen & Pettigrew; and Erlenmeyer-Kimling & Stern and reply by Scarr-Salapatek originally appeared in *Science,* 1973, *182*, 1042–1047. Copyright © 1973 by the American Association for the Advancement of Science. Reprinted by permission.

Scarr-Salapatek's restriction of explanations to two models tends, albeit unintentionally, to affirm the above fallacious view and to perpetuate the widespread idea that genetic factors set limits on an individual's potential, while the environment determines how closely he will approach these limits. Neither heredity nor environment sets absolute limits on quantitative traits.

If we discard simplistic formulations, many more than two models have to be considered in any attempt to understand racial and class differences in intelligence. A complete and testable model should predict at least three things: the effect of socioeconomic environment on intelligence test scores, the relative magnitude of the phenotypic (total) variance in different classes, and class differences in the proportion of that variance which is genetic (heritability in the broad sense). Scarr-Salapatek's two models make very simple predictions: Either favorable environments increase the mean, the variance, and the heritability of intelligence or environments do not significantly affect intelligence at all.

Another hypothesis that might be as easy to test is that environmental advantages increase the mean and variance of intelligence, while reducing its heritability. Different favorable conditions might provide people with different mental skills almost independently of their genetic endowment, and the genetic endowment would be expressed most distinctly in basic or deprived cultures. However, if disadvantaged monozygotic twins are no more similar in intelligence than Scarr-Salapatek has estimated, we must agree with her that "genetic factors cannot be seen as strong determinants of aptitude scores in the disadvantaged groups" (1, p. 1292). One might then modify this hypothesis or look at a few others.

Several models could be proposed in which lower-class environments, more than upper-class environments, contain diverse stimuli that produce deviations from an individual's "most probable" IQ. The diversity and magnitude of stresses in some economically deprived groups are formidable, and, unlike chronic deprivation, stresses may have positive behavioral consequences (2). If some stresses in a lower-class environment produce positive, and others negative, deviations in intelligence, this could account for its low heritability in low socioeconomic classes. Particular models would further specify whether a low mean IQ in these social classes reflected cultural impoverishment or economic selection, and what effect either phenomenon might have on variance. One such particular model would invoke the effects of stress in a lower-class environment to modify the hypothesis, proposed in the preceding paragraph, that environmental advantages tend to lower the heritability of intelligence.

These hypotheses are all more complicated than the two discussed by Scarr-Salapatek, but some of them might be closer to reality.

Failure to list other alternatives would not detract from an effective exclusion of one hypothesis, Scarr-Salapatek's main purpose. When one examines her calculations, one is forced to doubt whether she did, in fact, demonstrate lower heritability in disadvantaged groups, and this doubt can be made more explicit than was done by Dawes (*3*). Estimates obtained from differences between statistics may have relatively large errors because they combine the two sampling errors of the statistics from which they were calculated. Scarr-Salapatek has compounded her sampling errors by taking differences between differences. First, to estimate the intraclass correlation coefficient for the monozygotic twins, Scarr-Salapatek subtracted the coefficient of the opposite-sex pairs from that of the same-sex pairs, after converting to Fisher *z* scores and weighting them according to the estimated proportions of monozygotic and dizygotic same-sex twins (*l*, p. 1287). The same-sex pairs were, by her estimates, approximately equally divided between monozygotic and dizygotic pairs, and the error of the transformed monozygotic coefficient in her formula is therefore at least twice the error of the transformed same-sex coefficient. The formula for heritability again subtracts the correlation coefficient of opposite-sex twins, this time from the indirectly obtained coefficient of monozygotic twins (p. 190). When at last she compares heritabilities, the observed differences may be explained by chance variation.

To appreciate the degree of uncertainty surrounding Scarr-Salapatek's estimates, consider the 95 percent confidence interval for her estimates. The limits of this interval can be calculated for her intraclass correlation coefficients by adding ± 1.96 times the square root of the sampling variances of the corresponding Fisher *z* scores. The conventional large-sample variances may be used for the coefficients of same-sex and opposite-sex twins. The estimated coefficient for monozygotic twins requires a different calculation, its sampling variance (*var*) being a weighted sum of the variances of the two coefficients from which it was calculated:

$$var(Z_{rims}) = \left(\frac{1}{SS_{ms}}\right)^2 var(Z_{riss}) + \left(\frac{SS_{dz}}{SS_{mx}}\right)^2 var(Z_{rios})$$

where z_{rimz} is the transformed correlation coefficient for monozygotic twins, z_{riss} that for same-sex twins, and z_{rios} that for opposite-sex twins; SS_{mz} is the proportion of monozygotic twins among same-sex pairs, and SS_{dz} is the proportion of dizygotic twins among same-sex pairs. This assumes the validity of her method of estimating the monozygotic intrapair correlation.

The coefficient for the middle and above median group of dizygotic black twins with respect to verbal aptitude scores, calculated by Scarr-Salapatek as .460, has 95 percent confidence limits at .241 and .635. For monozygotic twins in the same group, on the same tests, with a correlation coefficient estimated by her as .753, the possible range is .492 to .890. The wide overlap with the range for dizygotic twins would be even wider if one took into account the negative correlation between the coefficient of dizygotic twins and the derived coefficient of monozygotic twins. Yet this comparison was one of the most reliable (*4*). It is therefore not surprising that several of the groups in her study appeared to have negative heritabilities. Eaves and Jinks have presented a detailed mathematical criticism of this point (*5*).

Finally, Scarr-Salapatek's attempt to estimate the intraclass correlation coefficient of monozygotic twins by an extension of Weinberg's difference method, attributed to Burt (6), is of considerable methodological interest. Before other workers make the same attempt, the pitfalls should be noted, even though they do not affect Scarr-Salapatek's conclusions.

Burt's approach assumed that partitioning the z-transformation of the same-sex intraclass correlation coefficient was equivalent to partitioning the components of variance represented in that coefficient. This is only approximately correct, and it seems more appropriate to partition the mean squares, also available. The formula used by Scarr-Salapatek (1, p. 1287) can be applied separately to between-pair and within-pair mean squares instead of to converted correlation coefficients. The adjusted mean squares are then used in the usual formula for the intraclass correlation coefficient. This procedure yields corrections ranging from − .028 to + .050 in the coefficients estimated for monozygotic twins, but these corrections are smaller than the presumed sampling errors. Sampling variances of the improved estimates can be obtained only by approximation (7), but are probably rather similar to those we calculated for Scarr-Salapatek's estimates.

Both methods of estimating intraclass correlation coefficients of monozygotic twins require three assumptions: (i) the usual Weinberg assumption, that same-sex dizygotic twins occur in the same number as opposite-sex twins or in a proportion that can be estimated from the sex ratio; (ii) that monozygotic and dizygotic twins have the same mean value (intelligence in this instance); and (iii) that variance within same-sex dizygotic pairs is equal to that within opposite-sex dizygotic pairs in all social classes. We are most interested in the third assumption. Actually, the variance among same-sex dizygotic pairs is almost always smaller than that among opposite-sex pairs, and subtracting the variance of opposite-sex twins from that of all same-sex pairs will remove too much of the variance. The remaining variance attributed to monozygotic twins will be an underestimate, and the intraclass correlation coefficient estimated by either method will be an overestimate. This exaggerates the heritability of the trait in question. It is an error in the conservative direction for Scarr-Salapatek's purpose of demonstrating low heritability of intelligence in the disadvantaged class.

In summary, Scarr-Salapatek has presented a plausible model and a helpful approach to a difficult problem, but her data are insufficient. The approach might permit the exclusion of not one, but several significant hypotheses if the blood types of such a series of twins were determined or, given a much larger series, even if they were not.

REFERENCES

1. S. Scarr-Salapatek, *Science* **174**, 1285 (1971).
2. V. H. Denenberg and A. E. Whimbey, *Develop. Psychobiol.* **1**, 55 (1968).

3. R. M. Dawes, *Science* **178**, 229 (1972).
4. S. Scarr-Salapatek, *ibid.*, p. 235.
5. L. J. Eaves and J. L. Jinks, *Nature* **240**, 84 (1972).
6. C. Burt, *Brit. J. Psychol.* **57**, 137 (1966).
7. O. Kempthorne, *An Introduction to Genetic Statistics* (Wiley, New York, 1957), p. 246.
29 November 1972

GORDON ALLEN
Mental Health Intramural Research
Program, National Institute of Mental
Health, Bethesda, Maryland 20014

KAREN D. PETTIGREW
Biometry Branch,
National Institute of Mental Health

Considerable heat, 1 or 2 million words of discussion, and several pounds of printed paper have been generated during the past few years in controversy over genetic versus environmental interpretations of racial and social class differences in mean IQ scores. No satisfactory resolution has been possible because of the inadequacies of available data. The latest major article, Scarr-Salapatek (*1*), furnishes a fresh set of data collected in a study of school-aged black and white twins grouped by social class. Studies of twins are frequently used to derive estimates of a trait's heritability (that is, the ratio of the genetic variance to the phenotypic variance) within a given population. That approach has yielded relatively consistent estimates of the heritability of IQ within white populations in the course of a number of investigations, but such estimates have been lacking for blacks and members of lower social classes. Scarr-Salapatek proposes that by filling the gap and by comparing the heritabilities estimated for each race and for the different social classes, competing predictions of simple nature and nurture hypotheses about the origins of between-group IQ differences can be put to the test. Thus, at first glance, this new study seems to promise the kinds of data that are needed to settle the issue at last.

Indeed, some readers will be tempted to believe that Scarr-Salapatek's report contains the definitive answer, especially because the sentiments expressed in the concluding paragraphs are so clearly fair-minded. Scarr-Salapatek states (and who would disagree with her?) that "Group differences in IQ scores and phenotypic variability that exist because of environmental deprivation can and should be ameliorated" (p. 206). We wish we could as readily agree that her data convincingly establish that the between-group differences in IQ observed in her study do exist largely *because of* environmental deprivation. Nevertheless, we are compelled to question whether such a conclusion—or, in fact, any conclusion—can be drawn from these data, just as we seriously doubt that conclusions can be based upon the lines of evidence that other authors (2) have assembled in attempting to demonstrate the existence of group differences *because* of genetic factors.

Several technical difficulties in Scarr-Salapatek's material will be obvious to most readers. They include: the loss of one-third of her starting sample, with the reasons for the losses apparently being differently distributed in the two racial groups (3); the need to estimate social class from census tract data rather than from known characteristics of the individual twins' families; and the extreme nonnormality of the test score distributions mentioned by the author. All combine to introduce into the analyses an unknown, but possibly substantial, amount of "noise." Confusion is added, too, by a number of discrepancies in the tables (4). Yet, we are troubled chiefly by another problem, one that is less likely to be recognized by many readers but that is more fundamental than the above shortcomings: All of Scarr-Salapatek's main analyses are based on the twin method, which, in turn, depends upon comparisons between monozygotic and dizygotic pairs and, hence, upon accurate zygosity determinations. But no tests of zygosity were made on this sample (5); not a single same-sex pair can be classified as to zygosity.

The author has sought to cope with this important omission by calling upon Weinberg's differential rule (6), which postulates that same-sex and opposite-sex pairs occur in about equal frequency among dizygotic twins. Presumably, therefore, one has only to subtract twice the number of opposite-sex pairs from the total sample size to find the number of monozygotic pairs in the sample. This is the procedure that Scarr-Salapatek follows. Reliance on the Weinberg rule, however, has been called into question by several authors (7). A recent review (8) of eight studies of twins shows that the proportion of same-sex dizygotic pairs predicted by the differential rule may be considerably less than the proportion actually found when blood-grouping is done. If the proportion of dizygotic pairs is underestimated, then, of course, monozygotic pairs are proportionately overestimated. In that case, analyses like Scarr-Salapatek's will almost certainly undervalue the genetic contribution to phenotypic variance.

We see three specific reasons to believe that the Weinberg rule fits Scarr-Salapatek's sample poorly.

1. The correlations reported for the test scores of opposite-sex twins are frequently—in three out of nine comparisons within the black group and four out of nine comparisons within the white group—*higher* than the correlations for same-sex pairs as a whole and than the estimated correlations for monozygotic twins (tables 5 to 8, pp. 197–199). In a letter on Scarr-Salapatek's article, Dawes (9) points out that such a finding is not to be expected on genetic grounds. We would add that it is not to be expected on environmental grounds either.

2. As Scarr-Salapatek correctly notes, "The heritability of intelligence in white, middle-class populations . . . has been repeatedly estimated to account for

60 to 80 percent of the total variance in general intelligence scores. . . .'' (*1*, p. 1285). For her own group of white, middle-class children, however, the heritabilities of the test scores (tables 9 to 12, pp. 200–201) range between only 4 and 44 percent. Problems with the Weinberg differential rule mentioned above could account for the failure to obtain figures in line with most other studies. In the absence of previous data on black and disadvantaged subjects, it is of course not possible to judge whether Scarr-Salapatek's data minimize the genetic contribution to differences in IQ as drastically within those groups as they appear to do for middle-class white subjects.

3. Finally, the sex distributions presented in table 13 (p. 202) make it evident that, for the black group at least, the Weinberg rule is inappropriate. The rule rests on the assumption that the distribution of sexes is nearly equal among twins in any population. That assumption is certainly not met in the sample of black twins, which contains 194 female–female and 139 male–male pairs. (Carrying through on the Weinberg formula for this sample with 169 opposite-sex pairs, one would obtain estimates of 109 female and only 55 male monozygotic pairs. Or, if the basic assumption of the Weinberg rule is waived, the deviation in sex ratio of 41 percent males to 59 percent females found among the same-sex black pairs may be assigned equally to monozygotic and dizygotic pairs, yielding 67 male to 97 female monozygotic pairs and 69 male to 100 female dizygotic pairs—a biased sample at best. And, then, how much further distortion occurs when this sample is subdivided by estimated ratings of social class?)

For the foregoing reasons, we believe that the zygosity estimates in Scarr-Salapatek's study cannot be accepted with any degree of certainty. It is difficult to see how the analyses, which hinge upon such estimates, can be considered meaningful.

Perhaps it is just as well that the data are not to be taken too seriously, for, otherwise, a true puzzle might confront us all. According to her own formulation, Scarr-Salapatek would have to demonstrate that heritabilities of the test scores are higher in whites than in blacks, and higher in middle than in lower social classes, in order to support the theoretical model, which attributes group differences to the depressing effects of environmental disadvantages rather than to genetic differences. The author holds that her data on social class are consonant with the environmental disadvantage hypothesis. Actually, as noted by Dawes' letter (*9*) and in the author's reply (*10*), heritability estimates are missing for lower-class whites on both the verbal and nonverbal aptitude tests and for lower-class blacks on the nonverbal tests owing to the methodological problems detailed above. Hence, we contend that hypotheses about social class differences in IQ are untestable with Scarr-Salapatek's data.

For blacks and whites within social classes, however, some comparisons are possible, and there is where the puzzle would come in. Of the four possible comparisons [using either h_r^2 or h_a^2 in table 9 (p. 200)], three show the estimated heritability ratios for blacks to exceed, by at least 50 percent, those for the white group. The environmental disadvantage explanation of black and white differences in IQ would predict the reverse. Fortunately, the methodological difficulties that we have noted make it unnecessary to worry over the seeming contradiction between the reported results and expectations of the environmental hypothesis.

Emotionally and intellectually, we concur in the belief that the environmental hypothesis is the correct explanation for observed differences in IQ between groups, at least between blacks and whites. Our point, however, is that Scarr-Salapatek's data do not provide the longed-for evidence in support of that hypothesis.

REFERENCES AND NOTES

1. S. Scarr-Salapatek, *Science* **174**, 1285 (1971).
2. A. R. Jensen, *Harv. Educ. Rev.* **39**, 1 (1969); H. J. Eysenck, *The IQ Argument: Race, Intelligence and Education* (Library Press, New York, 1971).
3. According to Scarr-Salapatek's note 26 (*1*, p. 1295), exclusion of twins enrolled in special classes for the "retarded" accounted for 23 percent of the lost black pairs and 10 percent of the lost white pairs.
4. For example, there are unexplained small fluctuations in N's. From table 1 (*1*, p. 1288), it appears that 506 black pairs and 282 white pairs took the aptitude tests on which the main statistics are based. In tables 5 through 8 (*1*, pp. 1290–1291), N's shown for black pairs range between 501 and 504, and N's shown for white pairs range from 274 to 282. No explanation is given for these differences. It is especially difficult to understand why the number of pairs listed for the total aptitude scores consistently exceeds the number shown for either the verbal or the nonverbal sections of the tests alone.
5. We fully appreciate the tactical difficulties that Scarr-Salapatek mentions in connection with differentiating monozygotic and dizygotic twins in large samples. Nevertheless, we believe that this must be done. Many large twin studies were carried out before blood-grouping was generally available. Data from those studies are often criticized for that reason, but at least some effort was made by the investigators to classify individual pairs by one of the phenotypic similarity methods.
6. W. Weinberg, *Arch. Gesamte Physiol. Menschen Tiere (Pfluegers)* **88**, 346 (1902).
7. I. I. Gottesman and J. Shields, in *Progress in Experimental Personality Research* (Academic Press, New York, 1966). vol. 3. pp. 1–84; P. P. S. Nylander and G. Corney. *Ann. Hum. Genet.* **33**, 31 (1969); K. O. Renkonen, *ibid.* **30**, 277 (1967).
8. W. H. James, *Nature* **232**, 277 (1971).
9. R. M. Dawes, *Science* **178**, 229 (1972).
10. S. Scarr-Salapatek, *ibid.*, p. 235.
11. We thank Arthur Falek, Leonard L. Heston, and Jacques Rutschmann for their helpful comments and suggestions.

27 November 1972

L. ERLENMEYER-KIMLING
Department of Medical Genetics,
New York State Psychiatric Institute,
New York 10032

SAMUEL E. STERN
Department of Sociology, Georgia
State University, Atlanta 30303

REPLY

My first attempt to explore possible differences in the sources of variance in aptitude scores among children from several populations (*1*) has been roundly, and often correctly, criticized because it failed to settle all of the methodological, statistical, ethical, and social issues arising from the observation of individual and group differences in intelligence.

Further, the discussion section seems to have enraged some hereditarians by its emphasis on environmental differences, even though the sentiments expressed have been labeled as "fair-minded." First, let me discuss briefly the difficulties of model testing in human populations and, second, deal with specific criticisms raised by the two technical comments.

Model Testing

The posing and testing of competing models to explain the human data on intellectual variation is an extremely difficult task, made nearly impossible by the requirement that each study meet all possible criticisms. Many potential investigators, especially the biometricians (*2, 3*), can specify ideal designs for genetic research on behavior. Their specifications for ideal studies are so extraordinary, however, that no research is likely to meet their criteria of sample size, composition, minimum standard errors of estimate, and so forth, unless a giant, collaborative effort were launched. To predict from past performance, the critical research will certainly not be done by those who demand such rigor from others.

There is also an irony in their demands: as Barker (*4*) has pointed out, the higher the estimated heritability, the fewer the pairs of related persons needed to detect statistically significant genetic variance, because the power of the test increases as heritability estimates increase. Thus, if heritabilities are low, as predicted for disadvantaged populations, their detection is nearly impossible by biometrical standards. There is an overwhelming bias in favor of accepting the results of studies with high heritability estimates.

There has never been a study of the effects of genetics on human behavior that could withstand all of the criticisms leveled at mine. Does this mean that we know nothing about the effects of genetic and environmental differences on behavior? Nonsense. I believe we do know that genetic differences play an important role in the distribution of individual differences for many characteristics in some populations. Our knowledge is based not on one critical study, but on the accumulated weight of evidence from many partially flawed investigations. Strong inferences can often be made on the basis of such data (*5*).

I agree that we do not yet have a sufficiently sound basis for making strong inferences about possible differences in the expression of genetic variants within and between many populations and subgroups. The pattern of results I obtained suggested one set of interpretations regarding environmental differences, but more definitive studies are obviously needed.

I agree with Allen and Pettigrew that more models than the two simple ones proposed can and should be tested. In fact I said so (p. 189), but not as eloquently or explicitly as they have. My choice of the two simple and opposing models was not random, however, but was based on prevailing views in the controversy over the relative importance of genetic and environmental differences in intellectual differences.

The environmental disadvantage model is supported by Tanner's (6) analysis of variation in physical growth. He concluded (6, pp. 40–41):

> The rate of growth at any age is clearly the outcome of the interaction of genetic and environmental factors. The child inherits possible patterns of growth from his parents. The environment, however, dictates which (if any) of the patterns will become actual. In an environment where nutrition is always adequate, where the parents are caring, and where social factors are adequate, it is the genes that largely determine differences between members of the population in growth and adult physique. In an environment that is suboptimal and perhaps changes from time to time, as in periodic famines characteristic of much of the world, differences between members of the population reflect the social history of the individuals as much as their genetic endowment.

Tanner went on to discuss the fact that the growth of some individuals is affected more severely by deprivation than the growth of others. In other words, environmental deprivation—in this case nutritional, social, and emotional disadvantages—has a generally depressing effect on average physical growth in a total population and both a depressing and variable effect on the expression of genetic differences among individuals. A principal effect is lowered heritability of differences in physical growth in disadvantaged populations.

To the extent that intellectual growth is similar to physical growth (by being cumulative and subject to the effects of continuous or periodic deprivation), the same simple environmental disadvantage model may well apply. I hope that more studies of intellectual differences within and between populations will further test the appropriateness of this model.

Specific Criticisms

Both technical comments question the appropriateness of the Weinberg rule, which was used to estimate the monozygotic twin correlations and, subsequently, the heritabilities. Interestingly, Allen and Pettigrew conclude that limitations on the appropriateness of the Weinberg rule probably led to an *overestimate* of genetic variance in my study, while Erlenmeyer-Kimling and Stern conclude that the Weinberg rule probably led to an *underestimate* of the genetic variance in the same data. The reasoning behind their criticisms is sufficiently different to lead to conflicting opinions on the effects of the Weinberg rule.

The technical comments agree, however, in questioning the statistical significance of the pattern of results I reported and interpreted to support primarily the environmental disadvantage hypothesis. In response to the same criticism from Dawes (7), I professed ignorance of any known statistical technique to calculate the reliability of an estimated correlation coefficient. By ignoring the unreliability introduced by estimation, I calculated the usual Fisher formula to show that the advantaged groups of both races had (statistically) "significantly" higher monozygotic than dizygotic correlations, while the disadvantaged groups did not. Since then, several statisticians have contributed error terms that preclude any statistical significance without samples consisting of many thousands of pairs. I stand corrected on the parametric front. The only other comment I would make is that the distribution of monozygotic:dizygotic correlations is still quite interesting: the monozygotic coefficients exceeded the dizygotic in all six comparisons in advantaged groups, but in only one comparison in the disadvantaged groups. This is the pattern of results that I discussed.

Several "technical difficulties" are cited by Erlenmeyer-Kimling and Stern as criticisms of the study. Some of these I acknowledged in the article: (i) individual zygosity could not be determined for each pair because the twins were not seen; (ii) social class ratings depended upon census tract data and thus described neighborhood, not individual, characteristics (which may have been an asset, not a liability, if one goal is to describe the school-aged child's environment); (iii) the raw test data were skewed and had to be normalized; and (iv) small fluctuations in sample size (of less than .02 percent) occurred in the tables. This "bias" occurred because a few children failed to correctly answer a sufficient number of items on a particular subtest to obtain a scaled score; total scores were extrapolated from other subtests by the school testing service (a very trivial point).

Less obvious "technical difficulties" cited by Erlenmeyer-Kimling and Stern pertain to sample losses and to the appropriateness of the Weinberg method.

1. Sample losses, they say, may be differently distributed in the two racial groups. In fact, the total public school twin population, as reported, was 64 percent black and 36 percent white; the final sample with aptitude scores was 64.7 percent black and 35.3 percent white. There was no differential loss by racial group. It is true that more black children than white were lost to special classes where standard tests were not given. A larger portion of the lower tail of the black tested-ability distribution was probably lost. As noted (note 26), the results can only be applied to children in normal, public school classrooms.

2. They state that one-third of the starting population was lost. This is not true. As explained in note 27, the aptitude tests were given in *every other* grade from 2 through 12. Thus, 282 pairs were too young to take the tests, and five grades were not tested in the year we collected data. We actually tried to go back to the previous year's records to obtain aptitude scores on those not currently tested, but this was only possible if a child had not changed schools (because test records were kept only by school building at that time). Of the 1115 pairs in regular classrooms of grades 2 through 12, the sample tested should have

included six-elevenths of the total (660) plus some others who remained in the same school building. Since we had aptitude test scores on both members of 778 pairs, I cannot concede that one-third of the sample was lost for biased reasons.

3. Erlenmeyer-Kimling and Stern suggested that the Weinberg differential rule, based on equal numbers of same-sex and opposite-sex dizygotic twins, may be inappropriate. If James (8) is correct in saying that the ratio of same-sex to opposite-sex dizygotic twins is 7 : 6, then the proportion of monozygotic twins was lower than calculated. Therefore, the estimated monozygotic correlations should have been slightly higher than calculated in all groups. The pattern of results would remain exactly the same, however.

4. They assert that higher opposite-sex than same-sex correlations were sometimes obtained, a finding not to be expected on genetic or environmental grounds. I certainly agree, except that Erlenmeyer-Kimling and Stern must recognize that these slight differences fall well within the range of the sampling errors they apply so rigorously to other aspects of the study. Furthermore, I replied to this point previously (7).

5. They correctly note that the sex ratio in the black sample was not the ideal 1 : 1, and they claim that the unusual sex ratio makes the Weinberg rule inapplicable. Let me examine the consequences of this bias.

As noted earlier, the ratio of black to white pairs was the same in the total twin population and in the final sample. The ratio of same-sex to opposite-sex pairs (the central requirement of the Weinberg rule) was also the same in the twin population and in the final sample. Black opposite-sex pairs were 34 percent of the original population and 33.6 percent of the tested sample; white opposite-sex pairs were 30 percent of both groups. Upon further examination, we discovered that proportionally fewer black males and more black females had actually been tested. For unknown reasons, the larger number of black same-sex females tested had compensated for the loss of black same-sex males, thereby maintaining the racial balance and the same-sex to opposite-sex ratio. One could speculate about the reasons for the unequal sex ratio of black pairs in the public schools and in the tested sample, but the main concern here is how the overrepresentation of female pairs could affect the Weinberg rule. Since the same-sex to opposite-sex ratio was constant, and since there were no sex differences in test scores, I do not believe that the final sample was biased in any important way.

6. Erlenmeyer-Kimling and Stern criticize the study's failure to replicate the high heritabilities often reported for general IQ scores in studies of white, middle-class samples. Upon closer inspection of the reported twin studies, one finds the claimed unanimity of results to be highly misleading, based primarily on the questionable reports of Burt's studies (3, 9) and on the use of median data (10). Erlenmeyer-Kimling has unfortunately perpetrated the view that the heritability of IQ can be calculated for any population. Others have long ago shown that multifactorial approaches to intellectual skills yield not only different heritabilities for different measures at different ages in the same population, but also

that various components of intelligence may have different sources of genetic variance (*11*).

7. They ridicule the suggestion that disadvantaged and black children have lower heritabilities for aptitude scores than advantaged and white children. I agree that statistically the pattern of results I obtained was not strictly defensible, but a new study, with improved methodology, is forthcoming. Four hundred pairs of adolescent twins, stratified by race and social class, were studied in Philadelphia (*12*). Five cognitive skills and many other variables of personality, self-esteem, physical growth, and medical-dental status were assessed. All twins were given extensive blood tests. Several models of genetic and environmental differences will be tested. The study will surely not settle all of the issues raised by Allen and Pettigrew and Erlenmeyer-Kimling and Stern, but our preliminary results do add weight to the environmental disadvantage hypothesis.

Let me emphasize that other partially flawed studies can increase our knowledge of the roles of genetic and environmental differences in relatively unexplored populations and environments. Studies of separated siblings, half-siblings, and adopted children will be particularly valuable contributions to our knowledge, even if no one study can include 10,000 pairs. Over the next several years my colleagues and I plan to collect data on the similarities in intellectual skills among adopted and natural children and separated siblings to add to our twin data. No one study will settle all of the issues, but I hope that others will join us in seeking new knowledge about diverse human groups.

REFERENCES AND NOTES

1. S. Scarr-Salapatek, *Science* **174**, 1285 (1971).
2. L. J. Eaves and J. L. Jinks, *Nature* **240**, 84 (1972); J. L. Jinks and D. W. Fulker, *Psychol. Bull.* **73**, 311 (1970); L. J. Eaves, *ibid.* **77**, 144 (1972). For very different reasons, a perfectionist stance has also been adopted by Kamin (*3*).
3. L. Kamin, "Heredity, intelligence, politics, and psychology," paper presented at the Eastern Psychological Association, May 1973.
4. W. F. Barker, "The relationship between sample size, power, and heritability estimates," paper presented at Behavior Genetics Association, Chapel Hill, N.C., April 1973.
5. For example, A. R. Jensen, *Educability and Group Differences* (Harper & Row, New York, 1973).
6. J. M. Tanner, *Sci. Amer.* **229**, 34 (1973).
7. R. M. Dawes, *Science* **178**, 229 (1972); S. Scarr-Salapatek, *ibid.*, p. 235.
8. W. H. James, *Nature* **232**, 277 (1971). James claims that the ratio of same-sex to opposite-sex DZ twin pairs at birth is 7 : 6 rather than 1 : 1. If true, the bias introduced into the estimated proportion of MZ twins in the same-sex group was about 9 percent. Whether the bias persists into middle childhood is unknown because twin studies never begin by ascertaining whether all pairs in the population are living later.
9. A. R. Jensen, *Behav. Genet.*, in press.
10. L. Erlenmeyer-Kimling and L. F. Jarvik, *Science* **142**, 1477 (1963).
11. For example, see J. B. Block in *Progress in Human Behavior Genetics*, S. G. Vandenberg, Ed.

(Johns Hopkins, Baltimore, 1968), pp. 221–228; R. D. Bock and S. G. Vandenberg, *ibid.*, pp. 233–260; J. C. Loehlin and S. G. Vandenberg, *ibid.*, pp. 261–278; R. D. Bock and D. Kolakowski, *Amer. J. Hum. Genet.* **25**, 1 (1973); R. S. Wilson, *Science* **175**, 914 (1972). (1972).

12. In collaboration with Solomon H. Katz, William B. Barker, and others. Reports of the entire study are in preparation in two volumes: *Black and White Children: A Study of Physical, Intellectual and Personality Development at Adolescence* and *Black and White Children: Biomedical Aspects of Development at Puberty.*

SANDAR SCARR-SALAPATEK
Institute of Child Development,
University of Minnesota,
Minneapolis 55455

INSIGNIFICANCE OF EVIDENCE FOR DIFFERENCES IN HERITABILITY OF IQ BETWEEN RACES AND SOCIAL CLASSES*

During the last few years, Jinks, Fulker and Eaves[1,6] have systematically reanalysed many of the available data on IQ and from a combination of this experience, biometrical model-building and computer simulations we have defined both the qualitative and quantitative minimal requirements for such data if they are to yield estimates of heritability and of the genetical, environmental and interactive components of variation. We have also described kinds of data and laid down guidelines for the future collection of data that would be adequate to answer the kinds of question that have been posed but so far inadequately answered.

Dr. Scarr-Salapatek[7] has attempted to go beyond what we have shown to be possible with the minimal set of data we considered, doing so on the basis of analyses of data which fall short of this minimal set in both quality and quantity. It is necessary, therefore, to examine the consequences of doing so.

Qualitative Inadequacies

Qualitatively, the minimal set of data considered by Jinks and Fulker[1] consists of a number of pairs of monozygotic (MZ) and dizygotic (DZ) twins, the individuals in each pair having been raised together. Such data provide an estimate of the ratio of genetical variation within families (pairs) to the total variation arising

---

from all sources within families[1]—the H statistic of Holzinger. This statistic is not a heritability estimate in any meaningful sense as it omits all information about the genetical, environmental and interactive sources of variation that arise between different families (pairs). It is an estimate of broad heritability only where the ratio of genetical to all sources of variation is the same both within and between families. In addition, the minimal set of data also provides test for the presence of interactions and correlations of the genotype with the within family environment and interactions of the environmental components of variation within the between families. Such data, however, will not provide estimates of the four basic components of the total variation, namely, the genetical and environmental variation within and between families, that is, the G_1, E_1 and G_2, E_2 of Jinks and Fulker which are directly relatable to the σ_{wg}^2, σ_{we}^2 and σ_{bg}^2, and σ_{be}^2 of Scarr-Salapatek.

The data presented by Dr. Scarr-Salapatek fall short of this minimal set in that there is no complete classification of twin pairs into monozygotic and dizygotic. They are classified into twins of unlike sex that must be dizygotic in origin and twins of like sex that may be either monozygotic or dizygotic. With a notional partitioning of the twins of like sex into proportions that are monozygotic and dizygotic in origin, of the kind used by Scarr-Salapatek, the data become equivalent to the minimal set in one respect but fall short in all others. They provide an estimate of Holzinger's H statistic, but with a larger standard error, and no test for genotype–environmental interactions or correlations. In relating Scarr-Salapatek's derivation of the H statistic (her "restricted heritability", h_r^2) to that of Jinks and Fulker[1] and Eaves[5] it should be noted that the σ^2s of Scarr-Salapatek are not the variance components of the conventional analysis of variance but are the mean squares of the latter.

From the estimate of the H statistic and the corresponding total variance Scarr-Salapatek proceeds to estimate the genetical and environmental components of the variances within and between family. With only the equivalent of the minimal set of data this procedure is not possible without making assumptions[1]. The nature of these assumptions can be seen from the simplest of all models (which assumes random mating and no genotype–environmental interactions or correlations) in which G_1, E_1 and G_2, E_2 represent the genetical and environmental components of variation within and between families as follows (see Scarr-Salapatek, Table 10):

Component	Within family	Between family	Row total
Genetical	G_1	G_2	$G_1 + G_2$
Environmental	E_1	E_2	$E_1 + E_2$
Column total	$G_1 + E_1$	$G_2 + E_2$	$G_1 + G_2 + E_1 +$ E_2 = total variance (V_T)

Because

$$\frac{\text{Row 1 total}}{\text{Total variance}} = \frac{G_1 + G_2}{G_1 + G_2 + E_1 + E_2}$$

is the true broad heritability, h_i^2, and

$$\frac{\text{Column 2 total}}{\text{Total variance}} = \frac{G_2 + E_2}{G_1 + G_2 + E_1 + E_2}$$

is the intraclass correlation, r_{dz}, for dizygotic twins, the row totals equal $h_b^2 V_r$ and $(1 - h_b^2)V_r$ and the columns totals $(1 - r_z)V_r$ and $r_{dz}V_T$, respectively. From Scarr-Salapatek's data we can estimate only $h_b^2 = G_1/(G_1 + E_1)$ and to equate this statistic to h_b^2 we must assume that $G_1/G_2 = E_1/E_2$. This is also a necessary assumption for the next step in Scarr-Salapatek's analysis which is the estimation of G_1, G_2, E_1 and E_2 from the row and column totals.

The relative magnitudes of G_1 and G_2 depend on the kinds of gene action underlying the variation and the mating structure of the population[1]. In the absence of both dominance and assortative mating $G_1 = G_2$, with dominance alone $G_1 > G_2$ and with assortive mating along $G_1 < G_2$. Both dominance and assortative mating are known to occur for IQ[1,6,8,9] and since they affect the relative magnitudes of G_1 and G_2 in opposite directions we neither expect nor find large differences between them.

The relative magnitudes of E_1 and E_2 cannot be predicted from any *a priori* model; they can only be established empirically by observation. The minimal set of data which allows the estimation of E_1, if we assume the present model, cannot provide a direct estimate of E_2. Thus, the assumption that $G_1/G_2 = E_1/E_2$, that underlies the analyses and interpretations of Scarr-Salapatek, is neither testable from the data she provides nor can it be justified on theoretical grounds. These arguments are, of course, made more complex if we attempt, as does Dr. Scarr-Salapatek, to correct $h_r{}^2$ and the components of the total variation for the effects of assortative mating (her $h_a{}^2$) but this extension does not invalidate the principle we have sought to illustrate by reference to the simpler situation, namely, that her analysis involves untestable assumptions about the relative magnitudes of the genetical and environmental components.

Quantitative Inadequacies

Having commented upon the limitations imposed on the analysis and interpretation arising from the qualitative aspects of the data, we can now turn our attention to the limitations that arise from the quantitative aspects which depend on the number of twin pairs that fall within each of the racial, sex and socio-economic sub-groups. While it is the qualitative properties of the data that determine the kinds of analyses and conclusions that can be validly applied, it is the quantitative properties that determine the standard errors of the estimates, their significance levels and hence the confidence that can be placed on the conclusions.

Dr. Scarr-Salapatek provides no errors for her estimates of "heritability" (H statistics) and she compares and interprets these estimates with no regard to their likely errors. Elsewhere it has been argued that even data which are qualitatively adequate will not yield convincing and significant results unless sample sizes are much larger than those employed in this study[5]. It is no surprise, therefore, that when we attempt to derive standard errors for some of the comparisons made by Dr. Scarr-Salapatek we find that little confidence can be placed in individual "heritability" estimates and even less upon comparisons between them.

In deriving conclusions from the raw correlations, Dr. Scarr-Salapatek combines correlations firstly to estimate the intraclass correlation for monozygotic twins, (r_{mz}), secondly to estimate the "heritability", (h_a^2), and finally to compare "heritability" estimates from different subpopulations. We shall show that the tests of significance, which should be applied before strong conclusions are claimed, are practically powerless with sample sizes used in her study. Indeed, even gross effects could not be detected.

Consequences of Indirect Estimation of r_{mz}

The correlation between monozygotic twins is estimated from the z values obtained for same-sex (ss) and opposite sex (os) pairs. If the proportion of OS pairs in the population is p, then:

$$Z_{ss} = \frac{pz_{os} + (1 - 2p)z_{mz}}{1 - p}$$

giving:

$$Z_{mz} = \frac{(1 - p)z_{ss} - pz_{os}}{1 - 2p}$$

Dr Scarr-Salapatek uses r instead of z in connexion with these formulae[7] (p. 1287), although her estimates of the MZ correlations are, in fact, correctly based on the z's. The variance of z_{mz} is given by:

$$\sigma_{z_{mz}}^2 = \left(\frac{1 - p}{1 - 2p}\right)^2 \sigma_{z_{os}}^2 + \left(\frac{p}{1 - 2p}\right)^2 \sigma_{z_{os}}^2$$

assuming p to be known exactly.

For whites p is given (p. 1288) as 0.3, which yields

$$\sigma_{z_{mz}}^2 = 3.0625\sigma_{z_{ss}}^2 + 0.5625\sigma_{z_{os}}^2$$

and for blacks ($p = 0.34$):

$$\sigma^2_{z_{mz}} = 4.2539\sigma^2_{z_{ss}} + 1.1289\sigma^2_{z_{os}}$$

These values of σ^2_z are inversely related to the sample sizes only. For a given number of SS and OS pairs, it is a simple matter to calculate σ^2_{zmz} since $\sigma^2_z = 1/(N - 3) = 1/N$ for large samples, where N = number of pairs. In Dr Scarr-Salapatek's samples, SS pairs are approximately twice as frequent as OS pairs, so $\sigma^2_{z_{ss}} = 1/2N_{os} = {}^1/_1 \, \sigma^2_{z_{os}}$ where N_{os} is the number of OS pairs in the sample.

Thus,

$$\sigma^2_{z_{mz}} = 2.09\sigma^2_{z_{os}} \text{ for whites and}$$
$$\sigma^2_{z_{mz}} = 3.26\sigma^2_{z_{os}} \text{ for blacks.}$$

The standard error of the restricted heritability (h^2_r) cannot be estimated directly for reasons already stated, but it is arguably pointless to produce such an estimate unless the difference $z_{mz} - z_{dz}$ is itself significant, because this difference is the numerator in the estimation of h^2_r.

The variance of the difference is:

$$\sigma^2_{z_{mz}} + \sigma^2_{z_{dz}}$$
$$\sigma^2_{z_{mz}} + \sigma^2_{z_{os}}$$
$$3.09\sigma^2_{z_{os}} \text{ for whites}$$

and $4.26\sigma^2_{z_{os}}$ for blacks.

given samples of the same proportions as before. This estimate of σ^2_d applies only when the indirect method of estimating r_{mz} is used. Given accurate zygosity determination on the other hand, and assuming equal numbers of monozygotic and dizygotic twins:

$$\sigma^2_d = \sigma^2_{z_{dz}} + \sigma^2_{z_{mz}}$$
$$= 2\sigma^2_{z_{os}}$$

Thus, a sample of N MZ pairs and N DZ pairs gives a value of σ^2_d which is approximately half that obtained for a sample of N OS pairs and $2N$ SS pairs of unknown zygosity. If zygosity determination is not undertaken, therefore, the size of the experiment has to be increased by a factor of, approximately, three to avoid loss of power in testing for a genetical component. This is a very damaging consequence of the indirect method of estimating the correlation between MZ twins which it may be difficult to justify on economic grounds.

Power of the Test for a Genetical Component

For a given true heritability, with certain assumptions about gene action, the mating system and environmental variation, expected values of the correlations between MZ and DZ twins can be derived. Knowledge of the standard error of the difference $z_{mz} - z_{dz}$ and the expected value of the difference enables the power of the test to be calculated for samples of a given size. That is, we can calculate for a given sample structure the probability of correctly rejecting the null hypothesis that there is no genetical component of variation. If this probability is low then the test is poor since the null hypothesis will be generally retained even though false (type II error).

There is a prior expectation that $z_{mz} \geq z_{dz}$, so the test of the difference $d = z_{mz} \times z_{dz}$ is a one-tail test. That is, if

$$c = (z_{mz} - z_{dz})/\sigma_d \geq 1.65$$

we reject at the 5% level the null hypothesis that there is no heritable variation. For a given expected $z_{mz} - z_{dz}$, which depends upon the true heritability, and for a given σ_d, which depends upon the sample size, the expected value of c can be calculated, c_e. The power of the test is then the area under a normal curve with zero mean and unit variance between the limits $(1.65 - c_e)$ and infinity.

If 60% of the variation is genetically determined and there are no common environmental effects, the expected value of r_{mz} would be 0.6. This is approximately the mean value of r_{mz} given in Dr Scarr-Salapatek's study, and is an upper limit to the true broad heritability of the trait. If, further, there is no dominance, the expected value of r_{dz} will be 0.3, providing mating is at random. Under conditions of assortative mating the DZ correlation will be higher, being 0.45 if there is a correlation of 0.5 between the additive genetical deviations of spouses.

The expected value of $z_{mz} - z_{dz}$ will then be 0.3836 in a randomly mating population and 0.2084 under assortative mating of the kind just defined.

Consider the sample of upper socio-economic status (SES) whites, consisting of 70 OS pairs[7] (Table 8, page 1291). Assume, for approximation, that the number of SS pairs, actually 155, is exactly twice that of OS pairs, so that $\sigma_d^2 = 3.09\sigma_{z_{os}}^2$ as above.

Now $\sigma_{z_{os}}^2 = 1/70$
   $= 0.014286$
so that $\sigma_d^2 = 0.044143$
and $\sigma_d = 0.2101$.

For the randomly mating population the expected value of c is thus

$c_d = 0.3836/0.2101$
   $= 1.8258$, when $h_b^2 = 0.6$.

The power of the test, α, is thus the area under a normal curve having zero mean and unit variance, between the limits $- 0.18$ and infinity. In this case α can be found from tables to be 0.57. That is, a significant genetical component of variation will only be detected in randomly mating populations in 57% of all possible samples of this size, even when the broad heritability is as high as 0.6. Under conditions of assortative mating a similar calculation shows that samples of this size would only produce a significant genetical component in 25% of studies. Table 1 gives the power of the test for the four separate subclasses of Scarr-Salapatek's study by race and SES, and the value of α for tests for each race separately after pooling over social classes. The sample sizes hardly provide powerful tests of a genetical component when the subgroups are considered separately, and do not provide a very rigorous test even when a pooled "heritability" estimate is obtained for each race. It is noticeable that a moderate degree of assortative mating reduces the power of the tests to values which would inevitably provide non-significant estimates more often than not. To provide more convincing tests (say, $\alpha = 0.95$), between 800 and 1,000 pairs are needed for randomly mating populations, and between 2,000 and 3,500 pairs are needed for assortatively mating populations depending on race. If we remove the simplifying assumptions of no dominance or E_2 we find that the presence of either will tend to improve the power of the test, dominance by reducing r_{dz} relative to r_{mz}, and E_2 by increasing the overall correlation between relatives and thus, on the transformed scale, increasing the difference $z_{mz} - z_{dz}$.

Comparing "Heritabilities"

The conclusions reached so far relate only to the existence or otherwise of a genetical component of variation. We have seen that even a relatively large genetical component, corresponding to a true broad heritability (h_b^2) of 0.60, can only be detected unreliably with samples of this size. Dr Scarr-Salapatek's conclusions, however, are based on the comparison of estimates of h_b^2 for different subpopulations so we must enquire to what extent statistical unreliability is increased by attempting to draw comparative conclusions about different groups of individuals. We will concern ourselves only with a comparison between races.

TABLE 1
The Power of the Test for a Genetical Component of Variation

| | Subpopulation | | | | | |
| | Black | | | White | | |
	Low SES	High SES	Pooled	Low SES	High SES	Pooled
Total sample size (N)	321	186	507	48	210	258
Power of test (a)						
Random mating	0.61	0.43	0.78	0.22	0.57	0.64
Assortative mating	0.27	0.20	0.37	0.14	0.25	0.29

Sample sizes approximately equal to those in Scarr-Salapatek. A broad heritability (h) of 0.6 is assumed, and values are tabulated for randomly mating and assortatively mating populations. For simplicity no dominance or E_2 has been assumed.

The null hypothesis, that there is no racial difference in "heritability", is only rejected if the comparison $k = (z_{mz} - z_{dz})$, white; $(z_{mz} - z_{dz})$, black, differs significantly from zero.

The variance of this comparison is

$$\sigma_k^2 = \sigma_d^2, \text{ white } + \sigma_d^2, \text{ black.}$$

For samples in which like-sex twins are twice as frequent as unlike sex pairs

$$\sigma_k^2 = 3.09\sigma_{z_{os}}^2, \text{ white } + 4.26\sigma_{z_{os}}^2, \text{ black.}$$

There is no prior expectation about the direction of the difference so the null hypothesis will only be rejected by the 5% level if $k/\sigma_k \geq 1.96$.

With the sample sizes used in the study, $\sigma_{z_{os}}^2$, white $= 0.011628$ and $\sigma_{z_{os}}^2$ black $= 0.005917$, so that

$$\sigma_k^2 = 0.061137$$

and $\sigma_k = 0.2473$.

In an extreme case, where the true heritability in one population is 0.6, and there is no heritable variation in the other

$$c_e = 0.3836/0.2473 = 1.55$$

under conditions of random mating. The power of the test is thus the area under a normal curve of unit variance between the limits $(1.96 - 1.55)$ and infinity. That is, the power of the test (α) is 0.34. Thus, even in this extreme case, we shall find, more often than not, that there is no significant difference in the genetical structure of the two populations with the sample sizes in Dr. Scarr-Salapatek's study. With equal numbers of black and white pairs, nearly 4,000 pairs would be needed altogether to be 95% certain of detecting a difference of the grossest kind between the heritabilities of a trait in the two populations. If the difference is less marked, say $h_b^2 = 0.3$ in one population and 0.6 in the other, over 3,000 pairs are required for the power of such a test to be even 0.5, and upwards of 11,000 pairs would be needed before we could be 95% certain of detecting a difference between the two heritabilities. On purely theoretical grounds, therefore, we suggest that this particular experimental design, with the small samples available, could not be expected to lead to the conclusions which were drawn and indeed could only be drawn from it by omitting proper tests of significance.

THE SIMPLEST MODEL

We reanalysed Dr. Scarr-Salapatek's data using a more rigorous approach to see whether any statistical significance could be attached to the strong conclusions she draws from the tabulated correlations. We describe an analysis of variation of the z values for the cells of a table of correlations for the two types of twin in each race and SES combination (derived from Scarr-Salapatek's Tables 6 and 7, p. 1291). We observe, firstly, that such a detailed analysis is not strictly justified by the data because the eight raw correlations are homogeneous for the non-verbal scores ($\chi^2_{(7)} = 5.63$, $50\% < P < 75\%$) and they are barely heterogeneous for the verbal scores ($\chi^2_{(7)} = 15.63$, $2^1/_2\% < P < 5\%$). This means that all the correlations given by Dr Scarr-Salapatek are really nothing more than estimates of the same population value of the correlation between twins, irrespective of their classification as SS or OS. We give, however, a more detailed analysis of the correlations for the verbal scores because of the slight indication of heterogeneity. The variation in the z for the eight correlations can be predicted by the linear model given in Table 2. The model includes, besides the overall mean value of z, the effects due to race, SES, and the difference between SS and OS twins. Of particular interest in the light of Dr Scarr-Salapatek's analysis, however, is the possibility of attaching tests of significance to the first order interaction between the SS/OS dichotomy and social class and that between SS/OS and race which provide the crucial tests of differences in heritability between races and social classes.

Because the z values are based on different numbers of observations they do not have the same variance so the estimated components of the linear model are not orthogonal. The method of weighted least squares, however, yields maximum likelihood estimates of the effects and gives their variance–covariance matrix. These estimates are given in Table 3 with their standard errors derived from the diagonal elements of the variance–covariance matrix. All the estimates have the same standard error since every z enters into each comparison. The fact

TABLE 2
Linear Model for Predicting the Observed Degree of Similarity
between Twins (Measured by z) in Terms of Race, Social Class and
Concordance for Sex

	Black				White			
	Low OS	SES SS	High OS	SES SS	Low OS	SES SS	High OS	SES SS
Mean	1	1	1	1	1	1	1	1
Race	1	1	1	1	−1	−1	−1	−1
Socio-economic status (SES)	1	1	−1	−1	1	1	−1	−1
Same sex $v.$ opposite-sex pairs (SS, OS)	1	−1	1	−1	1	−1	1	−1
Race × SS/OS	1	−1	1	−1	−1	1	−1	1
Race × SES	1	1	−1	−1	−1	−1	1	1
SES × SS/OS	1	−1	−1	1	1	−1	−1	1
Race × SES × SS/OS	1	−1	−1	1	−1	1	1	−1

TABLE 3
Effects Contributing to Variation in the
Similarity Between Twins for Verbal IQ

Effect	Estimate
Mean	0.597*
Race	−0.048 NS
SES	0.052 NS
SS/OS	−0.069 NS
Race × SS/OS	0.025 NS
Race × SES	0.008 NS
SES × SS/OS	−0.053 NS
Race × SES × SS/OS	0.018 NS

The estimates are obtained by weighted least
squares from the observed values of z. The standard
error of every estimate is 0.051.
*Significant at the 0.1% level.
NS = Not significant at the 5% level.

that the only significant effect is the overall mean suggests that the slight
heterogeneity of the z values cannot be assigned to any particular cause.

We find, first, that there is no significant overall difference between the
correlations for SS and OS twins. This implies that the data cannot even support
the well-established conclusion that there is a genetical component of individual
differences in intelligence. We find further that the interactions of the SS/OS
difference with race and SES are not significant. This confirms that there is no
evidence that the size of any heritable component depends on race or social
advantage. This finding contradicts the main conclusion of Dr Scarr-Salapatek's
analysis which is based on a comparison of the numerical values of the correlations.

As there is no detectable heritable component, we cannot, on the basis of this
study, suppose that the similarity between twins is due to anything other than
common environmental effects. Such a conclusion is clearly inconsistent with
other, more secure, evidence on this matter[1,6,9-12]. The fact that the overall
correlations for both types of twin depend neither on race nor on socio-economic
status indicates that there is no difference in the magnitude of a common environmental component between the races or the two social groupings. Furthermore, the absence of a race × socio-economic status interaction implies that
the magnitude of any common environmental effect does not depend on the joint
effects of race and social class.

The only tenable conclusion to be drawn from the data is that there is a highly
significant correlation between twins of all kinds for verbal IQ ($z = 0.597$, $P <
0.001$, $r = 0.54$). We are in no position to decide the cause of such similarity.

There is no evidence that it has a genetical basis as far as this study goes, but as we have shown above, the likelihood of detecting such an effect with this experimental design and with these samples is very small. There is certainly no evidence in Scarr-Salapatek's studies that the proportion of genetical variation in either verbal or non-verbal IQ depends on race or social class. In view of this conclusion, and having regard to the general absence of genotype–environmental interactions for IQ[1,13,14], there is little justification for detailed consideration of the particular models suggested by Dr Scarr-Salapatek.

We thank Professor P. L. Broadhurst for helpful comments on the manuscript. This work is part of a research project in psychogenetics supported by the Medical Research Council.

Received August 3, 1972.

REFERENCES

1. Jinks, J. L., and Fulker, D. W., *Psychol. Bull.*, **73**, 311 (1970).
2. Fulker, D. W., *Symposium on Methodology in Human Behaviour Genetics, 4th Int. Cong. Hum. Genet.* (1971).
3. Eaves, L. J., *Brit. J. Math. Statist. Psychol.*, **22**, 131 (1969).
4. Eaves, L. J., *Brit. J. Math. Statist. Psychol.* **23**, 189 (1970).
5. Eaves, L. J., *Psychol. Bull.*, **77**, 144 (1972).
6. Eaves, L. J., *Heredity* (in the press).
7. Scarr-Salapatek, S., *Science*, **174**, 1285 (1971).
8. Reed, E. W., and Reed, S. C., *Mental Retardation: A Family Study,* 57 (Saunders, Philadelphia, 1965).
9. Burt, C., *Brit. J. Psychol.*, **57**, 137 (1966).
10. Jensen, A. R., *Harv. Educ. Rev.*, **39**, 1 (1969).
11. Erlenmeyer-Kimling, L., and Jarvik, L. F., *Science*, **142**, 1477 (1963).
12. Nichols, R. C., in *Methods and Goals in Human Behaviour Genetics* 231 (edit. by Vandenberg, S. G.) (Academic Press, New York, 1965).
13. Jensen, A. R., *Behavior Genetics*, **1**, 133 (1970).
14. Eaves, L. J., PhD thesis, University of Birmingham (1970).

L. J. EAVES

J. L. LINKS

Department of Genetics
University of Birmingham, England

EVIDENCE AGAINST A GENETICAL
COMPONENT TO PERFORMANCE ON
IQ TESTS*

Eaves and Jinks[1] have failed to note the significance of Scarr-Salapatek's[2] data, which provides important evidence against the heritability of IQ performance. A straightforward overall evaluation of this study, together with a review of evidence[3-7] which Eaves and Jinks consider to be more secure in establishing a genetical component to IQ performance shows that: (1) the upper limit of IQ heritability in Scarr-Salapatek's study is 15% ± 16%. This is consistent with zero heritability and directly contradicts the higher figures claimed by other studies[3-7]; (2) other studies[5-7] which use identical-fraternal comparisons to derive apparently higher upper limits to heritability do not take into account the more similar treatment frequently given to identical twins. When this is adjusted for, these studies are consistent with low or zero heritability; (3) the similarity between separated identical twins, used by Jinks and Fulker[3] to derive an 80% heritability estimate, can be quantitatively accounted for by highly correlated placement (ref. 8 and L. J. Kamin, Invited Address, Eastern Psychological Association, Washington DC, March 1973) with little or no genetical component.

We use the methods of Jinks and Fulker for our evaluation. The difference in correlation coefficients for identical twins raised together (MZ) and fraternal twins raised together (DZ) is

$$r_{MZ} - r_{DZ} = [G_1 + E_1(DZ) - E_1(MZ)]/\sigma_T^2 \text{ (a)}$$

where

$$\sigma_T^2(DZ) = \sigma_T^2(MZ) \text{ and } G = G_1 + G_2$$

In general $E_1(DZ) > E_1(MZ)$ since identical twins are treated more similarly than fraternal twins. Identical twins are of the same sex, are frequently dressed alike, given the same toys and mistaken for one another. Thus, large differences in correlation of identical and fraternal twins do not necessarily mean high heritability, or any heritability[4,8], and studies of MZ-DZ differences can only give upper bound estimates for G_1

$$G_1/\sigma_T^2 \leq r_{MZ} - r_{DZ}$$

To obtain the upper limit heritability from Scarr-Salapatek's data we have, for the error in z scores of MZ twins, $\sigma_{zMZ}^2 = a\sigma_{zss}^2 + b\sigma_{zos}^2$. The coefficients a and b are given in Eaves and Jinks[1]. With $\sigma_{z_{os}}^2 = 1/(N_{SS} - 3/2)$ (ref. 9) where N_{SS} is the number of same sex pairs and similarly for σ_{zos}^2 and with $\sigma_r = (1 - r^2)\sigma_z$ we

---

compute the standard deviation of the correlation coefficient r_{MZ}. Assuming $Z_{DZ} = Z_{os}$ (this raises the heritability estimate since in general same sex DZ twins are treated more similarly than opposite sex DZ twins) we then compute the variance, σ_d^2, of the difference, $r_{MZ} - r_{DZ}$, $\sigma_d^2 = \sigma_{r_{MZ}}^2 + \sigma_{r_{DZ}}^2 + 2(1 - r_{MZ}^2)(1 - r_{DZ}^2)(P/(1 - 2p))\sigma_{z_{os}}^2$ where $p = 0.30$ for whites and $p = 0.34$ for blacks. For Scarr-Salapatek's Table 8 we obtain four independent estimates of the difference $r_{MZ} - r_{DZ}$ as follows: black, lower socio-economic status (SES) $= -0.165 \pm 0.185$; blacks higher SES $= 0.109 \pm 0.184$; whites, lower SES $= -0.046 \pm 0.340$; whites, higher SES $= 0.160 \pm 0.110$. Using least squares the overall best fit is

$$r_{MZ} - r_{DZ} = 0.075 \pm 0.082 \; \chi^2 = 2.4(3 \; \text{d.f.})$$

or

$$G_1 \leqslant 7.5\% \pm 8.2\%$$

Estimating the heritability depends on the relative magnitudes of G_1 and G_2. Previous work has used $G_1 = kG_2$ with $k \simeq 1$ (refs 1,2,5,6). For purposes of comparison we choose $k = 1$ and obtain

$$h^2 \leqslant 15 \pm 16\%$$

which is a new upper limit to the heritable component to performance on IQ tests.

This result is to be compared with other estimates[5-7] cited by Eaves and Jinks derived from the identical approach. It is 4.0 standard deviations lower than the figure of $h^2 = 80\%$ quoted by Jensen[5,6] and promulgated in popular accounts[10]. The probability of a discrepancy this large occurring by chance is less than 10^{-4} if the true heritability is $h^2 = 80\%$.

We fail to understand why Eaves and Jinks are prepared to discard this result. To do so only perpetuates the apparently common practice in this field of ignoring or failing to report evidence against the genetic hypothesis. As Scarr-Salapatek describes it "there are few published reports of null results unless a major theoretical point is at issue. I, for one, obtained the same correlation (0.61) for blood-grouped MZ and DZ twins on an individually administered test of non-verbal IQ and did not submit the results for publication (because no one would believe that MZ twins were not more similar, there were only sixty pairs and so on)"[11].

The apparent discrepancy between $h^2 \leqslant 15 \pm 16\%$ and the higher figures reported elsewhere[5,6] is resolved by estimating the size of the 'treatment' effect, caused by the more similar treatment of MZ twins. By comparing the correlations of groups with the same G_1 we obtain pure treatment effects of expected magnitude less than $E_1(DZ) - E_1(MZ)$. From Wictorin[12] $\Delta r_{DZ}(\text{male} - \text{female}) = 0.12 \pm 0.05$ and $\Delta r_{MZ}(\text{male-female}) = 0.15 \pm 0.09$. (For comparison $\Delta r(\text{males})$ (MZ–DZ) $= 0.18 \pm 0.09$ and $\Delta r(\text{females (MZ–DZ)}) = 0.15 \pm 0.05$ in the same data). Similarly from Huntley[13] Δr_{DZ}(same sex–opposite sex) = 0.21 ± 0.09 and from Jinks and Fulker[3] Δr_{MZ}(boys–girls) = 0.17 ± 0.16. From Erlenmeyer-Kimling and Jarvik[7] we see that the range in correlations for studies of the same groups is large. For parent–child Δr = 0.6, for siblings Δr = 0.5, and for same-sex DZ twins Δr = 0.45. Since in Jensen's method[6] Δr(MZ–DZ) ~ 0.35 yields 70% heritability, these figures demonstrate that the treatment effect acting alone is enough to produce the Δrs observed between MZ and DZ twins.

We now consider the four studies of separated twins. Kamin has demonstrated gross errors in methodology and analysis in these studies but the Shield's data is still useful for a quantitative comparison of genetic and environmental models. Jinks and Fulker[3] analyse this data in terms of the components G_1, G_2, E_1, E_2, and $G = G_1 + G_2$. Naming a variance component G, however, does not mean that it is genetic. A model with the substitutions $E_T \leftrightarrow E_1$, $E_F \leftrightarrow E_2$, $E_A \leftrightarrow G_1$ E_s(DZ) $\leftrightarrow G_2$ and E_s(MZ) $\leftrightarrow G$ is an environmental model formally identical to the simple genetic model where the sources of variance are: E_T, differences in treatment of identical twins; E_A, additional differences due to the different appearance of DZ twins; E_F, between pairs family differences; E_s, differences in social environment. The results are shown in Table 1.

The large value of E_s(MZ) means there is a high degree of similarity in the environments of separated MZ twins. Such a conclusion is born out by Fehr's[8] and Kamin's analysis of Shield's data. The null E_2 in the genetic model contradicts the known fact that social environments have a large effect on IQ performance[14] while the null F_F in the environmental model means that differences in the way families in the same social environment treat children have little effect on IQ performance compared to differences in the way the social environment treats children. The environmental model is actually more consistent with the data than the conventional genetic model.

In summary, we note the following. The upper limit obtained from Scarr-Salapatek's data of $h^2 \leq 15\% \pm 16\%$ ($G_1 \leq 7.5 \pm 8.2\%$) is evidence against the heritability of IQ performance. Other low results go unreported[11] and this lends additional weight to her results. This 15% figure and every higher estimate

TABLE 1
Comparison of Variances of Environmental and Genetic Models Based on Analysis of Shield's Data

Environmental model		*Genetic model*
Variance due to differences in		Variances due to differences in
Social environment (E_s[MZ])	71% ± 12%	Genetics (G)
Family (E_F)	0%	Family and social environment (E_2)
Within family treatment (E_t)	29% ± 12%	Within family treatment (E_1)

reported in MZ–DZ studies contains an uncontrolled environmental component deriving from the more similar treatment accorded identical twins. Estimates indicate that this effect is large enough to make other upper limits derived from MZ–DZ comparisons consistent with zero. The separated twin studies when properly analysed also give heritability estimates which are low or consistent with zero.

We conclude that the evidence used to support high heritability of IQ performance actually yields low estimates of heritability consistent with zero and not larger than the upper limit of $h^2 \leqslant 15\% \pm 16\%$. Zero heritability of IQ performance means that the individuals in the population all have the same genetic potential for the expression of this trait.

We thank Professor Leon Kamin for making his results available prior to publication and Professors John Gibbon, Sonia Ragir and Eugene Weinstein for critical readings of the original manuscript.

Received December 12, 1972; revised November 5, 1973.

REFERENCES

1. Eaves, J. J., and Jinks, J. L., *Nature*, **240**, 84 (1972).
2. Scarr-Salapatek, S., *Science, N.Y.*, **174**, 1285 (1971).
3. Jinks, J. L., and Fulker, D. W., *Psych Bull.*, **73**, 311 (1970).
4. Burt, C., *Br J. Psychol.*, **57**, 137 (1966).
5. Jensen, A. R., *Harv. Educ. Rev.*, **39**, 1 (1969).
6. Jensen, A. R., *Proc. Natn. Acad. Sci. U.S.A.*, **58**, 149 (1967).
7. Erlenmeyer-Kimling, L., and Jarvik, L. F., *Science, N.Y.*, **142**, 1477 (1963).
8. Fehr, F. S., *Harv. Educ. Rev.*, **39**, 57 (1969).
9. Snedecor, G. W., and Cochran, W. G., *Statistical Methods*, 295 (Iowa State, 1967).
10. Herrnstein, R., *Atlant. Mon.*, **228**, 43 (1971).
11. Scarr-Salapatek, S., *Science, N.Y.*, **178**, 236 (1972).
12. Vandenberg, S. G., in *Genetics* (edit. by Glass, D. C.), **3** (Rockefeller University Press, New York, 1968).
13. Huntley, R. M. C., in *Genetic and Environmental Factors in Human Ability* (edit. by Meade, J. E., and Parkes, A. S.), 208 (Plenum, New York, 1966).
14. Klineberg, O., *Negro Intelligence and Selective Migration* (Columbia University Press, New York, 1935).

M. SCHWARTZ
Department of Sociology,
State University of New York, Stony Brook

J. SCHWARTZ
Division of Pure and Applied Sciences,
Richmond College,
City University of New York

GENETIC DIVERSITY AND HUMAN EQUALITY

Class and race differences in IQ averages may be ascribed to inequalities in educational opportunities and living standards. This explanation is traditionally favored by most social scientists and by political liberals. On the other hand, the differences may be genetic, which is pleasing to racists and reactionaries, but not espoused by any reputable scientist. Finally, both environmental and genetic conditionings may be involved. The bone of contention is then not environment versus heredity, but how much environmental relative to genetic conditioning.

The controversy is growing hotter because of the finding that individual IQ differences have large genetic components. Racists try to obtain maximum propaganda mileage from this fact. Yet the differences between race and class averages need not be genetically conditioned to the same degree as individual differences. Nobody, not even racists, can deny that living conditions and educational opportunities are disparate in races and classes. Jensen (1969), after recognizing explicitly that the heritability of individual differences within a population cannot validly be used as a measure of the heritability of the population means, tries to do just that. In fairness to him, it must be conceded that he presents a most detailed analysis of the environmental factors which could be instrumental in bringing about the divergence of IQ averages in the white and black populations of the United States. His conclusion is that none of the factors, or combinations of factors, give an adequate explanation of this divergence, which accordingly must be largely genetic. I remain unconvinced by his argumentation.

Scarr-Salapatek (1971a,b) may have achieved a breakthrough in heritability studies. The assumption made heretofore in IQ analyses has been that the action of genetic and environmental factors is simply additive. In other words, genetic and environmental agencies that bring about increments and decrements of intelligence (and other mental traits) act independently of one another, and always in the same way. This need not be so at all. Genetic differences may manifest themselves conspicuously in people who develop in favorable and stimulating environments, and remain undisclosed in adverse or suppressive environments. Carriers of genetic endowments who could unfold high IQs under favorable conditions will fare no better than genetically less well endowed people in suppressive environments. If this is so, the heritability of IQ should be lower among disadvantaged socioeconomic groups (classes as well as races) than among the privileged ones. On the other hand, the heritabilities should be uniform if the simple additivity hypothesis is valid. The two hypotheses are empirically testable, and Scarr-Salapatek has made an ingenious and discerning effort to test them.

---

*This comment by Th. Dobzhansky originally appeared in T. Dobzhansky, *Genetic Diversity and Human Equality*. New York: Basic Books, 1973. Copyright © 1973 by Basic Books, Inc. Reprinted by permission of Basic Books, Inc.

Among 250,258 children in Philadelphia schools, from kindergarten to the twelfth grade, 3,042 twin pairs were found; 36 percent of the twins were white and 64 percent black. Regrettably, tests could not be made to identify the monozygotic and the dizygotic pairs (presumably because of the expense involved). Obviating this handicap involved resorting to a rather complex statistical operation. Among the twins, 1,028 pairs were of the same sex and 493 were of opposite sexes. These latter were dizygotic. Among the same-sexed twins, there must also have been approximately 493 dizygotics, with the rest monozygotic. This group was, accordingly, a mixture of not individually identifiable mono- and dizygotic twins. The families of the twins were classified according to their socioeconomic status: above median, median, and below median. As expected, the black families were more often disadvantaged:

	Below	Median	Above
Black	634	236	134
White	114	106	340

Aptitude and scholastic achievement test scores of the twins were analyzed statistically. On aptitude tests (where the national mean is 50) the following socioeconomic class and race averages were found:

	Below	Median	Above
Black	27.7	29.7	33.0
White	34.8	43.4	50.9

Differences between the upper- and the lower-class children among the blacks are much smaller (5.3) than among the whites (16.1). What is more important is that the variance of the test scores is greater in the advantaged than in the disadvantaged groups, among both blacks and whites. A greater proportion of the variances found in the relatively privileged than in the underprivileged socioeconomic classes is attributable to genetic causes. This is what the hypothesis of interaction between the genetic and environmental factors (see above) has predicted. The conclusion of Scarr-Salapatek is worth quoting:

From studies of middle-class white populations, investigators have reached the conclusion that genetic variability accounts for about 75 percent of the total variance in IQ scores of whites. A closer look at children reared under different conditions shows that the percentage of genetic variance and the mean scores are very much a function of the rearing conditions of the population. A first look at the black population suggests that genetic variability is important in advantaged groups, but much less important in the disadvantaged. Since most blacks are socially disadvantaged, the proportion of genetic variance in the aptitude scores of black children is considerably less than that of the white children, as predicted by model 1 [environmental determination].

Evolutionary Genetics of Caste and Class

The question is sometimes asked: How do you define "man"? Biologically the answer is simple. All human beings are members of a single species, *Homo sapiens*. Though some pathological variants seem to be less than human, they belong to our species. Their genes come from the same gene pool as everybody else's. Inhabitants of the whole world share in the common gene pool of the species. Perhaps no hybrids of Eskimos and Tungus with Hottentots and Aboriginal Australians have ever been produced, but there are unbroken chains of intercrossing of geographically intermediate populations. Assuredly, this does not mean that mankind is a single uniform breeding population, wherein every individual would have equal chance to mate with any individual of the opposite sex anywhere. The population of our species is complexly subdivided into a variety of subordinate Mendelian breeding populations. In each of these, the probability of marriage within is greater than between populations.

Geographic, national, linguistic, religious, economic, and other factors keep the gene pools of the subordinate breeding populations partly, but probably never entirely, separate. Mendelian breeding populations within a species are more often than not overlapping, which does not make them unreal. The population of New York City has WASPs, Jews, Catholics, and blacks; wealthy, moderately well-off, poor, and destitute; educated and ignorant; people of English, Irish, Italian, Greek, and other ethnic groups, partly preserving their cultural backgrounds. Many individuals belong at the same time to two or more of these subpopulations or "isolates."

All these subdivisions are not only social and economic but also biological—a fact which may not be pleasing to social scientists who would like to make their field entirely autonomous from biology. But in man sociological and biological factors are almost always intertwined. The social subdivisions have biological consequences because they influence the choice of marriage partners. Marriages within each subpopulation are more frequent than are intermarriages. The subordinate Mendelian populations may become and may be maintained genetically distinct. The distinctions are almost always quantitative rather than qualitative. That is, gene variants which control some traits, from blood groups to intelligence, may be species-wide in distribution, and yet be found more frequently in some subpopulations than in others. This is not a biological technicality but a fact of cardinal ethical and political importance. Every person must be rated according to his individual qualities, regardless of the subpopulation from which his genes came.

All human societies, even the allegedly "classless" ones (e.g., the Soviet-type communist societies), are stratified into classes. People of a class have life chances in common, as determined by their power to dispose of goods and skills for the sake of income (Lipset, 1968). Classes are not only socioeconomic groups but also breeding populations, to a greater or lesser extent separate from other populations. It is therefore legitimate to ask whether their gene pools are different, and, if so, to what extent (Eckland, 1967; Gottesman, 1968b).

REFERENCES

Ecklund, B. K. Genetics and sociology: A reconsideration. *American Sociological Review*, 1967, *32*, 173–194.

Gottesman, I. I. Biogenetics of race and class. In M. Deutsch, I. Katz, & A. R. Jensen (Eds.), *Social class, race, and psychological development*. New York: Holt, Rinehart, & Winston, 1968.

Jensen, A. R. How much can we boost IQ and scholastic achievement? *Harvard Educational Review*, 1969, *31*, 1–123.

Lipset, S. M. Social class. *International Encyclopedia of Social Sciences*, 1968, *15*, 296–316.

Scarr-Salapatek, S. Race, social class, and IQ. *Science*, *174*, 1285–1295. (a)

Scarr-Salapatek, S. Unknowns in the IQ equation. (Review). *Science*, *174*, 1223–1228. (b)

REPLY: SOME MYTHS ABOUT HERITABILITY AND IQ*

Things have gone too far. Estimates of the heritability of IQ reported in *Nature* have assumed a distinctly bimodal distribution. First, Eaves and Jinks[1] decried my data on the heritability of scholastic aptitudes[2] as a failure to detect the high heritability of IQ. In a sample of urban, public-school twins, I found that Black and economically disadvantaged children from both races seemed to have lower heritabilities for verbal and quantitative aptitudes than white and middle-class children. In some cases heritabilities were not calculable, because the correlations of opposite-sex twins were slightly larger than those of same-sex twins. Now, Schwartz and Schwartz[3] proclaim zero heritability for IQ as the obvious conclusion to be drawn from the same study and from Kamin's iconoclastic efforts (L. J. Kamin, Invited Address, Eastern Psychological Association, Washington DC, March 1973). I beg to differ with both extremes and to argue against any simple conclusions on the issue.

Uniformity

The notion that there is a single answer to the question, "What is the heritability of IQ?" is patently false. Heritability estimates vary according to what skills are

---

*This reply by Scarr-Salapatek originally appeared in *Nature*, 1974, *251*, 463–464. Copyright © 1974 by MacMillan Publishing Co. Reprinted by permission.

TABLE 1
Heritability Estimates for Four Tests of Cognitive Abilities in Two
Adolescent Twin Populations

Tests	Black h^2* (N = 160 pairs)	White h^2 (N = 211 pairs)
Raven standard progressive matrices	.59	.87
Peabody picture vocabulary test	.28	.49
Columbia test of mental maturity	.42	.58
Revised test of figural memory	.61	.71
First principal component	.48	.63

*$h^2 = 2(r_{\text{IMZ}} - r_{\text{IDZ}})$, where r_{IMZ} is the intraclass correlation for mono-
zygotic twins and r_{IDZ} for dizygotic twins.

measured as intelligence, by how they are tested, by the age at which abilities are measured, and by the genetic and environmental composition of the population tested. To claim that there is a single estimate for the genetic contribution to human abilities is to deny, first, a half century of evidence on differential abilities. Some aspects of intelligence, such as vocabulary, have consistently higher heritability estimates than, say, numerical reasoning. Even if one concluded, with Burt, that general intelligence (g) is more important than specific abilities, different test of g will still yield different heritability estimates.[4,5]

Differences in heritability estimates across abilities and tests are exceeded only by differences across age groups and populations. Bayley Infant Intelligence Test scores for the first two years have been found to have generally lower heritabilities than larger scores. Even early heritabilities vary enormously: from .2 to .4 for siblings (R. B. McCall, American Psychological Association, Honolulu, September 1972), .75 for some twins (P. Nichols and S. Broman, preliminary report of the Collaborative Perinatal Study, 1973), and .3 for other twins.[6] Across populations, Nichols (PhD dissertation, University of Minnesota, 1970) reported a significantly lower correlation for black than white siblings on the Stanford-Binet at age 4. Another twin study (S. Scarr-Salapatek, S. Katz, and W. Barker, *Black and White Twins*, in preparation) found lower heritabilities for adolescent black than white twin pairs on each of four tests of cognitive abilities and for the first principal component from the four tests. These data are presented in Table 1.

Not only are heritabilities lower for black children on all four measures, the heritabilities are not uniformly .80 or .00 in either group.

The Panorama of High Heritability

If one observes an array of data from studies of related and unrelated people, the IQ scores of those more closely related generally correlate more highly than those more distantly related. This is undeniable. The view from afar reveals important regularities in the results. If the proponents of a uniformly high heritability would look more closely, however, at the constellation of human differences, they would find important inconsistencies as well.

A recent reanalysis of data on the heritability of Stanford–Binet IQ scores questions the very high heritability estimate that Eaves and Jinks[1] propose. Jencks[7] reanalyzed U.S. family correlations and obtained heritability estimates between .45 and .60, far below the .8 claimed by Burt,[8] Jensen,[9] Eaves and Jinks,[1] and Herrnstein.[10] If Burt's data are included, the heritability estimates rise, in large part because his observed (?) correlations fit genetic expectations so perfectly. As Jensen[11] has recently shown, however, there are serious inconsistencies in Burt's reports. If one relies primarily upon Burt's data, one could be grossly misled as to the proper range of heritability estimates.

A reanalysis of Jencks' reanalysis[12] suggests that the best fit to the U.S. data is a heritability of about .68. But Eaves and Jinks ignore Jencks' major point: that the data from parent–child, twin, sibling, and adopted child pairs do not fit any simple model! There are sufficiently serious disagreements in the data that forcing them into a biometrical model is to risk a nonsense solution—however mathematically elegant.

In addition, twin data on which the proponents of high heritability rely have been shown to overestimate heritability values,[13] presumably because twin environments, particularly those of monozygotic twins, have less variability (pre- and postnatally) than the environments of ordinary siblings. The variance between monozygotic co-twins is further reduced by genotype–environment covariances and interactions. There has not yet been a serious test of the magnitude of covariance and interaction effects on human intelligence. Although Jinks and Fulker[14] suggest a test for interaction (the correlation of ½ the sum and ½ the difference between IQ scores of separated monozygotic twins), their marginal to insignificant results are based on very small samples.

Further evidence on the exaggeration of heritability values comes from Newton Morton.[15] He revived Sewell Wright's[16] reanalysis of Burks'[17] adoption study. Burks' faulty path analysis model yielded a heritability estimate for general IQ (in white California adoptees) of .75 to .80, Wright's more adequate path model resulted in a heritability of .50 from the same data. Morton's additional calculations for sibs and foster sibs gave a heritability solution of .52.

Microscopic Critiques to Deny Heritability

The idea of zero heritability strikes most geneticists and biologists as odd (J. L. Fuller, presidential address, Behavior Genetics Association, Minneapolis, June 1974). How can there be any biological characteristic for which genetic variability makes no contribution to phenotypic variability? As Morton[15] remarked, "... the experience of biometrical genetics [is] that a trait heritable at its extremes has never been found to have zero heritability within the normal range.'' [p. 257] Certainly IQ is affected by many single gene and chromosomal anomalies. There are four possibilities to explain a finding of zero heritability: first, the measurement of the phenotype is invalid or unreliable; second, there is no genetic variability underlying the phenotype; third, all genotypes are functionally equivalent in producing the phenotype; or fourth, other effects overwhelm genetic variability. The first two possibilities for the heritability of human abilities can be dismissed out of hand. The third is what Schwartz and Schwartz[3] want to argue. There is simply too much evidence to the contrary, however, from studies other than those that Kamin and the Schwartz's would dismiss. While every human family study may be criticized on one or more methodological grounds, their flaws are varied and nonoverlapping. The weight of evidence suggests that genetically related persons *are* more similar intellectually than unrelated persons, whether they are reared together or apart. The microscopic examination of research flaws has blinded some critics of heritability to the obvious pattern of results.

The fourth is what Henderson[18] and I[19,20] argued for some populations. Other effects can include rearing conditions, growth patterns at a particular age, the skills tested, and many unspecified conditions that will affect sources of variability. The negligible and low heritabilities reported for aptitude scores among disadvantaged, school-aged twins in Philadelphia[2] were a function of the environments sampled, the tests, the populations, and possibly the age group. The point is that genetic differences did not seem to contribute much to variability in aptitude scores in those populations. Different tests, ages, populations, and cohorts may well yield other results. Since these tests are very widely used to make life decisions for children, however, their low heritabilities have considerable implications.

There is no single answer to the question, ''What is *the* heritability of IQ?'' because it is a pseudo-question. Heritability estimates range between .00 and .9 in reported research, but most values are in a middle range. An accurate view of genetic contributions of differences in IQ cannot be obtained from the proponents of extreme positions. In fact, the best view of human variability can be obtained by getting off the political platform and out there to study families. With the notable exception of Arthur Jensen, not many advocates of high or low heritability are adding to our store of knowledge about human intelligence.

REFERENCES

[1]Eaves, L. J., and Jinks, J. L., *Nature,* **240,** 84 (1972).
[2]Scarr-Salapatek, S., *Science,* **174,** 1285 (1971).
[3]Schwartz, M., and Schwartz, J., *Nature,* **248,** 84 (1974).
[4]Vandenberg, S. G., in *Intelligence: Genetic and Environmental Influences* (edit. by Cancro, R.), 182 (Grune & Stratton, New York, 1971).

[5]Vandenberg, S. G., in *Genetics, Environment, and Behavior* (edit. by Ehrman, L., Omenn, G. S., & Caspari, E.), 276 (Academic Press, New York, 1972).

[6]Wilson, R. S., and Harpring, E. B., *Developmental Psychology,* **7,** 277 (1972).

[7]Jencks, C., *Inequality* (Basic Books, New York, 1972).

[8]Burt, C., *British Journal of Psychology,* **57,** 137 (1966).

[9]Jensen, A. R., *Educability and Group Differences* (Harper & Row, New York, 1973).

[10]Herrnstein, R., *IQ in the Meritocracy* (Atlantic, Little, Brown, Boston, 1973).

[11]Jensen, A. R., *Behavior Genetics,* **4,** 1 (1974).

[12]Eaves, J. J., and Jinks, J. L., *Nature,* **248,** 287 (1974).

[13]Layzer, D., *Science,* **183,** 1259 (1974).

[14]Jinks, J. L., and Fulker, D. W., *Psychology Bulletin,* **72,** 311 (1970).

[15]Morton, N. E., in *Genetics, Environment, and Behavior* (edit. by Ehrman, L., Omenn, G. S., & Caspari, E.), 247 (Academic Press, New York, 1972).

[16]Wright, S., *Journal of the American Statistical Association Suppl.,* **26,** 155 (1931).

[17]Burks, B. S., *Yearbook Nat. Soc. Stud. Educ.,* **27,** 219 (1928).

[18]Henderson, N., *Journal Comp. Physiol. Psychol.,* **3,** 505 (1970).

[19]Scarr-Salapatek, S., *Science,* **178,** 229 (1972).

[20]Scarr-Salapatek, S., *Science,* **182,** 1044 (1973).

The Effects of Family Background: A Study of Cognitive Differences Among Black and White Twins

II.4

The Philadelphia Twin Study was conceived to help answer a very complicated question: Why do black children score so badly on standard tests of intellectual skills? Although it may seem foolhardy to pose so large and ill formed a question, we have never believed that bits and pieces of answers to smaller and better-formed questions were likely to add up to the information one *really* wanted to know. So we felt it was better to fall short of answering completely an important question than to answer satisfactorily a question one did not want to ask.

Both common sense and the research literature on kinships support the view that the causes of cognitive differences are both genetic and environmental differences among people. Although there is continuing controversy over the magnitude of genetic and environmental effects, there is a general consensus in the behavioral and biological sciences that individual differences in brain function and behavior must follow the same laws of variability as other human characteristics.

Whether or not genetic individual differences aggregate in groups that differ in their average values is a matter of less consensus and no direct evidence. Certainly, phenotypic differences in intellectual test scores are well known. Two major hypotheses have been advanced to account for racial differences in IQ scores: the *genetic-differences* hypothesis and the *environmental-differences* hypothesis. The genetic-differences hypothesis states that observed racial differences in mean IQ scores result primarily from racial differences in genotype distributions and that the environment plays a minor role in determining

This chapter, written by Scarr, is based on research conducted with William B. Barker and supported by NICHHD (HD06502) and The William T. Grant Foundation.

phenotypic group differences. The environmental-differences hypothesis proposes that observed racial differences in IQ are determined primarily by environmental factors that produce poorer phenotypes in disadvantaged circumstances and not by any substantial genetic differences between groups.

Earlier reports by Henderson (1970) on mice and by Scarr-Salapatek (1971) on human twins have supported the predictions of the environmental disadvantage hypothesis. Mice reared under deprived conditions showed reduced mean scores on a learning task, reduced phenotypic variability in scores, and a reduced amount of genetic variance in scores when compared to littermates reared under enriched conditions. The findings on disadvantaged and advantaged, black and white twins suggested similar conclusions. Disadvantaged children were found to have little or no genetic variation in their aptitude scores, whereas advantaged children showed considerable genetically determined variation (Rao, Morton, & Yee, 1974).

Two recent studies, in a series of investigations on the origins of racial differences in intelligence, brought new evidence on the issue. A study of transracial adoption (Scarr & Weinberg, 1976) showed that black and interracial children reared by socioeconomically advantaged white families score very well on standard IQ tests and on school achievement tests. Being reared in the culture of the test and the schools resulted in intellectual achievement levels for black children that were comparable to those of adopted white children in similar families. Therefore, it is highly unlikely that genetic differences between the races could account for the major portion of the usually observed differences in the performance levels of the two groups.

A second study on the relation of black ancestry to intellectual skills within the black population (Scarr, Pakstis, Katz, & Barker, in press) showed that having more or less African ancestry was not related to how well one scored on cognitive tests. In other words, holding social identity and cultural background constant, socially classified blacks with greater amounts of white ancestry did not score better than other blacks with more African ancestry. A strong genetic-differences hypothesis cannot account for this result.

Both the study of socially classified black children reared in the culture of white families and the study of socially classified blacks of varying degrees of African ancestry indicate that genetic racial differences cannot account for the magnitude of usually observed differences in performance between the races. Previous research on socioeconomic differences within the two racial groups indicates that SES differences are also an insufficient explanation (Jensen, 1973). Cultural differences have been invoked as an explanation of racial differences in intellectual performance, but Jensen (1974b) has shown that there is little *differential* cultural bias in tests.

The twin study reported here was designed to answer questions about the sources of individual differences in cognitive skills within the black and white groups. The major hypothesis is that black children are culturally less familiar with the kinds of skills and materials required for high performance on typical intellectual tests. This generalized unfamiliarity with such materials and skills would result in several outcomes of a twin study—outcomes that are not predicted by the genetic-differences hypothesis. The three major predictions of the generalized cultural-differences hypothesis are:

1. Black children will score relatively worse on those tests that are more culturally loaded than on more "culture-fair" tests when the instructions for all tasks are equally understood.

2. The cultural differences of the blacks constitute a "suppressive environment" with respect to the development of the intellectual skills sampled by typical tests, and therefore black children will show less genetic variability in their scores and more environmental variability (Scarr-Salapatek, 1971).

3. Differences among black children will be more dependent on differences among their family environments in the extent to which they aid children in the development of test-relevant skills; therefore: (a) The twin correlations will be higher for black twins; and (b) there will be less difference between MZ and DZ coefficients in the black groups than in the white groups.

Three major predictions of a genetic-differences hypothesis are:

1. Black children will score relatively worse on those tests that are loaded more highly on a g factor than on more verbal, culturally loaded tests.
2. The proportions of genetic and environmental variability will be the same in both racial groups.
3. Family environments will be no more important in black than in white racial groups in determining individual variation.

METHOD

Subjects

Four populations were to be sampled in the study: "advantaged" and "disadvantaged," black and white adolescents. Our knowledge of socioeconomic status in Philadelphia alerted us to the obvious fact that on the average, black families were far more disadvantaged than whites. In the previous study (Scarr-Salapatek, 1971), only a quarter of the white families of twins in the public schools lived in census tracts with as low income and educational level as half the blacks, and only a quarter of the blacks had as high census-tract characteristics as half the whites. Now that we were to include suburban and parochial school twins as well as the city public school sample, we expected even less overlap in the income and education levels of the two racial groups.

To draw representative samples of the two racial groups, we began with the Philadelphia public schools. A list of pairs of twins, matched for same last name,

TABLE 1
Recruitment of Sample from Twins in Public
School

All Same-Sex Twin Pairs, Ages 10–15		702
No contact possible	236	
Positive response but no show	92	
Positive response but couldn't come	54	
Not interested	74	
In final sample	246	
Total		702

same address, and same birthdate, was obtained from the Philadelphia public school system. From this list were selected same-sex pairs born between October, 1956 and June 1962. The resulting population consisted of 702 twin pairs and 2 sets of triplets between the ages of 10 and 15 years, as shown in Table 1. Letters describing the study were sent to parents of all children in the population, and phone interviews supplemented the initial written correspondence. From this original population, 246 twin pairs and 1 set of triplets are in the final sample. Of the remaining 456 pairs, no contact was made with 236; 92 responded positively (by returning consent forms and/or making appointments for a testing date) but did not show up for testing; 54 had no objections to the study but indicated that external circumstances (vacation, illness, jobs, and so forth) prevented their participation; and 74 indicated that they were not interested in participating in the study.

In late June 1972, an article describing the study appeared in a widely circulated, Philadelphia daily newspaper. Responses to this increased the sample size by 153 same-sex twin pairs and 1 set of triplets. Sixty twin pairs and the set of triplets attended schools in the Roman Catholic Archdiocese of Philadelphia, and 93 pairs attended schools in the suburban areas surrounding Philadelphia.

TABLE 2
Characteristics of Final Sample[a]

	Black			White		
	Male	*Female*	*Total*	*Male*	*Female*	*Total*
Philadelphia public school	73	84	157	54	35	89
Philadelphia other	5	13	18	23	19	42
Suburban	0	0	0	42	51	93
Totals	78	97	175	119	105	224

[a] Total number of twin pairs = 399 plus 2 sets of black female triplets.

TABLE 3
Distribution of Median Income and Education
by Census Tracts with Twin Subjects

	Income		Education	
	Black	White	Black	White
Quartile 1	$6,310	$ 9,450	9.6 years	10.5 years
Quartile 2	7,910	11,000	10.2	11.9
Quartile 3	9,450	12,500	11.2	12.4

The final sample, therefore, consisted of 399 pairs of twins and 2 sets of triplets, as shown in Table 2.

Socioeconomic characteristics of the twins' neighborhoods were taken from census tracts. The median income of the tracts in which black twins reside is $7910, and the median adult educational level is 10.2 years (see Table 3). Both figures are very close to the average 1970 census figures for urban black families. The subjects ranged in age from 10 years to 15 years, 11 months.

Procedures[1]

The children were each paid $10 to participate, and they received a free dental checkup, physical growth assessment, and refreshments. They were brought after lunch by chartered bus from the elementary schools nearest their homes and returned to school after approximately 5 hours at the Dental School, University of Pennsylvania.

Co-twins were separated into different small groups, each with an adult leader who explained the procedures, answered questions, and gave assistance. An average of 28 children, divided into 4 small groups, were tested each weekday afternoon from late June to early August 1972.

For the psychological assessments, the small groups were assembled in a large auditorium. Seating was arranged in alternate seats and rows. Test materials were presented on 35-mm slides on a large screen. Instructions and test items were presented on audiotape and coordinated automatically with the slide presentations. No reading skills were required. All the material had been pretested with 30 black, inner-city children who were paid a consultant fee to criticize the procedures and tests (see Appendix A). Based on the pretest, all test instructions were made more redundant than standard instructions to help the disadvantaged black children to understand the nature of the tasks. Group leaders monitored the children's use of the simplified answer sheets for the tests.

Blood samples were drawn at the end of the day, just before the payments

---

[1]For fuller details, see Appendix A.

were given out. Although some children were reluctant to have blood drawn, peer pressure and the promise of $10 produced excellent cooperation and minimal distress.

Intellectual Skills

Five measures of intellectual skills were administered as parts of two 1.25-hour psychological assessments that also included personality and self-esteem measures. The two sessions were separated by approximately 1 hour in which dental, taste, dermatoglyphic, radiological, physical-growth, and other assessments were made. Refreshments were served during a break between sessions.

The Raven Standard Progressive Matrices,[2] Sets A, B, C, and D (Raven, 1958), were included to measure abstract reasoning skills. Seventy items from the Peabody Picture Vocabulary Test (Dunn, 1959) were used to measure knowledge of standard English vocabulary. Thirty items from the Columbia Mental Maturity Scale (Burgemeister, Blum, & Lorge, 1959) were used to assess conceptual skills. The Revised Visual Retention Test, Form C (Benton, 1963), was included to test conceptual memory for designs. Finally, a paired-associated task (Stevenson, Hale, Klein, & Miller, 1968) was included to test rote, associative learning skills.

Socioeconomic Status

Two measures of socioeconomic status were obtained. The Home Index (Gough, 1970), a 24-item measure of family SES, was administered as part of the first test battery. It was found to be unreliable for young adolescents, because co-twins often disagreed about information on their families. A revised scale of the 10 most reliable items was included in this study. Census-tract median values for educational level and income were obtained on all census tracts in which black twins lived. The census tract in an urban area is fairly homogeneous with respect to socioeconomic characteristics, but it is an imperfect measure of individual SES. It is a good measure of some neighborhood and school characteristics that are related to children's intellectual development.

Blood Group Markers

Two 10-cc blood samples were obtained from each child—one in EDC solution, one in a clot tube. Blood samples were shipped daily by air in refrigerated cartons to the Minneapolis War Memorial Blood Bank for typing. The following marker loci were assessed: ABO (A_1, A_2, B O), MNSs, Kidd (JK^a, JK^b), Kell (K, k), Rhesus (r, r^1, R^o, R^1, R^2), Ceruloplasmin (Cp^a, Cp^b, Cp^c), Group Specific (Cc^1,

---

[2]For full details of the administration of the measures, see Appendix B.

Cc^2), Transferring (Tf^C, Tf^D), Duffy (Fy^a, Fy^b), Hemoglobin (Hb^A, Hb^S, Hb^C), Haptoglobin (Hp^1, Hp^2), Adenylate Kinase (AK^1, AK^2), Gm (a, x, b, c), and Inv (1).

Twin zygosity was established by comparing co-twins' blood groups at each of the loci. If dizygosity was determined by only one blood group difference, the tests for that locus were redone to affirm the diagnosis.

A Critical Assumption

The comparison of MZ and DZ twins is the basis of inferences about the effects of genetic differences on phenotypic differences. If the differences observed between DZ co-twins exceed those between MZ co-twins, it is usually thought to be evidence for the effects of genetic differences. There is a critical assumption in this procedure—that the environmental differences of MZ co-twins are equal to those of DZ twins.

The possibility of greater environmental similarity for MZ twins is based on the hypothesis that their physical similarity will lead others to treat them more similarly than DZ twins, who more often look less alike in appearance. If MZ twins are treated more alike because of their striking physical resemblance, then their higher correlations in behavior traits may not reflect simply greater similarity.

To examine the validity of this assumption, we used the twins' own beliefs about their zygosity. In a brief interview, each twin was asked whether he or she was a fraternal or identical twin. As reported elsewhere (Carter-Saltzman & Scarr, 1976, 1977), only about 60% of the twin pairs were in agreement and correct about their zygosity. The critical cases were those whose beliefs differed from true zygosity based on blood groups. In addition, we asked the twins whether or not they looked as alike as carbon copies, whether they were mistaken for each other by teachers and friends, and whether or not they dressed alike. Further, we had ratings of the similarity in appearance of the co-twins made by eight graduate students—two each, male and female, black and white.

The ratings by the twins and others of their zygosity and physical resemblance were combined into a single index by principal components analysis with verimax rotation. The first factor is shown in Table 4. The loadings of the variables are in the order of their simple correlations with true zygosity; so although we did not specify a criterion for the factor, it does represent a proper weighting of the ratings to predict actual zygosity.

To check further on the validity of the twin differences as perceived by self and others (TWPSO factor), we correlated the factor scores with twin differences in physical growth, as shown in Table 5. In comparison with blood group similarities, scaled by the number of blood group phenotype matches out of 12 systems, the TWPSO factor is highly correlated with physical differences, as are the blood groups. (The signs of the correlations differ because the blood groups

TABLE 4
Co-Twin Similarity as Perceived by Themselves and Others
(Factor Analysis, Verimax Rotation)[a]

	Factor 1
Average of twins' ratings of their zygosity	.84
Average of eight ratings of co-twin similarity in appearance	.81
Average of twins' responses to question of looking alike	.72
Average of twins' responses to question of being mistaken for each other	.74
Average of twins' responses to question of dressing alike	.11

[a] Eigenvalue = 2.61, % variance = 52.2.

are scaled as matches instead of differences.) The correlation of perceived differences with differences on the cognitive test, Raven matrices, is nearly zero, whereas the coefficient for blood groups is significant ($-.235$).

When the factor scores for perceived differences (the high end of the factor) are entered into a regression to predict co-twin absolute differences in Raven matrices scores, little of the intellectual difference is predicted by perceived differences, as shown in Table 6. When both blood group matches between co-twins (MZ = 12, DZ = 11 to 0—at least theoretically) are entered along with perceived differences, the blood group matches significantly predict co-twin intellectual differences, whereas the perceived differences actually go in the opposite direction from that predicted. It looks as though the less similar appearing twins score more similarly once blood group differences are controlled.

TABLE 5
Correlation Coefficients: Co-Twin Differences as Perceived by Self
and Others, Number of Blood Group Matches, and Differences in
Physical and Intellectual Scores

/d̄/	Blood Group Matches (N = 293)	Perceived Differences (N = 264)
Stature	−.205	.182
Skeletal age	−.446	.434
Upper arm circumference	−.357	.407
Tricept skin fold thickness	−.270	.343
Sitting height	−.362	.328
Weight	−.407	.437
Skin reflectance	−.158	.137
Raven matrices scores	−.235	.065
Perceived differences	−.744	

TABLE 6
Regression of Co-Twin Differences in Scores on the Raven Standard
Progressive Matrices on the Perceived Differences and Blood Group
Similarities

Step	Variable	Beta	R	R^2	p
1	Co-twin differences as perceived by self and others	.065	.065	.004	.36
2	Number of blood group matches	−.417	.235	.055	.001
	Co-twin differences as perceived by self and others	−.245	.286	.082	.02

Finally, using the factor scores to divide the twin pairs into perceived MZ and DZ groups (arbitrarily around the mean), we did a two-way ANOVA to test for the reactive effects of true and actual zygosity on Raven scores. As Table 7 shows, only true zygosity has a significant effect, although the interaction term shows an interesting nonlinear trend, with the mistaken MZs and DZs being very confused!

The last analysis was done for all four cognitive measures (Peabody Picture Vocabulary Test, Columbia Mental Maturity Scale, Raven Standard Progressive Matrices, and Revised Visual Retention Test). Using the reduced sample size necessitated by the perceived-differences factor and the multivariate treatment of the cognitive test, neither true nor perceived zygosity is significantly related to co-twin differences in Peabody or Columbia scores, and only true zygosity approaches significance on the figural memory test (see Table 7).

The overall point to be made from these data is that perceived similarity between MZ twins does not explain their sometimes greater cognitive similarity. In fact, when entered into the regression with true zygosity, perceived similarity goes the wrong way.

TABLE 7
Average Absolute Differences in Co-Twins' Scores on the Raven
Standard Progressive Matrices as a Function of True (Blood Groups)
and Perceived (Ratings by Self and Others) Zygosity

True	Zygosity Perceived	N	/ả/	SD		
MZ	MZ	84	.66	.50	$F_{True} = 4.24,$	$p = .04$
MZ	DZ	19	.80	.70	$F_{Perc.} = 0.17,$	$p = .68$
DZ	MZ	15	1.10	.78	$F_{P \times T} = 3.23,$	$p = .07$
DZ	DZ	86	.82	.69		

RESULTS

Because this is a twin study, the results are multipurpose. The test scores are reported, first, as profiles of performance for the racial and socioeconomic groups, with attendant concerns for reliability and validity. Second, sex and age effects are considered. Finally, twin analyses are reported to evaluate the sources of variability within the two racial groups.

Patterns of Cognitive Performance of Race and SES

The means and standard deviations of the four conceptual tests are given in Table 8 for blacks and whites. As reported in many other studies, the difference between the two average test scores is enormous—of the magnitude of .75 to 1 standard deviation in these large and representative groups of twins.

Although racial differences are large, there are also socioeconomic differences with both races. More advantaged whites score about .33 of a standard deviation above the less advantaged. Social-class differences are less extreme among blacks; only the Raven and the Peabody show marked SES performance differences, although all of the mean differences are statistically reliable. Table 9 gives these results.

When the raw scores on the cognitive tests were standardized by 1-year age intervals to a mean of 0 and a standard deviation of 1, the racial and socioeconomic differences could be compared across tests. As Table 10 shows, the largest differences in performance between the races occurred on the vocabulary test, and the smallest differences, on the memory and concept tests. Socioeconomic differences were also greatest on the vocabulary test but equally large on the Raven matrices. These results are in direct contrast to the findings of Jensen (1973), who reported that blacks do relatively worse on the less culturally loaded reasoning test and better on the vocabulary test.

Because SES effects were more extreme among the white children, there was

TABLE 8
Means and Standard Deviations by Race

Cognitive	Black			White		
	(N)	M	SD	(N)	M	SD
Peabody	(348)	29.0	8.4	(436)	39.7	10.0
Raven	(352)	22.1	11.3	(446)	31.5	9.6
Columbia	(351)	19.4	3.4	(447)	21.5	3.3
Benton	(344)	4.9	2.0	(441)	6.2	2.0
Benton error	(344)	8.3	4.3	(441)	5.8	3.7
P–A task	(183)	21.4	9.2	(401)	24.6	8.7

TABLE 9

Means and Standard Deviations of Cognitive Test Scores by Race and
Social Class (Using the Home Index with a Common Cutting Score for
the Two Racial Groups)

			Black				White		
	Total Sample		Lower (226)		Middle (114)		Lower (138)		Middle (292)	
Age (mos.)	154.7	(20.8)	153.5	(21.5)	156.2	(21.5)	149.7	(20.1)	158.7	(19.9)
Raven	27.2	(11.5)	21.3	(11.6)	23.7	(10.8)	27.9	(10.7)	33.2	(8.8)
Columbia	20.5	(3.6)	19.1	(3.6)	20.1	(3.3)	19.8	(3.3)	22.3	(3.0)
Peabody	34.9	(10.8)	28.1	(7.3)	30.9	(10.1)	34.6	(9.0)	42.4	(9.5)
Benton	5.6	(2.1)	5.0	(1.9)	4.9	(2.2)	5.5	(2.0)	6.5	(1.9)

Ranges of Cognitive Test Scores by Race and Social Class (Using the
Home Index with a Common Cutting Score for the Two Racial Groups)

		Black		White	
	Total Sample	Lower (226)	Middle (114)	Lower (138)	Middle (292)
Age (mos.)	109–191	115–187	119–190	109–190	115–191
Raven	1–44	1–44	3–41	3–43	1–44
Columbia	3–29	3–26	12–27	7–27	12–29
Peabody	9–67	15–52	9–58	11–55	16–67
Benton	0–10	0–10	1–10	0–10	1–10

a significant race × SES interaction effect. The scores of more advantaged whites exceeded those of less advantaged whites to a greater degree than the scores of higher-SES blacks exceeded those of lower-SES blacks. The interaction effect is also shown in Table 10.

Two measures of socioeconomic status were collected—the Home Index that the twins filled out about their families, and the census-tract information on the educational and income medians of the neighborhoods in which the twin families resided. Table 11 presents the correlations of the two measures of family and neighborhood SES and the cognitive test scores.

It is readily apparent that the SES differences among whites are far more correlated with their performance on cognitive tests than the SES differences among blacks. Both the census-tract data and the home information of white children are more predictive of their cognitive performance than are those for black children. Several explanations may be given for this result. First, the Home Index was found to be less reliable and valid for the black children than for the white children; that is, two members of the same family (the twins) gave more conflicting reports (Carter-Saltzman, Scarr-Salapatek, & Barker, 1975). But that

TABLE 10
Mean Differences in Performance on Five Cognitive Tests by Race
and SES[a,b,c]

	White–Black	White Hi–Lo	Black Hi–Lo
Raven Standard Progessive Matrices	.82	.37	.27
Columbia Mental Maturity Scale	.61	.24	.05
Peabody Picture Vocabulary Test	1.05	.38	.29
Revised Visual Retention Test	.65	.39	.04
Paired-associate	.41	.33	.07

F Tests for Race on Standardized Scores

	F	P
Raven	59.8	.0001
Columbia	32.2	.0001
Peabody	100.6	.0001
Benton	21.5	.0001

F Tests for SES on Race Scores

Raven	13.3	.001
Columbia	7.7	.006
Peabody	29.6	.001
Benton	8.1	.005

F Tests for Race × SES on Race Scores

Raven	7.2	.007
Columbia	4.6	.03
Peabody	3.6	.06
Benton	8.9	.003

[a] $N = 440$ white, 350 black (invalid tests eliminated).
[b] Mean $= 0$, $SD = 1$.
[c] SES measured by median census-tract educational levels and income.

TABLE 11
Correlations of Two SES Measures with Scores on the Cognitive
Tests by Race

Test	Black		White	
	Home Index	Census Tract	Home Index	Census Tract
Raven	.12	.05	.26	.24
Columbia	.06	.00	.33	.17
Peabody	.20	.14	.35	.23
Benton error	.03	−.01	−.29	−.22
P–A task	.15	−.01	.22	.19

does not explain the lower correlation of census-tract information among the blacks. Second, it may be that residential segregation keeps more socioeconomically heterogeneous blacks in the same neighborhood in Philadelphia. Although we do not have quantitative information on this point, it is our impression that the census tracts from which black families were drawn were no more heterogeneous with respect to income and educational characteristics than those with white twins. In fact, it seemed to be the reverse. Like the age effects, which are discussed in the next section, the usual age and SES effects found for whites on cognitive measures are attenuated for blacks, for reasons we discuss later.

It is clear from the arrays of mean scores that black children perform far worse on the tests than white children, and even the more advantaged blacks do very poorly. Although the *less* advantaged whites are better off socioeconomically than the *more* advantaged blacks, the difference in their average scores is startlingly large. Another, and slightly perverse, way to look at the data on race, SES, and cognitive test scores, however, is to show the relative disadvantage of black children who score well on the tests. If we array scores on the Raven matrices in .5-standard-deviation units and look at the average income and educational levels of the neighborhoods from which the twins are drawn, it becomes clear that even high-scoring blacks come from relatively disadvantaged areas. Within each racial group, however, the association between SES and average scores is clear, less so for blacks than for whites, as shown in Table 12.

The ranges of scores were essentially identical in all groups, and the variances of the groups were equal as well (see Table 9). The means were very different, however, and the distributions tell the story graphically.

TABLE 12
Census-Tract Median Income and Educational Levels for Raven Scores by Race

| | Census-Tract Income and Educational Level | | | | | |
| | Black | | | White | | |
Raven Score (SD Units)	Ed	Income	N	Ed	Income	N
+2.0–2.5				11.9	$12,622	18
+1.5–2.0	10.6	$8321	13	11.8	11,908	31
+1.0–1.5				11.7	11,871	48
+0.5–1.0	11.3	9240	22	11.6	11,671	79
0.0–+0.5	10.8	8531	50	11.4	11,160	102
−0.5–0.0	10.6	7979	77	11.5	11,252	75
−1.0––0.5	10.2	7879	54	11.3	11,023	43
−1.5––1.0	10.3	7412	46	11.4	10,991	18
−2.0–1.5	10.5	7853	24	10.8	9,705	12
−2.5–2.0	10.1	7375	11			

Score Distributions

For three of the four cognitive tests, normal distributions with a single mode were obtained. Figures 1 through 12 in Appendix C show the distributions of scores for two SES groups within each race for the Peabody, the Columbia, the visual retention, and the Raven Standard Progressive Matrices.

The Raven, however, yielded a very peculiar bimodal distribution for three of the four racial, SES groups. Only higher-SES whites failed to have a strong mode distributed around a "guessing" score of 8.5. It looked to us as though about half the black children were "guessing" on the matrices. To evaluate the degree of randomness in their responses, we established a priori criteria for a "guessing" protocol. Any child who had a total score of less than 15 (8.5 ± 2 SD) had to have at least 5 items correct on the easiest set of problems (A). Of the 135 children with fewer than 15 total correct, only 42 were found to have fewer than 5 correct on Set A. By our criteria, the vast majority were not randomly guessing on the whole task. They were somehow unable to answer more difficult items, and there were too few items in a middle range of difficulty for them. Had the colored matrices been used, the Set AB would have provided a better distribution of scores for the black and lower-SES white children, because that set is inter-mediate to Sets A and B. It would have given a more even and normal distribution of scores for the matrices.

The scores of the 42 who were "guessing" by our criterion were eliminated from further analysis. In doing this, we doubtless lost some low-ability children, particularly among the low-SES blacks, who constituted 75% of the lost subjects. But the range of the test was clearly inappropriate for them. Their "motivation" was not an issue, for they scored at least 7 correct on the PPVT and the Columbia and completed all the personality materials.

The 42 individuals eliminated from the Raven analyses constituted 5% of the total twin sample. If they were randomly distributed in twin pairs, it is probable that only .25% of the co-twin pairs would both score below 15 total correct and less than 5 correct on Set A. On this basis, we should expect 1 twin pair with both members eliminated. Instead, there are 12 twin pairs with both members rejected from the sample. Among the low-scoring group of 135, there are 31 twin pairs, again far in excess of randomly assorted low scores.

What Do the Cognitive Tests Measure?

There are several ways to examine what tests measure in several populations. Many accusations are current about the cultural bias inherent in tests constructed by white, middle-class professionals. The most common references are to language differences (Labov, 1967) and differential validity (Williams, 1970). Jensen (1974b) examined the most popularly cited issues of test bias and found them all wanting.

Four methods were chosen to assess what our cognitive tests measure: (1) reliability coefficients; (2) intercorrelations of measures, factor analysis; (3) profiles of performance; and (4) correlations of item difficulty. The first, reexamination of reliability coefficients, is designed to answer the question: "Are the tests internally consistent—that is, graded in difficulty in a fairly consistent manner?" The second, intercorrelation of the tests themselves, shows the pattern underlying the tests. Similar test intercorrelations suggest that the tests are measuring roughly the same dimensions with various samples. The factor analysis is included to formalize the second concern. Third, the pattern of mean scores is included to test a cultural bias hypothesis—a prediction that verbal, culturally loaded tests should show higher average differences between the races than nonverbal, culturally "fair" measures like the Raven matrices. Jensen (1974b) rejected the cultural bias hypothesis, in part because of his finding that black children perform relatively worse on nonverbal tests than on verbal tests. The fourth, item difficulty, permits a close look at the relative difficulty of the items based on the percentage of respondents who pass each item. If black and white children respond differently to the test because black children are unfamiliar with some aspects of the performance called for, then item difficulties should have a different rank order in the two populations. If black children respond similarly but at a lower level than white children, then the rank order of item difficulty should be quite similar.

Reliability and Validity

When vast mean differences appear between groups' scores on cognitive tests, it is appropriate to ask if the measures are equally reliable and valid in the two groups. First, the internal consistencies of the three tests amenable to this kind of analysis were considered. In Table 13 the Kuder–Richardson Formula-20 reliabilities are given by race and social-class group (census tract). Both the PPVT and the Raven matrices have reliability above .85 in all groups. The Columbia test has lower reliabilities in the white groups and in the black, advantaged

TABLE 13
KR-20 Reliability Coefficients by Race and
Social Class for Cognitive Measures

	Black		White	
	Higher	Lower	Higher	Lower
Raven	.95	.95	.92	.95
Peabody	.88	.88	.93	.92
Columbia	.82	.88	.73	.75

TABLE 14
Correlations Among Cognitive Measures by Race

		Black (350)			
		Raven	Peabody	Columbia	Benton	P-A Task
White (440)	Raven		.49	.45	.53	.28
	Peabody	.50		.45	.48	.30
	Columbia	.52	.55		.43	.33
	Benton	.51	.45	.50		.32
	P-A task	.36	.34	.31	.30	

group. Thus, the results of the Columbia should be viewed as less reliable than those of the matrices and the PPVT. Scoring reliability of two scorers for the Benton Revised Visual Retention Test was .94 for total errors.

Another important measurement question is whether or not the tests measure the same underlying dimensions of performance in the various racial and SES groups. Correlation matrices and a principal component analysis of the four conceptual tests and the paired-associate reasoning task for the two racial groups showed a very similar first principal component in the two groups. As Table 14 and Figure 1 indicate, the first factor accounts for about half the variance in both groups and has loadings of about .7 to .8 for each of the conceptual measures. The "rote" learning measure loads less highly on the first principal component. Thus, the structure of the major dimension of test performance is quite similar in the two racial groups. There were too few subjects to divide the sample into SES groups for the factor analysis.

A third way to look at the comparability of measurement, however, does allow both racial and SES comparisons. The four conceptual tests were each standardized, and the rank orders of individuals' scores on the four tests were calculated regardless of the level of those scores. That is, each test was given a score of 1, 2, 3, or 4 for each individual, depending on the order of the individual's standard scores. Ranks were summed for each test within the racial and SES groups to show a profile of performance for the group. The profiles clearly show that white children score relatively well on vocabulary or culturally loaded material compared to more loaded material. This result, shown in Figure 2, is in direct contrast to Jensen's (1973) report.

A fourth method to evaluate the comparability of measurements in the racial and SES groups was suggested by Jensen (1974a). The rank orders of item difficulty of the racial and SES groups were correlated. In this case our results are in close agreement with those reported by Jensen. The same items that are difficult for black children are also difficult for whites; easy items are easy for both groups. The lowest correlations are between the most disparate groups—lower-SES blacks and higher-SES whites—but even for these groups, the correlation that reflects the order of item difficulty is .9 or above for the three tests that are amenable to this analysis. As shown in Table 15, the item correlations are lower for the more culturally loaded PPVT than for the matrices or the concept test, but they are in all cases indicative of quite similar measurement dimensions in the racial and SES groups.

From these analyses of the reliability and validity of the measures in the study, we concluded that whatever intellectual skills were being measured in the white, middle-class group were also being assessed in the other groups. We had no external criteria of validity, such as school grades or achievement test scores, but previous research has amply demonstrated the comparable predictive validity and concurrent validity of IQ and aptitude scores in different racial and SES groups (Cleary, Humphreys, Kendrick, & Wesman, 1975; Scarr-Salapatek, 1971).

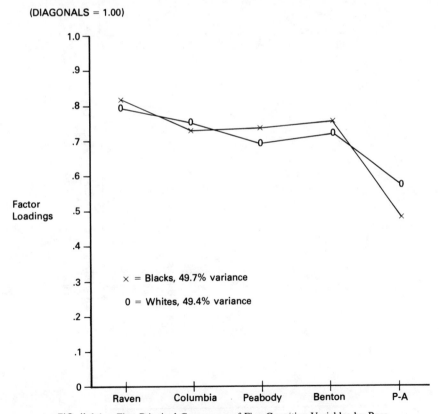

FIG. II.4.1.   First Principal Component of Five Cognitive Variables by Race

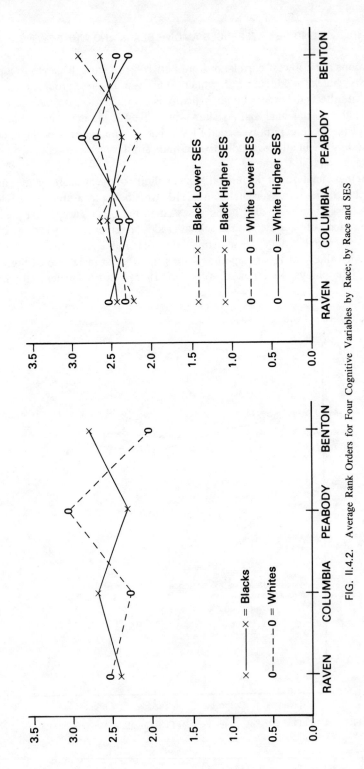

FIG. II.4.2. Average Rank Orders for Four Cognitive Variables by Race; by Race and SES

TABLE 15
Correlations by Race and SES

Peabody

	Black		White		
	Lower	Higher	Lower	Higher	
Lower Black		.97	.95	.90	P
					e
Higher	.94		.96	.92	a
					r
Lower White	.90	.96		.97	s
					o
Higher	.86	.91	.97		n
		Spearman Rank			

Columbia

	Black		White		
	Lower	Higher	Lower	Higher	
Lower Black		.99	.98	.97	P
					e
Higher	.99		.98	.97	a
					r
Lower White	.98	.99		.99	s
					o
Higher	.97	.98	.99		n
		Spearman Rank			

Raven Matrices

	Black		White		
	Lower	Higher	Lower	Higher	
Lower Black		.99	.96	.92	P
					e
Higher	.99		.97	.94	a
					r
Lower White		.97		.99	s
					o
Higher	.98	.98	.99		n
		Spearman Rank			

AGE TRENDS IN COGNITIVE SCORES

One sure result of studying complex cognitive skills over the period of 10 to 16 years is that one will find scores increasing with age. If scores did not improve with chronological age, the validity and reliability of the measures would be in question. Therefore, it is not surprising that for both blacks and whites, at all socioeconomic levels, age correlated with performance on the four cognitive measures. What is surprising is the systematically lower correlations of age with cognitive skills for black children than for white children and for disadvantaged children than for advantaged children.

As Table 16 shows, the correlation of age with scores on the four conceptual measures is about .40 to .60 in the white group and only .20 to .40 for the blacks. The pattern of higher and lower correlations with age is quite similar in the two racial groups, with the vocabulary test being most highly correlated with age, the figural memory test next highest, and the reasoning and concept tests least highly correlated.

The same pattern is repeated by social class: Lower-SES youngsters in both racial groups have smaller correlations of age with test scores, and virtually the same order of magnitude holds for the tests within each of the four groups. One exception is the reversal of vocabulary and memory tests in the lower-SES white group.

These correlational patterns are not a function of the variances of the tests for the different racial and SES groups. In fact, as Tables 2 and 3 in Appendix D show, the variances of the test scores of the blacks more often exceed the variance of the whites than the reverse. In both groups, the mean scores generally increase from age 10 to 13 or 14, after which they either reach a plateau or decline slightly. The largest increases in scores occurred in the 10-to-12 age

TABLE 16
Correlations of Age with Cognitive Variables by Race and SES
(Census Tracts with Common Median)

	Black			White		
	All	Lower	Higher	All	Lower	Higher
	(349)	(215)	(110)	(410)	(128)	(266)
Raven	.23	.19	.25	.39	.33	.37
Columbia	.22	.17	.24	.41	.36	.38
Peabody	.36	.27	.51	.58	.42	.62
Benton	.29	.24	.34	.41	.40	.36
Benton error	−.30	−.23	−.40	−.44	−.45	−.39
P-A task	.35			.22		

groups, with the exception of vocabulary, which had a slightly larger increase for whites from 13 to 14.

Sex Differences in the Age Trends

Although there were some statistically significant sex differences in scores at some ages, the overall patterns of increasing scores are quite similar. Indeed, overall there were no sex differences in cognitive scores on any test. Tables 4 through 7 in Appendix D give the score distributions by age and race for the two sexes. Neither were there systematic racial differences in the pattern of increasing scores for the sexes. It has been reported (Jensen, 1973) that black females consistently outscore males throughout development, but that result was not obtained with our testing procedures and measures.

Racial Differences in Age Effects

At every age, black children score lower than whites. The white 10-year-olds score as well or better than the black 14- or 15-year-olds on all the conceptual tests, but the slope of the increase in scores is similar in the two racial groups. Jensen's (1974b) developmental lag hypothesis could explain these results, in that black children have the same but a delayed developmental pattern. Another hypothesis, of overall cultural differences, would also explain the lower scores of black children at each age.

It should be noted that the only measure with a higher age–score correlation for blacks than whites is the paired-associate task (see Table 16). This rote learning, or Level I, task is also the only measure to show higher heritability for blacks than whites, as is shown in a later section. For conceptual measures, black and lower-SES children of both races have scores that are less related to age than the white and higher-SES children.

These findings also suggest that the test measures are not discontinuous in the way described by Earl Hunt (1974) or else that there are two discontinuities that happen to coincide with average performance levels of black and white 10 to 12 year olds.

Twin Correlations

The proper comparison of differences between co-twins is with randomly paired individuals in the sample of twins. The calculation is called an intraclass correlation, because it is a ratio of the variance within pairs to that between pairs. Differences between pairs of twins can readily be attributed to age differences, whereas no differences within pairs can arise from age differences, because co-twins are always exactly the same age! Thus, it is extremely important to control for age effects before calculating a comparison of differences within and between pairs.

To control for age effects, we divided the twin pairs into 1-year age bands and standardized the scores separately for each test. There were at least 100 individuals in each age band except for a few age bands for the paired-associate learning task. After standardization, we combined all the scores and correlated the new distribution with age. The coefficient was an insignificant − .03. Thus, the twin correlations reported in this study are not inflated by the identical ages of co-twins.

In Table 17 the twin correlations by race are shown. The MZ coefficients range from a low of .39 for white scores on the (not very reliable) Columbia test to .66 for blacks on the PPVT. The black MZ-twin coefficients slightly exceed the white MZ correlations for all five tests. The black DZ coefficients greatly exceed the white DZ values for the four conceptual tests, but not for the paired-associate learning task.

The differences between the MZ and DZ correlations are statistically significant for all four conceptual tests for the whites, but only for the Raven matrices and the memory test for the blacks. Scores on the paired-associate task are significantly more similar for black MZs than DZs, but not for whites. The

TABLE 17
Comparisons of MZ and DZ Correlations and Heritabilities for
Normalized Standard Scores on Five Cognitive Measures by Race

| Test | Black | | | |
	MZ (65)	DZ (95)	t	MZ–DZ
Raven	.63	.36	2.07*	.27
Columbia	.46	.25	1.51	.21
Peabody	.66	.52	1.37	.14
Benton error	.61	.31	2.49**	.30
P-A task	.65	.40	1.66*	.25

| Test | White | | | |
	MZ (121)	DZ (91)	t	MZ–DZ
Raven	.59	.15	3.65***	.44
Columbia	.39	.11	2.25*	.28
Peabody	.64	.40	2.44**	.24
Benton error	.57	.22	3.05**	.35
P-A task	.56	.49	.64	.07

*$p < .05$.
**$p < .01$.
***$p < .001$.

TABLE 18
Within- and Between-Pair Variances of MZ and DZ Twins for Cognitive
Tests by Race

	White				Black			
	MZ		DZ		MZ		DZ	
Test	MS_w	MS_b	MS_w	MS_b	MS_w	MS_b	MS_w	MS_b
Raven	.36	1.36	.73	.99	.27	1.21	.42	.89
Columbia	.60	1.39	.73	.91	.45	1.22	.62	1.04
Peabody	.28	1.28	.44	1.02	.21	1.03	.31	.97
Benton error	.40	1.47	.77	1.20	.45	1.84	.65	1.23
P-A task	.40	1.41	.52	1.53	.32	1.49	.43	1.00

differences between the MZ and DZ correlations are greater for the whites than the blacks for the conceptual tests, but not for the rote learning task.

The largest racial difference in the pattern of these correlations lies in the DZ group. To evaluate the source of the DZ correlational differences between the white and black groups, we looked at the mean square variances. As Table 18 shows, the within-pair variances for the white DZ twins are consistently larger than those for the black twins, but the between-pair variances are quite similar. From this comparison, we conclude that the black DZ co-twins are more similar than their white counterparts because of smaller differences within the families, not because of larger differences between families.

The mean squares of the black MZ twins are also smaller than those of the white MZs for four of the five tests. The between-pair variances are also smaller in the black MZ group. Thus, as was evident in the table of twin correlations, the black MZs' coefficients are of approximately the same magnitude as those of the white twins, but the similar coefficients result from smaller total variances in the black MZ group.

In the black group, then, the twins of both zygosities have fewer differences in scores within families than do twins in the white group. The black DZs, however, are particularly similar in that their within-pair variances are considerably smaller than those of the white DZs.

Twin Correlations by Race and SES

Dividing the twin sample by both race and social class reduces the sample sizes to dangerously small numbers, as small as 32 pairs of lower-SES black twins. Thus, the standard errors around the correlation coefficients are large. Nevertheless, as Table 19 shows, there are some interesting differences in the patterns of MZ and DZ correlations when the sample is divided by social class. First the

TABLE 19
Comparisons of MZ and DZ Correlations for Normalized Standard
Scores on Five Cognitive Measures by Race and SES (Census Traits)

	Blacks					
	Higher SES			Lower SES		
Variables	MZ (36)	DZ (35)	t	MZ (32)	DZ (56)	t
Raven	.64	−.09	3.11***	.63	.47	.98
Columbia	.57	.53	.27	.32	.05	1.24
Peabody	.54	.63	−.56	.76	.42	2.41**
Benton error	.61	.27	1.79*	.62	.34	1.74*
P-A task	.50(30)	.27(28)	.85	.71(24)	.57(46)	.75

	Whites					
	Higher SES			Lower SES		
Variables	MZ (60)	DZ (34)	t	MZ (61)	DZ (57)	t
Raven	.55	.23	1.71*	.56	.09	2.82**
Columbia	.40	−.08	2.35**	.35	.18	1.02
Peabody	.57	.50	.42	.61	.35	1.84*
Benton error	.38	.03	1.69*	.70	.28	3.02**
P-A task	.54	.46	.51	.56	.49	.50

$*p < .05.$
$**p < .01.$
$***p < .001.$

PPVT correlations were as high for DZ twins as for MZ twins in both black and white, higher-status groups. The two lower-SES groups had substantially higher MZ than DZ correlations for the vocabulary test. Second, only the memory test had significantly higher MZ than DZ correlations in all the groups, the Raven matrices in three groups, and the Columbia test in only one—in part because of the lower variability and poorer reliability of the Columbia. The paired-associate task had such small samples of blacks that it is not discussed.

The two least culturally loaded tasks—the Raven matrices and the figural memory test—have the most consistent patterns of larger MZ than DZ correlations. Although the sample sizes are small in each racial, SES-group comparison, the overall pattern of results suggests that these measures sample consistently heritable dimensions of performance. The more culturally loaded vocabulary test is clearly not tapping a heritable performance in the more advantaged groups. Family membership is important for the development of vocabulary in the higher-SES groups of both races, as demonstrated by the comparably high MZ and DZ correlations. In the lower-SES groups, however, the Peabody Picture

Vocabulary Test scores are more similar in the MZ than DZ groups of both races. In all the groups, the DZ correlation for vocabulary is high relative to the other tests—suggesting, therefore, that family environment is more important in determining vocabulary than other skills. This result is consonant with the results of our adolescent adoptive sample, who resemble their parents and each other only on vocabulary measures (Scarr & Weinberg, 1977).

Twin Correlations by Race and Sex

The division of the twin sample by race and sex again results in small samples, and the reader is reminded to consider all numbers to have large standard errors. In general, the MZ correlations exceeded the DZ coefficients in both sexes and racial groups. Black female DZs and white male DZs had larger correlations than black male and white female pairs. This may be because of small sample fluctuation. Table 20 gives these results.

Of the four conceptual tests, the DZ correlation for vocabulary is the largest in all groups, and the MZ vocabulary coefficient is as large or larger than any other

TABLE 20
Comparisons of MZ and DZ Correlations for Normalized Standard
Scores on Five Cognitive Measures by Race and Sex

	Blacks					
	Males			Females		
Variables	MZ (31)	DZ (40)	t	MZ (37)	DZ (51)	t
Raven	.70	.32	2.03*	.57	.41	.89
Columbia	.43	.16	1.20	.49	.31	1.01
Peabody	.74	.40	2.16*	.60	.58	.15
Benton error	.73	.37	2.27*	.51	.26	1.38
P-A task	.62(24)	.30(32)	1.21	.67(30)	.45(45)	1.15

	Whites					
	Males			Females		
Variables	MZ (63)	DZ (50)	t	MZ (59)	DZ (40)	t
Raven	.61	.32	1.93*	.54	−.06	3.11***
Columbia	.47	.22	1.51	.32	−.02	1.74*
Peabody	.60	.39	1.44	.68	.42	1.83*
Benton error	.40	.31	.52	.70	.13	3.56***
P-A task	.59	.63	−.34	.54	.29	1.40

*p < .05.
***p < .001.

test correlation. As in the previous comparison of twin correlations by race and SES, the race × sex group results suggest that family membership is more determinative of differences in vocabulary than other skills. The Raven matrices have the most consistent pattern of larger MZ than DZ correlations when the samples are divided by race and sex.

DISCUSSION

The twin study was designed to look at the sources of variance within samples of young, black and white adolescents' cognitive test scores. The data generally support the view that individual differences in the intellectual skills sampled by these tests are to some extent heritable in both black and white groups. Individual differences arise from both environmental and genetic differences, between and within families. The magnitude of the effects differs in the two racial groups. Two major hypotheses were used to generate different predictions about three aspects of the results: (1) the relative performance of black children on more culturally loaded versus less loaded tasks; (2) the amount of environmental variability in the scores of black versus white children; and (3) the importance of family environments for the development of intellectual skills in the black versus white groups.

On the first prediction, black children were shown to perform relatively better on *less* culturally loaded material once the instructions were made more comprehensible to them. This result, in contrast to Jensen (1973), suggested that a general unfamiliarity with the tasks and instructions for such tasks may be at the root of the previously reported better performance of black children on more culturally loaded material. Because the instructions for the verbal, culturally loaded tests are simpler than those of the less obvious, less culturally loaded tests, we conclude that the former result can largely be attributed to the level of difficulty in the instructions, not to the task itself. At least if the simple alteration of the instructions can reverse the previous profile of performance, one has to conclude that finding better black performance on culturally loaded material is a trivial result and no support for the idea of genetic racial differences. If it is true, as we found, that black children perform worst on the most culturally loaded material, it is evidence for a generalized cultural unfamiliarity with the material on the culturally loaded tests. Although we agree with Jensen that there is no evidence for *differential* cultural bias within the tests we used, we do not agree that black children as a group have equal access with white children to the material sampled by culturally loaded tests.

On the second hypothesis—that black environments fail to enhance the development of the skills sampled by these tests (and by the schools)—we found less genetic variability and more environmental variability in the scores of black children. The differences between the MZ and DZ correlations are greater in the white group, an indication that the effect of genetic differences or cognitive differences is greater in the white group.

To test the third hypothesis—that twin correlations will be higher in the black group because family membership is more important in determining the degree of exposure to the intellectual skills we sample—we looked at the magnitude of the MZ and DZ correlations. The DZ correlations are clearly higher in the black group for all conceptual tests, and this higher black correlation is based on smaller within-family variances, not on larger between-family variances. One possible cause of the different variance between blacks and whites could be a higher degree of assortative mating among the black twins' parents. A higher degree of assortative mating would reduce the genetic variability within families, but it would also increase the genetic variance between families. There is no evidence for the latter point; only the within-family variances are smaller in the black than white DZ pairs. Another possibility is that black twins are treated more similarly by their parents, particularly the DZ pairs. The increased similarity of treatment of black, as compared to white, twins would explain the results, but we have no speculations on why this might occur.

The importance of family membership in determining individual differences among the black children should be seen in the context of two other trends: the lower correlations of age and SES with differences among the blacks. Although the reliabilities of the tests are as high for the black children as for the white children, the test scores of the blacks are not consistently related to age differences. The variability of scores within the 1-year age bands was higher for the black group, especially for the Raven matrices and the figural memory test. For unexplained reasons, the mental progress that children make with increasing age is not only slower for black children than white children; it is also less correlated with increasing age in the black group. Speculations on this result lead us to believe that other, environmental determinants of differences in cognitive performance among black children are overwhelming the generally recognized age effect.

Family membership explains more of the differences among the black twins than the white ones. Belonging to a particular family seems to create more similarity among black DZ twins than white DZs and relatively smaller differences among black MZs than white MZs. Paradoxically, the measures of social-class differences are less strongly associated with cognitive differences among the black children than the white. Whatever factors make for greater similarity among black than white co-twins are not associated with social-class variables as measured by census-tract data or by individual reports about the twins' families. It may be that parental intellectual characteristics and child-rearing practices are not as highly associated with the usual SES ratings in the black community. Given the history of racial discrimination in employment, housing, and education, and given the variability in length of time spent in the North, it may well be that the educational and income characteristics of a neighborhood are not as predictive of intellectual differences among black children, whereas unmeasured characteristics of their individual families determine more of their cognitive differences.

Although we offer no explanation that readers should feel compelled to accept, we believe that the pattern of results supports a general cultural-differences hypothesis far better than a genetic-differences view. The data are not sufficiently good nor the results clear enough to demand that one accept one view and reject the other. In summary, however, we present the following account of the results:

1. Black children have lower scores on all the cognitive tests, but they score relatively worse on the more culturally loaded of the conceptual tests.

2. The cognitive differences among the black children are less well explained by genetic individual differences, by age, and by social-class differences than those of the white children.

3. The similarity of the black co-twins, particularly the DZs, suggests that being reared in different families determines more of the cognitive differences among black than white children, but that those between-family differences are not those usually measured by SES variables in the white community.

4. Therefore, we conclude that the results of this study support the view that black children are being reared in circumstances that give them only marginal acquaintance with the skills and the knowledge being sampled by the tests we administered. Some families in the black community encourage the development of these skills and knowledge, whereas others do not. In general, black children do not have the same access to these skills and knowledge as white children, which explains the lower performance of black children as a group. The hypothesis that most of the differences among the cognitive scores of black and white children are due to genetic differences between the races cannot, in our view, account for this pattern of results.

ACKNOWLEDGMENTS

Supported by NICHD Grant #HD-06502 and the W. T. Grant Foundation. We wish to thank Dr. Herbert Polesky, Director of the Minneapolis War Memorial Blood Bank, for the extensive blood-grouping analyses and Solomon H. Katz, William Thompson, and Valerie Lindstrom for their help in collecting and analyzing the data.

REFERENCES

Benton, A. L. *The Revised Visual Retention Test, Form C*. Dubuque, Iowa: William C. Brown, 1963.
Burgemeister, B. B., Blum, L. H., & Lorge, I. *Columbia Mental Maturity Scale*. New York: Harcourt, Brace & World, 1959.

Carter-Saltzman, L., & Scarr, S. Blood group, behavioral, and morphological differences among dizygotic twins. *Social Biology*, 1976, *22*(4), 372–374.

Carter-Saltzman, L., & Scarr, S. MZ or DZ? Only your blood grouping laboratory knows for sure. *Behavior Genetics*, 1977, 4, 273–280.

Carter-Saltzman, L., Scarr-Salapatek, S., & Barker, W. B. Do these co-twins really live together? An assessment of the validity of the Home Index as a measure of family socioeconomic status. *Educational and Psychological Measurement*, 1975, *35*, 427–435.

Cleary, T. A., Humphreys, L. G., Kendrick, S. A., & Wesman, A. Educational uses of tests with disadvantaged students. *American Psychologist*, 1975, *30*(1), 15–41.

Dunn, L. M. *Peabody Picture Vocabulary Test*. Circle Pines, Minn.: American Guidance Service, 1959.

Gough, H. G. *The Home Index*. Berkeley: University of California, 1970.

Henderson, N. D. Genetic influences on the behavior of mice can be obscured by laboratory rearing. *Journal of Comparative and Physiological Psychology*, 1970, *72*(3), 505–511.

Hunt, E. Quote the Raven? Nevermore! In L. W. Gregg (Ed.), *Knowledge and cognition*. Potomac, Maryland: Lawrence Erlbaum Associates 1974.

Jensen, A. R. *Educability and group differences*. New York: Harper & Row, 1973.

Jensen, A. R. Cumulative deficit: A testable hypothesis? *Developmental Psychology*, 1974, *10*(6), 996–1019. (a)

Jensen, A. R. How biased are culture-loaded tests? *Genetic Psychology Monographs*, 1974, *90*, 185–244. (b)

Labov, W. Some sources of reading problems for Negro speakers of nonstandard English. In *New directions in elementary English*. New York, National Council of Teachers of English, 1967.

Rao, D. C., Morton, N. E., & Yee, S. Analysis of family resemblance. II. A linear model for familial correlation. *American Journal of Human Genetics*, 1974, *26*, 331–359.

Raven, J. C. *Standard Progressive Matrices: Sets A, B, C, D, & E*. London: Lewis, 1958.

Scarr, S., Pakstis, A. J., Katz, S. H., & Barker, W. B. Absence of a relationship between degree of white ancestry and intellectual skills within a black population. *Human Genetics*, 1977, *39*, 69–86.

Scarr, S., & Weinberg, R. A. IQ test performance of black children adopted by white families. *American Psychologist*, 1976, *31*, 726–739.

Scarr, S., & Weinberg, R. A. Intellectual similarities within families of both adopted and biological children. *Intelligence*, 1977, *1*(2), 170–191.

Scarr-Salapatek, S. Race, social class and IQ. *Science*, 1971, *174*, 1285–1295.

Stevenson, H. W., Hale, G. A., Klein, R. E., & Miller, L. K. Interrelations and correlates in children's learning and problem solving. *Monographs of the Society for Research in Child Development*, 1968, *33*(7, Serial No. 123).

Williams, R. L. Danger: Testing and dehumanizing black children. *Clinical Child Psychology Newsletter*, 1970, *9*(1), 5–6.

APPENDIX A

THE PRETEST

Few testing procedures have been standardized on disadvantaged children. We were concerned about the appropriateness of test instructions that had not been tried on inner-city, black children. If they could not understand the instructions, they could not be expected to score well on the tests. We were not interested in the level of difficulty of the *instructions,* but we wanted to be certain they were appropriate.

In addition, we wanted to choose test items at an appropriate range of difficulty so that neither "floor" nor "ceiling" effects would occur. Thus, both task levels and instructions were pretested on black, inner-city children.

In 2 days of pretesting, we paid $5 each to 30 inner-city, black 10- to 16-year-olds to tell us what was wrong with our tests and procedures. The children were recruited through a neighborhood center and were bused from North Philadelphia to the University of Pennsylvania for the pretest. After an introduction to the purposes of the twin study, we emphasized that they were hired to help us revise our measures. They soon responded critically when they realized that we were seriously interested in their opinions. We wrote down their suggestions and repeatedly tried test procedures in alternate ways, asking for feedback about the changes. The children were vocal in their criticism, and we thank them for saving us much wasted effort.

It was clear from the 1st pretest day that many standard instructions for the intellectual tasks were not appropriate for inner-city, black children. They seemed to need more redundancy. The task instructions had to be simple and clear, with examples of correct responses given, and they had to be repeated. As a result of the children's help, one measure of spatial abilities was eliminated; the Raven matrices were shortened to four sets instead of five; a film produced for the paired-associate task was revised; and most other instructions were made more redundant. We do not know how much these changes reflected our slide-tape presentation rather than written tests and how much they reflected differences between our subjects and standardization samples. The slide–tape presentation was designed to eliminate the effects of reading difficulties on many of the tests, but it may also have complicated test taking in unknown ways.

What follows is an impressionistic account of the pretest sessions that led us to construct the test battery as we did. The study was not constructed to assess the effects of task instructions on the intellectual performance of inner-city children. It was critically important that the subjects understood what they were to do if we were to have fair measures of their current performance levels on intellectual tasks. Thus, we used essentially clinical methods to get feedback on why the children were having difficulties and on how we could best arrange the tasks and instructions to minimize their problems.

The spatial abilities test, the Surface Development Test, was too difficult in concept. The task is to fold mentally a two-dimensional figure into a solid and to identify which edges become which edges of the solid. We tried every kind of instructions we could think of to make it simpler, but the task was just too difficult. We even used paper models to illustrate the concept of edge identification. The children tried, and we tried—but to no avail.

Their response to the Raven matrices was quite different from that to the Surface Development Test. They understood the early problems but got frustrated toward the end. We gave them more and more time but got more and more boredom rather than correct answers. On this basis we decided finally to eliminate Set E, the most difficult series. In retrospect, the older suburban children could have increased their scores somewhat if Set E had been retained, but we could have tortured the majority of our subjects with material that was far too difficult.

The time allowed for the matrix problems was set by having the children raise their hands when they had made a selection. We told them not to hurry but to concentrate on finding the correct answer. When nearly all the children—there were always a few compulsive ones—had raised their hands, we noted the time. By averaging across problems, we arrived at an interval of 15 seconds for each problem in Sets A and B and 25 seconds for C and D. The children seemed most comfortable with these intervals, which were a trade-off between rushing them and boring them. Too much time seemed to disrupt performance on subsequent problems.

The Peabody Picture Vocabulary Test provided still another problem. The children did not seem to hear the words they did not know. The tape said "Obelisk, Obelisk," and the children said "Whaat?" When an experimenter repeated the stimulus word again and again, the children stopped asking what it was. But when asked how many were helped by the repeated presentations, few said that they were. When we gave the correct answer, very few said they got it because it had been repeated a third or fourth time. Thus, we concluded that two presentations were generally enough, but we continued to say the word again if the twins asked for it. The time for the vocabulary test was set according to the same procedure used for the matrices.

The paired-associate task was a fascinating error. Harold Stevenson and his associates (1968) had successfully used the film to test some 800 fourth-, fifth-, and sixth-grade children in the Twin Cities area. The film stars an educational TV commentator who explains the P-A task to the children with examples and instructions for the first trial. Subsequent trials require the children to generalize from the instructions for the first trial. The pretest children did not seem to generalize; they were lost by the second trial. We stopped the film and paraphrased the commentator's instructions for Trial 2. They were lost again by Trial 3. We told them to use the same instructions for every subsequent trial. Nothing seemed to work. We tried a prefilm tape to supplement the filmed instructions. More but not most of the children understood the task on Pretest Day 2. Contrary to our better judgment, we decided to go on with the film and even more elaborate prefilm instructions in the early days of twin testing. Later we had to eliminate those data and switch to slide and tape presentation, repeating the instructions for each trial. The times for trials given in the film were retained in the slide–tape presentation.

A similar experience occurred with the instructions for the Revised visual retention test (Benton, 1963). The manual's instructions are very simple: Look at the figure for 10 seconds, and when it is removed, draw what you have seen. For tape and slide presentation, the instructions were essentially the same. A second prompt is given before the third card (slide) when multiple geometric figures appear for the first time: Do not forget to draw everything you see. After the third stimulus, no further instructions are indicated by the manual.

In the pretest, we discovered that instructions were not generalized from one trial to the next. The children were genuinely confused about what to do. Thus, we devised a set of instructions that told them for each of the 10 slides: "Here is slide number ____. Look but do not draw. (10 seconds) Now draw. (45 seconds) Turn the page. Here is slide number ____. Look but do not draw. . . .

The interval allowed for drawing was based on the feedback of the pretest children who raised their hands when they were satisfied that they were through. The vast majority of the children found 45 seconds an ample, even lengthy, interval for drawing the figures.

In contrast, the task required by the Columbia Mental Maturity Scale presented no apparent conceptual problems for the pretest children. To find one figure that does not belong with the other four is popularly known as "The Sesame Street Task," one with which they were all familiar. The ease with which they comprehended the instructions for the CMMS suggests that they profit from experiences with tasks. The other tasks were far less familiar problems. As the results show, the inner-city children performed somewhat better on the CMMS than on some other tasks.

The pretest days were enormously valuable in providing information about how to assess inner-city children. There is simply no point in giving children tests that are conceptually too difficult, such as the Surface Development Test, or tests for which the instructions are inappropriate. Although we did not approach the problems of task level and instructions in a full-fledged study, we did ascertain a great deal of helpful information that altered the course of our assessments. The pretest children were wonderfully cooperative and helpful, and we are grateful to them.

The Implications of the Pretest

The initial selection of task levels had been made with a range of MA 7 to adult in mind. For children of chronological age 10 to 16 in the sample, we needed a wide range of difficulty. Although we hoped to eliminate some of the easier items, this was not possible. The pretest indicated that discriminations at the lower end of the performance distributions required 7-year items from the PPVT, Sets A and B from the Raven matrices, and 7-year items from the CMMS. Besides providing discriminations, they also provided some success experiences for children who did not perform at their age level on aptitude tests.

One wonders about the efficacy of school-administered aptitude and achievement tests whose ranges are far more restricted than those chosen for this study.

As noted in an earlier study (Scarr-Salapatek, 1971), many of the black, inner-city children "pile up" in the first percentile on standard tests. Whether task level, task instructions, or reading skills are one or all implicated we do not know. But it is clear that some aspects of the school testing program are not adequate to assess the level at which many children are functioning.

In addition, we had the opportunity to pretest 851 seventh-grade children in the Philadelphia public schools as part of an assessment of the usefulness of the Raven matrices to the school district. Sets A to E were administered by booklet; so the results are not entirely comparable to our slide-and-tape presentation. Individual children could proceed with the problems at their own pace in the school setting, to a limit of about 45 minutes, compared to our limit of 25 minutes for the first four sets. What the pretest showed us, however, was that even under self-paced conditions, Set E of the standard matrices added very little information. The average number of correct responses to the 12 problems in each set was: A = 9.9; B = 7.4; C = 6.1; D = 6.4; E = 2.1. Random responses to Set E would result in 1.5 correct answers.

PROCEDURES WITH THE TWINS

Twin subjects came to the study in two ways—by chartered bus and on their own. For children within the city, whether from public or parochial school, bus transportation from the elementary school nearest their homes was offered. The bus schedule was arranged to provide at least two dates during the testing period for each elementary school. A chartered SEPTA bus made the rounds of five to eight elementary schools daily, picking up and later returning the twins.

The twins were notified by telephone or by mail to appear at a given time at the local elementary school. These arrangements seemed clear to us, but there were numerous confusions about the time, date, and place. There is no doubt that more inner-city children could have been obtained for the study if door-to-door service could have been provided and if home visitors could have been sent out to make contact with the families on the day of testing. It was decided, however, that it was too dangerous to send the group leaders into many areas of the city where they were not known.

Some city twins and all suburban twins came to the study under their own arrangements. Some rode buses and trains; about one-third were accompanied by their parents, who sat in on the testing procedures. Unfortunately, we did not expect enough parents to have planned to test them at the same time. In retrospect, we should have tested the 30 to 35 parents who came. A few suburban children were given transportation money when they requested it by telephone. Most, however, paid their own way to come.

The twins arrived at the dental school auditorium around 1 o'clock. They were greeted with name tags and small-group assignments written on the tags. The two members of each twin pair were assigned to different small groups to prevent collaboration on tests or interviews. We had also discovered in the pretest that young adolescents make lots of noise when surrounded by their friends. The twin groups were quiet and orderly, for they rarely knew anyone in their small groups.

Once the twins-for-the-day were assembled in their groups and seated in alternate seats and rows, they were given an introduction to the study. They were told that we were interested in the similarities between co-twins in a variety of psychological and physical. Approximate times and schedules were given for the afternoon. Questions, if any, were answered. They were told to do their best and that although the results would not be reported to their schools or parents, it was important to know how well twins could do and how similar their abilities and personalities were.

Small Groups

Upon arrival at the testing site, the twins were divided into small groups, each with an adult leader. On the 30 days of testing, there were a total of 109 groups for the 810 children tested. The average number of children per group was 7.4, the median 7, and the mode 8. The smallest group was 2; the largest was 26 on one wild day when an excessive number of suburban children showed up to participate. Fortunately, the suburban children had fewer problems with following instructions than the city children, and the large groups functioned satisfactorily for the psychological assessments. Data were lost, however, for dental assessments, photographs, dermatoglyphics, and some X rays. These individually administered measures could not be handled for so many children on a single afternoon.

Each small group had an adult leader who escorted them through the afternoon's assessments and who answered questions about the tests and procedures. The leader also checked on every child's use of the answer sheets for the psychological tests. Occasionally, a child needed help to find the correct column or row for an answer. Once or twice, a whole answer sheet had to be transcribed by the leader because the child had used the wrong one.

ANSWER SHEETS

The answer sheets were custom-made versions of standard IBM scoring forms. Each answer sheet was labeled for the test in large primary-grade type. Only the proper number of questions and answer alternatives appeared on the sheet. If there were 24 questions to be answered "yes," "no," or "don't know," as in the Home Index, the answer sheet contained only 24 questions and three alternative responses for each question. The answer alternatives were also given on the bottom right, such as "1 = no, 2 = yes, 3 = don't know." In this way, confusion over the use of answer sheets was kept to a minimum.

APPENDIX B

RAVEN[3]

Turn to the second answer sheet, the Raven Standard Progressive Matrices. There are four sets of problems, marked A, B. C, and D. Each set has 12 questions. Here is the first problem in set A.

Number A-1. The upper part is a pattern with a piece missing. Each of the pieces below is the right shape to fit the space, but they do not all complete the pattern. Number 1 is the wrong pattern. Numbers 2 and 3 are wrong. They fit the space, but they are not the right pattern. What about number 6? It is the right pattern, but the pattern does not fill in the whole space. Number 4 is the right one. So fill in the brackets to cover the number 4 for number 1 in set A. On every slide you will see a pattern with a piece missing. You have to decide each time which of the pieces below is the right one to complete the pattern. When you have found the right piece, fill in the brackets to cover the number on your answer sheet. They are simple at the beginning and get harder as you go on. There is no catch. If you pay attention to the way the easy ones go, you will find the later ones less difficult. Please mark an answer for every question even if you have to guess. See how many you can get right. Try the next one. *Pause of 9 seconds.* The right one is number 5. See that you have marked the number 5 in the bracket under question A-2. Go on like this to the end of the test.

Question A-3 through A-12.

Timing: 10 seconds after question till buzzer. 13 seconds between buzzers (took 3 seconds to say "Question A-10," etc.).

Set B. Question B-1 through B-12.

Timing: Same as for Set A.

Set C. Question C-1 through C-12.

Timing: 25 seconds between buzzers.

Set D. Question D-1 through D-12.

Timing: Same as in Set C.

Please stop.

PEABODY[4]

This is a picture vocabulary test. There are four pictures on every slide. Each of them is numbered. You will hear a word, then you should mark the number of the picture which best tells the meaning of the word. Let's try number 1. Which

---

[3]From Raven (1958).
[4]From Dunn (1959).

picture goes with *capsule*? Fill in the brackets on your answer sheet to cover the number of the picture for capsule, capsule. Number 1 is the correct answer. Here is question 2. Which picture goes with thermos, thermos? Number 4 is correct. Each time you hear a word, you should mark your answer sheet with the number of the picture which best tells the meaning of the word. As the test goes on, the words get harder. If you are not sure of the answer, please guess anyway. Be sure to mark an answer for every word.

Question 3. group, group—pause of 7 seconds—bell—pause of 5 seconds—next word.

Question 4. Transportation, transportation

Examiner repeats every word once.

5. ceremony	22. kayak	39. precipitation	56. tartan
6. bronco	23. sentry	40. gable	57. obelisk
7. funnel	24. furrow	41. amphibian	58. entomology
8. lecturer	25. beam	42. graduated	59. dormer
9. archer	26. fragment	43. hieroglyphic	60. consternation
10. excavate	27. hovering	44. orate	61. gauntlet
11. stunt	28. bereavement	45. cascade	62. cupola
12. meringue	29. crag	46. illumination	63. burnishing
13. appliance	30. tantrum	47. nape	64. eminence
14. chemist	31. submerge	48. genealogist	65. senile
15. arctic	32. descend	49. embossed	66. raze
16. destruction	33. hassock	50. mercantile	67. cravat
17. porter	34. canine	51. encumbered	68. marsupial
18. coast	35. probing	52. concentric	69. incertitude
19. hoisting	36. angling	53. sibling	70. homunculus
20. wailing	37. appraising	54. waif	Please stop
21. coil	38. confining	55. timorous	

Timing: After word was given, a pause of 7 seconds before bell. After bell, a pause of 5 seconds before next word was given.

COLUMBIA[5]

Please turn to the next answer sheet—the Columbia Test.

This is a reasoning test. You will see five pictures on each slide. One of the pictures does not belong there—does not go with the others. Here is a practice one. Try to find the one which does not belong. Mark the number of the picture that does not belong on your answer sheet below question number 1. If you chose number 4, the red circle, you are correct. There are two solid blue circles that go together and two outlined circles that go together. The red circle does not belong

[5]From Burgemeister, Blum, and Lorge (1959).

with any other part of the picture. Here is another example. Try to find the picture which does not belong. Pause of 9 seconds. Mark your choice on your answer sheet below the question number 2. The right answer is number 4, the hat. All the others are things to wear on your foot. They all go together, but the hat does not belong. *You will have 25 seconds for each problem—then you will hear the sound.* If you have not marked an answer, be sure to mark your answer sheet before the next problem appears.

Here is question number 3.

Mark your answer sheet with the number of the picture that does not belong. Do the rest in the same way. Pause of 25 seconds, then the buzzer.

Question 4. Pause of 25 seconds. . . .

Question 30.

Please stop.

PAIRED-ASSOCIATE TEST[6]

There are some things we want you to do for us while you watch these slides. Each of you will need a booklet. Make sure it's on your desk in front of you, and check to see if your name is on the front of the booklet. Do not open the booklet. Now let me tell you what we are going to do. We want to see how well you can remember things that go together. I am going to show you some made up words and some pictures. First you will see a made up word on the screen. Then you will see the same word paired with a picture. Your job is to remember which word and picture go together. The same made up word and picture always go together. At first you will make some mistakes, but I will show you the pairs several times, and if you pay close attention you will be able to remember which ones go together. I will show you all the pairs so that you can see which ones go together. After we have gone through all of them you will open your booklets, and I will say, now you may begin. In the booklet you will see the made up words and all of the pictures. You are to try to remember which one of the pictures goes with each made up word. I will tell you more about this after we have seen some slides. Now I will show you the first made up word and the picture that goes with it. Then I will show you the second made up word and the picture that goes with it. Watch very carefully. Now we will go through the list. Please watch the screen.

Pause of 65 seconds.

Open your book to the first page. Look at the made up words on the left. Now, look at the pictures on the right. You must try to remember which picture goes with each made up word. Draw a circle around the picture you think goes with

---

[6]From Stevenson, Hale, Klein, and Miller (1968).

each made up word. Start with the one at the top, and go down the list circling the one which you think is correct each time. Make a guess if you're not sure. Now you may begin on the first yellow page.

Pause of 37 seconds, bell, pause of 3 seconds before next instruction.

Please turn to the next blank page even if you have not finished. Now watch the screen. Pause of 67 seconds.

Turn to the next page, the red page, and circle the picture you think goes with each made up word. Pause of 38 seconds, bell.

Please turn to the next blank page even if you have not finished. Now watch the screen. Pause of 65 seconds.

Turn to the next page, the green page, and circle the picture you think goes with each made up word. Pause of 35 seconds, bell.

Please turn to the next blank page even if you have not finished. Now watch the screen. Pause of 68 seconds.

Turn to the next page, the yellow page, and circle the picture you think goes with each made up word. Pause of 39 seconds.

Please turn to the next blank page even if you have not finished. Now watch the screen. Pause of 69 seconds.

Turn to the next page, the pink page, and circle the picture you think goes with each made up word. Pause of 40 seconds.

Please turn to the next blank page even if you have not finished. Now watch the screen. Pause of 68 seconds.

Turn to the next page, the blue page, and circle the picture you think goes with each made up word. Pause of 40 seconds.

Please stop.

BENTON[7]

This is a visual memory test. You have ten blank white pages in your booklet. You should draw one slide on each page. You will be shown the slide on which there is one or more figures. You will see each slide for ten seconds. Do not draw while the slide is being shown. As soon as the slide is removed, please draw what you have seen on the slide. Be sure to look at the slide for the full ten seconds. Here is slide number 1. Look but do not draw—pause of 13 seconds. Now draw—pause of 31 seconds.

Turn the page. Here is slide number 2. Look but do not draw. Pause of 13 seconds. Now draw—pause of 30 seconds.

Turn the page. Here is slide three. Do not forget to draw everything you see. Now look but do not draw—pause of 13 seconds. Now draw. Pause of 31 seconds.

---

[7]From Benton (1963).

Turn the page. Here is slide number four. Look but do not draw. 13 seconds.
Now draw—44 seconds.
Turn the page. Here is slide 5. Look but do not draw. 13 seconds.
Now draw—42 seconds.
Turn the page. Here is slide number 6. Look but do not draw. 13 seconds.
Now draw—43 seconds.
Turn the page. Here is slide number 7. Look but do not draw. 13 seconds.
Now draw—43 seconds.
Turn the page. Here is slide number 8. Look but do not draw. 13 seconds.
Now draw—44 seconds.
Turn the page. Here is slide number 9. Look but do not draw. 13 seconds.
Now draw—43 seconds.
Turn the page. Here is slide number 10. Look but do not draw. 13 seconds.
Now draw—45 seconds.
Please stop.

HOME INDEX[8]

Please look at the first answer sheet. You can see that there are numbers from 1 to 24 along the top row. These are the numbers of the questions you will be asked to answer. Below each question number there are three small numbers in brackets. If you look at the lower right hand corner of your answer sheet, you will see that the number zero means yes, 1 means no, and 2 means that you don't know. Here is the first question on the home index. Is there an electric or gas refrigerator in your home? If you have a refrigerator in your home please fill in the brackets to cover the number zero. If you do not have a refrigerator in your home fill in the brackets to cover the number 1. If you are not sure of the answer to any question fill in the brackets to cover the number two. *You will have ten seconds to answer each question.* Just before the next question appears you will hear this sound. If you have not yet marked an answer, please mark one. Please make your marks nice and dark because a machine will score your answer sheet.

Question 2. Is there a telephone in your home?
     3. Do you have a bathtub in your home?
     4. Is your home heated with a central system such as by a furnace in the basement?
     5. Does your family have a car?
     6. Did your mother go to high school?
     7. Did your mother go to college or university?
     8. Did your father go to high school?

---

[8]From Gough (1970).

9. Did your father go to a college or university?
10. Do you have a fireplace in your home?
11. Do you have a piano in your home?
12. Does your family have a radio?
13. Does your family have a phonograph? (record player, stereo)
14. Does your family have any servants such as a cook or maid?
15. Does your family leave town every year for a vacation?
16. Does your mother belong to any clubs or organizations such as study, art, or civic clubs?
17. Does your father belong to any civic, study, service, or political clubs, such as the Chamber of Commerce, the Lions Club, etc?
18. Have you ever taken private lessons in music, dancing, art, etc. outside of school?
19. Do you have your own room at home?
20. Does your family subscribe to a daily newspaper?
21. Do you belong to any club where you have to pay dues?
22. Does your family have more than 500 books?
23. Does your family own its own home?
24. Does your family have a color television set?

Please stop.

APPENDIX C

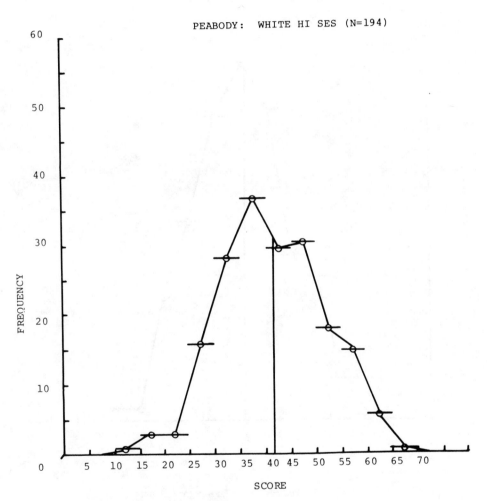

FIG. A.1.   Peabody: White Hi SES (N = 194).

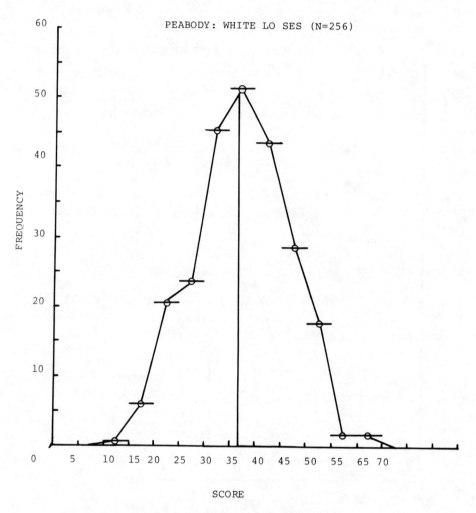

FIG. A.2.   Peabody: White Lo SES (N = 256).

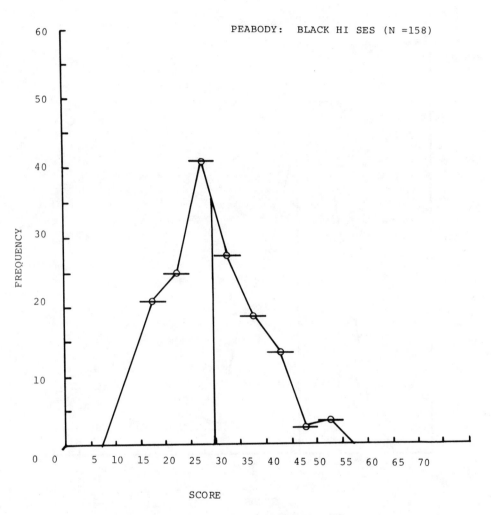

FIG. A.3. Peabody: Black Hi SES (*N* = 158).

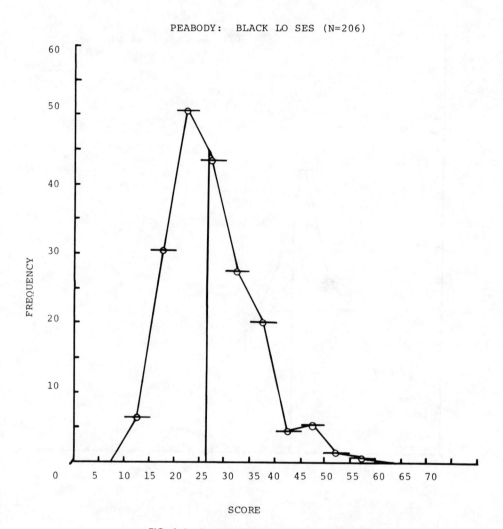

FIG. A.4. Peabody: Black Lo SES (N = 206).

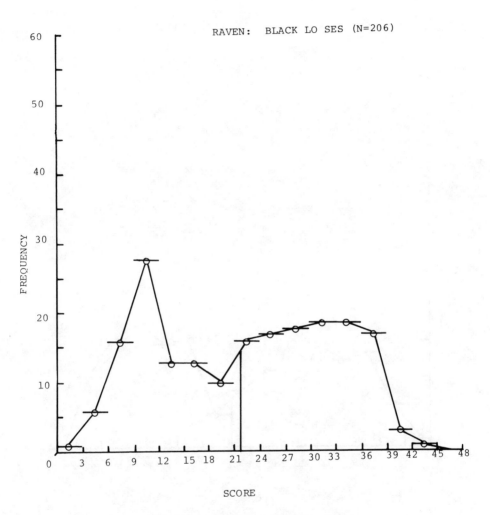

FIG. A.5.   Raven: Black Lo SES (*N* = 206).

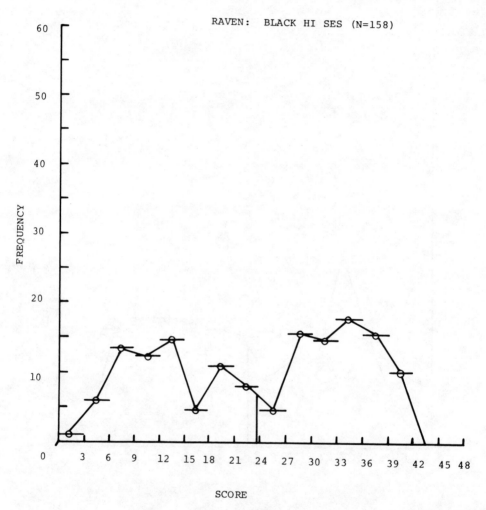

FIG. A.6.   Raven: Black Hi SES (N = 158).

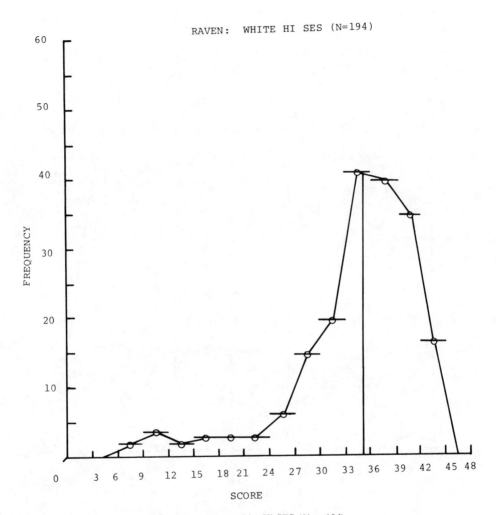

FIG. A.7.   Raven: White Hi SES (N = 194).

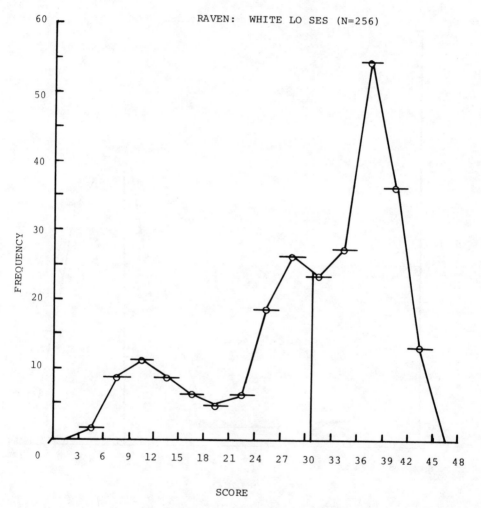

FIG. A.8.   Raven: White Lo SES ($N = 256$).

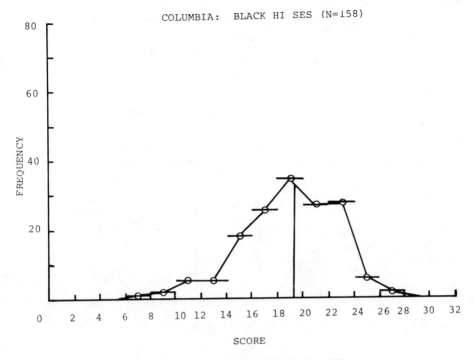

FIG. A.11. Columbia: Black Hi SES (N = 158).

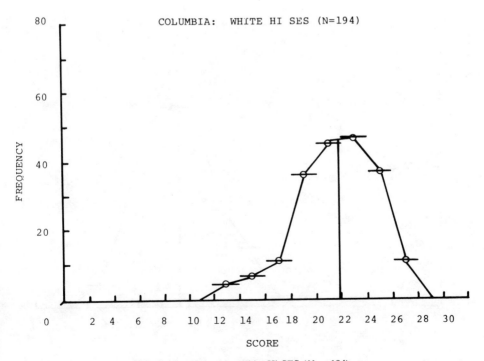

FIG. A.12. Columbia: White Hi SES (N = 194).

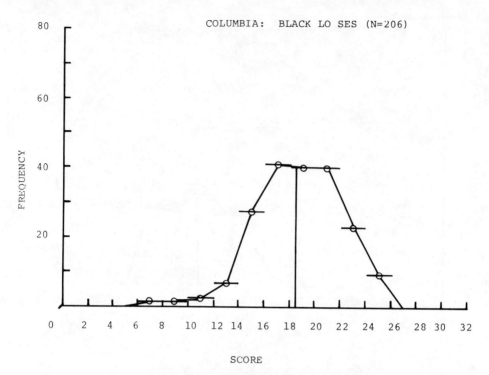

FIG. A.9. Columbia: Black Lo SES ($N = 206$).

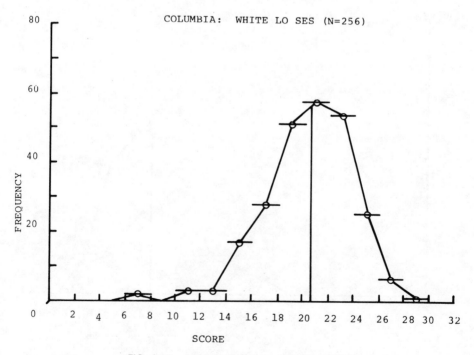

FIG. A.10. Columbia: White Lo SES ($N = 256$).

APPENDIX D

TABLE 1
Age Effects: Means and *SD*s of Raw scores on Five Cognitive Tests
for All Subjects[a]

		Age in Years					
		10	11	12	13	14	15
Corrected Raven	$\overline{M}$	23.8	28.8	31.1	31.6	31.3	31.9
	SD	(8.9)	(8.8)	(9.4)	(8.8)	(8.9)	(8.2)
	N	142	117	113	131	131	103
Peabody	$\overline{M}$	29.4	32.0	35.2	36.9	37.7	41.4
	SD	(8.6)	(8.3)	(9.5)	(10.1)	(11.1)	(12.3)
	N	176	126	114	128	134	106
Columbia	$\overline{M}$	18.9	19.9	20.8	21.2	21.5	21.8
	SD	(3.1)	(3.2)	(3.2)	(3.4)	(3.7)	(3.5)
	N	180	129	117	130	136	105
Benton E	$\overline{M}$	8.3	7.6	6.3	6.3	5.7	5.3
	SD	(3.6)	(3.5)	(3..2)	(3.4)	(3.6)	(3.1)
	N	166	121	112	119	122	97
PA	$\overline{M}$	20.5	21.3	25.4	26.1	25.1	25.3
	SD	(8.8)	(8.4)	(8.1)	(8.5)	(9.2)	(7.9)
	N	122	96	84	92	102	85

[a] Ages 10–12 = great leap forward in skills.

TABLE 2
Age Effects: $\bar{X}$ and *SD* Raw Scores for All Whites

		Age in Years					
		10	*11*	*12*	*13*	*14*	*15*
Raven	$\bar{X}$	27.4	30.6	33.5	34.3	36.6	35.5
	SD	(8.3)	(8.3)	(7.7)	(6.9)	(5.6)	(5.4)
	N	73	79	73	81	59	64
Peabody	$\bar{X}$	31.3	35.9	39.3	41.2	46.7	47.6
	SD	(7.0)	(7.6)	(8.6)	(9.1)	(6.3)	(10.1)
	N	77	83	73	81	56	64
Columbia	$\bar{X}$	19.4	20.3	21.5	22.2	23.3	23.1
	SD	(3.3)	(3.1)	(3.0)	(3.0)	(2.5)	(2.8)
	N	78	86	75	83	59	64
Benton C	$\bar{X}$	5.1	5.6	6.2	6.5	6.8	7.3
	SD	(2.0)	(1.9)	(1.8)	(1.8)	(1.8)	(1.5)
	N	77	85	76	80	57	64
Benton E	$\bar{X}$	8.2	6.8	5.4	5.1	4.4	3.6
	SD	(4.1)	(3.8)	(3.1)	(3.1)	(2.8)	(2.4)
	N	77	85	76	80	57	64
PA	$\bar{X}$	21.4	23.0	25.3	27.0	26.9	26.4
	SD	(8.4)	(8.0)	(8.4)	(7.8)	(9.6)	(7.9)
	N	70	82	64	73	53	58

TABLE 3
Age Effects: $\bar{X}$ and SD Raw Scores for All Blacks

		Age in Years					
		10	11	12	13	14	15
Raven	$\bar{X}$	19.9	25.5	26.9	27.2	27.1	26.2
	SD	(7.9)	(9.0)	(10.0)	(9.8)	(8.9)	(9.8)
	N	69	38	40	50	72	39
Peabody	$\bar{X}$	24.2	27.3	29.0	30.7	31.8	32.4
	SD	(5.4)	(6.9)	(7.4)	(8.2)	(9.7)	(8.9)
	N	78	50	45	52	80	44
Columbia	$\bar{X}$	18.1	19.1	19.8	19.6	20.2	20.0
	SD	(2.7)	(3.1)	(3.1)	(3.3)	(3.9)	(3.7)
	N	81	50	46	52	79	44
Benton C	$\bar{X}$	4.0	4.4	4.9	5.3	5.6	5.4
	SD	(1.7)	(1.9)	(2.0)	(2.2)	(2.2)	(2.0)
	N	80	54	46	52	74	44
Benton E	$\bar{X}$	10.7	9.2	8.0	7.7	7.0	7.4
	SD	(4.2)	(4.1)	(2.0)	(4.4)	(4.6)	(4.0)
	N	80	54	46	52	74	44
PA	$\bar{X}$	17.1	16.0	25.5	23.4	24.1	23.1
	SD	(7.7)	(7.2)	(7.0)	(10.4)	(7.9)	(7.9)
	N	39	24	24	25	57	27

TABLE 4
Age Effects: $\bar{X}$ and SD Raw Scores for Black Females

		Age in Years					
		10	11	12	13	14	15
Raven	$\bar{X}$	19.2	27.7	28.7	25.9	26.6	26.3
	SD	(7.8)	(9.5)	(9.8)	(8.8)	(8.1)	(9.7)
	N	39	20	26	18	41	25
Peabody	$\bar{X}$	23.7	27.1	29.9	29.5	28.9	30.7
	SD	(4.9)	(7.6)	(7.2)	(7.9)	(8.6)	(8.1)
	N	47	28	27	20	45	30
Columbia	$\bar{X}$	18.0	18.7	20.2	19.8	20.2	19.3
	SD	(2.7)	(3.5)	(2.8)	(3.1)	(4.0)	(3.7)
	N	50	28	28	20	46	30
Benton E	$\bar{X}$	11.1	8.7	7.5	7.8	7.6	7.8
	SD	(3.4)	(4.2)	(3.7)	(4.4)	(4.5)	(4.2)
	N	46	30	28	20	40	30
PA	$\bar{X}$	18.0	15.8	25.6	22.7	25.4	22.8
	SD	(7.6)	(4.8)	(6.2)	(13.0)	(7.2)	(8.0)
	N	26	10	16	11	35	21

TABLE 5
Age Effects: $\overline{X}$ and *SD* Raw Scores for Black Males

		Age in Years					
		10	11	12	13	14	15
Raven	$\overline{X}$	20.7	23.1	23.8	28.0	27.8	26.1
	SD	(8.2)	(8.1)	(10.3)	(8.9)	(9.8)	(9.7)
	N	30	18	14	32	31	14
Peabody	$\overline{X}$	24.9	27.6	27.6	31.5	35.4	36.0
	SD	(5.9)	(6.0)	(7.1)	(7.3)	(9.4)	(9.0)
	N	31	22	18	32	35	14
Columbia	$\overline{X}$	18.3	19.5	19.0	19.4	20.2	21.3
	SD	(2.5)	(2.4)	(3.5)	(3.2)	(3.8)	(2.6)
	N	31	22	18	32	33	14
Benton E	$\overline{X}$	10.2	9.8	8.8	7.6	6.2	6.5
	SD	(4.9)	(3.9)	(3.9)	(4.3)	(4.2)	(3.5)
	N	34	24	18	32	34	14
PA	$\overline{X}$	15.1	16.1	25.4	24.0	22.1	24.5
	SD	(5.3)	(8.6)	(6.2)	(8.5)	(8.9)	(8.2)
	N	13	14	8	14	22	6

TABLE 6
Age Effects: $\overline{X}$ and *SD* Raw Scores for White Females

		Age in Years					
		10	11	12	13	14	15
Raven	$\overline{X}$	29.7	31.3	32.4	33.9	36.6	36.6
	SD	(7.3)	(8.7)	(8.4)	(7.0)	(5.3)	(4.6)
	N	18	47	30	41	27	34
Peabody	$\overline{X}$	32.6	36.6	41.5	39.7	44.9	49.3
	SD	(6.5)	(7.8)	(8.2)	(8.4)	(5.9)	(10.4)
	N	20	50	29	41	27	34
Columbia	$\overline{X}$	19.1	20.6	21.9	21.6	22.8	23.6
	SD	(3.5)	(2.9)	(3.2)	(3.2)	(2.9)	(2.7)
	N	20	52	31	43	27	34
Benton E	$\overline{X}$	8.7	7.0	6.4	5.2	4.0	3.0
	SD	(5.3)	(3.9)	(3.3)	(3.2)	(3.2)	(2.4)
	N	20	52	32	40	27	34
PA	$\overline{X}$	20.6	23.6	25.9	29.2	27.6	27.9
	SD	(8.1)	(7.8)	(8.6)	(6.4)	(10.7)	(6.8)
	N	20	50	30	35	25	30

TABLE 7
Age Effects: $\overline{X}$ and SD Raw Scores for White Males

		Age in Years					
		10	11	12	13	14	15
Raven	$\overline{X}$	26.6	29.5	34.2	34.7	36.7	34.2
	SD	(7.9)	(7.8)	(6.2)	(6.9)	(5.2)	(5.6)
	N	55	32	43	40	32	30
Peabody	$\overline{X}$	30.8	34.8	37.9	42.8	48.4	45.6
	SD	(6.9)	(6.6)	(8.8)	(9.5)	(6.1)	(8.5)
	N	57	33	44	40	29	30
Columbia	$\overline{X}$	19.5	19.9	21.2	22.8	23.7	22.6
	SD	(3.1)	(3.4)	(2.7)	(2.7)	(2.1)	(2.8)
	N	58	34	44	40	32	30
Benton E	$\overline{X}$	8.0	6.6	4.7	5.0	4.8	4.4
	SD	(3.5)	(3.7)	(2.9)	(3.0)	(2.5)	(2.1)
	N	57	33	44	40	30	30
PA	$\overline{X}$	21.8	21.9	24.8	25.1	26.2	24.9
	SD	(8.5)	(8.2)	(8.1)	(8.4)	(8.7)	(8.0)
	N	50	32	34	38	28	28

III SOCIAL CLASS AND INDIVIDUAL VARIATION

Intellectual Similarities within Families of Both Adopted and Biological Children*

III.1

The effects of genetic and environmental differences on intellectual differences among children were examined in a study of families with both biological and adopted children. IQ scores of all family members and education of natural parents were used to estimate intellectual similarities among related and unrelated persons, living together and apart. Comparisons of correlations between related and unrelated siblings produced negligible heritability values, whereas the parent–child data suggested moderate heritability for the children's IQ differences. The high mean values of the adopted children's IQ scores and the high degree of similarity among unrelated sibs suggest that IQ scores are more malleable than previously thought.

Recent interest in the social ecology of intellectual development has focused on the family context. Implicit in studies of home environments is the assumption that the development of intellectual differences among children is strongly influenced by the behavior of their parents and other family members, as well as aspects of their physical environments (Wachs, 1975).

The primary emphasis in studies of family effects has been on differences *between* families in child rearing practices, parent–child interaction, social class variables, and the like (e.g., Baumrind, 1969). Loehlin and Nichols (1976) have indicated the lack of studies on variation *within* families, which may be more important in determining individual differences than between-family effects. Birth order is one of the few within-family variables that has received any attention (Zajonc & Markus, 1975). There is little research on genetic or environmental differences among siblings or between parents and children.

The comparison of adoptive and biologically related families provides a framework for studying both within- and between-family effects on intellectual development. Furthermore, related and unrelated persons, living together and apart, offer an opportunity to estimate genetic and environmental effects on individual variation. Ideally, one should study related and unrelated children and their parents in the same families.

The present study is an investigation of the similarities in IQ scores among

*This chapter by Sandra Scarr and Richard A. Weinberg originally appeared in *Intelligence*, 1977, *1*(2), 170–191. Copyright © 1977 by Ablex Publishing Co. Reprinted by permission.

members of families with adopted and biological children. In past adoption studies, few families had both adopted and biological children (Burks, 1928; Freeman, Holzinger, & Mitchell, 1928; Leahy, 1932; Munsinger, 1975; Skodak & Skeels, 1949), because most adoptions result from parental infertility. The present sample is unusual in several respects: first, the families adopted children from a variety of racial backgrounds; second, they adopted many children past infancy; and third, the majority also have their own biological children.

The data presented in this article are family correlations, which reflect rank order resemblances among related and unrelated siblings and parent–child pairs. Resemblances among family members can be measured in two ways: *means* and *rank orders*. While similarities in the averages and distributions of scores are presumably responsive to the *average* values of the genotypes and environments in which the children are reared, the rank orders of scores reflect the *relative* values of individuals' genotypes and environments.

Resemblances in average scores and distributions were reported in another paper (Scarr & Weinberg, 1976). The study of intellectual similarities is part of a larger investigation of the psychosocial functioning of transracial adoptive families.

The purposes of this paper are (1) to describe the correlations in intellectual performance between parents and children, whether related or not and whether living together or not; (2) to analyze the effects of rearing together on sibling resemblance, whether the sibs are genetically related or not; and (3) to investigate the effects of selective placement of adopted children in families that resemble intellectually their natural parents.

While, in the world of real families, relationships—both interpersonal and statistical—are full of problems, the value of a study of related and unrelated families is to clarify the roles of genetic and environmental differences in creating the intellectual diversity we observe.

METHODS

The Adoptive Families

The 101 participating families were recruited through the Newsletter of the Open Door Society and by letters from the Minnesota State Department of Public Welfare Adoption Unit to families with Black adopted children, 4 years of age and older, who were adopted throughout the state of Minnesota through the Lutheran Social Service and the Children's Home Society. These agencies have placed the majority of adopted Black children in the state. We were unable to ascertain how many transracial adoptive families learned about the study from the Newsletter since the mailing list of about 300 includes agencies, social workers, and interested citizens. In addition, we do not know how many of these families were also contacted by the State Department of Public Welfare. The support of the Open Door Society was important, however, in affirming the legitimacy of the study.

The State Department of Public Welfare mailed 230 letters to transracial adoptive families. In some cases a family received more than one letter if they had adopted more than one child.

The mailings of the Newsletter and the State Department of Public Welfare yielded 201 replies. Of these 65 were ineligible to participate, mostly because their children were less than 4 years of age; 28 declined to participate, 14 because they lived too far away, and 14 for various personal reasons; and 108 agreed to participate. Of the 108 volunteers, 101 families eventually took part in the study. Thus, of the 136 families known to be eligible for the study, 74% were actually studied.

The 101 participating families included 145 biological children and 176 adopted children, of whom 130 were socially classified as Black (29 with two Black natural parents and 101 with one Black natural parent and one natural parent of other or unknown racial background), and 25 as white. The remaining 21 included Asian, North American Indian, and Latin American Indian children. All of the adopted children were unrelated to the adoptive parents. Adopted children reared in the same home were unrelated, with the exception of four sibling pairs and one triad adopted by the same families, who were excluded from the analyses.

The sample of families live within a 150 mile radius of the Minneapolis/St. Paul, Twin Cities metropolitan area. Although nearly all of the children were adopted in Minnesota, 68 were born outside of the state. Through interstate cooperation, the child placement agencies arranged for the adoption of many Black and Indian children from other states.

Early Adoptees and Natural Children

To study family similarity, we decided to restrict the present study to three types of families:

1. *Families who adopted children during the first year of life* (early adoptees): Of the 176 adopted children, 65 were adopted after 12 months of age. Because early experience elsewhere can reduce the similarity of adopted children to their adoptive parents, *this report includes only the 111 children adopted in the first year of life*. The group included 13 children with 2 Black parents, 9 with 2 white parents, 3 Asian/Indian children, and 86 with one Black parent and one parent of other or unknown racial background.

2. *Adoptive families with natural children:* Of the 101 adoptive families, 72 have biological children, but they do not necessarily have *early* adopted children as well. Correlations between natural children reared together and between parents and their own children can be compared to sibling and adoptive parent–child correlations in families that adopted children in infancy.

3. *Adoptive families with both natural and early adopted children:* Because adoptive families with natural children may differ in significant demographic or intellectual ways from other adoptive families, we calculated family similarity for both adoptive and biologically related pairs within the same families.

Procedures

Most of the information was obtained directly from members of the adoptive families at the time of testing (1973–1975). Some additional data on the natural parents and the children's preadoption history were obtained by Minnesota State Department of Public Welfare personnel from the adoption records. Achievement and aptitude test scores were supplied by school districts for all of the school-aged children to whom such tests had been administered.

The IQ Assessment

Both parents and all children in the family over four years of age were administered an age-appropriate IQ test as part of an extensive battery of intellectual, personality, attitudinal, and demographic measures. The tests were administered in the family home during two visits by a team of trained testers. The examiners were all graduate students who had completed at least a year-long course in psychoeducational assessment and who had participated in a training session on assessment for this study. Among the 21 examiners were 7 males and 15 females, including 2 Blacks. Testers were assigned randomly to members of the family. Race and sex of examiner were unrelated to children's or parents' IQ scores (all r's $<$ .06). Eighteen testers assessed 5 or more parents and 5 or more children. The standard deviation of the mean IQ scores they each obtained was 4.0 for children and 2.8 for parents. For the 11 testers who assessed 15 or more children, the standard deviation of the scores obtained was also 4. These tester differences were normally distributed and well within the limits of sampling error for Ns of 5 to 33.

Both parents and all children 16 years of age and older were administered the Wechsler Adult Intelligence Scale (WAIS). Children between 8 and 15 were given the Wechsler Intelligence Scale for Children (WISC), and children between 4 and 7 were administered the Stanford–Binet Intelligence Scale, Form L-M (S-B).

All scoring of protocols and computations of IQ scores were done by a graduate student with extensive experience in administering and scoring IQ measures. This student had no contact with the families and with the examiners except to clarify questionable responses. In no case was the scorer aware of the child's race or adoptive status.

The Adoption Records

The Director of the Adoption Unit, Minnesota State Department of Public Welfare, abstracted the following information from the records of the adopted children and their families:

1. The child: *a*. birthdate; *b*. number and dates of preadoption placements, unless the child was in the adoptive home at 2 months of age; *c*. evaluation of the quality of preadoption placements, rated by the authors on a scale of 1 = poor to 3 = good; 4 = placement only in the adoptive home; *d*. date of placement in adoptive home.

2. The natural parents: *a*. age at birth of child; *b*. educational level at birth of child as an estimate of intellectual functioning, since IQ scores were not available; *c*. occupation of mother; *d*. race.

Family Demographics

In the interview portion of the testing session, each parent was asked his or her birthdate, last school grade completed, occupation and whether it was full time or part time, range of income, and date of marriage.

Statistical Analysis

To eliminate mean and distributional differences between the adoptive parents' and the adopted and natural children's IQ scores, the scores were standardized to a mean of 0 and a standard deviation of 1 separately for parents, for adopted, and for natural children by test and within the three types of family constellations. Similarity, therefore, reflects only rank order resemblance and not similarity in mean scores.

Regression analyses were applied to the parent–child IQ scores. Pearson correlations were calculated for sibling pairs. All parent–child and sibling data were also analyzed by intraclass correlations.

When scores are standardized, the results of the various correlational and regression analyses are entirely equivalent. Therefore, only the intraclass correlations are reported in this paper.

RESULTS

Family Characteristics

The adoptive families who participated in the study can be characterized as highly educated, above average in occupational status, and in income. Table 1 is a summary of selected demographic characteristics of the adoptive and natural parents in the three family constellations.

Generally, in all family constellations, the educational level of the adoptive parents exceeded that of the adopted children's natural parents by 3–5 years. The typical occupations of the adoptive fathers were clergyman, engineer, and teacher. Nearly half (46.5%) of the adoptive mothers were employed at least part time at the time of the study, typically as teachers, nurses, and secretaries. The median educational level of the natural parents was high school graduation, which is close to the median for that age cohort of the general population. In

TABLE 1
Income and Educational Characteristics of the Adoptive
and Natural Parents of the Adopted Children by Family
Constellation

	N	Mean	SD
Adoptive families with natural children			
Income	71	$15,250	$4,500
Education			
Adoptive mother	72	15.0	2.2
Adoptive father	72	16.8	3.0
Adoptive families with early adopted children			
Income	73	$15,250	$4,500
Education			
Adoptive mother	73	15.4	2.0
Adoptive father	73	17.5	2.7
Natural mother	94	12.6	1.9
Natural father	23	12.6	1.9
Adoptive families with both natural and early adopted children			
Income	51	$14,750	$4,750
Education			
Adoptive mother	51	15.4	2.0
Adoptive father	51	17.5	2.6
Natural mother	41	12.3	1.8
Natural father	12	12.2	.8

contrast, the mean educational level of the adoptive parents was atypically high. Typical occupations of the natural mothers were office workers, nurses' aides, and students. Insufficient information was available on the occupations of natural fathers. There were no significant differences among the three family types in demographic characteristics.

IQ Scores of Family Members

As indicated in Table 2, the mean WAIS IQ scores of the adoptive parents in all three family constellations were in the high average to superior range of intellectual functioning. The distributions of scores extended from the "low average" to the "very superior," with considerable restriction of range. The scores were congruent with the very high educational level of the group. Within occupational classes, one expects a restricted range of IQ. Burt (1961) reported that within six classes, the standard deviation for IQ was 9.6 instead of the population value of 15. The variability of IQ scores of children whose fathers were found within the various occupational classes was greater (SD = 14.0).

The mean IQ scores (presented in Table 2) of the natural children of the

TABLE 2
Mean IQ Scores of Adoptive Family Members
by Child Test and Family Constellation

	N	Mean	SD	Range
Adoptive families with early adopted children				
Adoptive mother's WAIS IQ	71	118.5	10.0	97–139
Adoptive father's WAIS IQ	73	122.3	9.1	98–140
Early adopted child's Stanford–Binet IQ	92	110.3	11.9	86–144
WISC + WAIS IQ	19	115.2	11.6	92–138
Total IQ	111	111.1	12.0	86–144
Adoptive families with natural children				
Adoptive mother's WAIS IQ	71	117.7	9.7	96–140
Adoptive father's WAIS IQ	71	120.2	10.6	93–140
Natural child's Stanford–Binet IQ	47	113.8	16.7	81–148
WISC + WAIS IQ	96	118.1	12.4	87–150
Total IQ	143	116.7	14.0	81–150
Adoptive families with both natural and early adopted children				
Adoptive mother's WAIS IQ	50	118.7	9.4	98–134
Adoptive father's WAIS IQ	51	121.5	9.7	98–140
Early adopted child's Stanford–Binet IQ	56	109.0	12.5	86–144
WISC + WAIS IQ	11	113.6	12.8	92–133
Total IQ	67	109.8	12.6	86–144
Natural child's Stanford–Binet IQ	32	115.6	16.9	81–148
WISC + WAIS IQ	70	119.8	12.2	93–150
Total IQ	102	118.5	13.9	81–150

adoptive families were in the high average range of intellectual functioning, as predicted by their parents' high IQ scores and their enriched home environments. The standard deviation of 14 matches Burt's (1961) finding. The mean IQ scores of the early adopted children were also in the high average range, reflecting their superior family environments. The standard deviation of 12 represents considerable restriction of range. One possible explanation for the smaller standard deviation of adopted children's IQ scores is the lack of genotype–environment correlation for adopted children. Another is a bias that might affect the study: the self-selection of participating families whose children have less conspicuous sibling differences. To test this hypothesis, we calculated absolute IQ differences between natural and adopted sib pairs, as shown in Table 3.

Natural–natural and adopted–adopted sib pairs do not differ in their average absolute differences in IQ scores, although their differences are smaller than one would expect among sibs in the population at large (~ 13 IQ points). An argument against the self-selection by families with small sib differences is the larger than expected sibling differences for natural–adopted pairs. In fact, the average

TABLE 3
Mean Absolute Differences in IQ between
Related and Unrelated Sibling Pairs

Sib pair types	N	d	SD	$t_{1 \text{ vs. } 2}$ / $t_{1 \text{ vs. } 3}$	p	$t_{2 \text{ vs. } 3}$	p
1 Natural–natural	107	11.4	9.2				
2 Adopted–natural	134	14.6	10.4	−2.45	.02		
3 Adopted–adopted	53	10.8	6.6	.49	.63	2.49	.01

difference between all sibs in the adoptive families is 13.1 IQ points, the difference expected between sibs in all families in the population.

Other kinds of self-selection are also used to criticize the results of adoption studies. Munsinger (1975) noted that obviously retarded and damaged infants are not likely to be adopted, a fact which raises the mean IQ of adoptees above the population average. This bias is slight, however: If all infants with eventual IQ scores of less than 60 (at most 3% of children) were eliminated from the adoption pool, the mean IQ of adoptees would be raised by only 1 IQ point.

Another bias could be the self-selection of families whose children appear normal in intelligence and school work. The range of IQ scores in this study contraindicates a strong bias in this regard, since 15 of the 176 adopted children have IQ scores of 85 and below. Furthermore, since 74 per cent of those families known to be eligible did participate and the average IQ of all 176 adoptees was 106, the average IQ of children in the 26% of families who did not participate would have to be unreasonably low to explain the mean results. If we consider the sample to be composed entirely of interracial children, with white adoptees offsetting those with two Black parents, their average IQ might fall between those of Black and white children in the region, namely, 95. To obtain this figure, the nonparticipants would have to have IQ scores that average 64, or in the retarded range. This is highly unlikely for any sample of adopted children.

For all the groups of children, the Stanford–Binet (1972 norms) yielded a slightly lower mean score than the WISC or WAIS. Had the 1960 Stanford–Binet norms been used, the average IQ scores of the children would have been 7 points higher. In families with either or both natural and early adopted children, the total IQ score of the adopted group was five to six points lower than that of the natural children, in part because a large number of natural children were old enough to take a Wechsler test. The average differences between all adopted and all natural children by test were about three points, not statistically significant differences. In the families with both natural and adopted children, the differences by test were also not significant. The average total IQ scores were statistically different in comparisons between all natural and adopted children ($t = 3.43, p < .01$) and between natural and adopted children in families with both ($t = 4.21, p < .01$).

THE PARENT–CHILD IQ CORRELATIONS

Table 4 shows the intraclass correlations of standardized IQ scores by test between the adoptive parents and their children, both adopted and biological. Regression analyses were also done on the same data. The beta weights never differed from the intraclass correlations by more than .01 (e.g., .38 versus .37). Therefore, the regression analyses are not reported. Also not reported are any values based on Ns of 20 or fewer pairs.

The correlations between the adoptive parents and their biological children were higher than those between the adoptive parents and their adopted children in every comparison, although the differences between the correlations were not usually statistically significant.

Table 5 gives the same parent–child correlations based only on those families with both natural children and early adoptees. Similarly, in every case the correlations between biologically related parents and children were higher than those between unrelated parent–child pairs. Again, the differences were not generally statistically significant.

If one assumes, with Jensen and Munsinger, a polygenic model in which the major (or only) source of similarity between parents and children is their shared genotypes, and one further assumes an assortative mating coefficient of .25, test reliability of .90, and no genotype–environmental correlation, then the predicted intraclass correlation (t_1) between a single parent and a child will be about .50. This correlation is predicted because a parent and a biological child share half of their segregating genes, resulting in their sharing one-half of the genetic variance due to additive effects, none of the dominance effects, less than one-quarter of any effects of epistasis, and half of the variance due to assortative mating (Jencks, 1972, pp. 274–275; Jensen, 1973, p. 371; Munsinger, 1975, pp. 624–625). In this model the predicted correlation between parent and child does not depend upon any environmental transmission from parent to child.

In this study, the adoptive parents' IQ scores were correlated .21, and the educational levels of the natural parents of the adopted children were correlated .27. Both data are consistent with an assortative mating coefficient of .25; however, the obtained values of the parent–child correlations did not reach .50. The biological parent–child correlations in these transracial adoptive families were between .17 and .50, with most of the values in the .30s.

Because adoptive parents and their adopted children share no genes, any similarity between them could only be attributed to similarity in their environment and/or selective placement. The correlations between the unrelated parent–child pairs were found to range between .07 and .29, with the majority below .20.

Under the assumptions outlined above, the biological midparent–child correlation would be about .71; that is, $\sqrt{1/2}$ (Falconer, 1960) or slightly less, if one assumes a test reliability of .90. Since the biological offspring share genes from

TABLE 4
Intraclass Correlations of Children's IQ Scores by Test, Adoptive Parents' IQ Scores, and Natural Parents' Education for All Early Adopted and Natural Children

Child test	Natural children					Early adopted children								
	N	r_i	MS_W	MS_B	$(\hat{r}_i)^a$	N	r_i	MS_W	MS_B	$(\hat{r}_i)^a$	$(\hat{r}'_i)^b$	h^2	$(\hat{h}^2)^a$	$(\hat{h}'^2)^b$
Stanford–Binet														
Adoptive mother IQ	45	.38	.63	1.4	(.52)	90	.18	.83	1.2	(.26)	(.13)	.40	(.52)	(.78)
Adoptive father IQ	46	.27	.74	1.3	(.39)	92	.17	.84	1.2	(.25)	(.05)	.20	(.28)	(.68)
Midparent IQ	44	.42	.58	1.4	(.57)	90	.23	.77	1.2	(.33)	(.26)	.38	(.48)	(.62)
WISC + WAIS														
Adoptive mother IQ	96	.33	.68	1.3	(.46)				^{c}					
Adoptive father IQ	96	.50	.51	1.5	(.65)									
Midparent IQ	96	.57	.44	1.6	(.72)									
All IQ scores														
Adoptive mother IQ	141	.35	.65	1.3	(.49)	109	.23	.78	1.2	(.33)	(.26)	.23	(.32)	(.58)
Adoptive father IQ	142	.39	.61	1.4	(.54)	111	.15	.85	1.2	(.22)	(.11)	.47	(.64)	(1.06)
Midparent IQ	140	.51	.49	1.5	(.66)	109	.25	.75	1.3	(.36)	(.33)	.50	(.60)	(.72)
Natural mother education	114	.14	.86	1.1	—	94	.32	.68	1.3	—	(.25)	.36	—	—
Natural father education	48	.21	.80	1.2	—	23	.52	.50	1.6	—	(.41)	.62	—	—
Midparent education	44	.07	.94	1.1	—	23	.58	.44	1.6	—	(.55)	.96	—	—

^{a} Corrected for restriction of range in parents' IQ scores.
^{b} Corrected for both selective placement *and* restriction of range.
$^c N < 20.$

TABLE 5
Intraclass Correlations of Children's IQ Scores by Test, Adoptive Parents' IQ Scores, and Natural Parents' Education for Families with Both Natural and Early Adopted Children

Child test	Natural children					Early adopted children								
	N	r_1	MS_W	MS_B	$(\hat{r}_1)^a$	N	r_1	MS_W	MS_B	$(\hat{r}_1)^a$	$(\hat{r}'_1)^a$	h^2	$(\hat{h}^2)^a$	$(\hat{h}'^2)^b$
Stanford–Binet														
Adoptive mother IQ	30	.39	.62	1.4	(.54)	55	.23	.77	1.2	(.33)	(.19)	.31	(.38)	(.70)
Adoptive father IQ	32	.17	.85	1.2	(.25)	56	.11	.90	1.1	(.16)	(−.01)	.11	(.18)	(.52)
Midparent IQ	30	.38	.63	1.4	(.52)	55	.24	.76	1.3	(.35)	(.30)	.27	(.34)	(.44)
WISC + WAIS														
Adoptive mother IQ	70	.31	.70	1.3	(.44)				c					
Adoptive father IQ	70	.49	.51	1.5	(.64)								c	
Midparent IQ	70	.57	.43	1.6	(.72)									
All IQ scores														
Adoptive mother IQ	100	.34	.65	1.3	(.48)	66	.29	.72	1.3	(.41)	(.34)	.12	(.14)	(.40)
Adoptive father IQ	102	.34	.67	1.3	(.48)	67	.07	.93	1.1	(.10)	(.01)	.53	(.76)	(1.12)
Midparent IQ	100	.49	.51	1.5	(.64)	66	.26	.74	1.3	(.37)	(.34)	.46	(.54)	(.66)
Natural mother education	111	.15	.86	1.2	—	41	.30	.71	1.3	—	(.23)	.31	—	—
Natural father education	47	.18	.83	1.2	—				c					
Midparent education	43	.07	.95	1.1	—				c					

[a] Corrected for restriction of range in parents' IQ scores.
[b] Corrected for both selective placement *and* restriction of range.
[c] $N < 20$.

both parents, the combination of information in the midparent IQ should yield a better prediction of the child's IQ than either parent's score alone. The midparent–offspring correlations were around 0.50; that is, higher than the single parent–child values, but lower than the prediction from the polygenic model.

The midadoptive parent–adopted child IQ correlations were all between .23 and .26, about half of the midparent and natural child values.

Family Constellations

Contary to Kamin's (1974) speculations, there were no consistent differences in family similarity between parents and children in families with natural or adopted children and those with both.

Sex Differences in Parent–Child Similarity

Regressions were calculated for natural and adopted children by sex of parent and child. There was no consistent pattern of differences in beta coefficients by sex. The range of mother–child coefficients was .20–.36; the range of father–child coefficients was .21–.41. The range of son–parent coefficients was .21–.36; the range for daughters was .20–.41. Again, despite Kamin's (1974) comments about past adoption studies, there were no sex differences in the degree of family similarity.

Correction for Restriction of Range ($\hat{r}_i$)

The correlations between parents and children were all depressed by the restricted range of the parents' IQ scores, as shown in Table 2. The standard deviations of the parents' scores were approximately two-thirds those of the standardization population. Therefore, the intraclass correlations, corrected for restriction of range (McNemar, 1962), are also presented in Tables 4 and 5.

In Table 4, the corrected correlations ($\hat{r}_i$) for all biologically related parent–child pairs were considerably higher than the uncorrected values. The single, related parent–child correlations rose to about .5 for all IQ scores, and the midparent value was .66. The adoptive parent–adopted child coefficients rose to the .22 to .33 range, with a midparent value of .35. The midparent–child IQ regression for biologically related pairs is sometimes seen as an estimate of the narrow heritability of IQ scores in a sample, because it does not include variance due to assortative mating or dominance effects. The midparent–child correlation does include common environment, however, which can certainly increase the resemblance of parents and children for behavioral traits.

The adopted children's IQ scores had a more restricted range than those of the natural children (SD = 12.0 and 12.6 versus 14.0 and 13.9). This restriction reduced the unrelated parent–child correlations more than the related parent–child pairs. Because no reliable correction for restriction of range in two variables exists (McNemar, 1962), the further correction of the parent–child correlations was not attempted. One should bear in mind, however, that the adopted child–parent correlations are probably underestimates of their true values in the population.

Natural Parents' Education and the Children's IQ Scores

Two sets of analyses were done to compare the natural parent–child correlations, including natural parents who were students or excluding them. Since the category "student" included parents who were attending college as well as high school, there were no differences in the educational mean or standard deviation when students were included or excluded from the analysis. There were also no differences in correlations of children's IQ scores with parents' education, whether or not the "student" category was included. Therefore, the larger sample including students is reported here.

Also presented in Tables 4 and 5 are the intraclass correlations between the educational level of the adopted children's natural parents and the children's IQ scores. Although the children have never lived with their natural parents, these correlations were similar to those between the adoptive parents' IQ and their biological children's IQ scores. The single parent correlations ranged from .30 to .52, and the midparent value was .58. Educational level is not as good an estimate of intellectual level as an individual IQ score; therefore, these correlations are underestimates of the intellectual similarity between natural parents and their children who were adopted into other families.

A Correction for Selective Placement

To test for the effects of selective placement on the adoptive and natural parent-child correlations, an ingenious procedure was suggested by Horn, Loehlin, and Willerman (1975): correlating the education of the adoptive children's natural parents and the IQ scores of the biological children of the adoptive parents. Since the natural parents of the adopted children are neither genetically related to the natural children of the adoptive families, nor live with them, any similarity exists because of selective placement—brighter natural parents of the adopted children have been paired with brighter adoptive parents who have brighter natural children. Therefore, both the adopted and biological children reared by those parents are genetically brighter and environmentally more advantaged. The correlations between the education of the natural parents of the adopted children and the IQ scores of the biological children of the adoptive family measure the degree to which selective placement affects rank order similarity between the adoptive parents and their adopted children.

The same correlations also measure the degree to which the natural parent–adopted child correlations are inflated by selective placement. When the children of brighter natural parents are adopted by brighter adoptive families, their relative genotypic advantage is enhanced by the relative environmental advantages provided by the adoptive home. In a sense, the adoptive family provides an environmental program for development, the rank of which is similar to that the natural parents would have provided. Thus, the adopted children come to resemble their natural parents by environmental as well as genetic means (Cavalli-Sforza & Feldman, 1973).

The correlations between the education of the natural parents of the adopted children and the IQ scores of the biological children of the adoptive parents ranged from .14 to .21, indicating some effect of selective placement. The midparent value, however, was small (.07), probably due to restriction of range. The standard deviations of the individual parent education levels were 1.9 compared to 1.5 for the midparent value.

Parent–Adopted Child Correlations Corrected for Selective Placement

The correlations between adoptive parents and their adopted children and between natural parents and their children who have been adopted can be corrected for the effects of selective placement. By Fisher's z transformation the parent–child correlations can be corrected for the correlation between natural parents' education and the IQ scores of the biological children of the adoptive family.

The Horn–Loehlin–Willerman correction will vary depending upon the underlying assumptions: (a) if similarity between the biological parents of the adopted children and the natural children of the adoptive parents is predominantly genetic, then the subtraction of that correlation from the natural parent–adopted child correlation would not be appropriate, because the procedure underestimates the heritable correction in the scores of biologically related parents and children; the same correction, however, would be appropriate for the adoptive parent–adopted child correlations; (b) if, however, the similarity between the biological parents of the adopted children and the biological children of the adoptive parents is predominantly environmental, then the correction is appropriate for biological and not adoptive correlations.

Since one cannot decide which assumption is correct, it has been suggested (Willerman, 1976) that half of the correlation between the biological parents of the adopted children and the natural children of the adoptive parents be subtracted from both biological and adoptive parent–child correlations. This correction can be interpreted to mean that both genetic and environmental factors are contributing to the similarity of the natural parents of the adopted children and the natural children of the adoptive parents. In Tables 4 and 5, the parent–child correlations which have been corrected for restriction of range ($\hat{r}_i$) have been further corrected for selective placement ($\hat{r}_i'$).

The adoptive parent–adopted child correlations corrected for restriction of range and selective placement ranged from nearly zero for father–child pairs to moderately positive for mother–child pairs. The midparent values of .33 and .34 were moderate. The natural parent education–adopted child IQ correlations were

similarly reduced in magnitude as a result of the correction for selective placement. However, these correlations generally exceeded those of the adoptive
parents and adopted children.

Another method for correcting parent–child correlations for selective placement is path analysis. Path analysis provides standardized partial regression
coefficients for a specified model. Using the data provided in Scarr & Weinberg
(1976), Robert Plomin (1976) calculated the weighted average correlation between natural parents' education and adopted child's IQ as .38; the weighted
average correlation between adopted parents' education and adopted children's
IQ as .28; and the correlation between natural and adoptive parents' education
was .22. Figure 1 is the path model, where Ed_{NP} and Ed_{AP} are the educational
levels of natural and adoptive parents; IQ_{AC} is the IQ level of the adopted
children; g is the genetic path, and e the environmental path.

Solving for paths g and e, he found that path g was .34 and path e .21. The .34
value of path g was in the range of the natural parent–adopted child correlation
corrected for selective placement. By the previous method this value was between .25 and .41. The .21 value for path e falls between the adoptive parent–
adopted child correlations of .11 and .26.

Heritabilities Based on Parent–Child Correlations

The comparison of related and unrelated pairs of parents and children can
provide an estimate of the proportion of genetic variance in the distribution of
children's IQ scores. The degree to which the correlations of genetically related
parent–child pairs exceed those of unrelated parent–child pairs is used to calculate a heritability coefficient. The heritability coefficient is an estimate of the
proportion of variance in a phenotypic distribution (e.g., IQ) which is attributed
to genetic differences among individuals. Parent–child correlations yield *narrow*
heritabilities, based only on additive genetic variance. Because heritability estimates contain the unreliability of two correlation coefficients, they tend to fluc-

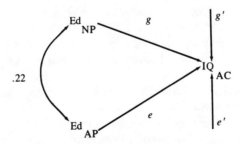

FIG. 1   Path model of the relationship of natural and adoptive parent educational levels to
adopted child IQ (Plomin, 1976).

tuate due to sampling error. The estimates, therefore, should not be taken as point values.

Tables 4 and 5 include three heritability estimates for each comparison of related and unrelated parent–child pairs. The first heritability estimate is 2 $(r_{i\ RP-C} - r_{i\ UP-C})$, where $r_{i\ RP-C}$ is the intraclass correlation of genetically related, parent–child pairs, and $r_{i\ UP-C}$ is for unrelated parent–child pairs. To estimate the additive genetic variance the remainder is doubled because parents and children share only half of their genes in common. The heritability estimate from the adoptive parent–child correlations obtained in this sample varied between .11 and .53, a low to moderate range. Taking assortative mating into account reduces the h^2 values by 20% but does not change the basic picture.

The second heritability estimates were calculated by the same formula on the intraclass correlations corrected for the restriction in range in the parents' IQ scores ($\hat{h}^2$). These values were all higher, ranging from .18 to .76. Since the correction for restriction of range had a larger effect on the biologically related, parent–child correlations, the degree to which they exceeded those of unrelated parent–child pairs increased.

The third heritability estimates were calculated by the same formula on the intraclass correlations corrected for both restriction of range in the parents' IQ scores and selective placement. When selective placement bias was eliminated, heritabilities ranged from moderate to high, including a value around 1.0.

Heritability estimates were also generated using the correlations of natural parents' education and children's IQ scores. (In this case, the adopted children are in the *related* parent–child pairs, and the natural children of the adoptive family are *unrelated* to the natural parents of the adopted children.) The heritability estimates based on natural parent–child correlations were in the moderate to high range (.31–.96). Since the sample sizes for natural fathers were small, the higher heritability values were based on the smaller Ns. Since the correction for selective placement is subtracted from the natural parent–adopted child correlation in the first heritability estimate (h^2), there is no need to calculate corrected values.

A commonly used method for estimating narrow heritability is the regression of single child on midparent IQ. In Tables 4 and 5, the biologically related parent–child pairs living together yielded heritability estimates of .52 to .72 (corrected for range restriction). The related pairs living apart yielded an estimate of .58.

The corrected heritability estimates ($\hat{h}'^2$) are most generalizable to the Minnesota population from which these families are sampled, because it has neither a restricted range of IQ scores nor a selective placement bias. They are, however, statistically manipulated values with inflated error possibilities. Therefore, one should not take any one figure too literally. The range of .40 to .70 most probably includes the best estimate of the heritability of children's IQ scores, *based on parent–child data,* in the population sampled.

SIBLING CORRELATIONS

Table 6 shows the intraclass correlations for related and unrelated sibling pairs by family constellation. Pairs of adopted children reared together (A/A), pairs of adopted and natural children of the same adoptive parents (A/N), and pairs of natural siblings reared together (N/N) are included. Only the IQ scores combined across tests are presented because there were too few sibling pairs who were of similar age to take the same IQ test.

The IQ scores of the genetically related siblings (N/N) correlated .42 for all natural sibs and .37 for natural sib pairs in families with early adopted children. Biological siblings share one-half of the additive variance, one-quarter of the dominance variance, one-half of the variance due to assortative mating, and less than one-quarter of the epistatic variance. Given an assortative mating coefficient of about .25 and a test reliability of .90, the sibling correlation should be about 0.55 (Jensen, 1973; Jencks, 1972). Sibling correlations should exceed parent–child correlations.

The pairs of adopted and natural children in the same families were slightly less similar with a correlation coefficient of .30, a value that is surprisingly high for unrelated pairs of children. Even more astonishing are the still higher correlations of unrelated, adopted siblings.

The within-family variance (MS_W) of the early adopted sib pairs was as small as the within-family variance of related sibs ($\sim$ .6). The between-family variances were the same (1.4). Since nearly all of the genetic variance (and some of the environmental variance) in unrelated pairs occurs within families, while only half of the genetic variance (and some of the environmental variance) in related sibs occurs within families, these results imply that genetic variance has nothing to do with similarities in siblings' IQ scores.

Compared to the parent–child pairs, both related and unrelated siblings have slightly smaller within-family differences and larger between-family differences, resulting in higher intraclass correlations. The largest difference in variances, however, occurred for adopted siblings, compared to adoptive parent–adopted child pairs (.62 to .81 for within-family effects and 1.4 to 1.2 for between-family effects). Since the unrelated siblings share no more genes than the unrelated parent–child pairs, the changes in variance must mean that environmental differences between families and similarities within families have greater effects on sibling than on parent–child similarities in IQ scores.

Correction for Restriction of Range ($\hat{r}_i$)

Because the standard deviation of the adopted children's IQ scores was restricted by 20%, as shown in Table 2, corrected intraclass coefficients ($\hat{r}_i$) were calculated for those correlations involving adopted children (A/A and A/N). After correction, as shown in Table 6, the correlations of unrelated children were even higher.

TABLE 6
Intraclass Correlations of IQ Scores for Sibling Pairs by Family Constellation

	Natural/natural				Sibling pairs in families with natural *and/or* early adopted children											h^2 NN/AN	$(\hat{h}^2)^a$ NN/AN	h^2 NN/AA	$(\hat{h}^2)^a$ NN/AA
					Adopted/natural					Adopted/adopted								
	N	r_i	MS_w	MS_B	N	r_i	MS_w	MS_B	$(\hat{r}_i)^a$	N	r_i	MS_w	MS_B	$(\hat{r}_i)^a$				
All IQ scores	107	.42	.58	1.4	134	.30	.70	1.3	(.37)	53	.39	.62	1.4	(.47)	.25	(.10)	.06	(.00)
					Sibling pairs in families with *both* natural *and* early adopted children													
All IQ scores	75	.37	.63	1.4	134	.30	.70	1.3	(.37)	21	.49	.53	1.5	(.58)	.15	(.00)	.00	(.00)

[a] Corrected for restricted range in adopted children's IQ scores

One cause of the exceptionally high IQ correlations between adopted siblings may be similarity in their natural parents' education and preplacement histories. If agencies match natural and adoptive parents for two children adopted into the same family, they also create a correlation in background variables between the unrelated sibs. Table 7 gives the correlations of background variables among adopted siblings reared in the same homes. Although three of the four correlations in background characteristics were not statistically significant, there is a suggestion that selective placement has increased the A/A correlations to some extent. Although there was no obvious way to correct for any effects of the selective placement of two adopted children in the same family, one should bear in mind that the adopted–adopted sibling correlations should be a little lower.

Heritabilities Based on Sibling Correlations

Heritability estimates calculated from comparisons of the correlations of related and unrelated sibling pairs were low or negligible. When the intraclass correlations were corrected for restriction of range in the adopted children's IQ scores, the heritability estimates (h^2) were zero. If the natural children's IQ scores were corrected for a slight restriction of range (SD $= 14$), there would be no essential change in these results.

DISCUSSION

The traditional biometrical approach to calculating heritability estimates, based on related and unrelated parent–child and sibling data, yielded conflicting results. Whereas the parent–child correlations suggested moderate heritabilities for children's IQ scores, the sibling data yielded negligible values.

Jencks (1972) and Scarr-Salapatek (1974) have noted the same trend in data from past adoption studies. Although few pairs of unrelated siblings had been studied, their IQ correlations were too high to yield heritability estimates in the same range as parent–child and twin comparisons. The results of this study confirm previous suspicions that the IQ scores of unrelated siblings are nearly as

TABLE 7
Early Adopted Sibs: Correlations in Placement
Histories and Natural Mothers' Education

	N (pairs)	r	p
Length of time in home	52	.34	.01
Number of placements	37	.21	.10
Quality of placements	37	.21	.10
Natural mother's education	36	.14	.21

similar as those of natural sib pairs. Rather than force an immediate biometrical solution onto the combined parent–child and sibling data (see Eaves & Jinks, 1974; Jencks, 1972; Scarr-Salapatek, 1974) we prefer to puzzle about the lack of fit.

Sibling and Parent–Child Data

We propose that the major explanation for the unusually high correlations between unrelated sibs lies in their common rearing environments. Children adopted in the first year of life spend their developing years together, whether they are related or not. The relative advantages of their common environment— in home, neighborhood, school—can create strong pressures toward similar intellectual performance.

Parents and children do not share a common rearing environment. Parents' relative intellectual level is fairly constant in adulthood. While their intelligence influences the rearing environment they provide for their related and unrelated "offspring," the parents are probably not greatly influenced by it. Thus, the relative similarity of related and unrelated children to their parents may depend almost equally on within-family environments and on genetic relatedness—the degree to which the children genotypically respond to the environment afforded by the parents.

In the case of unrelated siblings, the within-family IQ variance was reduced to levels similar to those of related parent–child and natural sibling pairs ($\sim .6$). Since the genetic variance between unrelated siblings is nearly 100%, even given a slight degree of selective placement, the correlations in their IQ scores must come from their rearing environments.

Not all children in the same family are treated in the same way by their parents, however, Parents can provide "compensatory programs" for children who threaten to intellectually lag behind other siblings in the family. Therefore, the within-family environments for adopted sib pairs may appear quite different to an observer but produce more similar intellectual outcomes than identical treatments of genetically different children would produce.

In our interviews with the parents there were many anecdotal accounts of special tutoring and enrichments offered to adopted children who were suspected not to be intellectually as proficient as other children in the family. Several families with adopted children in the low average range of IQ scores were engaged in periodic evaluations of their progress in raising the child's intellectual level (with reported success, we might add). Similar compensatory programs were not offered to other siblings in the families. Nor were most families engaged in such active interventions.

The general effects of successful parental efforts to alter some adopted children's intellectual levels would be to reduce the within-family IQ variance for unrelated sib pairs. The IQ rank of compensated children could change with respect to uncompensated ones in other families, thereby increasing the between-family variance.

The parents in our sample who compensated their lower IQ adopted children did not themselves have higher IQ scores than other parents. Therefore, parent–child correlations would be unaffected by the parents' extra environmental manipulations, even if their efforts decreased the IQ variance among their unrelated children.

Because this was not a longitudinal study, we cannot verify the claimed effectiveness of some parents' attempts to produce higher IQ levels in their adopted children. Nor can we demonstrate that these efforts explain, even partially, the high correlations among unrelated siblings. All that can be said is that the reported parental interventions, if successful, would produce the effects observed in the study.

Heritability Estimates

Heritability estimates are not safely generalized from the sibling data to the general population. Adoptive parents have special investments in their adopted children, or they would not have bothered to adopt. In the case of transracial families, there are even more keenly felt responsibilities for the intellectual (and other) development of their children. In other words, the families in this study were, we feel, highly invested in the intellectual success of *all* of their children, natural and adopted. We believe that siblings reared in these families have had intensive and extensive experiences that have pushed all of them toward similar levels of intellectual precocity. This is hardly typical of the entire Minnesota population.

Heritability estimates, based on the parent–child data, are probably less biased against genetic variance. Intellectual differences among the parents did correlate with intellectual differences among their children, more highly for natural than adopted "offspring." In addition, the natural parent data provide a crucial check on the degree of selective placement and the heritability estimates from adoptive parent data. It is remarkable that the natural parent–adopted child correlations were only slightly smaller in magnitude than the biologically related, adoptive parent–natural child pairs, even though the former do not live together while the latter do, and the educational levels of the natural parents are not as good an estimate of intellectual level as the IQ scores of the adoptive parents.

Since the natural parent–child correlations yield heritability estimates comparable to the adoptive parent–child values, more credence should be placed on the range of h^2 values (.4 to .7) estimated from parent–child data. There are still some biases in these data, both for and against genetic variance, as noted in the results. On balance, we concluded that they provide reasonably coherent support for the moderate heritability of IQ scores in a racially mixed sample of children in Minnesota.

ACKNOWLEDGMENTS

We are grateful for the assistance of Louise Carter-Saltzman, Harold Grotevant, Margaret Getman, Marsha Sargrad, Patricia Webber, Joanne Bergman, William Thompson, and Carol Nelson. The research was supported by the Grant Foundation and NICHD (HD-08016).

REFERENCES

Baumrind, D. Authoritarian vs. authoritative parental control. *Adolescence*, 1969, **3** (1), 1–20.

Burks, B. S. The relative influence of nature and nurture upon mental development. A comparative study of foster parent–foster child resemblance and true parent–true child resemblance. *27th Yearbook of the National Society for the Study of Education*, 1928, Pt. 1, 219–316.

Burt, C. Intelligence and social mobility. *British Journal of Statistical Psychology*, 1961, **14**, 3–24.

Cavalli-Sforza, L. L., & Feldman, M. W. Cultural versus biological inheritance: Phenotypic transmission from parents to children (a theory of the effect of parental phenotypes on children's phenotypes). *American Journal of Human Genetics*, 1973, **25**, 618–637.

Eaves, J. J., & Jinks, J. L. IQ and inequality. *Nature*, 1974, **248**, 287.

Falconer, D. S. *Introduction to quantitative genetics*. New York: Ronald Press, 1960.

Freeman, F. N., Holzinger, K. J., & Mitchell, B. C. The influence of environment on the intelligence, school achievement, and conduct of foster children. *27th Yearbook of the National Society for the Study of Education*, 1928, Pt. 1, 103–217.

Horn, J. M., Loehlin, J. C., & Willerman, L. The Texas adoption project. In L. Carter-Saltzman (Chair), *Adoption studies: Similarities of children to adoptive and natural parents*. Symposium presented at the meeting of the Behavior Genetics Association, Texas, 1975.

Jencks, C. *Inequality: A reassessment of the effect of family and schooling in America*. New York: Basic Books, 1972.

Jensen, A. R. *Educability and group differences*. New York: Basic Books, 1973.

Kamin, L. J. *The science and politics of IQ*. Hillsdale, N.J.: Lawrence Erlbaum Assoc., 1974.

Leahy, A. M. A study of certain selective factors influencing prediction of the mental status of adopted children. *Journal of Genetic Psychology*, 1932, **41**, 294–329.

Loehlin, J. C., & Nichols, R. C. *Heredity, environment, and personality: A study of 850 twins*. Austin: University of Texas Press, 1976.

McNemar, Q. *Psychological statistics*. Wiley: New York, 1962.

Munsinger, H. The adopted child's IQ: A critical review. *Psychological Bulletin*, 1975, **82**, 623–659.

Plomin, R. Personal communication, July 1976.

Scarr-Salapatek, S. Some myths about heritability and IQ. *Nature*, 1974, **251**, 463–464.

Scarr, S., & Weinberg, R. A. IQ test performance of Black children adopted by white families. *American Psychologist*, 1976, **31**, 726–739.

Skodak, M., & Skeels, H. M. A final follow-up study of one hundred adopted children. *Journal of Genetic Psychology*, 1949, **75**, 85–125.

Wachs, T. Proximal experience and early cognitive-intellectual development: 1. The physical environment. Unpublished manuscript, 1975.

Willerman, L. Personal communication, July 1976.

Zajonc, R. B., & Markus, G. B. Birth order and intellectual development. *Psychological Review*, 1975, **82** (1), 74–88.

Comments and Replies

CRITIQUE OF SCARR AND WEINBERG'S IQ ADOPTION
STUDY: PUTTING THE PROBLEM IN PERSPECTIVE*

In the first part of this article, Scarr and Weinberg's results are compared to those of similar studies and there is found to be considerable congruence despite the uniqueness of the Scarr and Weinberg sample. This comparison provides a perspective for understanding some of the problems raised by Scarr and Weinberg. The second part looks to the future and suggests that the major contribution of behavioral genetics in psychology may be to increase our understanding of the environment. Examples supporting this prediction are the concepts of genotype–environment interaction, genotype–environment correlation, environmental variance between and within families, and the "structure" of environmental influences in behavior.

After reading Scarr and Weinberg's article, the newcomer to the behavioral genetic literature will probably conclude that research on hereditary factors influencing IQ has produced a veritable jungle of contradictory conclusions and a welter of wildly varying estimates of the importance of heredity. In the first part of this review, an attempt is made to temper such an interpretation by placing Scarr and Weinberg's paper in a proper perspective. Some general issues in behavioral genetic research will then be discussed at the suggestion of this journal's editor.

Scarr and Weinberg conclude that "the traditional biometrical approach to calculating heritability estimates, based on related and unrelated parent–child and sibling data, yielded conflicting results. . . . Rather than force an immediate

*This comment by Plomin originally appeared in *Intelligence*, 1978, 2, 74–79. Copyright © 1978 by Ablex Publishing Corp. Reprinted by permission.

341

biometrical solution onto the combined parent–child and sibling data . . . we prefer to puzzle about the lack of fit.'' There is, however, a considerable body of adoption research on IQ. Comparing the Scarr and Weinberg design and results to the other studies provides a useful perspective that simplifies the complexities and resolves the perplexities raised by Scarr and Weinberg.

The goal of behavioral genetic research is to sample representative populations that have representative genetic and environmental variability. Scarr and Weinberg's study, however, is different. It is a spin-off from a transracial adoption study of black children adopted into white homes (Scarr & Weinberg, 1975). Generalizations about the etiology of individual differences are very hazardous in such a unique group with its unusual sampling of environmental and genetic variability. On the environmental side, the study is limited by the fact that the adoptive parents are of above average income, education, and IQ. On the genetic side, the sample is also unrepresentative: Of the 111 early adopted children in this study, most were the progeny of black–white matings (with the exception of 13 who had two black parents and 9 who had two white parents). However, the extent to which the results agree with other, more representative, behavioral genetic studies on IQ is surprising.

Table 1 shows a comparison of correlations from Scarr and Weinberg's study with results from other behavioral genetic studies. *None* of the correlations in the Scarr and Weinberg study is significantly different (at the .01 level) from the comparable correlation in other studies. Moreover, the average correlations from the other studies document a significant genetic component in IQ for *both* parent–offspring and sibling data. The correlation for parents and offspring sharing both genes and environment (.48) is significantly greater ($p < .001$) than the correlation for parents and offspring who share only environment (.20). Similarly, the correlation for siblings who share both genes and environment (.52) is significantly greater ($p < .001$) than the correlation for siblings who share only environment (.27). The large sample size for the average correlations yields our best guess of the relative influence of genetic and environmental factors. The parent–offspring correlations suggest a heritability of .56, and the sibling correlations suggest a heritability of .50, although these estimates do not attempt to correct for complicating but often counterbalancing factors.

What does this review suggest about the Scarr and Weinberg study? The correlation for parents and offspring sharing only environment was .19, which is very close to the usual correlation of .20. For parents and offspring sharing both genes and environment, the correlation in Scarr and Weinberg's study was .37, lower than the usual correlation of .48. Because of Scarr and Weinberg's lower-than-usual correlation for genetically related parents and offspring, their estimate of heritability $[2(\hat{r}_{1\ \text{RP-C}} - \hat{r}_{1\ \text{UP-C}})]$ is lower than usual.

The real power of a full adoption study lies in the clean separation of genetic and environmental influences. This is accomplished by comparing genetically unrelated individuals living together to genetically related individuals living apart. The Scarr and Weinberg study provided only a weak test of the second half

TABLE 1
Comparison of Scarr and Weinberg's Results to Other Studies

Relationship	Scarr and Weinberg		Weighted mean of other studies	
	r^a	N	r	N
Parent–offspring correlations				
IQ parent–IQ offspring (living together)	.37	(283)	.48[b]	(1,250)
IQ adoptive parent–IQ adopted child (living together)	.19	(220)	.20[c]	(2,101)
Education natural parent–IQ adopted child (living apart)	.36	(117)	.35[d]	(152)
Sibling correlations				
IQ sib–IQ sib (living together)	.42	(107)	.52[b]	(2,215)
IQ unrelated children (living together)	.33	(187)	.27[c]	(793)

[a] Weighted uncorrected mean correlations from Tables 4 and 6 of the Scarr and Weinberg article.

[b] Weighted uncorrected mean correlations adapted from Jencks (1972).

[c] Weighted uncorrected mean correlations adapted from Jencks (1972) with the addition of the preliminary results (June, 1976, N = 461 adoptive families) from the largest adoption study, the Texas Adoption Project (Horn et al., 1976).

[d] Weighted uncorrected mean correlation from Skodak and Skeels (1949).

of this two-part comparison, because the only available characterization of the natural parents' intelligence was years of education. Nonetheless, the correlation of .36 between the education of the natural parents and the IQ of their adopted-away children is as high as the comparable correlation in Skodak and Skeel's (1949) classic study. Two adoption studies (Skodak & Skeels, 1949; Horn, Loehlin & Willerman, 1976) have reported correlations between IQ (not just education) of natural mothers and IQ of their adopted-away children. The weighted mean correlation was .31 (N=425), suggesting a narrow heritability of .62 for IQ.

Turning to the sibling data, the Scarr and Weinberg sibling IQ correlation of .42 was lower than usual (.52), and the unrelated sibling correlation of .33 was higher than usual (.27). Together, these discrepancies combined to produce a heritability estimate of .18, considerably lower than the usual estimate of .50. Although the authors emphasized that the unrelated sibling correlation was high, it should be noted that the natural sibling correlation was even more discrepant. Because neither correlation differs significantly from the mean correlation of other studies, it is prudent to attribute these dual discrepancies to sampling error.

Thus, a quite different interpretation of the Scarr and Weinberg study emerges from consideration of the fact that the agreement between their results and the results of other behavioral genetic adoption studies is more impressive than the statistically insignificant differences, especially noting the uniqueness of their sample. Because Scarr and Weinberg sampled a mix of genetic differences and environmental differences not sampled by the other studies, the similarity in results suggests that behavioral genetic estimates of environmental and genetic influences on IQ may be *more* robust than previously thought.

The tide seems to be flowing toward acceptance of a substantial role for genes in the development of individual differences in IQ, although undertows and backwaters are still frequent (as discussed by Plomin & DeFries, 1976). In the near future (perhaps with the completion of the large-scale Texas Adoption Study, see Horn *et al.*, 1976), we will need no more studies demonstrating that genes affect IQ. But then what? Two obvious directions for future research are to sharpen our tools for more precise analysis and to broaden our study to include other phenotypes. More precise analysis will come, for example, from larger and more representative adoption samples without problems such as selective place- ment and from adoption studies that attempt to assess characteristics of unwed fathers as well as those of unwed mothers so that we can control for the effects of assortative mating (Plomin, DeFries, & Roberts, 1977). Such methods will also be applied to the analysis of a wide variety of important traits other than IQ. For example, in the cognitive domain, specific cognitive abilities and different views of intelligence (such as Piagetian or information processing approaches) are being subjected to behavioral genetic analyses (DeFries, Vandenberg, & McClearn, 1976). Other realms of behavior such as personality are also being studied (Buss & Plomin, 1975).

These studies have begun and will continue as a necessary first step in under- standing the etiology of behavior. The long-range significance of such research will be to open doors to new areas of research on genetic *and* environmental effects. On the genetic side, questions such as the following will be addressed: What physiological mechanisms mediate the genetic effects? How many inde- pendent genetic pathways are involved? Are there any major or single gene systems and, if so, can they be mapped? When and how are the genes turned on during development?

However, the major contribution of behavioral genetics in psychology may well be to increase our understanding of the environment. This prediction is based on the likely importance of four topics: genotype–environment interaction, genotype–environment correlation, environmental variance between and within families, and the ''structure'' of environmental and genetic influences in be- havior. A brief description of each will suggest the potential power of behavioral genetic studies to extend our knowledge of how the environment affects be- havior.

Genotype–Environment (GE) Interaction

The mistaken notions of the nature–nurture controversy are too often replaced with the equally mistaken notion that genes and environment are somehow hopelessly enmeshed in interaction. Discussion of GE interaction has been confused by the failure to distinguish the population concept from that of the individual. This issue has recently been discussed (Plomin, DeFries, & Loehlin, 1977). Once the clouds of confusion are blown away, the really important implication of GE interaction can be popularized as "different strokes for different folks." More prosaically, individuals of different genotypes may respond differently to environments or, looking at it from the other side, different environments may be differentially effective for individuals of different genotypes. My colleagues and I (Plomin, DeFries, & Loehlin, 1977) have discussed the importance of GE interaction and concluded that "the use of adoption data to screen for GE interaction is an unusually promising tool for the more refined analysis of environmental effects in psychology."

Genotype–Environment Correlation

GE correlation occurs if individuals of different genotypes are selectively exposed to different environments. For example, musically gifted children may receive or select musically rich environments. Three types of GE correlation (passive, reactive, and active) provide a new way of thinking about transactions between organisms and their environments, and behavioral genetics provides the tools needed to pin down these transactions (Plomin et al., 1977).

Environmental Variance between and within Families

Behavioral genetics can also be used to separate environmental factors into those that operate within families (to make family members different from one another) and those that operate between families (to make family members similar to one another and different from other families). Although Scarr and Weinberg imply that their study tapped within-family environmental influences, it should be noted that their major correlational analyses of parents and offspring and of siblings are actually focusing on between-family influences. Loehlin and Nichols (1976) have shown how to use twin studies to separate environmental influences into these two types, and they have come up with a surprising finding from their study of 850 pairs of twins: For cognitive abilities, most of the environmental variance operates *between* families; for personality traits, most of the environmental variance operates *within* families. The latter finding is particularly important because psychologists have rarely considered within-family environmental influences.

The "Structure" of Environmental and Genetic Influences

When the traditional univariate behavioral genetic analysis is generalized to the multivariate case, it assesses the relative contributions of genetic and environmental factors to the *covariance* among behaviors rather than to the variance of behaviors considered one at a time (Plomin, DeFries, Rowe, Horn, & Rosenman, 1977). This multivariate approach has the unique ability to reveal the structure and nature of environmental and genetic effects upon behavior. Just as factor analysis of phenotypic correlations yields a phenotypic factor structure, the structure of the genetic and environmental influences can be derived from factor analyses of genetic and environmental correlations among behaviors. Although the usual phenotypic factor structure of behavior (which mixes environment and genes in unknown proportions) is often studied, hardly anything is known about the environmental or genetic influences that underlie the "finished" phenotypic structure.

ROBERT PLOMIN
University of Colorado, Boulder

ACKNOWLEDGMENTS

I am grateful to S. G. Vandenberg, J. C. DeFries, and E. S. Gollin for their comments on an earlier draft of this review.

REFERENCES

Buss, A., & Plomin, R. *A temperament theory of personality development.* New York: Wiley–Interscience, 1975.

DeFries, J. C., Vandenberg, S. G., & McClearn, G. E. Genetics of specific cognitive abilities. *Annual Review of Genetics,* 1976.

Horn, J. M., Loehlin, J., & Willerman, L. Personal communication describing the Texas Adoption Project, 1976.

Jencks, C. *Inequality: A reassessment of the effect of family and schooling in America.* New York: Harper & Row, 1972.

Loehlin, J. C., & Nichols, R. C. *Heredity, environment, and personality: A study of 850 twins.* Austin: University of Texas Press, 1976.

Plomin, R., & DeFries, J. C. Letter in response to "The Heritability Hang-up," by M. Feldman & R. C. Lewontin (*Science,* 19 December 1975). *Science,* 1976.

Plomin, R., DeFries, J. C., & Loehlin, J. C. Genotype-environment interaction and correlation in the analysis of human behavior. *Psychological Bulletin,* 1977, **84,** 309–322.

Plomin, R., DeFries, J. C., & Roberts, M. K. Assortative mating by unwed biological parents of adopted children. *Science,* 1977, **196,** 449–450.

Plomin, R., DeFries, J. C., Rowe, D. C., Horn, J. M., & Rosenman, R. Genetic and environmental influences on human behavior: Multivariate analysis. Paper presented at the Seventh Annual Meeting of the Behavior Genetics Association, April 27–30, 1977. Louisville, Kentucky.

Scarr, S., & Weinberg, R. A. When black children grow up in white homes. *Psychology Today,* 1975, December, 80–82.

Skodak, M., & Skeels, H. M. A final follow-up on one hundred adopted children. *Journal of Genetic Psychology,* 1949, **75,** 85–125.

Comments and Replies

NATURE AND NURTURE STRIKE (OUT) AGAIN*

This is a reply to the critique of the Scarr and Weinberg paper by Plomin. In addition, Munsinger's review of the adopted child literature is challenged as inaccurate and misleading. The need to discern mean effects in adoptions studies is highlighted by noting that mean scores show more malleability than rank order of individual scores, when the environments of adoptive families are well above the mean and when the variability with the group of families is restricted. Also discussed are alleged selective bias in the current pool of adoptees, the implicit assumptions in models that lead to heritability estimates, and the problems produced by the lack of a generally accepted model of environmental transmission.

It has been difficult to entertain genetic hypotheses about individual differences in IQ and still remain on speaking terms with many of one's psychological colleagues. It has been even harder to maintain agnosticism about the sources of group differences in intellectual performance. Thus, we welcome the calm discussion of the issue that appears in comments by Professors Munsinger and Plomin. Their positions in the nature–nurture spectrum are not as popular as more thoroughly environmentalist loci, but the merit of positions is not determined by popular vote. Naturally, we do not agree with many of the points they have made.

---

*We are extremely grateful to Professor Arthur Goldberger for his extraordinarily helpful suggestions and comments. He is in no way responsible, however, for any errors of thought or act that may lie within this piece. This reply by Sandra Scarr and Richard A. Weinberg originally appeared in *Intelligence*, 1979, *3*, 31–39. Copyright © 1979 by Ablex. Reprinted by permission.

THE MATH OF IQ MALLEABILITY

With sweeping generalizations, based on his surveys of the literature on adoptions and twins, Munsinger dismisses the notion that intellectual development is affected by the rearing environment. He would have the reader believe that the variance analysis of IQ differences among adopted children and twins settles the issue of malleability because the heritability of IQ is so high as to preclude substantial environmental effects. Let us examine first his reviews of literature and second the conclusions he draws from those reviews.

Munsinger's (1975) review of the adopted child literature should not be accepted as authoritative. It is inaccurate and misleading on several accounts. (See Goldberger, 1976) For example, Munsinger says:

> Burks also computed a multiple correlation between [nine variables listed] and the child's IQ in the adoptive families. When all these nine variables were entered into a multiple correlation with the child's IQ... (p. 635).

Burks herself said:

> To have gone through the operation of computing multiple correlations that utilized all nine of the variables in question would have been enormously time-consuming. To save labor, certain variables were eliminated... (1928a, p. 287).

In fact, Burks was unable to take more than a few variables at a time because there were no computers in 1928. Her extraordinary diligence in calculating the multiple correlations of 3 and 4 variables by hand is amazing enough.

On Burks' conclusions about IQ malleability, Munsinger says (p. 636):

> Burks rightly concluded nothing from the fact that the group mean IQ of the adopted children in her sample was 107.4 rather than 100 because she was aware of the many selective biases operating on her initial sample.

Burks herself said:

> A group of 214 foster children, whose average inheritance was judged to be close to normal or slightly above, had an average I.Q. of 107. The average environment of their foster homes was markedly superior, and the conclusion was drawn that 5 or 6 points of the excess over 100 I.Q. could be explained by environment (1928b, p. 318).

And so on through the literature....

The more important issue is the basis for his conclusion that adoptive family environments have little effect on their children's levels of intellectual performance. As is typical of behavioral geneticists, Munsinger finds considerably more comfort in discussing variances than means. The methods of variance analysis, correlations, and related techniques are well established in the field. Methods for discerning mean effects are less well established (Cavalli-Sforza & Feldman, 1973; Lewontin, 1974; Feldman & Lewontin, 1975). Unfortunately, Munsinger errs in discounting the environmental effects on the above average IQ scores of adopted children, because he says, biological background is more highly related to individual differences than are social environmental variables. A more proper interpretation is that mean scores show more malleability than rank orders of individual scores, when the environments of adoptive families are well above the mean and when the variability within the group of families is restricted.

To discount the intellectually stimulating effects of the adoptive families on the IQ levels of their adopted children, Munsinger points to selective biases in the pool of adoptees. In the past, illegitimate children who were relinquished for adoption came from mothers with somewhat higher educational and occupational levels than those who were retained by their mothers (Leahy, 1935). But Munsinger omits from his review the one substantial study in recent years on the critical issue of natural parents' IQ scores. Pearson & Amacher (1956) studied nearly 3,600 women in Minnesota who relinquished their infants for adoption. By law the mothers were required to take IQ tests. Their IQ scores averaged 100.0 with a standard deviation of slightly over 15. Although fathers were not tested, there is no good reason to assume that their IQ's would be distributed differently from their mothers.

If natural parents have normal IQ distribution around a mean of 100, why do their offspring deviate upward? One reason, properly cited by Munsinger, is that clearly damaged and potentially retarded infants are not adopted. Let us suppose that 3 percent of available infants are not adopted, because either the natural parents or the infants appear to be mentally at risk. If the rejected infants have a mean IQ of 50, then the mean IQ's of the adoptable 97 percent is raised by 1.6 IQ points ($.97x + .03(50) = 100$, $x = 101.6$).

A second, and more obvious reason for upward deviation in the mean IQ's of adopted children, is the adoptive family environment. As a group, adoptive families are self-selected for their interest in child rearing and further selected by agencies for their stability, mental health, and abilities to provide good rearing environments. *One cannot look for the effects of variation among adoptive families on virtues that the whole group shares.* The environmental determinants of variation in the general population are surely underestimated when studied in adoptive samples where important determinants vary over a quite restricted range. One virtue of the present study was to sample adopted and biologically-related children in the same *adoptive* families. Their restricted range of environmental variation would not affect the *comparison* of genetically-related and unrelated pairs. The restriction of environmental variation does affect the conclusions that can be drawn about the sources of variation in the scores of adopted children alone, however. Munsinger confuses the analysis of variance with the analysis of causes (Lewontin, 1974).

What, then, happens when a group of adopted children, (whose natural parents' IQ's would predict a mean of 101 in the children), reach adoptive families, whose socioeconomic status is above average and whose interest in child rearing, no doubt, exceeds the population average? The adopted children achieve IQ scores of 107 to 110, on the average (Burks, 1928a; Leahy, 1935; Scarr & Weinberg, 1976).

Two new adoption studies, reported on the same symposium in 1975—the first cited by Munsinger and the second not cited—speak to the issue of mean IQ scores. The Texas project (Horn, Loehlin, & Willerman, Note 2) includes a selected sample from a private home for unwed mothers, whose IQ scores average about 108. The adoptive parents, it so happens, have a similar level of IQ. Thus, no mean effects of parental IQ level can or ever could be observed.

The Minnesota project (Scarr & Weinberg, 1976) has a quite different population. The 99 Black and interracial children adopted in the first year by white families have average IQ scores of 110. The natural parents of the adoptees are educationally average for their population or, in the case of Black mothers, a little below average. The predicted IQ level for these children, based on intellectually average natural parents, would be in the mid-90's at best. Instead, there is no individual with an IQ score below 85 (the population average for Blacks), and the mean equals that of white adoptees in previous studies. Can Munsinger possibly conclude that the adoptive families have had no effect on IQ levels of these Black children?

To test for the relative effects of adoptive and natural parents' educational levels on the IQ levels of the adopted children, we did a simple two-way ANOVA. (Parents were divided *a priori* around their respective mean educational levels.) The biological effects of having brighter natural parents is roughly estimated by the natural parents' educational level. The social environmental effect of having brighter adoptive parents is roughly estimated by the educational level of the adoptive parents. Table 1 shows that having adoptive parents above their educational mean, by regression estimate, adds about 6 points to the child's IQ, whereas having natural parents above their educational mean increases the child's IQ by only 3 points. In fact, the effect of the adoptive family is the only statistically significant effect on the children's intellectual performance ($t = 2.24$, $p < .05$). Since arranging the data in this form eliminates the problem of selective placement, it is impossible to explain the adoptive family effect without recourse to environmental influences on the development of children's intellectual skills.

In the Minnesota study, as in other adoption studies, there is indeed a correlation between natural parents' intellectual level and adopted children's IQ scores. The rank order of IQ scores in the adopted group bears more

TABLE 1

The Effects of Higher and Lower Educational Levels of Natural
and Adoptive Parents on the IQ Scores of Early Adopted Black
and Interracial Children

Education of Natural Parents[a]	Education of Adoptive Parents[a]		
	Higher > 16	Lower ≦ 16	
Higher > 12	113.5	108.1	112.3
	N = 24 (11.7)	N = 7 (8.1)	
Lower ≦ 12	111.1	104.5	107.9
	N = 22 (11.2)	N = 21 (11.3)	
	112.4	105.4	

Regression model: $\hat{y} = b_0 + b_1x_1 + b_2x_2$
    where x_1 = natural parents' education (1 = higher, 0 = lower)
           x_2 = adoptive parents' education (1 = higher, 0 = lower)
           y = child's IQ
           $\hat{y} = 104.7 + 2.8x_1 + 6.2x_2$

[a]Midparent education used for all adoptive parents and for 28 of the 74
natural parents; educational data on at least the natural mothers were
available on 74 of the 99 early adopted black and interracial children.

resemblance to their biological parents than to their adoptive parents. The
variance approach that Munsinger espoused is important to our understanding of genetic and environmental effects on individual differences. But
the mean of the IQ distribution seems to be far more malleable than
Munsinger admits.

THE MYTH OF THE SEPARATED TWINS

On separated, identical twins, Munsinger (1977) reaches the incredible and
singular conclusion that the heritability of IQ is close to 1.00, if one controls
for birth weight differences among identical twins. Despite the fact that many
of the pairs of MZ twins were reared by branches of the same family and that
many were childhood friends, sharing school and neighborhood, Munsinger,
like Jensen, treats the correlation in their rearing environments as zero,
despite clear evidence to the contrary. It is quite possible that the identical
twins who were reared in closely correlated environments were the ones with
the small birth weight differences and those reared apart were those with large
weight differences. This pattern would explain his data in terms quite
different from a heritability of nearly 1.00. Comparisons of MZ and DZ twins
do not generally yield heritability estimates of .86, as Munsinger claims,
unless one is referring to Burt's dubious data (Jensen, 1974; Kamin, 1974).

Most recent studies of twins yield heritability estimates (by the simplest but possibly incorrect assumptions) of closer to .60, and some yield lower values (Nichols, 1976).

MORE MAGIC MODELS

The major problems for the occasional reader of this tangled literature are to sort out the facts, which are embedded in impenetrable polemics, and to figure out the assumptions that are usually implicit in the models that lead to heritability estimates.

As Plomin indicates in his opening paragraph, we do indeed see the literature on family correlations as a veritable jungle of uninterpretable results, but perhaps not entirely for the reasons he cites. On the nature of the data themselves, a new review (MacAskie and Clarke, 1976) raises many questions about the quality of the parent–child data.

Competing biometrical models (Cavalli-Sforza and Feldman, 1973; Jencks, 1972; Jensen, 1973; Jinks and Eaves, 1974; Jinks and Fulker, 1970; Taubman, Behrman and Wales, Note 4; Wright, 1931) make conflicting assumptions about the nature of family influences, but they all produce heritability estimates that lie between 0 and 1. Although no one except Kamin (1974) seriously suggests that the heritability of IQ could be zero, and none except Munsinger believes it is virtually one, there is certainly no point estimate that would achieve general consensus from the cognoscenti in the field, present authors included. For example, the consensus between Munsinger and Plomin is hardly ovewhelming!

A major problem in fitting kinship models to the existing data on parent–child, twin and sibling pairs is that the assumptions are nearly always questionable. There is no generally accepted model of environmental transmission, comparable to Mendelian genetics (to which we all subscribe). There are existing models to satisfy every taste, contrary to the brief sermon that Plomin gives on the topic. Are children's intellectual environments more influenced by their parents' IQ phenotypes or by the education–income–occupational characteristics of the parents? Is the child's environment more correlated with the parents' genotypes, or the parent's own rearing environment. Are childrens' genotypes as highly correlated with their parents' environments as with their own environments? Are adopted children's genotypes as correlated with their adoptive parents' environments as natural children's with their biological parents? (Munsinger would have us believe they are.) Are the common environments of parents and children as similar as those of siblings or twins? These and many other questions become assumptions that only full time devotion to biometrical models will suffice to disentangle.

We do not agree that Plomin's excellent *discussion* of the problems of genotype-environment correlations has provided "the tools needed to pin down these transactions." Neither he nor anyone else has put forth a compelling case for the acceptance of one version of covariance than another in models. Moreover, there are no compelling reasons to choose one model over another for empirical reasons, because the data can be made to fit, more or less, any and all models, whose estimates of heritability vary from .45 (Jencks, 1972) to .86 (Munsinger, 1975).

As we said in the article, a value between .4 and .7 seems most likely to us, which puts us in the mainstream of our colleagues.

UNREPRESENTATIVE GENES?

Plomin raises some issues of representativeness of our sample on both environmental and genetic bases. As in all adoption studies, the families whom agencies permit to adopt are an unrepresentative sample of child–rearing environments, both demographically above average and self-selected for interest in child rearing. We are not sure what genetic unrepresentativeness means to Plomin, however. The "unique" group to whom he refers are the progeny of varied racial backgrounds, representing humanity to a greater extent than other studies that have been limited to "white" children. In fact, the 222 natural parents of the early adopted children were comprised of 112 socially–classified blacks, 64 whites, 11 Asian or Indian parents and 35 parents of unknown classification.

What *is* unique about the sample is that all of the adopted and biologically related children in this study have parents who *adopted*. This qualification makes the biologically–related parent–child and sibling correlations far more comparable to the correlations of adopted parent–child and sibling pairs, because the family characteristics are similarly restricted in the related and unrelated comparisons. These families may not be representative of biological families in general, but as a comparison sample for adopted relatives we feel they are far superior to a socioeconomically-matched group of controls, who may well differ on motivational and personality character-istics that affect children's development.

THE FAMILY CORRELATIONS

We agree with Plomin that our parent–child correlations are quite similar to others reported earlier, although our coefficients corrected for attenuation are an even better match to the corrected values from U.S. studies, summarized by Jencks. Our sibling results are also a close match to Jenck's summary of the literature on unrelated children reared together. For 259 published pairs of unrelated children reared together, Jencks calculated a weighted mean correlation of .32, in close agreement with the .33 obtained in the present study.

To the published data summarized by Jencks, Plomin has added 534 cases that are either unpublished or from Burt's highly questionable reports. Plomin did include Burt's 264 cases of full siblings living together in the 2,215 cases he reports in his Table 1, but their presence does not affect the results. If he added Burt's "data" on 136 cases with a reported correlation of .25 for the "London Binet," then the remaining 398 unrelated sib pairs from the Texas Adoption Project must correlate .244. Based on the 1975 symposium report, our understanding is that in the Texas study the standard deviations of the Stanford–Binet and WISC IQ scores were about 11. If so, a substantial correction for restriction of range is required. Corrected to a standard deviation of 15, the Texas coefficient for unrelated siblings would come closer to the Jencks and Scarr and Weinberg values than Plomin implies.

In commenting on Jencks' heritability analysis, Loehlin, Lindzey and Spuhler (1975, Appendix I) noted that the obtained correlations for unrelated children reared together did not fit the heritability estimates based on other kinships. Two of the four American studies have yielded results so discrepant from the other two that little sense can be made of the literature. Jencks himself said that there was no set of values for heritability, environmental variance and covariance of GE that could satisfy a kinship model if unrelated children reared together were included:

> How can we explain this? The basic data on parents and on children and siblings is probably fairly accurate. This means that either the correlation between unrelated children in the same home is overestimated, or the analytic model is wrong. The reader will recall that the data on unrelated children also raise problems when we used Jensen's simpler analytic model. . . . A large careful study of unrelated children in the same home is badly needed. (Jencks, 1972, p. 307).

We agree heartily with Jencks' sentiments. The full report of the Texas Adoption project will be eagerly awaited. In addition, our own study of older adolescents, half of them adopted in early infancy, provides new information on parent–child and sibling resemblance after the rapid intellectual changes of the childhood period are over (Scarr & Weinberg, 1978). Several large studies of differential abilities, in samples of varying age and location, by investigators with differing hypotheses, will be a great benefit to our knowledge of intellectual development and the roles of genes and environments in that development.

SANDRA SCARR
Yale University

RICHARD A. WEINBERG
University of Minnesota

REFERENCES

Burks, B. S. The relative influence of nature and nurture upon mental development. A comparative study of foster parent-foster child resemblance and true parent-true child resemblance. *27th Yearbook of the National Society for the Study of Education,* 1928, Pt.1, 219–316 (1928a).

Burks, B. S. Comments on the Chicago and Stanford Studies of foster children, *27th Yearbook of the National Society for the Study of Education,* 1928, 317–321 (1928b).

Cavalli-Sforza, L. L., & Feldman, M. Cultural versus biological inheritance: Phenotypic transmission from parents to children (a theory of the effect of parental phenotypes on children's phenotypes). *American Journal of Human Genetics,* 1973, *25,* 618–637.

Feldman, M. and Lewontin, R. The heritability hang-up. *Science,* 1975, *190,* 1163–1168.

Goldberger, A. S. Jensen on Burks. *Educational Psychologist,* 1976, *12,* 64–78.

Goldberger, A. S. Statistical inference in the great IQ debate. Institute of Research on Poverty, Discussion Papers, University of Wisconsin, 1975.

Horn, J., Loehlin, J., Willerman, L. The Texas Adoption Project. Paper presented at the meeting of the Behavior Genetics Association, Austin, Texas.

Jencks, C. *Inequality: A reassessment of the effect on family and schooling in America.* New York: Basic Books, Inc., 1972.

Jensen, A. R. *Educability and Group Differences.* New York: Harper & Row, 1973.

Jensen, A. R. Kinship correlations reported by Sir Cyril Burt. *Behavior Genetics,* 1974, *4,* 1–28.

Jinks, J. L. & Eaves, J. J. IQ and inequality. *Nature,* 1974, *248,* 287.

Jinks, J. L. & Fulker, D. W. A comparison of the biometrical genetical, MAVA, and classical approaches to the analysis of human behaviour, *Psychological Bulletin,* 1970, 73, 311–349.

Kamin, L. J. *The science and politics of IQ.* Potomac, Md.: Lawrence Erlbaum Associates, 1974.

Leahy, A. M. Nature-nurture and intelligence. *Genetic Psychology Monographs,* 1935, *17,* 236–308.

Lewontin, R. The analysis of variance and the analysis of cause. *American Journal of Human Genetics,* 1974, *26,* 400–411.

Loehlin, J. C., Lindzey, G. & Spuhler, J. N. *Race Differences in Intelligence,* San Francisco: Freeman, 1975.

McAskie, M. & Clarke, A. M. Parent-Offspring resemblance in intelligence: Theories and evidence. *British Journal of Psychology,* 1976, *67,* 243–273.

Munsinger, H. The adopted child's IQ: A critical review. *Psychological Bulletin,* 1975, *82*(5), 623–659.

Munsinger, H. The identical-twin transfusion syndrome: A source of error in estimating IQ resemblance and heritability. *Annals of Human Genetics,* 1977, 40, 307–321.

Nichols, R. C. Heredity and Environment: Major Findings from Twin Studies of Ability, Personality and Interests. Invited address, American Psychological Association, Washington, D. C. September 4, 1976.

Pearson, J. S., & Amacher, P. L. Intelligence test results and observations of personality disorder among 3594 unwed mothers in Minnesota, *Journal of Clinical Psychology,* 1956, *12,* 16–21.

Scarr, S. & Weinberg, R. A. The influence of "family background" on intellectual attainment. *American Sociological Review,* 1978, *43,* 674–692.

Taubman, P., Behrman, J., and Wales, T. The roles of Genetics and Environment in the Distribution of Earnings. Unpublished manuscript, 1976.

Wright, S. Statistical methods in biology. *Journal of the American Statistical Association,* 1931, *26,* Supplement, 155–163.

III.2 The Influence of "Family Background" on Intellectual Attainment*

"Family background" has been frequently found to have long-term effects on adult intellectual, occupational, and economic outcomes. Since families differ both genetically and environmentally, it has been difficult to interpret family effects in studies of individuals or biological relatives. This study includes samples of adoptive and biologically related families with children between 16 and 22 years of age. We regressed child IQ on several family demographic variables, on parental IQ, and on natural-parent characteristics (for the adopted children) to estimate the degree of genetic bias in the coefficients on measured family background. The results indicate that there is little effect of those family *environmental* differences studied on IQ differences among the adolescents in the SES range of working to upper middle class. Parent–child and sibling correlations further indicate that genetic differences among families account for the major part of the long-term effects of "family background" on IQ.

Family background has been much discussed and studied recently as a source of inequality among American adults (Behrman, Taubman, & Wales, 1978; Duncan, Featherman, & Duncan, 1972; Duncan, 1968; Grilliches & Mason, 1972; Jencks, 1972; Jencks & Brown, 1978; Sewell & Hauser, 1975; Taubman, 1976; Taubman & Wales, 1972, 1974). That accidents of birth leave us at the mercy of our families' fortunes, and that home environments can affect life chances, strike most social scientists as unfair, undemocratic, and even morally wrong. Even

---

*This chapter by Sandra Scarr and Richard A. Weinberg originally appeared in *American Sociological Review*, 1978, *43*, 674–692. Copyright © 1978 American Sociological Association. Reprinted by permission.

more difficult for some to accept is the idea that genetic differences among individuals and families can control some of our differences in adult achievements. The impact of family environmental and genetic differences on intellectual outcome of children is the subject of this study.

It has been frequently reported in recent years that "family background" continues to affect intellectual, educational, occupational, and income differences long after children have grown up and left home. Some vaguely specified characteristics of the offspring are differentially rewarded by employers, and those offspring traits are correlated with parental and home characteristics, even 30 years after the offspring have left home. Although there are substantial differences among studies in the magnitude of the effects they find for family variables (Crouse, 1978; Leibowitz, 1978), there is no sign that the effects diminish with time; in fact, Taubman (1977a) reported stronger effects of "family background" and own IQ as one approaches middle age.

Studies of outcome differences among the offspring of biologically related families confound four sources of variance: within- and between-family, environmental, and genetic differences. Regressions of individual outcomes on differences in family background are not illuminating as to the genetic or environmental sources of outcome differences, because parents transmit both genes and family environments that are likely to be correlated with each other and with genetic differences between families. In other words, the genetic variance in the predictors is likely to be correlated with the genetic variance in the outcomes. As unreconstructed liberals, we get upset about the long-term *environmental* effects of families on their offspring's life chances. When individual outcomes are shown to be affected by "family background," we don't know how upset to be.

Behavior Genetic Methods

As Taubman and his collaborators (Behrman, Taubman, & Wales, 1978) have shown, twin study methods can help to define what is subsumed by the term *family background*. Behavior genetic methods have long included the study of genetically and environmentally related and unrelated people (and mice, dogs, and so forth). The contrast of effects from similar and different treatments on similar and different genotypes has been a continuing fascination for the field. Families are the usual source of human beings aggregated in related groups. Fortunately, for behavior genetic studies, there are also families who are genetically unrelated but aggregated through adoption. Also beneficial to the field has been the tendency of human populations to produce occasional litters of offspring, some of them genetically identical and others no more alike than sibs. Adoptive families and twins offer unique but different opportunities to study the effects of genes and environments on the outcomes of offspring. The confluence of behavior genetic and social science methods to study the effects of "family background" will provide new insights into true environmental effects.

As Jencks and Brown (1978) have indicated, there are two basic approaches to estimating the importance of environmental differences in determining differences in outcomes. First, they say, one should begin by offering some meaningful definition of what one means by environment. One strategy is to specify what one means by *measured* environment and to study the effects of differences in home background on unrelated children, adopted into the home. A second strategy is to look at only those environmental influences shared by children reared together. One can estimate the contribution of such influences to phenotypic inequality by calculating the correlation between the phenotypes of genetically unrelated parents and children and unrelated children reared together.

A third way to obtain an estimate of the "true" environmental effects of family background would be with identical twins reared apart in uncorrelated environments. Genetic differences would be controlled, but both within- and between-family environmental effects would be free to vary. Unfortunately, child development experts have repeatedly warned about the psychological hazards of giving away one of a pair of twins, and there are simply too few cases, too peculiarly sampled, to make these subjects useful to social science.

Adoptive Families

Adopted children, on the other hand, provide almost as useful data as the rare identical twins reared apart, and they are far more available. Adopted children are not genetically descended from the family of rearing; so environmental differences between families are not confounded with genetic differences in the children if the adopted children are randomly placed by adoption agencies. Theoretically, regressions of adopted-child outomes on adoptive-family characteristics will provide genetically unbiased estimates of true environmental effects in the population. Unfortunately, adoptive families are selected by agencies for being above average in many virtues, including socioeconomic status. Thus, they are always an unrepresentative sample of the population to which one would like to generalize. Although it is possible that the adoptive-family coefficients on background are good estimates of the population values, it is difficult to know without modeling the way in which the families were selected. An easier corrective for the possible bias of selected adoptive families is to have a comparison sample of biologically related families who are similarly selected.

The study reported in this paper includes both adoptive and biologically related families. The comparison of regression coefficients on measured family background for adoptive families with those of biological families is an estimate of the extent of the genetic bias in studies of family background effects in the usual sociological and psychological studies of families. An additional focus of the paper is on family correlations for IQ. The comparison of similarities among related and unrelated children, and the comparison of related and unrelated parent–child correlations, is the best estimate of the "true" environmental effects of total, shared family background. The children reported here are the oldest adoptive sample ever studied. The study was designed to assess the cumulative impact of family environments at the end of the child-rearing period. If differences in family environments have lasting impact on individual differences in intellectual functioning, the study of adolescents adopted in the first few months of life should reveal those differences.

METHOD

Subjects

The 845 subjects in this report are members of 120 biological and 104 adoptive, white families in Minnesota. The adoptive families included 194 adopted and 15 biological children between the ages of 16 and 22. In the first section of this report, only the 150 adopted children whose natural mothers' educational levels were known are included. In the second section, all adoptees are included. The biological families include 237 children with complete data and 268 with IQ data. Adoptive families were recruited through the Department of Public Welfare (DPW), whose director sent letters on behalf of the study to 1620 families who had adopted children between 1953 and 1959. We were particularly interested in families who had adopted at least 2 children; so our recruitment concentrated on those volunteers with 2 available children between the ages of 16 and 21 at the time of testing. Table 1 gives the details of the adoptive-family recruitment.

Table 1. Recruitment of Adoptive and Biological Families

Adoptive Families		
Letters sent by DPW		1,620
Letters returned undelivered		477
No Response		345
Eligible to participate		798
Said No	327	
Said Yes	471	
Participate		
By mail		164
By interview		110*
Biological Families		
Eligible to participate		?
Recruited by adoptive families		41
Recruited by media		153
Participated		
By interview		122*

* The samples reported in this paper.

Of the 1620 letters sent by DPW, 477 were returned to us without forwarding addresses, hardly surprising since the addresses were 15 to 20 years old. Another 345 letters evoked no response, which may mean that they were not received or that the family chose not to acknowledge our attempted contact, even though follow-up letters were also sent. Of the 798 families known to be eligible to participate, 471 agreed to come to the university for a half-day testing session. Many of those who refused lived far across the state and were unable to join the study. Others did not choose to subject themselves to such extensive scrutiny. The final interview sample who came to the university consisted of 115 families; nearly all of these families had 2 children in the designated age range and were conveniently located relative to the university. An additional 164 families, most of whom had only 1 child in the prescribed age range, participated in the mail sample that will not be discussed in this paper. Other willing families were not recruited because of funding and time limitations.

To check on the representativeness of the sample recruited for the study, we compared the socioeconomic characteristics of participants and nonparticipants at the time of adoption. Since we had no data on the nonparticipants in later years, this was the best comparison we could manage. There were no age, income, educational, occupational differences between the participants and non-participants (refusals or nonrespondents) at the time of adoption, but of course, there may be some current differences in the outcomes of their adoptions or family life histories that we are unable to detect by this method.

The biological families were recruited through newspaper articles and advertisements, word of mouth, and the adoptive families. Approximately 153 biological families came from public media contact and about 41 from recommendations of the adoptive families. Of these, 122 were randomly chosen to come to the university for the full evaluation.

All families who participated in the interview procedure received small payments for their time and transportation and bonuses for recruiting other families. The data were collected from July 1974 to June 1976.

A crucial methodological consideration for any adoption study is the age at which the children are placed with their adopting families. Only early placements can guarantee that potentially confounding, early environmental experiences are minimized. All of the children in this study were in their homes before 12 months of age. Exact age of placement was available for 171 of the 194 adopted children. The mean age of placement into the adopted children's present homes was 2.6 months. Of these 171 children, 109 were placed before 2 months of age; 158 were placed at or before 6 months. All but 6 of the 171 were placed by age 9 months. Of all the children for whom placement data were available, there is only 1 case in which the natural mother may have had social contact during the first 68 days. In all other cases the child left the maternity hospital for the adoptive home or a foster placement. All adopted children were genetically unrelated to their adoptive parents and to each other. The biological children were all full siblings and claimed to be the biological offspring of both parents tested.

Procedure

Subjects in the sample were administered a 3-hour battery of tests and interviews at the University of Minnesota as part of a behavior genetic study of intellectual, personality, and attitudinal similarities within families. The data reported here are from the Wechsler Adult Intelligence Scale (WAIS; Wechsler, 1955), an individually administered IQ test. Four subtests of the WAIS were administered: vocabulary, arithmetic, block design, and picture arrangement. The combination of these four subtests has been shown to correlate above .90 with the full-scale test score and is generally accepted as a shortened version of the adult test (Doppelt, 1956). The test protocols were scored by an experienced psychometrician who was unaware of the respondents' adoptive status.

After scoring all of the tests, we became aware of a substantial sex difference on three of the four subtests, a fact seldom reported in the literature, but of which the Psychological Corporation seems to have been aware for some time (Herman, 1977). From the point of view of regression analysis, these mean sex differences are not critical, because there are about the same proportions of male and female children in the adoptive and biological samples (47% and 45% male, respectively).

RESULTS

Socioeconomic Variables

The socioeconomic characteristics of the biologically related and adoptive families are shown in Table 2. Parental educational levels in both kinds of families are .75 to 1 standard deviation above the averages of their cohorts in the population. The occupational prestige of the fathers, rated on the expanded NORC scale (Reiss, 1961), is about 60 in both types of families. Since less than half the mothers were employed, their occupational ratings were not used in the analyses. Family income averages $25,000 to $26,000 in both types of families.[1]

---

[1]Occupations of the fathers in the two samples varied from janitor, auto mechanic, small farmer (income < $10,000), telephone installer, and sheet metal worker at the low end to physician, engineer, college professor, and radio station owner at the high end of the scale. Most occupations were in the middle range of carpenter and printer to insurance agent and building contractor.

The income levels of the families may appear to be higher than they are unless parental age is taken into account. In 1974, the median family income in the North Central region was $14,017, but the median family income for families headed by workers aged 45 to 55 was approximately $18,000. The families in this sample are less than 1 standard deviation above that value.

TABLE 2
Means, Standard Deviations, and Correlations of Adoptive and Biological Family Characteristics

Biological Children (N = 237) — correlations above the diagonal; **Adopted Children (N = 150)** — correlations below the diagonal.

Variable	1	2	3	4	5	6	7	8	9	10	Mean	S.D.
1 Child's IQ		.26	.24	.10	.22	-.19	-.21	.39	.39		112.82	10.36
2 Father's Education	.10		.51	.61	.44	.01	-.36	.56	.24		15.63	2.83
3 Mother's Education	.10	.51		.36	.39	.02	-.36	.43	.46		14.68	2.24
4 Father's Occupation	.12	.57	.25		.47	.01	-.30	.37	.13		62.47	24.73
5 Family Income	.06	.50	.40	.46		.00	-.25	.38	.19		24,987.34	8,770.43
6 Birth Rank	-.19	.05	.03	.06	.15		.08	-.00	.03		1.62	0.63
7 Family Size	-.05	.04	.11	-.00	.21	.10		-.30	-.10		3.85	1.48
8 Father's IQ	.15	.53	.30	.40	.45	.08	.14		.20		118.02	11.66
9 Mother's IQ	.04	.29	.44	.19	.21	.07	.12	.30			113.41	10.46
10 Natural Mother's Age	-.10	.04	.03	.12	-.02	-.11	-.04	-.10	.03			
11 Natural Mother's Education	.21	.33	.24	.29	.43	.09	.14	.20	.10	.07		
12 Natural Mother's Occupation	.12	-.00	.13	.11	.06	-.06	.11	.11	.15	.28	.33	

Adopted Children (N = 150)

	1	2	3	4	5	6	7	8	9	10	11	12
Mean	106.19	14.90	13.95	60.30	25,935.00	1.43	2.87	116.53	112.43	22.46	11.97	30.44
S.D.	8.95	3.03	2.06	24.14	10,196.78	0.57	1.20	11.36	10.18	5.80	1.66	23.24

$r \geqq .16$, $p < .05$.

The variance of the educational, occupational, and income measures is not as restricted as the high means might imply. In fact, the standard deviations are roughly comparable to the population figures (Taubman's veteran twin sample, 1977b). Two points should be made, therefore, about the socioeconomic characteristics of these families: First, the adoptive and biological families are fairly comparable; and second, they both represent selected portions of the SES range in the United States, both regionally and within the region from which they are drawn. It is well known that volunteers in social science research are self-selected for better-than-average characteristics of all kinds, and the sample of biological families is at least as biased in SES characteristics as the adoptive one. This is what we hoped would happen, without the statistically hazardous procedure of matching individual families.

The adoptive and biological parents are also comparable in mean IQ scores and in the variance of their scores. Compared to the standardization sample for the WAIS (Wechsler Adult Intelligence Scale), the fathers are more than a standard deviation above the mean and the mothers, about .75 of an *SD* above. It is not accidental, of course, that samples with above-average income, education, and occupational status also score above the average on a standard IQ test. The standard deviation of the parental IQ scores is only 75% of that of the population, a significant restriction. Their scores are significantly restricted in range, with the lowest scores in the mid-90s.

The children of the two types of families are quite comparable in age, the mean being about 18½ in both groups. The range of ages is 16 to 22 in both groups (with a few older or younger exceptions). There was no correlation between age and IQ. The IQ scores of the adopted children are about 6.5 points lower than those of the biological children, however. These results are also shown in Table 2. If IQ is heritable to any extent, one should expect the biological offspring of bright parents to have higher IQ scores than unselected people. The adopted children are not a genetically selected group. Their natural mothers averaged 12 years of education at a present average age of 41. The median educational level for women, aged 25 to 44 in the Minnesota area, is 12.5 years of education. Education is an indirect measure of intellectual ability, but as we have shown in another study, there is good reason to expect that intellectual level of the natural mothers is reasonably well indexed by their educational levels (Scarr & Weinberg, 1976, 1977a, 1977b). Furthermore, there was a large study of unmarried mothers in the state of Minnesota during the years 1948 to 1952, when IQ tests were mandated for all women giving up children for adoption. The average IQ score of 3600 women was 100.00, with a standard deviation of 15.4 (Pearson & Amacher, 1956). Since our mothers were sampled from 1953 to 1959, there is no reason to expect them to differ significantly from the normal population. Fathers, of course, should not be expected to deviate from the average of the population any more than mothers. Thus, the adopted children are genetically a sample of an intellectually average population, whereas the biological children are more selected.

Correlations Among Parental Characteristics

The parental educational levels, family income, and father's occupation are similarly correlated in the biological and adoptive families. Despite the above-average means on all of these variables, the correlations are either greater than, or of the same magnitude as, those reported from more representative samples by Sewell and Hauser (1975), Jencks (1972), and others. These two facts—the comparability of correlations in the two samples and their comparability with more representative samples—encouraged us to proceed with the regression analyses.

As Table 2 shows, mothers and fathers in the adoptive and biologically related families are assortatively mated for educational level with a correlation of about .50. Sewell and Hauser (1975, p. 72) reported .52. Father's education correlated with his own occupational status (NORC scale) about .59. Sewell and Hauser reported .43 (Duncan SEI). Father's occupational status correlated with family income about .46, the same figure obtained by Sewell and Hauser. Mother's education is somewhat more correlated with father's occupational prestige in biological than adoptive families (.36 vs. .25), and Sewell and Hauser reported .29. In these samples, mother's education correlated more highly with family income (.40) than in Sewell and Hauser's study (.24), perhaps because our mostly urban mothers may be more likely to be contributing to that income.

From an examination of the means, variances, and correlations of family demographic characteristics, we concluded that there were no important differences between the adoptive and biological families in the study. The correlation patterns were sufficiently similar to those for more representative samples that the regression analyses are probably more directly generalizable to the general population than we had feared from the selected characteristics of the families.

Parental IQ Correlations

Fathers' and mothers' IQ scores were moderately correlated with the family demographic characteristics, as might be expected. In both the adoptive and biological families, father's IQ was more highly correlated with his educational attainment than mother's was with hers. We suppose this says something about selection for advanced education for women in the cohort that is now 45–55 years of age. Adoptive fathers' correlation of IQ score with occupational prestige is a bit lower than the biological fathers' (.39 vs. .51). Adoptive parents' IQ scores correlated .31 and biological parents,' .24—a moderate difference in assortative mating for IQ. There are no other striking differences in the correlations by family type.

Family Size and Birth Rank

The adoptive families have on the average fewer children than the biological families (2.9 versus 3.9). The average birth rank of those children who were of appropriate age to participate in the study, however, did not differ much in the two types of families. In both cases, the participants were between first- and second-borns, on the average (1.4 and 1.6 in the adoptive and biological families, respectively). This means that the participants from the biological families have a larger number of younger siblings than the adopted children.

Parental characteristics are surprisingly correlated with family size in the biological families. Although it has often been reported in the general population that family size is negatively correlated with parental IQ, occupational status, education, and income, we did not expect to find such relationships in a socioeconomically advantaged sample. Yet number of children is significantly negatively correlated with all the family demographic characteristics and with father's IQ in the biological families. As we did expect, adoptive families with more children (the range of family size was from 1 to 6 children) were slightly more advantaged than those with fewer children, presumably because adoptive agencies select parents who can afford to rear more children.

Correlations with Children's IQ Scores

It is clear from Table 2 that parental education, family income, family size, and parental IQ tend to be more highly correlated with biological than adopted adolescents' IQ scores. (Father's occupation and birth rank are not.) The greater resemblance between adolescents' IQ scores and their parents' characteristics in biological families presumably results largely from the genetic resemblance, since both types of families share the home environment (at least after the first 2 months of the child's life.) The slight correlation between adopted child IQ and family demographic characteristics is confounded by the selective placement of children of better educated (probably brighter) natural mothers into adoptive families with higher levels of parental education, income, and occupational status. Since natural mother's educational level is moderately correlated with the adopted child's IQ, the correlations between adoptive-family demographics and child IQ are inflated by the natural-mother–child resemblance via selective placement.

Family size is unrelated to child IQ in adoptive families, but negatively correlated in biological families, probably because of the negative correlation between family size and parental characteristics in the biological families. From the adoption data, however, it is clear that family size per se is not a detriment to IQ in the range of adoptive-family sizes represented in this study and at the socioeconomic levels of these families. Birth rank, on the other hand, is clearly related to IQ in both the adoptive and biological families. Later-born or adopted children are at a slight disadvantage in IQ.

Selective Placement

Adoption agencies are not uninformed. They have information about the natural mothers' educational level, occupational prestige, and age, and they use it to match the children of the natural mothers to adoptive families. As shown in Table 2, there are substantial correlations between natural mothers' educational levels and the adoptive families' demographic characteristics, particularly family income and fathers' education. Fortunately for the study, the agencies do not have information on the IQ levels of the adoptive parents or the natural mothers; so their effective matching for IQ is quite poor. The correlations of adoptive parents' IQ and natural mothers' education are only .20 and .10 for mother and father, respectively. If the correlation between natural mothers' educational and IQ levels is .70, as Jencks (1972) believes, then the average of the correlations between natural mother's education and adoptive parents' IQ levels is only (.15) (.70) = .105. Since the agencies have little or no information about the natural fathers, the correlation between the IQs of natural and adoptive parents is undoubtedly lower than .10. This creates a small shared genetic variance in adoptive families, accounting for less than 1% of the genetic variance in the population, compared to biologically related families, who share half the genetic variance.

Regression of Adolescent IQ Scores on Family Characteristics

The major concern of this paper is with the predictability of children's intellectual outcomes from their family's demographic and intellectual characteristics. In the first set of equations, shown in Tables 3 and 4, father's education, occupation, mother's education, and family income were used to predict the child's IQ. In the biological families, parental education and family income are positive coefficients, and father's occupation is negative. This last, seemingly anomalous, result probably reflects the multicolinearity of the family demographic variables, as shown in Table 2. Once all of these intercorrelated variables are in the regression equation, one or more are likely to be pulled in a negative direction. More attention, therefore, is given to the R^2's than to the particular regression coefficients. The total R^2 for the regression of biological children's IQ scores on their families' demographic characteristics in this sample is .107.

Table 3. Unstandardized Regression Coefficients of Adolescent IQ on Family Demographic Characteristics and Parental IQ in Biologically-Related and Adoptive Families

Family Characteristics/N	Bio. 237	Adopt. 150	Bio. 237	Adopt. 150	Bio. 237	Adopt. 150	Adopt. 150	Adopt. 132
Father's Education	.855	*	.795	*	.262	−.153	−.248	−.074
Mother's Education	.551	.362	.465	.343	−.525	.378	.336	.282
Father's Occupation	−.065	.040	−.069	.038	−.059	.032	.035	.014
Family Income	.170	−.020	.160	.010	.100	−.020	−.090	−.085
Birth Rank			−2.699	−3.063	−2.724	−3.078	−3.419	−4.077
Number of Children			−.720	−.303	−.751	−.390	−.528	−.605
Father's IQ					.274	.125	.115	.091
Mother's IQ					.357	−.020	*	−.021
Natural Mother's Education							1.325	1.554
Natural Mother's Age							−.226	−.121
Natural Mother's Occupation								.009
R^2	.107	.019	.145	.059	.309	.075	.138	.157

* $F < .01$, variable did not enter the equation.

The total R^2 for the adopted child regression on the same variables is much lower—only .019.[2] The positive coefficients on parental education are lower than those in the biological-family regression; family income is slightly negative; and father's occupation is moderate and positive.

When birth rank and family size are added to the equation, the R^2's for both the biological and adoptive children increase by about .04, to .145 for the biological offspring and .059 for the adopted children. (The "birth rank" of the adopted children is their social, sibling order in the adoptive family; nearly all adopted children are firstborn of their natural mothers.) Family size is a larger negative coefficient for biological children's IQ scores than for the adopteds, because family size is negatively correlated with demographic characteristics only in the biological families. The coefficients on the demographic characteristics in biological families are reduced slightly when birth rank and family size are added. In the adoptive families, the demographic coefficients are also slightly reduced, except family income, which is pulled from slightly positive to slightly negative by the addition of birth rank and family size. Birth rank has a higher coefficient for adopted children's IQ than for biological, thereby demonstrating that it is entirely a social effect within families.

[2]It was suggested by one reviewer that the differences between the pairs of regression equations be tested by the Chow test. We have resisted calculating yet another statistic, because our goal was magnitude estimation, not testing all possible null hypotheses. More importantly, the unequal sample sizes of the adoptive and biological families yield different expected mean squares, and any result would only be approximately correct, with unknown distributions and standard errors. Two leading textbooks on regression analysis (Cohen & Cohen, 1975; Kerlinger & Pedhazur, 1973) either do not mention the test or are opposed to its being done, even with equal sample sizes.

The addition of parental IQ scores has dramatically different effects on the regression equations in the biological and adoptive families. First, the R^2 for biological children's IQ scores is doubled to .309, whereas the R^2 for adopteds is increased by only .016, to .075. This striking difference in the overall effect of adding parental IQ to the equation must reflect the genetic contribution of biological parental IQ to their offspring's IQ scores. There are also striking changes in the coefficients on biological-family demographic characteristics once parental IQ has been added. Father's educational coefficient drops to .33 its former value, and mother's education is pulled to a negative coefficient. The coefficients on father's occupation and family income are reduced. Birth rank and family size coefficients remain virtually unchanged, however. The addition of parental IQ to the adopted children's regression changes the demographic coefficients very little, with the exception that the coefficient on father's education is now slightly negative.

The addition of natural mother's education, age, and occupation doubled the R^2 for the adopted children, from .075 to .157. The coefficients on adoptive-family demographic characteristics are reduced, reflecting a degree of selective placement, with the exception of family income, which is more negative than in the equation without natural mother's characteristics. It is natural mother's education that contributes most to the changes in the equation.

Adding information on the natural mother's education level, occupation, and age increased the R^2 of adopted children by about .09 over the R^2 with just family

Table 4. Standardized Regression Coefficients of Adolescent IQ on Family Demographic Characteristics and Parental IQ in Biologically-Related and Adoptive Families

	Bio.	Adopt.	Bio.	Adopt.	Bio.	Adopt.	Adopt.	Adopt.
Family Characteristics/N children	237	150	237	150	237	150	150	132
N families	120	104	120	104	120	104	104	99
Father's Education	.233ª	*	.217ª	*	.072	−.052	−.084	−.025
Mother's Education	.119	.083	.101	.079	−.113	.087	.077	.066
Father's Occupation	−.155ª	.108	−.166ª	.102	−.140	.085	.094	.037
Family Income	.145	−.027	.139	.015	.089	−.019	−.104	−.099
Birth Rank			−.162ª	−.195ª	−.166ª	−.196ª	−.218ª	−.253ª
Number of Children			−.103	−.041	−.107	−.052	−.071	−.079
Father's IQ					.308ª	.158	.146	.116
Mother's IQ					.361ª	−.023	*	−.024
Natural Mother's Education							.246ª	.293ª
Natural Mother's Age							−.147	−.074
Natural Mother's Occupation								.023
R^2	.107	.019	.145	.059	.309	.075	.138	.157
$F_{R^2 > 0}$ (d.f. = # families	3.44ª	0.48	3.19ª	1.01	6.20ᵇ	0.96	1.49	1.68

* $F < .01$, variable did not enter the equation.
ª $p < .05$.
ᵇ $p < .001$.

demographic, birth order, and family size information. The final R^2 of about .15 is comparable in size to the R^2 of the biological children equation with family demographic, birth order, and family size information (.145).

Conclusions from Regression Analyses

Since the social environment is equally well (or poorly) measured for the biological and adopted children, the impact of direct measures of intellectual functioning for the parents is primarily accounting for the genetic contribution of parents to their biological offspring. In this regard, it is noteworthy that the addition of adoptive parental IQ data to the equation for the adopted children has little impact on the adoptive-family demographic coefficients, whereas the demographic coefficients for the biological children are greatly changed. Adding parental IQ scores to the equation for the biological children increases R^2 by .16. Presumably, having IQ data for the natural parents of the adopted children would cause a similar increment, even though these parents do not rear their children.

From these regression equations, it is evident that significant regression coefficients of child IQ on family variables in studies using only biologically related parents and children are based largely on genetic variance, as indicated by the different R^2's for the biological and adoptive families.

FAMILY CORRELATIONS

For the second approach to deciphering the meaning of the term *family background,* we used all the subjects for whom IQ data were available, regardless of what other information might be missing. Thus, the samples of both adoptive- and biological-family members are considerably larger, ranging from 270 parent–child pairs in biological families to about 180 pairs in adoptive families. Significance levels for the data have been calculated on the numbers of pairs. A more conservative approach would be to use the number of independently sampled families. Which approach is more defensible is not agreed on in the literature, and the reader can consult any table of significance levels for correlation coefficients and Fisher's z formula for the calculation of significance levels based on the number of families. Sample sizes for pairs of family members are given in the middle of Table 5 and sample sizes for families at the top.

By calculating the correlations for related and unrelated family members, we hoped to get an estimate of the degree to which similarity in intellectual outcome is conditioned by similarity in the rearing environment. This entails a comparison of biological and adoptive families and a comparison of parent–child with sibling correlations. Parents and children do not share the same rearing environment, whereas siblings do—regardless of their genetic relatedness.

In an earlier study of young adopted and biologically related children, we

Table 5. Correlations among Family Members in Adoptive and Biologically-Related Families (Pearson Coefficients on Standardized Scores by Family Member and Family Type) for Intelligence Test Scales

	Reliability	Biological (120 families)				Adoptive (104 families)			
	(*)	MO	FA	CH	MP	MO	FA	CH	MP
Child Score									
Total WAIS IQ	(.97)	.41	.40	.35	.52	.09	.16	−.03	.14
Subtests									
Arithmetic	(.79)	.24	.30	.24	.36	−.03	.07	−.03	−.01
Vocabulary	(.94)	.33	.39	.22	.43	.23	.24	.11	.26
Block Design	(.86)	.29	.32	.25	.40	.13	.02	.09	.14
Picture Arrangement	(.66)	.19	.06	.16	.11	−.01	−.04	.04	−.03

___ = biological>adoptive correlation, $p < .05$.

	Sample Sizes: Pairs of Family Members							
	Biological				Adoptive			
	MO	FA	CH	MP	MO	FA	CH	MP
Children	270	270	168	268	184	175	84	168

	Assortive Mating	
	Biological FA-MO	Adoptive FA-MO
WAIS IQ	.24	.31
Arithmetic	.19	−.04
Vocabulary	.32	.42
Block Design	.19	.15
Picture Arrangement	.12	.22
Sample Size	120	103

MO = mother-child; FA = father-child; CH = child-child; MP = midparent-child.
* Reliability reported in the WAIS manual for late adolescents.

found that parent–child correlations were much greater for the biologically related pairs (yielding "heritability" estimates in the range of .4 to .7), but the sibling correlations were quite similarly high for both related and unrelated pairs (Scarr & Weinberg, 1977a, 1977b). We speculated that similarities among these young children were greatly influenced by their families' common rearing environments.

In this sample of late adolescents, we were able to check on the degree of family environmental influence at the end of the child-rearing period. The results for the parent–child pairs are quite similar to the earlier study, whereas those for the siblings are very different. The adopted siblings at the average age of 18½ hardly resemble each other at all.

The evidence for genetic effects is striking in all comparisons of correlations among members of the adoptive and biological families. Even though the scores of both biological- and adoptive-family members have restricted variance, the coefficients for the biological-family pairs usually exceed those of the adoptive-family members by a statistically significant amount. As Table 5 shows, in total IQ the biological parent–child pairs, the midparent–child, and the child–child pairs are significantly more similar than the adoptive-family members. Only in vocabulary are the adoptive-family members similar at a level different from zero. It is no accident that vocabulary differences are most amenable to social environmental influence. Language is the mode of social exchange among human beings—genetically related or not; so people who live together develop more similar verbal skills than random members of the population. Other skills are not notably similar among people who live together unless they are genetically related. It is also not surprising that the skill most amenable to mate selection is vocabulary. Evidently, courting couples spend some time talking to each other but are not as concerned with other intellectual skills!

From these family correlations, one can calculate the differences between the adoptive and biological correlations and, depending upon the model, the "heritabilities." Genetically related persons in ordinary families share about half their genes. Unrelated people share none of their genes except through the selective placement of adopted children for IQ, of which there is only a slight bias in this study, as explained earlier. Even though they have always lived together, the correlations of adoptive fathers' and mothers' IQ with adopted children's IQ scores are .15 and .04, respectively; thus there is little evidence for either selective placement or social environmental influence on IQ differences.

Table 6 gives the differences between the IQ correlations of biological and adoptive relatives and the "heritabilities," based on a simpleminded model—multiplying the difference between the correlations of biologically related and unrelated pairs by 1.6, based on biological families sharing half of the total genetic variance plus that portion due to assortative mating ($r = .25$ for parents). A footnote to the table explains this calculation. This naive model throws the genotype–environment (GE) covariance (if any) into the genetic term, because only biologically related parents transmit both genes and environments to their offspring. The "heritability" terms calculated here are really additive genetic variance plus GE covariance in the parent–child comparisons and broad heritability (including some dominance) in the sibling comparisons. The inexactitude of the measures, however, makes this distinction academic, in all probability.

The differences between biological- and adoptive-family correlations in total IQ range from .24 to .38. Multiplying this difference, then, we find that the values for the combination of genetic variance and GE covariance range from .38 to .61. Although this range of "heritability" values is a far cry from .80, it is substantially different from 0.

In the simplest-minded genetic model that assumes no environmental transmission or genotype–environment covariation, the regression of offspring value on midparent value is an estimate of narrow heritability or the proportion of additive genetic variance in the total variance (Falconer, 1970). The value of the midparent regression coefficient for total IQ is .52, as shown in Table 7. By a more sensible model for behavioral traits, one that allows for environmental transmission, the regression of adopted offspring on adoptive midparent values is subtracted from the biological midparent–child regression. The resulting value of

Table 6. Differences between the Correlations of
Genetically-Related and Unrelated Family
Members and "Heritabilities"

Child Score	Related-Unrelated				$1.6(r_{np-c} - r_{ap-c})$*		
	MO	FA	CH	MP	MO	FA	CH
Total WAIS IQ	.31	.24	.38	.38	.50	.38	.61
Subtests							
Arithmetic	.27	.23	.27	.37	.43	.37	.43
Vocabulary	.10	.15	.11	.17	.16	.24	.18
Block Design	.16	.30	.16	.26	.26	.48	.26
Picture Arrangement	.20	.10	.12	.14	.32	.16	.19

MO = mother-child; FA = father-child; CH =
child-child; MP = midparent-child.
* The usual calculation for heritability would be to
multiply the difference between the biological and
adoptive family correlations by two, because the resemblance of bio members depends on sharing half
their genes and home environments and that of adoptive members on sharing only the family environment; thus, the difference equals half of the genetic
variance in the populations from which the families
were sampled. But biological parents and their children (and siblings) are genetically related by half
only when parents are mated randomly for the trait
being measured. Because parents are not randomly
mated for intelligence (the correlation being about .25
in this sample), there is less genetic variability within
the biological families, which leads to a higher correlation among the biological family members. To correct for this in the comparison of biological and
adoptive family pairs, it is necessary to multiply the
difference between the pairs by 1.6 rather than two
based on the following formula:

$$r_{bio} - r_{adopt} = \frac{1+m}{2} h^2$$

where m is the phenotypic correlation between the
parents.

the midparent heritability estimate for total IQ is .38 in the population from
which we sampled.

We have focused on the total IQ score for several good reasons. First, the
other tests are parts of this larger whole. Second, the subtests are less reliable
than the total score. And, last, the meaning of the whole is greater than the parts
taken singly. It is also clear that total IQ has the highest heritability as estimated
from the parent–child correlations and from the sibling comparison. These results
lead to the same conclusion reached earlier from the regression of child IQ on the
family background and parent IQ data—namely, that half or more of the con-

tribution that parents make to differences in their offspring's intellectual level is genetic.

We have resisted so far, from ignorance and fear of some formidable critics, the temptation to analyze our data in more sophisticated ways. We cannot defend all the assumptions that must be made to justify elaborate models and therefore have hesitated to throw ourselves into an inevitable fray.[3] Nonetheless, it seems evident to us that the study of adoptive and biological families provides extensive support for the idea that half or more of the long-term effects of "family background" on children's intellectual attainments depend upon genetic, not environmental, transmission. Furthermore, in the range of environments sampled in this study, there is little evidence for any measured environmental effects in "family (SES) background." Birth order is the only variable with substantial effects in the adoptive families, and that accounts for about 4% of the IQ variation among the adolescent children.

DISCUSSION

Accidents of birth do leave us at the genetic mercy of our parents, it seems. Different people have different responses to the same environment, and the effects of differences in environments within the range we sampled are very small. The comparison of the coefficients of child IQ on family background would lead one to conclude that in unrelated families, the effects of the demographic variables we measured are nearly nil. Even adding a direct measure of social parental IQ does not substantially increase the explained variance for adopted children's IQ differences.

The IQ coefficients for biologically related children are highly biased in

---

[3]At the time of writing, Morton and Rao (1977), Cavalli-Sforza and Feldman (1973, 1977), and the Birmingham group in genetics (Eaves, 1975, 1976; Jinks & Fulker, 1970; Martin & Eaves, 1977) have all proposed various models for the transmission of family effects. Goldberger (1975, 1978) has questioned the assumptions and specifications of most of them. There is no one set of assumptions or parameters that is satisfactory to convince unbelievers. Therefore, we have presented our data in a form that can be modeled by the various groups, who may then defend their own models.

An analysis of means from this adoption study in relation to biological and cultural transmission of intellectual skills has recently been done by Cavalli-Sforza and Feldman (1977). Using parental education as an environmental index, they obtain an estimate of cultural transmission (n) of intellectual skills in the adoptive families as follows: "We can obtain an estimate of n from the mean IQ of adopted children (which is 6.2/15 = 0.41 standard deviations above the general mean of the population):

$$n = 0.41/0.74 = 0.55 \pm 0.06$$

The indication from this preliminary analysis is that the results from means make cultural inheritance about as important as biological inheritance. [p. 10]." Their analysis is in agreement with a "heritability" estimate of .5, the value we propose from our family correlations (Table 6).

regression equations, because the demographic variables are indirect measures of the parents' abilities, which are transmitted to the offspring genetically, as well. Adding demographic information about one of the natural parents of the adopted children doubles the explained variance, even though that parent has never had social contact with the child after the first few days in the hospital nursery. If we had information about the other parent, there is every reason to believe that the R^2 would rise considerably. Thus, the final equation for the biologically related children, with an R^2 of .31, is about four times as great as that of the adopted children with comparable information about the social-class environment alone (even including some selective placement).

It may be thought by some readers that some unmeasured variables that *really* matter in determining children's intellectual development do not vary in these adoptive families, who were selected by the adoption agencies. To argue that the lack of effect of differences among the demographic and intellectual characteristics of the adoptive families is due to this underlying lack of variation, one must simultaneously explain the considerable regression of child IQ on the same family variables, in the same ranges, in the biologically related families. Presumably, the argument would be that the biological families were not screened by agencies and do vary on those unmeasured family characteristics that *really* matter.

Fortunately, in a younger sample of transracially adopted children, we have the same data on adoptive families with their own biological children. Table 7 gives these data. For 143 biological offspring of the adoptive parents, the R^2 from the regression of child IQ (at an average age of 10) on family demographic and parental IQ is .301. For the adopted children *in the same families* ($N = 111$, at an average age of 7), the R^2 is .156, or about half the coefficient for the

Table 7. Regressions of Child IQ on Family Demographic Characteristics, and Parental IQ in Transracial Adoptive Families with Their Own Children

	Biological Children (143)		Early Adopted Children (111)	
	B	beta	B	beta
Mother's IQ	.474	.32	.141	.13
Father's IQ	.513	.40	−.028	−.02
Father's Education	.682	.14	.389	.09
Mother's Education	−.943	−.15	1.501	.25
Father's Occupation	−.174	−.23	.008	*
Family Income	.445	.06	−.371	−.06
Total R^2	.301		.156	

* F < .01, variable did not enter the equation.

biologically related children. This result is in accord with Burks' (1928) regression of adopted and biologically related children's IQ scores at an average age of 7 years on family background indicators. She found R^2's of .37 and .18 for the biological and adoptive families, respectively.

We have argued (Scarr, 1977) that the younger adopted children's intellectual skills are more affected by their parents' characteristics and family environments than the adolescents in the present study, who—at the average age of 18½ years—have "gone their own ways" in school and community settings and are less subject to the effects of family differences than are younger children. Nonetheless, the selection of adoptive parents by agencies does not decrease the impact of family differences upon their biological children, and differences among the same parents have less impact on their adopted children.

Compared to the regression equations for biologically related adolescents, the magnitude and signs of the regression coefficients for young biologically related children are suprisingly similar. The regressions of biologically related children on measures of their family background are found to be rather stable across samples and greatly inflated by the shared genetic variance in families.

One could argue that the range of environments sampled here is not sufficiently great to bear the weight of any conclusions about the effects of environmental variation in the population. Our counterargument is twofold. First, the comparison with similarly sampled biological families reduces the force of the argument. Second, the coefficients of the biological families are much like those in other studies with more representative samples.

Even if differences in several demographic measures of family environments do not contribute much to differences in offspring's IQ scores, however, one must not conclude that the levels of environments in general make no difference for the development of intelligence. Obviously, the average performance level of the adopted children depends on the average value of their environments. In this sample, the average level of the environments is above average, and so is the average IQ level of the unrelated children. Presumably, if they had been reared in below-average homes, their average IQ levels would also be below average.

The average IQ of 106 for the adopted children can be explained partially by selection and partially by SES advantages. First, children who are obviously damaged or genetically defective are less likely to be placed for adoption. If agencies eliminated from the pool of potential adoptees all of the retarded—possibly 3% of the population with a mean of IQ 60—the average IQ score of the adoptable 97% would be 101. Second, if the actual regression of adopted children's IQ scores on family demographic variables is used to predict IQ improvement, an R of .138 yields 2.1 IQ points. Thus, the adoptees would be predicted to have an IQ average of 103.1, not 106.2, given an SES advantage 1 standard deviation above the population mean. By the same token, the average IQ scores of the biological children would be predicted from SES alone to be 104.9. With the addition of their genetic advantage, the average IQ of biological-family adolescents should be 108.0. This is 4.8 points below their obtained average IQ of 112.8. Where do the extra 3 to 5 points come from?

One hypothesis is that SES is not a perfect indicator of the child-rearing advantages enjoyed by families who volunteer for social science research; they are also above average in their interest in their children. Since we have no reason to believe that working-class families are on the average less interested in their children's welfare than professional families, volunteers would not bias the *slope* of the SES regression but would affect the intercept. Another hypothesis is that the regression of child IQ on family characteristics is not linear over its entire range. In the range we measured—from working to upper middle class—the slope is relatively flat, but it falls off sharply in the lower-SES groups. Based on the obvious negative effects of very impoverished environments on children's development, we prefer the latter, although our data do not discriminate the two hypotheses.

The Evidence on Individual Differences as Genes and Environment

From our family studies, the evidence for *some* genetic individual differences in IQ is simply overwhelming. Especially if one considers the past literature, there are literally dozens of studies that support that mild conclusion. When one attempts to get quantitative about proportions of genetic variance in IQ scores, one has to establish a range of probable values rather than any point estimate. There are several reasons for this. First, there may be real developmental differences in the degree to which environmental influences are potent determinants of individual differences. It seems from limited evidence that younger children may resemble their parents more on environmental grounds, because they are more exclusively influenced by their parents before they are launched into the world of schools, social institutions, and many individual choices.

Second, different cognitive skills that are sampled by different measures may be more or less environmentally influenced, such as vocabulary compared to other skills. Thus, different age groups using different measures may well get somewhat different results. And, third, there are all the measurement and reliability questions that pertain to any study of cognitive abilities.

Going straight to the heart of the matter, we think that most evidence points to a "heritability" for IQ of about .4 to .7, given that "heritability" here means the proportion of variance among individuals sampled in twin and family studies, which—as we have repeatedly noted—are not representative of lower-SES, neglectful, or abusive environments. If one could include people with really poor environments, the proportion of environmental variance might rise; on the other hand, the genetic variance might also be increased. It is hard to predict whether the proportions of variance would change or not, and in which direction.

It is important to note the lack of systematic, measured, environmental differences among the adolescents. This suggests that within a range of "humane environments," from an SES level of working to upper middle class, there is little evidence for differential environmental effects. The average level of these environments is such that the children perform intellectually somewhat above the population average, even though they have average biological parents. Thus, the environments sampled in family studies are better than average at fostering intellectual development. But why are the relatively poor families rearing adopted children whose IQ scores are nearly as high as those of the children in professional families? It must be that all of these seemingly environmental differences that predict so well to outcome differences among biological children are not primarily *environmental* differences, but indices of genetic differences among the parents and their biological offspring. This brings us to social class.

The Evidence on Social-Class Differences as Genes and Environment

In 1938 Barbara Burks compared her California adopted and biological children to those studied by Alice Leahy in Minnesota. Grouping the children by the occupational status of their adoptive families, Burks computed the average effects of being born to and reared by, or only reared by, families at different locations in the social structure. As in all adoption studies, the families do not vary over the whole SES range; in fact, adoptive samples always omit those lower portions of the income and educational distributions where big negative effects can occur. Nonetheless, it is interesting to examine the overall effects of being reared by a skilled working-class family, or a white-collar family, or a professional family. As we already know, the intellectual levels of parents in those groups differ on the average. What about the children?

For biological children of these occupational classes, the average difference between working-class and professional families was 12 IQ points in Burks' study and 17 IQ points in Leahy's. Children adopted by families of the same occupational classes, however, differed far less—about 5 IQ points in both studies. Adopted children in professional families scored below biological offspring; in working-class families, adoptees scored above the natural children—a very predictable genetic outcome. In our Minnesota studies, we found that the natural children of the transracial adoptive families averaged 4 to 6 IQ points above their adopted siblings (Scarr & Weinberg, 1976, 1977a). The adolescent adoptees averaged 6 IQ points below the biological children of comparably advantaged families. As in the other studies, there is a far greater relationship between parental social class and child IQ in the biological than adoptive families.

Since there is always some selective placement of adopted children into families that resemble their biological parents, the actual effect of differences in this middle-to-high range of social-class environments may be less than the 5 or 6

IQ points cited. Again, let us emphasize that none of these studies speak to lower-class, deprived, abusive, or any other kind of abominable environments. We are only saying that in that portion of the SES range where so many studies report intellectual differences among children reared in such circumstances, the differences observed among the children may not be primarily of environmental origin at all. From the older studies, Burks estimated that genetic differences among the occupational classes account for about .67 to .75 of the average IQ differences among the children born into those classes. Our studies support that conclusion.

If this had been a longitudinal study from the 1st year of the children's lives to the 18th—with detailed observations of the children's environments—the regression coefficients of adolescents' IQ scores on a better set of environmental variables may well have been higher. SES variables are far from perfect indices of children's experiences. Presumably, more of the total variance in adolescent IQ would have been accounted for if better environmental measures had been available. The effect of such a change would be similar in the adoptive and biological families, since the environments of both were equally represented by the SES measures. Thus, the amount of variance explained by *measured* rather than unmeasured environments might be increased in both kinds of families, but the genetic variance estimated would remain the same.

Why Study Genetic Differences in Behavior?

Some readers may conclude that family research supports pessimistic conclusions. What is left to the systematic environment? (A lot is left to random events or is otherwise unexplained!) We do not see these research outcomes as pessimistic in the slightest. On the contrary, these family studies permit behavioral scientists and social policymakers to sort out important differences in people's environments. There are three major reasons that behavior genetic studies of families are useful.

The first, and weakest one for social policy, is that we need to gain a fuller understanding of the nature of human behavior. The naive environmentalism of the past three decades locked us into assumptions that are simply untenable, useless, and wrongheaded. The average layman had better intuitions about the nature of human differences than many social scientists purported to have. We have the suspicion, however, that most environmentalists privately explained behavioral differences much as the rest of the population does. But why should we continue to be publicly wrong?

The second reason for behavior genetic studies of families is more "relevant," to use a phrase of the sixties. These studies can and do provide diagnostic clues about the nature of some developmental problems. Just as a good family history in medicine and clinical psychology expresses a concern for individual risks, so tracing family patterns of behaviors affords us a look at human behavior in the making, and often a more optimistic prognosis. So father was a "hyperactive boy"; today he is a successful businessman. So when mother was a child, she had a difficult time meeting new people; today she is a respected member of community groups. Social scientists can afford to have more respect for the individual patterns of development that make us different from one another. Biological diversity is a fact of life; respect for individual differences comes very much from that biological perspective and is not a trivial victory.

Third, and most important to us, are the implications for intervention programs. In its baldest form, naive environmentalism has led us into an "intervention fallacy." By assuming that all of the variance in behavior was environmentally determined, we have blithely promised a world of change that we have not delivered—at great cost to the participants, the public, and ourselves. The fallacy runs like this: If people who do X without our intervention have more desirable outcomes than people who do not do X, then we should persuade, or compel, all people to do X. This is unwise, because some of the reasons for the naturally occurring differences between those who do and do not do X are not just environmental differences. Many of these seemingly environmental variations are actually genetic differences or gene–environment correlations. People who are different do things differently.

But here is the most costly part of the intervention fallacy—the erroneous belief that small variations in environments within the "humane range" have meaningfully different outcomes for children. If we observe that professional families take their children to the theater more often than working-class families, or hang mobiles above their cribs more frequently, some social scientists feel justified in recommending to everyone that they take in plays frequently—rather than playing baseball in the backyard—or hang mobiles over the crib—rather than carrying the baby about wherever the parents go. Since these are the child-rearing practices of the professional class, whose children excel at IQ tests and in school, all parents are advised to alter their child-rearing practices to follow suit. *It has not been demonstrated that these variations in child rearing are functionally different in their effects on the children,* and we argue that most "humane environments" are in fact functionally equivalent. Behavior genetic studies of families can spare us all a homogeneity of environmental practices imposed by an "omniscient" professional class.

We can do a better job of designing and implementing effective intervention programs if we know which variations in the environment make a difference and which ones do not. We can shift our resources to the improvement of those circumstances that have clear, environmentally deleterious effects on people. Many of these we know: We do not have to do research to know that hunger is not good for children or that child abuse leaves scars. Most of the worst environments are obviously deleterious. But there are many other marginal and less obvious practices and conditions that we can only judge from sophisticated research on the effects of those environments. So it is important to know what aspects of the environment have consequences for behavioral differences and which ones are only apparent variations, based on cultural preferences, genetic differences, or on gene–environment correlations. People deserve respect for self-expression and their own modes of child rearing unless there is clear environmental reason to intervene. Behavior genetic methods will help us to gain a far clearer understanding of which environmental variables to worry about.

But let us recall that *the average level of our environment is the most important determinant of the level of behavioral development.* Therefore, by providing better schooling, nutrition, health care, psychological services, and the like, we can raise the average level of the environment and of behavioral development in the whole population. But some of you will argue that there are real dangers for social policy from research on individual and group differences. We see no necessary connections between the scientific results reported here and *any* social policy. Science is *not* politics; nor are social policies primarily dependent on scientific evidence, however much we might wish sometimes that they were. Policy matters depend mostly on values, and in this society, many groups compete over the translation of their values into policies.

Frankly, we think such pluralism is healthy, because as scientists we have no special wisdom in policy matters. Our unique gift to the society is the most objective look we can manage at the nature of the human condition. Hopefully, that information will be noticed and used to improve human lives. As citizens, we can try to be heard, so that our work will have the effects we personally value; but in doing so, we must be very careful not to throw away our unique contribution—a set of methods and standards of truthfulness that distinguish us from many other groups.

Conclusion

The conclusion that we feel is justified by our data is that intellectual differences among children at the end of the child-rearing period have little to do with environmental differences among families that range from solid working class to upper middle class. These results have important implications for sociological and economic studies of the long-range effects of family background on adult achievements. The persistent finding that differences in class background bias adult achievements has been interpreted to mean that differences in family environments during the child-rearing period enhance or impede the intellectual, educational, and occupational achievements of the offspring, for a lifetime. From our data, it appears to us that these linkages should be reinterpreted to mean that differences in family background that affect IQ are largely the result of genetic differences among parents that affect their own status attainments and that are passed on genetically to their offspring, whose status attainments are subsequently affected. The implications of these results are that social scientists should be very wary of interpreting the causes and effects of class differences in studies of biological families. We should also be sensitive to the genetic transmission of family characteristics.

ACKNOWLEDGMENTS

The present study was supported by the William T. Grant Foundation and the National Institute of Child Health and Human Development (HD-08016). The manuscript was prepared while the first author was a Fellow at the Center for Advanced Study in Behavioral Sciences, with support from the Spencer Foundation and the National Institute of Mental Health.

This study was conducted with the full collaboration of the Minnesota State Department of Public Welfare, Adoption Unit, directed by Ruth Weidell and assisted by Marjorie Flowers. Their help was invaluable. The additional support of the Open Door Society, Lutheran Social Service, and The Children's Home Society, all of Minnesota, facilitated the study.

We are very greatful for the assistance of Louise Carter-Saltzman, Harold Grotevant, Margaret Getman, Marsha Sargrad, Patricia Webber, Joanne Bergman, William Thompson, and Carol Peterman in the collection of the data and the preparation of this report. Special thanks go to Arthur R. Goldberger for his extensive help with the data analyses.

REFERENCES

Behrman, J., Taubman, P., & Wales, T. Controlling for the effects of genetics and family environment in equations for schooling and labor market success. In P. Taubman (Ed.), *Kinometrics: The determinants of economic success within and between families.* New York: North Holland-Elsevier, 1978.

Burks, B. S. The relative influence of nature and nurture upon mental development: A comparative study of foster parent–foster child resemblance and true parent–true child resemblance. *Yearbook of the National Society for the Study of Education,* 1928, *27* (I), 219–316.

Burks, B. S. On the relative contribution of nature and nurture to average group differences in intelligence. *Proceedings of National Academy of Sciences,* 1938, *24,* 276–282.

Cavalli-Sforza, L. L., & Feldman, M. W. Cultural versus biological inheritance: Phenotypic transmission from parents to children (A theory of the effect of parental phenotypes on children's phenotypes). *American Journal of Human Genetics,* 1973, *25,* 618–637.

Cavalli-Sforza, L. L., & Feldman, M. W. *The evolution of continuous variation III: Joint transmission of genotype, phenotype, and environment.* Unpublished paper, Stanford University, 1977.

Cohen, J., & Cohen, P. *Applied multiple regressions/Correlation analysis for the behavioral sciences.* Hillsdale, N.J.: Lawrence Erlbaum Associates, 1975.

Crouse, J. Effects of academic ability. In C. Jencks (Ed.), *Who gets ahead?* New York: Basic Books, 1978.

Doppelt, J. E. Estimating the full scale on the Wechsler Adult Intelligence Scale from scores on four subtests. *Journal of Consulting Psychology,* 1956, *20,* 63–66.

Duncan, B., Featherman, D. L., & Duncan, O. D. *Socioeconomic background and achievement.* New York: Seminar Press, 1972.

Duncan, O. D. Ability and achievement. *Eugenics Quarterly,* 1968, *15,* 1–11.

Eaves, L. J. Testing models for variation in intelligence. *Heredity*, 1975, *34*, 132–136.

Eaves, L. J. The effects of cultural transmission on continuous variation. *Heredity*, 1976, *37*, 51–57.

Falconer, D.S. *Introduction to quantitative genetics*. New York: Ronald Press, 1970.

Goldberger, A. *Statistical inference in the great IQ debate*. Madison, Wisconsin: Institute for Research on Poverty (Discussion Paper), 1975, 301–375.

Goldberger, A. Twin methods: A skeptical view. In P. Taubman (Ed.), *Kinometrics: The determinants of economic success within and between families*. New York: North Holland-Elsevier, 1978.

Grilliches, A., & Mason, W. M. Education, income, and ability. *Journal of Political Economy*, 1972, *80*, S74–S103.

Herman, D. Personal communication, April 1977.

Jencks, C. *Inequality: A reassessment of the effects of family and schooling in America*. New York: Basic Books, 1972.

Jencks, C., & Brown, M. Genes and social stratification. In P. Taubman (Ed.), *Kinometrics: The determinants of economic success within and between families*. New York: North Holland-Elsevier, 1978.

Jinks, J. L., & Fulker, D. W. A comparison of the biometrical genetical, MAVA, and classical approaches to the analysis of human behavior. *Psychological Bulletin*, 1970, *73*, 311–349.

Kerlinger, F. N., & Pedhazur, E. J. *Multiple regression in behavior research*. New York: Holt, Rinehart & Winston, 1973.

Leibowitz, A. Family background and economic success. In P. Taubman (Ed.), *Kinometrics: The determinants of economic success within and between families*. New York: North Holland-Elsevier, 1978.

Martin, N. G., & Eaves, L. J. The genetical analysis of covariance structure. *Heredity*, 1977, *38*, 79–95.

Morton, N. E., & Rao, D. C. *Genetic epidemiology of IQ and sociofamilial mental defect* (PGL paper). University of Hawaii: Population Genetics Laboratory, 1977.

Pearson, J. S., & Amacher, P. L. Intelligence test results and observations of personality disorder among 3594 unwed mothers in Minnesota. *Journal of Clinical Psychology*, 1956, *12*, 16–21.

Reiss, A. J., Jr. *Occupations and social status*. New York: Free Press, 1961.

Scarr, S. *Genetic effects on human behavior: Recent family studies*. A Master Lecture delivered at the annual meeting of the American Psychological Association, San Francisco, 1977.

Scarr, S., & Weinberg, R. A. IQ test performance of black children adopted by white families. *American Psychologist*, 1976, *31*, 726–739.

Scarr, S., & Weinberg, R. A. Intellectual similarities within families of both adopted and biological children. *Intelligence*, 1977, *1*(2), 170–191. (a)

Scarr, S., & Weinberg, R. A. *Nature and nurture strike (out) again*. Unpublished paper, Yale University, 1977. (b)

Sewell, W. H., & Hauser, R. M. *Education, occupation, and earnings: Achievment in the early career*. New York: Academic Press, 1975.

Taubman, P. The determinants of earnings: Genetics, family, and other environment; a study of white, male twins. *American Economic Review*, 1976, *66*, 858–870.

Taubman, P. *Ability, IQ, and earnings*. Unpublished manuscript, University of Pennsylvania, 1977. (a)

Taubman, P. Personal communication, May 1977. (b)

Taubman, P., & Wales, T. *Mental ability and higher educational attainment in the twentieth century*. Berkeley, Calif.: National Bureau of Economic Research-Carnegie, 1972.

Taubman, P., & Wales, T. *Higher education and earnings*. New York: McGraw-Hill, 1974.

Wechsler, D. *Wechsler Adult Intelligence Scale*. New York: Psychological Corporation, 1955.

Comments and Replies

THE NON-INFLUENCE OF 'FAMILY BACKGROUND' ON INTELLECTUAL ATTAINMENT: A CRITIQUE OF SCARR AND WEINBERG

This critique places a recent article by Scarr and Weinberg into the eugenic or hereditarian school of studies which have examined the relative impacts of genetics and environment on I.Q. Because of the tremendous policy implications of the resolution of the I.Q. debate, studies bearing on the question should be closely scrutinized for scientific rigor and objectivity. The Scarr and Weinberg article fails to meet rigorous scientific standards for several reasons. The theoretical concepts of genetics and environment are not explicitly and satisfactorily operationalized. The authors explain only a very small portion of the variance of the dependent variable, adolescent I.Q., yet make conclusions based upon these insignificant results. Sampling bias undercuts environmental variation and jeopardizes external validity. The use of regression analysis is unclear, and correlation 'heritability' analysis is arbitrarily and unfoundedly employed.

The perpetual debate in social science concerning the relative contributions of genetic inheritance and environment upon individual development in general and intellectual achievement in particular is not only intrinsically interesting, but also has social policy implications. So great are the policy implications of this debate for the distributions of rewards within society that two clearly indentifiable camps have emerged on the issue, despite a lack of rigorous application of

This comment by Marcia Whicker Taylor originally appeared in *American Sociological Review*, *1980*, *45*, 912–916.

scientific methodology in developing causal links and despite inconclusive data. One school of authors of studies of IQ test scores and of factors causing score differentials between groups is the eugenic or hereditarian school and includes the works of Burt, McDougall, Davenport, Eysenck, Jensen, and Reed and Reed. Into this camp also falls the recent study by Scarr and Weinberg (1978). This school argues that the impact of heredity upon IQ is great and exceeds the impact of environment upon IQ. The other camp, called the environmental school, or the 'naive environmental' school by its critics, remains skeptical that importance of heredity in IQ development exceeds the importance of environment. These authors cite the known deleterious effects of malnutrition, disease, and deprivation from poverty upon IQ development as proof of the potency of environmental factors. Into this second camp fall on-going studies by the National Center for Health Statistics examining links between family income and well-being and standardized test and outcomes; Drillien's work examining social class, birth weight and IQ scores in all-Nordic child populations; Sexton's examination of the entire school population of Detroit; the explanation of group differences by Pasamanick and Knobloch, Mercer, and Mayeske; and the studies of Eichenwald and colleagues of mental retardation prevention through the control of infectious diseases.

To the degree that the impact of genetic inheritance is greater than that of environmental factors, dominant groups in society may not only be expunged of guilt for disparities in intellectual attainment with minority groups, but they are also alleviated of responsibility for compensatory education and other environmental mechanisms to close the gaps. Throughout history, the policy consequences of this intellectually unresolved question have already been great. Dominance of the eugenic or hereditarian school has helped to establish the racial immigration quotas in the U.S. Immigration Act of 1924. Between 1925 and 1941, the effect of this act was to reduce by over six million the immigration flow of groups labeled inferior by IQ test results, such as Jews, Italians and Greeks. During the same time period in Germany and Europe, eugenicism run rampant contributed the horrific genocide of the Holocaust. In the U. S., the Supreme Court doctrine of 'separate but equal' education for blacks in practice was often separate, unequal, and justified by eugenic philosophy. More recently the environmental school has provided justification for compensatory education programs. Because of the obvious emotionalism of the debate and the magnitude of its outcome for public policy, both historically and in the future, academic research on the subject should strive for impeachable objectivity, avoiding conclusions which are unsupported by scientifically collected and analyzed data. Thus, each new piece of evidence bearing on the genetic inheritance-environment question should be scrutinized with great interest for scientific rigor and legitimacy. The Scarr-Weinberg article (1978) is no exception to this rule.

Scarr and Weinberg employ data collected on two samples of families: "biological" families, or those who have children by the birth process and whose offspring are consequently genetically related, and "adoptive" families whose children are adopted shortly after birth and are consequently not genetically related to the adopted parents or sibblings. On the basis of analysis of these data, Scarr and Weinberg conclude "it seems evident to us that the study of adoptive and biological families provides extensive support for the idea that half or more of the long-term effects of 'family background' on children's intellectual attainments depend on genetic, not environmental, transmission." (1978:686) This conclusion is incredible since none of their data, nor their analysis of the data, supports this conclusion. Furthermore, their tortuous analyses often obfuscate rather than clarify the evidence bearing on the basic question of genetic inheritance versus environmental impacts. The conclusions that seem so evident to Scarr and Weinberg may not appear so obvious to others, for these reasons:

1. Lack of Explicit Operationalization of Theoretical Concepts Employed. What is being measured and tested in the Scarr-Weinberg research is ambiguous and slippery. While the authors begin their presentation by discussing the potential saliency of "family background" on intellectual attainment, they quickly switch to a discussion of "behavior genetic" methods and argue that "theoretically, regressions of adopted child outcomes on adoptive family characteristics will provide genetically unbiased estimates of true environmental effects in the population." (1978:675) While the regressions of adopted child outcomes on adoptive family characteristics do provide estimates of the environmental effects of the particular family characteristics measured and employed in the analysis, those family characteristics employed by Scarr and Weinberg are by no means inclusive of all relevant environmental effects. Indeed, the Scarr-Weinberg family variables are not even inclusive of all relevant familial environmental effects, as any attempts to measure the nature and intensity of nurturing or parental interest in child learning and intellectual attainment have been precluded. To imply, as do Scarr and Weinberg, that because the biological and adoptive families have slightly different R^2's in the regressions that genes and not environment are the source of family background transmissions is inappropriate. More precisely, the authors never clarify what specifically operationalizes the concepts family genetic transmission, and family environment transmissions. Are all of family characteristies of the biological sample measures of family genetic transmission? If all of these variables (eg. father's education, mother's education, father's occupation, family income, birth rank, number of children, father's IQ, and mother's IQ) are indeed indirect measures of family genetic transmission in the biological family sample, why are they not more highly correlated? No correlation of family background characteristics exceeds .61 (Table 2, 1978:678), the correlation for father's occupation and father's education, and most correlations of family characteristics in the biological sample are considerably less. One could argue that the relationship of father's occupation to father's education, for example is a greater reflection of labor market demand than of family genetic transmission to adolescent IQ.

Whether the family background characteristics of the biological sample measure genetic tranmissions at all is doubtful at worst and conjecture at best. If one concedes that at least some portion of these background characteristics measure genetic inheritance, the thoughtful reader must conclude that the family background characteristics for the biological sample in the Scarr-Weinberg study are a mixture of genetic and environmental transmissions, to the degree that genetic inheritance is measured at all. How the authors can then conclude, as they do, that these family background characteristics actually understate rather than overstate measured genetic transmissions (1978:688) is most perplexing.

2. *Very Small Explained Variance in the Dependent Variable.* Even to the casual reader familiar only with the rudiments of regression analysis, the aspect of the Scarr-Weinberg regression equations totally ignored by the authors but, nonetheless, so obvious and compelling, is the paltry amount of variance in the dependent variable, even by social science standards, explained by the independent variables they employ. The bulk of the article is spent arguing about the relative contributions of various independent variables, as well as the larger meaning of those variables for the gene-environment debate, when the reported R^2's show that all of the independent variables combined explain almost none of the variance in adolescent IQ. For the biological sample, the highest R^2 obtained is .31, while for the adoptive sample, an even lower .16 is the best obtained. Eight independent variables are used to obtain the model explaining 31% of the biological sample dependent variable variance, while 11 independent variables are used to obtain the model explaining 16% of the adoptive sample dependent variable variance. The obvious conclusion from these R^2's is that family background characteristics explain almost nothing about adolescent IQ variation—an incredible finding, which should have lead the authors to comment, as does this reply on the non-influence of family background, at least as measured by Scarr and Weinberg, on intellectual attainment. With so little of the total variation in the dependent variable explained, to dwell at length, as do the authors on the relative contributions of independent variables is to make "much ado about nothing". Despite R^2's which never explain more than .31 of the variance, and despite the fact that these low R^2's were generated by mixture of environmental and genetic transmission measures, the authors blithely conclude that genetic transmissions account for 40 to 70% of adolescent IQ variation, a finding totally unsupported by the data.

3. *Sampling Bias Undercuts Environmental Variation and Jeopardizes External Validity.* Random sampling is not employed to extract an unbiased sample for the Scarr-Weinberg study. Consequently external validity —— that is, the extent to which conclusions from the data can be generalized to a broader population —— is limited. An analysis of the socio-economic characteristics of both samples reveals that the largely self-selected samples were atypical of the general population in several potentially salient ways (eg. family income, parental education levels, etc.). Furthermore, the sampling procedure compressed the variance

for environment, if socio-economic characteristics were meant to measure environment. In essence, environment is held fairly constant at enriched levels for both samples. The subsequent finding that observed variation in the dependent variable is based on inheritance transmission is not startling, given that environmental variance was compressed, while genetic variance, especially for the adoptive sample, was not.

    4.   Unclear Use of Regression Analysis.   If the authors intended for birth rank and family size to measure environment and the remainder of family background characteristics to measure genetic inheritance for the biological sample, the rationale underlying the order in which the regression variables were loaded when analyzing the two samples is unclear. Standard procedure when a researcher is attempting to demonstrate the greater significance of one variable or set of variables, as Scarr and Weinberg implicitly if not explicitly are trying to demonstrate the greater potency of genetic transmission measures, is to load all other independent variables first. The variable or variables in which one has the greatest interest are then loaded in a second stage and are regressed into the residuals resulting from the first stage regression with all other variables. Not only do Scarr and Weinberg not follow this procedure, but they intersperse the "environmental" variables of birth rank and family size with "genetic" variables.

    Secondly, the relative contributions of any independent variable in a regression equation to explaining dependent variable variation depends in part on what other independent variables are in the equation. Hence, one can only compare independent variable effects across regression equations if the exact same variables are employed in each equation, a procedure which is violated when additional variables for natural mother characteristics are loaded into the adoptive sample, in addition to other family background characteristics. A more appropriate comparison would be to compare the natural parent characteristics for both samples. While IQ scores may not have been readily available for natural mothers of adopted children, surely additional data on the natural mothers in the biological sample equivalent to the data obtained for natural mothers of adopted children could have been secured. However, only education for the former group was used and data on age and occupation which was collected for natural mothers of adopted children was not obtained for the natural mothers of the biological sample —a puzzling omittance, despite the fact that some mothers did not "work." (Housewives would counter that they do work.)

    Thirdly, because the signs of some regression coefficients are opposite from the sign from the direction anticipated, the authors ignore them in the analysis and discuss total R^2's. This is compounded, however by the invalidation of cross-regression equation comparisons since family back-ground characteristics are not measuring, by the authors assertion, the same kind of transmissions in the two samples. Had equivalent measures been loaded for the two samples simultaneously, two-sample significance tests testing for the cross-equation differences in equations might have been conducted.

5. *Arbitrariness in Correlation "Heritability" Analysis.*   Having failed with regression analysis at showing that family background characteristics are salient to adolescent IQ, the authors launch into bivariate correlation analysis. That correlations among related family members of the biological are generally higher than the equivalent correlations among unrelated family members of the adoptive sample is interesting, although given that no control variables are employed, the possibility that spurious relationships which might account for the higher biological sample correlations cannot be discounted. Then, however, on the basis that related family members share half of their genes, the authors arbitrarily decide to multiply the difference in correlations between samples by 1.6 (2 adjusted for "assortive mating") in a calculation that makes no theoretical sense. If adolescents in the adoptive sample share no genes with adoptive parents and biological sample adolescents share all genes with their natural parents, half with the mother and half with the father, then the difference between sample correlations alone should reflect genetic transmissions. If one is concerned about assessing the combined effect of both parents, midparent-child correlation differences would be more appropriate. Unfortunately, for Scarr & Weinberg midparent correlation differences are less than those obtained by the arbitrary multiplications.

6. *Unexplained Sample Differences.*   Scarr and Weinberg use enlarged samples for their correlation analysis. Given the ability of most regression programs to handle missing data in a pair-wise fashion, the rationale for the smaller sample sizes for the regression analysis are never explained.

In conclusion, what began as an interesting and imaginative piece of research did not live up to its original promise, primarily due to the lack conceptual clarity in specifying the operationalization of key concepts, and the author's haste to prove the potency of genes.

REFERENCES

Scarr, S. and Weinberg, R. A. The influence of 'family background' on intellectual attainment. *American Sociological Review,* 1978, *43,* 674–692.

MARCIA WHICKER TAYLOR

REPLY

CALLING ALL CAMPS! THE WAR IS OVER*

We appreciate the opportunity to address again the readership of *ASR*, because the journal is central to the social sciences. Contrary to Taylor's muddled chauvinism, we propose that the Hundred Years War between nature and nurture is over. Her last-ditch skirmishes with genetic differences in behavior bear as little resemblance to current thinking in the social sciences as Shockley's sperm bank bears to contemporary thought in the biological sciences.

The problem we studied, the effects of "family background", is of concern to both social and biological scientists. A multi-disciplinary perspective provides more complex models, which can lead to more complete explanations of the phenomena of parental influence on their children. Although there are advantages to viewing the same problem through several conceptual lenses, there are inherent difficulties in communication among people from several disciplines.

Taylor, like most social scientists, seems to be familiar with the concept of "family background", as it is used in the social sciences, to mean the total biasing effects of family membership on long-term outcomes of children. The focus of social science research is on *how much* bias, regardless of the sources of the bias. Most social scientists state or imply that family *environmental* differences are the source of "family background" effects.

Evolutionary biologists and behavior geneticists focus on *how* "family background" affects long term outcomes of children. "Family background" is considered to include the effects of shared genes *and* shared environments. Taylor evidently does not understand that questions about sources of bias in "family background" for children who are genetically-related to their parents must include a consideration of both genetic and environmental transmission from parent to child. In our study of adoptive and biologically related families, we attempted to answer both social and biological questions of "how much" and "how".

As psychologists, sympathetic to both social and biological perspectives, we are concerned with sources of individual differences and with the application of developmental psychology to the welfare of children and their families. (e.g., Scarr, 1969 on birth weight and IQ; Scarr and Williams, 1973 on early intervention for low birth weight infants; Scarr, 1979 special issue of the *American Psychologist* on psychology and children's welfare; Scarr and Schwarz, 1979 on an early intervention program; Weinberg, 1979 on preschool intervention programs; Weinberg and Moore, 1975 on the evaluation of early intervention programs.) We are committed to the *realistic* use of environmental interventions on behalf of children. An integral part of our conceptual framework is the under-

---

*This reply by Sandra Scarr and Richard A. Weinberg originally appeared in the *American Sociological Review*, 1980, *45*, 859–865. Copyright © 1980 by American Sociological Association. Reprinted by permission.

standing that human variation depends most often on both genetic and environmental differences.

Differences versus Development

A common error among social scientists is the failure to distinguish genetic and environmental sources of individual *differences* in behavior from the necessary roles of both genes and environments in behavioral *development*. One cannot assess the relative impact of heredity or environment on intelligence per se, because everyone must have both a viable gene complement and an environment in which the genes can be expressed over development. No genes, no organism; no environment, no organism.

Behavioral *differences* among individuals, on the other hand, can arise in any population from genetic differences, from variation among their environments, or both. Imagine a population of genetically identical clones who are reared in family environments that vary from working to upper middle class. Any behavioral differences among the clones would necessarily arise from developing within those different environments. Next imagine a genetically diverse human population reared in laboratory cages. All members experience exactly the same environments. Naturally, all differences among these individuals are accounted for by their genetic variability. Notice that in the two fantasies, the organisms all have *both* genes *and* environments for *development*. In human populations, behavioral differences among people arise most often from both genetic and environmental diversity.

Theory and Operations

The theoretical bases of the research we reported are both population genetics and principles of socialization. Individual genetic differences in populations result from the evolutionary history of selection and variation and the transmission of genes from one generational pool to the next — from parents to their children. Concepts in population genetics were operationalized by studying families of different degrees of genetic relatedness —parents who transmit half of their genes to their children compared to parents who transmit none of their genes to their children. From the theoretical perspective of socialization, human parents provide the rearing environment for their children, regardless of their genetic relatedness. In adoption studies, however, the natural parents of adopted-away children transmit only their genes and not their social environments to their offspring. Thus, adoption provides a naturally-occurring experiment for studying the effects of genetic variation and differences in socialization.

The study of adoptive families provides an opportunity to estimate the effects of environmental differences on individual behavior. The fact that all adoptive families provide environments in the normal species range means that all adopted children's genotypes have the opportunity to be expressed (with genetically variable results). Adoptive parents transmit no genes to their children, although selective placement creates a very small ($\leq .01$) genetic correlation in adoptive families.

In our study, the biological families provided similar environmental opportunities for the development of their children. In biological families, however, each parent contributes a random half of his or her genotype to each child.

We operationalized the concept of genetic IQ differences in the population of working to upper-middle class whites in the U.S. by comparing IQ resemblance among members of the biological and adoptive families drawn from this population. We compared pairs of family members who share about half of their genes with pairs who share virtually none of their genes. That is, by subtracting the IQ correlation of adoptive pairs from that of biological pairs, one subtracts the effects of environmental differences among families, measured by adoptive pair resemblance. The remaining, surplus resemblance of biologically-related pairs must be due to their greater genetic resemblance.

Because biologically-related parents and children share about *half* of their genes, the remaining covariance is an estimate of about *half* of the genetic variance in the population from which the families were drawn. To estimate the *total* effects of genetic differences one must nearly double the difference between the correlations of biological versus adoptive relatives.

To calculate the genetic influence of *both* parents on each child (midparent-child correlation), one does not merely add up the genetic correlation of each parent with the child. Although the explanation of the midparent-child correlation is complex (see Falconer, 1970, pp. 179–181; Munsinger, 1975, pp. 624–625), the value is predicted by the term $\sqrt{2}r_{po}$, where r_{po} is the correlation of one parent with the child. The calculation is affected by the assortive mating of parents.

When the same parents have more than one child, the siblings share about half of their genes, because each child receives a random half from each parent. Some siblings will have by chance as few as 40 per cent or as many as 60 per cent shared genotypes.

When parents are not mated at random for a trait, as they are not for IQ, then the genetic correlations in biological families average more than 0.50, a fact that should be used to adjust estimates of genetic differences, as we did in our non-arbitrary multiplier of 1.6. The theoretical reasons for this multiplier are given in the lengthy footnote to Table 6 in the original article.

The midparent-child correlation is the best estimate of that portion of the genetic variance that is additive. Any effects of the parents' particular gene *combinations* are not included in the midparent-child or parent-child correlations. Thus, the differences between parent-child and midparent-child correlations in biological and adoptive families are measures of additive genetic variance or *narrow* heritability. Sibling correlations do include portions of the dominance and other non-additive genetic effects. The estimate of *broad* heritability from the sibling correlation (0.61) was naturally larger than the estimate of *narrow* heritability from the midparent or parent-child correlations (0.38–0.50). As we also indicated, sibs share a common rearing environment, not shared by parents and their children.

Representative Sampling

The population from which the adoptive and biological families were drawn was certainly not the entire U.S. white population. As we emphasized repeatedly, these families do not include lower class or economically deprived or abusive, neglectful environments. Nor are the families representative of racial minorities.

We agree with Taylor, that the range of SES sampled by families in this study was necessarily restricted. Although the correlations among parental income, education, and occupational prestige were as high as those reported by studies with more representative samples (see p. 365), all of the children were reared in non-deprived, non-abusive environments. We agree that, "the subsequent finding that observed variation in the dependent variable is based on inheritance transmission is not startling, given that environmental variance was compressed, while genetic variance, especially for the adoptive sample, was not" (Taylor, this volume p. 388). The fact that the SES range of these families includes at least two-thirds of the U.S. white population in this age cohort makes the results of some interest, however.

Even within the range of working class to upper middle class U.S. white families, the regression equations included only SES, parental IQ, sibling order and family size measures of "family background", which "are far from perfect indices of children's experiences" (p. 379). But these are a more complete set than most social science studies of "family background" include. Furthermore, with the inclusion of a better set of such measures, "the amount of variance explained by *measured* rather than unmeasured environments might be increased in both kinds of families, but the genetic variance estimated would remain the same" (p. 379). Given the nature of the "family background" measures, "much of the variance is still unexplained, of course!" (p. 379).

Unmeasured Environments

The *unmeasured* effects of differences among family environments are in fact estimated as part of the total environmental variance by the adoptive family correlations. That is, the slight IQ resemblance between adoptive parents and adopted children and between adopted siblings necessarily means that 18 years of being reared in *different* family environments (measured and unmeasured) has only slight effects on the children's IQ differences. And it is from the comparison of correlations between biological relatives and correlations between adoptive family members (not from the regression equations) that we were able to estimate that 40 to 70 per cent of the adolescents' IQ differences resulted from genetic differences among them (see Tables 5 and 6). By contrast, the median correlation among adoptive parents, children, and siblings shows that only 9 per cent of the IQ variance results from total differences among family environments in this SES range.

Regression Equations

Tables 3 and 4 presented three sets of comparable regression equations for biological and adopted adolescents' IQ scores, in columns 1-6. The first set, columns 1 and 2, gives the family SES variables usually considered in social science studies of "family background". For the adopted children, these measures index differences in only their family environments. For children biologically related to their rearing parents, the same SES variables represent both genetic and environmental transmission, as Taylor notes. It is precisely the comparison of the equations for the adopted and the biological adolescents that permits an estimate of the relative importance of genetic and environmental differences in these indices of "family background".

In columns 3 and 4, sibling order and family size have been combined with the SES measures, but not in a stepwise fashion, as indicated by the changes in the coefficients on SES. The set of variables in these equations represents indices of both between and within-family differences in "background".

In columns 5 and 6, the IQ scores of the rearing parents have been included with the previous variables. Parental IQ has rarely been available in social science studies of family effects on offspring, but is of great interest to behavior genetic studies of family effects. Again, it can be seen by changes in coefficients from the preceding columns that the variables entered the equation simultaneously to produce the best weighted combination of predictors.

The last two equations, columns 7 and 8, are unique to the adopted children, because their rearing parents are not their genetic parents. When some information about the adopted child's genetic background was introduced, the variance explained in the children's IQ scores was doubled over that explained by differences in adoptive rearing environments alone.

As Taylor notes, the measures of differences in rearing *environments* (both between and within family indices) accounted for only 7.5 per cent of the adopted adolescents' IQ variance. By contrast, the *same* variables accounted for 31 per cent of the IQ variance among biologically-related adolescents, *because* parents in this SES range transmit their intellectual and social status achievements to their offspring by genetic as well as environmental means. Taylor's evaluation of the importance of 31 per cent of the variance should be seen in the context of the expected R^2. Because parents and their children neither share all of their genes, nor all of their experiences, random, individual genetic variance and experiences unique to individuals should account for at least one third of the IQ variance. We do not know of any studies of "family background" that accounted for more than 35 per cent of the children's IQ variance (see Burks, 1928; Leahy, 1935, Sewell & Hauser, 1975; Duncan, Featherman, and Duncan, 1972; Grilliches and Mason, 1972; Jencks, 1972; Jencks and Brown, 1978).

The "Same" Equations

Taylor requests comparable regression equations of child IQ on "family background" characteristics for adoptive and biological families, using pairwise deletion. We chose casewise deletion to avoid the suspicion that we had unfairly weighted partial information on employed mothers and natural fathers of the adopted children. Table 1 shows comparable sets of equations for biological and

TABLE 1
Standardized Regression Coefficients of Adolescent IQ on Demographic
Characteristics of Rearing and Genetic Parents in Biologically-Related
and Adoptive Families (Pairwise Deletion)

			Adolescents' IQ Scores				
		Biological				*Adopted*	
			Zero order				Zero order
	(N)	beta	r	(N)	beta	beta	r
Rearing Parents							
Father's Education	262	.26	.25***	179	−.04	−.53	.07
Mother's Education	262	.17	.28***	188	.02	−.40	.09
Father's Occupation	269	−.12	.10	182	.09	.12	.11
Mother's Occupation	183	.03	.09	114	.11	.57	.12
Father's Age	269	.13	.11	182	.07	−1.25	.12
Mother's Age	269	−.06	.11	191	.05	.92	.13
Genetic Parents							
Father's Education				24		1.15	.43*
Mother's Education				184		.00	.28***
Father's Occupation				<10			
Mother's Occupation				154		.08	.17*
Father's Age				23		.00	.17
Mother's Age				184		.04	−.06
R²		*.11*			*.037*	*.483*	
Adj. R²		.08			−.021	−1.238	
F		3.63			0.638	0.281	
df		6,173			6,99	10,3	

*p < .05.
***p < .001.

adoptive families, including the educational, occupational, and age differences of rearing and genetic parents.

Three regression equations have been calculated, two that contain the same variables for the adopted and biological adolescents (rearing family only) and two that contain the same information — sort of. As Taylor requested we show the regression of adolescent IQ on the educational, occupational, and age levels of both the rearing and genetic parents for both groups of adolescents. Unfortunately, as we reported in the article, there is insufficient information on the natural fathers and on the occupational prestige of employed, rearing mothers. Using pairwise deletion, the regression equations for child IQ on rearing family background are much the same as they were in the original report. The inclusion of information about the natural mothers and fathers of the adopted children greatly increased the R^2 (from .037 to .483), but the latter is an absurd result because of the degrees of freedom. We were not hiding these results, but, rather, chose not to subject the readers to nonsense.

More informative are the zero order correlations between adolescents' IQ scores and the background characteristics of the rearing and genetic parents. The adolescent IQ correlations with the educational levels of parents who are genetically related to their children reach statistical significance whether or not those parents had social contact with the children. In the biological families, where the parents are both the rearing and the genetic parents, mothers' and fathers' educational levels are related to their offsprings' IQ scores. Similarly the educational levels of the natural parents of the adopted children are correlated with the IQ scores of children whom they did not rear. In addition, natural mothers' occupational level has a small but statistically reliable coefficient with child IQ. No characteristic of the adoptive parents is significantly correlated with the IQ scores of the adopted adolescents.

We hasten to reiterate that the average level of IQ in the adopted group is higher than would be predicted from the intellectual levels natural parents, because they have, as a group, been reared by adoptive families above average in SES and interest in children. Differences among adoptive family environments in the range of working to upper middle class had negligible effects on differences in the adolescents' IQ scores, however.

Unexpected Results

"This study was designed to assess the cumulative impact of family environments at the end of the child-rearing period" (p. 360). We expected to find that the differences among family environments would prove to be of *greater* importance by late adolescence then they had been for several samples of young adopted children (Burks, 1928; Leahy, 1935; Scarr and Weinberg, 1977; Horn, Loehlin, and Willerman, 1978). Just the opposite was found. In retrospect, our prediction seems unreasonable, because by early to late adolescence, children are subjected to many extra-familial influences (schools, peers, TV, etc.), and they are far freer than younger children to select their own environments. Parental influences are diluted by the more varied mix of adolescent experience.

Our interpretation of the results now emphasizes the kind of "niche building" that is called *active genotype-environment correlation* (Plomin, DeFries, and Loehlin, 1979). Different people select different aspects of their environments, which they find compatible, live in them, enlarge them and deepen them. Part of what they bring to the selection of niches is genetic differences in what they are good at, what they enjoy, and what makes them comfortable. Adopted children, who are not genetically related to their parents or to each other, build niches that are correlated with their own genotypes but not with those of their family members. Biologically-related children also build niches that are correlated with their own genotypes, but their choices continue to be correlated with those of their genetically-related family members. We have found continuing resemblance among the biological but not adoptive family members in interests (Grotevant, Scarr, and Weinberg, 1977), personality (Scarr, Webber, Weinberg, and Wittig, 1981), attitudes (Scarr and Weinberg, 1981), and specific cognitive skills (Carter, 1976). Genetic resemblance and genotype-environment correlations continue to affect IQ resemblance into later adolescence, whereas the effects of common family rearing environments wane.

Calling a Truce Between "Camps"

We detailed here our theoretical framework and operational methods, drawn from both social and biological science in the hope that *ASR* readers will return to the original article to reconsider the evidence. Although it may be distasteful to some social scientists to acknowledge genetic sources of individual and SES differences, it appears to us important to recognize the biosocial nature of human variation.

We strongly oppose a eugenic strategy that interferes with people's civil liberties; we propose that understanding the nature of human variation will facilitate the design and implementation of effective environmental interventions to improve people's lives.

REFERENCES

Burks, B. S. The relative influence of nature and nurture upon mental development, a comparative study of foster parent — foster child resemblance and true parent — ture child resemblance." *Yearbook of the National Society for the Study of Education*, 1928, *27(1):* 89–99.

Carter, S. L. *The structure and transmission of individual differences in patterns of cognitive ability.* Unpublished doctoral dissertation. University of Minnesota, 1976.

Duncan, O. D., Featherman, D. L., and Duncan, B. *Socioeconomic background and achievement.* New York: Seminar Press, 1972.

Falconer, D. S. *Introduction to quantitative genetics*. New York: Ronald Press, 1970.

Grilliches, Z. and Mason, W. M. Education, income and ability. *Journal of Political Economy*, 1972, *80:* S74–S103.

Grotevant, H. D., Scarr, S., and Weinberg, R. A. Patterns of interest similarity in adoptive and biological families. *Journal of Personality and Social Psychology*, 1977, *35(9):* 667–676.

Horn, J. M., Loehlin, J. C., and Willerman, L. Intellectual resemblance among adoptive and biological relatives: the Texas adoption project. *Behavior Genetics*, 1979, 177–207.

Jencks, C. *Inequality: A reassessment of the effects of family and schooling in America*. New York: Basic Books, 1972.

Jencks, C., and Brown, M. Genes and social stratification. In P. Taubman (ed.), *Kinometrics: The determinants of economic success within and between families*. New York: North Holland-Elsevier, 1978.

Leahy, A. M. Nature-nurture and intelligence. *Genetic Psychology Monographs*, 1935, *17:* 237–308.

Munsinger, H. The adopted child's IQ: a critical review. *Psychological Bulletin*, 1975, *82(5):* 623–659.

Plomin, R., DeFries, J. C., and Loehlin, J. C. Genotype-environment interaction and correlation in the analysis of human behavior. *Psychological Bulletin*, 1977, *84(2):* 309–322.

Scarr, S. The effects of birthweight on later intelligence. *Social Biology*, 1969, *16:* 249–255.

Scarr, S. Psychology and children: Current research and practice. Introduction to the special issue. *American Psychologist*, 1979, *34(10):* 809–811.

Scarr, S., and Schwarz, J. C. *Report to the Bermuda government on the evaluation of the Child Development Project*, October 1978 to August 1979.

Scarr, S., Webber, P. L., Weinberg, R. A., and Wittig, M. A. *Personality resemblance among adolescents and their parents in biologically-related and adoptive families. Journal of Personality and Social Psychology*, 1981, *40* (5).

Scarr, S., and Weinberg, R. A. ''Intellectual similarities within families of both adopted and biological children. *Intelligence*, 1977, *1(2):* 170–191.

Scarr, S., and Weinberg, R. A. The transmission of authoritarianism in families: genetic resemblance in social-political attitudes? In S. Scarr (ed.), *IQ: Race, social class and individual differences*. Hillsdale, N.J.: Erlbaum, 1981.

Scarr, S., and Williams, M. L. The effects of early stimulation on low-birth-weight infants. *Child Development*, 1973, *44,* 94–101.

Taylor, M. The non-influence of 'family background' on intellectual attainment: a critique of Scarr and Weinberg. *American Sociological Review*, 1980.

Weinberg, R. A., and Moore, S. G. *Evaluation of educational programs for young children*. Washington, D.C.: The Child Development Associate Consortium, 1975.

III.3 The Transmission of Authoritarianism in Families: Genetic Resemblance in Social-Political Attitudes?

ABSTRACT

Resemblance in authoritarian attitudes (F-scale scores) among family members has been explained most often by their similar life experiences, including socio-economic status. This explanation is challenged by the finding that genetically unrelated families do not share similar attitudes, whereas biologically related families in the same range of SES do. Middle-aged parents and their adolescent children resemble each other more in IQ, verbal ability, and authoritarianism according to their genetic relatedness than to their environmental relatedness. Within this sample, differences in sociopolitical attitudes, measured by the F scale, appear to be genetically transmitted from parents to their children in the form of verbal ability and personality and to show no effect of direct learning.

INTRODUCTION

This is the empirical history of a control variable that failed. In our study of adoptive and biologically related families, the main focus of the research was on the transmission of family patterns of intellectual skills, personality, and attitudes. We hypothesized that genetic resemblance would be more important in accounting for intellectual than for personality similarities and that genetic similarity would have nothing to do with the resemblance of family members' political and social attitudes. The pattern of results expected was as follows: (1) significantly greater intellectual similarity in biological than adoptive families; (2) somewhat greater personality resemblance in biological than adoptive families; and (3) equal similarity on attitudinal measures.

Naively, we chose the California F-scale as our measure of social and political attitudes, failing to notice in the literature the correlations (often explained away) between authoritarianism and IQ (see Badgett, Fair, & Hunkler, 1974; Berkowitz & Wolkon, 1964; Himmelweit & Swift, 1971; Kayser, 1972; Thompson & Michel, 1972; and Trachtman, 1975). The strong correlation between IQ and authoritarianism (about $-.50$ in several large, representative samples) led Christie (1954) to conclude that the partial correlation between IQ and F-scale scores had to be about $-.20$, even with education partialed; educational differences are, of course, largely confounded with intellectual differences.

> The relationship between the cultural sophistication of a subject and the nature of his response to a question or scale item is a highly complicated matter. Through long experience, social scientists have come to be especially sensitive to this factor. Consistently high correlations between attitudinal dimensions and years of education, scores on intelligence tests (based largely on what is learned in school) and various other socio-economic criteria have been found [p. 167].

The standard explanation of these results was that socioeconomic factors determined life experiences that lead to higher authoritarianism, lower IQ scores, and lower educational levels. The implicit causal model led from social status to the other three variables. "It is a tenable hypothesis that a basic reason for the greater acceptance of F-scale items among members of lower socio-economic groupings as contrasted with middle-class individuals is related to the reality of the referent in the items" (Christie, 1954, p. 175).

There were some dissensions from this view, notably by Kelman and Barclay (1963) and by Himmelweit and Swift (1971), who claimed that a lack of cognitive complexity was an important contributor to high F scores, apart from life circumstances. However, a prevailing view of authoritarianism has been that it is largely determined by one's location in the social structure.

Our results disconfirm that explanation and require a reexamination of the nature of authoritarianism (1) among middle-aged parents and their adolescent children; (2) in the SES range from working class to upper middle class; and (3) in the mode of transmission of such attitudes from one generation to the next. Differences in social-political attitudes, measured by the F-Scale, appear to be genetically transmitted from parents to their children in the form of verbal ability and personality and to show no effect of direct learning.

The Adoption Study Design

How important are differences in parents' attitudes in shaping the beliefs of their children? The answer to this question depends methodologically on separating the differences in attitude learning that may occur in the home environment from the possible transmission of genetic differences in abilities and personality that can affect the acquisition of social and political attitudes.

Studies of individual differences across families confound four sources of variance: Within-family, between-family, environmental, and genetic differences. Regressions of individual outcomes on differences in family background are not illuminating as to the genetic or environmental sources of outcome differences, because the differences in family background are correlated with parental differences. Parents' differences are transmitted to their biological children both genetically and environmentally. Therefore, the differences among offspring reflect the correlated differences in their parents' genetic and environmental contributions.

Adopted children are not genetically related to the family of rearing; so environmental differences among the families' rearing environments are not confounded with genetic differences among the children, as they are in biological families. To estimate the total effect of being reared by parents who differ in social and political attitudes, the scores of the adopted children can be correlated with those of the genetically unrelated, adoptive parents. The magnitude of the correlations is a direct estimate of the environmental transmission of attitudes.

The problem with this simple method, however, is that adoptive families are not a random sample of the population to which one would like to generalize, because they have been selected by agencies for being above average in many virtues, including socioeconomic status and, probably, benign attitudes toward others. Thus, adoptive families are always a biased sample. To estimate the true environmental effects of differences in parental attitudes, one needs a comparison sample of biological families who have been similarly selected to be biased toward above-average characteristics, including attitudes. Any greater similarity among members of the biological families than among those of the adoptive families would be attributed to their genetic relatedness if the families are otherwise similar in the means and variance of their relevant characteristics and scores. To the extent that the selected adoptive- and biological-family samples do not represent the full range of attitudinal (and other) variation, the absolute level of their correlations will be biased downward, but the comparison of the similarly selected adoptive and biological parent–child coefficients will not be affected.

This study included both adoptive and biologically related families to estimate "true" environmental determinants of differences among children in their intellectual, personality, and attitudinal outcomes. The "children" to be reported here are the oldest adoptive sample ever studied. The study was designed to assess the cumulative impact of family environments over the entire child-rearing period. If differences in family environments have lasting impact on individual differences in intellectual functioning, personal adjustment, interests, and attitudes, the study of late adolescents who were adopted in the first few months of life should reveal those differences.

METHOD

Subjects

The subjects in this sample are members of 120 biological and 112 adoptive white families in Minnesota. The adoptive families include 194 adopted and 15 biological children between the ages of 16 and 22. Of the 194 adoptees, 186 have complete attitudinal and IQ data. The biological families include 252 children with attitudinal and IQ data. Adoptive families were recruited through the Department of Public Welfare (DPW), whose director sent letters on behalf of the study to all families who had adopted children between 1953 and 1959. We were particularly interested in families who had adopted at least two children; so our recruitment concentrated on those volunteers with two available children between the ages of 16 and 21 at the time of testing.

The biological families were recruited through newspaper articles and advertisements, word of mouth, and the adoptive families. Approximately 153 biological families came from public media contact and about 41 from recommendations of the adoptive families. Of these, 122 were chosen to come to the university for the full evaluation on the basis of convenient scheduling and location.

All families who participated in the interview procedure received small payments for their time and transportation and bonuses for recruiting other families. The data were collected from July 1974 to June 1976.

A crucial methodological consideration for any adoption study is the age at which the children are placed with their adopting families. Only early placements can guarantee that potentially confounding, early environmental experiences are minimized. All the children in this study were in their homes before 12 months of age. Exact age of placement was available for 171 of the 194 adopted children. The mean age of placement into the adopted children's present homes was 2.6 months. Of these 171 children, 109 were placed before 2 months of age, and 158 were placed at or before 6 months. All but 6 of the 171 were placed by 9 months. All adopted children were genetically unrelated to their adoptive parents and to each other. The biological children were all full siblings and claimed to be the biological offspring of both parents tested.

IQ Assessment

Subjects in the sample were administered a 3-hour battery of tests and interviews at the University of Minnesota as part of a behavior genetic study of intellectual, personality, and attitudinal similarities within families. The data reported here are from the Wechsler Adult Intelligence Scales (WAIS; Wechsler, 1955), an individually administered IQ test, and the California F-Scale (Adorno, Frenkel-Brunswik, Levinson, & Sanford, 1950). Four subtests of the WAIS were

TABLE 1
Attitude Questionnaire
Instructions and Answer Sheet[a]

Listed below are 20 statements of opinion. We are interested in the degree to which you agree or disagree with the statements. Your answers should reflect your own point of view; there are no right or wrong answers.

Please write a number in the left margin by each statement, according to how much you agree or disagree with it. *Please mark every statement* with one of the following numbers.

1 = I disagree very much
2 = I disagree pretty much
3 = I disagree a little
4 = no opinion
5 = I agree a little
6 = I agree pretty much
7 = I agree very much

1. _____ It is essential for learning or effective work that our teachers or bosses outline in detail what is to be done and how to do it.
2. _____ One of the most important things children should learn is when to disobey authorities.
3. _____ People ought to pay more attention to new ideas, even if they seem to go against the American way of life.
4. _____ Most people don't realize how much our lives are controlled by plots hatched in secret places.
5. _____ Most of our social problems could be solved if we could somehow get rid of the immoral, crooked, and feebleminded people.
6. _____ Human nature being what it is, there will always be war and conflict.
7. _____ It is highly unlikely that astrology will ever be able to explain anything.
8. _____ What youth needs most is strict discipline, rugged determination and the will to work and fight for family and country.
9. _____ No weakness or difficulty can hold us back if we have enough will power.
10. _____ If it weren't for the rebellious ideas of youth there would be less progress in the world.
11. _____ Most honest people admit to themselves that they have sometimes hated their parents.
12. _____ Books and movies ought to give a more realistic picture of life, even if they show that evil sometimes triumphs over good.
13. _____ Every person should have complete faith in a supernatural power whose decisions he obeys without question.
14. _____ The artist and professor are probably more important to society than the business man and the manufacturer.
15. _____ The findings of science may some day show that many of our most cherished beliefs are wrong.
16. _____ An urge to jump from high places is probably the result of unhappy personal experiences rather than anything inborn.
17. _____ Nowadays more and more people are prying into matters that should remain personal and private.
18. _____ In spite of what you read about the wild sex life of people in important places, the real story is about the same in any group of people.
19. _____ No sane, normal, decent person could ever think of hurting a close friend or relative.
20. _____ Sex crimes, such as rape and attacks on children, deserve more than mere imprisonment; such criminals ought to be publicly whipped or worse.

[a] From Adorno, Frenkel-Brunswik, Levinson, and Sanford (1950).

administered: vocabulary, arithmetic, block design, and picture arrangement. The combination of the four subtests has been shown to correlate above .90 with the full-scale test (Doppelt, 1956). The test protocols were scored by an experienced psychometrician who was unaware of the respondents' adoptive status.

The F Scale

The 20-item version of the California F-Scale administered in this study is reproduced in Table 1. The scoring was straightforward: $F-$ and $F+$ scores were obtained by summing the numbers assigned by the respondents to each of the 10 negative and 10 positive items. A total F score was obtained by reversing the item scores for the negative items.

RESULTS

Socioeconomic Variables

Parental educational levels in both kinds of families are well above the averages of their cohorts in the populations. The occupational prestige of the fathers, rated on the expanded NORC scale (Reiss, 1961), is about 60 in both types of families. Because less than half of the mothers are employed, their occupational ratings are not used in the analyses. Family income averages $25,000 in both types of families. The variance of the educational, occupational, and income measures is not as restricted as the high means might imply. In fact, the standard deviations are roughly comparable to the population figures. Two points should be made, therefore, about the socioeconomic characteristics of these families: First, the adoptive and biological families are fairly comparable; second, they both represent selected portions of the SES range in the United States, both regionally and within the region from which they are drawn. It is well known that volunteers in social science research are self-selected for better-than-average characteristics of all kinds, and the sample of biological families is at least as biased in SES characteristics as the adoptive one. This is what we hoped would happen, without using the statistically hazardous procedure of matching individual families.

WAIS IQ Levels

The adoptive and biological parents are also comparable in mean IQ scores and in the variance of their scores, as shown in Table 2. Compared to the standardization sample for the WAIS (Wechsler Adult Intelligence Scale), the fathers are more than a standard deviation above the mean, and the mothers, about .75 of an *SD* above. It is not accidental, of course, that samples with above-average income, education, and occupational status also score above the average on a

TABLE 2
Means and *SD*s for WAIS IQ

Biological	$\overline{M}$	SD	N	Range
Father	117.6	11.9	120	91–144
Mother	113.1	10.5	121	87–140
Son	115.2	10.5	116	94–135
Daughter	110.0	10.0	145	84–132
Adoptive	$\overline{M}$	SD	N	Range
Father	116.5	10.9	106	92–142
Mother	112.9	10.2	111	91–138
Son	107.8	9.0	88	79–134
Daughter	105.3	9.3	103	75–128

standard IQ test. The variance of the parental IQ scores is only 50% of the population variance, a significant restriction. Their scores are significantly restricted in range, with the lowest scores in the mid-90s.

The children of the two types of families are quite comparable in age, the mean being about 18½ in both groups. The range of ages is 16 to 22 in both groups (with a few older or younger exceptions). There was no correlation between age and IQ. The IQ scores of the adopted children are about 6.5 points lower than those of the biological children, however. These results are also shown in Table 2. If IQ is heritable to any extent, one should expect the biological offspring of bright parents to have higher IQ scores than unselected people. The adopted children are not a genetically selected group (Scarr & Weinberg, 1978).

F-Scale Levels

Given a 20-item scale, scored from 1 to 7 for each item, the minimum score possible was 20 and the maximum, 140. The mean scores of the various biological- and adoptive-family members ranged from 71.5 to 81.5, with standard deviations from 10.9 to 15.6, indicating that there were neither ceiling nor floor effects for the scale. The mean item scores ranged from 3.57 to 4.05, a typical range for a largely middle-class sample (Adorno et al., 1950; Christie, 1954; Scarr, 1970). The means, standard deviations, and sample sizes of the *F*-Scale scores for the various members of the adoptive and biological families are given in Table 3.

In these samples, there are significant generation, sex, and family-type differences in mean F scores ($F = 5.35, 8.99, 39.31$) but no interaction effects. More of the adoptive families came from smaller towns and rural areas than the

TABLE 3
F-Scale: Means, Standard Deviations, and
Sample Sizes

	$\overline{M}$	SD	N
Biological			
Father	75.77	15.58	118
Mother	73.30	15.36	120
Son	73.27	12.59	112
Daughter	71.46	12.74	140
Adoptive			
Father	81.50	13.42	105
Mother	79.77	14.43	112
Son	78.55	10.93	85
Daughter	76.31	11.48	101

biological families, which may explain their higher *F* scores in both generations. Although the fathers tend to have higher IQ scores and are better educated than the mothers, they have slightly higher *F* scores—as do the sons, who have higher IQ scores but are not better educated than the daughters. The reason for the consistent 2-point sex difference and the 2-point generation difference is not clear, although they have often been reported (Badgett, Fair, & Hunkler, 1974). But because we standardized the scores for further analysis by sex, generation, and family type, the mean differences need not further concern us here.

Family Resemblance in Authoritarianism

The astounding result as shown in Table 4 was the lack of similarity in *F*-scale scores between adopted children and their parents and among adopted children reared together from early infancy. By contrast, the biological relatives' correlations ranged from .34 to .46 for the various combinations of mothers, fathers, sons, and daughters. The only statistically significant similarity in the adoptive families was between fathers and their daughters. With this exception, the parent–child and sibling correlations in the biological families significantly exceeded those of the adopted relatives in every case. Whereas we had included the *F*-Scale as a control variable, predicted to be as similar in adoptive families as in biological families, we were faced with startling evidence for the "heritability" of social and political attitudes, a seemingly incongruous result.

One explanation could be that the adoptive parents were not as similar to each other as the biological parents and, thus, presented their adopted children with diverse attitudinal models. That this is not the case can be seen in Table 4. Husbands and wives in the two types of families were similarly correlated in their attitudes, at the same level as the biological relatives. Marriage partners may well select each other in part for the similarity of their social and political attitudes (Byrne, 1966), or for whatever is measured by the *F*-Scale. The significant attitudinal similarity between the adoptive parents seemed to have little effect, however, on the attitudes of their adopted children, whereas in the biologically related families, the parental similarity in attitudes is reflected in the parent–child and sibling similarities.

A quick look at these results sent us directly to the comparable table for IQ scores. The family correlations for WAIS IQ scores are given in Table 5. The pattern of results for the IQ scores and the *F*-Scale were frighteningly similar, including the anomalous father–daughter resemblance in the adoptive families. Could this be accidental? Or the result of biased testing or sampling procedures?

A comparison of the IQ and *F*-scale results to those of the Eysenck Personality Inventory quickly assured us that a different pattern of results was possible with the same sample. As Table 6 shows, the correlations of biological-family members for introversion–extraversion were half (or less) their correlations for

TABLE 4
F-Scale: Family Correlations Based on Scores
Standardized by Sex, Generation, and Family Type

	Correlations			
	r_{bio}	r_{adopt}	$r_{bio}-r_{adopt}$	t_{corr}
Fa–Mo	.43	.34	.09	0.78
Fa–Child	.37	.14	.23	2.44**
Fa–Da	.34	.31	.03	0.24
Fa–Son	.44	−.05	.49	3.62***
Mo–Child	.41	.00	.41	3.45***
Mo–Da	.40	.06	.34	2.79**
Mo–Son	.41	−.06	.46	3.45***
MP–Child	.44	.06	.38	4.33***
MP–Da	.43	.20	.23	1.91*
MP–Son	.51	−.08	.59	4.35***
Child–Child	.36	.14	.22	1.71*
Son–Son	.46	—		—
Da–Da	.36	—		—
Son–Da	.41	.04	.37	2.26*

$*p < .05$, one-tailed.
$**p < .01$, one-tailed.
$***p < .001$, one-tailed.

TABLE 5
WAIS IQ: Family Correlations Based on Scores
Standardized by Sex, Generation, and Family Type

	Correlations			
	r_{bio}	r_{adopt}	$(r_{bio} - r_{adopt})$	t_{corr}
Fa–Mo	.24	.31	(.07)	−0.52
Fa–Child	.40	.16	.24	2.69**
Fa–Da	.31	.30	.01	.14
Fa–Son	.42	.05	.37	2.78**
Mo–Child	.41	.09	.32	3.68***
Mo–Da	.26	.10	.16	1.29
Mo–Son	.53	.09	.44	3.53***
MP–Child	.52	.14	.38	4.42***
MP–Da	.38	.20	.18	1.41
MP–Son	.60	.09	.51	4.17***
Child–Child	.35	−.03	.38	2.91*
Son–Son	.57	—		
Da–Da	.23	—		
Son–Da	.34	−.01	.35	2.19*

*$p < .05$, one-tailed.
**$p < .01$, one-tailed.
***$p < .001$, one-tailed.

the other two measures and often did not exceed the correlations of the adoptive-family members. The explanation of the peculiar similarity of IQ and F-scale correlations did not include any overall biases in the study (there were a number of other personality, interest, and cognitive measures that also served to reassure us; see Carter-Saltzman, 1976; Grotevant, 1977; Webber, 1976).

Then we discovered the high and consistent correlations between F-scale scores and the intellectual measures, particularly vocabulary, as shown in Table 7. The correlations between WAIS vocabulary, a highly reliable measure, and F-scale scores ranged from −.51 to −.57 in the biological families and from −.30 to −.47 in the adoptive families. The correlation of WAIS vocabulary and F-scale scores for all 914 subjects was −.42. In contrast, the F-scale correlation with a nonverbal measure of ability—the Raven's Standard Progressive Matrices (Raven, 1958)—was only −.27 in the whole sample and ranged from −.09 to −.32 for the various family members. Correlations with WAIS IQ were high (−.26 to −.50) but generally lower than those for vocabulary. Family correlations for WAIS vocabulary are shown in Table 8. Vocabulary appeared to be more influenced by common environment than either the WAIS IQ or F scale, because adoptive family correlations were higher; but the pattern of correlations still showed evidence of genetic differences.

Thus, we concluded that whatever the F-Scale was reputed to measure, it had two important characteristics: The pattern of correlations in the adoptive and biological families pointed to possible genetic differences in authoritarianism, and the correlations with verbal IQ suggested an explanation of that result; that is, F-Scale scores are similar only in biological families, because the F-Scale measures differences in intellectual skills that are partly heritable.

In addition to the intellectual correlates, the F-Scale could also be sampling personality dimensions, as claimed by its authors (Adorno et al., 1950). Indeed, in the biological and adoptive families, there were some statistically significant correlations of F-scale scores with measures of social anxiety (Lykken, Tellegen, & Katzenmeyer, 1973) and social potency (Tellegen, 1974), but not with introversion–extraversion, neuroticism, or physical anxiety. One could have predicted the pattern: Highly socially anxious people who feel low in social effectance score higher on the F-Scale, but the correlations were so low (.18 and .20) as to have little explanatory power.

TABLE 6
Introversion–Extraversion: Family Correlations Based on Scores Standardized by Sex, Generation, and Family Type (Eysenck Personality Inventory)

| | Correlations | | | |
	r_{bio}	r_{adopt}	$r_{bio}-r_{adopt}$	t_{corr}
Fa–Mo	−.13	.01	(.14)	1.03
Fa–Child	.21	.05	.16	1.72*
Fa–Da	.29	−.01	.30	2.37**
Fa–Son	.10	.10	.00	−0.03
Mo–Child	.04	−.03	.07	.66
Mo–Da	.03	−.08	.11	.84
Mo–Son	.06	.03	.03	.24
MP–Child	.19	−.00	.19	1.78*
MP–Da	.24	−.05	.29	2.22*
MP–Son	.12	.08	.04	.30
Child–Child	.06	.07	(.01)	−.04
Son–Son	.28	—		—
Da–Da	.02	—		—
Son–Da	.04	.04	.00	.00

*$p < .05$, one-tailed.
**$p < .01$, one-tailed.

TABLE 7
F-Scale Correlations with Abilities and Personality

	F-Scale								
	Biological				Adoptive				All Subjects
	Fa	Mo	Son	Da	Fa	Mo	Son	Da	
N	118	120	112	140	105	102	85	101	914
Abilities									
Education	−.54	−.49	−.17	−.37	−.46	−.44	−.27	−.24	−.27
Raven Matrices	−.31	−.31	−.16	−.27	−.25	−.32	−.09	−.25	−.27
Mill Hill Vocab.	−.54	−.47	−.33	−.46	−.44	−.43	−.29	−.31	−.36
WAIS Vocabulary	−.57	−.53	−.51	−.53	−.46	−.44	−.30	−.47	−.42
WAIS IQ	−.50	−.44	−.36	−.31	−.37	−.38	−.26	−.43	−.35
Personality									
Ey. Intro-Extra	.04	−.03	.11	.05	.12	.04	.11	.23	.05
Ey. Neuroticism	.04	.10	.03	.06	.14	.24	.04	.12	.06
Social Closeness	.04	−.11	−.00	.02	−.04	.05	.12	.29	.03
Social Potency	−.23	−.26	−.01	−.23	−.22	−.15	−.03	−.21	−.18
Impulsivity	−.21	−.31	−.17	.02	−.09	.04	−.15	−.15	−.14
Social Anxiety	.19	.19	.25	.23	.33	.30	.18	.23	.20
Physical Anxiety	.16	.03	.02	.15	.06	.17	.05	.29	.11
Total Anxiety	.22	.15	.15	.24	.24	.29	.14	.33	.20

$p \leq .05$, when:
$N = 85, r \geq .21$
$N = 100, r \geq .20$
$N = 125, r \geq .17$
$N = 914, r \geq .06$

TABLE 8
WAIS Vocabulary: Family Correlations Based on
Scores Standardized by Sex, Generation, and Family
Type

| | Correlations | | | |
	r_{bio}	r_{adopt}	$r_{bio} - r_{adopt}$	t_{corr}
Fa–Mo	.32	.42	−.10	
Fa–Child	.39	.24	.15	1.69*
Fa–Da	.33	.34	−.01	−0.06
Fa–Son	.46	.13	.33	2.51**
Mo–Child	.33	.23	.10	1.07
Mo–Da	.22	.27	−.05	−0.44
Mo–Son	.48	.20	.28	2.27*
MP–Child	.43	.26	.17	2.08*
MP–Da	.35	.32	.03	0.20
MP–Son	.56	.19	.37	3.03**
Child–Child	.22	.11	−.11	
Son–Son	.44	—	—	
Da–Da	.30	—	—	
Son–Da	.21	.14	.07	

*$p < .05$, one-tailed.
**$p < .01$, one-tailed.

The high correlations of the F-Scale with verbal skills, on the other hand, offered an opportunity to examine both the nature of authoritarianism, measured by the F-Scale, and the nature of the transmission of authoritarianism from one generation to the next.

Item Correlations

One way to examine the relationship between authoritarianism and verbal skills is to correlate the items of the F-Scale with F-Total score and with WAIS vocabulary scores, as shown in Table 9. The correlation between items and total scores on the F-Scale ought to exceed those between the F-Scale items and the vocabulary scale if the F-Scale has discriminant validity. If not, then one would have to conclude that the items on the F-Scale might as well be considered part of a vocabulary test! As Table 9 shows, the correlations of the F-Scale items with the F Total score do generally exceed those of the F items with the WAIS vocabulary score, with the exception of Item 7 ("It is highly unlikely that astrology will ever be able to explain anything"), which seems to be more of a sample of verbal skills than of "authoritarianism," and Item 16 ("An urge to

TABLE 9
F-Scale-Item Correlations with WAIS Vocabulary and F-Total Scores
for Biological-Family Members

F Item No.	(N = 500) All		(N = 117) Fa		(N = 118) Mo		(N = 120) Son		(N = 145) Da	
	WSV	F T	WSV	F T	WSV	F T	WSV	F T	WSV	F T
1	−.28	.51	−.26	.38	−.38	.53	−.31	.60	−.27	.46
2	.25	−.45	.22	−.46	.13	−.42	.27	−.32	.37	−.51
3	.22	−.57	.28	−.54	.24	−.54	.30	−.49	.37	−.52
4	−.22	.27	−.31	.40	−.18	.28	−.23	.44	−.12	.20
5	−.39	.41	−.34	.49	−.35	.37	−.43	.50	−.35	.47
6	−.08	.39	−.08	.35	−.12	.41	−.09	.36	.01	.30
7	.33	−.16	.37	−.25	.17	−.19	.33	−.22	.30	−.16
8	−.18	.57	−.25	.52	−.28	.62	−.30	.60	−.25	.54
9	−.26	.37	−.31	.43	−.30	.37	−.11	.38	−.10	.28
10	.18	−.35	.25	−.41	.34	−.43	−.00	−.26	.44	−.32
11	.10	−.29	.16	−.33	.14	−.34	−.08	−.16	.13	−.31
12	.08	−.30	.21	−.41	.08	−.33	.02	−.08	.05	−.33
13	−.08	.42	−.07	.34	−.04	.40	−.09	.40	−.01	.41
14	.10	−.29	.11	−.29	.16	−.38	.09	−.33	.07	−.14
15	.11	−.40	.19	−.39	.18	−.41	.07	−.18	.09	−.39
16	−.01	−.13	−.02	−.09	.00	−.15	−.03	−.00	.16	−.31
17	−.05	.35	−.00	.23	−.10	.27	−.19	.43	−.14	.43
18	.16	−.22	.12	−.29	.14	−.21	.18	−.05	.17	−.21
19	−.24	.46	−.32	.48	−.29	.49	−.38	.52	−.19	.40
20	−.26	.56	−.26	.56	−.33	.61	−.32	.58	−.27	.49

jump from high places is probably the result of unhappy experiences rather than anything 'inborn' ''), which seems to tap neither verbal skills nor "authoritarianism.''

Nine of the items were correlated with WAIS vocabulary at a ± .20 or greater level, as shown in Table 10. Of the nine, four items also had higher correlations in the biological families than in the adoptive families; the other five items did not. Three items (4, 15, 17) not correlated with WAIS vocabulary had significantly higher biological than adoptive correlations. They can easily be characterized as paranoid items.

Thus, the greater biological-family than adoptive-family correlations for the F scale can be partially explained by the item correlations with WAIS vocabulary; but a few items appeared to be "heritable" apart from the vocabulary resemblance in biological families, and a few items correlated with vocabulary without showing greater biological-family than adoptive-family resemblance, We hypothesized, therefore, that shared verbal skills could probably explain only part of the biological-family resemblance in authoritarianism.

For two items, the adoptive-family correlations significantly exceeded those

TABLE 10[a]

Relationship Between F-Scale and WAIS Vocabulary Scores and the
Magnitudes of Biological and Adoptive Family Correlations

A. *F*-Scale Items that Are Correlated with WAIS Vocabulary $\geq$ .20 and $r_{bio} > r_{adopt}$

---

   1. It is essential for learning and effective work that our teachers and bosses outline in detail what is to be done and how to do it. (−)
   7. It is highly unlikely that astrology will ever be able to explain anything. (+)
   8. What youth needs most is strict discipline, rugged determination, and the will to work and fight for family and country. (−)
   10. If it weren't for the rebellious ideas of youth there would be less progress in the world. (+)

B. *F*-Scale Items that Are Not Correlated with WAIS Vocabulary but $r_{bio} > r_{adopt}$

---

   4. Most people don't realize how much our lives are controlled by plots hatched in secret places. (+)
   15. The findings of science may some day show that many of our most cherished beliefs are wrong. (−)
   17. Nowadays more and more people are prying into matters that should remain personal and private. (+)

C. *F*-Scale Items that Are Correlated with WAIS Vocabulary but $r_{bio} = r_{adopt}$

---

   2. One of the most important things children should learn is when to disobey authorities. (+)
   3. People ought to pay more attention to new ideas, even if they seem to go against the American way of life. (+)
   5. Most of our social problems could be solved if we could somehow get rid of the immoral, crooked, and feebleminded people. (−)
   19. No sane, normal, decent person could ever think of hurting a close friend or relative. (−)
   20. Sex crimes, such as rape and attacks on children, deserve more than mere imprisonment; such criminals ought to be publicly whipped or worse. (−)

---

of the biological families. One is predictable, because it refers to inborn behavioral tendencies (Item 16), probably a salient topic for adoptive families; but the other, Item 12—"Books and movies ought to give a more realistic picture...."—is less easily understood.

One explanation for the inconsistent pattern of correlations of *F* items with WAIS vocabulary and with *F*-Total Score could be that some items are more reliable than others; perhaps those items that best sample authoritarianism (high item–total correlation) also are the items that are most closely related to verbal skills, because they are the most reliable items. Thus we correlated the *F*-item–*F*-total correlations with the *F*-item–WAIS vocabulary correlations. These coefficients ranged from .41 to .67, all statistically significant.

The consistency of the item–total and the *F*-item–WAIS vocabulary correlations across family members is shown in Table 11. The magnitude of the *F*-item–total correlations is quite consistent for all family members, and the *F*-item–WAIS vocabulary correlations are moderately consistent. The implica-

TABLE 11
WAIS Vocabulary–F-Item Correlations

		Fa	Mo	Son	Da
F-Item-F-Total Correlations	Fa	×	.73	.63	.52
	Mo	.82	×	.57	.58
	Son	.62	.80	×	.51
	Da	.59	.69	.66	×

tions of these analyses are that there is a consistent relationship between the contribution of the F item to the total score and its similarity to a measure of verbal skills, a kind of reliability test, and that different family members have fairly similar patterns of relationship between F-scale and WAIS vocabulary scores, indicating consistency for this effect.

MODELS OF FAMILY TRANSMISSION

How, then, do children come to resemble their parents' authoritarian attitudes? The similarity of biological-family members in both verbal skills and attitudes and the lesser resemblance of the adoptive-family members could be modeled in several ways. First, we decided to test the predictive value of various family background measures for adolescent attitudes. In the adoptive families, the predictive value of socioeconomic and adoptive parental characteristics would be nearly all environmental, whereas in the biological families the effects of family background would have both genetic and environmental bases. If one's location in the social structure—in this study, from working to upper middle class—were crucial to the level of authoritarianism, then adopted children reared in working-class families should have more authoritarian attitudes than those reared in upper-middle-class families. In biologically related families, on the other hand, such social-class effects could result from both genetic and environmental differences among parents and their children at different locations in the social structure (see Scarr, 1977; Scarr & Weinberg, in press).

Prediction of Adolescents' F-Scale Scores from Family Characteristics

To explore further the explanatory power of family background characteristics for F-Scale scores, we regressed the adolescents' scores on parental F-Scale scores, parental vocabulary scores, and a variety of standard measures of family socioeconomic status and composition. Table 12 shows the regression equations for the biological and adoptive families.

In the biologically related families, about a quarter of the variance among adolescents' F-Scale scores is predicted by this combination of family variables, and the equation is statistically significant overall. Given the intercorrelations of the predictors, it is difficult to assign importance to one or another coefficient (the problem of multicolinearity), but in this sample, both parents' F-Scale scores and sibling rank in the family are significant predictors of adolescents' F-Scale scores in the biological families.

In the adoptive families, only 12% of the adolescents' F-Scale score variance is predicted by the combination of the same set of adoptive-family predictors and three characteristics of the natural mothers of the adopted children. Because the natural mothers' education was an important predictor of adopted adolescents' IQ scores (Scarr & Weinberg, in press), we wanted to explore the relationship of biological parentage to authoritarianism as well. None of the coefficients in the adoptive family equation are statistically significant, for two reasons: They are smaller than the significant coefficients in the biological-family equation, and the sample size was greatly reduced in order to include data on the natural mothers. Even ignoring the problem of reduced sample size, resulting in statistical insignificance and a greatly shrunken R^2 value, the only predictors that come close to

TABLE 12a
Regressions of Adolescents' F-Scale Scores on Characteristics of Their
Parents and Family Backgrounds

Family Characteristics	Biological (N = 241)			Adoptive (N = 134)		
	B	beta	p	B	beta	p
Mother's F-Scale Score	.210	.254	.001	−.057	−.073	.484
Father's F-Scale Score	.191	.237	.003	.086	.098	.353
Mother's Education	.092	.016	.844	−.652	−.120	.320
Father's Education	−.541	−.121	.227	−.288	−.072	.593
Father's Occupation	.399	.076	.320	−.127	−.027	.827
Family Income	−.052	−.004	.958	−.710	−.064	.592
Mother's WAIS Vocabulary	−.496	−.084	.253	.593	.091	.421
Father's WAIS Vocabulary	.467	.083	.305	−.272	−.046	.687
Family Size	−.294	−.033	.605	1.389	.144	.111
Sibling Rank	4.156	.209	.001	.597	.029	.770
Natural Mother's Age				.980	.175	.127
Natural Mother's Education				−.539	−.048	.665
Natural Mother's Occupation				−.108	−.028	.767
R		.499			.347	
R^2		.249			.120	
Adjusted R^2		.216			.025	
F		7.610			1.260	
p		.001			.244	

TABLE 12b
Correlations Among Family Characteristics and F-Scale Scores in Biological and Adoptive Families

Biological Children (N = 241)

	1	2	3	4	5	6	7	8	9	10	11	12	13
1. Adolescent F Score		-.24	-.06	-.06	-.09	.21	.09	.36	.38	-.18	-.25		
2. Father's Education	-.19		.51	.61	.42	.01	-.33	-.59	-.30	.66	.22		
3. Mother's Education	-.14	.53		.36	.38	.03	-.33	-.36	-.52	.34	.53		
4. Father's Occupation	-.18	.54	.21		.46	.04	-.30	-.29	-.16	.39	.11		
5. Family Income	-.14	.49	.43	.46		.03	-.20	-.23	-.16	.35	.24		
6. Sibling Rank	.08	.00	.01	.03	.15		.04	.01	-.01	-.01	.02		
7. Family Size	.15	.01	.05	-.04	.22	.07		.20	.24	-.20	-.11		
8. Father's F Score	.18	-.44	-.28	-.43	-.22	-.03	.03		.42	-.57	-.23		
9. Mother's F Score	-.02	-.18	-.34	-.19	.04	.14	.01	.23		-.26	-.51		
10. Father's WAIS Vocabulary	-.18	.59	.34	.42	.39	-.05	-.01	-.45	-.10		.24		
11. Mother's WAIS Vocabulary	-.04	.38	.53	.14	.28	.01	.03	-.24	-.39	.35			
12. Natural Mother's Age	.11	.06	.11	.13	.03	.02	.06	.21	-.09	.03	.08		
13. Natural Mother's Education	.06	.30	.26	.31	.43	.00	.16	.27	-.09	.17	.21	.17	
14. Natural Mother's Occupation	-.04	-.01	.13	.10	.04	-.07	.11	.14	-.05	.14	.10	.31	.32

Adopted Children (N = 134)

statistical significance are family size and natural mothers' age. Neither the overall equation nor the adoptive-family characteristics are statistically significant in the adoptive families.

A comparison of the predictive value of family background for adolescents' F-scale scores reveals the continuing puzzle—the greater resemblance of biologically related children's attitudes to their parents' attitudes, and the surprisingly small relationship between family socioeconomic status and children's attitudes on an environmental basis, at least in these adoptive families that range from skilled workers to upper professionals.

Second, we decided to test several path models of family transmission of attitudes through intellectual resemblance between children and their parents. If the F-Scale were more a measure of intellectual status than of social structural experience, then a model of the family transmission of intellectual skills should best account for the differential attitudinal resemblance in the adoptive and biological families.

We tested the fits of three path models, all designed to account for the transmission of authoritarian attitudes as part of intellectual resemblance in families. Path models require the specification of causality, and different models yield different results. Indeed, other models might be proposed. The preference of one model over another depends on its predictive or explanatory power, measured by smaller residuals. On this basis, we tested the most reasonable a priori models we could conceive.

Model 1

Model 1, shown in Figure 1, states that the WAIS vocabulary (Q) scores of the parents determine their own F scores (F), the verbal skills of the children (Q'),

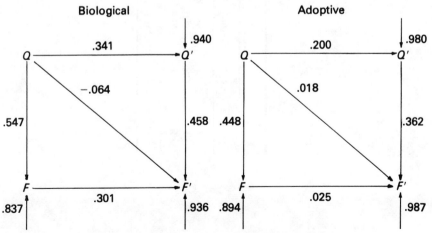

FIG. 1.   Average Model 1 fits—standardized coefficients.

TABLE 13
Model 1: Path Coefficients

	Biological					Adoptive				
	Fa–Son	Fa–Da	Mo–Son	Mo–Da	Mean	Fa–Son	Fa–Da	Mo–Son	Mo–Da	Mean
Q → F	.566	.566	.528	.528	.547	.455	.455	.442	.442	.448
Q' → F'	.476	.485	.414	.458	.458	.278	.408	.287	.475	.362
Q → F'	−.139	−.120	−.004	.055	−.064	.111	.039	−.074	−.006	.018
Q → Q'	.430	.288	.468	.179	.341	.082	.301	.163	.253	.200
F → F'	.392	.251	.340	.247	.301	−.123	.179	.075	−.030	.025

and the F scores of the children (F'). In addition, the children's verbal scores determine their own F scores. The path coefficients for the various related and unrelated parent–child pairs are shown in Table 13. Average coefficients and residuals are shown in Figure 1.

Both the Q and F transmission paths are larger in the biological families, as expected. What is surprising is that all the resemblance of adoptive-family members in authoritarian attitudes is accounted for by their similarity in vocabulary scores. In the biological families, however, there is a sizable path coefficient for the transmission of authoritarianism once verbal skills have been controlled.

The residuals for this model are quite large, however; so we tested another model.

Model 2

Model 2 specifies the indirect transmission of authoritarian attitudes through verbal skills. The verbal skills of both parents (Q) and children (Q') affect their own F scores (F, F'), and the authoritarianism of the parent affects the verbal development of the child and, thereby, his or her authoritarianism. This model and its path coefficients and residuals are shown in Figure 2 and Table 14. The residuals of this model are even larger than those of Model 1; so it is not further discussed.

Model 3

The final and most successful model, shown in Figure 3 and Table 15, states that there is some common skill or characteristic (C, C') underlying both verbal skills

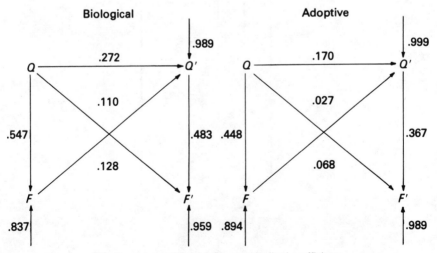

FIG. 2.   Average Model 2 fits—standardized coefficients.

TABLE 14
Model 2: Path Coefficients

	Biological					Adoptive				
	Mo–Son	Mo–Da	Fa–Son	Fa–Da	Mean	Mo–Son	Mo–Da	Fa–Son	Fa–Da	Mean
Q → F	.528	.528	.566	.566	.547	.442	.442	.455	.455	.448
Q' → F'	.431	.500	.473	.529	.483	.287	.473	.275	.434	.367
Q → F'	.167	.177	.085	.010	.110	−.041	−.019	.055	.112	.027
Q → Q'	.440	.058	.436	.153	.272	.168	.215	.070	.225	.170
F → Q'	.054	.229	−.011	.238	.128	−.011	.086	.027	.168	.068

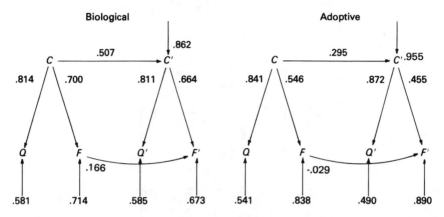

FIG. 3.   Average Model 3 fits—standardized coefficients.

and authoritarianism that is transmitted from parent (Q, F) to child (Q', F'). In addition, there is a direct transmission of authoritarianism from parent to child apart from the transmission of whatever is common to the two. The fit of this model to the data is far better, yielding much smaller residuals.

Note that the transmission from C to C', or from parent to child, of whatever is common to verbal skills and authoritarianism is far better specified in this model than in the others; that is, the path coefficients are considerably larger. Also, note that there is a statistically significant, though small, path from F to F' in the biological families but not in the adoptive families. Apart from the greater transmission of verbal skills among biological parents and children, there is evidence for the *genetic* transmission of a small part of what we call authoritarian attitudes. But there is no evidence for any environmental transmission from parent to child at all, because the *adoptive*-parent–child, F–F', path is zero.

The differences in the path coefficients, C–C' and F–F', between the biological and adoptive families are .212 and .165, respectively. The implication of this result is that whatever is measured by the F-Scale, apart from verbal skills, is almost as "heritable" as verbal skills. It must be emphasized, however, that the path from the biological parent's F score to the child's F score is quite small once verbal skills have been removed from the relationship.

There is a large sex difference in the path coefficients from F–F', as shown in Table 15. Sons show some transmission of a nonintellectual type of authoritarianism, and daughters do not. Whether this is a sampling fluctuation cannot be determined from these data.

DISCUSSION

People are not born with social and political attitudes; so one must explain how they are acquired. The content of any thought is, of course, learned from experience. But the thought processes that predispose or restrict what one learns from

TABLE 15
Model 3: Path Coefficients

	Biological					Adoptive				
	Fa–Son	*Fa–Da*	*Mo–Son*	*Mo–Da*	*Mean*	*Fa–Son*	*Fa–Da*	*Mo–Son*	*Mo–Da*	*Mean*
C → Q	1.016	.708	.930	.603	.814	.795	.712	1.069	.786	.841
C → F	.557	.799	.568	.876	.700	.572	.639	.413	.562	.546
C' → Q'	.872	.973	.803	.597	.811	.543	.761	1.100	1.083	.872
C' → F'	.584	.547	.634	.891	.664	.517	.615	.255	.432	.455
F → F'	.268	.158	.230	.007	.166	-.112	.089	-.075	-.019	-.029
C → C'	.485	.418	.627	.497	.507	.190	.555	.139	.297	.295

experiences may not themselves be so acquired. There is now ample evidence that different people learn different kinds and amounts of information from the same situations. Why should individual differences in learning social and political attitudes have a different basis from, say, differences in learning numerical skills?

To label authoritarianism as a personality or attitudinal "trait" is to avoid an explanation of the processes by which the "trait" is acquired. Although for some purposes, such as the prediction of political behavior, it may be legitimate to ignore a process explanation of authoritarianism, no theory of the "trait" is complete without it.

Turiel (1974) put it well when he spoke of the formation of moral judgments.

> The problem with character-trait explanations, as I see it, is that such traits do not reflect how people actually make moral decisions, nor how people act. That is, it does not reflect the psychological structures that children develop. It is for these reasons that character traits cannot be measured reliably and that programs of character education do not work. What I see as lacking in that work is the thinking, judgmental component—and the developmental component. From my point of view, to understand development it is, first, necessary to understand how children think. We must understand what kinds of judgments they make about right and wrong. Secondly, we must understand how the child constructs or generates his own values and conceptions out of his dealing with the world around him. In sum, it is necessary to study how the child organizes his social and emotional experiences and how transformations occur within this [pp. 4–5].

In our view, the only adequate explanation of the strong authoritarianism–IQ correlation is a cognitive one that interprets scores on the F-Scale as the products of social reasoning processes that are themselves clearly linked to more general intellectual or cognitive levels. The cognitive view rejects the social learning or modeling explanation; moral decisions and authoritarian views are not learned in rote fashion from one's associates (parents, teachers, colleagues) but rather represent conclusions one has reached by applying one's cognitive skills to social and political experiences.

Authoritarianism: A Manifestation of Social Reasoning

Intellectual or cognitive levels represent different kinds of reasoning about all the phenomena of everyday life, including moral, social, and political issues. Cognitive level, measured by Piagetian tasks, is closely tied to whatever is sampled by the individual IQ test (Keating & Bobbitt, 1978; Neimark, 1975; Tuddenham, 1970). Cognitive level is also closely related to level of moral judgment (Hoffman, 1970; Rest, 1974, 1976; Turiel, 1974) and authoritarianism. We propose, with Piaget and many other cognitive theorists, that common intellectual processes underlie the sample of school-related skills found on IQ tests, the cognitive tasks favored by Piagetians, and the social judgments studied by others, in and out of the Piagetian tradition (Keating, 1978).

Students of moral reasoning—notably Kohlberg (1969), Rest (1974), Hogan (1973), Hoffman (1970), and Turiel (1975)—and of other types of social cognition (Adelson, 1975; Selman & Damon, 1975; Turiel, 1975) argue that people construct their social realities. Judgments about moral, social, and political issues grow out of an *interaction* of person and environment—not from one or the other; therefore, moral judgments and authoritarian conclusions are not swallowed whole, nor do they emerge from the developing person. Turiel (1974) writes:

> Moral thought is not to be located in social objects nor in the subject. Our evidence indicates that there are stages of moral development and that children universally develop through these stages; saying that there are stages of moral development implies that morality is knowledge. It is knowledge, not in the sense of empirical facts, but in the sense of principles that are understood and applied [pp. 7–8].

In this view, cognitive level determines the "sophistication" a person can bring to the formation of certain social and political attitudes. Adelson (1975) confirmed this view in his work on the development of political reasoning, and Himmelweit and Swift (1971) supported it for authoritarianism.

We propose that the F-Scale is a sample of more and less "sophisticated"— in this sense, cognitively complex—judgments about social and political issues. The items are samples of *conclusions* that people have accepted or rejected about their social realities and ideals. Therefore, it is not surprising that the F scale should be found to correlate with measures of cognitive and intellectual functioning, sampled broadly by IQ tests. (IQ tests do often contain items tapping everyday, commonsense judgments about the social world, precisely for the reason that these applications of reasoning are part of the intellectual domain.)

Additional evidence on the constructive nature of moral judgments comes from attempts to enhance them. Rest (1974) and Turiel (1974) reported that people comprehend moral reasoning at their own level and at those below but that they neither comprehend, nor are able to adopt, levels of reasoning more "sophisticated" than their own. Less "sophisticated" adolescents and young adults, and presumably older adults, construct less universalistic ideals and realities; they have more rigid regard for established authority and therefore are more authoritarian, as defined by the F-Scale.

The Transmission of Authoritarianism as Intellectual Level

Our data clearly show that children do not model their parents' authoritarian attitudes or "trait." Adopted children scarcely resembled their adopted parents in F-Scale scores, and whatever small similarity there was could be entirely explained by their resemblance in verbal skills. In biological families, on the other hand, parent–child and sibling resemblance was strong and largely explainable by the intellectual similarity among these genetic relatives.

A model (Model 3) proposing that authoritarianism shares a common path with verbal skills in the transmission from parent to child succeeded in explaining a large portion of the resemblance in biological families and all of the similarity in adoptive families. Differences in intellectual skills, as measured by the IQ test and other cognitive measures, are far more closely related to genetic than to environmental differences in these samples of working- to upper-middle-class families (Carter-Saltzman, 1976; Scarr, 1977; Scarr & Weinberg, 1978). Because the F-Scale seems to be primarily a part of the intellectual domain, it is not surprising that the transmission of difference in these social and political "attitudes" should also have a strong genetic basis.

The Transmission of Authoritarianism as Personality

In the biological families, there was evidence of a small but significant path for the nonintellective transmission of authoritarianism, as measured by the F-Scale. Because this nonintellective transmission occurred only in the biological families, we concluded that some genetic differences in personality are the most likely explanation. We found small but significant correlations between social anxiety, social impotence, and authoritarianism. None of these personality scales were related to IQ. It seems likely that some dimension of fearfulness in social situations could explain the remaining resemblance among biological relatives, but we did not measure it sufficiently well to account for the remaining similarity in the genetic relatives. Or it may be that the paranoia sampled by several of the F-Scale items—for which there was significantly greater biological- than adoptive-family resemblance—constitutes an additional source of genetic variance. In general, however, our personality measures did not show sufficiently strong evidence for genetic or environmental explanations to tempt us to further speculations.

A Reinterpretation of Authoritarianism

Although people are not born with social and political attitudes, they seem to come equipped with an intellectual genotype that—in concert with their rearing environment—determines that they will interpret their social experiences in more or less sophisticated ways. None of our adolescents were reared in deprived or abusive environments. Nor do we have anything to say about the social realities of the *lower-class* life. It does appear, however, that being reared in a working-class family does not lead one to more authoritarian attitudes on an environmental basis. The parents and children of the biological families (and the adoptive parents) repeated the often-reported pattern of lower SES–lower educational level–lower IQ—and—higher authoritarianism. Although this correlational pattern has usually been explained by the powerlessness and poorer circumstance of the working class, our results require another explanation. Social-class differences among the adoptive families did not create any such differences among their children. Despite the obvious differences among the adoptive parents in intelligence, education, occupational status, and income, the adolescents and young adults of these families are not more or less authoritarian in relation to their social-class background or the intellectual characteristics of their adoptive parents. It must be that in the biological families, the transmission of authoritarian attitudes is largely a part of the more general, shared pattern of intellectual skills—transmitted more surely by their common genes than by their common environments.

ACKNOWLEDGMENTS

The research was supported by the W. T. Grant Foundation and NICHHD (HD-08016), the Center for Advanced Study in the Behavioral Sciences, the Spencer Foundation, the Graduate School of the University of Minnesota, and the National Institute of Mental Health.

REFERENCES

Adelson, J. The development of ideology in adolescence. In S. E. Dragastin & G. H. Elder, Jr. (Eds.), *Adolescence in the life cycle: Psychological change and social context.* New York: Wiley, 1975.

Adorno, T. W., Frenkel-Brunswik, E., Levinson, D. J., & Sanford, R. N. *The authoritarian personality.* New York: Harper, 1950.

Badgett, J. L., Fair, S., & Hunkler, R. F. The authoritarianism exhibited by intelligent men and women. *Journal of College Student Personnel,* 1974, *15,* 509–512.

Berkowitz, N. H., & Wolkon, G. H. A forced choice form of the F-Scale—free of acquiescent response set. *Sociometry,* 1964, *27,* 54–63.

Byrne, D. *An introduction to personality: A research approach.* Englewood Cliffs, N.J.: Prentice-Hall, 1966.

Carter-Saltzman, S. L. *The structure and transmission of individual differences in patterns of cognitive ability.* Unpublished doctoral dissertation, University of Minnesota, 1976.

Christie, R. Authoritarianism re-examined. In R. Christie & M. Jahoda (Eds.), *Studies in the scope and method of "the authoritarian personality."* Glencoe, Ill.: Free Press, 1954.

Doppelt, J. E. Estimating the full scale score on the Wechsler Adult Intelligence Scale from scores on four subtests. *Journal of Consulting Psychology,* 1956, *20,* 63–66.

Grotevant, H. D. *The development of interests: Studies of construct validity, profile differentiation, and family influence.* Unpublished doctoral dissertation, University of Minnesota, 1977.

Himmelweit, H. T., & Swift, B. Adolescent and adult authoritarianism re-examined: Its organization and stability over time. *European Journal of Social Psychology,* 1971, *1*(3), 357–384.

Hoffman, M. L. Moral development. In P. Mussen (Ed.), *Handbook of child psychology.* New York: Wiley, 1970.

Hogan, R.. Moral conduct and moral character: A psychological perspective. *Psychological Bulletin*, 1973, *79*, 217–232.

Kayser, B. D. Authoritarianism, self-esteem, emotionality, and intelligence. *Perceptual and Motor Skills*, 1972, *34*, 367–370.

Keating, D. B. A search for social intelligence. *Journal of Educational Psychology*, 1978, *70* (2), 218–223.

Keating, D. P. A search for social intelligence. *Journal of Educational Psychology*, 1978, *70*, 218–223.

Keating, D. P., & Bobbitt, Individual and developmental differences in cognitive processing components of mental ability. *Child Development*, 1978, *49*, 155–167.

Kelman, H. C., & Barclay, J. The F-scale as a measure of breadth of perspective. *Journal of abnormal and Social Psychology*, 1963, *67*(6), 608–615.

Kohlberg, L. Stage and sequence: The cognitive-developmental approach to socialization. In D. Goslin (Ed.), *Handbook of socialization theory and research*. Chicago: Rand McNally, 1969.

Lykken, D. T., Tellegen, A., & Katzenmeyer, C. *Manual for the Activity Preference Questionnaire (APQ)* (Report No. PR-72-4). Minneapolis: University of Minnesota, Reports from the Research Laboratories of the Department of Psychiatry, October 1973.

Neimark, E. D. Intellectual development during adolescence. In F. D. Horowitz (Ed.), *Review of child development research* (Vol. 4). Chicago: University of Chicago Press, 1975.

Raven, J. C. *Standard progressive matrices: Sets A, B, C, D, and E*. London: H. K. Lewis, 1958.

Reiss, A. J., Jr. *Occupations and social status*. New York: Free Press, 1961.

Rest, J. R. The cognitive-developmental approach to morality: The state of the art. *Counseling and Values*, 1974, *18*(2), 64–78.

Rest, J. R. *Moral judgment related to sample characteristics*. Final report to the National Institute of Mental Health, August 1976.

Scarr, S. How to reduce authoritarianism among teachers: The human development approach. *Journal of Educational Research*, 1970, *63*(8), 367–372.

Scarr, S. *Genetic effects on human behavior: Recent family studies*. A Master Lecture, delivered at the annual meeting of the American Psychological Association, San Francisco, August 26, 1977.

Scarr, S., & Weinberg, R. A. The influence of "family background" on intellectual attainment: The unique contribution of adoptive studies to estimating environmental effects. *American Sociological Review*, in press.

Selman, R., & Damon, W. The necessity (but insufficiency) of social perspective taking for conceptions of justice at three early levels. In D. J. DePalma & J. M. Foley (Eds.), *Moral development: Current theory and research*. Hillsdale, N.J.: Lawrence Erlbaum Associates, 1975.

Tellegen, A. *The Differential Personality Questionnaire, Form 9, DPQ*. Unpublished manuscript, University of Minnesota, 1974.

Thompson, R. C., & Michel, J. B. Measuring authoritarianism: A comparison of the F and D scales. *Journal of Personality*, 1972, *40*(2), 180–190.

Trachtman, J. P. Cognitive and motivational variables as predictors of academic performance among disadvantaged college students. *Journal of Counseling Psychology*, 1975, *22*(4), 324–328.

Tuddenham, R. D. A "Piagetian" test of cognitive development. In B. Dockrell (Ed.), *On intelligence*. Toronto: Ontario Institute for Studies in Education, 1970.

Turiel, E. *Cognitive theory of developmental stages*. Unpublished manuscript, Harvard University, 1974.

Turiel, E. The development of social concepts: Mores, customs, and conventions. In D. J. DePalma & J. M. Foley (Eds.), *Moral development: Current theory and research*. Hillsdale, N.J.: Lawrence Erlbaum Associates, 1975.

Webber, P. L. *The research utility of broad and component measures of introversion–extraversion*. Unpublished doctoral dissertation, University of Minnesota, 1976.

Wechsler, D. *Wechsler Adult Intelligence Scales*. New York: Psychological Corporation, 1955.

IV CONCLUSIONS AND IMPLICATIONS

IV.1

Testing Minority Children: Why, How, and with What Effects?*

To speak to issues of why, or why not, to test and how, one must examine briefly the nature of the overt and covert arguments on both sides. Unfortunately, "discussions" of the pros and cons of testing minority children are most often conducted in a Tower of Babel, where different languages and assumptions prevent productive discourse. Overtly, the opponents of the use of standard psychological and educational tests with minority children object primarily to the negative social outcomes of testing, for which they blame biases in the tests and testing procedures. Proponents of the use of standard tests defend the equal predictive validity of the measures for all groups. Some opponents of tests propose their elimination; others hope for culturally relative measures that will eliminate average group differences. Test supporters caution about the subjective and potentially more biased nature of other assessments and the lack of predictive use for ethnically adjusted scores. As Messick and Anderson have noted, the complaints of the testing opponents are not answered by the proponents; their respective arguments fly by like shells in the din of battle.

Covertly, two unjustified suspicions inflame the conflict about testing minority children: (1) that tests measure fixed, innate abilities, and (2) that minority children have less of this gene-given ability than majority children. I will, therefore, review briefly my own research to show that both fears are unfounded. Tests sample what has been learned, especially in relation to what is required by

*This chapter by Sandra Scarr originally appeared in R. M. Bossone (Ed.), *Proceedings of the National Conference on Testing: Major Issues*. New York: Center for Advanced Study in Education, 1978. Reprinted by permission.

current school programs; and as my research shows, there is no evidence in the mean test-score differences of genetic differences among ethnic groups.

If these two unfounded suspicions are allayed, I hope that a more rational look at the nature of standard tests can lead to their constructive use, and to the elimination of misuses that seem so common in current practice.

The Social and Philosophical Context of Testing

Testing on a broad scale was adopted by the schools to improve the opportunities of lower-SES and minority children for selection into educationally—and occupationally—advantaged positions and to reduce the pervasive class and ethnic biases of personal judgments. The incorporation of standard tests into the schools was an example of the American ethic of equality of opportunity. But one has to be very careful about the meaning of "equal opportunity"; it is a slippery term. The use of standard tests to give all children the same chance to compete is a case of equal opportunity construed as *identical treatment* for all, regardless of their initial differences in preparation.

It has always been clear, of course, that minority children were not equally prepared to compete, whether they were the Irish of the 1900s, the Southern and Eastern Europeans of the 1910s and '20s, or the blacks and Spanish-speaking groups of the mid-century. We should not ignore the upward mobility that has resulted for some minority children through test scores and educational opportunities, but the overwhelming fact is that minority children have, as a group, always scored lower on tests and performed more poorly in schools before the economic assimilation of their groups into American life (Sowell, 1977).

The use of standard ability and achievement tests in schools was primarily motivated by liberal views of equal opportunity as *identical treatment*. There are at least two other ways to construe the ethic of equality: Equality of opportunity can also mean "different strokes for different folks," a view that recognizes the advantages and disadvantages that individuals bring to the competition; and equality of opportunity can be stretched to mean the assurance of *equal outcomes,* the selection of equal proportions of all groups (however defined) into good and bad outcomes. For the use of standard tests, the second view of equal opportunity means different investments in and preparations for the eventual competition to meet the same standards. The third view implies different standards to insure equal outcomes.

I introduce the different meanings of the ethic of equal opportunity because current arguments about the use of standard tests revolve around these underlying differences in the philosophical meanings of the term. Opponents of the use of standard tests with minority children object primarily to the negative social outcomes in the differential selection of minority and majority children into socially desirable and undesirable life tracks. They argue that the abolition of tests and the adoption of ethnic quotas will improve equal opportunity construed as equal outcomes (meaning #3). Proponents of the use of standard tests base their support on the equal predictive validity of the measures for all groups, thereby interpreting equal opportunity as identical treatment (#1). Some middle ground of meaning is occupied by those who support "different strokes for different folks" to mean that truly equal opportunity for all requires more instructional and social investment in some who begin the competition with fewer chances of success. Eventually, however, all individuals must be held to the same standard of competitive achievement (#2).

Recognizing the different meanings of equal opportunity for the various opponents and proponents of standard tests does not resolve the problem, but it puts everyone on notice that they had better be prepared to defend their meaning of equality on a broader social scale than mere psychological testing. The use of standard tests in the schools cannot be attacked or defended without a correlated justification for one's view of social equity in all spheres of educational and economic life.

My own position is unequivocally in favor of "different strokes for different folks," by which I mean that individual differences must be taken into account in our investment in and training for all spheres of educational and economic life. Some individuals need more investment of time and resources to reach some Rawlsian lowest-acceptable-level of competence. We, as a society, must guarantee that investment. In addition, differences in life chances—be they socioeconomic disadvantage, cultural difference, or genetic endowment—should be compensated to assure that every individual has the most equal possible chance to achieve; This tenet of my value system calls directly for matching instruction to individual differences, whatever the person's group membership. The measures of achievement, however, are universally applied.

This brief statement of personal principles is included to alert you to the assumptions of the paper.

Why Should We Test Minority Children?

In my view, answers to questions of why and how to test minority children are predicated on the assumption that *testing should inform instruction*. The proper use of tests is to provide diagnostic information to teachers that alters instruction and improves the match of instruction to the child. On a broader scale, testing can inform the recruitment of children into educationally appropriate programs and settings that fit their current needs. Testing need not be used as an accomplice to biased selection procedures, but neither will children benefit from the denial that their school-related skills and instructional needs differ on the average by ethnic group. There are humane reasons to use tests appropriately *in the interests of the child,* whatever his ethnicity.

Covert Suspicion: Tests as Measures of Innate Intelligence

What we test as "intelligence" is based on the summation of an individual's learning experiences which prepare him to tackle new problems. All tests of intelligence presuppose past learning. Some items simply call for past learning; others require the use of past learning to solve a new problem. There is no intelligence without experience!

To use past learning as a basis for new problem solving does not imply that all individuals of the same chronological age have learned or are capable of learning the same quantity or quality of material at the same rate (genetic and biological differences exist in intelligence), but it does imply that what is tested as intelligence is not some magical "innate capacity" that is unaffected by experience. Without learning opportunities, we would all be equally stupid and ignorant. With equal learning opportunities, individuals vary enormously in what they have learned and in what skills they bring to the solution of new problems.

The Assumptions of IQ Testing

Alfred Binet was well aware that his practical device rested on several critical assumptions—assumptions that have too often been forgotten by those who followed him. The two most important assumptions are: (1) common experiences for those being compared on the test; (2) the test as a sample of intelligent behavior.

Common Experiences.   Today we recognize a profound problem in the use of intelligence tests with culturally different populations. The information sampled on IQ tests is general cultural knowledge. But whose culture—white, urban, middle-class culture? The skills sampled are those most likely to be taught by middle-class parents.

The Test as a Sample of Intelligent Behavior.   Many IQ test items seem arbitrary and ridiculous. Why should tracing a maze, arranging a sequence of pictures, knowing the capital of Greece, and defining the word "ballast" be used to measure intelligence? Tests are *samples* of information and skills, not complete inventories. The sampling rationale is that an individual who knows the capital of Greece is also more likely to have other kinds of rare information; a person who can repeat six digits backwards can also manipulate other information in his head, and a person who can abstract similarities between farming and manufacturing also knows how to think abstractly about other problems.

An obvious problem for minority children is the content of the test. Items are written by educated, urban, middle-class psychologists and educators to predict middle-class standards in schools and jobs. While the tests may predict well, they may not be fair samples of intelligence. At this point, we must define what we mean by "intelligence." An alternative definition is adaptability in "real-life" (not school or job) situations, such as neighborhood and family settings. Although sufficient space does not exist here to do justice to the issue of test validity, no one to date has devised a satisfactory substitute test of intelligence based on alternative criteria.

Part of the problem is the lack of agreement on what behaviors one would call intelligent in family and neighborhood settings. Is getting any job in a Black ghetto a good criterion? How about knowing how to milk a herd of cows in 30 minutes or finding your way home over ten miles of woods in West Virginia? The majority culture is not primarily interested in these feats of adaptation; we do not reward them with notable success or acclaim, but few would deny that they require "intelligence," broadly conceived.

To appreciate the difficulty in finding agreeable, alternative criteria, we have to recall the history of IQ tests; they were designed to select children who would not profit from the usual school curriculum, at a time when all children had to be served by the school system. Intelligence, as measured by IQ tests, is primarily *school-learning* ability, not general adaptation to life.

How Should We Test Minority Children?

Given that tests are samples of learned information and skills and that they predict well school performance for all groups, I will argue for a reeducation of school personnel and the public on the meaning of test scores, the elimination of any lingering suspicion about genetic racial differences in IQ, and the abandonment of culturally relative assessment in favor of culturally specific assessment.

To understand why minority children, on the average, score lower on all forms of standard tests—achievement, aptitude, and IQ varieties—school personnel must be educated to see that test scores only measure past learning of information and skills that are sampled by the tests and the schools, not as more global measures of intellectual functioning for minority children. And they must come to see that children's performance can change, particularly on those achievement measures most closely tied to instructional programs. It is not enough for academic psychologists and test writers to proclaim the correct interpretation of a test score as a *current* assessment of what a child has *learned* in relation to his peers or some criterion performance.

For a minority child, this means that unless his knowledge or skills get a big environmental boost, his low scores in first grade will predict his low scores in fourth grade. Since he has the same sociocultural environment, that is hardly surprising. But suppose the schools came up with a Big Boost program for the early grades. Presumably, both his school performance and his standard test scores would change upward.

Teachers and school psychologists must be educated to understand that a test score is not written in the child's brain. More importantly, they must understand that low scores are indicators for action—instructional action to fit the educational needs of the child. They are not excuses for labeling and discard.

THE "GOOD GUYS": DIAGNOSTIC AND CRITERION-REFERENCED TESTS

One does not have to extol the virtues of diagnostic and criterion-referenced tests. Nearly everyone in education is (or should be) in favor of diagnostic tests that inform teachers of the individual child's particular strengths and weaknesses in skill development, often without comparing him to any other children. Suzy has a 60-word sight vocabulary but needs help in word-attack skills. Jimmy's phonics are okay, but his reading speed could probably be improved by instruction in phrasing and reading for meaning. Johnny understands the concepts of addition and subtraction but needs help on the concepts of multiplication and division. Surely, we would all agree that this information is useful to *immediate* instruction. The lack of a normative basis for the instructional decisions about what to teach next to an individual child is no hindrance.

One clear advantage of criterion-referenced tests is that they require teachers to *specify the objectives* of instruction and to use the test items to judge whether or not the child has achieved a specific objective. Does Suzy understand and can she use the concepts "across" and "through"? Can Bill add two-digit numbers with carrying? If the child has not yet achieved that skill, the teacher is informed by the test to improve or increase her instruction of that skill.

One difficulty with such specificity is that not every criterion of an education can be so specified. For many reasons, test items must *sample* what a child knows and can do, not attempt an exhaustive inventory. Three problems that I will briefly mention are the *expanding universe* of knowledge and skills with development, the *substitution of thresholds* for quantification, and the dilemma of *incomparable measurements*.

In the early grades, the skills required for basic literacy can be relatively well specified, compared to those broader qualities of thinking and knowledge at later periods of development. To my knowledge, no one has tried to analyze all of the tasks involved in the interpretation of poetry or the development of a critical point of view about complex historical or social issues. Although there is still much excitement in psychology about the possibilities of specifying and organizing the learning steps in higher-level skills and knowledge, the only partially successful programming models are for young children's thinking and simple mental processes, neither of which describe or prescribe the instruction of literary or historical thought. Of course, you may object, computers can be programmed to play rather good chess, but that too is a limited domain with a finite number of possible moves, unlike most of the higher-level skills I am citing. I think it is safe to say that the prescription of instructional objectives is far more feasible for second than tenth graders, unless one is still prescribing the same primary-level objectives!

This brings me to the substitution of thresholds for quantification of the differences in skills and knowledge that children have learned. It is important to specify *minimal* criteria for achievements that nearly every child can and should attain. But this minimal threshold of literacy is no substitute for quantifying the remaining range of individual differences in achievements and designing appropriate instruction for *all* children, even those whose skills and knowledge far exceed the average of their age group. Criterion-referenced tests are simply not appropriate for this measurement problem, particularly at the older grade levels.

The final problem that I want to mention briefly is the incomparability of criterion measures from one setting to another. If we are serious about setting instructional objectives and using criterion-referenced tests to judge our effectiveness in helping children to reach those objectives, then the test items must be very closely tied to the curriculum. Because different schools teach different materials, in different orders, once a child is past the first few grades, how can tests be comparable from one school district, or building, to another? If South High in Oshkosh spends the fall semester of the eleventh grade on the poetry of e. e. cummings, a reasonable set of criterion items would test the student's comprehension, interpretation, and appreciation of that poetry. But Wilson High in Madison used the essays of Martin Luther King in their eleventh-grade curriculum; the criterion items for those students will necessarily be different. I think you can see the myriad problems that arise from such diverse criteria of achievement.

The approach of many norm-referenced tests is to sample the skills and knowledge that are usually imparted in the eleventh grade. Give the student a new passage (an attempt to provide equal environmental exposure or lack of same); test his comprehension, interpretation, and appreciation of "literature." There will be some poetry samples, on which the Wilson High students will have less experience, and some prose, for which the South High youngsters will have had less exposure. Although none of the students will probably have encountered the particular test samples before, the items will assess the students' approach to literature in a gross and global way that estimates how well individual students and groups can deal with new material of the kinds they have had some exposure to in the school curriculum. The hypothetical test will be more helpful to teachers if it reports separate scores for poetry and prose, for reading comprehension, vocabulary, and the like, than if it reports a general "literature" score.

Now it probably occurred to you that this same norm-referenced test could be used as a criterion-referenced one, by the simple expedient of reporting the item results to the teachers. The eleventh-grade English teachers at South High and Wilson High would receive profiles of performance for their students, presumably with differential achievements in the poetry and prose sections according to the curricular emphasis. In addition to receiving the norms of the individual students and the class, the teacher should be able to see whether his/her instruction affected the profile of performance and to see in which areas the students need further work.

For the purposes of immediate instruction, the teacher has no need for the norms at all. In fact, given the ways that too many teachers interpret norms, their absence is probably better. But in most ways, a criterion-referenced test is merely an unstandardized one; anything a criterion-referenced test can do could be done just as well if it were standardized. Conversely, the use of standardized test items as criteria of learning transforms it into a criterion-referenced test without changing an item.

It is all very well to eliminate norm groups for tests that diagnose next instructional steps and measure instructional objectives in the immediate teaching situation. But it is much less appropriate to eliminate norms for other kinds of assessment. Not all instructional decisions are or can be immediately applied to classroom strategies with children. Some instructional decisions involve planning months or years ahead, making educated guesses about the suitability of the program for the child. Of course, these decisions are less valid and reliable than those made for the immediate situation if the tests are equally well constructed (which of course they usually are not). But advice must be given about planning the child's curriculum for junior high or high school, planning for algebra, business math, Latin, or remedial English. Standard achievement tests are, in my knowledge, the best advice givers on these and similar matters, along with school grades and teachers' experiences with the child.

For an even more temporally remote kind of decision, selection for higher education is, I believe, most efficiently done with a combination of standard aptitude tests, school grades, and recommendations. The role of test scores in this process has been challenged, but I think that a dispassionate look at the data would convince most people that global samples of school-related knowledge and general intellectual functioning in school-related skills provide the best prediction of who should be where in postsecondary education. Note that I am not making judgments about non-school-related intelligence, just about who will be more likely to succeed in given instructional programs.

THE "BAD GUYS": EVEN GLOBAL ASSESSMENTS HAVE THEIR USES IN THE INTERESTS OF CHILDREN

Most criticism of testing has been leveled at the standard, group aptitude and individual IQ tests. The use of a single score or a few subtest scores to make life decisions for a child has been rejected by those who note that average group differences in test scores classify more minority children as retarded. Low test scores alone have been used to place them in special classes. Clearly, this is poor practice.

Let us consider possible legitimate uses of such tests. First, minority children who score well on standard tests are the forgotten 25 to 30%, whose above-average to high scores are tickets to educational advancement, particularly in these days of affirmative action. In every school building in Philadelphia there are black children scoring in the 99th percentile on standard aptitude tests (and achievement tests as well). For some of these children, whose reading and math skills are not well developed, their high aptitude scores will alert teachers and counselors to their instructional needs and potential selection into higher education.

A simple classification of children by above- and below-average aptitude and achievement tests will quickly show that the aptitude tests give additional information. There are sizeable numbers of children with specific learning disabilities whose reading and math scores are low but whose aptitude scores reveal general abilities to do well in scholastic skills, once the specific problems are remedied. These children can be said to be "saved" by the aptitude tests from being put into inappropriate, generally slower groups.

What about those who score low on both aptitude and achievement tests? This is the source of the angriest attacks on standard tests because many schools lump these heterogeneous children into a single slow or retarded group. Undoubtedly, many of the minority children in the low-scoring group should not be considered generally mentally retarded or even slow learners at nonschool tasks. No matter what the causes of their slow school learning, it is not useful to label them as mentally retarded because they will not be so considered when they leave school. The probable cause of their slow school learning is cultural difference and inappropriate instruction. This does not mean, however, that they will thrive in a regular classroom with 28 other children, many of whom were reared in the majority culture.

Their low scores on standard tests should be only the first clue that their varied performances should be further evaluated to obtain a more complete picture of what they *can do*, not what they cannot do on standard tests. But note that the tests are the first clue that something is amiss with the match of the school program to the child with low aptitude and achievement scores. Perhaps he cannot read well enough to take any of the tests, including math instructions. Perhaps he is in need of individual encouragement to try harder. Perhaps teachers have misunderstood his quietness or outbursts and turned him off entirely. Perhaps an auditory mode of instruction is better suited to his learning needs.

In other words, the only use of low standard test scores should be to alert school personnel to the need for further individual study of the child. They should not be used alone to make any decisions about special classes or even special instruction.

What Would We Do Without Tests?

There are two major suggestions for a world without standard tests. First, we could return to the turn of the century and teacher ratings. Second, we could try everyone at everything they wanted to try and eliminate those who fail at the criterion performance. The first, I will argue, is even more prejudicial than tests, less reliable, and likely to lead to some wretched wrangling over minority quotas, in perpetuity. Subjective judgments are no replacement for objective assessments, although teachers often have valuable, additional, qualitative information about a student's work habits, interests, personality, and the like. Recommendations should not supplant performance on a standard test.

The second, doing away with prediction and diagnosis and trying the criterion, may work reasonably well in immediate learning situations, but it is unlikely to be useful in selection of a few students from many applicants for higher education or desirable jobs. Those of you at CUNY know the experience of open admissions far better than I, but I have not heard of any great success stories emanating from the experiment. One likely outcome is that the exit criteria are simply adjusted downward to permit graduation for the majority who no longer can meet the old standards of excellence. When we insisted that everyone stay in high school to graduate, we found that a high school diploma now guaranteed only reasonably frequent attendance, not any minimum standard of achievement in reading, math, or cultural knowledge. Now, nationwide, the schools are rapidly returning to criteria of competency for the high school diploma, according to the *New York Times*. Can you guess which groups of children will suffer the highest failure rates?

Somehow, none of this is the answer for the instructional needs of minority children. To deny that we have a problem in educating minority children to the knowledge and skills of the majority culture is to hide one's head in the proverbial sand; to pretend that doing away with the tests will fix the ethnic disproportions in the various school curricula is to whistle Dixie in Harlem.

Covert Suspicion: Genetic Racial Differences in IQ

Research by genetically oriented psychologists, including myself, has shown repeatedly that individual differences in test scores are caused in part by genetic individual differences. Does this fact have anything to do with the average test-score differences among racial groups?

Three recent investigations on the possible genetic origins of racial differences in performance in school and on IQ tests reject the hypothesis of genetic differences as a major source of those differences in performance. The study of 130 transracially adopted black children (Scarr & Weinberg, 1976) showed that black and interracial children reared by socioeconomically advantaged white families score very well on standard IQ tests and on school achievement tests. Being reared in the culture of the test resulted in intellectual achievement levels for black children that were comparable to adopted white children in similar families. Therefore, it is highly unlikely that genetic differences between the races could account for the major portion of the usually observed differences in the performance levels of the two groups.

A second study on the relation of black ancestry to intellectual skills within the black population (Scarr, Pakstis, Katz, & Barker, 1977) showed that having more or less African ancestry was not related to how well one scored on cognitive tests. In other words, holding constant social identity and cultural background, socially classified blacks with greater amounts of white ancestry did not score better than other blacks with more African ancestry. A strong genetic-difference hypothesis cannot account for this result.

The third study was of black and white twins in Philadelphia. Briefly, the black 10- to 16-year-olds scored half to one standard deviation below the whites on every cognitive measure. The social-class differences between the races were not sufficiently large, as Jensen has reminded us, to account solely for the magnitude of this performance difference between the racial groups. The major hypothesis was that black children have less overall familiarity with the information and the skills being sampled by the tests and the schools. By using twins in this study, we were able to examine three implications of cultural differences compared to a genetic-differences hypothesis.

We believe that the pattern of results supports a general cultural-difference hypothesis far better than a genetic-differences view. The major intellectual results are:

1. Black children have lower scores on all of the cognitive tests, but they score relatively worse on the more culturally loaded of the conceptual tests.
2. The cognitive differences among the black children are less well explained by genetic individual differences, by age, and by social-class differences than those of the white children.
3. The similarity of the black co-twins, particularly the DZs, suggests that being reared in different families determines more of the cognitive differences among black than white children, but that those between-family differences are not those usually measured by SES variables in the white community.

Therefore, we conclude that the results of this study support the view that black children are being reared in circumstances that give them only marginal acquaintance with the skills and the knowledge being sampled by the tests we administer. Some families in the black community encourage the development of these skills and knowledge, while others do not. In general, black children do not have the same access to these skills and knowledge as white children, which explains the lower performance of black children as a group. The hypothesis that most of the differences among the cognitive scores of black and white children are due to genetic differences between the races cannot, in our view, account for this pattern of results. Therefore, in three studies the hypothesis of genetic differences between the races fails to account for the IQ performance differences.

Culturally Relative Assessment

Thus, we know that the major causes of the lower scores of black children reared in the black community are cultural differences and socioeconomic disadvantage. The mean scores of minority children are lower than they would be if they had equal access to the majority culture.

But that does not mean that the performance of minority children on other types of school tests or school grades will be less well predicted. Nor does it mean that adding points to their test scores will fix their later achievement difficulties. As many others have noted, the attacks on testing will not improve the match between instruction and the child.

What then about minority youths who on the average do not score as high on standard aptitude tests or in school grades; should they be given compensatory scores, padded to take into account their cultural differences? It may be cosmetic, but it does not answer the challenge of matching instruction to the educational needs of the minority youth. Their lower scores *do* predict lower postsecondary school performance, and fudging them upward will not in itself help anyone to provide more appropriate teaching or program selection. It may well be true that outside of school, the minority youths with low scores can do better than majority youths with similarly low scores because the lower scores of the minority youths result in large part from their culturally different rearing. But that fact will not help them in scholastic settings where the standards are majority norms. If you adjust standard test scores according to the home background of the child, you fall into the trap of defining tests scores as measures of intelligence in the most offensive way; in other words, you have bought the *misuse* of IQ tests.

Culturally Specific Assessments

There are good reasons, on the other hand, to develop *culturally specific,* not culturally relative, assessment procedures. To assess the strengths of a minority child in terms of functioning within his own community can be useful in predicting his adaptation *to that community.* By culturally specific assessments, I mean those measures that discriminate the more from the less skillful in the terms of the minority community. It is doubtful, however, that such culturally specific assessments will improve the prediction made by standardized tests to adaptation in the majority community, because as the predictors vary, so do the criteria. But culturally specific assessments can remind the schools and others that the current IQ and aptitude tests are better predictors of school than life performance and are probably more closely tied to life in the majority than minority communities.

The more compelling reason I see for the development of culturally specific assessments is to better understand the bases of achievement in minority communities, the differences in expectations between minority and majority cultures, and to use that information to help children bridge the gulf between community and school. At present, we really do not understand the variety of skills that minority children bring to school that may be equivalent to, but different from, those of the majority group, whose skills the school capitalizes upon. Something called "social competence" may capture what I mean here, but it is poorly defined at present and not well measured in any community. Whatever we call this culturally specific set of skills, it is a fairly safe bet that the skills developed in the majority community are more fully sampled by the current school programs than any culturally specific set of competencies from minority communities. Knowing what their differences are will help educators to capitalize more fully on what minority children *can* do, rather than always approaching their instruction as deficient members of the majority culture.

Toward an Informed Instruction

The norm of a year's progress for a year spent in school is often not met by minority children, and when it is, they are still behind because they came to school in kindergarten well behind their majority peers in the skills that schools expect. There is no evidence that minority children fall farther behind the majority group through the school years, once one takes into account the larger individual variation in school performance later in the school career. That is, second graders cannot be 4 years behind in reading skills, whereas eighth graders can, and often are. Once these individual variations are scaled in standard deviation units, the gap between minority and majority children is the same from kindergarten to twelfth grade. Thus, the schools do not aggravate the performance gap, but neither do they narrow it. Perhaps one ought to ask what kind of special programs could be applied to narrow the academic gap, so well predicted by the early tests and so well recognized by kindergarten and first-grade teachers.

A different kind of special instruction is required, one that is not equally applied to all children by race and color, but one that is applied to those children who need it. Equal opportunity need not be construed as equal treatment for all, because if it is, it ignores the large individual differences in learning rates and does nothing to remedy the performance gaps between groups. If we want to give more minority children an equal opportunity, we will have to give them more time and instruction in the school skills that will make them literate citizens in the majority culture.

Perhaps more minority children do need special instruction than children whose home cultural environment shares more features with the school culture. Perhaps there ought to be a new category of special instruction. Call it what you like—majority cultural instruction, the culturally different hour, whatever. The problem with the instruction of minority children in the current schools lies not with the teachers, who as a group are usually dedicated, hard-working adults; nor with standard tests that evaluate children according to their *performance* levels, regardless of why they perform that way; nor with the children, whose task it is to comprehend and learn what the schools have to offer. The problem is with the mismatch of instructional norms and strategies to many minority children and our ignorance about the skills they do have.

AUTHOR'S NOTE

The controversial nature of this paper does not lend itself to traditional citations of the literature. I am especially indebted to the following articles, whose authors, however, do not necessarily share my views:

Bennett, V. D. C. Intelligence Testing. *Clinical Child Psychology Newsletter*, 1970, *9*(3), p. 8.

Gordon, E. W. Human Diversity, Program Evaluation and Pupil Assessment. *IRCD Bulletin*, 1977, *12*(1), pp. 1–7.

Gordon, R. A. Examining Labelling Theory: The Case of Mental Retardation. In Walter R. Gove (Ed.), *The Labelling of Deviance: Evaluating a Perspective*. New York: Wiley Press, 1976.

Messick, S., & Anderson, S. Educational Testing, Individual Development, and Social Responsibility. *Counseling Psychologist*, 1970, *2*(2), pp. 80–88.

Milgram, N. A. Danger: Chauvinism, Scapegoatism, and Euphemism. *Clinical Child Psychology Newsletter*, 1970, *9*(3), pp. 2–3.

Newland, T. E. Testing Minority Group Children. *Clinical Child Psychology Newsletter*, 1970, *9*(3), p. 5.

Samuda, R. J. *Psychological Testing of American Minorities: Issues and Consequences*. New York: Dodd, Mead and Company, 1975.

Wikoff, R. L. Danger: Attacks on Tests Unfair. *Clinical Child Psychology Newsletter*, 1970, *9*(3), p. 4.

Williams, R. L. Danger: Testing and Dehumanizing Black Children. *Clinical Child Psychology Newsletter*, 1970, *9*(1), pp. 5–6.

Williams, R. L. From Dehumanization to Black Intellectual Genocide: A Rejoinder. *Clinical Child Psychology Newsletter*, 1970, *9*(3), pp. 6–7.

BIBLIOGRAPHY

Anastasi, A. (Ed.). Assessment in a pluralistic society. *Proceedings of the 33rd Invitational Conference on Testing Problems*. Princeton, N.J.: Educational Testing Service, 1973.

Boehm, A. E. Criteria-referenced assessment for the teacher. *Teachers College Record*, 1973, *75*, 117–126.

Brim, O. G., Jr. American attitudes toward intelligence tests. *American Psychologist*, 1965, *20*, 125–130.

Caldwell, M. B., & Knight, D. The effect of Negro and white examiners on Negro intelligence test performance. *Journal of Negro Education,* 1970, *39,* 177–179.

Cleary, A. T. Test bias: Prediction of grades of Negro and white students in integrated colleges. *Journal of Educational Measurement,* 1968, *5,* 115–124.

Costello, J. Effects of pretesting and examiner characteristics on test performance of young disadvantaged children. *Proceedings of the 78th Annual Convention of the American Psychological Association,* 1970, *5,* 309–310.

Crown, P. J. *The effects of race of examiner and standard vs. dialect administration of the Wechsler Preschool and Primary Scale of Intelligence on the performance of Negro and white children.* Doctoral dissertation, Florida State University. Available through University Microfilms, Ann Arbor, Michigan, 1970, No. 71–18, 356.

Ebel, R. L. The social consequences of educational testing. *School and Society,* 1964, *92,* 331–334.

Goslin, D. A. Standardized ability tests and testing. *Science,* 1968, *159,* 851–855.

Holtzman, W. H. The changing world of mental measurement and its social significance. *American Psychologist,* 1971, *26,* 546–553.

Kohlberg, L., & Zigler, E. The impact of cognitive maturity on the development of sex role attitudes. *Genetic Psychology Monogram,* 1967, *75,* 89–165.

Sattler, J. M. *Assessment of children's intelligence.* Philadelphia: Saunders, 1974.

Scarr, S. *Genetic effects on human behavior: Recent family studies.* A Master Lecture, delivered at the annual meeting of the American Psychological Association, San Francisco, August 26, 1977.

Scarr, S., Pakstis, A. J., Katz, S. H., & Barker, W. B. The absence of a relationship between degree of white ancestry and intellectual skills within a black population, *Human Genetics,* 1977, *857,* 1–18.

Scarr, S., & Weinberg, R. A. IQ test performance of black children adopted by white families. *American Psychologist,* 1976, *31,* 726–739.

Sowell, T. (Ed.). *American ethnic groups.* Washington, D.C.: The Urban Institute, 1977.

Thorndike, R. L. Concepts of culture-fairness. *Journal of Educational Measurement,* 1971, *8,* 63–70.

Valentine, C. A. Deficit, difference, and bicultural models of Afro-American behavior. *Harvard Educational Review,* 1971, *41,* 137–157.

Williams, E. B. Testing of the disadvantaged: New opportunities. In F. H. Wright (Chair), *Uses and abuses of psychology: A program for constructive action.* Symposium presented at the American Psychological Association meeting, Washington, D.C., September 1971.

Zigler, E., & Butterfield, E. C. Motivational aspects of changes in IQ test performance of culturally deprived nursery school children. *Child Development,* 1968, *39*(1), 1–14.

IV.2 From Evolution to Larry P., or What Shall We Do About IQ Tests?*

IQ tests are a dilemma in that great morality play, "Who Shall Enjoy Society's Privileges?" Legal authorities battle over IQ tests as heroes or villains. The stages are courts around the nation, jammed with plaintiffs whose test scores were used to reject them from desired educational and occupational positions or whose scores exceeded those of others who were selected for desired positions on nonintellective bases. Larry P., Bakke, and Griggs are but a few of the plaintiffs whose names may become household words in the late '70s. Judges know little about the technical construction of IQ tests, their appropriate use and interpretation, and about the underlying issues of inequality that bring the adversaries to court. But the judges will decide how, when, and for whom IQ tests may be used to make life decisions.

As in most decisions in which morality plays an important role, there is conflicting "evidence" from the scientific community about the meaning, value, validity, and most of all, *legitimacy* of IQ measures. The history of IQ tests, for example, can be told as one of psychology's greatest achievements (Herrnstein, 1973) or as one of its most shameful (Kamin, 1974). Proponents of the use of IQ tests cite their exemplary statistical virtues; opponents strike at their role in perpetuating social and economic injustice. If the experts lined up in support of or against IQ tests, as physicians stand up for antibiotics and against VD, there would be no moral dilemma. It is the absence of scientific consensus that leaves IQ tests at the doubtful mercy of the legal system.

IQ TESTS AND EQUAL OPPORTUNITY

Historically, at the time IQ tests were being developed, there were widespread fears in the U.S. about assimilating hoards of linguistically different peasants from the poorest parts of Europe. Calling them feebleminded could help to stem the tide. By the 1930s, there were strong political forces toward increasing the participation of the common man (and woman) in the democratic process, toward greater equality of rights, and toward more nearly equal distribution of social and economic benefits (that are, of course imperfectly distributed to this day). The selection of an educational and occupational elite by IQ tests came in conflict with the prevailing environmentalist ethic. That ethic largely denies that individuals

---

*This chapter by Sandra Scarr originally appeared in *Intelligence*, 1978, 2, 325–342. Copyright © 1978 by Ablex Publishing Corp. Reprinted by permission.

differ importantly in any but unfortunate circumstances in their family backgrounds and subsequent opportunities to develop into intellectually competent adults.

Philosophically, the meaning of equality has changed over the past century. "Equal opportunity" used to be construed to mean an equal chance to compete for desirable positions, regardless of one's initial handicaps, be they biological or sociocultural. Fairness, therefore, depended on the lack of bias in selection procedures not in selection criteria.

In the majority of cases brought today against IQ tests, equal opportunity has been recast to include the selection criteria. Everyone, it is now said, should have equal access to the knowledge and skills being sampled by the selection criteria. In the case of IQ tests, this means that all groups in the society must have their cultures equally sampled, or the courts must know why not.

On the periphery (and heading for the mainstream) is the view that selection criteria must admit equal proportions of all groups to desirable locations in the social structure, or the selection criteria are de facto biased. Equal opportunity is thereby recast to mean equal outcome. Since no IQ test so far devised can assure this meaning of the term equal opportunity, IQ tests must go.

The use of IQ tests to sort and select individuals for various educational and occupational niches in society brings into conflict four separable issues: (1) civil rights for all citizens and equal protection under the law; (2) the distribution of economic and social benefits in the population; (3) subcultural differences in life-style and child rearing that affect equal access to the skills and knowledge measured by IQ tests; and (4) genetic and biological differences in intelligence. Sources of test score differences, (3) and (4), come crashing against equal protecton, (1), in courtroom battles over the justice or injustice of IQ tests and their applications to educational and occupational selection, (2).

If we sit far back in the audience and contemplate the legal play, we find it has some aspects of a tragedy and some of a comedy. The tragic part is the web of conflicting values that assert, on the one hand, that all men are created equal (before the law) and, on the other hand, that social and economic benefits shall be allocated in this society according to scales of individual merit in achievements, some of which are intellectual. How to assess individual merit? Given the usual criteria and the tests used for selection, it is easy to see that everyone in the society does not have equal access to the environmental, genetic, or biological requisites for high intellectual achievement. Some pigs on this *Animal Farm* are more equal than others, by being better prepared to compete.

The comic part of the play is that IQ tests are blamed for the educational, social, and economic inequalities of society, and their good-riddance is proposed as a remedy for inequities that are firmly embedded in the capitalist system as a whole. Without attacking or defending free enterprise, I think it is ridiculous to suppose that abolishing intellectual measurement will revolutionize anyone's life chances. Furthermore, the existence of individual differences in IQ scores has led some zealots to deny that genetic differences play any role in those differences. It is as though biological diversity must be denied to defend universal civil liberties and to obtain greater equality in the distribution of social and economic benefits. IQ tests must be eliminated because they aid and abet inequalities.

It is on this central theme of the morality play that I wish to linger to develop an evolutionary argument to fit our knowledge of human history and development into the political arena of IQ tests and the courts.

In outline, the argument is as follows:

1. As a species, we have evolved a common genetic program for intellectual development in a pan-human environmental context.

2. The evolutionary process virtually guarantees that genetic diversity will account for some of the intellectual differences among us.

3. A just society is one that provides humane developmental environments for all of its children and thereby maximizes genetic individual differences.

4. Humane developmental environments can appear to be very different in their particulars, but they will be effectively the same for the development of species-typical intellectual skills.

5. Samples of intelligent behavior on IQ tests are necessarily culturally bound, but genetic differences among individual and between social groups with intellectual mobility will be prominent.

6. The appropriate use of IQ tests is to infer probable success on a criterion that is sampled from the same cultural context as the text.

7. IQ tests, therefore, are appropriately used in educational and occupational contexts that share the same culture, regardless of the culture of the individual being tested; but no sure inference can be made to the intellectual functioning of that person is another cultural context.

8. One could well question the exclusive representation of mainstream American culture in the criteria for academic and occupational success.

9. Civil liberties belong to all of us as citizens, and represent a great human achievement, given biological diversity.

10. The distribution of social and economic benefits need not depend to the current degree upon difference in intellectual and academic achievement.

ASPECTS OF AN EVOLUTIONARY VIEW

Two aspects of an evolutionary view of human intelligence deserve some emphasis in this essay: first, the sociocultural context in which human brains and behavior evolve and develop; and second, the necessary genetic implications of an evolutionary view. Many other sources provide a more complete and scholarly account of these issues (e.g., Dobzhansky, 1962, 1973; Mayr, 1970, 1974), but I want to set the stage for a discussion of contemporary conflicts about IQ tests.

We are compromise organisms. The evolution of intelligence cannot be separated from all of the other characteristics that make us viable, functioning beings in our human environments. Brains and intelligence had to be coadapted with reproductive requirements, life-span limitations, motor functions, etc.

Every genetic change, as Mayr (1970) has pointed out, must be fit into the existing genetic program, rather more like adding a violin to an orchestra than expecting a solo performance. The final arrangement of instruments is that which makes the best adapted compromise with all of the requirements of the environment, without unduly favoring one function over any others that are necessary for survival and reproduction. So, brains and intelligence could not evolve willy-nilly, without being part of the coadapted gene complex that determines all of the organisms' development.

In each generation there is a feedback system for genetic change. Individuals are more or less successful at procreating and rearing their offspring to reproductive age. Since the gene pool of the next generation depends on the frequency of successful reproduction of the parental genotypes, differential fertility and mortality of the preceding generation will directly determine the genetic character of the next.

Through most of human history both differential fertility and mortality changed the gene pool from one generation to the next. Some people were more desirable as mates than others, some produced more offspring, and some were more successful in parenting those offspring to adulthood, when the parental genes could extend into yet another generation. As long as genetic differences in intelligence had even the slightest part in this drama of human fertility and mortality, some genes would be increased and others decreased in frequency over time.[1] Presumably, increases in the neocortex and associated behaviors were determined by the evolutionary process.

Because human intelligence evolved by directional selection toward bigger brains, symbolic thought, and more complex communication, there *must* be a

---

[1]In the twentieth century differential mortality of parents and offspring has decreased as an evolutionary factor, because most babies now survive to reproductive age in most of the world. (This is not to say that public health and infant mortality are no longer issues even in the United States, but that differential mortality by nation, class, race, and probably IQ level have declined.) Differential fertility, on the other hand, has increased for the moment, as the more modernized and affluent were the first deliberately to limit family size effectively. It is still quite likely, however, that human intelligence is holding its own, with the more intelligent in every group outreproducing the retarded by a slight margin, as in the U.S. white population (Bajema, 1968; Higgins, Reed & Reed, 1962). Fertility is a volatile measure, however, as more and more peoples around the world achieve some measure of reproductive control.

genetic basis for the development of these behaviors to account for the regular appearance of intellectual changes in childhood. The species genetic program must include a timed, turning-on of the capacity to acquire these skills. There may also be a timed, turning-off of the easy learning of these skills, as Lenneberg (1967) found for primary language acquisition.

With the exception of a few severely impaired individuals, all human beings have more intellectually in common with one another than with any other species. This is one way to say that individual differences within the species are very small compared to our differences from even our closest relatives, the great apes. Variations in the developmental genetic program are not so large as to allow any human child to resemble a chimp more than another child. Even severely isolated children do not resemble great apes; such children are sadly deficient in human or any other skills. And a chimp reared in a chimp environment does not become a human child. So, to become a functioning human being clearly requires both the species genetic program and a rearing environment within the range that was evolutionarily typical for the species. However platitudinous, this fact is too often debated by the cold warriors of the nature–nurture controversy.

Since there is a species genetic program for intellectual development there is also very likely to be genetic variability for intelligence; that is, individual differences that depend in part on genotypic differences. Certainly, during the millions of years of human evolution, selection acted on genetic variability or there would have been no evolutionary change. That there was change is demonstrated by the fossil record.

Some geneticists, such as Lewontin, question whether there is any genetic variance left for intelligence in contemporary populations. Maybe it was all used up in our struggle to become homo sapiens, an achievement of the last 50,000 years. Studies of sibling differences, adopted children, and twins deny this speculation. Within every group studied, there is genetic variability in intelligence. I will return to this point later.

If one is either convinced or willing to assume for the sake for argument that there is some genetic variance for intelligence left in contemporary human populations, then the more profitable question is *how* is that variance likely to be affected by environmental variations? Are all of the possible combinations of genes and environments likely to produce linear increases or decreases in intelligence—so much of a linear slope for genetic differences, so much for environmental differences?

Some obscurantists (e.g., Hirsch, 1975) who think that questions about genetic differences are either unanswerable or immoral, have argued that gene–environment interactions (nonlinear effects) produce wild discontinuities in the phenotypes produced by various gene–environment combinations. Are there really genotypes that flourish in less humane, less invigorating environments? Poor Jake, if only he had less protein and fewer books in childhood, he'd be a genius today, instead of just a little above average. Lucky

Sal, her parents gave her just the right amount of abuse and neglect to optimally foster her low IQ. Is this likely? I suppose that within some normal limits on nutrition, opportunities to learn, adult stimulation, etc., some genotypes would develop better with less rather than more. But are these large effects? I would guess that the discontinuities produced by such combinations produce little static on the linear regression of gene–environment combinations.

INTELLIGENCE: BIOLOGICAL AND CULTURAL EVOLUTION WORK TOGETHER

In recent years, public discussions of "sociobiology" have polarized biological and sociocultural accounts of human behavior. E. O. Wilson (1975), the synthesizer of the field is not to blame for this regrettable cleavage; rather, his more vociferous critics have misrepresented his views repeatedly (see *Science*, 1976; Wilson, 1977), making it appear that the new field of sociobiology explains all of human behavior in biological terms—a gross form of reductionism. Instead, my reading of Wilson's thesis is that the evolution of human behavior occurred in the sociocultural context of small bands of hunters and gatherers, for whom certain selective forces increased the probability that some kinds of social and intellectual behaviors would be favored by increasing the fitness of those who developed them. (Fitness is, of course, defined by the number of offspring surviving to reproductive age.) So far, the argument is traditional to. evolution thought. The relatively new, though not unique, twist in Wilson's argument is that biases in learning develped for the human species, biases that make it more likely that some things would be learned than others. Hinde (Hinde & Sevenson-Hinde, 1973), Seligman (1970), and the Brelands (Breland & Breland, 1961) told us the same thing about infrahuman behavior. And, though Chomsky has not specified the nature of his "language acquisition device," it can be seen as a bias in the human species toward learning a language. Language is recognized by infants from certain properties that are shared by all human languages. Thus, Wilson's message is hardly news in the intellectual domain.[2]

Once one considers the notion that human intelligence evolved in the sociocultural context of small human groups, of mixed ages and sexes, who traveled around gathering food and sometimes hunting, one can begin to question the implications of this environment for the kinds of human intelligence that evolved. And one can look at the pan-human context for intellectual development (e.g., Chapter I-3, this volume).

---

[2]His thesis applied to human social behavior, parent–child relations, aggression, territoriality, and sex differences created the larger storm, but are fortunately beyond the scope of this essay!

The development of these typically human skills depends both on evolved biases in learning that make it easier to acquire these skills than others (such as the use of sonar to locate objects in space) and proper environmental conditions for development. Some environmental conditions are very generally available for all members of the species, such as opportunities to communicate with others, to manipulate objects, and to move about in space. Children cannot learn any language without its being present in their environments, nor can they learn to locomote in space without the opportunity to do so. But all normal humane environments provide these opportunities. More particular environments may be required for the development of literacy, such as formal instruction of reading and writing skills (See Cole, Gay, Glick, & Sharpe, 1971). But the human species has evolved to be capable of acquiring such skills with the provision of requisite environmental supports. Even children in those groups that only recently acquired writing readily learn literacy skills. The major point is that environments of almost all groups, not undergoing disasters from plague, starvation or war, provide the necessary opportunities and instruction for the young to acquire the local culture and to develop into species-typical human beings.

IS THE GENETIC PROGRAM SENSITIVE TO ENVIRONMENTAL VARIATIONS?

Several remarkable cases of extreme isolation in early childhood have been reprinted and reviewed recently by the Clarkes (Clarke & Clarke, 1976). Isolated children, when discovered around the ages of six or seven, were extremely retarded in their intellectual development, having been reared in environments that deviated disastrously from those of normal members of the species. These children had little or no exposure to language, opportunities for sensorimotor development, or interpersonal affection. Like cage-reared, isolated monkeys, they were sadly deficient in the usual childhood skills, until patient tutoring and exposure over the next few years succeeded in in bringing all but one (the famous Anna, reported by Kingsley Davis) up to average levels of intellectual performance. There is no question that being reared in environments outside of the range that is normal for the species will have deleterious consequences for intelligence.[3]

Environments outside of the optimal range, at the margins of those that are normal for the species, can also have measurable deleterious effects. Poor protein–calorie nutrition, cultural isolation (such as that of the canal boat

---

[3]The genetic program is also sensitive to genetic effects, such as chromosomal and single gene effects that can distort normal intellectual development.

children in England and the Appalachian children of the 1930s), being reared in an unstimulating institution, and not attending school for at least a few years all seem to depress intellectual functioning, as measured by both Western IQ tests and more culturally suitable assessments (Cole et al., 1971).

As a species, our developmental program is best suited to profiting from the learning and problem-solving opportunities that occur in some rather broad range of human environments. Peoples around the world do not rear children in the same ways. The many variations of caretaking (who does it?), cultural patterns of sleeping and eating (what, with whom, and when?), food production or gathering, are the delight of cultural anthropologists. But are there any societies where children are typically excluded from interacting with other speakers of the human language, refused opportunities to explore material objects, and denied opportunities to learn the culture into which they have been born?

HUMANE ENVIRONMENTS FOR ALL

An evolutionary view of human intelligence leads one to expect that there are common skills that develop in all normal members of the species reared in typical human environments. The developmental psychologists of this century have spent most of their efforts in detailing the nature of that intelligence and its developmental course. To my knowledge, there is no evidence that different human groups have different *kinds* of intellectual skills, although adequate assessment across diverse languages and cultures has proved very difficult, if not impossible. Claims have been made that some groups have more intellectual skill(s) than others, but not different kinds of memory, reasoning, or categorization skills. (There is, however, no IQ test that will show our common humanity, because each is bound to the culture from which the particular sample of knowledge and skills is drawn.)

Given our pan-human profile of intelligence, we may rightfully ask that all environments be humane enough to foster the development of the universal skills. Arbitrary environmental differences among people are unfair advantages for the intellectual development of some and unfair disadvantages for others. There is, then, some absolute scale on which we can rate the effectiveness of any given group in fostering intelligence in its young. Please keep in mind that I am not judging all environments by their effectiveness in instilling any particular culture, just by their giving all children the opportunity to learn their own culture. In this view, *an enlightened social policy ought to maximize the heritability of intelligence in all groups.* Populations with low heritabilities are those with the greatest environmental inequalities.

The necessary implication of this absolutist–developmental view is that environmental differences among people and peoples ought to be eliminated.

Horrifying, you say! Yes, horrifying, if all of the current diversity of cultural practices and personal preferences were to be homogenized into a uniform environmental standard for the species.[4] Fortunately, however, most human cultural practices, however apparently different are probably not effectively different in creating large, human intellectual differences.

RACIAL VS. SOCIOECONOMIC GROUPS

More than forty years ago, Davis and Dollard (1937) contrasted the social systems of *caste* and *class*. Among castes there is no individual mobility; one is born into a caste and stays there regardless of individual merit. Races are castes in the United States. Social classes exist within castes, and individuals can move up or down the class structure according to criteria of individual merit. Dobzhansky (1962) spelled out the implications of this differentiation for genetics: Genetic differences are less likely to arise between castes, because all of the genetic individual variability is kept within them—there are few ways out of one racial group into another. By contrast, there are permeable boundaries among social class groups, not perfect mobility according to individual merit, allowing some 30 to 40% change of status in each generation. The individuals who move socially take their genes with them, mate, and reproduce in their achieved status. Thus, there is a far higher probability of social class than racial group differences in those characteristics that contribute to individual mobility (Scarr-Salapatek, 1971a,b).

The implication of this difference between race and social class for intellectual achievements is that there are more likely to be genetic differences in IQ scores between social class than racial groups. Let us review the recent research on this issue.

THE EVIDENCE ON RACIAL DIFFERENCES
AS ENVIRONMENT AND GENES

Three recent investigations on the possible genetic origins of racial differences in performance in school and on IQ tests reject the hypothesis of genetic differences as a major source of those differences in performance. First, a

---

[4]There is an ironic implication of two views most often held by the same radical environmentalists: that all human beings have equal genetic endowment for the development of intelligence and that all human differences arise because of environmental inequities. Since we know how intellectual development ought to proceed under optimal conditions and how to identify those particularly well-developed intellects, all those other people in all those other environments must be impaired by the diversity of their sociocultural environments. This leads to a pernicious cultural imperialism by the professional class in Western societies, whose child-rearing and home-neighborhood environments promote, it seems, higher intellectual achievements in their young.

study of transracial adoption (Scarr & Weinberg, 1976) showed that black and interracial children reared by socioeconomically advantaged white families score very well on standard IQ tests and on school achievement tests. Being reared in the culture of the test and the school resulted in intellectual achievement levels for black children that were comparable to adopted white children in similar families. Therefore, it is highly unlikely that genetic differences between the races could account for the major portion of the usually observed differences in the performance levels of the two groups.

A second study on the relation of black ancestry to intellectual skills within the black population (Scarr, Pakstis, Katz, & Barker, 1977) showed that having more or less African ancestry was not related to how well one scored on cognitive tests. In other words, holding constant social identity and cultural background, socially classified blacks with greater amounts of white ancestry did not score better than other blacks with more African ancestry. A strong genetic difference hypothesis cannot account for this result.

Briefly, blood groups were used to estimate the proportion of each person's African and European ancestry. This is roughly possible because the parent populations differ in the average frequencies of many alleles at many loci and differ substantially at a few loci. Therefore, if a person has a particular allele, we were able to assign a probability that he got that gene from one of the two populations. While there is undoubtedly a large error term in these estimates, they had several satisfactory characteristics, such as appropriately large sibling correlations and correlations with skin color. What is most important here is that the estimates of ancestry did *not* correlate with any measures of intellectual performance in the black sample. Thus, we concluded that degree of white ancestry had little or no effect on individual levels of performance within the black group. We must look to other explanations.

The third study was of black and white twins in Philadelphia (Scarr & Barker, 1981). Briefly, the black 10-to-16-year-olds scored one-half to one standard deviation below the whites on every cognitive measure. The social class differences between the races were not sufficiently large, as Jensen has reminded us, to account solely for the magnitude of this performance differences between the racial groups. The major hypothesis was that black children have less overall familiarity with the information and the skills being sampled by the tests and the schools. By using twins in this study, we were able to examine three implications of cultural differences compared to a genetic differences hypothesis. The major predictions of the cultural differences hypothesis are:

1. Black children will score relatively worse on these tests that are more culturally loaded than on more "culture-fair" tests when the instructions for all tasks are equally understood.

2. The cultural differences of the blacks constitute a "suppressive environment" with respect to the development of the intellectual skills

sampled by typical tests, and therefore black children will show less genetic variability in their scores and more environmental variability (Scarr-Salapatek, 1971).

3. Differences among black children will be more dependent on differences among their family environments in the extent to which they aid children in the development of test-relevant skills, and therefore (a) the twin correlations will be higher for black twins, and (b) there will be less difference between MZ and DZ coefficients in the black than white groups.

Three major predictions of a genetic differences hypothesis are:

1. Black children will score relatively worse on those tests that are loaded more highly on a "g" factor than on more verbal, culturally-loaded tests.

2. The proportions of genetic and environmental variability will be the same in both racial groups.

3. Family environments will be no more important in black than in white racial groups in determining individual variation.

We believe that the pattern of results supports a general cultural difference hypothesis far better than a genetic differences view. The major intellectual results are:

1. Black children have lower scores on all of the cognitive tests, but they score relatively worse on the more culturally loaded of the conceptual tests.

2. The cognitive differences among the black children are less well explained by genetic individual differences, by age, and by social class differences than those of the white children.

3. The similarity of the black co-twins, particularly the DZ's, suggests that being reared in different families determines more of the cognitive differences among black than white children, but that those between-family differences are not those usually measured by SES variables in the white community.

Therefore, we conclude that the results of this study support the view that black children are being reared in circumstances that give them only marginal acquaintance with the skills and the knowledge being sampled by the tests we administered. Some families in the black community encourage the development of these skills and knowledge, while others do not. In general, black children do not have the same access to these skills and knowledge as white children, which explains the lower performance of black children as a group. The hypothesis that most of the differences among the cognitive scores of black and white children are due to genetic differences between the races cannot, in our view, account for this pattern of results. Therefore, in three studies, the hypothesis of genetic differences between the races fails to account for the IQ performance differences.

THE EVIDENCE ON INDIVIDUAL DIFFERENCES
AS GENES AND ENVIRONMENTS

From a review of recent family studies (Scarr, 1977), I think that the evidence for some genetic individual differences in behavior is simply overwhelming. Especially if one considers the past literature, there are literally dozens of studies that support that mild conclusion in all groups studied.

Going straight to the heart of the matter, I think that most evidence points to a "heritability" of about .4 to .7 in the U.S. white population and .2 to .5 in the black, given that "heritability" here means the proportion of genetic variance among individuals sampled in twin and family studies, which, as I have repeatedly noted, are not representative of bad environments. If one could include people with really poor environments, the proportion of environmental variance might rise; on the other hand, the genetic variance might also be increased. It is hard to predict whether or not the proportions of variance would change, and in which direction.

It is important to note here the small effects of environmental differences on IQ scores among the people in our white family samples. This suggests that within the range of "humane environments," from an SES level of working to upper-middle class, there is little evidence for differential environmental effects within the whole group. The average level of these environments in such that the black and white children reared by these families perform intellectually somewhat above the population average, even though they have average biological parents. Thus, the environments sampled in family studies are better than average at fostering intellectual development. But why are the relatively poor families rearing black and white *adopted* children whose IQ scores are nearly as high as those in professional families? It must be that all of these seeming environmental differences that predict so well to outcome differences among biological children are not primarily *environmental* differences, but indices of genetic differences among the parents and their biological offspring. This brings us to social class.

THE EVIDENCE ON SOCIAL CLASS DIFFERENCES
AS ENVIRONMENT AND GENES

In 1938, Barbara Burks compared her California adopted and biological children to those studied by Alice Leahy in Minnesota. Grouping the children by the occupational status of the adoptive families, Burks computed the average effects of being born to *and* reared by, *or only reared by,* families at different locations in the social structure. As in all adoption studies, the families do not vary over the whole SES range; in fact, adoptive samples always omit those lower portions of the income and educational distributions where big negative effects on intellectual development can occur. Nonetheless, it is interesting to examine the overall effects of being reared by a skilled working-class family, or a white collar family, or a professional family. As you already know, the intellectual levels of parents in those groups differ on the average. What about the children?

For biological children of these occupational classes, the average difference between working-class and professional families was 12 IQ points in Burks's study and 17 IQ points in Leahy's. Children *adopted* by families of the same occupational classes, however, differed far less—about 5 IQ points in both studies. Adopted children in professional families scored *below* biological offspring; in working-class families, adoptees scored *above* the natural children, a very predictable genetic outcome.[5] In our Minnesota studies (Scarr, 1977, note 1; Scarr & Weinberg, 1976, 1977, 1978, 1979), we found that the natural children of the transracial adoptive families averaged 6 IQ points above their adopted siblings. The adolescent adoptees also average 6 IQ points below the biological children of comparably advantaged families. As in the other studies, there is a far greater relationship between parental social class and child IQ in the biological than adoptive families.

Since there is always some selective placement of adopted children into families that resemble their biological parents, the actual effect of differences in this middle to high range of social class environments may be less than the 5 or 6 IQ points cited. Again, let me emphasize that none of these studies speak to lower-class, deprived, or abusive environments. I am only saying that in that portion of the SES range where so many studies report intellectual differences among children reared in such circumstances, the differences observed among the children may not be primarily of environmental origin at all. From the older studies, Burks estimates that genetic differences among the occupational classes account for about two-thirds to three-quarters of the

---

[5]The genetic prediction for the IQ scores of adopted children, compared to biological offspring of the same or similar families, is based on random assignment of genotypically bright and dull adoptees to families at all locations in the social structure. Although this assumption is not perfectly met, because agencies selectively place infants of educationally-advanced natural mothers with adoptive families of higher educational levels (and lower with lower), the effects on IQ resemblance between adoptive parents and their children is small, since educational level is an imperfect estimator of IQ scores of the adoptive parents, and the natural mother's education is certainly a distal estimate of the genetic contribution of both natural parents to their offspring's eventual intellectual level. Therefore, the genetic prediction is that children adopted into professional families will be environmentally advantaged but genotypically average, whereas the biological offspring of the same or similar parents will be both environmentally and genotypically advantaged. Similarly, the children adopted by working-class families will be environmentally less advantaged but genotypically average, whereas the children born into such families will be both environmentally and genotypically disadvantaged. Selective placement of the adopted children works against the genetic prediction.

average IQ differences among the children born into those classes. Our recent studies support that conclusion.

Suppose, then, that the usual 15–point IQ difference between children born into the top and lower-middle of the white social structure is two-thirds due to genetic differences and one-third due to environmental inequalities. Suppose, in addition, that the entire 15–point black–white differential is explained by sociocultural factors. What does that recommend to us about IQ tests and their use in educational and occupational selection?

THE IQ TEST AS A SAMPLE OF
INTELLEGENCE IN A CULTURE

There is no need to recite the sampling biases of IQ tests. They are not exhaustive inventories of what people known and can do, but samples of important aspects of intellectual functioning in a particular cultural context.

The degree to which current IQ tests sample culturally specific information and skills is a matter of considerable debate. No one would wonder why the WISC had to be translated into Japanese to be administered to Japanese children; at least the comprehension and vocabulary sections would be useless samples of intelligent behavior in a totally different linguistic and cultural context. To sample other, less obviously different cultural milieu with the Weschler test has been a matter of great debate. Is American black culture sufficiently different to require a different sample of skills and knowledge? Whether it is or not is probably irrelevant for the purposes of the test, since the criteria to which the American version of the test is designed to predict are equally as biased away from black culture as the tests (e.g., schools and occupational settings). Whereas in the Japanese case, the criteria are also Japanese schools and jobs, in the United States blacks control few jobs and determine little about the criteria of school performance. The cultural context of the tests is that of the criteria. Similarly, if one wants to select African students to attend Oxford University, it is quite appropriate to administer the Oxford entrance examination in English, because it reflects the cultural milieu and skills predictive of success in the Oxford environment.

It is not justified, however, to infer anything about an African's level of general intelligence from such an entrance exam, or from an American IQ test administered to a culturally different group. In fact, one should wonder about the efficacy of inferences from IQ tests to general intellectual functions in any population more diverse than the standardization sample, and I even wonder about the environmental–cultural diversity within that group. Why, really, do rural children score lower than urban children on even the newest tests? Isn't it that the tests are a less adequate sample of their skills and knowledge? Do we know that they have less skill and cultural knowledge in their own context?

The test manuals are clear in their assumption of equal exposure to the material to be sampled by the test. How can that requirement be met by different geographic and cultural groups?

The only way out of this dilemma, it seems to me, is to limit the meaning of test scores to their predictive value for the criteria of school and jobs where the skills and knowledge of the majority culture are essential to good performance in those contexts.

Now, it may seem that we have escaped the major objections of the opponents of IQ tests in the selection of minority group members for school programs and jobs. These are not tests of intelligence in some abstract, culture-free way; they are measures of the ability to function intellectually by virtue of knowledge and skills in the culture of which they are a sample. But that is the *narrowest possible victory*.

CULTURAL PLURALISM AND CULTURALLY-SPECIFIC ASSESSMENT

One consideration that is often overlooked in the debate over the elimination of IQ tests is whether the same biases in the criteria of school and job performance can and should be changed. Should the majority culture be so exclusively represented in these criteria? Ought there to be more Latino, Black, and Asian culture represented in our American scheme? Generations of immigrant children became "real" Americans by learning the WASP way, but that largely occurred in the early decades of this century when most Americans had little idea of, or use for, cultural diversity. Are we not now a more worldly, sophisticated people, whose children could be permitted to learn more than their own culture and language, without fear of contamination? In the near future, Spanish-speaking Americans will be a larger group than blacks in the United States, and very significant portion of the school-age population in Florida and California (about one-third to one-half). Are we to continue to ignore their life-style and literature in the hope that they, too, will melt into the American pot?

Some geneticists today are quite concerned about the loss of genetic diversity in plants and animals, as standard hybrid seeds and artificial insemination replace the local plantings and herds. (Too much loss of genetic diversity will make epidemic losses in agriculture a major threat.) On the cultural side, anthropologists lament the loss of exotic local groups, whose cultures are swallowed by a cannibalistic Western culture. Within our own nation, we are eating away at any remaining cultural diversity with fast food chains, mass media, and uniform standards for schools and jobs. Let us ask ourselves if this meal is necessary.

Should we be so wise as to encourage cultural pluralism, we will need culturally appropriate ways of assessing intellectual adaptation in different cultural communities. Since we are all human beings, most skills will be common to every culture, but the ways in which they are manifest and the relative emphasis given to various skills may well vary from one group to another. At this time we simply do not know how various groups teach their children different things, what it is important to know, and how to solve common and local problems. To coin a phrase, more research on these problems will be needed.

SOCIAL POLICY, CIVIL LIBERTIES, AND THE GREAT IQ DEBATE

Intelligence, and individual variations on that species theme, has been argued to have both an evolutionary history and a common developmental pattern. Arguments have been made about the cultural loading of IQ tests, the likelihood of genetic individual differences in whatever is sampled by tests in any culture, the problems of the cultural boundedness of the current criteria for school and job performance, and the necessarily associated cultural bias in IQ tests.

A word is needed about the role of IQ tests in the distribution of educational, social and economic benefits. Given the present uniform American standard for intellectual achievement and its use for selection into desirable niches in the society, it would appear to many that getting rid of the tests might enhance the chances of those who are not currently in the mainstream in gaining access to many of the goodies. Such is not the case, as demonstrated by California, where, despite the injunction against the use of IQ tests for educational selection more than two years ago, there are still as many minority children in classes for the retarded as when the tests were used. Other, less objective assessments will be found and used as long as the bias in the criteria remains. Halting the use of the tests will not solve the problem. Nor will adding points to the scores of those who come from disadvantaged and culturally different backgrounds. They will still fail at the criterion, just as the tests would predict, for the aforementioned reasons of shared cultural loading.

So, what should the courts decide about the current use of IQ tests in educational and occupational decisions? Fortunately, I do not have to make any such decisions, but I would advise them to look much further into American life than the tests. Just as schools cannot singlehandedly solve the problems of inequality in the country, abandoning the tests cannot make the society more pluralistic, insure equal rights, or redistribute social and economic benefits.

It is unlikely that the solution to the unequal distribution of social and economic rewards can be found in the educational system at all. For reasons too numerous to cite here, the relationship of schooling to later achievements is tenuous, and, more importantly, there are more efficient ways to redistribute prestige, income, and wealth.

Jencks and his colleagues (Jencks, 1972) suggested that economic and social benefits be allocated with less regard for the existing inequalities in performance. That, they said, would be the only way to bring about a more egalitarian society in the face of such large differences among people. John Rawls (1971) has suggested a similar remedy: Bring up the bottom level to a socially just standard by approving any social or economic changes that benefit those least afforded a decent life now, and disapproving any changes that increase the inequalities and lower the standard of those at the bottom of the social structure. In other words, these social philosophers, and others, propose that individual inequalities in performance be less linked than to the allocation of social and economic rewards and more tied to ideas of social justice. The use of IQ tests in the selection of educational and occupational elites need not lead inexorably to grossly disproportional social and economic benefits.

The late and very humane Professor Dobzhansky published a long essay on genetic diversity and human equality in which he differentiated the political nature of human equality and the natural fact of biological diversity (Dobzhansky, 1973). The achievement of universal human rights in the face of such human differences is one of the great achievements of mankind. If there were no biological diversity we would not need legal civil liberties, because it is easy to afford rights to those who are most like us. The very fact of our differences make the achievement of human rights for all a supreme accomplishment. Everyone should read Dobzhansky's essay for inspiration and immunity against those whose fears for such rights tempt them to suppress the truth about human differences.

REFERENCES

Bajema, C. J. Relation of fertility to occupational status, IQ, education attainments, and size of family of origin: A follow up study of a male Kalamazoo public school population. *Eugenics Quarterly*, 1968, *15*, 198–203.

Breland, K., & Breland, M. The misbehavior of organisms. *American Psychologist*, 1961, *16* 681–684.

Burks, B. S. On the relative contribution of nature and nurture to average group differences in intelligence. *Proceedings of the National Academy of Sciences*, 1938, *24*, 276–82.

Clarke, A. M., & Clarke, A. D. B. *Early experience: Myth and evidence*. New York: Free Press, 1976.

Cole, M., Gay, J., Glick, J. A., & Sharpe, D. W. *The cultural context of learning and thinking*. New York: Basic Books. 1971.

Davis, A., & Dollard, J. *Caste and class in a southern town*. London: Oxford University, H. Milford Press, 1937.

Dobzhansky, T. *Genetic diversity and human equality*. New York: Basic Books, 1973.

Dobzhansky, T. *Mankind evolving: The evolution of the human species.* New Haven: Yale University Press, 1962.

Herrnstein, R. J. *I.Q. in the meritocracy.* Boston: Little, Brown, 1973.

Higgins, J., Reed, E. W., & Reed, .S. Intelligence and family size: A paradox resolved. *Eugenics Quarterly,* 1962, *9,* 84–90.

Hinde, R. A., & Sevenson-Hinde, J. *Constraints on learning: Limitations and predisposition.* New York: Academic Press, 1973.

Hirsch, J. Jensenism: The bankruptcy of "science" without scholarship. *Educational Theory,* 1975, *25,* 3–27.

Jencks, C. *Inequality: A reassessment of the effect of family and schooling in America.* New York: Basic Books, 1972.

Kamin, L. J. *The science and politics of IQ.* Hillsdale, N.J.: Lawrence Erlbaum Associates, 1974.

Lenneberg, F. H. *Biological foundations of language.* New York: Wiley, 1967.

Mayr, E. Behavior programs and evolutionary strategies. *American Scientist,* 1974, *62* 650–665.

Mayr, E. *Populations, species and evolution.* Cambridge, Mass.: Harvard Univ. Press, 1970.

Rawls, J. *A theory of justice.* Cambridge, Mass.: Belknap Press 1971.

Scarr, S. Genetic effects on human behavior: Recent family studies. A Master Lecture delivered at the Annual Meetings of the American Psychological Association, San Francisco, August 26, 1977. Note 1

Scarr, S., & Barker, W. B. The effects of family background: A study of cognitive differences between black and white twins. In S. Scarr, *IQ: Race, Social Class and Individual Differences.* Hillsdale, N.J.: Lawrence Erlbaum Associates, 1981.

Scarr-Salapatek, S. Unknowns in the IQ equation. *Science,* 1971, *174,* 1223–1228. (b)

Scarr-Salapatek, S. An evolutionary perspective on infant intelligence. In M. Lewis (Ed.), *Origins or intelligence: Infancy and early childhood.* New York: Plenum, 1976. Pp. 165–197.

Scarr, S., Pakstis, A. J., Katz, S. H., & Barker, W. B. The absence of a relationship between degree of white ancestry and intellectual skills within a black population. *Human Genetics,* 1977, *39,* 69–86.

Scarr, S., & Weinberg, R. A. The influence of "family background" on intellectual attainment: The unique contribution of adoptive studies to estimating environmental effects. *American Sociological Review,* 1978, *43,* 674–692.

Scarr, S., & Weinberg, R. A. Nature and nurture strike (out) again. *Intelligence,* 1979, *3,* 31–39.

Scarr, S., & Weinberg, R. A. IQ test performance of black children adopted by white families. *American Psychologist,* 1976, *31,* 726–739.

Scarr, S., & Weinberg, R. A. Intellectual similarities within families of both adopted and biological children. *Intelligence,* 1977, *1,* 170–191.

Science, Sociobiology: Troubled birth for new discipline, 1976, *191,* 1151–1155.

Seligman, M. E. P. On the generality of the laws of learning. *Psychological Review,* 1970, *77,* 406–418.

Sociobiology: Troubled birth for new disciplines. *Science* 1976, *191,* 1151–1156.

Wilson, E. O. *Sociobiology; The New Synthesis.* Cambridge, Mass.: Belknap Press, 1975.

Wilson, E. O. Review of "Unnatural Science" by P. B. Medawar. *New York Times Review of Books.* March 31, 1977.

V COMMENTARIES

V.1 Commentary

Leon J. Kamin[1]
Princeton University

The invitation by an author to comment critically on her work, in the pages of her own book, is an act of considerable generosity. The fact that I have taken Professor Scarr at her word will not, I hope, appear as incivility on my part. There is much disagreement between us—not only about the interpretation of IQ data but even about the usefulness and advisability of carrying out the kind of research to which she is committed. This was of course known to Professor Scarr, and her inviting me to comment bears testimony to her fairmindedness and sense of responsibility. The issues to which IQ research at least *appears* to be relevant are large enough that Scarr's scrupulous seeking out of critical response is a precedent that all might do well to consider. Professor Scarr has been notably generous as well in making her raw data and computer printouts freely available to me for inspection and reanalysis. The willingness to make one's data available for critical scrutiny may strike some readers as a normal and obvious procedure among working scientists. With regret, I must report that some prominent workers in the field of IQ heritability have refused to make their raw data available. There can be no question concerning Scarr's competence, energy, fairness, and integrity, and I am pleased to record my appreciation of these (and her many other) virtues.

The position that Scarr occupies in the Great IQ Debate, consistent with these virtues, is that of a centrist, a moderate, and a liberal. Where extremists have claimed that the heritability of IQ among whites in the United States is .80, or .00, Scarr guesses that the figure probably lies between .40 and .70. Where the incautious, and the racist, have asserted that the black–white difference in mean

---

[1]This chapter was written by Leon Kamin for this volume at the invitation of the author.

IQ is a sign of black genetic inferiority, Scarr correctly points to the inherent ambiguity of the data. To claim a genetic cause, granted the social context, is likened by Scarr to a scream of "FIRE! . . . I think" in a crowded theater. Then, without "fear of unpopular results," Scarr collects new data on black–white differences, which she interprets as unfavorable to a genetic hypothesis. The Scarr right hand, however, promptly taketh away what the Scarr left hand giveth. To interpret the similarly confounded and ambiguous data on social-class differences in IQ, "a genetic hypothesis is almost a necessity. . . ." The fire in this case is no more certain than in her racial example, but the theater may be less crowded.

The commitment to civil liberties for all and a repulsion toward censorship are evident in much of Scarr's writing. These values, in contrast to the tone of her scientific judgments, appear absolutist—much more so than the views of Justice Holmes and many other American jurists. Thus, "political radicals and blacks" are upbraided, without qualification, for their "ugly" efforts to deny the "right to speak" to Shockley or to Jensen. The speech of these martyrs, however, has been compared by Scarr to a cry of "fire" in a crowded theater. (This is not to argue that campus talks by Shockley and Jensen *should* be suppressed. What I want to say is that the nice sense of balance and of evenhandedness so characteristic of Scarr's science does not always inform her politics. That may follow from the certitude with which she declares—as I cannot—that "science is *not* politics. . . .")

The fearless gathering of more data appears to be an unquestioned good in Scarr's view. The ideologues concerned with the Great IQ Debate are urged to get "off the political platform and out there to study families. With the notable exception of Arthur Jensen, not many advocates of high or low heritability are adding to our store of knowledge about human intelligence." The battle that has broken out on the barricades is to be resolved peacefully at the computers. There is evidently no intended rhetorical exaggeration in Scarr's comment: "I am also in favor of additional research on any problem. . . ."

Well, I am not. The great merit of Scarr's plentiful empirical research lies, in my view, in the demonstration that no scientific gain is to be had from further "behavior genetic" research on the heritability of IQ. The same data set from which Scarr concludes that IQ is substantially heritable can also be used—as Scarr is willing to share her raw data—to show that IQ is not at all heritable. The data are not, after all, the product of clearly designed and well-controlled experimentation. They are necessarily correlational data, collected in difficult and inevitably flawed field settings. The patterns discerned within such data are many and complex. The interpretation of these complex patterns, I believe, must reflect the investigator's theoretical bias.

The confounding of variables is only one avenue for the emergence of the investigator's (and the critic's!) bias. The sheer quantity of the data collected makes selective reporting inevitable, as well. Thus Scarr, with characteristic honesty, tells us that she had never published identical MZ and DZ correlations of .61 that she obtained in a twin study employing Goodenough's nonverbal Draw-a-Person IQ test. That study was in fact Scarr's Ph.D. thesis, and many other results from it—results consistent with a genetic interpretation—were published in a series of papers. The anomalous result, Scarr indicates, failed to see the light of day because it didn't make much sense. The same Goodenough test was also employed in an English twin study by Mittler (1969). That study also found virtually identical correlations: .61 for MZs and .68 for DZs. The Mittler study, like Scarr's, was a Ph.D. thesis from which a number of subsequent publications arose. The "anomalous" twin correlations are available only in Mittler's unpublished thesis, however. Thus, two genetically oriented researchers—for wholly innocuous and understandable reasons—failed to communicate the *same* anomalous fact. Perhaps I am the only person who has read the two unpublished theses; at least I am the first to report that in replicated studies, this highly regarded and much used nonverbal IQ test has been found to have zero heritability.

The pages that follow are an attempt to reanalyze some of the raw data that Scarr has so generously made available to me. The focus is, in turn, on three of her recent and major studies: the Minnesota transracial adoption study, the Minnesota adolescent adoption study, and the Philadelphia twin study. The conclusions that I reach on the basis of Scarr's data are very different from hers. They are also, I think, more nearly correct. What is a reader to make of the fact that in The Great IQ Debate, competent scientists so often disagree in this way?

THE TRANSRACIAL ADOPTION STUDY

This study demonstrates, for those obtuse enough to have doubted it, that the IQ scores of black children, like those of others, are highly malleable. That is doubtless a point worth making, but the more interesting data in the study derive from the fact that most families contained *both* an adopted and a natural child of the same parents. Traditionally, adoption studies (Burks, 1928; Leahy, 1935) compared the IQ correlation of adoptive parent–adopted child with the parent–child correlation obtained in a "matched control group" of normal, biological families. The correlation within adoptive families was found to be lower, and this was said to indicate the heritability of IQ. There is, however, no adequate way to "match" adoptive and control families. The rigorous selective filter through which adoptive families must pass produces a set of highly favored families, with sharply restricted environmental variance. The nexus of intercorrelated environmental indices may differ systematically between adoptive and demographically "matched" families. These considerations led me to suggest (Kamin, 1974) that a more adequate adoption study would examine a single set of families, each containing both an adopted and a biological child. The transracial study was the first adoption report to contain a reasonably sized sample of such families. To be sure, the sample is atypical. The parents and biological children are white, and the adopted children are black.

For her own data analyses, Scarr properly distinguished between early adoptees (placed before 1 year of age) and late adoptees. The mean IQ of early adoptees was a full 15 points higher than that of late adoptees. Therefore, late adoptees were excluded from the various heritability calculations. However, Chapter III-1 presents two different sets of correlational analyses. Within one set, early adoptees are compared to *all* natural children in the study. Within the other set, the comparison is made only in families containing *both* early adoptees and natural children. The latter analysis is by far the more appropriate. That is so because families who receive late adoptees differ substantially from those who contain early adoptees. The *natural* children in families containing late adoptees had mean IQs of 110.1 (Stanford–Binet) or 113.3 (Wechsler). The natural children in families containing early adoptees had significantly higher IQs—115.6 (Stanford–Binet) or 119.8 (Wechsler). The same kind of difference occurs between parents in the two kinds of families. For families with late adoptees, mean midparent IQ was 116 and mean midparent education, 14.6 years. The same figures for families with early adoptees were IQ 120 and 17.4 years of education. Thus the adoptive parents and adoptive sibs of late adoptees are obviously drawn from different populations than those of early adoptees. They should not be lumped together in analyses that, correctly, distinguish between early and late adoptees themselves. Throughout my own analyses and citations of Scarr's data, I have excluded both late adoptees *and* the parents and natural children in the families containing them.

Scarr notes that within families of early adoptees, the IQs of adoptive parents appear more similar to those of their natural children than to those of their adopted children. Pooling Binet and Wechsler tests, adoptive mother correlates .34 with her natural child and .29 with her adopted child. The difference seems more impressive in the case of fathers, who correlate .34 with their natural children and .07 with their adopted children. These figures were taken by Scarr to indicate a substantial heritability of IQ. The heritability estimates, depending on what "corrections" were employed, varied between .53 and 1.12 [*sic*] for fathers' data and between .12 and .40 for mothers' data. The suggestion of a difference between fathers and mothers may be more than coincidental. The Texas Adoption Project (Horn, Loehlin, & Willerman, 1979) has also reported correlations between adoptive parents and their adopted and biological children. For mothers, the correlation with adopted child was actually a trifle *larger* than that with biological child (.22 vs. .20). For fathers, the correlation with biological child was higher (.28 vs. .12). The maternal data from these two studies not only suggest a lower heritability than the paternal data; they are clearly consistent with zero heritability.

Though Scarr obtained data on the educational level of the adoptive parents and employed them in an illustrative path analysis, she did not report the correlations between adoptive parents' education and the IQs of their adopted and natural children. These correlations are of interest, because parental educational level has often been employed as an index of parental intelligence. The classic study by Skodak and Skeels (1949), for example, reported a correlation of only .02 between adoptive mother's education (no IQs were available) and adopted child's IQ. The biological mother's education, in contrast, correlated .32 with the IQ of her adopted-away child. That significant difference has routinely been interpreted as strong evidence for the heritability of IQ. The transracial adoption study provides a welcome opportunity for replication.

The computer printout kindly made available by Scarr indicates the following correlations, employing her procedure of computing intraclass correlations from separately normalized Stanford–Binet and Wechsler scores. The adoptive mother's education correlates .17 with the IQ of her natural child and .28 with that of her adopted child. The adoptive father's education, similarly, correlates .24 with the IQ of his natural child and .28 with that of his adopted child. Thus, the unreported data on adoptive parents' education offer no support at all to a heritability interpretation. The educational data, it might be noted, are not so much at variance with the parental IQ data as may at first appear. The only IQ correlations approaching a statistically significant difference were those involving adoptive fathers and their two kinds of children. The totality of these data, in my view, do not constitute even suggestive evidence for any heritability of IQ—particularly when they are combined with Scarr's own analysis of the sibling data from this same study. The unrelated sib pairs reared together were correlated just as highly in IQ as were biologically related sibs. The sib data were regarded by Scarr as puzzlingly discrepant from the parent–child data because, as she noted, they suggest zero heritability. The parent–child data, it seems to me, suggest about the same.

There are also available educational data for the biological mothers of the adopted-away children. (There were no IQ scores for these women, who—to simplify subsequent discussion—are referred to as "unwed mothers.") The education of unwed mother, as reported by Scarr, correlated .32 with the IQ of her adopted-away child—a value identical to that reported by Skodak and Skeels. This correlation, however, cannot be taken as an unambiguous indicator of heritability. The correlation might be an artifact produced by selective placement of children of well-educated mothers into superior adoptive homes. Thus Scarr sensibly compared this correlation to that between the education of the same unwed mother and the IQ of the natural children of the adoptive parents with whom the unwed mother's child had been placed. This latter correlation, which can reflect nothing but selective placement, was reported by Scarr to be .15. The fact that .32 appears to be larger than .15—together with Scarr's apportionment of half the selective placement effect to genes and half to environment—suggests substantial heritability. The same data, however, can be made to suggest a very different story.

The Scarr calculations, it will be recalled, combined Stanford–Binet and Wechsler IQ's in a single analysis. The great majority of the (younger) adopted children had been given Binet tests, whereas most of the natural children had been Wechsler tested. What happens if we examine correlations with unwed mother's education separately by test? The correlations, computed by me from Scarr's raw data, are product moment. With the Stanford–Binet, unwed mother's education correlates .28 with the IQ of her adopted-away child ($N = 79$) and .33 with that of the natural child of her child's adoptive parents ($N = 29$)! Thus, the correlation between unwed mother and her adopted-away child appears to be *entirely* a consequence of selective placement—at least for Binet-tested children. The data for Wechsler-tested children, with a very small sample of adoptees, provide little evidence for anything beyond a selective placement effect. The unwed mother's education correlates .27 with her adopted-away child's Wechsler IQ ($N = 14$) and .18 with that of the natural child of her child's adoptive parents ($N = 78$). The apparent demonstration of a heritability effect by Scarr is evidently a consequence of the fact that the predominantly employed test differed markedly between adoptees and natural children. The two types of children also differed systematically, of course, both in age and in race.

While touching on the often neglected topic of selective placement, it might be noted that unwed mother's education correlated .27 with the Wechsler *verbal* IQ of the natural child of her child's adoptive parents. The correlation with the same child's *performance* IQ was only .02. This difference, based on a substantial N of 78, suggests that selective placement matches the unwed mother to aspects of the adoptive home that primarily affect verbal, rather than performance, IQ.

The data on the *mean* IQs of adopted and natural children, in Scarr's hands, also provide evidence for heritability. Within families containing both early adoptees and natural children, the natural children have higher IQs by about 9 points. This, as Scarr notes, is partly a consequence of the fact that most natural children received Wechsler tests, which consistently produced higher IQs than did the Stanford–Binet. There were, however, 56 early adoptees and 32 natural children who were given Binet tests. With test thus held constant, the natural children had a significantly higher IQ by 6.6 points. (With Wechsler tests, natural children outscored adoptees by 6.2 points, but only 11 adoptees were Wechsler tested.)

The different mean IQs of the two types of children were attributed by Scarr to the superior genetic endowment of the (highly selected) adoptive parents. The adoptive parents, in Scarr's view, could transmit environmental advantages to their adopted children. That was said to have increased the adoptees' mean IQ over what it would have been if they had been reared by their less environmentally favored natural parents. The superior genes of the adoptive parents, however, could be transmitted only to their biological children.

The different observed means are in fact open to several interpretations. The great majority of the adopted children were black, and it is at least conceivable that a black child reared by white parents does not reap as many of the home's environmental advantages as does a white child. Further, recall that Scarr's definition of "early adoptee" included all children placed any time before *1 year* of age. The IQs of late adoptees, we have seen, were 15 points lower than those of early adoptees. Perhaps age of placement also has an effect *within* the 1st year of life. This is at least suggested by an arbitrary division of Stanford–Binet-tested "early adoptees" into the 25% ($N = 14$) placed between 8 and 12 months of age and the 75% ($N = 42$) placed earlier. The earlier-placed children had a mean IQ of 111.0, compared to 103.0 for the later-placed "early adoptees." (Though this difference would be significant by a conventional test, the division into two groups was conveniently arbitrary.) The 32 natural children in these same families who were Binet-tested had a mean IQ of 115.6.

These data suggest the possibility—one with considerable a priori likelihood—that the mean IQ of adopted children is affected by placement age even within the 1st year of life. The fact that the gap between adopted and natural child appears to increase with the adoptee's placement age makes it plausible to speculate that the mean difference may be entirely attributable to delayed placement in the adoptive homes. That would reconcile an apparent discrepancy between Scarr's data and analogous data from the Texas Adoption Project. The Texas study included only adoptees who were placed directly from the hospital. The mean IQs of such truly "early-adopted" children were, in the Texas study, *identical* to those of the natural children of the adoptive parents. That fact, as Horn et al. (1979) noted, suggests zero heritability, because the IQs of the unwed mothers were significantly lower than those of the adoptive parents.

The reanalysis of the transracial adoption data has at several points "equated" early adoptees and natural children by focusing exclusively on younger children, all tested with the Stanford–Binet. The final point to be made reflects the inevitable difficulties that beset all studies carried out in a natural or "field" setting. Though Scarr consistently employed the Stanford–Binet with all children under 8, early adoptees and natural children who were Binet tested were *not* matched for age. The mean ages, in fact, differed significantly—75.9 months for natural children and 61.5 months for early adoptees in the same families. Thus, if mean IQ or the parent–child IQ correlation varies with child's age, new and disturbing confounds are suggested. Within the Texas Adoption Project, unfortunately, adoptees were also significantly younger than natural children in the same families. Presumably, my calling attention to such problems is what Scarr had in mind when she referred to my "perfectionist stance." The point I want to make is that such confounds, like unreported "anomalies," tend to occur *consistently* across studies. The failure to think seriously about them might lead us into grave errors of interpretation. The repeated replication of confounded results will do nothing to advance theoretical understanding.

THE ADOLESCENT ADOPTION STUDY

This study examined a cohort of adoptees who, when they were given Wechsler IQ tests, were between 16 and 22 years of age. This is the oldest adoptee sample ever studied and is thus of special interest. There was a special emphasis on attempting to recruit families who contained at least two adoptees within the specified age range. The major finding was that within the adoptive families, IQ correlations were very low. The adoptive parent–adopted child correlation averaged only .13. The correlation between pairs of (unrelated) adoptive sibs was actually −.03.

The adoptive families evidently contained very few biological children. Thus—unlike the transracial study—the sensitive within-family comparison of adoptive versus biological relations could not be made. To replace it, Scarr falls back on a rather haphazardly assembled group of volunteering biological families, each containing at least two children of appropriate ages. Though statistical matching of individual families was not attempted, Scarr concludes that the two groups of families are in fact appropriately matched. There is of course a bias toward upper-middle-class representation, but it seems much the same in both groups. The mean parental IQ is about 115 in each group, with similarly restricted variance in each. The intercorrelations among a set of demographic variables appear reasonably similar within the two groups. Thus, to Scarr, comparisons of correlations (and multiple regressions) across groups serve to disentangle genetic from environmental factors. Within the biological families, the parent–child correlation in IQ averaged .41. The biological sib correlation was .35. These correlations are obviously higher than those observed in the adoptive families. These data, and this design, are very similar to those reported by Burks (1928) and by Leahy (1935). The present question, as with the classical studies, is whether the environmental variance within the two types of families is really comparable.

There were, in fact, some significant differences between the two types of families, even in respect to *measured* environmental variables. Thus, parents in the biological families were significantly more educated than those in the adoptive families—a fact very likely related to the somewhat higher IQs (about 6 points) observed in the biological children. The F-scale (authoritarianism) scores were lower, and consistently appeared more variable, in the biological families. To explain the significant difference in F scores, Scarr points out that more of the adoptive families came from smaller towns and rural areas. That difference between biological and adoptive samples had not been pointed to as a possible explanation of the lower IQ scores of the adopted children. The more rural nature of the adopted sample is mentioned only in a separate paper, dealing with the *F*-scale data. Within the biological families, there are significant negative correlations between family size and parental IQ, education, occupation, and income. Within the adoptive families, the same correlations are positive and significantly different from those observed in the biological families. The number of tested children per family—presumably related to family size—in turn differs significantly between the two types of families. For example, 38% of the adoptive families and none of the biological families had only one tested child. The fact that family size was significantly and differentially related to IQ and demographic variables in the two family types poses some complexities.

The major tack taken by Scarr is to stress that IQ correlations are much higher in the biological families and that there is scarcely any relation between environmental variables and child's IQ in the adoptive families. Particularly—and in contrast to the transracial study of younger adoptees—there is literally no IQ correlation between adolescent adoptive sibs reared in the same household.

These facts lead Scarr, to conclude—once again—that the heritability of IQ is between .4 and .7; and that "seeming environmental differences that predict so well to outcome differences among biological children are not primarily *environmental* differences, but indices of genetic differences. . . ." That is, although superior biological parents provide superior environments for their offspring, it is the transmission of superior genes that is related to high IQ. The Scarr conclusions, however, ignore a vitally salient fact. The adopted children, who are shown to be "genetically a sample of an intellectually average population," have a grossly restricted IQ *variance*. The IQ variance of the adoptees is a mere 80—even smaller than the variance of 107 observed among the biological children. This can *only* mean that between- and/or within-family environmental variance is enormously diminished in the sample of adoptive families. (The restricted IQ variance of the biological children could conceivably reflect restricted genetic, as well as environmental, variance.)

The within-pair IQ variance for 168 biological sib pairs is given in Scarr's computer printout as 74.13, and the within-pair variance of 84 adoptive sib pairs is 96.23. The two variances do *not* differ significantly, although the two intraclass correlations into which they enter differ very significantly. Thus, the correlations differ because the *between-family* variance in the adoptive families is very much smaller than in the biological families. To be specific, it seems clear that there is much less between-family *environmental* variance among the adoptive families. This would of course serve to lower the parent–child, as well as the sib, IQ correlation in the adoptive families. The demographic "environmental" variables actually measured by Scarr, which do not greatly differ between the two types of family, seem very poorly related to unmeasured, genuinely IQ-relevant environmental variables characteristic of adoptive families. That, of course, was the a priori argument against any attempt to "match" adoptive and biological families.

The plausibility of such an argument has in fact been explicitly recognized by Scarr, who wrote: "It may be thought by some readers that some unmeasured variables that *really* matter in determining children's intellectual development do not vary in these adoptive families, who were selected by the adoption agencies." To refute such a suggestion, Scarr refers to data from the transracial adoption study. "For 143 biological offspring of the adoptive parents, the R^2 from the regression of child IQ . . . on family demographic and parental IQ is .301. For the adopted children *in the same families* ($N = 111$) . . . the R^2 is .156." This is, however, a very misleading comparison. The two groups of children, as Scarr notes, differed significantly in age. The reader will doubtless remember that they also differed in race. They *also* differed with respect to the IQ test employed. Further, despite Scarr's italics, the biological and adopted children were *not* "in the same families." For this regression analysis, Scarr has employed the data from *all* natural children in the adoptive families, including those families who did not contain one of the 111 *early*-adopted children. We have seen earlier that these natural children and their parents differed significantly from the natural children and parents of families containing early adoptees. This systematic difference shared by parent and child in Scarr's sample of "143 biological offspring" clearly inflates any difference in the R^2 between biological and adoptive children. The data from the transracial study, in fact, make it obvious that within families containing early adoptees, any difference in the R^2 between biological and adoptive children would not approach statistical significance. This would be even more true if the samples were equated for test or for age.

There are, it seems to me, a number of problems having to do with Scarr's use of stepwise multiple regression in this study and with the multicolinearity of her data. There seems little sense in detailing them, because even if my doubts were to be resolved, I would not accept at face value any comparison between her adoptive and biological families. We might note in passing that nine of the biological families in the present study in fact contained 11 adopted children, together with 11 natural children of the same parents. *Within* these families, the mean IQ of the biological children was 110.5, compared to 113.1 for the adopted children. The sample size is trivial, but—in contrast to the comparison *between* adoptive and biological families—there is clearly no suggestion that the IQs of the adoptive children are lower.

We ought also to comment on the strong evidence for selective placement—and the clues concerning its nature—provided by Scarr's data. The education of the unwed biological mother correlated fully .43 with the income of the family into which her child had been placed. The unwed mother's education correlated only .29 with the education of the adoptive parents and only .15 with their IQ. The fact that adoptive parents' education guides placement more than their IQ does is scarcely surprising. The education of the adoptive parents is known to the agencies, whereas their IQ is not. There is considerable ground for speculation, however, in the fact that the highest selective placement correlation involves adoptive parents' income. The measure of income was obtained by Scarr some 18 years *after* the child had been placed, whereas the educational levels must have been almost entirely fixed at the time of placement. The data thus suggest that adoption agencies somehow succeed in placing the children of highly educated unwed mothers into adoptive households that, many years in the future, will be relatively wealthy. The magnitude of the selective placement phenomenon in adoption studies has often been overlooked. When any effort is made to assess it, the measures of adoptive families utilized by investigators have typically been education and a rough assessment of occupational status. There are doubtless many unmeasured criteria of selective placement sufficient to account for the relatively modest correlation of .21 reported by Scarr between unwed mother's education and adopted-away child's IQ.

THE PHILADELPHIA TWIN STUDY

The major focus of this study is on a comparison of blacks and whites, but the twin data are employed by Scarr to address a question with wider implications for the study of heritability. Particularly, Scarr is concerned with a "critical assumption" that underlies the very use of twins in heritability analyses. The point has often been made that MZ twins, who tend to be strikingly similar physically, experience more similar environmental treatment than do same-sexed DZ twins. The similarity of treatment, rather than their genetic identity, might thus account for the higher IQ correlation observed among MZs. There is no attempt by Scarr to deny the often-documented greater similarity of treatment experienced by MZs. The Philadelphia twin data, however, are said to demonstrate that the *perceived similarity* of twins—presumably the determiner of similar treatment— is *not* related to their IQ resemblance. This, if true, would indicate that the MZ–DZ difference in IQ correlations is a valid index of heritability.

The study includes both black and white twin pairs, all of whom are pooled together for Scarr's analysis of the "critical assumption." There were several different cognitive tests administered to all subjects, most of which resulted in rather low twin correlations and relatively weak evidence for heritability. The most satisfactory test, in terms of indicating a real MZ–DZ difference, was Raven's Standard Progressive Matrices. This test was thus the main focus of Scarr's analysis of the role of perceived similarity.

To measure "perceived similarity," Scarr employed a factor score emerging from a principal components analysis of several different measures. The factor score weighted the following measures: twins' beliefs about their own zygosity, twins' similarity of appearance rated by judges, twins' statements as to whether they looked alike, twins' reports about whether they had been mistaken for each other, and twins' reports of whether they dressed alike. The factor thus amalgamates judgments of the twins' physical similarity, made both by themselves and others, together with (in the case of dressing) a direct measure of similar experience. The factor loading of the dressing measure was by far the lowest.

The perceived similarity factor score was of course related to true zygosity, as determined by blood group loci. Thus the factor score, like the number of blood group matches, was significantly related to various physical measures of the twins. The Raven difference score (standardized) was calculated for each twin pair. The correlation between factor score and Raven difference score was a mere .07. This was compared to the correlation between number of blood group matches and Raven difference score—a significant .24. Thus an index of genetic similarity (number of blood group matches) significantly and appropriately predicts Raven-score resemblance, and a measure of perceived similarity does not. The overall conclusion reached by Scarr is that perceived similarity (and, presumably, similarity of treatment) is not an important source of bias in twin studies.

The correlations reported by Scarr, however, have some special and peculiar properties. First, they *pool* MZ and DZ twin pairs into a single distribution. This implicitly maintains that perceived similarity, if it is an important variable, is linearly related to IQ similarity over the full range of perceived similarity—from the striking similarity characteristic of most MZs to the minimal similarity of the most genetically diverse DZs. From an environmentalist standpoint, a more reasonable position is that it is the *striking* physical resemblance of most MZs that results in a marked similarity of treatment and thus a high IQ correlation. There is no reason to suppose that variation in the relatively modest physical similarity of DZs will be related to IQ similarity. Thus, a more appropriate test of an environmentalist position would relate perceived similarity to Raven difference score *within MZs only*. There are 108 MZ pairs who have both factor scores and Raven difference scores. The correlation between these two variables is a significant .19. Thus, within a group of genetically identical pairs, perceived similarity *does* appropriately predict IQ resemblance! This makes it plausible to regard the different IQ correlations of MZs and DZs as attributable to their differential similarity of experience.

Second, it should be noted that the factor score and the number of blood group matches are measures with very different properties. The number of blood group matches had a maximum possible value of 12; and by definition, all MZ pairs had precisely 12 blood group matches. There was no such constraint on the values for DZ pairs, who varied in the number of blood group matches. The situation with respect to the perceived similarity score was very different. This could and did vary within MZs, as well as within DZs. This different property of the two measures makes the comparison of correlations pooling MZs and DZs a hazardous enterprise at best. Thus, for example, any unmeasured environmental variables that make MZs alike in IQ, unless they are wholly confounded with Scarr's factor score, will inflate the correlation between blood group matches and IQ resemblance.

Third, most of the measures that enter Scarr's factor score seem very insensitive. The twins' responses to questions concerning their similarity were scored on a 2-point scale—yes or no. There seems little doubt that more sensitive measures would relate more strongly to IQ differences. This possibility can in fact be assessed with respect to one of the items included in Scarr's factor score. The twins were asked: "Do you and your twin dress alike? If so, how often?" The answers were dichotomized into yes (ever) and no (never). This blunt dichotomy was unrelated to Raven difference score. For twins who stated that they did dress alike, however, scores ranging from 4 to 1 were assigned to "almost always," "frequently," "sometimes," and "seldom," respectively. There were 17 MZ twin pairs who agreed that they almost always dressed alike and 43 MZ twin pairs who agreed that they never dressed alike. The Raven difference score for MZs who agreed that they almost always dressed alike averaged .38—equivalent to 5.7 IQ points. The mean Raven difference score for MZs who agreed that they never dressed alike was .71, or 10.7 IQ points. The two means differed significantly ($p < .001$). Thus, again, within a group of twin pairs—all of whom are genetically identical—a measure of similarity of experience appropriately and very significantly predicts IQ resemblance.

The same kind of environmental effect can be demonstrated using a simpler and less derived measure than Scarr's factor score. Photographs of the twins had been rated for similarity of physical appearance by eight independent judges, using a 6-point scale. For 121 MZ pairs, similarity of appearance correlated .26($p < .01$) with Raven difference score. The physically similar twins resembled one another more in test scores. This effect varied systematically with age. For 71 MZ pairs 13 years of age or older, the correlation was .40; for the 50 younger pairs, the correlation was $-.03$. The two correlations differ significantly. This suggests that, as the twins grow older, physical resemblance plays a larger role in determining the similarity of IQ-relevant environment experienced by members of a pair.

These significant environmental effects that emerge from the reanalysis of Scarr's data are not without precedent. Thus Loehlin and Nichols (1976), like Scarr, analyzed twin data and reported that "the greater similarity of our identical twins' experiences . . . cannot plausibly account for more than a very small fraction of their greater observed similarity on the . . . ability variables [p. 52]." That is, like Scarr, they argued that the "critical assumption" that underlies the use of twin data had been empirically sustained. They reached this conclusion, however, by analyzing only a subset of their data. The full data, happily, were made publicly available on a computer tape. When the full data were analyzed (Kamin, 1979), it developed that MZs whose parents tried to treat them "exactly the same" were significantly more alike in ability than were MZs whose parents did not treat them exactly the same. The parents of MZs, of course, were far more likely to try to treat their twins alike than were the parents of same-sexed DZs. These facts powerfully support the suggestion that the MZ–DZ difference in IQ correlations might reflect nothing more than their differential similarity of experience. *These* facts, however, tend not to be noticed or reported by researchers with a behavior genetic orientation. Presumably there is a moral involved in the fact that the same data sets that—in the hands of the original researchers—sustained the critical assumption of twin studies can be made—in less sympathetic hands—to refute it. The least that can be said is that in view of the differing possible conclusions, there is a clear obligation on researchers in this area to make their data available to critics for reanalysis. The obligation has of course been met by Scarr and by Loehlin and Nichols. The other point I would stress is that in this area, the fact that most active investigators agree on the interpretation of the data is not very convincing. The investigators, after all, tend to analyze their data in the same ways, reflecting the same theoretical preconceptions. The problem is nothing so simple as the suppression of embarrassing data. Theoretical commitment makes it unlikely that embarrassing patterns within the data will even be noticed.

The major portion of Scarr's report on the Philadelphia Twin Study is concerned with comparing the results obtained among blacks and whites. The higher mean IQ of whites, in Scarr's view, is best explained as an environmental effect. The particular environmental hypothesis supported by Scarr asserts that genetic variability in cognitive test performance among blacks will be relatively small. This, it is said, leads to an expectation of higher twin correlations among blacks than among whites; further, the MZ–DZ difference in IQ correlations should be larger within whites than within blacks. Though Scarr cautions readers about the large standard errors involved, and about the quality of the data, she indicates that the results are consistent with these expectations.

There is, however, a fundamental problem with Scarr's analysis, which vitiates any such conclusion. The ages of the twins varied between 10 and 16 years; of course, raw scores on the cognitive tests were positively related to age. The fact that Scarr employed only portions of standardized tests—and administered the tests with a slide presentation technique plus special instructions—compelled her to standardize scores by age within her own sample. To do so, she divided the subjects into six different age bands, each containing over 100 individuals. This age standardization, however, *pooled blacks and whites into a single distribution.* This, I think, cannot be defended—for several reasons.

The black mean was, invariably, lower than the white mean. Further, at least for Raven's test, the black raw-score variance was larger. This was particularly, and significantly, true at the older age levels. That, in turn, reflects a phenomenon noted by Scarr: The correlations between raw score and age were lower for blacks than for whites. Further, the proportions of the two races represented at the six age levels differed significantly. To make matters worse, there was a significant correlation between age and socioeconomic status within whites, but not within blacks. Thus, within whites only, the observed increase in raw score with age is at least in part attributable to increasing SES levels. The suburban whites whom Scarr added to her inner-city, public school sample appear to have been significantly older, as well as of higher SES. For all these reasons, the normalized, age-standardized scores assigned by Scarr to her subjects can have no generalized meaning. They depend upon the unique mixture of races and ages (as well as sexes and zygosities) contained in Scarr's nonrepresentative sample. Though score means and variances—as well as age distributions—differed between races, race was of course constant within each twin pair. Thus no significance can be attached to the different intraclass correlations reported by Scarr for blacks and whites, nor can those correlations be compared to those reported by investigators who employed standardized versions of the same tests.

Perhaps a more defensible procedure would have been to standardize scores by age within each race—though this would not have eliminated the confounding of age and SES within whites. To approximate what would happen if this were done, I calculated intraclass correlations on *raw scores*—separately for six age bands and separately by race. Then, for each race, I weighted the six separate obtained correlations. For Raven's test, I obtained the following correlations: white MZs, .60; white DZs, .30; black MZs, .57; black DZs, .23. The difference between the MZ and DZ correlations was a trifle larger among blacks than among whites. The correlations reported by Scarr, based on her inappropriate standardization, were: white MZs, .59; white DZs, .15; black MZs, .63; black DZs, .36. The MZ–DZ difference here appears substantially larger among whites. That kind of apparent result led Scarr to suggest that the data indicated less genetic variability within the black population. There is clearly no real evidence for such an effect in Scarr's data.

We should note that the data analyses relevant to the "critical assumption," reported earlier, made use of Scarr's standardized scores. To check on whether similar effects could be observed without the use of those scores, I calculated the raw-score, within-pair variances (Raven's test) for MZs who always dressed alike and for MZs who never dressed alike. The within-pair variance was significantly greater for those MZs who never dressed alike—a clear environmental effect. Presumably, if more valid ability scores were available, the reported environmental effects would have been larger and even more clearly detectable.

CONCLUSION

There is little point in reiterating what I have already stressed repeatedly. The empirical data can be reanalyzed in such a way as to suggest an IQ heritability close to zero. There are some difficulties and embarrassments for such a view posed by some bits of the data, but embarrassments of at least equal gravity abound for the view that heritability is high. To my mind, a refusal to reject a null hypothesis of zero heritability is a more prudent and realistic conclusion than Scarr's assertion that heritability lies somewhere between .4 and .7.

Though I have tried to avoid political argument in this commentary, I cannot resist the temptation to jump (perhaps unfairly) on a remark made by Scarr in the introduction to the Minnesota Adolescent Adoption Study. The introduction points out that observed effects of family background on IQ and on life success (income, SES, etc.) may be either environmental or genetic. Then, a frankly political statement intrudes: "As unreconstructed liberals, we get upset about the long-term environmental effects of families on their offsprings' life chances. When individual outcomes are shown to be affected by 'family background,' we don't know how upset to be."

Perhaps this remark was intended as a kind of parody of the liberal position—but it strikes perilously close to home. Why should a liberal *not* be upset if there are long-term *genetic* affects of families on their offsprings' life chances? Are "genetically" produced differences more just, good, or true than "environmentally" produced differences? Can the two types of differences be meaningfully distinguished? Are "genetic" differences more fixed and irreversible than "environmental" differences? To argue that we should be upset by cultural-familial retardation, while cheerfully accepting the genetically determined (but easily preventable) PKU, would be obviously absurd. Though in other contexts Scarr has recognized that social rewards need not, and perhaps ought not, to be contingent on "heritable" differences, it seems to me that the basic social function of research on IQ heritability is revealed in the sentiment Scarr ascribes to "unreconstructed liberals." To attribute the inequitable distribution of worldly goods to "genetic" causes is thought, somehow, to legitimize it.

REFERENCES

Burks, B. S. The relative influence of nature and nurture upon mental development: A comparative study of foster parent-foster child resemblance and true parent-true child resemblance. *Yearbook of the national society for the study of education* (Part 1), 1928, *27*, 219–316.

Horn, J. M., Loehlin, J. C., & Willerman, L. Intellectual resemblance among adoptive and biological relatives: The Texas adoption project. *Behavior Genetics*, 1979, *9*, 177–207.

Kamin, L. J. *The science and politics of IQ*. Potomac, Maryland: Lawrence Erlbaum Associates, 1974.

Kamin, L. J. Psychology as social science: *The Jensen affair, ten years after*. Presidential address to Eastern Psychological Association, Philadelphia, April, 1979.

Leahy, A. M. Nature-nurture and intelligence. *Genetic Psychology Monographs*, 1935, *17*, 241–306.

Loehlin, J. C., & Nichols, R. C. *Heredity, environment, and personality*. Austin: University of Texas Press, 1976.

Mittler, P. *Psycholinguistic skills in four year old twins and singletons*. Unpublished Ph.D. thesis, University of London, 1969.

Skodak, M., & Skeels, H. M. A final follow-up study of one hundred adopted children. *Journal of Genetic Psychology*, 1945, *66*, 21–58.

V.2 Obstacles, Problems, and Pitfalls in Differential Psychology

Arthur R. Jensen
University of California, Berkeley

Sandra Scarr is one of the leading thinkers and researchers in human behavioral genetics, particularly the analysis of individual and group differences in mental abilities. Her unusual industry in empirical research, guided by her keen eye for the crucial issues, has resulted in numerous articles that provide a wealth of stimulating food for thought for students of behavioral genetics and differential psychology. It is a boon to have these many articles, with critical commentaries, all collected in one volume. I plan to use it as the main collateral reading in my graduate course on the behavior genetics of human abilities.

But why only as collateral reading rather than as the main textbook? Two reasons: First, the collection does not attempt a comprehensive review of the empirical findings in this field or a systematic exposition of the theory and methodology of quantitative genetics, on which so much of the argumentation rests. Second, some of the research articles are of such a pioneering nature— dealing with the untamed frontiers of the field—as to be regarded as still too highly controversial to serve the purpose of a general textbook. (For the same reasons, I would not use either of my own books in this field—*Genetics and Education* and *Educability and Group Differences*—as the main textbook in such a course.)

Students can read books such as the present one much more intelligently and profitably after they have gained a systematic overview of the issues, methods, and findings in this field. The two books I most highly recommend for that purpose (and as excellent prerequisite reading for the present volume) are: first, Philip E. Vernon's *Human Intelligence: Heredity and Environment* (1979), which is a quite general, admirably lucid, and thoroughly balanced exposition of virtually all the issues in the so-called IQ controversy; and second, *Race Dif-*

ferences in Intelligence (1975) by John Loehlin, Gardner Lindzey, and J. N. Spuhler, which is more narrowly specialized but highly readable and informative.

Many of the articles and detailed arguments in the present volume also presuppose a higher level of background in statistical methods than can generally be expected for undergraduate students in psychology, education, or the other social sciences. It is hard to imagine how some of this material could be comprehended by readers who are not familiar with correlation and regression, multiple regression, the analysis of variance, and at least the main concepts of factor analysis and components analysis. These are the essential tools for research in differential psychology and quantitative genetics. For readers with this background, the present volume affords much engrossing and rewarding reading and study. I hope it will stimulate graduate students in the behavioral sciences to investigate further the many important problems highlighted by Scarr's own work.

The challenge of gaining a more complete scientific understanding of the role of genetic and environmental factors in individual and group differences in mental abilities is, I fear, often made unattractive to research students more by the *extrinsic* obstacles to research on these topics—in the doctrinaire academic climate of the recent past—than by the *intrinsic* scientific difficulties in the subject matter itself. Students are advised to try to distinguish, at all times, as clearly as possible between the extrinsic obstacles and the intrinsic problems in research on the genetics of mental ability. To this end, I think it would be helpful to make explicit briefly some of the main obstacles to clear thinking in this field, so that students can be on guard against them, both in their own thinking about these issues and in the many writings on these topics in the past decade.

EXTRINSIC OBSTACLES TO GENETIC RESEARCH ON IQ

1. *Antipathy Toward the Objective Measurement of Human Qualities.*   Scientific research on human abilities (or other traits) necessarily involves the objective measurement of traits and the application of quantitative methods to such measurements. Measurement is itself a part of the scientific enterprise. There need not be agreement that one particular method of measurement is the best or even adequate. But allowing the *principle* of measurement and the possibility of improving our measurements through the continuing interaction of empirical results and theoretical formulations is the sine qua non of any advanced science. Unfortunately, acceptance of even this basic principle may be too much to expect of many persons in psychology and other social sciences at present. Much of psychology today is unfortunately more akin to social ideology than to natural science.

2. *Fear of Predestination.*   The notion that the genes determine one's fate seems unacceptable to some persons, who therefore bring a negative attitude

toward any discussion of genetic influence on behavioral traits. This attitude is largely a result of faulty analysis. The remedy is the important concept of *reaction range*. It needs to be emphasized for beginning students of behavioral genetics. *Reaction range* is the fact that a given genotype (a gene or combination of genes) does not necessarily have a one-to-one correspondence with the resulting phenotype (the observed characteristic) but can give rise to a considerable variation in phenotypes depending on various *nongenetic* influences in the course of development.

Genotypes for various traits differ in the malleability of their corresponding phenotypes in response to the range of variation that occurs in the natural environment. But there are probabilistic *limits* to the reaction range, and one of the tasks of genetic analysis is to explore the extent of those limits in the natural environment and to discover specifically the environmental agents that affect them.

Everyone agrees that our fates are determined *in some degree* by genetic factors. The parents of one species, for example, do not bear offspring of a different species. This, of course, is predetermination of the offspring's fate to a drastic degree. *Within* a species, however, the degree of predetermination is less drastic and differs markedly from one characteristic to another. Behavioral characteristics are among the most malleable, in the sense of having quite a broad range of reaction. But the concept of the reaction range implies that it is a perfectly *continuous* variable. Thus, from a purely scientific standpoint, there is no dividing line on this continuum that should warrant emotional resistance to the idea that the genes control some amount of the observed individual variability in many characteristics—physical and behavioral. One's personal feelings about this fact should be viewed as a separate issue.

The notion of *determinism,* in general, is intrinsic to the nature of scientific explanation, regardless of genetics. The facts of prediction and control of variables, in accord with a scientific understanding of them, clearly justify determinism as a valid working hypothesis where scientific study is concerned, whatever one's personal religious or philosophic beliefs about free will may be.

3. *Confusion of Genes and Genotypes.* A genotype is a particular, often unique, combination of genes. Individuals are products of their own genotypes and their unique environmental experiences. As parents, they cannot pass on either their own genotypes (or unique environmental experiences, either) to their offspring; they can pass on only a random sample of one-half their genes, which are reconstituted in new combinations in the conception of the offspring. There seems little rational justification for extending the concept of the sacredness of the individual to a random assortment of the individual's genes (i.e., the gametes—ovum or sperm). Because one has no responsibility for one's own genotype and therefore deserves no credit (or blame) for it, it is impossible to find any rational justification for being ego-involved with one's own genetic

makeup. Yet this is a common human failing, expressed in such sentiments as "my *own* flesh and blood" in reference to one's offspring. Genetic factors are thus often unjustly denied or belittled when an offspring falls short of some desired expectation in terms of the parents' or society's values regarding particular traits. The trait of intelligence, with all its educationally, occupationally, and socially important correlates, is probably the most liable in this respect.

I believe that this erroneous ego identification with one's own genotype is in part responsible for such widely popular but mistaken beliefs (and the need for their constant reassurance) that genetic factors are not involved in most mental retardation and in the most severe types of mental illness, such as schizophrenia and manic-depressive psychosis. The obvious emotional resistance to the findings of genetical research on these topics needs to be explained and would be an interesting subject for psychological investigation in its own right.

4. *Personified Blame for Misfortune.*   In the era of prescientific thinking, as in many primitive cultures today, all the mysterious forces of nature become personified, with the attribution of causes to humanlike actions and motives. We still see this tendency today in regard to the explanations of behavioral, educational, and social problems that seem related to traits that may be conditioned, in part, by genetic factors. The possible role of genetic factors in the complex causal network is often shunned or belittled; but nefarious, humanly motivated factors such as social injustice, neglect, economic greed, political oppression, social snobbery, prejudice, racism, ill will, and humanity's inhumanity to its own are emphasized as the major or even the only causes. Such causes can be blamed with emotion, as one blames a person for committing a malicious act, and one's angry emotions at injustice may be recruited for political action. But this should never be confused with the scientific analysis of the causes of educational, social, and economic problems.

Yet science cannot ignore the "human factor" in its study of social problems. The fallacy to be avoided is the belief that all human problems are entirely a product of willful motives. Those who ardently cling to this belief cannot allow the consideration of genetic factors in the causal network.

5. *Belief in the Personal Beneficence of Nature.*   Human inequalities are all too obvious and may occasionally take forms that are commonly perceived as misfortune, arousing the natural sympathy of those who feel that they themselves have been more fortunate. Many persons strongly resist the belief that God or nature could perpetrate what they view as a great injustice on another human being. As a result, they cannot admit human misfortune as being in any way connected with humankind's biological evolution and the genetic mechanisms involved therein. We may wish to think that an all-wise nature, like a good parent watching over beloved children, will forever, unfailingly take benevolent care of

the human race and its genetic makeup. But that is a scientifically unwarranted and, in the long run, probably dangerous belief.

6. *Fear of Racism.* Genetical research on socially important human traits, especially intelligence, is scorned by some persons who fear that it could lead to the discovery of a genetic component in observed racial differences; or that such investigation, whatever its eventual outcome, lends scientific respectability to the question of racial differences in IQ or other behavioral characteristics. The question itself, they would declare, is to be scorned as insulting and racist. This fear reflects a gross failure to observe the important distinction between racism and the scientific study of racial variation, which logically must apply to *all* characteristics, physical as well as mental.

Racism has proved to be one of the major hindrances to the scientific study of racial variation in intelligence and other behavioral traits. Racism is the belief that human races can be distinctly ordered in a simple hierarchy in terms of some global evaluation of inferior–superior; and that individuals are justifiably treated differently—socially, educationally, legally, and politically—solely according to their racial origin or socially defined racial-group membership.

I know of nothing in genetics or in the scientific study of racial variation that would lend support to these racist beliefs. In fact, already well-established findings in genetics and differential psychology clearly contradict the essential tenets of racism. Racism must be fought where it actually exists—through education and enforced legal sanctions when necessary. The cause of racial justice is not furthered by putting down scientists who inquire into the nature and causes of racial variation in the same manner in which they might investigate any other natural phenomenon. Where certain racial differences are generally acknowledged to be of considerable social and educational importance, attempts to understand these phenomena warrant the best scientific effort we can bring to bear on them.

7. *Political and Social Ideologies.* Advocates of certain political and economic ideologies, most notably neo-Marxist and similar collectivist and totalitarian philosophies, are intolerant of the idea that not all of a person's behavior and not all social conditions are potentially amenable to the control of the political and economic system. To maintain the belief in complete economic determinism of the conditions of life, the importance of genetic factors—which are not directly subject to political or economic control—must be denied. This was the philosophic underpinning of Lysenkoism, which prevailed for many years in the Soviet Union, with ultimately disastrous consequences for the science of genetics and for its applications in agriculture in the U.S.S.R. Despite this lesson, in recent years we have seen a good deal of Lysenkoist thinking in the so-called nature–nurture controversy over IQ—most blatantly promulgated, of course, by

left-wing groups such as the Progressive Labor Party, the Students for a Democratic Society, the American Communist Party, and other minor, but highly vocal, political and social activist groups.

8. *Fear of Eugenics.*   Forced sterilization, instituted during Hitler's Nazi regime, with political overtones in connection with the Nazi persecution of Jews, became identified in the popular mind with *eugenics* and gave this term a terribly bad name. This was capitalized on by those who, for a variety of reasons, are opposed to the genetical study of human differences. As a result, even the highly respectable Eugenics Society and the *Eugenics Quarterly* saw fit to change their names, respectively, to the Society for Social Biology and *Social Biology.*

Eugenics refers to planned attempts to improve the human condition through the control of reproduction. The definition of *improve* and the means of control are not themselves intrinsic to the concept of eugenics but are separate issues in their own right, involving profound philosophic, ethical, and moral questions. But advocacy of eugenics really does not depend on a scientific consensus regarding the heritability of IQ or any other trait.

The very substantial correlation (between .50 and .70) between parents' IQs and their children's IQs is an empirical fact, *whatever* its cause. At our present stage of knowledge, the surest statistical prediction or control of unborn children's IQs could be achieved by selection of the parents on the basis of their own IQs. This would be eugenics, or the control of reproduction. But it does not necessarily have anything to do with genetics or our knowledge of the heritability of IQ. Yet proposals for the voluntary control of reproduction—even when justified by strictly environmental arguments—are today branded as "racist," as when Dr. Wilson Riles, California's State Superintendent of Public Instruction, referred to a statement by psychologist Lloyd Humphreys as "absolutely one of the most racist statements that I've ever heard." Humphreys, in his testimony as an expert witness in the Larry P. ("test bias") trial in California, had stated that "the surest and most effective social action the Negro community could take by itself to achieve equality and education and jobs would be to limit dramatically the birthrate in those families providing the least effective environment for intellectual development" (quoted by Ristow, 1978, pp. 48–50). Because Humphreys says nothing about genetics and emphasizes the environment, it is obviously the control of reproduction that is being objected to by Riles (and others) rather than its connection with genetics. Both the "environmentalist" and the "hereditarian" agree that the average IQ of the next generation could be most surely altered by selecting the parents, whatever the disagreement as to the desirability of such a course of action.

Seemingly implicit in the opposition to any suggestions for control of reproduction, whatever its purported benefits, is the belief that human ingenuity can solve any problems in the human condition without taking either genetic inheritance or reproductive rates into consideration. Behavioral genetics per se is completely neutral on such social-ethical issues, and it should not have to bear the brunt of emotional reactions to popularly disapproved opinions expressed in the social-ethical sphere.

9. *Fear of Scientism.*   It is a mistake to confuse the scientific study of genetics or of human behavior (or of anything else) with *scientism,* which is the erroneous belief that science itself imposes values or leads directly to the imposition of solutions to social problems.

The aims of science are to discover facts and to understand them within a systematic or theoretical framework. The alteration or betterment of conditions is not the goal of science per se. The facts of science, and the potential control over nature that scientific knowledge makes possible, lead to solutions to real-life problems only in the company of values, implicit or explicit, over which persons may markedly disagree.

Proposed solutions to human and social problems should be thought of, not as *Science* → *Solutions,* but as *Solutions* = *f* (*Facts, Values, Costs*). Science makes its contribution to the equation by reliably establishing the facts that must be taken into consideration to achieve a workable solution. Arguments about values and costs, though crucially important in their own right, should not be mixed up with the scientific issues. This, of course, in no way implies that scientists, in obtaining their data for scientific research, are exempt from responsibility for protecting the personal rights and welfare of the individuals involved.

10. *Psychology's Vested Interest in "Environmentalism."*   Although "hollow organism" S–R behaviorism is now largely a curio of the history of psychology, we still see a strong tendency among the majority of psychologists to look first (or even exclusively) for the causes of individual differences in circumstances *external* to the individual. The first impulse is to hypothesize some past or present environmental factor as the source of variance in all psychological phenomena, as if one believed that all individuals begin life as equivalent tabulae rasae and that all behavioral differences are learned, even differences in the *rate* of learning itself. This common tendency reflects the strong environmentalist bias in psychology.

Many psychologists with whom I have discussed these matters speak almost as if they are defending their professional domain from encroachment by other types of theories that invoke biological, genetic, and evolutionary concepts—in addition to the individual's experience—for the explanation of behavior. The advent of the field of sociobiology has had to face this strongly entrenched behaviorist-environmentalist bias in the social sciences. However, our science is beginning to show signs of change in this respect.

Scientific psychology is becoming largely a subdivision of biology. Those aspects of the field that do not put down roots in the biological sciences are doomed to becoming backwaters outside the mainstream of scientific progress, surviving only as discredited relics of scientific history, like astrology and phrenology.

11. *The Double Standard of Research Criticism for "Environmentalist" and "Hereditarian" Findings.*   There is simply no doubt about it: There is a double standard among journal editors, referees, book review editors, textbook writers, and reviewers of research proposals when it comes to criticizing and evaluating articles that appear to support what the readers may interpret as either "hereditarian" or "environmentalist" conclusions. I have had plenty of experience with this, for I have published many articles that range widely on this spectrum. I approve the thorough critical scrutiny to which "hereditarian" articles are subjected but deplore the fact that many "environmentalist" articles receive much more lax reviews. There is unquestionably much more editorial bias favoring "environmentalist" findings and interpretations. For example, I was recently told by a journal editor that one of my articles—which took all of seven months to be reviewed—had to be sent to seven reviewers in order to obtain *two* reviews of the article itself; the rest were merely diatribes against "Jensenism"; the editor apologized that they were too insulting to pass on to me.

Many young Ph.D.'s just starting their academic careers and in need of favorable reviews, publications, and research grants are understandably discouraged by this climate from embarking on research programs that might result in "hereditarian" findings. Research efforts in this field are still popularly perceived very much as the battle of the "good guys" versus the "bad guys," and this is reflected even in editorial reviews by some of our technical journals.

But I think these attitudes are now dying out with the upcoming generation of students in psychology, who today show little of the religious fervor in defense of doctrinaire environmentalism that was so prominent five or ten years ago. If my article, "How Much Can We Boost IQ and Scholastic Achievement?" (which raised a storm of protests in 1969, were published today, it would hardly raise an eyebrow. I found that most university students ten years later were surprised and puzzled in learning of the events on campus following publication of that article in 1969. The present volume fortunately will find a much more open-minded and inquiring audience in colleges than existed only a few years ago. This trend augurs well for progress in the behavioral sciences.

12. *Belittling or Dismissing the Heredity–Environment Question.*   As a desperate last resort of doctrinaire environmentalists, the whole question of the relative roles of genetic and environmental factors in individual and group differences is dismissed as a scientifically unworthy, useless, or forever unanswerable question. This position still occasionally finds expression, as in J. McVicker Hunt's statement (1979): "The failure of Project Head Start to achieve the unrealistic goals set for it prompted Jensen to revisit the faith and methodology of

predeterminism and to reawaken the useless controversy over the relative importance of heredity and environment [p. 104]."

If the present volume is not a sufficient antidote for this nihilistic attitude, I
fear the patient is beyond hope. Fortunately, the dormant era of nature–nurture
research that existed from about 1940 to 1970 is most definitely history, and
nothing like that is apt to recur in the foreseeable future. Behavioral genetics is
one of the most rapidly growing fields in the behavioral sciences.

SUGAR COATING THE ISSUES

There is still another category of beliefs that are often entertained to mollify some
of the possible perceived implications of the findings of behavior genetic analysis
regarding the heritability of general mental ability. This sugarcoating of the
issues is often at best a form of self-deception, and although it may temporarily
make certain facts seem more acceptable to a wider audience, it usually runs into
conflict with other facts. In science, no well-established findings should need to
be "sold" at the expense of other well-established findings; nor should other,
highly speculative counterbalancing factors have to be suggested that might
conceivably nullify any findings that are at risk of being viewed by someone as
"bad news." A few of the most commonly encountered sugarcoatings used in
the hopes of making life easier in the nature–nurture controversy are listed next.

1. *Belittling the IQ.*   This takes many forms; most of them are either straw
men or are invalid in light of all the evidence on the nature and correlates of IQ.

One can point to deficiencies in tests, particularly those in the early history of
psychometrics, and to the misuses of tests by uninformed, unwise, or unscrupu-
lous persons. But almost exact parallels can be found in the history of medicine,
or automotive engineering, or any other applied science. This line of argument
has virtually no relevance to the scientific issues in present-day research on
behavioral genetics.

It is misleading to suggest that there is an equal trade-off between IQ (i.e.,
general intelligence), on one hand, and other abilities (uncorrelated with IQ), on
the other, for educational and occupational achievement. So far, no hint of any
substitute for the intelligence measured by IQ tests has been found that can be
brought to bear on scholastic performance as we now know it. Also, IQ seems to
act as a *threshold* variable for the realization of special talents. That is to say,
probably at least an average level of intelligence is *necessary*, although not
sufficient, for a high level of achievement in fields requiring special talents.

Another ploy, often made in response to empirical demonstrations of the
predictive validity of the IQ for educational, occupational, and social criteria, is
to try to belittle the many *correlates* of IQ. If these are really all so unimportant,

one may wonder: Why should anyone be concerned with the conspicuous individual inequalities in all the correlates of IQ? Yet such concern is one of the most generally conspicuous features of our present society.

2. *Obscuring the Connection Between the Population Mean and the Proportion of the Population Falling Above (or Below) a Given Selection Cutoff.*   When a variable is at least roughly normally distributed on a fixed scale of measurement, there is a definite relationship between the mean of the distribution and the proportion of the total distribution that falls above or below a given cutting score on the scale. This elementary statistical relationship is too often obscured, forgotten, or ignored in discussions of group differences. For example, people who know there is approximately a 1-standard-deviation difference (about 15 IQ points) between the means of the white and black IQ distributions in the United States and who say "So what?" nevertheless seem alarmed to find that the percentage of blacks who contribute to school statistics on mental retardation (with IQs below 70) is five to six times greater than the percentage of whites. (The very opposite occurs at the top portion of the IQ distribution, in the selection of the academically gifted.) These large percentage differences at the extremes of IQ are, of course, an integral part of the very same phenomenon as the difference between the population means.

3. *Exaggerating the Probable Results of Environmental Manipulation.*   In the formulation $P = f(G,E)$, where G is genotype and E is environment, and the heritability of the trait is fairly high, it is tempting to suggest: Never mind, E can be manipulated so as to override any effects of G. This is the notion that whatever the variance attributable to G is, it can be neutralized by proper manipulation of E or by discovering such optimal $G \times E$ interactions ("different strokes for different folks") as to render all phenotypes practically equivalent. This is what Scarr aptly refers to as the *"intervention fallacy."* Although these are, of course, *theoretical* possibilities, there is no generally accepted evidence yet that anyone knows how to accomplish this, beyond the modest results of providing normally stimulating, supportive, and wholesome environments for children who would otherwise suffer physical and psychological neglect and deprivation. But we should want to do that anyway, regardless of any question of genetics. Its justification does not depend on research findings in behavior genetics.

4. *Escaping Hard Questions by Looking at Only One Set of Facts at a Time.*   This is the tendency to leave the impression that any given finding, if it is apt to be viewed unfavorably by someone, can be explained away by some other equally cogent findings. If it is found, for example, that hypothesized nutritional differences do not exist and therefore cannot explain any part of the IQ difference

between two subpopulations, one can claim that the tests were probably culturally biased, or that the subjects were tested by examiners of a different race, etc.,
which "explains" the difference between the subpopulations. When these
hypothesized effects are later investigated and found to be negligible sources of
between-group variance, one can ignore the previous nutrition research and
suggest that nutritional factors could be responsible for the observed group differences. One can always easily escape from facing the really hard questions by
not viewing all the key findings *simultaneously*. When we do take a simultane-
ous view, the most popular environmentalist explanations of social-class and
racial-group differences in IQ begin to appear unsupportable (Jensen, 1973;
1977b).

5. *Emphasizing Genetic Commonality as a Smoke Screen for Genetic Differences Between Groups.*   The fact that any two groups may have a very large
proportion of genes in common should in no way minimize the possibility or
importance of genetic differences in particular characteristics. Many genes are
nonsegregating; that is, all individuals within a species inherit the same alleles at
certain loci, and the characteristics affected by those alleles therefore show no
variation except for possible rare mutants. If it is a particular *difference* between
groups that we are interested in analyzing, the fact of overwhelming genetic
commonality in many other characteristics is quite irrelevant. It does not matter
whether the difference of interest is attributable to less than 1% of the total gene
pool or to more than 99%.

The fact is that a great deal of human variability in a multitude of characteristics involves genetic differences, even though a preponderant proportion of *all*
the genes is common to all persons of all races.

In fact, the human species even has a large proportion of genes in common
with the anthropoid apes. In terms of genetic commonality, the genetic distance
between Homo sapiens and the chimpanzee is not much different from the
genetic distance between the chimpanzee and the gorilla. The average probability
that any two humans will possess the same allele (i.e., any one of the alternate
forms of the gene at a given locus on the chromosome) is only about twice as
great as the average probability that a chimpanzee and a human will possess the
same allele at a randomly selected locus.

It should also be kept in mind that the human differences of greatest interest
are complex characteristics or traits involving polygenic systems in which combinations of many genes are simultaneously subjected to selection in the course
of evolution. It is these polygenic characteristics that are the most salient features
of racial differences. They are not in any way contradicted by evidence that a
purely *random* sample of single genes from *all* genetic loci show much greater
genetic commonality than genetic differences. The great average difference in
height between the Pgymy and the Watusi, for example, is not at all diminished
by the fact that some 95% or more of the total genes in these groups are the same.

6. *Middle-of-the-Road Fallacy.*   Theoretical eclecticism, which may sometimes be a virtue in the early stages of scientific investigation of complex and
poorly understood phenomena, is occasionally confused with the fallacious notion that some ''middle position'' with respect to apparently conflicting theories
or findings is most probably the correct position. One textbook writer, for example, pointed out that Jensen (1969) had claimed the heritability of IQ to be .80
whereas Kamin (1974) claimed it to be 0; the writer concluded that therefore the
true heritability of IQ is most likely close to the *average* of the values claimed by
Jensen and Kamin—that is, .40! Whatever the scientific truth of the matter is,
this form of illogical argument could never lead to it. One is reminded of the
16th-century astronomers who tried to reconcile the conflicting theories of
Ptolemy and Copernicus by claiming that some of the planets revolve around the
earth whereas others revolve around the sun! Scientific knowledge, of course,
does not advance by ''averaging'' expert opinions or theories or by tallying box
scores of empirical findings that seem to favor conflicting theories.

The illogic of believing that a middle-of-the-road position will more closely
approximate the truth than any of the conflicting positions, however, should not
be confused with scientific *agnosticism* regarding the point in question. Agnosticism is simply an admission of doubt and open-mindedness, and of resistance to
premature judgment where the evidence is inadequate or inconclusive.

PHILOSOPHY OF SCIENCE

Investigations in behavioral genetics, as in any other field, differ in their research
styles, and even in their philosophy of science, while agreeing on the main tenets
of appeal to objective evidence and statistical inference.

My own view is that the essential purpose of scientific theories and hypotheses is the discovery of new knowledge. Theories that can only order existing
knowledge or hypotheses that can only explain already established facts in an ad
hoc manner (that is, *after* the fact) are not as prized as theories or hypotheses that
lead us to new, previously unexpected or even counterintuitive phenomena.
Many alternative theories can usually be concocted to explain a single fact or
small set of facts that we already know. A more important criterion of a progressive theory is that it should lead to new knowledge and fresh insights. This often
requires that a theory boldly ''stick its neck out,'' so to speak. From the
standpoint of scientific progress, it is much more important that a theory promote
the acquisition of new facts—even though these may deal a deathblow to the
theory itself—than that the theory be true. A theory that cannot be falsified by
evidence, at least in principle, is not a theory at all in the scientific sense.

Knowledge can be advanced most rapidly by the practice of ''strong inference,'' which means proposing limited but clearly formulated theories from
which competing hypotheses can be unambiguously derived. The theories are in

competition in the sense that they give rise to hypotheses or predictions that are contradictory to one another. The data, then, if relevant and adequate and free of artifact, can result in the rejection of one or the other hypothesis. Psychologists often fail to narrow their hypotheses sufficiently to permit a clear-cut test of the hypothesis; or the hypothesis is so loosely linked to the theory in question that rejection of the hypothesis has no forceful implications for the theory, which continues to live on without real risk of empirical refutation. Thus the theory is preserved by ad hoc hypotheses concerning possible uncontrolled variables, previously unsuspected artifacts, or inadequacy of the measurements or experimental techniques. We should be wary of theories that are too vague or too general to risk falsification.

A modest and limited hypothesis that can be crucially tested seems to me far preferable to a much more sweeping hypothesis that cannot be subjected to a compelling test, for whatever reason. The answers to large questions usually depend importantly on having clear answers to a number of subsidiary questions that, if left unanswered, render any answer to the larger question quite ambiguous and uncompelling. It seems to me that this has been the rule rather than the exception in science. Usually, one must momentarily turn one's back on the Big Question in order to settle certain subsidiary issues that need to be understood before the Big Question can be adequately formulated in terms of a coherent theory yielding fruitful, testable hypotheses. Darwin's theory of the origin of species, for example, has become generally established, with certain modifications, by firmly establishing many more limited but crucially relevant issues.

I believe that much the same approach will be necessary to reach any scientific consensus on the question of racial differences in intelligence. It is on this point that I seem to find myself in most marked disagreement with Scarr and Barker (Part II, Chap. 4) when they state: "We have never believed that bits and pieces of answers to smaller and better-formed questions were likely to add up to the information one *really* wanted to know. So we felt it was better to fall short of answering completely an important question than to answer satisfactorily a question one did not want to ask." Answers to small questions, of course, do not "add up" to the answer to a Big Question, but they may well be crucial prerequisites for answering the Big Question. Small questions are nontrivial to the degree that they are clearly connected in a theoretical structure with the Big Question.

One should also distinguish between *strong* and *weak* tests of a hypothesis. A single study may formulate several hypotheses but be designed in such a way as to provide a strong test for only one (or some) of the proposed hypotheses. By a *strong* test of a hypothesis, I simply mean that the known relevant conditions have been adequately controlled and that the power of the statistical inference is sufficient that a failure of the hypothesized effect is substantially damaging to the theory from which the hypothesis was derived. A *weak* test of a hypothesis is one that, because of uncontrolled or confounded variables or rather weak statistical power, cannot carry much weight for or against the theory, whatever the empirical outcome. Weak tests allow easy "escape hatches" for explaining away any result if it does not accord with one's particular theoretical predilection.

Also, the tests of many respectable hypotheses are only one-directional with respect to two competing theories, such that if an empirical failure of the hypothesis damages one theory, this does not necessarily mean it supports the presently opposing theory. But the one-directional test may be an important gain in knowledge nevertheless. For example, showing that a particular IQ test is not culture biased in terms of some commonly agreed-upon criterion may definitively rule out one hypothesis put forth to explain a mean difference between two groups (which is worth knowing), but it does not definitively support some other hypothesis, such as that the difference is the result of nutritional factors or of genetic factors. It is a rare test of a hypothesis that has equally definitive implications for two opposing theories.

Students should be alerted to a common fallacy in evaluating evidence. It is what I term the *temporal order fallacy*—that is, the failure of a later study to replicate the findings of an earlier study. The fallacy consists of according more weight to the second (more recent) study than to the first. This is terribly common in psychology. We often read that Dr. A's study found such and such and then Dr. B's study failed to replicate Dr. A's finding. Dr. A's finding is dismissed, and often that ends the matter. We can just as logically claim that Dr. A's study failed to replicate Dr. B's finding. The temporal order of the studies is irrelevant, other things being equal. If one study is superior in terms of design, statistical power, representativeness of samples, and the like, then of course it should be accorded more weight, regardless of its temporal order in relation to a contradictory study.

It is a rare study, however, that can legitimately contradict a general finding based on a consensus of a number of other studies. There is scarcely any generally established theory or fact of science for which one cannot find at least some few studies reporting contradictory results.

INTRINSIC PROBLEMS

Like every other field of scientific study, behavioral genetics has its own intrinsic problems. The overriding problem of human behavioral genetics, as contrasted with animal behavioral genetics, is of course the severe ethical and practical limitations on experimental control. In this respect, human behavioral genetics is more like astronomy or paleontology than like experimental genetics.

In experimental genetics, with plants and infrahuman animals, important components of phenotypic variance can be brought directly under experimental control, whereas in human genetics, they must be teased out from a variety of kinship measurements with the aid of complex mathematical models and statistical estimations. This often requires very large samples of kinds of data that are hard to obtain, and it requires replication. So progress is slow and difficult.

Discrepancies in h² Estimates

Estimates of heritability (h^2) often vary widely when estimated from different combinations of kinship data—for example, twins, siblings, parent–child, and adopted children. They even differ more widely than we would like from one study to another using the same kind of kinship data. The reasons for the discrepancies must be sought in three main categories: (1) population sampling error, (2) psychometric sampling and measurement error, and (3) genetic model inadequacies.

1. *Population Sampling Error.*   Estimation of h^2 or other components of phenotypic variance are derived from measurements on two or more kinship samples, each having some degree of sampling error, which becomes compounded in taking the differences, products, and ratios of the kinship correlations or covariances involved in the quantitative manipulations for estimating different components of variance. Standard errors of the final results are often shockingly large. Unfortunately, they are too seldom computed in past work in behavioral genetics. It is a good rule to accompany every variance component that we estimate in our quantitative genetic analyses by its standard error. Unfortunately, the means for doing this are not readily at hand. It remains as a task for mathematical statisticians to work out the formulas for determining the standard errors of heritability estimates or any other components of phenotypic variance derived from any particular combinations of kinship data. It is surprising that so little systematic attention has been given to the estimation of sampling error in this field until recently.

2. *Psychometric Sampling and Measurement Error.*   Not all tests nominally measuring a particular trait are psychometrically equivalent. They may differ in factor composition and in reliability, which will contribute to variability in the results of genetical analyses. More careful attention needs to be paid to these sources of variation in results. Greater use of factor scores, in place of raw test scores, should be considered. Correction of covariances, correlations, and the like for attenuation (i.e., errors of measurement) are warranted where theoretical issues are at stake. Age attenuation should be determined, where possible, when kinship correlations are based on different-aged persons, such as siblings and parent–child. Standardization and scale artifacts for different age groups can seriously attenuate certain kinship correlations. In the absence of substantial longitudinal test–retest data from which we could determine the test's reliability across the age range in question, I would suggest seeking transformations of the test-score scales that will maximize the kinship correlations. Or at least we

should convert all the raw-score measurements to simple ordinal scales or normalized standard scores separately within each of the to-be-correlated kinship samples.

3. *Genetic Model Inadequacies.* A seemingly faulty model cannot be properly diagnosed without first taking account of the sources of error already mentioned. It seems to me that the best strategy is to keep the genetic model no more complex than the statistical "resolving power" of the available data will allow. If we cannot statistically discriminate between the results of fitting a simple model and a more complex model, we should either settle temporarily for the simple model or increase the size or precision of the study to permit discrimination between the two models at some acceptable level of statistical significance. Such an approach, I believe, will tend to enforce more rigorous hypothesis testing and model development in behavioral genetics.

Unfortunately, the research strategy of "strong inference" is still hindered in this field by the relative dearth of competing models, especially of precise models for environmentalist explanations of kinship data. Environmentalists have been limited to criticizing genetic models and results; they have not suggested comparably detailed or comprehensive models of their own. In this respect, genetical models of intelligence variation really have no scientifically worthy competitor on the environmental side. Merely nitpicking a theory or the data that seem to support it is not really competitive in the strong-inference sense. Every theory and finding in science can be nitpicked without major effect. We still see this to some extent in the case of the natural selection theory of evolution; and apparently there are always a few people who still argue that the earth is flat. But they offer no coherent theory that can explain the generally established observations or, more importantly, that could have led to those observations.

STUDY OF RACE DIFFERENCES

Research on race differences in mental abilities has its own peculiar difficulties. I believe that if a scientific consensus regarding the causes of observed racial differences in IQ can never be reached, it will be because of nonscientific obstacles—political or ideological.

It must seem disillusioning to many who have devoted their careers to the development of psychology as a natural science to think that there may still be such dogmatically held beliefs about certain natural phenomena that the intrusion of the normal methods of science into the investigation of these phenomena is a taboo even among behavioral scientists. That the study of race differences is still a strong taboo cannot be doubted. It is only a question of how quickly and thoroughly it can be overcome. One argument for the study of racial differences, which is rarely mentioned, is that it will test whether psychology can actually behave as a science on a question of social importance or if, in the final analysis, psychology can only rationalize popular prejudices and social ideologies.

It seems to be exceedingly difficult for psychologists, or perhaps anyone else for that matter, to be *openly agnostic* regarding the causes of the racial IQ difference. Some critics will simply not tolerate agnosticism on this issue and insist on classing everyone either as a true believer in the environmentalist dogma or as a hereditarian racist. Yet an openly agnostic position is all that anyone can scientifically justify at the present time. If there is compelling evidence to the contrary, I have yet to see it pointed out. So I am rather shocked to read (Part IV, Chap. 1) that Scarr advocates "reeducation of school personnel and the public on the meaning of test scores, [and] the *elimination of any lingering suspicion about genetic racial differences in IQ* [italics added]." Unfortunately, the state of our scientific knowledge about racial differences in IQ at present falls far short of warranting any such advocacy. I ask, what is so wrong with openly advocating agnosticism until we really know the answers?

Students should realize that among psychologists and social scientists in general, there is an overwhelming preference for purely environmental and cultural explanations of racial IQ differences, despite the fact that a theory invoking genetic factors, in addition to environmental ones, is a priori at least as plausible.

One may classify positions on the nature/nurture issue in terms of a 6×3 matrix, as shown in Table 1. I have entered Scarr's name and mine in those cells that seem to me to represent our positions in this matrix. In terms of social policy questions, I classify myself in cell 4C (Agnostic on race differences); but in terms of research strategy, I advocate position 3C [i.e., $P = f(G,E)$ for race dif-

TABLE 1

Matrix for the Classification of Positions in the Nature–Nurture IQ Debate

Position[a]	A. Individual Differences Within Race and SES[b] Groups	B. SES Differences Within Race	C. Race Differences
1. $P = f(E)$			Scarr
2. $P = f(G)$			
3. $P = f(G,E)$	Scarr/Jensen	Scarr/Jensen	
4. Agnostic			Jensen
5. Dismiss question as meaningless			
6. Unqualified to express opinion			

[a] P is phenotypic difference; E is environmental difference; G is genotypic difference; (G,E) represents some combination (additive or nonadditive) of G and E.

[b] SES is socioeconomic status.

ferences]. It is only my *personal hunch* (which is really of no general scientific importance) that, assuming the question is adequately researched, a preponderance of the various lines of evidence will *most probably* converge on $P = f$ (G,E) for the explanation of the presently observed, mean white–black "IQ" difference in the United States.

Let me now mention several technical matters we should try to be clear about in studying race differences in mental ability.

Magnitude and Attenuation of Mean Differences Between Groups

So that the mean difference between groups is not expressed in the quite arbitrary units of the raw scores on various tests of mental ability, it is customary to express the difference in terms of standardized units. The standard deviation is most often chosen as the unit of measurement, thereby expressing the group mean difference on the scale of standard or z scores. But if we are comparing two groups, A and B, should we express the difference between them in terms of the standard deviation of A, or of B, or of a weighted average of the two SDs? I believe some convention should be uniformly adopted so as to permit direct comparisons between various studies. It is hard to see any justification for using the SD of only one of the groups unless it is very much larger than the other group. Statistically, a weighted composite of the within-group SDs is the most reliable estimate of the true (i.e., population) value. So I recommend that group mean differences be expressed as:

$$\bar{D} = (\bar{X}_A - \bar{X}_B)/s_w,$$

where $\bar{X}_A$ and $\bar{X}_B$ are the raw-score means of Groups A and B and s_w is the average (weighted) within-groups standard deviation:

$$s_w = [(N_A s_A^2 + N_B s_B^2)/(N_A + N_B)]^{1/2},$$

where s_A and s_B are the standard deviations of Groups A and B and N_A and N_B are the numbers of individuals in Groups A and B.

It is often forgotten that a group mean difference expressed in standard scale units is *attenuated* (i.e., diminished) by errors of measurement or unreliability of the test scores in the same way that a correlation coefficient is attenuated by unreliability. We cannot properly compare group differences across different tests without taking the tests' reliability coefficients into account, because—other things being equal—the test with the higher reliability will show a larger difference between two groups. The mean difference should be corrected for attenuation (unreliability of measurement) by dividing the difference $\bar{D}$ (as defined earlier) by the geometric mean of the tests' reliability coefficients in the two groups—that is, $(r_A r_B)^{1/2}$. The corrected difference $\bar{D}_c$ will, of course, always be greater than $\bar{D}$.

Interval Scale of Test Scores

If we have no reason to believe that the test scores are an equal-interval scale, the interpretation of any given mean difference $\bar{D}$ (in standard score units) is problematic. But this may not be a serious problem unless we wish to compare values of $\bar{D}$ across different tests, such as the question of whether Group A and Group B differ more on Test X than on Test Y. The question is not unambiguously answerable unless we presume that the measurement scale represents equal units on the trait throughout the range of scores of the combined groups. Scaling of test scores by means of latent-trait models helps to insure this, provided it can be shown that the item-characteristic curves are nonsignificantly different in the two groups.

Another type of evidence that increases the reasonableness of our presumption that the scores are an interval scale is the demonstration (in both groups) that the absolute differences between siblings are the same throughout the entire range of scores subtended by the combined groups. This can be demonstrated by testing the hypothesis that the linear and nonlinear correlations between sibling means and sibling absolute differences do not differ significantly from zero. (An example of the use of this method can be found in Jensen, 1977a.) If the correlations are close to zero in both groups, it is a good indication that the test scores have the same scale properties in both groups. And if this is the case for two (or more) tests, we can feel more confident in concluding that an observed group difference (i.e., $\bar{D}_c$) is greater on one test than on another.

On Just What Do the Groups Differ?

It impresses me that thus far in the study of racial differences, we have not been as clear as we could be concerning the purely *psychometric* nature of group differences in mental abilities. For example, not all mental ability tests, or even standard "IQ" tests, show the same degree of difference between whites and blacks. The various subscales of the Wechsler show significantly different mean white–black differences, as do many other cognitive tests. We need more studies of the nature of this observed significant variation in mean white–black differences across various cognitive tests.

Spearman (1927, p. 379) originally suggested the interesting hypothesis that the magnitude of the mean white–black difference on any mental test is directly related to the test's g loading—that is, the degree to which the test measures the general factor common to a number of different tests. Spearman characterized g psychologically as a capacity for grasping relationships, reasoning, and problem solving.

To check Spearman's hypothesis, I have factor analyzed several different batteries of highly diverse tests, verbal and nonverbal, in large white and black samples (Jensen, 1979). Spearman's hypothesis is very significantly borne out: The various tests' g loadings (whether g is extracted in the white, black, or combined samples) are directly related to the size of the mean white–black difference (expressed in standard units). Where it is possible to correct the g factor loadings and the mean differences for attenuation, the parallel is even more striking. I have not found any evidence that would seriously contradict this conclusion. It thus appears that the white–black difference is essentially a difference in Spearman's g, which means that the difference does not depend on any of the highly specific features, types of content, knowledge, or acquired skills required by any *particular* test or test items. The g factor (or first principal component) is that aspect of test variance that best discriminates among individuals *within* each racial group; it is the same g factor that best discriminates *between* the two racial groups. Thus the white–black difference seems to be a difference in g or the *general* factor common to an extremely wide diversity of test items.

Within- and Between-Group Heritability

There has been considerable confusion in the literature over the relationship between estimates of the heritability of individual differences *within* each of two populations and the possible inference of the heritability of the difference *between* the two populations (i.e., the difference between the population means). (For brevity, I refer to the heritability coefficients *within* and *between* populations as h_W^2 and h_B^2, respectively.)

There is, in fact, a formal relationship between h_W^2 and h_B^2, which I have explicated elsewhere (Jensen, 1973, p. 146; 1977b, pp. 228–232; see also Loehlin, Lindzey, & Spuhler, 1975, pp. 75; 116; 290–291). If the value of h_W^2 can be empirically estimated (e.g., from data on twins and other kinships), the value of h_W^2 implies a definite constraint on the possible range of values of h_B^2, a range that may not include $h_B^2 = 0$ if the phenotypic group difference is substantially greater than zero. This inference holds true, however, *only* on the assumption that all the nongenetic sources of variance *between* the groups are also sources of variance *within* each of the groups.

The constraining implication of h_W^2 for h_B^2 can be escaped only by making a different assumption (note that it is presently also an *assumption*)—namely, that the phenotypic difference between the groups is attributable to a source of nongenetic variation (other than measurement error and sampling error) that does not contribute to phenotypic variation (i.e., individual differences) *within* either group. (This becomes immediately obvious through consideration of the hypothetical case of complete heritability of the trait—i.e., $h_W^2 = 1$—*within* each of two groups; then any difference between the means of the two groups must be attributed either to genetic factors, *or* to environmental factors that do not contribute to the phenotypic variance *within* the groups, *or* to some combination of both factors.) In other words, if the value of h_W^2 for IQ (or, more specifically, Spearman's g) is about .50 to .75 (i.e., the range of most empirical estimates of the heritability) in the white and black populations, the range of possible values for the heritability of the phenotypic difference between the racial groups (which differ about 1σ in IQ) may not include 0 *unless* it is hypothesized that there is some nongenetic factor(s) that affect(s) mental development (as indexed by g-loaded tests) for all members of one group or the other but does not affect individual differences within either group. Because such a factor has not been clearly identified or agreed upon by those who insist upon the genetic equality of all races with respect to "IQ," I have labeled it Factor X (Jensen, 1973, Chap. 5). The empirically demonstrated existence of such a factor would not, of course, rule out a genetic difference between the groups unless the factor could be shown to account for all the phenotypic difference that remains after the known (within-group) sources of environmental variation that also contribute to between-group differences have been accounted for.

Factor X could conceivably take many forms—for example, specific cultural biases in the tests, the effect of being a racial minority, having a history of slavery, being aware of racism in the society, lack of effort or "learned helplessness" in the face of cognitive demands because of assumed "racial" inability to compete intellectually, and so forth. Unless such hypothesized effects have some psychological generality (i.e., are not confined to minority groups of sub-Saharan African descent) and are clearly linked to mental development within some theoretical framework, or can be empirically tested (as in the case of test bias), they must be regarded as only ad hoc conjectures that have no theoretical justification independent of the particular observation they are specially invoked to explain.

An ad hoc hypothesis, of course, may be developed into something better; it can become integrated into a theoretical framework that suggests lines of support that are experimentally independent of the particular observation that originally gave rise to the hypothesis. But for a hypothesis merely to remain ad hoc is a scientifically undesirable state of affairs. Of course, *any* hypothesis, ad hoc or otherwise, that in principle cannot be empirically tested is useless and outside the pale of science. Scientific progress is won through an unrelenting battle against ad hoc explanations of natural phenomena.

It seems to me that it is much less ad hoc to hypothesize that the observed difference in "IQ" *between* racial populations is due to the same factors that are known causes of "IQ" variation *within* populations—that is, some combination of genetic and environmental factors. We already know with considerable scientific certainty that some substantial proportion of IQ variation is attributable to genetic variation, which is independent justification for hypothesizing that this known important factor in the development of individual differences is also involved in racial differences, just as the known environmental factors involved in individual differences in IQ can be reasonably hypothesized to contribute to racial differences.

Therefore, I reiterate what I originally said in 1969: The hypothesis of genetic factors in the mean white–black IQ difference is a scientifically reasonable *hypothesis*.

The fact that races differ in a great many other polygenic characteristics in which the differences are indisputably genetic reinforces the reasonableness of this hypothesis. The vehement objections to it that we have seen in much of the literature in recent years simply have no scientific justification. It can only be explained as an emotional or ideological reaction—of interest perhaps to social psychologists but not to behavioral geneticists as such.

If we dispense with hypothesizing an unknown Factor X and make what seems to me scientifically the simplest assumption—that the IQs of blacks and whites in the United States today are similarly influenced by genetic and environmental factors (i.e., the genetic and environmental variance in white and black IQs are comprised of the same genetic and environmental factors that affect IQ within both groups)—then it is reasonable to hypothesize that some substantial fraction of the between-groups variance in IQs of blacks and whites is attributable to genetic factors. How else, without hypothesizing some unknown, nongenetic Factor X, can one account for the observed difference in IQ between groups of blacks and whites who have been reared in the range of average environments where the between-families environmental variance is but a relatively small fraction of the total phenotypic IQ variance within either racial group? Strict environmentalists on the race–IQ question invariably seem forced to invoke cultural bias in the tests or some "Factor X." But as I have pointed out, as neither of these explanations has been empirically substantiated, they are quite limited ad hoc hypotheses. My recent extensive review (Jensen, 1979) of research on the culture bias hypothesis leads me to the conclusion that in the United States today, the average white–black difference on the most widely used, *g*-loaded standard mental tests *cannot* be attributed to cultural bias in the tests (or the test situation) in any objectively meaningful sense of the term.

A CLOSER LOOK AT THREE KEY STUDIES BY SCARR ET AL

Three of the empirical studies by Scarr et al. included in this volume seem to me especially important. The studies of the effect of cross-racial adoption and of racial admixture on IQ are among the very few studies of these types. In fact, there has been no other cross-racial adoption study involving American blacks. (For reviews of other studies, see Loehlin, Lindzey, & Spuhler, 1975, pp. 116–118; 120–125.) The adolescent adoption study is particularly important in this context for the light it throws on the cross-racial adoption study.

Adolescent Adoption Study

This study (Part III, Chap. 2) raises an important question concerning adoption studies in general. It can be called the question of a threshold of environmental adequacy beyond which environmental variation makes very little or no contribution to variance in IQ; or it can be thought of as the nonlinear regression of the environmental component of IQ on the quality of the environment. On the full continuum of possible environments in which a child could at least survive, there would obviously be some point of environmental deprivation below which the undesirable effects on intellectual development would be relatively drastic. And there could also be some favorable point on the environmental continuum above which additional environmental advantages would add no appreciable gains in the level of intellectual development.

We are not at all sure just where these "threshold" points of the nonlinearity of environmental effects on IQ occur on some criterion-referenced scale of natural environments, from the worst to the best. I suspect there is a very low threshold below which environmental effects may take a drastic toll on IQ. Such environmental conditions, involving abuse, neglect, social isolation, and malnutrition, are what Scarr refers to as "inhumane" environments. They are rare conditions within every racial group in our society, but such bad environments are certainly not unknown to social workers in many large cities and in some poor rural areas.

For "humane" environments that are above the threshold of abuse, neglect, social isolation, and malnutrition, I suspect there is a roughly linear regression with a very gradual slope extending all the way up to what we might consider the best natural environments for cognitive development—say, the childhood environments of Sir Francis Galton and John Stuart Mill, two of the most famous prodigies. But the slope of the regression is quite small, and therefore one cannot find impressive correlations between environmental indices and IQ in the range of environments found in the bulk of the population—and especially in the range of environments found in adoption studies, for adoption agencies do not place children for foster care or adoption in homes that are below the threshold of a "humane" environment.

If I am correct in these conjectures, we should expect to find that the average quality of the environments of adopted children selected from some restricted segment of the total range of environments would have some slight effect on the IQs of the children. Existing evidence suggests that the total range of naturally occurring *humane* environments can shift IQ over a range of some 6 to 10 IQ points.

This is also what Scarr and Weinberg have found in a large group of adopted children who were adopted in infancy and were IQ tested on the Wechsler Adult Intelligence Scale when they were 16 to 22 years of age. Scarr and Weinberg found even slightly less correlation of the adoptees' IQs with adoptive-family-background variables than has been found in some other studies based on younger children. The evidence suggests that environmental factors become a less important source of individual differences in IQ as children mature. This is accounted for not only by the widening sphere of environmental influences outside the home (much of which is probably due to self-selected genotype ×

environment covariance) but also by genetically conditioned maturational factors that are not fully in evidence before adolescence. Because this study by Scarr and Weinberg is focused on late adolescence and early maturity (i.e., ages 16 to 22), it is one of the most valuable of all adoption studies.

Some of their conclusions from this adolescent adoption study seem to me highly germane to consideration of the cross-racial adoption study. Their preferred explanation of their finding of only a slight multiple correlation (R^2 = .156) between adoptive-family demographic variables and adoptees' IQs is that in the range of the adoptive environments in this study—from working class to upper middle class—the slope of the regression of IQ on environmental quality is relatively flat. They state: "This suggests that within a range of 'humane environments,' from an SES level of working to upper middle class, there is little evidence for differential environmental effects [p. 378, this volume]." And they go on to note that even when children are adopted into relatively poor working-class families, their IQs are nearly as high as those of children adopted into professional families. Scarr and Weinberg argue that most "humane environments" are *functionally equivalent* with respect to their effects on IQ, despite what may appear to be different styles of child rearing. They conclude that "intellectual differences among children at the end of the child-rearing period have little to do with environmental differences among families that range from solid working class to upper middle class [p. 381]."

These conclusions are consistent with the results of a large number of other adoption studies. The reader should keep them in mind while examining the study of interracial adoptions.

Interracial Adoptions

In commenting on Chapter 1, Part II, by Scarr and Weinberg, I shall try to avoid repeating the points made by other commentators. I merely wish to raise a number of questions and implications inherent in this research report, so that future investigators in a similar vein may be made more aware of the problems.

1. *Liabilities of Different Statistics to Selection Biases.*   The authors claim that the significant correlations between the education level of the natural parents and the IQs of the adopted children (who were not reared by their natural parents), and the fact of a significant difference between the IQs of the adopted children and the IQs of the natural children in the same adoptive families, are explainable in terms of genetic inheritance and are quite consistent with other studies of the heritability of IQ. Their major conclusion, however, is that the mean IQ level of the black and interracial adopted children is much higher (by 10 to 20 points, they claim) than would be expected if the children had not been reared in intellectually superior, white families. This combination of conclusions implies that the environmental variation among the adoptive families is much less than the variation between the average adoptive environment and the average

environment these children would have had if they had remained with their biological parents. The IQ gain that is claimed (10 to 20 IQ points) implies (if we are to believe the other adoption studies) that the difference between the typical white, adoptive environment and the typical natural-family environment of black children must involve a greater environmental difference than exists within the range of environments that Scarr and Weinberg describe (in their adolescent adoption study) as going from "solid working class to upper middle class"—a range within which between-family environmental effects on IQ were shown to be almost negligible.

The mean IQs of the adopted children were 96.8 for those with two black parents (black/black) and 109.0 for those with a black father and a white mother (black/white). (The mean IQ of the natural children of the adoptive parents was 118.9.) Consider only the black/black adoptees for the moment, for we can compare them with black children reared by their own families. How extraordinary is a mean IQ of 98.6 for blacks? The national mean for blacks is about 85; but there are great regional variations and even variations from one city to another, depending on the cost of living, the types of employment available, the level of education required for the types of jobs, and so on. If the white, upper-middle-class adoptive environments were responsible for any gain in IQ, it would seem to be due mostly to their "whiteness" rather than their SES per se, because we find, for example, in the Berkeley population (Jensen, 1974b), that the approximately 7% of black children reared by their own parents who are in the top SES category (described as having jobs requiring a college degree: high-level administrators, supervisors, college teachers, high-level professionals—e.g., engineers, physicians, and so forth) obtain a mean IQ significantly (0.21σ) *below* the mean IQ of white children from low-SES backgrounds (described as having manual labor and unskilled jobs requiring less than a high school diploma). (This is not a unique finding; essentially the same finding has turned up in several other large-scale studies.) The question, then, is what advantage specifically is conferred by being reared by white parents, regardless of their educational and occupational status? At present, the purported advantage of the "white environment" must be classed as a Factor X.

Scarr and Weinberg point to evidence that a parental "expectancy effect" does not appear to affect the IQ. Also, if their claim of an overall IQ gain by the adoptees is valid, it would mean that such a gain is not precluded by negative attitudes toward blacks in the more general social environment outside the home. It would seem, then, that black children, on the average, can have IQs on a par with white children's if only the black children are reared by white parents; even being reared by low-SES white parents with only high school educations and unskilled jobs would seem preferable to being reared by black parents with college educations and professional-level jobs—or so it would seem if a "white" environment is the main factor responsible for the improvement in IQ and its correlates.

Are the white and black environments really all that different? Fine-grained observations and ratings of child-rearing styles in white and black families of roughly comparable SES have revealed no significant differences in parent–child interaction with the one exception that white mothers seem more relaxed about their children's academic futures (Baldwin & Baldwin, 1973). What could Scarr and Weinberg say to conscientious, well-educated, upper-SES black parents that they are *not* doing for their own children that apparently even relatively less educated, middle- and low-SES white parents *are* doing for their children? In short, what is Factor X?

I believe that the effect of "white environment" on "black IQ" has probably been overdrawn. Selective biases could be an explanation, and the adopted children's IQs may be about the same as they would have been if these same children had been reared by their natural parents.

One reason that I put more stock in the correlational data in this study, and in the *relative* differences between groups (i.e., the differences between the adopted and natural children of the adoptive parents) rather than in the absolute values of the group means, is that I suspect that *first-order* statistics (such as the mean) are more liable to various selection biases than are *second-order* statistics (such as correlations, relative differences, factor loadings, and heritabilities).

For example, if we should ask of a group of 1000 persons: "Will those 100 persons please volunteer who think they will get the highest scores on a battery of mental tests," we are certain to get a subgroup of 100 volunteers whose overall mean test performance is significantly higher than the mean of the total group of 1000 persons. But if we ask: "Will those volunteers come forward whose test scores will yield the highest intercorrelations, or produce the largest *g* loadings on certain tests, or show the highest heritabilities, or show the highest predictive validity, or have the highest reliability (or any other second-order statistic)," we are most likely to get results on these statistics that do not differ appreciably from what we would find in a sample selected at random from the total group.

When volunteers are requested for a study that involves mental testing, I suspect there is generally a tendency for the mean score to be biased upward. This cannot be contradicted by the fact that *some* low-scoring persons are found among the self-selected (or parent-selected) volunteers. In the Scarr and Weinberg study, 101 families volunteered to participate, but 59 technically eligible families refused or failed to respond to requests. We do not know the refusal rates of families with black/black adoptees as compared to families with black/white adoptees. Among the volunteers, only 29 adoptees were black/black as compared with 101 black/white adoptees.

In addition to some self-selection for IQ, selection by the adoption agencies seems highly probable, especially if the agencies had personal contact with the natural mothers, since expert judgments based on interviews are probably a better index of intelligence in high-school- or college-aged persons than years of schooling completed or type of employment. It would seem reasonable that adoption agencies might try to place the potentially brightest black and interracial adoptees in the upper-class white homes desiring to adopt children, especially when the adoptive parents already have children of their own.

It is interesting, too, to note where the adoptees were born; the majority are from Wisconsin (31%) and Massachusetts (21%). This is noteworthy because these are among the three states with the highest black means on the Armed Forces Qualification Test in 1968, the last year in which the test results were obtained on the entire male population of the United States between the ages of 18 and 26 (Office of the Surgeon General, 1969). Wisconsin blacks average highest in the country, with a mean AFQT score only 0.18σ (about 3 IQ points) below the white national average. (This would correspond to an IQ of about 97, assuming the white mean is 100.) The 29 black/black adoptees in the present study obtained a mean IQ of 96.8.

2. *Interracial Adoptees.*   The mean IQ of the interracial (i.e., black/white) adoptees was 109. With what population group can we compare that figure? Certainly not just the mean of whites and blacks in general, as if the interracial natural parents represented a random sample of the whites and blacks in the region. Black males involved in interracial mating are more likely to be above the black average in IQ. A study (Goldhammer, 1971) of interracial matings in Boston found that the black males were well above the average black male in occupational status, and it would seem safe to infer a higher average IQ as well. But we actually have no adequate comparison group for the black/white adoptees. The nearest I can find to it in the literature is a study by Willerman, Naylor, and Myrianthopoulos (1970), who found the offspring of black fathers and white mothers (who were reared by their own mothers) to have an average Stanford–Binet IQ of 95.9 at the age of 4 years. But there is no evidence that these particular interracial children are comparable to those whose mothers give them up for adoption.

In the Scarr and Weinberg study, judging from the means and standard deviations of the educational levels of the interracial children's natural parents, quite a few of them were college students, which could imply IQs above the general average for whites. But one is hard put to estimate what their offspring's IQs might have been if they had been reared by their own parents.

It should be noted, too, that the interracial children are, in any case, predominantly Caucasian, genetically speaking. Average American blacks have about 20% of their genes from Caucasian ancestors; and even if we assume that the blacks involved in these interracial matings are no more Caucasoid than blacks in general, the interracial offspring would have only about 40% of their genes from African ancestors, or only *half* as much African ancestry as the average black American—hardly an ideal group for comparison with black Americans in general.

3. *Confounding of Racial Parentage and Adoption History.*   The difference of 12.2 IQ points (or 1σ in the present sample) between the black/black and

black/white adoptees would seem consistent with a genetic hypothesis. But that interpretation is ambiguously weakened by the fact that the groups differed in their placement histories—the black/black children being in foster homes for a longer time and in a greater number of foster homes prior to legal adoption. (The lesser education of their natural mothers could be regarded as a part of the genetic prediction and so should not be invoked to "explain away" the IQ difference between the offspring of white and black mothers.)

The natural confounding of placement histories and racial admixture unfortunately cannot be *un*confounded statistically, by partial correlations or regressions, for that would be to commit the "sociologist's fallacy," which imputes causation to mere correlation. If the black/black children, or any potentially lower-IQ children (white *or* black), have poorer placement histories, in part, *because* of their own characteristics, these cannot properly be controlled in any *causal* sense by statistical regression techniques. To do so would be like arguing that cats and dogs, in general, differ in size because they eat different amounts of food; we could statistically "regress out" the amounts of food ingested by cats and dogs and reach the obviously fallacious conclusion that cats and dogs are genotypically the same size.

But just how convincing are differences in placement history as a *causal* explanation of the 12.2-IQ-point difference? The explanation seems to be quite ad hoc. It attributes a large effect on IQ to differences in environmental backgrounds of a type that have not been shown independently to affect IQ appreciably. I question whether the range of foster-care environments that the black/black children were reared in till the age of legal adoption, and the qualities of their final adoptive families, were at all outside the range of environments that Scarr and Weinberg, in their adolescent adoption study, refer to as "humane environments" and claim are functionally equivalent with respect to their effects on IQ: "The differences among children at the end of the child-rearing period have little to do with environmental differences among families that range from solid working class to upper middle class [p. 381]." No evidence is shown that any of the adopted children were reared outside the range of humane environmental conditions typical of foster and adoptive homes. Yet the 12.2-IQ-point mean difference between the black/black and black/white adoptees is greater than could be accounted for by any combination of the family background variables in the Scarr and Weinberg adolescent adoption study.

4. *Natural Mother's Age at Delivery.*   It is unfortunate that this variable, although available, was not taken into account in the analyses, for it is a potentially causal variable for the offspring's IQ. Prematurity adversely affects IQ; prematurity rates are higher among black mothers, and much of this higher rate is related to maternal age, teenage mothers contributing disproportionately to premature births. Therefore, when possible, we should include maternal age and prematurity (or birth weight) in our IQ analyses. I suspect they may be among the more potent environmental variables involved in the white–black IQ difference.

White Ancestry and Mental Ability of Blacks

The study by Scarr, Pakstis, Katz, and Barker (Part II, Chap. 2) illustrates even greater problems than the interracial adoption study. The basic idea of the study is to determine the correlation between an index of African ancestry (based on blood group analysis) in American blacks (who have about 20% of their genes from Caucasian ancestors) and scores on intelligence tests. The idea appears ingenious as a research strategy, but its practical execution and theoretical interpretation are fraught with problems.

The chief problem is that the sample size is not large enough to reject *either* the null hypothesis *or* almost any reasonable alternative genetic hypothesis.

Just to give the reader some idea of this, consider the correlation between the index of Caucasian ancestry ("Sample Odds") and scores on Raven's matrices—a correlation of -0.13. I chose the Raven, because it is known to be the best measure of Spearman's g (general intelligence factor) of any of the tests in the present battery; and as I noted earlier, the white–black difference seems to be essentially a difference in Spearman's g factor. (The first principal component of the five tests used by Scarr et al. is not as good an estimate of Spearman's g as the Raven alone, especially if the paired-associate test—which does not characterize Spearman's g,—is included in the components analysis.) We would not expect the Raven test scores to correlate any more highly with the index of African ancestry than does amount of skin pigmentation. After all, the heritability of the Raven scores is probably only about .60 or .70, whereas the heritability of the skin-color measurements of blacks in the present sample is over .90. Yet skin color (darkness) correlates only 0.27 with the same index of African ancestry that is correlated -0.13 with the Raven. So if we take the skin-color correlation as the upper limit that we should expect for the correlation between the Raven and amount of African ancestry, we can presumably also take this correlation as the upper limit of the correlation we should predict from any genetic hypothesis of the white–black difference in intelligence. The obtained correlation of -0.13 between the Raven and the index of African ancestry is nearly halfway between 0 (the null hypothesis) and 0.27 (the genetic hypothesis) and is nonsignificantly different from either extreme. In fact, if we corrected the Raven correlation for attenuation (because Raven scores are less reliable than skin-color measurements), the Raven correlation would be slightly closer to that for skin color than to 0. We could stop right there, for the data are incapable of rejecting either the null hypothesis or an alternative genetic prediction.

But this preliminary glimpse of the problem is rather oversimplified. We should aim for a better estimate of the most likely value for a genetic prediction. This cannot be decided purely in the abstract but must take account of the known parameters of the present samples and particular indices.

1. First, we need some idea of the correlation between our blood group indices and the true genotypic proportion of African genes. The best estimate of this can

be obtained from a path analysis of all correlations among the 3-loci and 9-loci ancestral and sample odds and skin color (given in Table 4 of Part II, Chap. 2). From this we can estimate the best linear combination (i.e., a multiple correlation coefficient) of the 3- and 9-locus indices for predicting the true proportion of African genes. The estimated multiple correlation is 0.49. In psychometric terminology we could say that the *validity* of the blood group index is 0.49. (I am indebted to Dr. Everett R. Dempster, a professor of quantitative genetics at Berkeley, for suggesting this and the following calculations.)

2. Second, we must take into account the amount of variation in African ancestry in our black sample. Obviously, restriction of variance limits the size of the correlation that a variable can have with another variable, and of course it is unlikely that any randomly selected black sample would have a range of variation (in the proportion of African ancestry) anywhere near approaching the full possible range between 0% and 100%. Scarr et al. divide the total distribution of variation in ancestry into thirds and suggest that the upper third of blacks has about .35 Caucasian ancestry and the lower third, about .15—for a difference of .20 in proportion of Caucasian genes. Using a normal curve approximation, the means of the upper and lower thirds of the distribution differ by approximately 2.2σ. Hence, if the difference of .20 in the proportion of Caucasian genes between the upper and lower thirds of the distribution is 2.2σ, then 1σ difference would be equivalent to $.20/2.2 = 0.09$—which then is an estimate of the standard deviation of the proportion of Caucasian admixture in the black population.

3. Next, consider the genetic hypothesis that I suggested several years ago: "All the major facts would seem to be comprehended quite well by the hypothesis that something between one-half and three-fourths of the average IQ difference between American Negroes and whites is attributable to genetic factors, and the remainder to environmental factors and their interaction with genetic differences" (Jensen, 1973, p. 363). To keep calculations to a minimum, let us take the midpoint between .50 and .75 (.625) for our example.

4. Scarr et al. give 0.9σ as the average white–black difference in mental test scores in their samples. Assume the black sample is typical of American blacks, with .20 of its genes from Caucasian ancestors, which is the average proportion cited by Scarr et al.

5. Then, if we hypothesize that .625 of the mean difference in test scores is genetic, the *genetic* difference in mental ability between whites and blacks—measured on the same scale as the test scores—should be $(.625)(.9\sigma) = 0.56\sigma$. But recall that we assumed the black sample has only 80% African genes. The genetic difference, then, between a black population with 100% African genes and an all-Caucasian population would be $0.56\sigma/.80 = 0.70\sigma$.

6. One interpretation of the correlation coefficient r_{xy} is that it is the amount of change (in σ units) in variable y for 1σ change in x. Given the standard deviation of 0.09σ for the proportion of Caucasian ancestry (as calculated in step 2), a shift of 1 standard deviation in genotypic ancestry would result in a $0.09 \times$

$0.70 = 0.063\sigma$ shift in test score, and 0.063 would also be the correlation (or path coefficient) between test scores and genotypic ancestry (i.e., proportion of Caucasian-derived genes).

7. From this figure (0.063), we can determine the *expected correlation* between test scores and the 12-loci blood group *index* of genotypic ancestry (with its validity of 0.49 [see step 1]). The expected correlation is the product of: (a) the correlation between test score and genotypic ancestry; and (b) the correlation between genotypic ancestry and the 12-loci index of ancestry—that is, $0.063 \times 0.49 = 0.031$.

Since the best expected value of the correlation between ancestry index and test scores is only 0.031 (which would be a negative correlation if the ancestral index increases with proportion of African ancestry), a sample size of almost 4000 would be required to detect such a correlation as significantly different from zero at the 5% level of confidence by a one-tailed t test.

8. By how much should we expect the top and bottom thirds of the ancestry-index distribution to differ in test scores? Given the expected correlation of 0.031 between ancestry index and test scores and the mean difference of 2.2σ between the top and bottom thirds in ancestral index, the expected mean test-score difference (in σ units) between the extreme thirds of the ancestry distribution would be only $.031 \times 2.2\sigma = 0.07\sigma$. This difference would not be significant with the present sample size, but then neither do the obtained differences (see Table 9 in Scarr et al.) deviate significantly from this theoretically expected value; most, in fact, are larger.

In terms of this analysis, the obtained correlations between skin color and ancestral index are remarkably high, suggesting that skin color is probably as good as or better an index of Caucasian/African ancestry than the blood groups. This raises a question about partialing the skin-color measurements out of the correlations between the blood group ancestral indices and test scores; removing the part of the correlation associated with skin color also substantially lowers the validity of the partialed blood group index of ancestry. Perhaps a better way of assessing the *social* effect of skin color on IQ would be to correlate skin-color differences (or other racial factors) between full siblings with the sibling differences in IQ. In any case, the value of the Scarr et al. chapter would be enhanced for future investigators if the correlations between skin color and test scores were reported in full.

An interesting point apparently not noticed by the authors is the *positive* correlation between amount of African ancestry and scores on the paired-associate test, in contrast to the *negative* correlations for the four other tests. Other studies have found small (or even zero) white–black differences in rote learning tasks. The fact that such tasks, when factor analyzed, show some g loading (usually about .3 to .5), plus the fact that blacks generally perform most poorly on the most highly g-loaded tests, suggests that blacks must be at least equal or even superior to whites in some of the non-g factors measured by the paired-associate task in order for them to differ as little as they do from whites, despite the moderate g loading of PA learning. This is consistent with the finding of a *positive* correlation between the PA test and the index of African ancestry.

Finally, it is my hope that these fascinating articles will not seem too daunting to students, but that the difficulties inherent in the study of human behavioral genetics—along with the obvious social importance of the questions it attempts to answer—will be seen as a challenge by students who seek to confront the more rugged and risky frontiers of behavioral science. If this book helps to inspire even a handful of able students to work in behavioral genetics with anything like the energy, ingenuity, dedication, and social conscience that are so well exemplified in its principal author's career, we can feel optimistic about the future of the field.

REFERENCES

Baldwin, A. L., & Baldwin, C. P. The study of mother–child interaction. *American Scientist*, 1973, *61*, 714–721.

Goldhammer, H. Letters. *Science*, 1971, *172*, 10.

Hunt, J. M. Psychological development: Early experience *Annual Review of Psychology*, 1979, *30*, 103–143.

Jensen, A. R. How much can we boost IQ and scholastic achievement? *Harvard Educational Review*, 1969, *39*, 1–123.

Jensen, A. R. *Genetics and Education:* New York: Harper & Row, 1972.

Jensen, A. R. *Educability and Group Differences*. New York: Harper & Row, 1973.

Jensen, A. R. Interaction of Level I and Level II abilities with race and socioeconomic status. *Journal of Educational Psychology*, 1974, *66*, 99–111. (b)

Jensen, A. R. Cumulative deficit in IQ of blacks in the rural South. *Developmental Psychology*, 1977, *13*, 184–191. (a)

Jensen, A. R. Race and mental ability. In A. H. Halsey (Ed.), *Heredity and Environment*. London: Methuen, 1977. (b)

Jensen, A. R. *Bias in mental testing*. New York: Free Press (Macmillan), 1979.

Kamin, L. J. *The science and politics of IQ*. Hillsdale, N.J.: Lawrence Erlbaum Associates, 1974.

Loehlin, J. C., Lindzey, G., & Spuhler, J. N. *Race differences in intelligence*. San Francisco: Freeman, 1975.

Office of the Surgeon General. *Supplement to health of the Army: Results of the examination of youths for military service, 1968*. Washington, D.C.: Medical Statistics Agency, Department of the Army, June 1969.

Ristow, W. Larry P. versus IQ tests. *The Progressive*, November 1978, pp. 48–50.

Spearman, C. *The abilities of man*. London: Macmillan, 1927.

Vernon, P. E. *Human intelligence: Heredity and environment*. San Francisco: Freeman, 1979.

Willerman, L., Naylor, A. F., & Myrianthopoulos, N. C. Intellectual development of children from interracial matings. *Science*, 1970, *170*, 1329–1331.

Comments and Replies

A REPLY TO SOME OF PROFESSOR JENSEN'S COMMENTARY*

Although I resist the temptation to respond to my two critics, point by point or blow by blow, there are a few provocative statements in Professor Jensen's commentary that I cannot let pass without rebuttal. On pages 506–513, he criticizes in detail the methods and interpretations of two studies: the transracial adoption study and the ancestry study. I take up his comments in that order.

ON THE TRANSRACIAL ADOPTION STUDY

As I have noted in several papers, the Factor X to which Jensen refers is none other than cultural differences in child-rearing styles, values, and emphasis on skills thought to be desirable for children to obtain. Not being a scientific romantic, if such is possible, I agree with Jensen that untestable hypotheses have no useful place in science. I fear, however, that we disagree about what constitutes a test of a hypothesis. There are many sources that document the different training practices of black families with their young children; for example, Virginia Young (1970) states from her extensive observations:

> The American Negro family is generally interpreted, ethnocentrically, as an impoverished version of the American White family, in which deprivation has induced pathogenic and dysfunctional features. This concept of the family is as-

---

*The following reply is by Sandra Scarr.

sumed in studies of Negro personality formation, which furthermore have relied entirely on clinical methods of research. Fieldwork among Negro town-dwellers in the southeastern United States plus a reassessment of the literature yield a sharply contrasting portrait and interpretation of the American Negro family in which organizational strength and functionality are found. Observations of parent–child relations show highly distinctive behavioral styles, some of which have remained undiscovered by psychoanalytically oriented studies and others of which differ markedly from the extrapolations of clinical research. These forms and styles are viewed as aspects of an indigenous American Negro culture. Finally, the formative effect of an indigenous culture is argued as a corrective to the common viewpoint of deprivation as the prime cause of Negro behavior [p. 269].

Black scholars and others interested in the varieties of child-rearing styles among cultural groups (The Laboratory of Comparative Human Development, University of California, San Diego; Janice Hale at Yale; Jean Carew at Stanford Research Institute, for example) are beginning to detail the child-rearing practices in black families. We know so far that the affective and communicative styles of parent–child interactions differ, as do probably the cognitive content, permission to explore the environment, interest in material objects as opposed to interpersonal contact, and possibly many other factors that affect the skills and knowledge that children bring to tests constructed by psychologists from the majority culture. It seems to me shameful to have to say this in 1981.

Socioeconomic differences *within* the racial groups may not contribute much environmental variability to children's IQ scores, but cultural differences between the racial groups seem to be of far greater importance than genetic differences between them.

Regional Differences in Blacks' IQ Scores

It is curious that Jensen brings up the putatively higher AFQT scores of young adult men who were tested by the Army in Wisconsin. Although he asserts that the majority of the black and interracial adoptees were from Wisconsin and Massachusetts (for which he does not give AFQT scores), the fact is that 78 of the 130 transracially adopted black and interracial children were born in Minnesota (see Table 2 in Part II, Chapter 1). Of the black and interracial adoptees, 16 were from parents in Wisconsin, 11 from Massachusetts, and 9 from Kentucky, which has one of the lowest average AFQT scores! The large majority of the adoptees were born in the North Central region, and it is to other black and interracial children in the area that we compared their performance on IQ tests and in school.

In the chapter on transracial adoption, we compared the performance of the black and interracial children reared in white families to that of those children reared in the black community. In school the performance of the transracially adopted children was vastly superior, as it was on IQ tests. We cited the latest data on black children who were included as a representative sample for the standardization of the WISC-R. The striking differences between the IQ test performance of children reared in black and white families deserves further elaboration.

In Table 4 of their article, Kaufman and Doppelt (1976) presented the IQ results for a representative sample of socially classified black and white children by region of the country. The full-scale WISC-R results are reproduced in Table 1.

Compared to white children from the same region, black children scored 10 to 16 points lower. In the North Central and Northeast regions—from which nearly all of our transracially adopted children came—the average IQ scores of whites and blacks are 103 and 90, respectively. By contrast, our black and interracial children reared by advantaged white families scored IQ 106 on the WISC, regardless of when they were adopted. I submit that this is a difference of 1 standard deviation from the average scores of black children reared in the black community. I still maintain that nearly all of this difference is due to the *socioeconomic* advantages of the adoptive families and to the *cultural relevance* of the rearing environments to the tests. Had these black and interracial adoptees been reared by average white families, I believe that their scores would have averaged about 102, as was found for white children in the North Central region. Because they were reared by more advantaged families, their scores exceed those of the whites. Of course, when we examined those who were adopted in the 1st year of life, the average IQ score was 110, considerably above whites in the region. Most of the scores for early-adopted children were obtained with the Stanford–Binet (1972 revised norms); so the scores are not entirely comparable to the WISC-R, but there is no evidence against a social-cultural explanation.

TABLE 1
Means and Standard Deviations of WISC-R IQs of
Standardization Sample by Geographic Region
and Race

	WISC-R Full-Scale IQ			
Group	*NE*	*NC*	*S*	*W*
Whites—6½ to 16½				
N	417	575	529	349
$\bar{M}$	103.7	101.9	100.7	103.5
SD	14.2	13.8	14.7	13.1
Blacks—6½ to 16½				
N	57	64	166	18
$\bar{M}$	93.0	88.1	83.4	87.3
SD	12.2	12.4	12.1	11.7

Note: The geographic regions are Northeast (NE), North Central (NC), South (S), and West (W).

The IQ scores of the transracially adopted children are entirely comparable to those of the young white adoptees in the Texas Adoption Project (Horn, Loehlin, & Willerman, 1979), who averaged 108, and to our white adolescent adoptees, who averaged 106. Nowhere do I see any evidence that the black and interracial adoptees of the Minnesota families are a select lot or that their performance on IQ tests can be explained by appeals to remote military data, when far more relevant data on children of the same ages collected in the same region at the same time with very similar instruments contradict Jensen's claims.

Jensen challenges me to give advice to black parents whose children do not score as well on the average as children of white parents at similar socioeconomic levels. (I'll bet he didn't think I'd take him up on that.) The articles of the last section of the book imply much of the advice I would give. In brief, I advise parents of ethnic minorities to examine their goals for their children, to state them clearly, and to choose the means most appropriate to these goals. If parents want their children to succeed in schools as they now exist and to be judged by the criteria of success that the majority group holds, then they should do their best to teach their children the majority culture, either as a second set of values and knowledges or as a replacement for their own. If they subscribe to the goals of the majority culture, most of their children will succeed only through thorough socialization into that culture. Some children in any group are bright enough to learn on their own what is required. The latter is an extraordinary burden on a child, one that only a few will shoulder successfully. It is this latter that I think is our current state of affairs.

The Myth of Damaged Children

Jensen suggested that natural mothers' ages may be implicated in the lower IQ scores of black and interracial children in the United States. Young mothers have a higher risk for pre- and perinatal complications that can damage infants, particularly through higher rates of premature delivery. We did not include natural mothers' ages as a variable in our report because it was not related to the children's IQ scores. Furthermore, extensive analyses of the (lack of) relationship between birth weight and other birth and perinatal complications in large and representative samples of blacks and whites in the United States (Broman, Nichols, & Kennedy, 1975) should discourage anyone from appealing to such variables for explanations of black–white cognitive differences. Although young mothers are slightly more likely to have infants at lower weights, there seem to be no long-term effects of these differences in the general population. Studies of very-low-birth-weight infants show that they are disadvantaged in growth and development (e.g., Scarr & Williams, 1973), but they are such a small minority of all children that the effects of early problems are not a significant portion of the IQ variance, even in samples of many thousands. Thus, it is not reasonable to appeal to events surrounding birth to explain the large difference in cognitive skills that is usually found on tests related to the majority culture.

ON THE ANCESTRY STUDY

For readers not adept at fancy statistical footwork, Jensen's comments on the study of degrees of white ancestry in a black population may seem confusing but convincing. Only the mother of such a study could love it enough to protect it from the arcane statistical threats that he presents. To protect readers from extended statistical infighting, I will respond only to the three major criticisms: (1) that g is best represented by a single test rather than the first principal component of four conceptual tests; (2) that the correlation of intellectual skills and ancestry cannot be expected to exceed that of skin color and ancestry, a direct contradiction of Jensen's own predictions (Jensen, 1973, pp. 222–224); and (3) that the correlation of ancestry estimates and intellectual skills cannot have been high enough to be detected in this study.

Is "g" a Single Test?

As reported in Part II, Chapter 4, Figure 1, the factor loadings of the four conceptual tests were equally high and between .7 and .8 for both blacks and whites. What is general to the four conceptual tests is found about equally in all of them and found less in the paired-associate learning task, as Jensen notes. I agree with Jensen that the Raven matrices may be the best *single* measure of g when one does not have other measures, but it is absurd to throw away vocabulary, concept development, and figural memory tests when one has them. The first principal component from these four tests accounted for about half of the variance in the individual tests and is surely the best measure of the g or general factor, given that the tests are equally intercorrelated. The first principal component reported in the ancestry study is based on the four conceptual tests and does not include the less-related learning task, as reported in the paper under *intellectual skills*.

A glance at Tables 7 and 8 of the ancestry chapter will suggest why Jensen has chosen to concentrate on the Raven matrices as the best intellectual measure. The correlations of the first principal component (g) and ancestry estimates are $-.01$ to $-.05$. His subsequent arguments about the indefinite results of the study depend on rejecting all measures but the Raven matrices, because as we demonstrated in the chapter, we could detect a correlation of $\pm$ .14 as different from 0.

The Correlation of Ancestry Estimates, Skin Color, and "g"

Jensen is correct that skin color is a highly heritable trait and that intellectual skills are less affected by genetic differences. In this sample of socially classified blacks, the h^2 estimate for the first principal component was .48. But is the correlation of ancestry with skin color the upper limit of the possible correlation of ancestry with intellectual skills? Jensen (1973, pp. 222–224) argued that because skin-color differences are determined by a few gene loci—three or four, most probably—and because differences in intelligence are determined by many loci—hundreds probably—intelligence is a better marker for ancestry than skin color! The logic is this: If African populations have fewer genes for high intelligence at hundreds of loci and more genes for dark pigmentation at a few loci, then lower intelligence will be more easily detected as a racial characteristic than skin color. Blood group estimates of greater degrees of African ancestry will be more highly correlated with lower intelligence than with darker skin color because of the more "reliable" sample of ancestral genes that determine intelligence than ancestral genes that determine pigmentation.

> Although skin color is definitely related to degree of African–Caucasian admixture for the average of *groups* having different degrees of admixture, skin color is not a highly reliable index of Caucasian admixture in individuals (Harrison *et al.*, 1967; Stern, 1970). When so few genes are involved in a characteristic, the individual variability of the characteristic among persons having exactly the same ancestry is great. The offspring to true mulattoes (who are the offspring of Caucasian and African parents), for example, show a wide range of skin color even within the same family. Estimates of the correlation of skin color in Negroes with amount of Caucasian ancestry are about 0.30 to 0.40. Thus, in terms of measurement theory, where the reliability of a measurement is the square of the correlation between true score and the observed score, the reliability of skin color ("observed score") as an index of Caucasian ancestry ("true score") would be at most about 0.40^2 or 0.16. If now we hypothesize that there is a correlation between Negroes' IQs and the amount of their Caucasian ancestry and that this correlation is slightly higher than for skin color (since more genes are involved in intelligence), say about 0.50 as an upper limit of the correlation, the reliability of IQ as an index of Caucasian ancestry would be about 0.50^2 or 0.25. The highest correlation that can be obtained between two measures is the square root of the product of their reliabilities. So the highest correlation we could expect to find between IQ and skin color would be about $\sqrt{(0.16)(0.25)} = 0.20$ [Jensen, 1973, pp. 222–223].

In the face of inconsistent evidence, Jensen has changed his predictions. Now the correlation between ancestry and skin color is said to be an upper-limit value for the correlation of ancestry with intelligence!

By Jensen's own logic, the correlation between a "true" measure of ancestry and a highly reliable measure of IQ ought to correlate above the .2 predicted for IQ and skin color on a genetic basis. Even given Jensen's low estimate of the validity of our odds coefficients as measures of "true" ancestry (.49), the predicted correlation between IQ and the odds coefficients would be detectably different from zero in this study:

Odds coefficient–"true" ancestry, $r = .49$ (Jensen's estimate)
IQ–"true" ancestry, $r = .50$ (Jensen's estimate)
Therefore, IQ–odds coefficient, $= \sqrt{(.24)(.25)} = .245$

This predicted value would be obtained in a population of hybrid blacks who varied from 0% to 100% African ancestry. In the Philadelphia population, the range was more likely .05% to 90% at the extremes; so the expected value would be somewhat smaller but well above the 14% that could be detected with the sample size.

Let us examine the validity of the odds coefficient. To estimate validity, Jensen manipulated the correlations of the 3- and 9-gene combinations that we used to test for genetic linkages between skin color and blood groups. These data do not provide an appropriate test of the validity of the ancestral or sample odds coefficients, because they do not represent their correlation with any criterion measure. Rather, as we reported in the chapter, we took two other tacks: (1) the correlation of the ancestry coefficients with the criterion of skin color, which were found to be .21 and .27; and (2) the DZ-twin correlation, which should be about .5 to reflect their half-shared genotypes. This is indeed what we found: The DZ-twin correlations for the two odds coefficients were .48 and .54—comfortably close to the predicted value.

If the odds coefficients lacked validity to the extent Jensen claimed, how could we have obtained these results? And if the correlations of skin color with our ancestry measures exceeded .2, why not the correlation of intelligence with ancestry? My answer is that intelligence is *not* a good marker for ancestry, because there are no substantial differences between the black and white gene pools for the development of intelligence, as there certainly are for the production of melanin in the skin cells.

Thus, Jensen's calculations of maximum correlations based on the validity he estimates for the odds coefficients is a statistical sleight of hand; the correlations of skin color, ancestry, and intellectual skills obtained are not limited, as he asserts, by the validity of the ancestry measure or any other. Even if the validity of the intellectual first principal component is not as high as the validity of the skin-color measurement, the vastly larger sample of the genotype involved in intellectual measures should, as Jensen originally said, make it a better correlate of ancestry than a measure of skin color.

Restriction of Range in Ancestry

Of the three major objections that Jensen raises, the greatest deception is involved in the assertion that correlations between the estimates of ancestry and the intellectual measures are severely restricted by the limited variation in ancestry. In one quick sentence, Jensen transforms our meaning into another. We said: "If we assume that the most extreme third of the black group *averages* 35% Caucasian ancestry, while the least admixed third *averages* 15% (based on data of MacLean *et al.*, 1974). . . . [emphasis added; too late, it seems].'' Jensen distorted this to mean: "Scarr *et al.* divided the total distribution of variation in ancestry into thirds and suggested that the upper third of blacks *has* about .35 Caucasian ancestry and the lower third about .15 for a difference of .20 in proportion of Caucasian genes [emphasis added].''

Correlation coefficients are dependent on the range of scores and the total variation. Imagine a positively skewed distribution of scores that range from .95 to .10, with a mean of .80. The upper third of scores *averages* .35, and the lower third *averages* .15. Now calculate one correlation coefficient based on the full distribution and another based on a distribution artificially truncated by the average values of the extreme thirds. I have not actually calculated these values, because it is obvious that the doubly truncated distribution will yield artificially lower values. I think that readers will agree that Jensen's calculations take advantage of a misunderstanding about the distribution of scores versus the comparison of average values of the extreme thirds.

After miscalculating the expected correlation coefficient between ancestry estimates and intellectual skills, Jensen uses his expected correlation to predict the differences between the extreme thirds—a circular convenience. I do not repeat our calculations, because they are given in the paper. By our estimates, the sample sizes were adequate to test Jensen's strong genetic hypothesis about race difference in intelligence and to reject it both on correlational grounds and by contrast of extreme thirds.

REFERENCES

Broman, S. H., Nichols, P. L., & Kennedy, W. A. *Preschool IQ: Prenatal and early development correlates.* New York: Wiley, 1975.

Horn, J. M., Lochlin, J., & Willerman, L. Intellectual resemblance among adoptive and biological relatives: The Texas adoptive project. *Behavioral Genetics,* 1979, *9,* 177–207.

Jensen, A. *Educability and group differences.* New York: Harper & Row, 1973.

Kaufman, A. S., & Doppelt, J. E. Analysis of WISC-R standardization data in terms of the stratification variables. *Child Development,* 1976, *47,* 165–171.

Scarr, S., & Williams, M. L. The effects of early stimulation on low-birth-weight infants. *Child Development,* 1973, *44,* 94–101.

Young, V. H. Family and childhood in a southern Negro community. *American Anthropologist,* 1970, *72,* 269–288.

SANDRA SCARR
Yale University

V.3 Having the Last Word

Sandra Scarr
Yale University

The delightful position of author is to have the last word! Professors Kamin and Jensen have expressed their views, as I requested, and they have done so in thoughtful and considerate ways. I thank them profusely for their commentaries that illuminate so many aspects of the genetics–IQ debate. Naturally, I do not agree with all they have said; there are legitimate differences of interpretation among us. Given the ambiguity of some data and the evident differences in orientation toward science and society, the reader can recognize that there are at least three sides to some issues.

On most points I have had my say in the text. Readers are respectfully requested to refer to relevant sections of the chapters, whose studies have been criticized or contradicted, for their own evaluations of the evidence. I stand by my interpretations of the data with which Professors Kamin and Jensen disagree—never, one may notice, with the same data. On several issues, however, I want to make additional comments—some philosophical, some theoretical.

ON PUBLISHING

There is an interesting agreement among the three of us on the difficulty of doing research and publishing material on genetic differences in human behavior. Jensen has, of course, suffered more than anyone from the widespread prejudice against genetic hypotheses, particularly racial ones. Standards of evidence are elevated when one is defying the zeitgeist. Although Jensen and I are well published, I would bet that each article has required 2 to 10 times more minute revision than is required from investigators of other topics and from other points of view. We are often required to examine all conceivable hypotheses, however ad hoc or unlikely, as alternatives to genetic differences. Needless to say, authors of articles with environmentalist interpretations are not usually asked to consider genetic differences as an alternative explanation of their results. Yes, we are complaining, not because of the final verdicts, but because the process is so manifestly unfair. Our work is subjected to the scrutiny of an electron microscope when the rest of psychology is examined through the wrong end of a telescope.

Leo Kamin sympathizes with the close scrutiny because he sees dire consequences in the possible errors of genetic claims. I am sympathetic with his politics in this case, but my civil-libertarian bias impells me to claim the right to make as many mistakes as anyone else in psychology. One purpose of reprinting in this volume the points and counterpoints of debate about genetics and IQ is to illustrate that the sky will not fall if honest scientists disagree about conclusions. It is a wonderfully egocentric illusion of scientists that what they find and what they believe about what they find matters so much to anyone else.

POLITICS AND SCIENCE

Sharp disagreement among the three of us can be seen in the discussion of the politics and science of the study of intelligence. For Kamin, science merges with politics; science is a political exercise in itself. For Jensen, there is an impermeable barrier between the activity of scientific investigation and the uses that are made of the data. Social policy implications that one might draw from data are not inherent in the research results, nor are the politics of the investigator at all relevant to the investigation. My position on this matter, as on so many others, lies in the middle of the road, where one is alleged to find either truth or.... I agree with Kamin that research questions are a product of one's times and politics. It is no accident, as I said in the introduction, that I chose to study genetic differences in behavior—even the possibility of race differences. From my social and educational background, those seemed to be pressing social issues, ones that had been neglected in scientific research. From another perspective, perhaps Kamin's, questions of genetic differences are dangerous and morally wrong. From Jensen's vantage point, the choice of research question seems to be guided by a quest for knowledge apart from one's sociocultural setting. I acknowledge that questions of genetic differences fascinated me because they loomed at me from the darkness, and I decided not to be afraid to ask them. This was a very personal and political decision.

Once I had decided to study genetic differences in human behavior, however, I tried to frame the questions in ways that could reveal the "true" nature of the human condition. That is, I was prepared to accept whatever results were obtained by the scrupulous exercise of the greatest objectivity I could manage. As my friends well know, I was prepared to emigrate if the blood-grouping study had shown a substantial relationship between African ancestry and low intellectual skills. I had decided that I could not endure what Jensen had experienced at the hands of colleagues.

Neither Rich Weinberg nor I were prepared to discover that adolescents at the end of the child-rearing period bear so little resemblance to those with whom they have lived for so many years. We were dismayed by the obvious implications of the adolescent adoption study for the nature of social-class differences. In fact, the adolescent adoption study was proposed and funded at the same time, in the same application, as the transracial adoption study; the goal of the adolescent study was to show the greater resemblance among adoptees and their parents at the end of the child-rearing period! Never did we contemplate that older adoptees would be *less* like their rearing families than the younger adoptees, who were, after all, of different races!

Perhaps even more telling is our experience with the transracial adoption study. In this case we did anticipate the result that black and interracial children reared in the culture of the tests and the schools would perform better on tests and in school than black children reared in the black community. Before beginning the data collection, we asked about 20 psychologists-friends across the country what they expected from our study: How well would the adopted black and interracial children perform on IQ tests? To our surprise, the overwhelming consensus of private opinion was that the adoptees would score about IQ 90! We told them they were not taking into account the more relevant and more enriched intellectual environments in which these children were being reared. We were told that black children could not benefit from such environments to the same extent as white children. The public and private zeitgeists were at variance. Perhaps this is backroom gossip, but we were amazed to find such discouragement with behavioral malleability. But then, it was 1973, and there was not much to be optimistic about.

The major point of all this personal history is to say that I have always tried to frame questions in such ways that my hypotheses could be falsified. This I understand to be a minimal requirement of scientific research. The black and interracial adoptees could have had low IQ scores; the adolescent adoptees could (and did) bear little resemblance to their families of rearing; the black twins could have performed worse on more "culture-fair" than on "culture-loaded" tests (but they did not, because we provided clearer instructions to make sure they understood the "culture-fair" task); the black children with more African ancestry could have performed worse on the intellectual tasks. Surely, I had personal and political reasons for pursuing such questions, but the results could have proven me wrong, and did in some cases.

THE MORALITY OF GENETIC DIFFERENCES

Another interesting point of disagreement among us in our evaluation of the moral good, bad, or neutrality of genetic differences. Clearly, Kamin deplores the very idea of genetic differences in behavior. He clings to the null hypothesis. Jensen takes a lofty, neutral position: It's no one's fault or credit that some of us are genetically better endowed than others. On other occasions, Jensen has extolled the virtues of genetic diversity in the human species, as have I. The difference between Jensen's position and mine is that I am bothered by the moral implications of genetic advantage for some. As John Rawls (1971) said, unfair advantages can be either environmental or genetic, and we should compensate both. I do not agree with all of Rawls' ethics, because they are impractical and have terrible implications for the effective use of social resources (Harsanyi, 1975), but I do think that social resources should be allocated with less different-ial benefit for the more able and more for the less able, regardless of why the differences exist.

Unlike Kamin, I do not deplore the idea of genetic diversity, because human-kind's future depends on the variety of adaptations the species can make. The genetic diversity among us is the guarantee that we can adjust as a species to the changing demands of our environments. It is hard, however, to observe human suffering that results from the poor adjustment of some in each generation. It is the suffering that should be addressed, not the genetic differences denied.

THE FOREST AND THE TREES

All of us find it easier to accept information that is congruent with our beliefs and prior conclusions than to admit evidence that is discrepant. For Jensen, accep-tance of the evidence *for* genetic differences among individuals and social-class groups and rejection of evidence *against* racial genetic differences fit his views. For Kamin, acceptance of the evidence *against* racial genetic differences and rejection of evidence *for* individual and social-class genetic differences are com-patible with his views. Both look at the forest of results in those studies that support their prior conclusions and examine the individuals trees in those that seem to contradict. (This human frailty is the basis of the closer scrutiny that Jensen's and my research receives from most reviewers and editors.) I am surely not exempt from this failing.

For me, the forests are the findings on individual and social-class variability. Not only my own work but research by many others also supports the modest conclusion that we are different from one another on both genetic and environ-mental bases—not only in intellectual ability but also in personality, cognitive style, gestural and postural communication, linguistic style, and probably all other measurable characteristics. I am hard pressed to think of any aspect of human behavior for which genetic as well as environmental differences will not explain part of the variability. Studies that have addressed the possibly different amount of genetic and environmental variability have failed to find consistently different degrees of "heritability" among any measured behavioral traits. Everything seems to have moderate "heritability." Perhaps the measures are not sufficiently fine-grained; perhaps most of our measurements and observations are sampling from a few domains of behavior and not sampling characteristics that are not heritable. Much remains to be resolved about the possibly different degrees of heritability of the many aspects of human behavior.

The aggregation of people with similar measured abilities in social-class groups within the U.S. white population is disturbing but comprehensible. As Herrnstein (1971) concluded in his much-maligned article, to the extent that individuals are upwardly and downwardly mobile according to their individual abilities, and to the extent that those differences in ability are partly heritable, there will be average ability differences among social-class groups of adults. It also follows that the children born to parents of different social-class groups will differ on the average in abilities. One does not have to be a philosopher to see the necessity of this logical chain.

Issues can be raised, however, about the magnitude of genetic differences among social-class groups of adults and of children born into those groups. The effect may be minuscule if: (1) mobility is only slightly associated with individual abilities; and/or (2) ability differences are only slightly related to genetic differences. I had assumed in previous reviews of Herrnstein's writings that the effect would be found to be quite small for the offspring of the different social-class groups, because social mobility was not closely related to ability differences.

Now I am reluctantly persuaded that within the white population in the United States, there are average genetic differences among the offspring in working-, middle-, and upper-middle-class families and that these genetic differences explain half or more of their average intellectual differences. (Note that I am referring to average differences among greatly overlapping distributions.)

I also think that social status is less likely to be associated with average differences in ability within the black population at this time, because blacks have a much briefer history of individual mobility by individual merit. The finding in the twin study that the common measures of SES were far less associated with ability differences among black than white adolescents is congruent with this hypothesis. One would predict that individual differences in ability will become increasingly associated with differences in social status as arbitrary, discriminatory barriers to blacks' mobility are removed.

In the forest of results that are congruent with the hypothesis of important genetic differences in intellect among individuals and social-class groups, I choose to ignore a few of my own discrepant trees—a couple of scrub pines in a forest of hardwoods. Kamin is right that one can find evidence of no heritability of IQ—particularly in the resemblances of young siblings, whether adopted or not. (Of course, if one dissects every sample of subjects into personally convenient subgroups, one can "prove" anything one wants.) Given what I see to be the weight of evidence for genetic differences, I choose to call my results a hardwood forest and not a heterogeneous collection of unlabelable trees. Anyone who believes in sampling theory and its application to studies, as well as measures and subjects, has to accept a distribution of results around some central tendency. The existence of a few scrub pines doesn't deter me from describing the central tendency in my distribution of trees as a hardwood forest.

On the other hand, I am willing to look at the trees in studies of racial differences. There are so few direct tests of a genetic-difference hypothesis that the results do not constitute a forest, or even a modest grove. So far, I see no evidence for the hypothesis that the average difference in intellectual performance between U.S. whites and blacks results primarily from genetic racial differences. Jensen's view is that there are no live trees in the grove. Mine is that there are three lines of evidence that are the beginnings of a forest, but we will need many more trees before we can be confident of the distribution or central tendency. In this area, I agree with Kamin that one should not reject the null hypothesis when there is no evidence against it. Agnosticism is more appropriate when there is evidence on neither or both sides.

THE FLAWS OF FIELD STUDIES

There are flaws in all the studies reported, and we have tried to indicate the limitations of inference that we think result. Critics have pointed to other flaws and other limitations they see in the studies. Readers can evaluate for themselves.

From my point of view, the most important fact is that the flaws of one study are not the same as those of another; there are nonoverlapping cracks in the evidence. Even though one adoption study confounds age of placement with preadoptive experience, the next does not; the second study compares samples of biological and adoptive families with different parents, whereas the first study sampled only adoptive parents—most of whom had their own biological children. Each study can be criticized for its lack of perfection, but laid on top of one another, the holes do not go clear through.

Apart from the (occasional, I think) mistakes in methodology or inference that could have been corrected, most of the flaws reside in the nature of field research. The characteristics of real people in the real world *are* messy and confounded. It is not possible to disentangle the correlated experiences of being working or middle class or of having an IQ or 120 or 80. *Life* is different for people at different locations in the social structure and for people with different abilities to comprehend and cope. I think we are stuck with a synthetic view of such variables; the option is to analyze them into bits and pieces that only partially capture the correlated experiences. For studying the phenomena of people's lives, my preference is for global index variables over analytic, proximal ones. I recognize that this is a personal preference not shared by most psychologists.

I have been criticized by developmental psychologists (not by the present commentators) for not measuring the *processes* by which children come to be different from one another. What socialization practices, what critical parent-child interactions created the intellectual differences that we so confidently index with IQ tests? What cognitive processes underlie those differences in IQ scores? Darned if I know.

In the first instance, that of socialization practices, I do not think we can separate biological parents' own intellectual and personal styles that affect their children environmentally from the genetic transmission of behavioral characteristics from parent to child. Hundreds of studies document the correlation between parental socialization practices and child behaviors and then leap to an environmental interpretation of parents' behaviors as the causes of children's behaviors. I hardly need to say that I think such leaps are not only unwarranted but scientifically suicidal. The hypothesis that parent socialization practices have anything to do with children's intellectual development must be tested with genetically unrelated families.

On the second point, cognitive processes, I think there may be hope of disentangling speed, complexity, rarity of cultural knowledge, and so forth from the global IQ score. There have, of course, been hundreds of studies and scores of models for intelligence. None so far comprehends all that is sampled on IQ tests. But I think there will be fruitful studies of genetic and environmental differences in cognitive processes. Such studies would naturally need to sample people with varied genetic and environmental similarities to assess the causes of variation.

WHERE DO WE GO FROM HERE?

Is the study of genetic differences in human behavior a frontier (Jensen) or a dead end (Kamin)? The answer depends, I think, on three issues: (1) How productive are studies of genetic differences for knowledge of human behavior; (2) how important is knowledge of human differences, and (3) how dangerous to society is such knowledge?

Because I have done and will continue to do studies of genetic differences in human behavior, I clearly side with Jensen in the view that accumulating knowledge from behavior genetic studies will advance our knowledge of human behavior. I do not agree with Kamin that the studies are so hopelessly confounded that no useful knowledge will result. Only if one has the illusion that people in the real world can be analyzed into neat, experimental variables is one disenchanted with the results of behavior genetic studies so far. I am quite excited about the regression models of individual differences that weight explanatory variables for outcomes that one cares about.

The philosophical difference between natural science, analytic models and social science, population models is that the former attempt to hold constant all variables but one and to assess experimentally the effect of that variable in isolation. Social scientists and population geneticists know that such models have little applicability to the operations of the human world, where variables are always confounded and act together to determine outcomes. It is the latter models to which I subscribe. One does not ask whether father's occupation or education—which are always correlated—has the "real" effect on children's IQ scores unless somewhere in some population it is possible to study them separately, and unless it is then possible to generalize from that population to the one one wants to study. That is a difficult pair of criteria to meet, as many cross-cultural studies have shown. Usually, one must model the effects of confounded variables across several populations to see if there is any generality to the regression coefficients one obtains in any one study.

I think that there is much to be learned from the continued pursuit of behavior genetic studies, especially if one takes into account developmental changes in genetic and environmental effects. We need studies of genetic differences across the life span.

Is knowledge of human differences important? To whom and why? I do not suppose that knowledge of how and why people differ from one another has the social importance of curing cancers, but in the behavioral sciences, individual differences have been underrated as a field of inquiry. This underevaluation is a legacy of the defunct, general laws of learning in psychology. It is no longer fashionable to study situations in which people can perform just as well as rats, and just as well as each other. We have come to recognize that this result can be obtained only under very restricted conditions, where people are made to act as dumb as rats and bright people, as dumb as dull people. Who cares? In the situations to which we want to generalize, humans behave differently from rats and bright people, differently from dull ones. Thus, the importance of understanding how and why people differ from one another is growing.

Theoretically, individual variation has great importance as one of the two major concepts of Darwinian evolution—selection and variation. Without variation, there could be no selection and no evolution. Populations are distributions of individual differences. From any measurement, we can abstract a mean or typical value, but we in psychology forget too often that what exists is a distribution of individual values—not a reified average. The importance of distributions and population thinking goes far beyond evolutionary theory. In developmental psychology, there are always individual differences on any measure one would care about. When we speak (too loosely) of "the 3-year old," usually in contrast to children of another age, we lose sight of the distribution of 3-

year-olds, whose average value is being used to typify the age group. It is rarely the case that all 3-year-olds have values that fall outside the range of another age group, such as "4-year-olds." To understand how and why children differ at these ages on some measured quantity, it is far more useful to study the correlates of individual variation than to contrast average values of the age groups. If extreme age groups whose distributions of values do not overlap—such as 3-year-olds and 13-year-olds—are contrasted, what can we possibly learn about why they differ? They differ, on the average, in every conceivable way. Thus, in brief, it seems to me that individual differences are, in Underwood's terms, the crucible of psychological theories; unless we can explain why individuals differ, we can not understand the processes underlying behavior.

On the third point—the possible danger to society of knowledge about genetic differences in behavior—my position is unequivocal. In my view, there is no danger so great as the suppression of knowledge. There is nothing we could learn about ourselves that would justify abridgment of scientific inquiry. There are methods of investigation that pose unconscionable threats to the participants in research. Methods should be subject to regulation. But there should be no regulation of scientists' rights to think, propose, and conduct ethical investigations on any question, however distasteful it might be to others.

Kamin is correct that I am absolutely against censorship in science. There is no more dangerous idea than the thought that someone, somewhere, can determine what I can study and say about my research. Who shall be the judge of my freedoms, or shall I be the judge of yours?

My absolutist view of freedom for scientific inquiry derives from my adherence to the First Amendment, the rights of which have been occasionally and regretably abridged. Even Justice Holmes regretted the implications of his decision that to cry "Fire" in a crowded theater was not protected by the First Amendment. His regret and that of contemporary constitutional experts is that once abridged, it is difficult to maintain the right to free expression. My remark about Jensen's claim of genetic racial differences was not an attempt at censorship, but a call for responsibility for the immediate and predictable implications of his views.

I do think that scientists are responsible for the proximal and predictable effects of their research reports, particularly to a wide audience. One has the responsibility to explain as best one can the limitations of one's research and the personal inferences one draws from the study, especially when the implications are socially relevant. If others do not like the implications and prefer others, they are free to disagree.

I believe in the free competition of ideas and in the evolution of a population of ideas that coexist at any one time in cultural history (Toulmin, 1972). The democracy of ideas may not be a perfect system, to paraphrase Thomas Jefferson, but it is the best one I know. We need not fear the competition of ideas as long as the proponents of one view do not have the power to suppress others. We should all tremble if the true believers of one position were to gain the power to silence dissent. And so, I do not believe that ideas are dangerous, however misguided and outlandish they may seem to me, but I quake at the self-appointed guardians of any orthodoxy.

REFERENCES

Harsanyi, J. C. Can the Maximin principle serve as a basis for morality? A critique of John Rawls's theory. *American Political Science Review*, 1975, *69*, 594–606.
Herrnstein, R. I.Q. *The Atlantic*, September 1971, pp. 43–64.
Rawls, J. *A theory of justice*. Cambridge, Mass.: Belknap Press, 1971.
Toulmin, S. *Human understanding*. Cambridge: Oxford University Press, 1972.

Author Index

Subject Index